W9-CPE-163

Experience Accounting Video Series

Developed by co-author Dan Heitger (Miami University), the new videos in the **Experience Accounting** video series center on cutting-edge success! These videos highlight progressive companies and allow students to more effectively visualize critical chapter concepts. The videos focus on how companies of today incorporate managerial accounting to fuel better business performance. Students are exposed to a wide variety of companies in both manufacturing and service sectors.

Critical thinking exercises accompany each video to test student comprehension of the video and to stimulate classroom discussion. An accompanying instructor manual offers discussion questions and answers, video synopses, learning goals, and experiential exercises to enhance the classroom experience!

The videos are delivered in 2 optional formats

- **ThomsonNOW™**

Within ThomsonNOW, the professor may assign the corresponding critical thinking questions to be graded online. The student can access the videos at any time, using them as part of an assignment or simply as a study tool.

- **Separate video website**

www.thomsonedu.com/accounting/eav

FUNDAMENTAL
CORNERSTONES
of Managerial Accounting

Dan L. Heitger
Miami University ~ Oxford

•

Maryanne M. Mowen
Oklahoma State University

•

Don R. Hansen
Oklahoma State University

THOMSON
™
SOUTH-WESTERN

Australia · Brazil · Canada · Mexico · Singapore · Spain · United Kingdom · United States

THOMSON
SOUTH-WESTERN

Fundamental Cornerstones of Managerial Accounting
Dan L. Heitger, Maryanne M. Mowen, and Don R. Hansen

VP/Editorial Director
Jack W. Calhoun

Editor-in-Chief
Rob Dewey

Acquisitions Editor
Keith Chassé

Developmental Editor
Aaron Arnsparger

Marketing Manager
Kristen Hurd

Senior Content Project Manager
Tim Bailey

Manager of Technology, Editorial
John Barans

Technology Project Manager
Scott Hamilton

Website Project Manager
Brian Courter

Senior Frontlist Buyer
Doug Wilke

Production House
GGS Book Services, Inc.

Printer
Transcontinental – Beauceville
Quebec, Canada

Art Director
Stacy Jenkins Shirley

Cover and Internal Designer
M. Stratton Design

Cover Image
© Getty Images

Photography Manager
Deanna Ettinger

COPYRIGHT © 2008
Thomson South-Western, a part of
The Thomson Corporation.
Thomson, the Star logo, and
South-Western are trademarks
used herein under license.

Printed in Canada
1 2 3 4 5 10 09 08 07

Student Edition
ISBN 13: 978-0-324-37806-1
ISBN 10: 0-324-37806-8

Instructor's Edition
ISBN 13: 978-0-324-65869-9
ISBN 10: 0-324-65869-9

ALL RIGHTS RESERVED.
No part of this work covered by
the copyright hereon may be
reproduced or used in any form or
by any means—graphic, electronic,
or mechanical, including
photocopying, recording, taping,
Web distribution or information
storage and retrieval systems, or in
any other manner—without the
written permission of the
publisher.

For permission to use material
from this text or product, submit a
request online at
http://www.thomsonrights.com.

Library of Congress Control
Number: 2007932304

For more information about our
products, contacts us at:

Thomson Learning Academic
Resource Center

1-800-423-0563

Thomson Higher Education
5191 Natorp Boulevard
Mason, OH 45040
USA

"CORNERSTONES"—
THE **PERFECT** FOUNDATION
FOR SUCCESSFUL LEARNING!

Carefully crafted from the ground up, this text's "Cornerstones" help you, the student, easily set up and solve fundamental managerial accounting calculations. Once you master these "Cornerstones," you can build on them and use them together to visualize the entire picture of managerial accounting.

"Cornerstones" are divided into three sections—*Information, Required,* and *Calculation*—and this format is consistent throughout the book. At each step along the way, you can see the concepts and theories at work behind the numbers.

- The Information portion of each "Cornerstone" provides the necessary data to solve the calculation.

- The Required section of each exhibit provides students with each step that must be calculated.

CORNERSTONE 4-5

HOW TO Solve for the Number of Units to Be Sold to Earn a Target Operating Income

Information: Whittier Company sells mulching mowers at $400 each. Variable cost per unit is $325, and total fixed costs are $45,000.

Required:
1. Calculate the number of units that Whittier Company must sell to earn operating income of $37,500.
2. Check your answer by preparing a contribution margin income statement based on the number of units calculated.

Calculation:
1. Number of units = ($45,000 + $37,500)/($400 − $325) = 1,100
2. Contribution margin income statement based on sales of 1,100 units:

Sales ($400 × 1,100)	$440,000
Total variable expense ($325 × 1,100)	357,500
Total contribution margin	$ 82,500
Total fixed expense	45,000
Operating income	$ 37,500

Indeed, selling 1,100 units does yield operating income of $37,500.

- The Calculation ends each "Cornerstone," showing the calculations for each of the required steps in the problem. Students can work through the math to ensure they understand the necessary calculations, or could try the problem on their own and refer back to the exhibit to check their answers.

Exercise 4-18 Calculating the Predetermined Overhead Rate, Applying Overhead to Production

OBJECTIVE ②

CORNERSTONE 4-1

At the beginning of the year, Badiyan Company estimated the following:

Overhead	$270,000
Direct labor hours	90,000

Badiyan uses normal costing and applies overhead on the basis of direct labor hours. For the month of January, direct labor hours equaled 8,150.

Required:
1. Calculate the predetermined overhead rate for Badiyan.
2. Calculate the overhead applied to production in January.

The "Cornerstones" are powerful references to help you work through your homework and prepare for tests & exams!

- End-of-chapter Exercises are linked to one or more specific "Cornerstone" features, allowing you to try a problem on their own that is similar to the in-chapter example.

EXPERIENCE
MANAGERIAL ACCOUNTING
IN THE REAL WORLD

The text, accompanying videos, and ThomsonNOW™ online learning resource will help you use accounting information to understand the *real issues* at hand in *actual companies.*

Experience Accounting Video Series

Including high-profile companies such as Washburn Guitar and Hard Rock Café, 14 new videos focus on how companies of today incorporate managerial accounting to fuel better business performance. You will be exposed to a wide variety of cutting-edge companies in service and manufacturing sectors to more effectively visualize critical chapter concepts. To further connect these concepts, each video correlates with the NEW *Experience Accounting Chapter Openers* in the text. To access or purchase the videos, please visit: www.thomsonedu.com/accounting/eav.

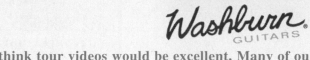

"I think tour videos would be excellent. Many of our students are very young and have no concept of a manufacturing facility."

—ELIZABETH T. COLE, JAMES MADISON UNIVERSITY

Save Time & Earn Your PERFECT Grade with ThomsonNOW™

ThomsonNOW™ for Heitger/Mowen/Hansen's *Fundamental Cornerstones of Managerial Accounting 1e* is a powerful and fully integrated online learning resource. It provides you with an efficient path to success, delivering the results you want—NOW! Ensure positive performance with online quizzing, tutorials, and much more!

Personalized Study Plan

- **Pre- and Post-Test Assessments** help you focus your study time
- **Integrated E-book** matches up to topics in the pre- and post test
- **Animated Cornerstones**—Each "Cornerstone" from the text is available as a problem demonstration with voice-over narration.
- **Audio Problem Reviews**—Students can view detailed, step-by-step explanations of selected problems from the text. (Must be assigned by the instructor.)
- **Full text PowerPoint® Presentation Slides**
- **Experience Accounting**—Video clips with exercises stimulate discussion.
- **Math Tutorials**—These tutorials offer remedial help in building math skills that are relevant to managerial accounting.

Online Graded Homework

Save time on homework and earn the grade you want when you take the most efficient path to understanding managerial accounting. ThomsonNOW helps you complete homework online. Your answers will be graded automatically, and you will receive immediate feedback, helping manage your time.

Just what you need to know and do NOW!
For more information, visit
www.thomsonedu.com/thomsonnow.

Acknowledgments and Thanks

We would like to thank the following reviewers for their valuable content feedback on *Fundamental Cornerstones*:

Nas Ahadiat, California State Polytechnic University

Sepeedeh Ahadiat, California State Polytechnic University

Elizabeth M. Ammann, Lindenwood University

Julie C. Chenier, Louisiana State University

Ken Fowler, San Jose State University

John Illig, Manatee Community College

Paul Jensen, University of Central Arkansas

Leslie Kren, University of WI-Milwaukee

Lois. S. Mahoney, Eastern Michigan University

Noel McKeon, Jacksonville Community College

David J. Medved, Eastern Michigan University

Barbara A. Reeves, Eastern Michigan University

T. Brian Routh, University of North Carolina at Wilmington

Akil Sanyika, Georgia Perimeter College

Marsha Scheidt, University of Tennessee—Chattanooga

Greg Thibadoux, University of Tennessee—Chattanooga

Kiran Verma, University of Massachussetts—Boston

We would also like to thank the following instructors who further helped shape the vision of the book through participation in marketing events and focus groups:

Markus Ahrens, St. Louis Community College—Meramec

Judy Beebe, Western Oregon University

Felicia Baldwin, Richard J. Daley College

Brenda Bindschatel, Green River Community College

Marvin Bouillion, Iowa State University

Anna Boulware, St. Charles Community College

Linda Chase, Baldwin-Wallace College

Star Ciccio, Johnson & Wales University

Andrea Drake, University of Cincinnati

Barbara Eide, University of Wisconsin—LaCrosse

Kurt Fanning, Grand Valley State University

Christopher Gilbert, Glendale Community College

Iris Jenkel, St. Norbert College

Becky Jones, Baylor University

David Juriga, St. Louis Community College—Forest Park

Rita M. Kingery Cook, University of Delaware

Mehmet Kocakulah, Southern Indiana University

Sang Kyu-Lee, Western New England College

Nastasha Librizzi, Milwaukee Area Technical College

William Link, University of Missouri—St. Louis

Brian McGuire, Southern Indiana University

Helen Miller, Baylor University

Barbara Norris, Johnson & Wales University

Yvonne Phang, Borough of Manhattan Community College

Aaron Reeves, St. Louis Community College—Forest Park

Randy Serrett, University of Houston—Downtown

Wendy Tietz, Kent State University

Mike Tyler, Barry University

Donna Viens, Johnson & Wales University

Anne Wessely, St. Louis Community College—Meramec

Cathy Xanthaky Larson, Middlesex Community College

Susan Young, Baruch College

Finally, we would like to thank the following past reviewers who helped refine the Cornerstones approach and theme.

Carl Allocca, Stony Brook University

Dan Bayak, Lehigh University

Karen Bird, University of Michigan

Blevins, Eastern New Mexico University

George H. Bodnar, Duquesne University

Steve Bucheit, Texas Tech University

Charles Caldwell, Tennessee Technological University

David M. Cannon, Grand Valley State University

Elizabeth T. Cole, James Madison University

Paul A. Copley, James Madison University

Sandy Devona, Northern Illinois University

Roger Doost, Clemson University

Peter G. Dorff, Kent State University—Stark

Robert Dunn, Auburn University

Barbara Durham, University of Central Florida

Richard Filler, Franklin University

Jim Groff, University of Texas—San Antonio

Sungkyoo Huh, California State University at San Bernadino

Marianne L. James, California State University—Los Angeles

Sharon Johnson, Kansas City Kansas Community College

David Juriga, Saint Louis Community College

Ronald C. Kettering, Columbus State University

Mike Klickman, University of Dallas

Mehemt Kocakulah, Southern Indiana University

Gregory J. Krivacek, Robert Morris University

Nancy Lamberton, University of Hartford

Natasha Librizzi, Milwaukee Area Technical College

Robert Lin, California State University, East Bay

Cathy Lumbattis, Southern Illinois University—Carbondale

David Marcinko, University of Albany—SUNY

Peter Margaritis, Franklin University

Barbara McElroy, Susquehanna University

Noel McKeon, Florida Community College

Cynthia Miglietti, Bowling Green State University

Paul Mihalek, University of Hartford

Susan Minke, Indiana University—Purdue University at Fort Wayne

J. Lowell Mooney, Georgia Southern University

Marilyn Okleshen, Minnesota State University—Mankato

Gail Pastoria, Robert Morris University

Janice Pitera, Broome Community College

Frederick W. Rankin, Colorado State University

Kelly Richmond, UNC—Greensboro

P.N. Saksena, Indiana University—South Bend

Howard Smith, Southwest Texas State University

Dwight Sneathen, Jr., Mississippi State University

Ron Strittmater, North Hennepin Community College

Tim Swenson, Sullivan University

Kun Wang, Texas Southern University

Charles Wellens, Fitchburg State College

Janice White, Kalamazoo Valley Community College

Marvin Williams, University of Houston—DowntownRonald

Jeff Yost, College of Charleston

Brief Contents

Contents

Chapter 6
Activity-Based Costing and Management 236

Chapter 7
Profit Planning 290

Dr. Dan L. Heitger is Associate Professor of Accounting and Co-Director of the Center for Governance, Risk Management, and Reporting at Miami University in Oxford, Ohio. He received his Ph.D. from Michigan State University and his undergraduate degree in accounting from Indiana University. He actively works with executives and students of all levels in developing and teaching courses in managerial and cost accounting, risk management and business reporting. He co-founded an organization that provides executive education for large international organizations. His interactions with business professionals, through executive education and the Center, allow him to bring a current and real-world perspective to his writing. His published research focuses on performance measurement and risk management issues and has appeared in Harvard Business Review, Behavioral Research in Accounting, Journal of Accountancy and Management Accounting Quarterly. His outside interests include hiking with his family in the National Park system.

Dr. Maryanne M. Mowen is Associate Professor of Accounting at Oklahoma State University. She received her Ph.D. from Arizona State University. She brings an interdisciplinary perspective to teaching and writing in cost and management accounting, with degrees in history and economics. She also teaches classes in ethics and the impact of the Sarbanes-Oxley Act on accountants. Her scholarly research is in the areas of management accounting, behavioral decision theory, and compliance with the Sarbanes-Oxley Act. She has published articles in journals such as Decision Science, The Journal of Economics and Psychology, and The Journal of Management Accounting Research. Dr. Mowen has served as a consultant to mid-sized and Fortune 100 companies, and works with corporate controllers on management accounting issues. Outside the classroom, she enjoys hiking, traveling, reading mysteries and working crossword puzzles.

Dr. Don R. Hansen is the Head of the School of Accounting and Kerr McGee Chair at Oklahoma State University. He received his Ph.D. from the University of Arizona in 1977. He has an undergraduate degree in mathematics from Brigham Young University. His research interests include activity-based costing and mathematical modeling. He has published articles in both accounting and engineering journals including. The Accounting Review, The Journal of Management Accounting Research, Accounting Horizons, and IIE Transactions. He has served on the editorial board of The Accounting Review. His outside interests include family, church activities, reading, movies, watching sports, and studying Spanish.

1

Managerial Accounting Concepts and Decision-Making Support

After studying Chapter 1, you should be able to:

1. Explain the meaning of managerial accounting and contrast it to financial accounting.

2. Explain the current focus of managerial accounting and the role of managerial accountants in an organization.

3. Explain the meaning of cost and how costs are assigned to products and services.

4. Define the various costs of manufacturing products and providing services.

5. Prepare income statements for manufacturing and service organizations.

6. Explain the importance of ethical behavior for managers and managerial accountants.

© BUYCOSTUMES.COM

Experience Managerial Decisions

with BuyCostumes.com

The greatest benefit of managerial accounting is also its biggest challenge—to provide managers with information that improves decisions and creates organizational value. This information helps inform managers about the impact of various strategic and operational decisions on key nonfinancial performance measures and their eventual impact on the organization's financial performance. The information is challenging to prepare and analyze because it requires an understanding of all value-chain components that affect the organization, including research and development, production, marketing, distribution, and customer service.

Since its inception in 1999, **BuyCostumes.com** has blended the right managerial accounting information and an innovative business model to provide costumes to customers in over 50 countries. Using the Internet and marketing creativity, BuyCostumes.com serves a market of 150 million U.S. consumers who spend $3.6 million dollars on costumes each year! According to CEO Jalem Getz, BuyCostumes.com measures key performance indicators to guide its decision making. For example, managerial accountants analyze measures of customer satisfaction, average time between order placement and costume arrival for each shipping method, and the profitability of individual customer types. As customer trends change, competitors emerge, and technological advances occur, BuyCostumes.com's managerial accounting information adapts to provide crucial insight into the company's performance and how its strategy should evolve to remain the world's largest Internet costume retailer!

In writing this textbook, we wanted to show our readers the importance and relevance of managerial accounting to decision making. Therefore, each chapter begins with a quick look (e.g., Experience Managerial Decisions with BuyCostumes.com) at how different companies—ones that you likely recognize—use the managerial accounting topics studied in that particular chapter. In addition, we teamed up with Kicker, a real company, and interviewed its top management extensively for stories about their firm and its use of accounting information. You will see boxes in each chapter called "Here's The Real Kicker," detailing how the company has used managerial accounting information in its operations. In addition, each chapter includes an exercise or problem based on actual Kicker experiences. Without further ado, let's get better acquainted with Kicker.

the web's most popular costume store!

Here's The Real Kicker

A division of Stillwater Designs and Audio Inc., Kicker makes car stereo systems. Their signature logo "Livin' Loud," gives you a hint as to the capabilities of the system. As the company website says, "Livin' Loud has always been the KICKER way—staying one step ahead of the pack—driven to create components that consistently raise the world's expectations for car stereo performance."

Twenty-five years ago, car stereos were underpowered, tinny affairs. They could power a radio or an eight-track tape deck. But the in-home listening experience coveted by audio buffs eluded the automobile market. In 1980, Stillwater Designs virtually invented the high-performance car audio enclosure market when company founder and president Steve Irby developed the Original KICKER®. It was the first full-range speaker enclosure designed specifically for automotive use.

Stillwater Designs began in 1973 as a two-person operation, custom designing and building professional sound and musical instrument speaker systems for churches, auditoriums, and entertainers. Building upon the success of the Original Kicker, the company concentrated on the car audio market, applying research and design skills to the development of a complete line of high-performance components for car audio. Once a company with two employees in a single-car garage, it is now a corporation with more than 200 employees in facilities totaling more than 500,000 square feet. World headquarters are in Stillwater, Oklahoma.

The Kicker brand has a variety of high-performance car stereo products, including subwoofers, midrange and mid-bass drivers, tweeters, crossovers, matched component systems, speakers, and power amplifiers. Kicker is proud to have won the prestigious AudioVideo International Auto Sound Grand Prix Award, sponsored annually by *AudioVideo International* magazine. Winners are selected by retailers based on fidelity of sound reproduction, design engineering, reliability, craftsmanship and product integrity, and cost/performance ratio. In 2003, seven Kicker products earned Grand Prix awards. Awards emphasizing the performance of the company include the 2000 Governor's Award for Excellence in Exporting and the 1996 Oklahoma City International Trade Association designation as its International Business of the Year.

While Stillwater Designs originally handled research and design (R&D), manufacturing, and sales, it now concentrates primarily on R&D and sales. The bulk of manufacturing has been outsourced (performed by outside firms on a contract basis), although the company still builds some products and plans to build even more as it moves into its new facility for factory-installed audio systems. Engineering and audio research is Kicker president and CEO Steve Irby's first love, and he still heads its design team. The day-to-day involvement of top management, coupled with an energetic workforce of talented individuals in all areas of the company's operations and an innate ability to create truly musical components, has been the reason for the company's remarkable success.

OBJECTIVE ①
Explain the meaning of managerial accounting and contrast it to financial accounting.

The Meaning and Purpose of Managerial Accounting

What is managerial accounting? **Managerial accounting** is the provision of accounting information for a company's various *internal* users. Internal users of managerial accounting information include managers of all levels; executives such as the chief executive officer (CEO), chief financial officer (CFO), chief risk officer, and the like; members of the company's board of directors; employees such as the production floor worker, delivery truck driver, and the like; union members; and members of the company's audit committee.

The purpose of managerial accounting is to generate information that helps managers and other internal users take actions that create value for the organization. To accomplish its purpose, managerial accounting has three broad objectives:

1. To provide information for planning the organization's actions.
2. To provide information for controlling the organization's actions.
3. To provide information for making effective decisions.

Using recent examples from many companies in both the for-profit and not-for-profit sectors, this textbook explains how all manufacturing (e.g., aircraft producer—**Boeing** Corporation), merchandising (e.g., clothing retailer—**Victoria's Secret**), and service (e.g., healthcare provider—**The Cleveland Clinic**) organizations use managerial accounting information and concepts. For instance, hospital administrators, presidents of corporations, dentists, educational administrators, and city managers all can improve their managerial skills by being well grounded in the basic concepts and use of managerial accounting information for planning, controlling, and decision making. It should be noted that many companies (over 2,000 large multinationals in total) increasingly are deciding to release on their websites large quantities of managerial accounting information, typically given only to internal users, to the public through optional reports known as corporate sustainability reports (e.g., **Starbucks**, **McDonald's**), social responsibility reports (e.g., **Tomkins PLC**, **Chiquita**), or citizenship reports (e.g., **General Electric**). The release of these reports often occurs because firms want to manage their reputation by preparing and releasing such information themselves rather than having Internet bloggers, newspapers, and 24-hour cable news networks publish their own estimates of such information. Therefore, the demand for managerial accounting information continues to grow.

Information Needs of Managers and Other Users

Managerial accounting information is needed by a number of individuals. In particular, managers and empowered workers need comprehensive, up-to-date information for (1) planning, (2) controlling, and (3) decision making. Exhibit 1-1 shows the relationship among these activities.

The detailed formulation of action to achieve a particular end is the management activity called planning. **Planning** requires setting objectives and identifying methods to achieve those objectives. For example, a firm may set the objective of increasing its short-term and long-term profitability by improving the overall quality of its products. **DaimlerChrysler** drastically improved the quality and profitability of its **Chrysler** automobile division during the beginning of the 21st century to the point where its quality surpassed that of **Mercedes-Benz** (at the time, DaimlerChrysler owned both Mercedes–Benz and Chrysler).[1] By improving product quality, firms like DaimlerChrysler should be able to reduce scrap and rework, decrease the number of customer complaints and warranty work, reduce the resources currently assigned to inspection, and so on, thus increasing profitability. To realize these benefits, management must develop some specific methods that when implemented will lead to the achievement of the desired objective. A plant manager, for example, may start a supplier evaluation program to identify and select suppliers who are willing and able to supply defect-free parts. Empowered workers may be able to identify production causes of defects and create new methods for producing a product that will reduce scrap and rework and the need for inspection. The new methods should be clearly specified and detailed.

Planning is only half the battle. Once a plan is created, it must be implemented and monitored by managers and workers to ensure that the plan is being carried out as intended. The managerial activity of monitoring a plan's implementation and taking corrective action as needed is referred to as **controlling**. Control is usually achieved by comparing actual performance with expected performance. This information can be used to evaluate or

Exhibit 1-1

Uses of Managerial Accounting Information

Planning   Controlling   Decision Making

---

[1]Sarah A. Webster, and Joe Guy Collier, "Fixing a Car Company: Zetsche on Mercedes: 'A Lot of Work Is Ahead'," *Detroit Free Press* (September 27, 2005): http://www.freep.com/money/autonews/zetsche27e_20050927.htm.

correct the steps being taken to implement a plan. Based on the feedback, a manager (or worker) may decide to let the plan continue as is, take corrective action of some type to put the actions back in harmony with the original plan, or do some midstream replanning.

The managerial accounting information used for planning and control purposes can be either financial or nonfinancial in nature. For example, Duffy Tool and Stamping saved $14,300 per year by redesigning a press operation.[2] In one department, completed parts (made by a press) came down a chute and fell into a parts tub. When the tub became full, press operators had to stop operation while the stock operator removed the full tub and replaced it with an empty one. Workers redesigned the operation so that each press had a chute with two branches—each leading to a different tub. Now, when one tub is full, completed parts are routed into the other tub. The $14,300 savings are a financial measure of the success of the redesign. The redesign also eliminated machine downtime and increased the number of units produced per hour (operational feedback), both of which are examples of nonfinancial information. Both types of measures convey important information. Often, financial and nonfinancial feedback is given to managers in the form of performance reports that compare the actual data with planned data or other benchmarks. The process of choosing among competing alternatives is **decision making**. Decision making is intertwined with planning and control in that a manager cannot successfully plan or control the organization's actions without making decisions regarding competing alternatives. For instance, **BMW** plans to offer by 2009 a car that runs on gasoline and hydrogen. Decisions can be improved if information about the alternatives (e.g., pertaining to gasoline vs. hydrogen vs. hybrid combinations of these two automobile fuel options) is gathered and made available to managers. One of the major roles of the managerial accounting information system is to supply information that facilitates decision making. For example, Kicker's vice president of sales and marketing was wondering whether or not to hold tent sales in certain cities. He had information on sales, as well as the expense of putting on the tent sale. This revenue and cost information, along with the manager's knowledge of competitive conditions and customers' needs, will improve his ability to select appropriate cities for the tent sales.

Financial Accounting and Managerial Accounting

A brief examination of the basic differences between financial accounting and managerial accounting is helpful for understanding the emerging trends and important managerial accounting concepts discussed in the remainder of the chapter. The two basic kinds of accounting information systems are financial accounting and managerial accounting. **Financial accounting** is primarily concerned with producing financial information and reports (financial statements) for *external* users, such as investors, creditors (banks), government agencies, customers, suppliers, and other outside stakeholders (environmental groups, human rights groups). It must conform to certain rules and conventions that are defined by various agencies, such as the Securities Exchange Commission (SEC), the Financial Accounting Standards Board (FASB), and the International Accounting Standards Board (IASB). These rules pertain to issues such as the recognition of revenues; timing of expenses; and recording of assets, liabilities, and stockholders' equity. Financial accounting information has a historical orientation and is used for such things as investment decisions, monitoring activities, and regulatory measures.

The managerial accounting system produces information for all *internal* users. Specifically, managerial accounting identifies, collects, measures, classifies, and reports financial and nonfinancial information that is useful to internal users in planning, controlling, and decision making. While investors look at a firm's overall profitability, managers need to know the profitability of individual products as well. The managerial accounting system should be designed to provide both total profits and profits for individual products and, thus, has a broad audience. Flexibility is crucial—the managerial accounting system

---

[2]George F. Hanks, "Excellence Teams in Action," *Management Accounting* (February 1995): 35.

should be able to supply forward-looking information for different purposes, as explained throughout this textbook. Unlike financial accounting, managerial accounting is *not* subject to the requirements of generally accepted accounting principles. When comparing managerial accounting with financial accounting, several differences can be identified. Some of the more important differences follow and are summarized in Exhibit 1-2 at the bottom of this page.

- *Targeted users.* Managerial accounting focuses on providing information for internal users, while financial accounting focuses on providing information for external users.
- *Restrictions on inputs and processes.* Managerial accounting is not subject to the requirements of generally accepted accounting principles. The SEC and the FASB set the accounting procedures that must be followed for financial reporting. The inputs and processes of financial accounting are well defined and, in fact, restricted. Only certain kinds of economic events qualify as inputs, and processes must follow generally accepted methods. Unlike financial accounting, managerial accounting has no official body that prescribes the format, content, and rules for selecting inputs and processes and preparing financial reports. Managers are free to choose whatever information they want—provided it can be justified on a cost-benefit basis.
- *Type of information.* The restrictions imposed by financial accounting tend to produce objective and verifiable financial information. For managerial accounting, information may be financial or nonfinancial and may be much more subjective in nature.
- *Time orientation.* Financial accounting has a historical orientation. It records and reports events that have already happened. Although managerial accounting also records and reports events that have already occurred, it strongly emphasizes providing information about future events. Management, for example, may want to know what it will cost to produce a product next year. Knowing this information helps in planning material purchases and making pricing decisions, among other things. This future orientation is needed to support the managerial functions of planning and decision making.
- *Breadth.* Managerial accounting is much broader than financial accounting. It includes aspects of economics, industrial engineering, management science, and psychology, as well as numerous other areas.

Emerging Trends in Managerial Accounting and the Role of Managerial Accountants in an Organization

OBJECTIVE ②
Explain the current focus of managerial accounting and the role of managerial accountants in an organization.

The business environment in which companies operate has changed dramatically over the past several decades. For instance, advances in technology, the Internet, the opening of markets around the world, increased competitive pressures, and increased complexity of

Exhibit 1-2

Comparison of Managerial and Financial Accounting

Management Accounting	Financial Accounting
1. Internally focused.	1. Externally focused.
2. No mandatory rules.	2. Must follow externally imposed rules.
3. Financial and nonfinancial information; subjective information possible.	3. Objective financial information.
4. Emphasis on the future.	4. Historical orientation.
5. Internal evaluation and decisions based on very detailed information.	5. Information about the firm as a whole.
6. Broad, multidisciplinary.	6. More self-contained.

strategy (e.g., alliances between **McDonald's** and the **Walt Disney Company** for promotional tie-ins) and operations all have combined to produce a global business environment. Effective managerial accounting systems also have changed in order to provide information that helps improve companies' planning, control, and decision-making activities. Several important uses of managerial accounting resulting from these advances include new methods of estimating product and service profitability, understanding customer orientation, evaluating the business from a cross-functional perspective, and providing information useful in improving total quality.

New Methods of Estimating the Profitability of Products and Services

Companies need focused, accurate information on the cost of the products and services they offer. Years ago, a company might have produced a few products that were roughly similar to each other. Only the cost of materials and labor differed from one product to another. Figuring out the cost of each unit was relatively easy. Now, however, with rapid increases in technology and automation, it is more difficult to generate the costing information needed by management to make a wide variety of decisions. As Peter Drucker, internationally respected management guru, points out:

> *Traditional cost accounting in manufacturing does not record the cost of nonproducing such as the cost of faulty quality, or of a machine being out of order, or of needed parts not being on hand. Yet these unrecorded and uncontrolled costs in some plants run as high as the costs that traditional accounting does record. By contrast, a new method of cost accounting developed in the last ten years—called "activity-based" accounting— records all costs. And it relates them, as traditional accounting cannot, to value-added.*[3]

Activity-based costing (ABC) is a more detailed approach to determining the cost of goods and services. ABC improves costing accuracy by emphasizing the cost of the many activities or tasks that must be performed to produce a product or offer a service. **United Parcel Service Inc.** (UPS) used ABC to discover and manage the cost of the activities involved with shipping packages by truck, as opposed to by plane, in order to beat **FedEx** at its overnight delivery business in quick mid-distance (up to 500 miles) overnight deliveries.[4]

Customer Orientation

Customer value is a key focus, because firms can establish a competitive advantage by creating better customer value for the same or lower cost than competitors or creating equivalent value for lower cost than that of competitors. Customer value is the difference between what a customer receives and what the customer gives up when buying a product or service. Customers receive basic and special product features, service, quality, instructions for use, reputation, brand name, and other important factors. On the other hand, customers give up the cost of purchasing the product; the time and effort spent acquiring and learning to use the product; and the costs of using, maintaining, and disposing of it.

Strategic Positioning
Effective cost information can help the company identify strategies that increase customer value. Generally, firms choose one of two general strategies: (1) cost leadership and (2) superior products through differentiation

---

[3]Peter F. Drucker, "We Need to Measure, Not Count," *The Wall Street Journal* (April 13, 1993): A14.
[4]Charles Haddad, and Jack Ewing, "Ground Wars: UPS's Rapid Ascent Leaves FedEx Scrambling," *Business Week* (May 21, 2001): 64–68.

(e.g., highest performance quality, most desired product features, best customer service, etc.). The objective of the cost leadership strategy is to provide the same or better value to customers at a *lower* cost than competitors. A differentiation strategy, on the other hand, strives to increase customer value by providing something to customers not provided by competitors. For example, Best Buy's Geek Squad of computer technicians creates a competitive advantage for **Best Buy** by providing 24-hour in-home technical assistance for its customers. Accurate cost information is important to see whether or not the additional service provided by the Geek Squad adds more to revenue than it does to cost.

The Value-Chain   Successful pursuit of cost leadership and/or differentiation strategies requires an understanding of a firm's value chain. The **value chain** is the set of activities required to design, develop, produce, market, and deliver products and services, as well as provide support services to customers. Exhibit 1-3 illustrates the value chain. A managerial accounting system should track information about a wide variety of activities that span the value chain. For example, prior to issuing final approval for its iPhone, **Apple** spent considerable effort researching the cost of developing and manufacturing the iPhone, as well as the amount of money potential customers would be willing to spend to purchase it. Also, customer value can be increased by improving the speed of delivery and response. FedEx exploited this part of the value chain and successfully developed a service that was not being offered by the U.S. Postal Service. Today, many customers believe that delivery delayed is delivery denied, which indicates that a good managerial accounting system should develop and measure indicators of customer satisfaction.

Cross-Functional Perspective

In managing the value chain, a managerial accountant must understand and measure many functions of the business. Contemporary approaches to costing may include initial design and engineering costs, as well as manufacturing costs, and the costs of distribution, sales, and service. An individual well schooled in the various definitions of cost, who understands the shifting definitions of cost from the short-run to the long-run, can be invaluable in determining what information is relevant in decision making. For example, strategic decisions may require a cost definition that assigns the costs of all value-chain activities. In a long-run decision environment, the banking industry (e.g., **Bank One**) spends an estimated $500 million per year across all functional areas to perform

Exhibit 1-3

The Value Chain

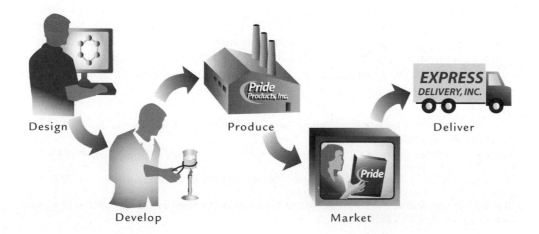

Design   Produce   Deliver

Develop   Market

customer profitability analyses that identify their most, and least, profitable customers.[5] However, a short-run decision to determine the profitability of a special order (e.g., an offer made to **Bridgestone Firestone North American Tire** at year-end to use idle machinery to produce 1,000 extra tires for a local tire distributor) may require only the incremental costs of the special order in a single functional area.

Total Quality Management

Continuous improvement is the continual search for ways to increase the overall efficiency and productivity of activities by reducing waste, increasing quality, and reducing costs. Managerial accounting information about the costs of products, customers, processes, and other objects of management interest can be the basis for identifying problems and alternative solutions.

Providing products with little waste that perform according to specifications are the twin objectives of world-class firms. A philosophy of **total quality management**, in which manufacturers strive to create an environment that will enable workers to manufacture perfect (zero-defect) products, has replaced the "acceptable quality" attitudes of the past. This emphasis on quality has also created a demand for a managerial accounting system that provides financial and nonfinancial information about quality. For example, in response to increasing customer complaints regarding its laptop computer repair process, **Toshiba** formed an alliance with UPS in which UPS picks up the broken laptop, fixes it, and returns the repaired laptop to the customer. In order for this alliance to work effectively, both Toshiba and UPS require relevant managerial accounting information regarding the cost of existing poor quality and efforts to improve future quality.[6]

Many companies, such as DaimlerChrysler, increasingly are using techniques like Six Sigma and Design for Six Sigma (DFSS) together with various types of cost information to achieve improved quality performance. Chrysler's goal is "to meet customer requirements and improve vehicle and system reliability while reducing development costs and cultivating innovation."[7] Many companies attempt to increase organizational value by eliminating wasteful activities that exist throughout the value chain. In eliminating such waste, companies usually find that their accounting must also change. This change in accounting, referred to as **lean accounting**, organizes costs according to the value chain and collects both financial and nonfinancial information. The objective is to provide information to managers that supports their waste reduction efforts and to provide financial statements that better reflect overall performance, using both financial and nonfinancial information.

Finally, one of the more recent charges of managerial accountants is to help carry out the company's **enterprise risk management** (ERM) approach. ERM is a formal way for managerial accountants to identify and respond to the most important threats and business opportunities facing the organization and is becoming increasingly important for long-term success. For example, **Wal-Mart**'s expert crisis management processes and teams repeatedly responded to the aftermath of Hurricane Katrina throughout Louisiana and Mississippi better and faster than did either local or federal government agencies (e.g., FEMA)![8] Matell's management of its recall involving 18 million toys as a result of the dangerous small magnets and lead paint used by Chinese manufacturers further illustrates the importance of managerial accounting information for decision making.

---

[5]Rick Brooks, "Unequal Treatment: Alienating Customers Isn't Always a Bad Idea, Many Firms Discover," *The Wall Street Journal* (January 7, 1999): A1.

[6]Thomas L. Friedman, "*The World Is Flat: A Brief History of the Twenty-First Century*," New York, New York, 2005. Farrar, Straus and Giroux, New York.

[7]Kevin Kelly, "Chrysler Continues Quality Push," WardsAuto.com. Retrieved September 30, 2005, from http://wardsauto.com/microsites/newsarticle.asp.

[8]Ann Zimmerman, and Valerie Bauerlein,"At Wal-Mart, Emergency Plan Has Big Payoff," *The Wall Street Journal*, (September 12, 2005): B1.

The Role of the Managerial Accountant—Preparing and Communicating Information

Managerial accountants must support management in all phases of business decision making. They must be intelligent, well prepared, up-to-date with new developments, and familiar with the customs and practices of all countries in which their firms operate. They are expected to be knowledgeable about the legal environment of business and, in particular, about the Sarbanes-Oxley Act of 2002.

Kicker's organization chart is shown in Exhibit 1-4. The **controller**, or chief accounting officer, for Kicker is located in the administration department. She supervises all accounting functions and reports directly to the general manager and chief operating officer (COO). Because of the critical role that managerial accounting plays in the operation of an organization, the controller is often viewed as a member of the top management team and is encouraged to participate in planning, controlling, and decision-making activities. As the chief accounting officer, the controller has responsibility for both internal and external accounting requirements. In larger firms, this charge may include direct responsibility for internal auditing, cost accounting, financial accounting (including SEC reports and financial statements), systems accounting (including analysis, design, and internal controls), and taxes. In larger companies, the controller is separate from the treasury department. The **treasurer** is responsible for the finance function. Specifically, the treasurer raises capital and manages cash and investments. The treasurer may also be in charge of credit and collection and insurance.

Finally, successful managerial accountants at all levels of the organization must communicate with other personnel—both accounting and nonaccounting—within the organization. Knowing how to "crunch the numbers" is necessary but not sufficient for managerial accounting information to be used successfully. CFOs increasingly expect managerial accountants to be able to help senior executives better understand

Exhibit 1-4

Kicker Inc. Organizational Chart

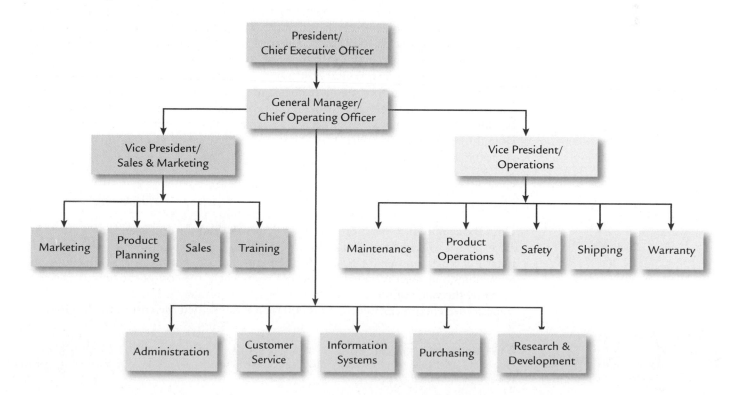

managerial accounting information in order to analyze complex business decisions.[9] This communications-based challenge for managerial accountants is growing in importance and offers exciting opportunities for well-versed managerial accountants to demonstrate their ability to add value to the organization.

Sarbanes-Oxley Act of 2002

In June 2002, Congress passed the **Sarbanes-Oxley Act (SOX)**. This legislation was passed in response to the collapse of Enron and the revelations of securities fraud and accounting misconduct associated with companies such as **WorldCom**, **Adelphia**, and **HealthSouth**. The SOX Act established stronger government control and regulation of public companies in the United States. SOX applies to **publicly traded companies**, which issue stock traded on U.S. stock exchanges. Major sections of SOX include establishment of the Public Company Accounting Oversight Board (PCAOB), enhanced auditor independence, tightened regulation of corporate governance, control over management, and assessment of the firm's internal controls. SOX also led to increased attention to corporate ethics, discussed later in this chapter. Managerial accountants, through the offices of internal auditing or the CFO, are the people in the organization who are expected to help their organizations comply with SOX.

OBJECTIVE ③
Explain the meaning of cost and how costs are assigned to products and services.

The Meaning and Uses of Cost

An important task of managerial accounting is to determine the cost of products, services, customers, and other items of interest to managers. Therefore, we need to understand the meaning of cost and the ways in which costs can be used to make decisions, both for small, entrepreneurial businesses and large, international businesses. For example, consider a small gourmet restaurant and its owner Courtney, who also is the head chef. In addition to understanding the complexities of gourmet food preparation, Courtney needs to understand the breakdown of the restaurant's costs into various categories in order to make effective operating decisions. Cost categories of particular interest would include direct costs (food and beverages) and indirect costs (laundry of linens). On a larger scale, local banks operating in college communities often look at the cost of providing basic checking account services to students. These accounts typically lose money—that is, the accounts cost more to service than they yield in fees and interest revenue. However, the bank finds that students already banking with them are more likely to take out student loans through the bank, and these loans are very profitable. As a result, the bank may actually decide to expand its offerings to students when the related loan business is considered. Now, let's define *cost* and more fully describe its managerial importance.

Cost

Cost is the amount of cash or cash equivalent sacrificed for goods and/or services that are expected to bring a current or future benefit to the organization. If a furniture manufacturer buys lumber for $10,000, then the cost of that lumber is $10,000 cash. Sometimes, one asset is traded for another asset. Then, the cost of the new asset is measured by the value of the asset given up (the cash equivalent). If the same manufacturer trades office equipment valued at $8,000 for a forklift, then the cost of the forklift is the

---

[9]Chris Rutledge, and Roseanne Williams, "A Seat at the Table," *Outlook Journal* (June 2004). Retrieved October 6, 2005, from http://www.accenture.com/Global/Research_and_Insights/Outlook/ By_Alphabet/ ASeatAtTheTable.htm.

$8,000 value of the office equipment traded for it. Cost is a dollar measure of the resources used to achieve a given benefit. Managers strive to minimize the cost of achieving benefits. Reducing the cost required to achieve a given benefit means that a firm is becoming more efficient.

Costs are incurred to produce future benefits. In a profit-making firm, those benefits usually mean revenues. As costs are used up in the production of revenues, they are said to expire. Expired costs are called **expenses**. On the income statement, expenses are deducted from revenues to determine income (also called *profit*). For a company to remain in business, revenues must be larger than expenses. In addition, the income earned must be large enough to satisfy the owners of the firm.

We can look more closely at the relationship between cost and revenue by focusing on the units sold. The revenue per unit is called **price**. In our everyday conversation, we have a tendency to use cost and price as synonyms, because the price of an item (e.g., a CD) is the cost to us. However, accounting courses take the viewpoint of the owner of the company. In that case, cost and price are *not* the same. Price must be greater than cost in order for the firm to earn income. Hence, managers need to know cost and trends in cost.

Accumulating and Assigning Costs

Accumulating costs is the way that costs are measured and recorded. The accounting system typically does this job very well. When a telephone bill comes into the company, the bookkeeper records an addition to the Telephone Expense account and an addition to the liability account, Accounts Payable. In this way, the cost is *accumulated*. At the end of the year, it would be easy to tell the total spending on telephone expense. However, that information usually is not enough. The company also wants to know why the money was spent. In other words, it wants to know how costs were assigned to cost objects.

Here's The Real Kicker

Kicker collects and analyzes many types of costs. In the manufacturing area, the company keeps track of direct materials, direct labor, and overhead. These costs, of course, make up the cost of goods sold that go on Kicker's monthly income statement. Nonmanufacturing costs include the costs of marketing and administration. However, this information is decomposed into a series of accounts that helps Kicker's management in budgeting and decision making.

The marketing function, for example, is broken down into three areas: selling, customer service, and marketing. Selling works directly with dealers and outside sales reps. Customer service handles calls from dealers and decides whether or not a problem is covered under warranty. Marketing is responsible for advertising, promotions, and the tent shows. One of the largest promotions is Kicker's annual Big Air Bash, an extravaganza of music, food, cars, and extreme sports demonstrations. Held in conjunction with the SEMA (Specialty Equipment Market Association) show, the Big Air Bash is held outside the Hard Rock Hotel and Casino in Las Vegas. The expenses associated with the show include the modification of show cars in Kicker's in-house garage. For the 2003 Big Bash, Kicker mechanics customized a new Dodge Neon. The trunk and back seat

area were virtually gutted to make room for 12 speakers and heavy-duty amps. With a souped-up engine, new fiberglass exterior, and trick paint, the car was ready for show. Other "veteran" show cars and pickup trucks were refreshed with additional trick paint, larger tires, and Kicker's newest amps and speakers. You could feel the music from outside a truck.

Tent shows are smaller scale affairs held several times a year in the central and south-central United States. Kicker brings its semitrailer full of products and sound equipment, as well as a couple show trucks. Then, a large tent is set up to sell Kicker merchandise, explain products, and sell the previous year's models at greatly reduced prices. Fun and relaxed, the tent shows appeal to Kicker's customer base and provide a chance for a look at the new models. The cost of each tent show is carefully tracked and compared with that show's revenue. Sites that don't provide sales revenue greater than cost are not booked for the coming year.

Like many companies today, Kicker tracks costs carefully to use in decision making. The general cost categories in this chapter help the company to organize cost information and relate it to decision making.

Assigning costs is the way that a cost is linked to some cost object. A cost object is something for which a company wants to know the cost. For example, of the total telephone expense, how much was for the sales department and how much was for manufacturing? *Assigning* costs tells the company why the money was spent. In this case, cost assignment tells the company whether the money spent on telephone expense was to support the manufacturing or the selling of the product. As we will discuss in later chapters, cost assignment typically is more difficult than cost accumulation.

Cost Objects

Managerial accounting systems are structured to measure and assign costs to entities called *cost objects*. A **cost object** is any item such as a product, customer, department, project, geographic region, plant, and so on for which costs are measured and assigned. For example, if **Fifth Third Bank** wants to determine the cost of a platinum credit card, then the cost object is the platinum credit card. All costs related to the platinum card are added in, such as the cost of mailings to potential customers, the cost of telephone lines dedicated to the card, the portion of the computer department that processes platinum card transactions and bills, and so on. In a more personal example, suppose that you are considering taking a course during the summer session. Taking the course is the cost object, and the cost would include tuition, books, fees, transportation, and (possibly) housing.

We will discuss various methods of assigning costs to cost objects in the succeeding chapters.

Concept Q&A

Make a list of the costs that you are incurring for your classes this term. Which costs are direct costs for your college course(s)? Which costs are indirect? Now, from your list of total costs, which ones are direct costs of this course? Which are indirect?

Answers will vary.

Assigning Costs to Cost Objects

Costs can be assigned to cost objects in a number of ways. Relatively speaking, some methods are more accurate, while others are simpler. The choice of a method depends on a number of factors, such as the need for accuracy. The notion of accuracy is a relative concept and has to do with the reasonableness and logic of the cost assignment methods used. The objective is to measure and assign costs as well as possible, given management objectives. For example, suppose you and three of your good friends go out to dinner at a local pizza parlor. When the bill comes, it totals $36. How much is your share? One easy way to figure it is to divide the bill evenly among you and your friends; you would each owe $9 ($36/4). But suppose that one of you had a small salad and drink (totaling $5) while another had a specialty pizza, appetizer, and beer (totaling $15). Clearly, it is possible to identify what each person had and assign cost that way. The second method is more accurate but also more work. Which method you choose will depend on how important it is to you to assign the specific meal costs to each individual. It is the same way in accounting. There are a number of ways to assign costs to cost objects. Some methods are quick and easy but may be inaccurate. Other methods are much more accurate but also much more work (in business, more work equals more expense).

Tracing Direct Costs
Direct costs are those costs that can be easily and accurately traced to a cost object. When we say that a cost is easy to trace, we often mean that the relationship between the cost and the object can be physically observed and is easy to track. The more costs that can be traced to the object, the more accurate are the cost assignments. For example, suppose that Chef Courtney, from our earlier discussion, wanted to know the cost of emphasizing fresh, in-season fruits and vegetables in her

entrees. The cost of the fruits and vegetables would be relatively easy to determine and, thus, would be direct costs with respect to the meals prepared and sold. Some costs, however, are hard to trace. **Indirect costs** are costs that cannot be easily and accurately traced to a cost object. For example, Courtney incurs additional costs in scouting the outlying farms and farmers markets (as opposed to simply ordering fruits and vegetables from a distributor). She must use her own time and automobile to make the trips. Farmers markets may not deliver, so Courtney must arrange for a co-worker with a van to pick up the produce. By definition, fruits and vegetables that are currently in-season will be out of season (i.e., unavailable) in a few weeks. This means that Courtney must spend much more time revising menus and developing new recipes that can be adapted to restaurant conditions. These costs are difficult to assign to the meals prepared and sold. Therefore, they are indirect costs. Exhibit 1-5 shows direct and indirect costs being assigned to cost objects.

Assigning Indirect Costs   Even though indirect costs cannot be traced to cost objects, it is still important to assign them. This assignment usually is accomplished by using allocation. **Allocation** means that an indirect cost is assigned to a cost object by using a reasonable and convenient method. Since no causal relationship readily exists, allocating indirect costs is based on convenience or some assumed linkage. For example, consider the cost of heating and lighting a plant in which five products are manufactured. How can we assign the utility cost to the five products? It is hard to see any causal relationship. A convenient way to allocate this cost is to assign it in proportion to the direct labor hours used by each product. This method is relatively easy and accomplishes the purpose of ensuring that all costs are assigned to units produced. Allocating indirect costs may be important for a variety of purposes. For example, allocating indirect costs to products is needed to determine the value of inventory and of cost of goods sold. Perhaps more important, as companies become more complex in the number and types of products and services they offer to customers, the need to understand, allocate, and

Exhibit 1-5

Object Costing

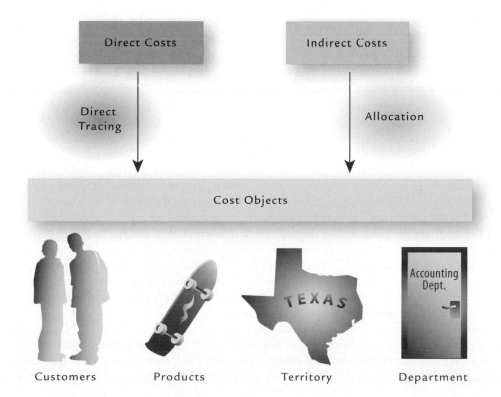

effectively control indirect costs becomes increasingly important. In addition, indirect costs represent an increasingly large percentage of total costs for many companies.

Direct and indirect costs occur in service businesses as well. For example, a bank's cost of printing and mailing monthly statements to checking account holders is a direct cost of the product—checking accounts. However, the cost of office furniture in the bank is an indirect cost for the checking accounts.

Other Categories of Cost
In addition to being categorized as either direct or indirect, costs also are analyzed with respect to their behavior patterns, or the way in which a cost changes when the level of the output changes. A **variable cost** is one that increases in total as output increases and decreases in total as output decreases. For example, the denim used in making jeans is a variable cost. As the company makes more jeans, it needs more denim. A **fixed cost** is a cost that in total does not increase as output increases and does not decrease as output decreases. For example, the cost of property taxes on the factory building stays the same no matter how many pairs of jeans the company makes. How can that be, since property taxes can and do change? While the cost changes, it is not because output changes. Rather, it changes because the city or county government decides to raise taxes. Variable and fixed costs are covered more extensively in Chapter 2.

Notice that you could also include the foregone earnings from a summer job. An **opportunity cost** is the benefit given up or sacrificed when one alternative is chosen over another. Thus, the foregone earnings from a summer job would be an opportunity cost. Opportunity cost differs from accounting costs in that the opportunity cost is never included in the accounting records because it is the cost of something that did not occur. Opportunity costs are important to decision making, and we will see that more clearly in Chapter 11.

We will discuss various methods of assigning costs to cost objects in the succeeding chapters.

Product and Service Costs

OBJECTIVE ④
Define the various costs of manufacturing products and providing services.

Output represents one of the most important cost objects. There are two types of output: products and services. **Products** are goods produced by converting raw materials through the use of labor and indirect manufacturing resources, such as the manufacturing plant, land, and machinery. Televisions, hamburgers, automobiles, computers, clothes, and furniture are examples of products. **Services** are tasks or activities performed for a customer or an activity performed by a customer using an organization's products or facilities. Insurance coverage, medical care, dental care, funeral care, and accounting are examples of service activities performed for customers. Car rental, video rental, and skiing are examples of services where the customer uses an organization's products or facilities. Organizations that produce products are called **manufacturing organizations**. Organizations that provide services are called **service organizations**. Managers of both types of organizations need to know how much individual products or services cost. Accurate cost information is vital for profitability analysis and strategic decisions concerning product design, pricing, and product mix. Incidentally, retail organizations, such as **J. Crew**, buy finished products from other organizations, such as manufacturers, and then sell them to customers. The accounting for inventory and cost of goods sold for retail organizations is much simpler than for manufacturing organizations and usually covered extensively in introductory financial accounting courses. Therefore, the focus here is on manufacturing and service organizations.

Services differ from products in many ways. First, a service is intangible. The buyers of services cannot see, feel, hear, or taste a service before it is bought. Second, services are perishable; they cannot be stored for future use by a consumer but must be consumed when performed. Inventory valuation, so important for products, is not an issue for services. In other words, because service organizations do not produce and sell products as part of their regular operations, they have no inventory asset on the balance sheet. Third, providers of services and buyers of services must usually be in direct contact for an exchange to take place. For example, an eye examination requires both the patient and the optometrist to be present. However, producers of products need not have direct contact with the buyers of their goods. Thus, buyers of automobiles never need to have contact with the engineers and assembly line workers who produced their automobiles. The overall way in which a company costs services in terms of classifying related costs as either direct or indirect is very similar to the way in which it costs products. The main difference in costing is that products have inventories and services do not.

Ethics Tracking costs can also act as an early warning system for unauthorized activity and possible ethical problems. For example, **Metropolitan Life Insurance Company** was dismayed to learn that some of its agents were selling policies as retirement plans. This practice is illegal, and it cost the company more than $20 million in fines as well as $50 million in refunds to policyholders. More accurate and comprehensive data tracking regarding sales, individual agents, types of policies, and policyholders could have alerted Metropolitan Life to a potential problem. Thus, we can see that tracking costs can serve many different and important purposes.◆

Determining Product Cost

Managerial accountants must decide what types of managerial accounting information to provide to managers, how to measure such information, and when and to whom to communicate the information. For example, when making most strategic and operating decisions, managers typically rely on managerial accounting information that is prepared in whatever manner the managerial accountant believes provides the best analysis for the decision at hand. Therefore, the majority of managerial accounting issues explained in this book do not reference a formal set of external rules but instead consider the context of the given decision (e.g., relevant vs. irrelevant cost information for make-or-buy decisions, full cost vs. functional cost information for pricing decisions, etc.).

However, there is one major exception. Managerial accountants must follow specific external reporting rules (i.e., generally accepted accounting principles) when their companies provide outside parties with cost information about the amount of ending inventory on the balance sheet and the cost of goods sold on the income statement. In order to calculate these two amounts, managerial accountants must subdivide costs into functional categories: production and period (i.e., nonproduction). The following section describes the process for categorizing costs as either product or period in nature.

Product (manufacturing) costs are those costs, both direct and indirect, of producing a product in a manufacturing firm or of acquiring a product in a merchandising firm and preparing it for sale. Therefore, only costs in the *production* section of the value chain are included in product costs. A key feature of product costs is that they are inventoried. Product costs initially are added to an inventory account and remain in inventory until they are sold, at which time they are transferred to cost of goods sold (COGS). Product costs can be further classified as direct materials, direct labor, and manufacturing overhead, which are the three cost elements that can be assigned to products for external financial reporting (e.g., inventories or COGS). Exhibit 1-6 on the next page shows how direct materials, direct labor, and overhead become product costs.

Direct Materials **Direct materials** are those materials that are a part of the final product and can be directly traced to the goods being produced. The cost of these materials can be directly charged to products because physical observation can be used to measure the quantity used by each product. Materials that become part of a product usually are classified as direct materials. For example, tires on a new **Porsche** automobile, wood in an **Ethan Allen** dining room table, alcohol in an **Estee Lauder** cologne, and denim in a pair of **American Eagle** jeans are all part of direct materials for manufacturers of these products.

Exhibit 1-6

Product Costs Include Direct Materials, Direct Labor, and Overhead

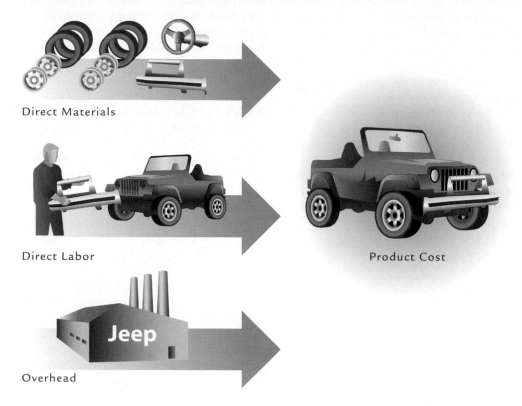

Direct Materials

Direct Labor

Overhead

Product Cost

A closely related term is *raw materials*. Often, the inventory of materials is called the *raw materials account*. Materials in the raw materials account do not become *direct materials* until they are withdrawn from inventory for use in production. The raw materials inventory account can include indirect materials as well as direct materials. Indirect materials are used in the production process, but the amount used by each unit cannot be easily determined, and as a result, these costs are treated as indirect costs (as discussed in the following section).

Direct Labor

Direct labor is the labor that can be directly traced to the goods being produced. Physical observation can be used to measure the amount of labor used to produce a product. Those employees who convert direct materials into a product are classified as direct labor. For example, workers on an assembly line at **Dell Computers** are classified as direct labor.

Just as there were indirect materials in a company, there may also be indirect labor. This labor is not direct labor, as these workers do not actually make the product. However, their contribution is necessary to production. An example of indirect labor in a production setting is the maintenance crew who performs regularly scheduled preventative maintenance every other Wednesday morning in **Georgia Pacific**'s plywood manufacturing plants. Indirect labor is included in overhead and, therefore, is an indirect cost rather than a direct cost.

Manufacturing Overhead

All product costs other than direct materials and direct labor are put into a category called **manufacturing overhead**. In a manufacturing firm, manufacturing overhead also is known as *factory burden* or *indirect* manufacturing costs. Costs are included as manufacturing overhead if they cannot be traced to the cost object of interest (e.g., unit of product). The manufacturing overhead cost category contains a wide variety of items. Examples of manufacturing overhead costs include depreciation on plant buildings and equipment, janitorial and maintenance labor, plant supervision, materials handling, power for plant utilities, and plant property taxes. The important thing to remember is that all costs in the factory are classified as direct materials, direct labor, or manufacturing overhead. No cost can be omitted from classification, no matter how far removed you might think it is from the actual production of a product. Earlier, we mentioned that indirect materials and indirect labor are included in overhead. In manufacturing, the glue used in furniture or toys is an example, as is the cost of oil to grease cookie sheets for producing cookies.

Concept Q&A

Look up and focus on any object in the room. What do you think the direct materials might include? What kind of direct labor might have worked on that item? Finally, what types of overhead costs might have been incurred by the company that produced it?

Answers will vary.

Total Product Cost   The total product cost equals the sum of direct materials, direct labor, and manufacturing overhead. The unit product cost equals total product cost divided by the number of units produced. Cornerstone 1-1 shows how to calculate total product cost and per-unit product cost.

Product costs include direct materials, direct labor, and manufacturing overhead. Once the product is finished, no more costs attach to it. That is, any costs associated with storing, selling, and delivering the product are not product costs but instead are period costs.

Prime and Conversion Costs   Product costs of direct materials, direct labor, and manufacturing overhead are sometimes grouped into prime cost and conversion cost. **Prime cost** is the sum of direct materials cost and direct labor cost. **Conversion cost** is the sum of direct labor cost and manufacturing overhead cost. For a manufacturing firm, conversion cost can be interpreted as the cost of converting raw materials into a final product. Cornerstone 1-2 on page 20 shows how to calculate prime cost and conversion cost for a manufactured product.

Determining Period Costs

The costs of production are assets that are carried in inventories until the goods are sold. There are other costs of running a company, referred to as period costs, that are not carried in inventory. Thus, **period costs** are all costs that are not product costs (i.e., all areas

---

HOW TO Calculate Product Cost in Total and Per Unit

Information: BlueDenim Company makes blue jeans. Last week, direct materials (denim, thread, zippers, and rivets) costing $48,000 were put into production. Direct labor of $30,000 (50 workers × 40 hrs. × $15 per hr.) was incurred. Manufacturing overhead equaled $72,000. By the end of the week, the company had manufactured 30,000 pairs of jeans.

Required: Calculate the total product cost for last week. Calculate the cost of one pair of jeans that was produced last week.

**CORNERSTONE
1-1**

Calculation:

Direct materials	$ 48,000
Direct labor	30,000
Manufacturing overhead	72,000
Total product cost	$150,000

Per-unit product cost = $150,000/30,000 = $5

Therefore, one pair of jeans costs $5 to produce.

**CORNERSTONE
1-2**

HOW TO Calculate Prime Cost and Conversion Cost in Total and Per Unit

Information: BlueDenim Company makes blue jeans. Last week, direct materials (denim, thread, zippers, and rivets) costing $48,000 were put into production. Direct labor of $30,000 (50 workers × 40 hrs. × $15 per hr.) was incurred. Manufacturing overhead equaled $72,000. By the end of the week, the company had manufactured 30,000 pairs of jeans.

Required: Calculate the total prime cost for last week. Calculate the per-unit prime cost. Calculate the total conversion cost for last week. Calculate the per-unit conversion cost.

Calculation:

Direct materials	$48,000
Direct labor	30,000
Total prime cost	$78,000

Per-unit prime cost = $78,000/30,000 = $2.60

Direct labor	$30,000
Manufacturing overhead	72,000
Total conversion cost	$102,000

Per-unit conversion cost = $102,000/30,000 = $3.40

Note: Remember that prime cost and conversion cost do NOT equal total product cost. This is because direct labor is part of BOTH prime cost and conversion cost.

of the value chain except for production). Period costs cannot be assigned to products or appear as part of the reported values of inventories on the balance sheet. Instead, period costs typically are expensed in the period in which they are incurred. The cost of office supplies, research and development activities, and the CEO's salary are examples of such period costs. However, if a period cost is expected to provide an economic benefit (i.e., revenues) beyond the next one year, then it is recorded as an asset (i.e., capitalized) and allocated to expense through depreciation over its useful life. The cost associated with the purchase of a delivery truck is an example of a period cost that would be capitalized when incurred and then recognized as an expense over the useful life of the truck. Exhibit 1-7 depicts the distinction between product and period costs and how each type of cost eventually becomes an expense on the income statement. As shown in the exhibit, product costs, which are capitalized as an inventory asset, are expensed on the income statement as cost of goods sold to match against the revenues generated from the sale of the inventory. However, capitalized period costs are depreciated to expense on the income statement over the asset's useful life to match against the revenues generated by the asset over its useful life.

In a manufacturing organization, the level of period costs can be significant (often greater than 25 percent of sales revenue), and controlling them may bring greater cost savings than the same effort exercised in controlling production costs. For example, in 2006, **Nike**'s period expenses were 35% of its revenue ($5,195,000,000/$14,954,900,000)! For service organizations, the relative importance of selling and administrative costs depends on the nature of the service produced. Physicians and dentists, for example, do relatively little marketing and thus have very low selling costs. On the other hand, a grocery chain may incur substantial marketing costs. Period costs often are divided into selling costs and administrative costs.

Exhibit 1-7

The Impact of Product versus Period Costs on the Income Statement

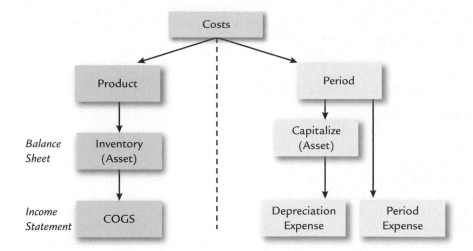

Selling Costs Those costs necessary to market, distribute, and service a product or service are **selling costs**. They are often referred to as *order-getting* and *order-filling* costs. Examples of selling costs include salaries and commissions of sales personnel, advertising, warehousing, shipping, and customer service. The first two items are examples of order-getting costs; the last three are examples of order-filling costs.

Administrative Costs All costs associated with research, development, and general administration of the organization that cannot reasonably be assigned to either selling or production are **administrative costs**. General administration has the responsibility of ensuring that the various activities of the organization are properly integrated so that the overall mission of the firm is realized. The president of the firm, for example, is concerned with the efficiency of selling, production, and research and development activities. Proper integration of these activities is essential to maximizing the overall profits of a firm. Examples of general administrative costs are executive salaries, legal fees, printing the annual report, and general accounting. Research and development costs are the costs associated with designing and developing new products and must be expensed in the period incurred.

As with product costs, oftentimes it is helpful for various purposes to distinguish between direct period costs and indirect period costs. Service companies also make this important distinction. For example, a surgical center would show that surgical gauze and anesthesia are direct costs used for an operation because it could be determined how much gauge or anesthesia was used for each procedure or patient. Other examples of direct costs in service industries include the chef in a restaurant, a surgical nurse attending an open-heart operation, and a pilot for **Southwest Airlines**.

Alternately, although shampoo and hair spray are used in a beauty shop, the exact amount used in each individual's hair cut or procedure likely is not easily determinable. As a result, the costs associated with shampoo and hair spray would be considered indirect, or overhead, costs and allocated, rather than traced, to individual hair cuts. Examples of indirect labor costs in a service setting include the surgical assistants in a hospital who clean up the operating room after surgery, dispose of certain used materials, and sterilize the reusable instruments. Indirect labor is included in overhead. The rental of a Santa suit for the annual company Christmas party would be an example of an indirect cost that would be expensed in the period incurred. Although these costs do not affect the calculation of inventories or cost of goods sold (i.e., because they are service companies), their correct classification as direct or indirect nonetheless affects numerous decisions and planning and control activities for managers, as we will discuss in detail in future chapters.

OBJECTIVE ⑤
Prepare income statements for manufacturing and service organizations.

Preparing Income Statements

The definitions of product, selling, and administrative costs are a good overview of the concepts of these costs. However, actually figuring these costs in practice is a bit more complicated. Let's take a closer look at just how costs are calculated for purposes of preparing the external financial statements.

Cost of Goods Manufactured

The **cost of goods manufactured** represents the total product cost of goods *completed* during the current period and transferred to finished goods inventory. The only costs assigned to goods completed are the manufacturing costs of direct materials, direct labor, and manufacturing overhead. So, why don't we just add together the current period's costs of direct materials, direct labor, and manufacturing overhead to arrive at cost of goods sold? The reason is inventories of materials or work in process. For instance, some of the materials purchased in the current period likely were used in production (i.e., transferred from materials inventory to work in process inventory during the period). However, other materials likely were not used in production and, thus, remain in materials inventory at period end. Also, some of the units that were worked on (and thus allocated labor and manufacturing overhead costs) in the current period likely were completed during the period (i.e., transferred from work in process inventory to finished goods inventory during the period). However, other units worked on during the period likely were not completed during the period and, thus, remain in work in process inventory at period end. In calculating cost of goods sold, we need to distinguish between the total manufacturing cost for the current period and the manufacturing costs associated with the units that were completed during the current period (i.e., cost of goods manufactured).

Let's take a look at direct materials. Suppose a company had no materials on hand at the beginning of the month, then bought $15,000 of direct materials during the month and used all of them in production. The entire $15,000 would be properly called *direct materials*. Usually, though, the company does have some materials on hand at the beginning of the month. These materials are the beginning inventory of materials. Let's say that this beginning inventory of materials cost $2,500. Then, during the month, the company would have a total of $17,500 of materials that could be used in production ($2,500 from beginning inventory and $15,000 purchased during the month). Typically, the company would not use the entire amount of materials on hand in production. Perhaps they use only $12,000 of materials. Then, the cost of direct materials is used in production this month is $12,000, and the remaining $5,500 of materials is the ending inventory of materials. This reasoning can be easily expressed in a formula.

$$\begin{matrix} \text{Beginning} \\ \text{inventory} \\ \text{of materials} \end{matrix} + \text{Purchases} - \begin{matrix} \text{Direct materials} \\ \text{used in production} \end{matrix} = \begin{matrix} \text{Ending inventory} \\ \text{of materials} \end{matrix}$$

While the above computation is logical and simple, it does not express the result that we are usually looking for. We are usually trying to figure out the amount of direct materials used in production, not the amount of ending inventory. Cornerstone 1-3 gives the "How To" to compute the amount of direct materials used in production.

Once the direct materials are calculated, the direct labor and manufacturing overhead *for the time period* can be added to get the total manufacturing cost for the period. Now, we need to consider the second type of inventory—Work in Process. **Work in Process**, often abbreviated as **WIP**, is the cost of the partially completed goods that are still on the factory floor at the end of a time period. These are units that have been started but are not finished. They have value but not as much as they will when they are done. Just as there are beginning and ending inventories of materials, there are

HOW TO Calculate the Direct Materials Used in Production

Information: BlueDenim Company makes blue jeans. On May 1, BlueDenim had $68,000 of materials in inventory. During the month of May, the company purchased $210,000 of materials. On May 31, materials inventory equaled $22,000.

Required: Calculate the direct materials used in production for the month of May.

Calculation:

Materials inventory, May 1	$ 68,000
Purchases	210,000
Materials inventory, May 31	(22,000)
Direct materials used in production	$256,000

**CORNERSTONE
1-3**

beginning and ending inventories of WIP. We must adjust the total manufacturing cost for the time period for the inventories of WIP. When that is done, we will have the total cost of the goods that were completed and transferred from work in process inventory to finished goods inventory during the time period. Cornerstone 1-4 shows how to calculate the cost of goods manufactured for a particular time period.

HOW TO Calculate Cost of Goods Manufactured

Information: Recall that BlueDenim Company makes blue jeans. During the month of May, the company purchased $210,000 of materials. On May 31, materials inventory equaled $22,000. During the month of May, BlueDenim Company incurred direct labor cost of $135,000 and manufacturing overhead of $150,000. Inventory information is as follows:

	May 1	May 31
Materials	$68,000	$22,000
WIP	50,000	16,000

Required: Calculate the cost of goods manufactured for the month of May. Calculate the cost of one pair of jeans, assuming that 115,000 pairs of jeans were completed during May.

Calculation:

Direct materials*	$256,000
Direct labor	135,000
Manufacturing overhead	150,000
Total manufacturing cost for May	$541,000
WIP, May 1	50,000
WIP, May 31	(16,000)
Cost of goods manufactured	$575,000

*Direct materials = $68,000 + $210,000 − $22,000 = $256,000
This was calculated in Cornerstone 1-3.

Per-unit cost of goods manufactured = $575,000/115,000 units = $5

**CORNERSTONE
1-4**

Cost of Goods Sold

To meet external reporting requirements, costs must be classified into three categories: production, selling, and administration. Remember that product costs are initially put into inventory. They become expenses only when the products are sold, which matches the expenses of manufacturing the product to the sales revenue generated by the product at the time it is sold. Therefore, the expense of manufacturing is not the cost of goods manufactured; instead, it is the cost of the goods that are sold. **Cost of goods sold** represents the cost of goods that were sold during the period and, therefore, transferred from finished goods inventory on the balance sheet to cost of goods sold on the income statement (i.e., as an inventory expense). Cornerstone 1-5 shows how to calculate the cost of goods sold.

The ending inventories of materials, WIP, and finished goods are important because they are assets and appear on the balance sheet (as current assets). The cost of goods sold is an expense that appears on the income statement. Selling and administrative costs are period costs and also appear on the income statement as an expense.

Income Statement: Manufacturing Firm

The income statement for a manufacturing firm is displayed in Cornerstone 1-6. This income statement follows the traditional format taught in an introductory financial accounting course. Notice that the income statement covers a certain period of time (i.e., the month of May in Cornerstone 1-6). However, the time period may well be a quarter or a year. The key point is that all sales revenue and expenses attached to that period of time appear on the income statement.

**CORNERSTONE
1-5**

HOW TO Calculate Cost of Goods Sold

Information: Recall that BlueDenim Company makes blue jeans. During the month of May, 115,000 pairs of jeans were completed at a cost of goods manufactured of $575,000. Suppose that on May 1, BlueDenim had 10,000 units in finished goods inventory costing $50,000, and on May 31, the company had 26,000 units in finished goods inventory costing $130,000.

Required: Prepare a cost of goods sold statement for the month of May. Calculate the number of pairs of jeans that were sold during May.

Calculation:

BlueDenim Company
Cost of Goods Sold Statement
For the Month of May

Cost of goods manufactured	$575,000
Finished goods inventory, May 1	50,000
Finished good inventory, May 31	(130,000)
Cost of goods sold	$495,000
Number of units sold:	
Finished goods inventory, May 1	10,000
Units finished during May	115,000
Finished goods inventory, May 31	(26,000)
Units sold during May	99,000

HOW TO Prepare an Income Statement for a Manufacturing Firm

Information: Recall that BlueDenim Company sold 99,000 pairs of jeans during the month of May at a total cost of $495,000. Each pair sold at a price of $8. BlueDenim also incurred two types of selling costs: commissions equal to 10 percent of the sales price and other selling expense of $120,000. Administrative expense totaled $85,000.

Required: Prepare an income statement for BlueDenim for the month of May.

Calculation:

**CORNERSTONE
1-6**

BlueDenim Company
Income Statement
For the Month of May

Sales revenue (99,000 × $8)	$792,000	
Cost of goods sold	495,000	
Gross margin	$297,000	
Less:		
Selling expense		
Commissions (0.10 × $792,000)	$ 79,200	
Fixed selling expense	120,000	199,200
Administrative expense		85,000
Operating income		$ 12,800

Look at the income statement in Cornerstone 1-6. First, the heading tells us what type of statement it is, for what firm, and for what period of time. Then, the income statement itself always begins with "sales revenue" (or "sales," or "revenue"). The sales revenue is the price multiplied by the units sold. After the sales revenue is determined, the firm must calculate expenses for the period.

Notice that the expenses are separated into three categories: production (cost of goods sold), selling, and administrative. The first type of expense is the cost of producing the units sold, or the cost of goods sold. This amount was computed and explained in Cornerstone 1-5. Remember that the cost of goods sold is the cost of producing the units that were sold during the time period. It includes direct materials, direct labor, and manufacturing overhead. It does *not* include any selling or administrative expense. In the case of a retail (i.e., a merchandising) firm, the cost of goods sold represents the total cost of the goods sold when they were purchased from an outside supplier. Therefore, the cost of goods sold for a retailer equals the purchase costs adjusted for the beginning and ending balances in its single inventory account. A merchandising firm, such as **Old Navy** or J. Crew, has only one inventory account because it does not transform the purchased good into a different form by adding materials, labor, and overhead, as does a manufacturing firm.

Gross margin is the difference between sales revenue and cost of goods sold. It shows how much the firm is making over and above the cost of the units sold. Gross margin does *not* equal operating income or profit. Selling and administrative expenses have not yet been subtracted. However, gross margin does provide useful information. If gross margin is positive, the firm at least charges prices that cover the product cost. In addition, the firm can calculate its gross margin percentage (gross margin/sales revenue), as shown in Cornerstone 1-7 on the following page, and compare it with the average gross margin percentage for the industry to see if its experience is in the ballpark with other firms in the industry. Gross margin percentage varies significantly by industry.

**CORNERSTONE
1-7**

HOW TO Calculate the Percentage of Sales Revenue for Each Line on the Income Statement

Information: Recall that BlueDenim Company's income statement for the month of May was shown in Cornerstone 1-6.

Required: Calculate the percentage of sales revenue represented by each line of the income statement.

Calculation:

BlueDenim Company
Income Statement
For the Month of May

			Percent*
Sales revenue (99,000 × $8)		$792,000	100.0
Cost of goods sold		495,000	62.5
Gross margin		$297,000	37.5
Less:			
Selling expense			
Commissions (0.10 × $792,000)	79,200		
Fixed selling expense	120,000	199,200	25.2
Administrative expense		85,000	10.7
Operating income		$ 12,800	1.6

*Steps in calculating the percentages:

1. Sales revenue percent = $792,000/$792,000 = 1.00 or 100% (sales revenue is always 100% of sales revenue)
2. Cost of goods sold percent = $495,000/$792,000 = 0.625 or 62.5%
3. Gross margin percent = $297,000/$792,000 = 0.375 or 37.5%
4. Selling expense percent = $199,200/$792,000 = 0.252 or 25.2% (this has been rounded)
5. Administrative expense percent = $85,000/$792,000 = 0.107 or 10.7% (this has been rounded)
6. Operating income expense percent = $12,800/$792,000 = 0.016 or 1.6% (this has been rounded)

For instance, **Kroger**'s gross margin percentage as determined from the income statement in its 2005 annual report was 24.8% ($14,988,000,000/$60,553,000,000). However, **Merck**'s gross margin percentage as determined from the income statement in its 2005 annual report was 76.6% ($16,862,300,000/$22,011,900,000)! One reason for Merck's extremely high gross margin percent is that a large percentage of its costs are related to marketing (e.g., advertising) and research and development ($7.1 million and $3.8 million, respectively) and, as such, are expensed as period costs in the period incurred. Thus, Merck's cost of goods sold was relatively small.

Finally, selling expense and administrative expense for the period are subtracted from gross margin to get operating income. This is the key figure from the income statement; it is profit and shows how much the owners are actually earning from the company. Again, calculating the percentage of operating income (i.e., operating income/sales revenue) and comparing it with the average for the industry gives the owners valuable information about relative profitability.

The income statement can be analyzed further by calculating the percentage of sales revenue represented by each line of the statement, as was done in Cornerstone 1-7. How can management use this information? The first thing that jumps out is that operating income is less than 2 percent of sales revenue. That's a very small percentage. Unless this is common for the blue jeans manufacturing business, BlueDenim's management should work hard to increase the percentage. Selling expense is a whopping 25.2 percent of sales! Do commissions really need to be that high? Or is the price too low (compared with competitors' prices)? Can cost of goods sold be reduced? Is 62.5 percent reasonable? These are questions that are suggested by Cornerstone 1-7, not answered. Answering the questions is the job of management.

Analytical Q&A

Your friend, Ted, mentioned that **Macy's** department store marks up sweaters by 100 percent. "Wow," said Ted, "so a sweater that costs them $25 is sold for $50—they're making $25 in profit (operating income)!" Is Ted correct? Refer to the income statement from Cornerstone 1-7. What line would include the $50 price of the sweater? What line would include the $25 original cost (to the store) of the sweater? What line would include the $25 that is over and above the cost?

Answer:

No, the $25 markup is not operating income. The $50 price is included in revenue, the $25 original cost is included in cost of goods sold, and the $25 over and above the cost to the store is in gross margin.

Income Statement: Service Organization

In a service organization, there is no product to purchase (e.g., a merchandiser like **The North Face**) or to manufacture (e.g., **Toshiba**), and, therefore, there are no beginning or ending inventories. As a result, there is no cost of goods sold or gross margin on the income statement. Instead, the cost of providing services appears along with the other operating expenses of the company. For example, Southwest Airlines' 2005 income statement begins with Total Operating Revenues of $7,584,000,000 and subtracts Total Operating Expenses of $6,764,000,000 to arrive at an Operating Income of $820,000,000. An income statement for a service organization is shown in Cornerstone 1-8.

HOW TO Prepare an Income Statement for a Service Organization

**CORNERSTONE
1-8**

Information: Komala Information Systems designs and installs human resources software for small companies. Last month, Komala had software licensing costs of $5,000, service technicians costs of $35,000, and research and development costs of $55,000. Selling expenses were $5,000, and administrative expenses equaled $7,000. Sales totaled $130,000.

Required: Prepare an income statement for Komala Information Systems for the past month.

Calculation:

Komala Information Systems Income Statement For the Past Month		
Sales revenues:		$130,000
Less operating expenses:		
Software licensing	$ 5,000	
Service technicians	35,000	
Research and development	55,000	
Selling expenses	5,000	
Administrative expenses	7,000	107,000
Operating income		$ 23,000

OBJECTIVE ⑥
Explain the importance of ethical behavior for managers and managerial accountants.

Managerial Accounting and Ethical Conduct

Ethical Behavior

Ethical behavior involves choosing actions that are "right," "proper," and "just." Traditionally, actions regarding the economic performance of the firm have been the overriding concern of managerial accounting. Yet, managers and managerial accountants should not become so focused on profits that they develop a belief that the only goal of a business is maximizing its net worth. The objective of profit maximization should be constrained by the requirement that profits be achieved through legal and ethical means. While this belief has always been an implicit assumption of managerial accounting, the assumption should be made explicit. To help achieve this objective, many of the problems in this text require explicit consideration of ethical issues.

Many of the recent accounting scandals, such as those involving Adelphia, WorldCom, HealthSouth, **Parmalat**, and **McKesson**, provide evidence of the pressures faced by top managers and accountants to produce large net income numbers. Unfortunately, such individuals often give into these pressures when faced with questionable revenue- and cost-related judgments. For example, the scandal at WorldCom was committed because the CEO, Bernie Ebbers, coerced several of the top accountants at WorldCom to wrongfully record journal entries into the company's books that capitalized millions of dollars in costs as assets (i.e., on the balance sheet) rather than as expenses (i.e., on the income statement) that would have dramatically lowered current period net income. In 2005, WorldCom was forced to pay hundreds of millions of dollars to the U.S. government and to shareholders for its illegal and unethical actions. In addition, several of the top executives were sentenced to extensive prison time for their actions.

Company Codes of Ethical Conduct

To promote ethical behavior by managers and employees, organizations commonly establish standards of conduct referred to as Company Codes of Conduct. For example, **Boeing**'s Code of Conduct[10] states that it will "conduct its business fairly, impartially, in an ethical and proper manner, and in full compliance with all applicable laws and regulations." All employees must sign the code of conduct, and the company "requires that they understand the code, and ask questions, seek guidance, report suspected violations, and express concerns regarding compliance with this policy and the related procedures."

As with the legal and medical professions, the accounting profession relies on certification to help promote ethical behavior, as well as to provide evidence that the certificate holder has achieved a minimum level of professional competence. The accounting profession offers three major forms of certification to managerial accountants: a Certificate in Management Accounting (CMA), a Certificate in Public Accounting, and a Certificate in Internal Auditing. In each case, an applicant must meet specific educational and experience requirements and pass a qualifying examination to become certified. These certifying organizations have responded to recent ethics scandals with their own policies. For example, in 2005, the Institute of Management Accountants (IMA), which sponsors the CMA, revised its Standards of Ethical Conduct for Management Accountants to reflect the impact of the Sarbanes-Oxley Act of 2002. Now called the Statement of Ethical Professional Practice, the revised code considers global issues and incorporates the principles of the code of the International Federation of Accountants, which is the global association of professional accounting groups. Perhaps the biggest challenge with ethical dilemmas is that when they arise, employees frequently do not realize either (1) that such a dilemma has arisen or (2) the "correct" action that should be taken to rectify the dilemma. Therefore, rather than attempt to study numerous ethical issues in one place, each chapter of this text includes an ethical dilemma or situation designed to increase student awareness of the types of conduct considered unethical in business.

---

[10]Taken from the Boeing website on August 27, 2007. http://www.boeing.com/companyoffices/aboutus/ethics/

Summary of Learning Objectives

1. Explain the meaning of managerial accounting, and contrast it to financial accounting.
    *   Managerial accounting information helps managers achieve their objectives of planning, controlling, and decision making. Planning is the detailed formulation of action to achieve a particular end. Controlling is the monitoring of a plan's implementation. Decision making is choosing among competing alternatives.
    *   Managerial accounting information is intended for internal users and typically is not subject to generally accepted accounting principles (GAAP), whereas financial accounting information is directed toward external users and is subject to GAAP.

2. Explain the current focus of managerial accounting and the role of managerial accountants in an organization.
    *   The nature of managerial accounting information depends upon the strategic position of the firm—cost leadership strategy, product differentiation strategy, and lean accounting.
    *   Information about value-chain activities and customer satisfaction is collected, including activity-based management information.
    *   Managerial accountants are responsible for identifying, collecting, measuring, analyzing, preparing, and interpreting information.
    *   Managerial accountants also must communicate—both orally and in writing—information to individuals inside and outside of the organization, including non-accountants.

3. Explain the meaning of cost and how costs are assigned to products and services.
    *   Cost is the cash or cash-equivalent value sacrificed for goods and services that are expected to bring a current or future benefit to the organization.
    *   Managers use cost information to determine the cost of objects, such as products, plants, geographic regions, and customers.
    *   Direct costs are traced to cost objects based on cause-and-effect relationships.
    *   Indirect (i.e., overhead) costs are allocated to cost objects based on assumed relationships and convenience.

4. Define the various costs of manufacturing and providing services.
    *   Products are goods that either are purchased or produced by converting raw materials through the use of labor and indirect manufacturing resources, such as plants, land, and machinery. Services are tasks performed for a customer or activities performed by a customer by using an organization's products or facilities.
    *   Product costs are those costs, both direct and indirect, of acquiring a product in a merchandising business and preparing it for sale or of producing a product in a manufacturing business. Product costs are classified as inventory on the balance sheet and then expensed as cost of goods sold on the income statement when the inventory is sold.
    *   The cost of goods manufactured (COGM) represents the total product cost of goods *completed* during the period and transferred to finished goods inventory. The cost of goods sold (COGS) represents the cost of goods that were sold during the period and, therefore, transferred from finished goods inventory to cost of goods sold. For a retailer, there is no COGM, and COGS equals the beginning inventory plus net purchases minus ending inventory.
    *   Selling costs are the costs of marketing and distributing goods and services, and administrative costs are the costs of organizing and running a company.
    *   Both selling and administrative costs are period costs.

5. Prepare income statements for manufacturing and service organizations.
    *   For manufacturing and merchandising firms, cost of goods sold is subtracted from sales revenue to arrive at gross margin. In addition, for manufacturing firms, cost of goods manufactured must first be calculated before calculating cost of goods sold.
    *   Service firms do not calculate gross margin because they do not purchase or produce inventory for sale and, as a result, do not have a cost of goods sold (i.e., inventory expense).
    *   All firms next subtract selling and administrative expenses to arrive at net income.
6. Explain the importance of ethical behavior for managers and managerial accountants.
    *   A strong ethical sense is needed to resist pressures to change economic information that may present an untrue picture of firm performance.
    *   Many firms have a written code of ethics (e.g., IMA) or code of conduct.
    *   Proper employee training, controls and regulation (e.g., Sarbanes-Oxley Act), and incentive systems can curb ethical problems.

Summary of Important Equations

1. Total product cost = Direct materials + direct labor + overhead
2. Unit product cost = Total product cost/number of units
3. Prime cost = Direct materials + Direct labor
4. Conversion cost = Direct labor + Overhead
5. Direct materials used in production = Beginning inventory of materials + Purchases − Ending inventory of materials
6. Cost of goods manufactured = Direct materials used in production + Direct labor used in production + Manufacturing overhead costs used in production + Beginning WIP inventory − Ending WIP inventory
7. Cost of goods sold = Beginning inventory + Cost of goods manufactured − Ending inventory

CORNERSTONES FOR CHAPTER 1

Cornerstone 1-1   How to calculate product cost in total and per unit, page 19

Cornerstone 1-2   How to calculate prime cost and conversion cost in total and per unit, page 20

Cornerstone 1-3   How to calculate the direct materials used in production, page 23

Cornerstone 1-4   How to calculate cost of goods manufactured, page 23

Cornerstone 1-5   How to calculate cost of goods sold, page 24

Cornerstone 1-6   How to prepare an income statement for a manufacturing firm, page 25

Cornerstone 1-7   How to calculate the percentage of sales revenue for each line on the income statement, page 26

Cornerstone 1-8   How to prepare an income statement for a service organization, page 27

Key Terms

Accumulating costs, 13
Administrative costs, 21
Allocation, 15
Assigning costs, 14
Continuous improvement, 10
Controller, 11
Controlling, 5
Conversion cost, 19
Cost, 12
Cost object, 14
Cost of goods manufactured, 22
Cost of goods sold, 24
Decision making, 6
Direct costs, 14
Direct labor, 18
Direct materials, 17
Enterprise risk management, 10
Ethical behavior, 28
Expenses, 13
Financial accounting, 6
Fixed costs, 16
Gross margin, 25

Indirect costs, 15
Lean accounting, 10
Managerial accounting, 4
Manufacturing organizations, 16
Manufacturing overhead, 18
Opportunity cost, 16
Period costs, 19
Planning, 5
Price, 13
Prime cost, 19
Product (manufacturing) costs, 17
Products, 16
Publicly traded companies, 12
Sarbanes-Oxley Act (SOX), 12
Selling costs, 21
Service organizations, 16
Services, 16
Total quality management, 10
Treasurer, 11
Value chain, 9
Variable cost, 16
Work in process (WIP), 22

Review Problem

Product Costs, Cost of Goods Manufactured Statement, and the Income Statement

Brody Company makes industrial cleaning solvents. Various chemicals, detergent, and water are mixed together and then bottled in 10-gallon drums. Brody provided the following information for last year:

Raw materials purchases	$250,000
Direct labor	140,000
Depreciation on factory equipment	45,000
Depreciation on factory building	30,000
Depreciation on headquarters building	50,000
Factory insurance	15,000
Property taxes:	
Factory	20,000
Headquarters	18,000
Utilities for factory	34,000
Utilities for sales office	1,800
Administrative salaries	150,000
Indirect labor salaries	156,000
Sales office salaries	90,000
Beginning balance, Raw Materials	124,000
Beginning balance, WIP	124,000
Beginning balance, Finished Goods	84,000
Ending balance, Raw Materials	102,000
Ending balance, WIP	130,000
Ending balance, Finished Goods	82,000

Last year, Brody completed 100,000 units. Sales revenue equaled $1,200,000, and Brody paid a sales commission of 5 percent of sales.

Required:
1. Calculate the direct materials used in production for last year.
2. Calculate total prime cost.
3. Calculate total conversion cost.
4. Prepare a Cost of Goods Manufactured Statement for last year. Calculate the unit product cost.
5. Prepare a Cost of Goods Sold Statement for last year.
6. Prepare an Income Statement for last year. Show the percentage of sales that each line item represents.

Solution:
1. Direct materials = $124,000 + $250,000 − $102,000 = $272,000
2. Prime cost = $272,000 + $140,000 = $412,000
3. First, calculate total overhead cost:

Depreciation on factory equipment	$ 45,000
Depreciation on factory building	30,000
Factory insurance	15,000
Factory property taxes	20,000
Factory utilities	34,000
Indirect labor salaries	156,000
Total overhead	$300,000

Conversion cost = $140,000 + $300,000 = $440,000

4.

Direct materials	$272,000
Direct labor	140,000
Overhead	300,000
Total manufacturing cost	$712,000
+ Beginning WIP	124,000
− Ending WIP	130,000
Cost of goods manufactured	$706,000

Unit product cost = $706,000/100,000 units = $7.06

5.

Cost of goods manufactured	$706,000
+ Beginning inventory, Finished goods	84,000
− Ending inventory, Finished goods	82,000
Cost of goods sold	$708,000

6. First, compute selling expense and administrative expense:

Utilities, sales office	$ 1,800
Sales office salaries	90,000
Sales commissions ($1,200,000 * 0.05)	60,000
Selling expense	$151,800
Depreciation on headquarters building	$ 50,000
Property taxes, headquarters	18,000
Administrative salaries	150,000
Administrative expense	$218,000

Brody Company
Income Statement
For Last Year

		Percent
Sales	$1,200,000	100.00
Cost of goods sold	708,000	59.00
Gross margin	$ 492,000	41.00
Less:		
Selling expense	151,800	12.65
Administrative expense	218,000	18.17
Operating income	$ 122,200	10.18

Discussion Questions

1. What is managerial accounting?
2. What are the three broad objectives of managerial accounting?
3. Who are the users of managerial accounting information?
4. Should a managerial accounting system provide both financial and nonfinancial information? Explain.
5. What is meant by controlling?
6. How do financial accounting and managerial accounting differ?
7. Explain the meaning of customer value. How is focusing on customer value changing managerial accounting?
8. Explain why today's managerial accountant must have a cross-functional perspective.
9. What is the value chain? Why is it important?
10. Explain the challenges faced by managerial accountants in effectively communicating managerial accounting information to various interested users.
11. What is a cost object? Give some examples.
12. What is the difference between accumulating cost and assigning cost?
13. What is a direct cost? An indirect cost? Can the same cost be direct for one purpose and indirect for another? Give an example.
14. Define *prime cost* and *conversion cost*. Why can't you add prime cost to conversion cost to get total product cost?
15. Explain the difference between cost and expense.
16. How does a period cost differ from a product cost?
17. Define *overhead*, and explain why it is sometimes referred to as a "catchall" category.
18. Explain the difference between direct materials purchases in a month and direct materials used for the month.
19. Why do firms like to calculate a percentage column on the income statement (in which each line item is expressed as a percentage of sales)?
20. What is the difference between the income statement for a manufacturing firm and the income statement for a service firm?
21. Define *marketing* (or *selling*) *cost*. Give five examples of marketing cost.
22. What is the difference between cost of goods manufactured and cost of goods sold?
23. What is ethical behavior? Is it possible to teach ethical behavior in a managerial accounting course?

Multiple-Choice Exercises

1-1 The provision of accounting information for internal users is known as

a. managerial accounting.
b. accounting.
c. financial accounting.
d. information provision.
e. accounting for planning and control.

1-2 The process of choosing among competing alternatives is called

a. controlling.
b. decision making.
c. planning.
d. performance evaluation.
e. none of the above.

1-3 Which of the following is a characteristic of managerial accounting?

a. There is an internal focus.
b. Subjective information may be used.
c. There is an emphasis on the future.
d. It is broad-based and multidisciplinary.
e. All of the above.

1-4 In terms of strategic positioning, which two general strategies may be chosen by a company?

a. Activity-based costing and value-chain emphasis
b. Revenue production and cost enhancement
c. Cost leadership and product differentiation
d. Increasing customer value and decreasing supplier orientation
e. Product differentiation and cost enhancement

1-5 Accumulating costs means that

a. costs must be summed and entered on the income statement.
b. each cost must be linked to some cost object.
c. costs must be measured and tracked.
d. costs must be allocated to units of production.
e. costs have expired and must be transferred from the balance sheet to the income statement.

1-6 Product (or manufacturing) costs consist of

a. direct materials, direct labor, and selling costs.
b. direct materials, direct labor, overhead, and operating expense.
c. prime costs and conversion costs.
d. prime costs and overhead.
e. selling and administrative costs.

Use the following information for Multiple-Choice Exercises 1-7 and 1-8.
Wachman Company produces a product with the following per-unit costs:

Direct materials	$15
Direct labor	6
Overhead	10

Last year, Wachman produced and sold 1,000 units at a price of $75 each. Total selling and administrative expense was $30,000.

1-7 Conversion cost per unit was

a. $15.
b. $21.
c. $31.
d. $16.
e. none of the above.

1-8 Total gross margin for last year was

a. $75,000.
b. $44,000.
c. $61,000.
d. $9,000.
e. $31,000.

1-9 The accountant in a factory that produces biscuits for fast-food restaurants wants to assign costs to boxes of biscuits. Which of the following costs can be traced directly to boxes of biscuits?

a.   The cost of flour and baking soda
b.   The wages of the mixing labor
c.   The cost of the boxes
d.   The cost of packing labor
e.   All of the above

1-10 Which of the following is an indirect cost?

a.   The cost of denim in a jeans factory
b.   The cost of mixing labor in a factory that makes over-the-counter pain relievers
c.   The cost of restriping the parking lot at a perfume factory
d.   The cost of bottles in a shampoo factory
e.   All of the above

1-11 Bobby Dee's is an owner-operated company that details (thoroughly cleans—inside and out) automobiles. Bobby Dee's is which of the following?

a.   Retailer
b.   Wholesaler
c.   Manufacturing firm
d.   Service firm
e.   None of the above

1-12 Kellogg's makes a variety of breakfast cereals. Kellogg's is which of the following?

a.   Retailer
b.   Wholesaler
c.   Manufacturing firm
d.   Service firm
e.   None of the above

1-13 Wal-Mart is which of the following?

a.   Retailer
b.   Wholesaler
c.   Manufacturing firm
d.   Service firm
e.   None of the above

1-14 Stone Inc. is a company that purchases goods (e.g., chess sets, pottery) from overseas and resells them to gift shops in the United States. Stone Inc. is which of the following?

a.   Retailer
b.   Wholesaler
c.   Manufacturing firm

d.   Service firm
e.   None of the above

1-15 Flame-Glo Company produces novelty candles for gift shops. Flame-Glo estimated the following average costs per candle:

Direct materials	$1.50
Direct labor	0.75
Overhead	2.00

Prime cost per unit is

a. $1.50.
b. $0.75.
c. $2.00.
d. $2.25.
e. $2.75.

1-16 Which of the following is a period expense?

a. Advertising
b. Factory supervision
c. Factory maintenance
d. Direct labor
e. All of the above

Use the following information for Multiple-Choice Exercises 1-17 through 1-22.
Last year, Barnard Company incurred the following costs:

Direct materials	$ 50,000
Direct labor	20,000
Overhead	130,000
Selling expense	40,000
Administrative expense	36,000

Barnard produced and sold 10,000 units at a price of $31 each.

1-17 Prime cost per unit was

a. $7.00.
b. $20.00.
c. $15.00.
d. $5.00.
e. $27.60.

1-18 Conversion cost per unit was

a. $7.00.
b. $20.00.
c. $15.00.
d. $5.00.
e. $27.60.

1-19 Cost of goods sold per unit was

a. $7.00.
b. $20.00.
c. $15.00.
d. $5.00.
e. $27.60.

1-20 Gross margin per unit was

a. $24.00.
b. $11.00.
c. $16.00.
d. $26.00.
e. $3.40.

1-21 Total period expense was

a. $276,000.
b. $200,000.
c. $76,000.
d. $40,000.
e. $36,000.

1-22 Operating income was

a. $34,000.
b. $110,000.
c. $234,000.
d. $270,000.
e. $74,000.

Exercises

Exercise 1-23 Customer Value, Strategic Positioning

OBJECTIVE ②

Adriana Alvarado has decided to purchase a personal computer. She has narrowed the choices to two: Drantex and Confiar. Both brands have the same processing speed, 6.4 gigabytes of hard-disk capacity, a 3.5-inch disk drive, and a CD-ROM drive, and each comes with the same basic software support package. Both come from mail order companies with good reputations. The selling price for each is identical. After some review, Adriana discovers that the cost of operating and maintaining Drantex over a three-year period is estimated to be $300. For Confiar, the operating and maintenance cost is $600. The sales agent for Drantex emphasized the lower operating and maintenance costs. The agent for Confiar, however, emphasized the service reputation of the product and the faster delivery time (Confiar can be purchased and delivered one week sooner than Drantex). Based on all the information, Adriana has decided to buy Confiar.

Required:
1.   What is the total product purchased by Adriana?
2.   How does the strategic positioning differ for the two companies?
3.   When asked why she decided to buy Confiar, Adriana responded, "I think that Confiar offers more value than Drantex." What are the possible sources of this greater value? What implications does this have for the management accounting information system?
4.   Suppose that Adriana's decision was prompted mostly by the desire to receive the computer quickly. Informed that it was losing sales because of the longer time to produce and deliver its products, the management of the company producing Drantex decided to improve delivery performance by improving its internal processes. These improvements decreased the number of defective units and the time required to produce its product. Consequently, delivery time and costs both

decreased, and the company was able to lower its prices on Drantex. Explain how these actions translate into strengthening the competitive position of the Drantex PC relative to the Confiar PC. Also discuss the implications for the management accounting information system.

OBJECTIVE ③   **Exercise 1-24 Cost Assignment**

The sales staff of Central Media (a locally owned radio and cable television station) consists of two salespeople, Derek and Lawanna. During March, the following salaries and commissions were paid:

	Derek	Lawanna
Salary	$25,000	$30,000
Commissions	6,000	1,500

Derek spends 100 percent of his time selling advertising. Lawanna spends two-thirds of her time selling advertising and the remaining one-third on administrative work. Commissions are paid only on sales.

Required:
1. Accumulate these costs by account by filling in the following table.

Cost	Salaries	Commissions
Derek		
Lawanna		
Total		

2. Assign the costs of salaries and commissions to selling expense and administrative expense by filling in the following table.

Cost	Selling Costs	Administrative Costs
Derek's salary		
Lawanna's salary		
Commissions		
Total		

OBJECTIVE ③   **Exercise 1-25 Products versus Services, Cost Assignment**

Holmes Company produces wooden playhouses. When a customer orders a playhouse, it is delivered in pieces with detailed instructions on how to put it together. Some customers prefer that Holmes puts the playhouse together, and they purchase the playhouse plus the installation package. Holmes then pulls two workers off the production line and sends them to construct the playhouse on site.

Required:
1. What two products does Holmes sell? Classify each one as a tangible product or a service.
2. Do you think Holmes assigns costs individually to each product? Why or why not?
3. Describe the opportunity cost of the installation process.

OBJECTIVE ③   **Exercise 1-26 Assigning Costs to a Cost Object, Direct and Indirect Costs**

Hummer Company uses manufacturing cells to produce its products (a *cell* is a manufacturing unit dedicated to the production of subassemblies or products). One manufacturing cell produces small motors for lawn mowers. Suppose that the motor manufacturing cell is the cost object. Assume that all or a portion of the following costs must be assigned to the cell.

a.   Salary of cell supervisor
b.   Power to heat and cool the plant in which the cell is located
c.   Materials used to produce the motors
d.   Maintenance for the cell's equipment (provided by the maintenance department)
e.   Labor used to produce motors
f.   Cafeteria that services the plant's employees
g.   Depreciation on the plant
h.   Depreciation on equipment used to produce the motors
i.   Ordering costs for materials used in production
j.   Engineering support (provided by the engineering department)
k.   Cost of maintaining the plant and grounds
l.   Cost of the plant's personnel office
m.   Property tax on the plant and land

Required:
Classify each of the above costs as a direct cost or an indirect cost to the motor manufacturing cell.

Exercise 1-27 Total and Unit Product Cost

OBJECTIVE ④

Weibring Manufacturing Inc. showed the following costs for last month:

Direct materials	$5,000
Direct labor	2,500
Overhead	3,700
Selling expense	6,000

Last month, 8,000 units were produced and sold.

Required:
1.   Classify the above costs as product cost or period cost.
2.   What is total product cost for last month?
3.   What is the unit product cost for last month?

Exercise 1-28 Cost Classification

OBJECTIVE ④

Loring Company incurred the following costs last year:

Direct materials	$216,000
Factory rent	24,000
Direct labor	120,000
Factory utilities	6,300
Supervision in the factory	50,000
Indirect labor in the factory	30,000
Depreciation on factory equipment	9,000
Sales commissions	27,000
Sales salaries	65,000
Advertising	37,000
Depreciation on the headquarters building	10,000
Salary of the corporate receptionist	30,000
Other administrative costs	175,000
Salary of the factory receptionist	28,000

Required:
1.   Classify each of the above costs using the table format given below. Be sure to total
the amounts in each column.
    Example: Direct materials, $216,000.

	Product Cost			Period Cost	
Costs	Direct Materials	Direct Labor	Overhead	Selling Expense	Administrative Expense
Direct materials	$216,000				

2. What was the total product cost for last year?
3. What was the total period cost for last year?
4. If 30,000 units were produced last year, what was the unit product cost?

OBJECTIVE ④   Exercise 1-29 Classifying Cost of Production

A factory manufactures jelly. The jars of jelly are packed six to a box, and the boxes are sold to grocery stores. The following types of cost were incurred:

Jars
Sugar
Fruit
Pectin (thickener used in jams and jellies)
Boxes
Depreciation on the factory building
Cooking equipment operators' wages
Filling equipment operators' wages
Packers' wages
Janitors' wages
Receptionist's wages
Telephone
Utilities
Rental of Santa Claus suit (for the annual Christmas party for factory children)
Supervisory labor salaries
Insurance on factory building
Depreciation on factory equipment
Oil to lubricate filling equipment

Required:
Classify each of the above costs as direct materials, direct labor, or overhead by using the following table. The row for "Jars" is filled in as an example.

Costs	Direct Materials	Direct Labor	Overhead
Jars	X		

OBJECTIVE ④   Exercise 1-30 Product Cost in Total and Per Unit

CORNERSTONE 1-1   Kyoto Company manufactures digital cameras. In January, Kyoto produced 10,000 cameras with the following costs:

Direct materials	$560,000
Direct labor	96,000
Overhead	220,000

There were no beginning or ending inventories of WIP.

Required:
1. What was total product cost in January?
2. What was product cost per unit in January?

OBJECTIVE ④   Exercise 1-31 Prime Cost and Conversion Cost

CORNERSTONE 1-2   Refer to **Exercise 1-30**.

Required:
1. What was total prime cost in January?
2. What was prime cost per unit in January?
3. What was total conversion cost in January?
4. What was conversion cost per unit in January?

Exercise 1-32 Direct Materials Used

OBJECTIVE ⑤
CORNERSTONE 1-3

Better Baker Company makes biscuits for fast-food restaurants. In July, Better Baker Company purchased $12,700 of materials. On July 1, the materials inventory was $2,300. On July 31, $4,900 of materials remained in materials inventory.

Required:

What is the cost of the direct materials that were used in production during July?

Exercise 1-33 Cost of Goods Sold

OBJECTIVE ⑤
CORNERSTONE 1-5

Portman Company makes tricycles. During the year, Portman manufactured 114,000 tricycles. Finished goods inventory had the following units:

January 1	1,430
December 31	2,650

Required:

1. How many tricycles did Portman sell during the year?
2. If each tricycle had a product cost of $15, what was the cost of goods sold last year?

Exercise 1-34 Direct Materials Used, Cost of Goods Manufactured

OBJECTIVE ⑤
CORNERSTONE 1-3
CORNERSTONE 1-4

In March, Chilton Company purchased materials costing $14,000 and incurred direct labor cost of $20,000. Overhead totaled $36,000 for the month. Information on inventories was as follows:

spreadsheet

Spreadsheet	March 1	March 31
Materials	$8,600	$2,300
Work in process	1,700	9,000
Finished goods	7,000	6,500

Required:

1. What was the cost of direct materials for March?
2. What was total manufacturing cost in March?
3. What was the cost of goods manufactured for March?

Exercise 1-35 Cost of Goods Sold

OBJECTIVE ⑤
CORNERSTONE 1-5

Refer to **Exercise 1-34**.

Required:

What was the cost of goods sold for March?

Exercise 1-36 Cost of Goods Sold, Sales Revenue, Income Statement

OBJECTIVE ⑤
CORNERSTONE 1-5

Landes Company provided the following information for last year:

Sales in units	200,000
Selling price	$ 14
Direct materials	$145,000
Direct labor	$335,000
Overhead	$670,000
Selling expense	$367,000
Administrative expense	$415,000

Last year, beginning and ending inventories of Work in Process and Finished Goods equaled zero.

Required:

Calculate the cost of goods sold for last year.

OBJECTIVE ⑤
CORNERSTONE 1-6

Exercise 1-37 Income Statement

Refer to **Exercise 1-36**.

Required:
1. Calculate the sales revenue for last year.
2. Prepare an income statement for Landes Company for last year.

OBJECTIVE ⑤
CORNERSTONE 1-7

Exercise 1-38 Income Statement

Refer to **Exercise 1-36**.

Required:
Prepare an income statement for Landes Company for last year. Calculate the percentage of sales for each line item on the income statement. Round percentages to the nearest tenth of a percent.

OBJECTIVE ⑥

Exercise 1-39 Ethical Behavior

Manager: If I can reduce my costs by $40,000 during this last quarter, my division will show a profit that is 10 percent above the planned level, and I will receive a $10,000 bonus. However, given the projections for the fourth quarter, it does not look promising. I really need that $10,000. I know of one way that I can qualify. All I have to do is lay off my three most expensive salespeople. After all, most of the orders are in for the fourth quarter, and I can always hire new sales personnel at the beginning of the next year.

Required:
What is the right choice for the manager to make? Why did the ethical dilemma arise? Is there any way to redesign the accounting reporting system to discourage the type of behavior that the manager is contemplating?

OBJECTIVE ⑥

Exercise 1-40 Ethical Issues

The Bedron Company is a closely held investment service group that has been quite successful over the past five years, consistently providing most members of the top management group with 50-percent bonuses. In addition, both the CFO and the CEO have received 100-percent bonuses. Bedron expects this trend to continue.

Recently, Bedron's top management group, which holds 35 percent of the outstanding shares of common stock, has learned that a major corporation is interested in acquiring Bedron. The other corporation's initial offer is attractive and is several dollars per share higher than Bedron's current share price. One member of management told a group of employees under him about the potential offer. He suggested that they might want to purchase more Bedron stock at the current price in anticipation of the takeover offer.

Required:
Do you think that the employees should take the action suggested by their boss? Suppose the action is prohibited by Bedron's code of ethics. Now suppose that it is not prohibited by Bedron's code of ethics. Is the action acceptable in that case?

OBJECTIVE ⑥

Exercise 1-41 Company Codes of Conduct

Required:
Using the Internet, locate the code of conduct for three different companies. Briefly describe each code of conduct. How are they similar? How are they different?

Problems

Problem 1-42 Manufacturing, Cost Classification, Income Statement Service Firm Product Costs and Selling and Administrative Costs, Income Statement

OBJECTIVES ④ ⑤

Pop's Drive-Thru Burger Heaven produces and sells quarter-pound hamburgers. Each burger is wrapped and put in a "burger bag," which also includes a serving of fries and a soft drink. The price for the burger bag is $3.50. During December, 10,000 burger bags were sold. The restaurant employs college students part-time to cook and fill orders. There is one supervisor (the owner, John Peterson). Pop's maintains a pool of part-time employees so that the number of employees scheduled can be adjusted to the changes in demand. Demand varies on a weekly as well as a monthly basis.

A janitor is hired to clean the building early each morning. Cleaning supplies are used by the janitor, as well as the staff, to wipe counters, wash cooking equipment, and so on. The building is leased from a local real estate company; it has no seating capacity. All orders are filled on a drive-thru basis.

The supervisor schedules work, opens the building, counts the cash, advertises, and is responsible for hiring and firing. The following costs were incurred during December:

Hamburger meat	$4,500	Utilities	$1,500
Buns, lettuce, pickles, and onions	800	Rent	1,800
		Depreciation, cooking equipment and fixtures	600
Frozen potato strips	1,250		
Wrappers, bags, and condiment packages	600	Advertising	500
		Janitor's wages	520
Other ingredients	660	Janitorial supplies	150
Part-time employees' wages	7,250	Accounting fees	1,500
		Taxes	4,250
John Peterson's salary	3,000		

Pop's accountant, Elena DeMarco, does the bookkeeping, handles payroll, and files all necessary taxes. She noted that there were no beginning or ending inventories of materials. To simplify accounting for costs, Elena assumed that all part-time employees are production employees and that John Peterson's salary is selling and administrative expense. She further assumed that all rent and depreciation expense on the building and fixtures are part of product cost. Finally, she decided to put all taxes into one category, taxes, and to treat them as administrative expense.

Required:

1. Classify each of the above costs for Pop's December operations by using the table format given below. Be sure to total the amounts in each column.
   Example: Hamburger meat, $4,500.

Cost	Direct Materials	Direct Labor	Overhead	Selling and Administrative
Hamburger meat	$4,500			

Total

2. Prepare an absorption-costing income statement for the month of December.
3. Elena made some simplifying assumptions. Were those reasonable? Suppose a good case could be made that the portion of the employees' time spent selling the burger bags was really a part of sales. In that case, would it be better to divide their time between production and selling? Should John Peterson's time be divided between marketing and administrative duties? What difference (if any) would that make on the income statement?

OBJECTIVE ③

Problem 1-43 Cost Assignment, Direct Costs

Harry Whipple, owner of an ink jet printer, has agreed to allow Mary and Natalie, two friends who are pursuing master's degrees, to print several papers for their graduate courses. However, he has imposed two conditions. First, they must supply their own paper. Second, they must pay Harry a fair amount for the usage of the ink cartridge. Harry's printer takes two types of cartridges, a black one and a color one that contains the inks necessary to print in color. Black replacement cartridges cost $25.50 each and print approximately 850 pages. The color cartridge replacement cost $31 and prints approximately 310 color pages. One ream of paper costs $2.50 and contains 500 sheets. Mary's printing requirements are for 500 pages, while Natalie's are for 1,000 pages.

Required:
1. Assuming that both women write papers using text only (i.e., black ink), what is the total amount owed to Harry by Mary? By Natalie?
2. What is the total cost of printing (ink and paper) for Mary? For Natalie?
3. Now suppose that Natalie illustrates her writing with many large colorful pie charts and pictures and that about 20 percent of her total printing is primarily color. Mary uses no color illustrations. What is the total amount owed to Harry by Natalie? What is the total cost of printing (ink and paper) for Natalie?

OBJECTIVE ⑤

Problem 1-44 Cost of Direct Materials, Cost of Goods Manufactured, Cost of Goods Sold

Bisby Company manufactures fishing rods. At the beginning of July, the following information was supplied by its accountant:

Raw materials inventory	$40,000
Work in process inventory	21,000
Finished goods inventory	23,200

During July, the direct labor cost was $43,500, raw materials' purchases were $64,000, and the total overhead cost was $108,750. The inventories at the end of July were:

Raw materials inventory	$19,800
Work in process inventory	32,500
Finished goods inventory	22,100

Required:
1. What is the cost of the direct materials used in production during July?
2. What is the cost of goods manufactured for July?
3. What is the cost of goods sold for July?

OBJECTIVE ⑤

Problem 1-45 Preparation of Income Statement: Manufacturing Firm

Laworld Inc. manufactures small camping tents. Last year, 200,000 tents were made and sold for $60 each. Each tent includes the following costs:

Direct materials	$18
Direct labor	12
Overhead	16

The only selling expenses were a commission of $2 per unit sold and advertising totaling $100,000. Administrative expenses, all fixed, equaled $300,000. There were no beginning or ending finished goods inventories. There were no beginning or ending work in process inventories.

Required:
1. Calculate the product cost for one tent. Calculate the total product cost for last year.
2. Prepare an income statement for external users. Did you need to prepare a supporting statement of cost of goods manufactured? Explain.

3.   Suppose 200,000 tents were produced (and 200,000 sold) but that the company had a beginning finished goods inventory of 10,000 tents produced in the prior year at $40 per unit. The company follows a first-in, first-out policy for its inventory (meaning that the units produced first are sold first for purposes of cost flow). What effect does this have on the income statement? Show the new statement.

Problem 1-46 Cost of Goods Manufactured, Cost of Goods Sold

OBJECTIVE ⑤

spreadsheet

Hayward Company, a manufacturing firm, has supplied the following information from its accounting records for the month of May:

Direct labor cost	$10,500
Purchases of raw materials	15,000
Supplies used	675
Factory insurance	350
Commissions paid	2,500
Factory supervision	2,225
Advertising	800
Material handling	3,750
Materials inventory, May 1	3,475
Work in process inventory, May 1	12,500
Finished goods inventory, May 1	6,685
Materials inventory, May 31	9,500
Work in process inventory, May 31	14,250
Finished goods inventory, May 31	4,250

Required:
1.   Prepare a statement of cost of goods manufactured.
2.   Prepare a statement of cost of goods sold.

Problem 1-47 Cost of Direct Materials, Prime Cost, Conversion Cost, Income Statement, Services versus Manufacturing

OBJECTIVES ④⑤

Lance Peckam owns and operates three Confiable Muffler outlets in Tucson, Arizona. Confiable is a franchise popular throughout the Southwest; it specializes in replacing old mufflers with new mufflers that have a lifetime guarantee. In April, purchases of materials equaled $200,000, the beginning inventory of materials was $26,300, and the ending inventory of materials was $14,250. Payments to direct labor during the month totaled $53,000. Overhead incurred was $120,000. The Tucson outlets also spent $15,000 on advertising during the month. A franchise fee of $3,000 per outlet is paid every month. Revenues for April were $500,000.

Required:
1.   What was the cost of materials used for muffler-changing services during April?
2.   What was the prime cost for April?
3.   What was the conversion cost for April?
4.   What was the total cost of services for April?
5.   Prepare an income statement for the month of April.
6.   Confiable purchases all its mufflers from Remington Company, a manufacturer of mufflers.
Discuss the differences between the products offered by Remington and Confiable.

Problem 1-48 Cost Identification

OBJECTIVES ③④

Following is a list of cost items described in the chapter as well as a list of brief descriptive settings for each item.

Cost terms:

a.	Opportunity cost	f.	Conversion cost
b.	Period cost	g.	Prime cost
c.	Product cost	h.	Direct materials cost
d.	Direct labor cost	i.	Overhead cost
e.	Selling cost	j.	Administrative cost

Settings:

1. Marcus Armstrong, manager of Timmins Optical, estimated that the cost of plastic, wages of the technician producing the lenses, and overhead totaled $30 per pair of single-vision lenses.
2. Linda was having a hard time deciding whether to return to school. She was concerned about the salary she would have to give up for the next four years.
3. Randy Harris is the finished goods warehouse manager for a medium-sized manufacturing firm. He is paid a salary of $90,000 per year. As he studied the financial statements prepared by the local certified public accounting firm, he wondered how his salary was treated.
4. Jamie Young is in charge of the legal department at company headquarters. Her salary is $95,000 per year. She reports to the CEO.
5. All factory costs that are not classified as direct materials or direct labor.
6. The new product required machining, assembly, and painting. The design engineer asked the accounting department to estimate the labor cost of each of the three operations. The engineer supplied the estimated labor hours for each operation.
7. After obtaining the estimate of direct labor cost, the design engineer estimated the cost of the materials that would be used for the new product.
8. The design engineer totaled the costs of materials and direct labor for the new product.
9. The design engineer also estimated the cost of converting the raw materials into its final form.
10. The auditor for a soft drink bottling plant pointed out that the depreciation on the delivery trucks had been incorrectly assigned to product cost (through overhead). Accordingly, the depreciation charge was reallocated on the income statement.

Required:

Match the items with the settings. More than one cost classification may be associated with each setting; however, select the setting that seems to fit the item best. When you are done, each cost term will be used just once.

OBJECTIVE ⑤ ### Problem 1-49 Cost of Goods Manufactured, Income Statement

W. W. Phillips Company produced 4,000 leather recliners during the year. These recliners sell for $400 each. Phillips had 500 recliners in finished goods inventory at the beginning of the year. At the end of the year, there were 700 recliners in finished goods inventory. Phillips' accounting records provide the following information:

Purchases of raw materials	$320,000
Beginning materials inventory	46,800
Ending materials inventory	66,800
Direct labor	200,000
Indirect labor	40,000
Rent, factory building	42,000
Depreciation, factory equipment	60,000
Utilities, factory	11,900
Salary, sales supervisor	90,000
Commissions, salespersons	180,000
General administration	300,000
Beginning work in process inventory	13,040
Ending work in process inventory	14,940
Beginning finished goods inventory	80,000
Ending finished goods inventory	114,100

Required:

1. Prepare a statement of cost of goods manufactured.
2. Compute the average cost of producing one unit of product in the year.
3. Prepare an income statement for external users.

Problem 1-50 Cost Definitions

OBJECTIVE ③

Luisa Giovanni is a student at New York University. To help pay her way through college, Luisa started a dog walking service. She has 12 client dogs—six are walked on the first shift (6:30 A.M. and 5:00 P.M.), and six are walked on the second shift (7:30 A.M. and 6:00 P.M.).

Last month, Luisa noted the following:

1. Purchase of three leashes at $10 each (she carries these with her in case a leash breaks during a walk).
2. Internet service cost of $40 a month. This enables her to keep in touch with the owners, bill them by e-mail, and so on.
3. Dog treats of $50 to reward each dog at the end of each walk.
4. A heavy duty raincoat and hat for $100.
5. Partway through the month, Luisa's friend, Jason, offered her a chance to play a bit role in a movie that was shooting on location in New York City. The job paid $100 and would have required Luisa to be on location at 6 A.M. and to remain for 12 hours. Regretfully, Luisa turned it down.
6. The owners pay Luisa $250 per month per dog for her services.

Required:

1. At the end of the month, how would Luisa classify her Internet payment of $40— as a cost on the balance sheet or as an expense on the income statement?
2. Which of the above is an opportunity cost? Why?
3. What price is charged? What is Luisa's total revenue for a month?

Problem 1-51 Cost Identification and Analysis, Cost Assignment, Income Statement

OBJECTIVES ③④⑤

Melissa Vassar has decided to open a printing shop. She has secured two contracts. One is a five-year contract to print a popular regional magazine. This contract calls for 5,000 copies each month. The second contract is a three-year agreement to print tourist brochures for the state. The state tourist office requires 10,000 brochures per month.

Melissa has rented a building for $1,400 per month. Her printing equipment was purchased for $40,000 and has a life expectancy of 20,000 hours with no salvage value. Depreciation is assigned to a period based on the hours of usage. Melissa has scheduled the delivery of the products so that two production runs are needed. In the first run, the equipment is prepared for the magazine printing. In the second run, the equipment is reconfigured for brochure printing. It takes twice as long to configure the equipment for the magazine setup as it does for the brochure setup. The total setup costs per month are $600.

Insurance costs for the building and equipment are $140 per month. Power to operate the printing equipment is strongly related to machine usage. The printing equipment causes virtually all the power costs. Power costs will run $350 per month. Printing materials will cost $0.40 per copy for the magazine and $0.08 per copy for the brochure. Melissa will hire workers to run the presses as needed (part-time workers are easy to hire). She must pay $10 per hour. Each worker can produce 20 copies of the magazine per printing hour or 100 copies of the brochure. Distribution costs are $500 per month. Melissa will receive a salary of $1,500 per month. She is responsible for personnel, accounting, sales, and production—in effect, she is responsible for administering all aspects of the business.

Required:

1. What are the total monthly manufacturing costs?
2. What are the total monthly prime costs? Total monthly prime costs for the regional magazine? For the brochure?

3. What are the total monthly conversion costs? Suppose Melissa wants to determine monthly conversion costs for each product. Assign monthly conversion costs to each product using direct tracing and driver tracing whenever possible. For those costs that cannot be assigned by using a tracing approach, you may assign them using direct labor hours.

4. Melissa receives $1.80 per copy of the magazine and $0.45 per brochure. Prepare an income statement for the first month of operations.

OBJECTIVES ③④

Problem 1-52 Cost Analysis, Income Statement

Five to six times a year, Kicker puts on tent sales in various cities throughout Oklahoma and the surrounding states. The tent sales are designed to show Kicker customers new products, engender enthusiasm about those products, and sell soon to be out-of-date products at greatly reduced prices. Each tent sale lasts one day and requires parking lot space to set up the Kicker semitrailer; a couple of show cars; a deejay playing music; and a tent to sell Kicker merchandise, distribute brochures, and so on.

Last year, the Austin tent sale was held in a far corner of the parking lot outside the city exhibition hall where the automotive show was in progress. Because most customers were interested more in the new model cars than in the refurbishment of their current cars, foot traffic was low. In addition, customers did not want to carry speakers and amplifiers all the way back to where they had originally parked. Total direct costs for this tent sale amounted to $14,300. Direct costs included gasoline and fuel for three pickup trucks and the semitrailer; wages and per diem for the five Kicker personnel who traveled to the show; rent on the parking lot space; depreciation on the semitrailer, pickups, tent, tables (in tent), sound equipment; and the like. Revenue was $20,000. Cost of goods sold for the speakers was $7,000.

Required:

1. How do you suppose Kicker accounts for the costs of the tent sales? What income statement items are affected by the tent sales?

2. What was the profit (loss) from the Austin tent show? What do you think Kicker might do to make it more profitable in the future?

Cases

OBJECTIVES ③④⑤

Case 1-53 Cost Classification, Income Statement

Gateway Construction Company is a family-operated business that was founded in 1950 by Samuel Gateway. In the beginning, the company consisted of Gateway and three employees laying gas, water, and sewage pipelines as subcontractors. Currently, the company employs 25 to 30 people; Jack Gateway, Samuel's son, directs it. The main line of business continues to be laying pipeline.

Most of Gateway's work comes from contracts with city and state agencies. All of the company's work is located in Nebraska. The company's sales volume averages $3 million, and profits vary between 0 and 10 percent of sales.

Sales and profits have been somewhat below average for the past three years due to a recession and intense competition. Because of this competition, Jack Gateway is constantly reviewing the prices that other companies bid for jobs; when a bid is lost, he makes every attempt to analyze the reasons for the differences between his bid and that of his competitors. He uses this information to increase the competitiveness of future bids.

Jack has become convinced that Gateway's current accounting system is deficient. Currently, all expenses are deducted from revenues to arrive at operating income. No effort is made to distinguish among the costs of laying pipe, obtaining contracts, and administering the company. Yet all bids are based on the costs of laying pipe.

With these thoughts in mind, Jack began a careful review of the income statement for the previous year (see below). First, he noted that jobs were priced on the basis of equipment hours, with an average price of $165 per equipment hour. However, when it came to classifying and assigning costs, he decided that he needed some help. One thing that really puzzled him was how to classify his own salary of $114,000. About half of his time was spent in bidding and securing contracts, and the other half was spent in general administrative matters.

Gateway Construction
Income Statement
For the Year Ended December 31, 2008

Sales (18,200 equipment hours @ $165 per hour)	$3,003,000
Less expenses:	
Utilities	$ 24,000
Machine operators	218,000
Rent, office building	24,000
CPA fees	20,000
Other direct labor	265,700
Administrative salaries	114,000
Supervisory salaries	70,000
Pipe	1,401,340
Tires and fuel	418,600
Depreciation, equipment	198,000
Salaries of mechanics	50,000
Advertising	15,000
Total expenses	2,818,640
Income before income taxes	$ 184,360

Required:
1. Classify the costs in the income statement as (1) costs of laying pipe (production costs), (2) costs of securing contracts (selling costs), or (3) costs of general administration. For production costs, identify direct materials, direct labor, and overhead costs. The company never has significant work in process (most jobs are started and completed within a day).
2. Assume that a significant driver is equipment hours. Identify the expenses that would likely be traced to jobs using this driver. Explain why you feel these costs are traceable using equipment hours. What is the cost per equipment hour for these traceable costs?

Case 1-54 Cost Information and Ethical Behavior, Service Organization

OBJECTIVES ③④

Jean Erickson, manager and owner of an advertising company in Charlotte, North Carolina, had arranged a meeting with Leroy Gee, the chief accountant of a large, local competitor. The two are lifelong friends. They grew up together in a small town and attended the same university. Leroy was a competent, successful accountant but currently was experiencing some personal financial difficulties. The problems were created by some investments that had turned sour, leaving him with a $15,000 personal loan to pay off—just at the time that his oldest son was scheduled to enter college.

Jean, on the other hand, was struggling to establish a successful advertising business. She had recently acquired the rights to open a branch office of a large regional advertising firm headquartered in Atlanta, Georgia. During her first two years, she had managed to build a small, profitable practice; however, the chance to gain a significant foothold in the Charlotte advertising community hinged on the success of winning a bid to represent the state of North Carolina in a major campaign to attract new industry and tourism. The meeting she had scheduled with Leroy concerned the bid she planned to submit.

Jean: Leroy, I'm at a critical point in my business venture. If I can win the bid for the state's advertising dollars, I'll be set. Winning the bid will bring $600,000 to $700,000 of revenues into the firm. On top of that, I estimate that the publicity will bring another $200,000 to $300,000 of new business.

Leroy: I understand. My boss is anxious to win that business as well. It would mean a huge increase in profits for my firm. It's a competitive business, though. As new as you are, I doubt that you'll have much chance of winning.

Jean: You may be wrong. You're forgetting two very important considerations. First, I have the backing of all the resources and talent of a regional firm. Second, I have some political connections. Last year, I was hired to run the publicity side of the governor's campaign. He was impressed with my work and would like me to have this business. I am confident that the proposals I submit will be very competitive. My only concern is to submit a bid that beats your firm. If I come in with a lower bid and good proposals, the governor can see to it that I get the work.

Leroy: Sounds promising. If you do win, however, there will be a lot of upset people. After all, they are going to claim that the business should have been given to local advertisers, not to some out-of-state firm. Given the size of your office, you'll have to get support from Atlanta. You could take a lot of heat.

Jean: True. But I am the owner of the branch office. That fact alone should blunt most of the criticism. Who can argue that I'm not a local? Listen, with your help, I think I can win this bid. Furthermore, if I do win it, you can reap some direct benefits. With that kind of business, I can afford to hire an accountant, and I'll make it worthwhile for you to transfer jobs. I can offer you an up-front bonus of $15,000. On top of that, I'll increase your annual salary by 20 percent. That should solve most of your financial difficulties. After all, we have been friends since day one—and what are friends for?

Leroy: Jean, my wife would be ecstatic if I were able to improve our financial position as quickly as this opportunity affords. I certainly hope that you win the bid. What kind of help can I provide?

Jean: Simple. To win, all I have to do is beat the bid of your firm. Before I submit my bid, I would like you to review it. With the financial skills you have, it should be easy for you to spot any excessive costs that I may have included. Or perhaps I included the wrong kind of costs. By cutting excessive costs and eliminating costs that may not be directly related to the project, my bid should be competitive enough to meet or beat your firm's bid.

Required:
1. What would you do if you were Leroy? Fully explain the reasons for your choice. What do you suppose the code of conduct for Leroy's company would say about this situation?
2. What is the likely outcome if Leroy agrees to review the bid? Is there much risk to him personally if he reviews the bid? Should the degree of risk have any bearing on his decision?

2

Cost Behavior

© RYAN STINER

After studying Chapter 2, you should be able to:

1. Explain the meaning of cost behavior, and define and describe fixed and variable costs.

2. Define and describe mixed and step costs.

3. Separate mixed costs into their fixed and variable components using the high-low method, the scattergraph method, and the method of least squares.

4. (Appendix) Use a personal computer spreadsheet program to perform the method of least squares.

xperience Managerial Decisions

with Zingerman's Deli

Have you ever walked by a bakery counter, or even Mom's kitchen, and been stopped in your tracks by the unmistakable aroma of freshly baked bread or home-made cookies? If so, cost behavior was probably the furthest thing from your mind. However, for the owners of **Zingerman's** deli and bakery, founded in 1982 in Ann Arbor, Michigan, cost behavior is critical in making decisions that improve Zingerman's profitability.

In total, Zingerman's tracks and manages over 3,000 distinct costs! For example, Zingerman's pays close attention to variable costs, such as the all-natural, nonalkalized cocoa powder ingredient used in its signature Hot Cocoa Cake, and the size of its hourly workforce, which varies by season. Zingerman's also closely manages its numerous fixed costs, such as recipe "research and development" creation and ovens, across different production and sales levels to be sure that it doesn't make decisions that increase costs to a greater extent than revenues. Still other costs are mixed in nature, and the variable and fixed components must be disentangled before Zingerman's owners can budget for future periods, set prices, and plan for growth in the businesses. So, the next time you bite into a warm chocolate chip cookie, think about—if only for a brief moment—all of the cost behaviors that went into producing, packaging, selling, and distributing that tasty bite of joy!

Chapter 1 discussed various types of costs and took a close look at manufacturing and service costs. However, at that time, the primary concern was organizing costs into production, selling, and administrative costs. Related schedules of the cost of goods manufactured, cost of goods sold, and income statements were built. Now, it is time to focus on cost behavior—the way costs change as the related activity changes.

Cost behavior represents the foundation upon which managerial accounting is built, much like the critical role played by the theoretical pyramid in financial accounting. The theoretical pyramid of financial accounting, which contains critical assumptions (e.g., economic entity assumption) and principles (e.g., matching principle), is necessary for helping financial accountants properly record transactions and prepare financial statements for parties external to the organization. In much the same way, managers must properly understand cost behavior in order to make wise decisions. For example, a 2006 Grant Thornton Survey of 300 U.S. business leaders and senior executives reported that 79% of CEOs focus on understanding and managing costs in an attempt to increase company value.[1] This textbook provides numerous examples of how understanding cost behavior improves managerial decision making.

Costs can be variable, fixed, or mixed. Knowing how costs change as output changes is essential to planning, controlling, and decision making. For example, suppose that BlueDenim Jeans Company expects demand for its product to increase by 10 percent next year. How will that affect the total costs budgeted for the factory? Clearly, BlueDenim will need 10 percent more raw materials (denim, thread, zippers, and so on). In addition, it will need more cutting and sewing labor because someone will need to make the additional jeans, so these costs are variable in nature. But the factory building will probably not need to be expanded. Neither will the factory need an additional receptionist or plant manager. So those costs are fixed in nature. As long as BlueDenim's accountant understands the behavior of the fixed and variable costs, it will be possible to develop a fairly accurate budget for the next year.

Budgeting, deciding to keep or drop a product line (e.g., **Converse**'s ongoing decision to keep, drop, or alter its Dwyane Wade shoe), and evaluating the performance of a segment (e.g., **Delta Air Lines** decided in late 2005 to discontinue its low-fare Song Airline business segment after only 3 years of operation) all benefit from knowledge of cost behavior. In fact, failure to understand cost behavior can lead to poor—even disastrous—decisions. This chapter discusses cost behavior in depth so that a proper foundation is laid for its use in studying other cost management topics.

OBJECTIVE ①
Explain the meaning of cost behavior, and define and describe fixed and variable costs.

Basics of Cost Behavior

Cost behavior is the general term for describing whether a cost changes when the level of output changes. A cost that does not change in total as output changes is a *fixed cost*. A *variable cost*, on the other hand, increases in total with an increase in output and decreases in total with a decrease in output. Let's first review the basics of cost and output measures. Then, we will look at fixed and variable costs.

Measures of Output and the Relevant Range

In order to determine the behavior of a cost, we need to have a good grasp of the cost under consideration and a measure of the output associated with the activity. The terms *fixed cost* and *variable cost* do not exist in a vacuum; they only have meaning when related to some output measure. In other words, a cost is fixed or variable with respect to some output measure or driver. In order to understand the behavior of costs, we must first determine the underlying business activity and ask ourselves "What causes the cost of this particular activity to go up (or down)?" A **driver** is a factor that causes or leads to a change in a cost or activity. The driver is the output measure for which we are looking.

Let's look at some examples. Suppose that BlueDenim Jeans Company wants to classify its product costs as either variable or fixed with respect to the number of jeans

---

[1]*Grant Thornton LLP Survey of U.S. Business Leaders*, 12th Edition, 2006.

produced. In this case, the number of jeans produced is the driver. Clearly, the use of raw materials (denim, thread, zippers, and buttons) varies with the number of jeans produced. So, we could say that materials costs are variable with respect to the number of units produced. How about electricity to run the sewing machines? That, too, is variable with respect to the number of jeans produced because the more jeans are produced, the more sewing machine time is needed, and the more electricity it takes. Finally, what about the cost of supervision for the sewing department? Whether the company produces many pairs of jeans or fewer pairs of jeans, the cost of supervision is unchanged. So, we would say that supervision is fixed with respect to the number of jeans produced.

How does the relevant range fit into cost relationships? The **relevant range** is the range of output over which the assumed cost relationship is valid. The relevant range limits the cost relationship to the range of operations that the firm normally expects to occur. Let's consider BlueDenim's cost relationships more carefully. We said that the salary of the supervisor is strictly fixed. But is that true? If the company produced just a few pairs of jeans a year, it would not even need a supervisor. Surely, the owner could handle that task (and probably a good number of other tasks as well). On the other hand, suppose that BlueDenim increased its current production by two or three times, perhaps by adding a second and third shift. One supervisor could not possibly handle three shifts. So, when we talk about supervision cost, we are implicitly talking about it for the range of production that normally occurs.

We now take a closer look at fixed, variable, and mixed costs. In each case, the cost is related to only one driver and is defined within the relevant range.

Here's The Real Kicker

Kicker uses information on cost behavior to guide new programs. For example, the variable cost of manufacturing speakers led Kicker to work with its manufacturers to both increase quality and decrease cost. Fixed costs at the Stillwater location also received attention. Eight years ago Safety Director Terry Williams faced a problem with worker safety. Cost information based on a number of indicators revealed the problem:

- The cost of workmen's compensation insurance was high.
- The workmen's compensation experience rating was high.
- The number of injuries was up.
- The number of injuries requiring time off was up.
- The number of back injuries (the most serious type) was up.
- The average cost per injury was up.

Terry looked for the root cause of the problem and discovered that improper lifting led to the more serious back injuries. He instituted a comprehensive safety program emphasizing 20 minutes of stretching exercises each day (five minutes before work, five minutes after each break, and five minutes after lunch).

Was the program a success? At first, the workers resisted the stretching. So, Terry got them weight belts. Workers hated them. They went back to stretching. But this time, any worker who refused to stretch had to wear the weight belt for 30 days. This was a highly visible sign of failure to adhere to the program. In addition, Kicker's president was a big proponent of the safety program. He explained the impact of the increased insurance premiums and lost work time on the Kicker profit sharing program. The profit sharing program is an important extra for Kicker employees; each employee makes it his job to contribute to the bottom line whenever possible.

Over several months, workers bought into the program. The indicators decreased dramatically. The cost of workmen's compensation insurance decreased by nearly 50 percent, the average cost per injury is less than 5 percent of the presafety program cost, and there is no lost work time.

Fixed Costs

Fixed costs are costs that *in total* are constant within the relevant range as the level of output increases or decreases. For example, **Southwest Airlines** has a fleet of 737s. The cost of these planes represents a fixed cost to the airline because, within the relevant range, the cost does not change as the number of flights or the number of passengers changes. Similarly, the rental cost of warehouse space by a wholesaler is fixed for the term of the lease. If the wholesaler's sales go up or down, the cost of the leased warehouse stays the same.

To illustrate fixed cost behavior, consider a factory operated by Colley Computers Inc., a company that produces unlabeled personal computers for small computer stores across the Midwest. The assembly department of the factory assembles components into a completed personal computer. Assume that Colley Computers wants to look at the cost relationship between supervision cost and the number of computers processed. The assembly department can process up to 50,000 computers per year. The assemblers (direct labor) are supervised by a production-line manager who is paid $32,000 per year. The company was established five years ago. Currently, the factory produces 40,000 to 50,000 computers per year. Production has never fallen below 20,000 computers in a year. The cost of supervision for several levels of production is as follows:

Colley Computers Inc.
Cost of Supervision

Number of Computers Produced	Total Cost of Supervision	Unit Cost
20,000	$32,000	$1.60
30,000	32,000	1.07
40,000	32,000	0.80
50,000	32,000	0.64

The cost relationship considered is between supervision cost and the number of computers processed. The number of computers processed is called the *output measure*, or *driver*. Since Colley Computers has been processing between 20,000 and 50,000 computers per year, the relevant range is 20,000 to 50,000. Notice that the *total* cost of supervision remains constant within this range as more computers are processed. Colley Computers pays $32,000 for supervision regardless of whether it processes 20,000, 40,000, or 50,000 computers.

Pay particular attention to the words *in total* in the definition of fixed costs. While the total cost of supervision remains unchanged as more computers are processed, the unit cost does change as the level of output changes. As the example in the table shows, within the relevant range, the unit cost of supervision decreases from $1.60 to $0.64. Because of the behavior of per-unit fixed costs, it is easy to get the impression that the fixed costs themselves are affected by changes in the level of output. But that is not true. Instead, higher output means that the fixed costs can be spread over more units and are thus smaller per unit. Unit fixed costs can often be misleading and may lead to poor decisions. It is often safer to work with total fixed costs.

Let's take a look at the graph of fixed costs given in Exhibit 2-1. We see that for the relevant range, fixed cost behavior is described by a horizontal line. Notice that at 40,000 computers processed, supervision cost is $32,000; at 50,000 computers processed, supervision is also $32,000. This line visually demonstrates that cost remains unchanged as the level of the activity driver varies. For the relevant range, total fixed costs are simply an amount. For Colley Computers, supervision cost amounted to $32,000 for any level of output between 20,000 and 50,000 computers processed. Thus, supervision is a fixed cost and can be expressed as:

Supervision cost = $32,000

Strictly speaking, this equation assumes that the fixed costs are $32,000 for all levels (as if the line extends to the vertical axis as indicated by the dashed portion in Exhibit 2-1). Although this assumption is not true, it is harmless if the operating decisions are confined to the relevant range.

Can fixed costs change? Of course, but this possibility does not make them variable. They are fixed at a new higher (or lower) rate. Going back to Colley Computers, suppose that the company gives a raise to the assembly department supervisor. Instead of being paid $32,000 per year, the salary is $34,000 per year. The cost of supervision within the relevant range is $34,000 per year. However, supervision cost is still *fixed* with respect to the number of computers produced.

By their nature, fixed costs are difficult to change quickly—that is why they are considered fixed. Two types of fixed costs are commonly recognized: discretionary fixed costs and

Analytical Q&A

In Exhibit 2-1, the fixed cost of supervision is drawn at $32,000. If the supervisor's salary is raised to $34,000 per year, can you draw in the new fixed cost line on Exhibit 2-1?

Answer:

The new line is above and parallel to the original one. The new line intersects the vertical axis at $34,000.

Exhibit 2-1

Colley Computers Fixed Cost of Supervision

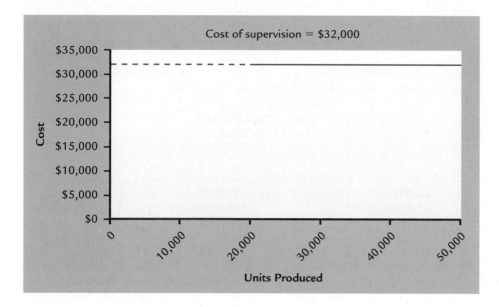

committed fixed costs. **Discretionary fixed costs** are fixed costs that can be changed relatively easily at management discretion. For example, advertising is a discretionary fixed cost. Advertising cost depends on the decision by management to purchase print, radio, or video advertising. The cost of advertising may depend on the size of the ad or the number of times it runs, but it does *not* depend on the number of units produced and sold. Management can easily decide to increase or decrease dollars spent on advertising.

Two days prior to the beginning of the 2006–07 season, the **National Football League** (NFL) was forced to make a decision involving discretionary costs. Specifically, the league realized that **Wilson Sporting Goods** had already manufactured 500,000 footballs (of the 900,000 total footballs that would be needed for the entire season) with the signature of the outgoing NFL commissioner—Paul Taglibue—instead of the incoming commissioner—Roger Goodell. The decision facing the NFL was whether to play the entire season or approximately only half of the season with the incoming commissioner's signature on the balls. If the 500,000 existing balls were given away to high schools (as the NFL eventually decided to do), then the $250,000 additional cost to produce another 500,000 balls with the new signature represents a discretionary cost to the league because it could be changed (i.e., avoided) relatively easily.[2] It is likely that this $250,000 discretionary cost is comprised heavily of fixed costs, as additional machinery will need to be purchased or leased to produce the footballs in such a short period of time.

A **committed fixed cost**, on the other hand, is a fixed cost that cannot be easily changed. Often, committed fixed costs are those that involve a long-term contract (e.g., leasing of machinery or warehouse space) or the purchase of property, plant, and equipment. For example, a construction company may lease heavy-duty earth-moving equipment for a period of three years. The lease cost is a committed fixed cost.

Variable Costs

Variable costs are defined as costs that in total vary in direct proportion to changes in output within the relevant range. The costs of producing and assembling the propeller on each boat

Concept Q&A

Consider the cost of a wedding reception. What costs are fixed? What costs are variable? What output measure did you use in classifying the costs as fixed or variable?

Answer:
Often, the number of guests is the output measure for a wedding reception. The cost of food and drinks varies with the number of guests. The relevant range for a wedding might be the approximate size—perhaps small (less than 100 guests), medium (100-200 guests), and large (200+ guests). Within a relevant range, fixed costs might include rental of the facility, flowers, and the cake.

[2]Tom Lowry, "Two-Minute Warning," *Business Week* (September 4, 2006): 12.

manufactured by **Boston Whaler** represent variable costs for a manufacturer. In a dentist's office, certain supplies, such as the disposable bib used on each patient, floss, and x-ray film, vary with the number of patients seen. **Binney & Smith**, the maker of Crayola crayons, finds that the cost of wax and pigments varies with the number of crayons produced.

To illustrate, let's expand the Colley Computers example to include the cost of the DVD-ROM drive that is inserted in each computer. Here, the cost is the cost of direct materials—the DVD-ROM drive—and the output measure is the number of computers processed. Each computer requires one DVD-ROM drive costing $40. The cost of DVD-ROM drives for various levels of production is as follows:

Colley Computers Inc.
Cost of DVD-ROM Drives

Number of Computers Produced	Total Cost of DVD-ROM Drives ($)	Unit Cost ($)
20,000	800,000	40
30,000	1,200,000	40
40,000	1,600,000	40
50,000	2,000,000	40

As more computers are produced, the total cost of DVD-ROM drives increases in direct proportion. For example, as production doubles from 20,000 to 40,000 units, the *total* cost of DVD-ROM drives doubles from $800,000 to $1,600,000. Notice also that the unit cost of direct materials is constant.

Variable costs can also be represented by a linear equation. Here, total variable costs depend on the level of output. This relationship can be described by the following equation:

Total variable costs = Variable rate × Amount of output

The relationship that describes the cost of disk drives is:

Total variable cost = $40 × Number of computers

Exhibit 2-2 shows graphically that variable cost behavior is represented by a straight line extending out from the origin. Notice that at zero units processed, total variable cost is zero. However, as units produced increase, the total variable cost also increases. Here, it can be seen that total cost increases in direct proportion to increases in the number of computers processed; the rate of increase is measured by the slope of the line. At 50,000 computers processed, the total cost of disk drives is $2,000,000 (or $40 × 50,000

Exhibit 2-2

Colley Computers Variable Cost of DVD-ROM Drives

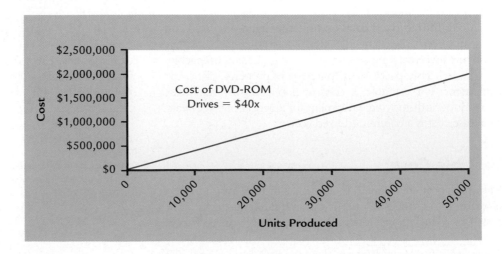

computers processed); at 30,000 computers processed, the total cost would be $1,200,000. Exhibit 2-2 illustrates variable cost behavior for the DVD-ROM drives.

The Reasonableness of Straight-Line Cost Relationships

The graphs of fixed and variable costs that were just reviewed show cost relationships that are straight lines. Is this reasonable; are real-world cost relationships linear?

In the Colley Computers example, the DVD-ROM drives cost $40 each—no matter how many were purchased. However, if only a couple drives were bought, surely the cost would be higher—perhaps more than double. So, there are economies of scale in producing larger quantities of output. For example, at extremely low levels of output, workers often use more materials per unit or require more time per unit than they do at higher levels of output. Then, as the level of output increases, economies of scale arise as workers experience a learning curve and figure out how to use materials and time more efficiently such that the variable cost per unit decreases as more and more output are produced. Therefore, when economies of scale are present, the true total cost function is increasing at a decreasing rate, as shown in Exhibit 2-3. Some managers refer to this type of cost behavior as **semivariable**.

When unit costs change in this way, how do we choose the correct variable rate? Fortunately, the relevant range can help us out. Recall that *relevant range* is defined as the range of activity for which the assumed cost relationships are valid. Exhibit 2-3 shows us how the relevant range can be used to see how well a straight line approximates variable cost. Note that for units of output before 20,000 on the x-axis, the approximation appears to break down. Therefore, managers must be extremely careful in applying cost behavior assumptions to decision making whenever the output level falls outside of the company's relevant range of operations.

Exhibit 2-3

Nonlinearity of Variable Costs

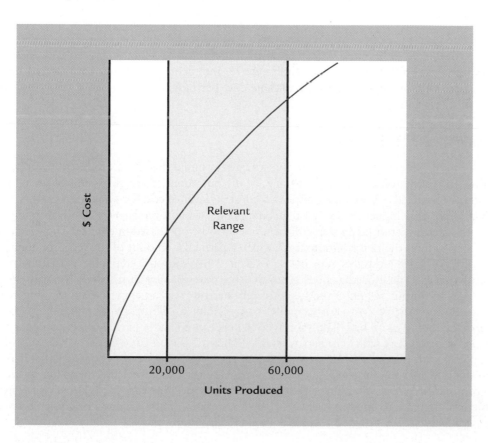

OBJECTIVE ②
Define and describe mixed and step costs.

Mixed Costs and Step Costs

While strictly fixed and variable costs are easy to handle, many costs do not fall into those categories. Often, costs are a combination of fixed and variable costs (mixed costs) or have an increased fixed component at specified intervals (step costs).

Mixed Costs

Mixed costs are costs that have both a fixed and a variable component. For example, sales representatives are often paid a salary plus a commission on sales. Suppose that Colley Computers has 10 sales representatives, each earning a salary of $30,000 per year plus a commission of $25 per computer sold. The activity is selling, and the output measure is units sold. If 50,000 computers are sold, then the total cost associated with the sales representatives is $1,550,000—the sum of the fixed salary cost of $300,000 (10 × $30,000) and the variable cost of $1,250,000 ($25 × 50,000).

The formula for a mixed cost is as follows:

Total cost = Total fixed cost + Total variable cost

For Colley Computers, the cost of the sales representatives is represented by the following equation:

Total cost = $300,000 + ($25 × Number of computers sold)

The following table shows the selling cost for different levels of sales activity:

Colley Computers Inc.

Fixed Cost of Selling ($)	Variable Cost of Selling ($)	Total Cost ($)	Computers Sold	Selling Cost per Unit ($)
300,000	500,000	800,000	20,000	40.00
300,000	750,000	1,050,000	30,000	35.00
300,000	1,000,000	1,300,000	40,000	32.50
300,000	1,250,000	1,550,000	50,000	31.00

The graph for our mixed cost example is given in Exhibit 2-4 (assuming a relevant range of 0 to 50,000 units). Mixed costs are represented by a line that intercepts the vertical axis (at $300,000 for this example). The y-intercept corresponds to the fixed cost, and the slope of the line gives the variable cost per unit of activity driver (slope is $25 for this example).

Step Cost Behavior

So far in our discussion of cost behavior, we have assumed that the cost function is continuous. In reality, some cost functions may be discontinuous; these costs are known as *step costs* (or semifixed). A **step cost** displays a constant level of cost for a range of output and then jumps to a higher level of cost at some point, where it remains for a similar range of output. Items that display a step cost behavior must be purchased in chunks. The width of the step defines the range of output for which a particular amount of the resource applies.

Exhibit 2-5 illustrates step costs. Exhibit 2-5A shows a step cost with relatively narrow steps. These narrow steps mean that the cost changes in response to fairly small changes in output. Often, if the steps are very narrow, we can approximate the step cost as a strictly variable cost. For example, Copy-2-Go, a photocopying shop, buys copy paper by the 20-ream box. The shop typically uses three boxes per day. The cost of copy paper is a step cost with very narrow steps. Exhibit 2-5B on page 62, however, shows a step cost with relatively wide steps. An example of this type of cost is a factory that leases production machinery. Suppose that each machine can produce 1,000 units per month. If production ranges from 0 to 1,000 units, only one machine is needed. However, if production increases to amounts between 1,001 and 2,000 units, a second machine must be leased. Many so-called fixed costs may be, in reality, step costs.

Exhibit 2-4

Mixed Cost Behavior

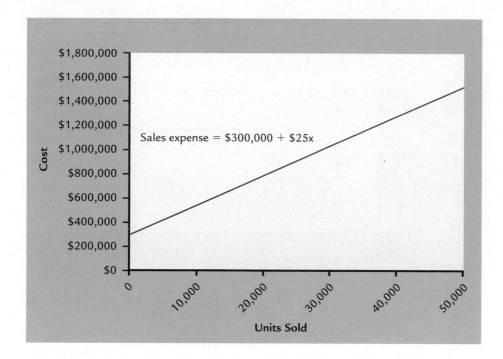

Sales expense = $300,000 + $25x

Exhibit 2-5A

Step Costs

A Step Cost with Narrow Steps

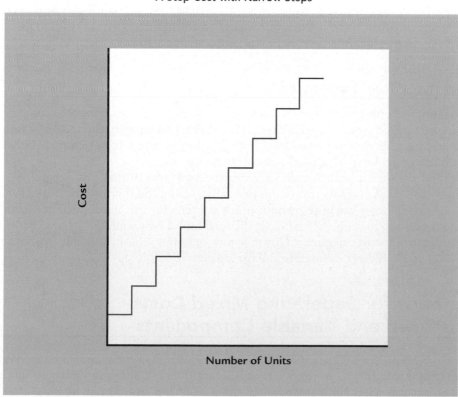

Exhibit 2-5B

Step Costs

A Step Cost with Wide Steps

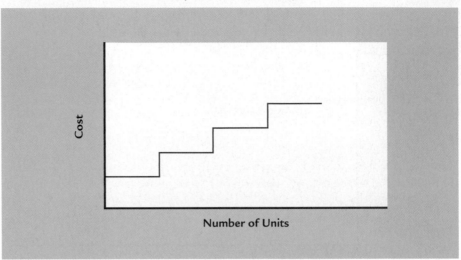

Accounting Records and Mixed Costs

Sometimes, it is easy to identify the variable and fixed components of a mixed cost, as in the example given earlier for Colley Computers' sales representatives. Many times, however, the only information available is the total cost and a measure of output. For example, the accounting system will usually record both the total cost of maintenance and the number of maintenance hours provided during a given period of time. How much of the total maintenance cost represents a fixed charge and how much represents a variable charge is not revealed by the accounting records. (In fact, the accounting records may not even reveal the breakdown of costs in the sales representative example.) Often, the total cost is simply recorded with no attempt to segregate the fixed and variable costs.

Need for Cost Separation

Accounting records typically show only the total cost and the associated amount of activity of a mixed cost item. Therefore, it is necessary to separate the total cost into its fixed and variable components. Only through a formal effort to separate costs can all costs be classified into the appropriate cost behavior categories.

   If mixed costs are a very small percentage of total costs, formal cost separation may be more trouble than it's worth. In this case, mixed costs could be assigned to either the fixed or variable cost category without much concern for the classification error or its effect on decision making. Alternatively, the total mixed cost could be arbitrarily divided between the two cost categories. However, this option is seldom available. Mixed costs for many firms are large enough to call for separation.

OBJECTIVE ③
Separate mixed costs into their fixed and variable components using the high-low method, the scattergraph method, and the method of least squares.

Methods for Separating Mixed Costs into Fixed and Variable Components

Three methods of separating a mixed cost into its fixed and variable components are commonly used: the high-low method, the scattergraph method, and the method of least squares. Each method requires the simplifying assumption of a linear cost relationship. Therefore, before we examine each of these methods more closely, let's review the expression of cost as an equation for a straight line.

Total cost = Fixed cost + (Variable rate × Output)

The **dependent variable** is a variable whose value depends on the value of another variable. In the above equation, total cost is the dependent variable; it is the cost we are trying to predict. The **independent variable** is a variable that measures output and explains changes in the cost or other dependent variable. A good independent variable is one that causes or is closely associated with the dependent variable. Therefore, many managers refer to an independent variable as a cost driver. The **intercept** corresponds to fixed cost. Graphically, the intercept is the point at which the cost line intercepts the cost (vertical) axis. The **slope** corresponds to the variable rate (the variable cost per unit of output); it is the slope of the cost line. Cornerstone 2-1 shows how to create and use a cost formula.

Since the accounting records reveal only total cost and output, those values must be used to estimate the fixed cost and variable rate. Three methods can be used to estimate these two items: the high-low method, the scattergraph method, and the method of least squares.

The following example with the same data will be used with each method so that comparisons among them can be made. The example focuses on materials handling cost

---

HOW TO Create and Use a Cost Formula

CORNERSTONE 2-1

Information: The art and graphics department of State College decided to equip each faculty office with an inkjet color printer (computers were already in place). Sufficient color printers had monthly depreciation of $250. The department purchased paper in boxes of 10,000 sheets (20 reams of 500 sheets each) for $35 per box. Ink cartridges cost $30 and will print, on average, 300 pages.

Required:
1. Create a formula for the monthly cost of inkjet printing in the art and graphics department.
2. If the department expects to print 4,400 pages next month, what is the expected fixed cost? Total variable cost? Total printing cost?

Calculation:
1. The cost formula takes the following form:

   Total cost = Fixed cost + (Variable rate × Number of pages)

   The monthly fixed cost is $250 (the cost of printer depreciation), as it does not vary according to the number of pages printed. The variable costs are paper and ink, as both do vary with the number of pages printed.

   Cost of paper per page is $35/10,000 = $0.0035
   Cost of ink per page is $30/300 = $0.10

   Variable rate per page is $0.0035 + $0.10 = $0.1035

   The cost formula is:

   Total cost of printing = $250 + ($0.1035 × Number of pages)

2. Expected fixed cost for next month is $250.
   Expected variable cost for next month is $0.1035 × 4,400 pages = $455.40
   Expected total printing cost for next month is $250 + $455.40 = $705.40

for Anderson Company, a manufacturer of household cleaning products. Materials handling involves moving materials from one area of the factory, say the raw materials storeroom, to another area, such as workstation 6. Large, complex organizations have found that the cost of moving materials can be quite large. Understanding the behavior of this cost is an important part of deciding how to reduce the cost.

Anderson's controller has accumulated data for the materials handling activity. The plant manager believes that the number of material moves is a good activity driver for the activity. Assume that the accounting records of Anderson Company disclose the following material handling costs and number of material moves for the past 9 months:

Month	Material Handling Cost ($)	Number of Moves
January	2,000	100
February	3,090	125
March	2,780	175
April	1,990	200
May	7,500	500
June	5,300	300
July	3,800	250
August	6,300	400
September	5,600	475

The High-Low Method

From basic geometry, we know that two points are needed to determine a line. Once we know the two points on a line, then its equation can be determined. Recall that the fixed cost is the *intercept* of the total cost line and that the variable rate is the *slope* of the line. Given two points, the slope and the intercept can be determined. The **high-low method** is a method of separating mixed costs into fixed and variable components by using just the high and low data points. Four steps must be taken in the high-low method.

Step 1: Find the high point and the low point for a given data set. The *high point* is defined as the point with the *highest activity* (*output level*). The *low point* is defined as the point with the *lowest activity* or *output level*. It is important to note that the high and low points are identified by looking at the activity levels and not the costs. In some cases, the highest (or lowest) activity level might also be associated with the highest (or lowest) cost, whereas in other cases it is not. Therefore, the managerial accountant must be careful to use the activity level in identifying the high and low data points for the analysis, regardless of whether or not the high (or low) activity level is associated with the high (or low) cost. In the data for maintenance cost, the high output occurred in May, with 500 material moves and total cost of $7,500. The low output was in January with 100 material moves and total cost of $2,000.

Analytical Q&A

When working high-low problems, it helps to circle the high and low points so that you don't become confused. Right now, go to the data given for materials handling cost and number of moves, and circle the high point and low point.

Answer:
The high point is May, with cost of $7,500 and 500 moves; the low point is January, with cost of $2,000 and 100 moves.

Step 2: Using the high and low points, calculate the variable rate. To perform this calculation, we recognize that the variable rate, or slope, is the change in the total cost divided by the change in output.

$$\text{Variable rate} = \frac{\text{High point cost} - \text{Low point cost}}{\text{High point output} - \text{Low point output}}$$

Using the high and low points for our example, that would be as follows:

Variable = ($7,500 − $2,000)/(500 − 100) = $5,500/400 = $13.75

Step 3: Calculate the fixed cost using the variable rate (from step 2) and either the high point or low point.

> **Fixed cost = Total cost at high point − (Variable rate × Output at high point)**

OR

> **Fixed cost = Total cost at low point − (Variable rate × Output at low point)**

Let's use the high point to calculate fixed cost.

$$\text{Fixed cost} = \$7,500 - (\$13.75 \times 500) = \$625$$

Step 4: Form the cost formula for materials handling based on the high-low method.

$$\text{Total cost} = \$625 + (\$13.75 \times \text{Number of moves})$$

Cornerstone 2-2 shows how to use the high-low method to construct a cost formula. Once we have the cost formula, we can use it in budgeting and in performance control. For example, suppose that the number of moves for November is expected to be 350. Budgeted materials handling cost would be $5,437.50, or $625 + ($13.75 × 350). Alternatively, suppose that the controller wondered whether or not October's materials handling cost of $6,240 was reasonably close to what would have been predicted. Our cost formula would predict October's cost of $6,469 (rounded). (This amount is found by multiplying $13.75 times the 425 actual moves and then adding fixed cost of $625.) The actual cost is just $229 different from the predicted cost and probably would be judged to be reasonably close to the budgeted cost. Cornerstone 2-3 on page 66 shows how to use the high-low method to calculate predicted total variable cost and total cost for budgeted output.

Let's look at one last point. Notice that monthly data were used to find the high and low points and to calculate the fixed cost and variable rate. This means that the cost formula is the fixed cost *for the month*. Suppose, however, that the company wants to use that formula to predict cost for a different period of time, say a year. In that case, the variable cost rate is just multiplied by the budgeted amount of the independent variable for the year. The

Analytical Q&A

Right now, calculate the fixed cost by using the *low* point and the variable rate calculated in step 2. (You will get the same fixed cost, $625.)

Answer:
Fixed cost = $2,000 − $13.75(100) = $625

HOW TO Use the High-Low Method to Calculate Fixed Cost and the Variable Rate and to Construct a Cost Formula

Information: BlueDenim Company makes blue jeans. The company controller wants to calculate the fixed and variable costs associated with electricity used in the factory. Data for the past eight months were collected:

Month	Electricity Cost ($)	Machine Hours
January	3,255	460
February	3,485	500
March	4,100	600
April	3,300	470
May	3,312	470
June	2,575	350
July	3,910	570
August	4,200	590

Required: Using the high-low method, calculate the fixed cost of electricity, calculate the variable rate per machine hour, and construct the cost formula for total electricity cost.

**CORNERSTONE
2-2**

**CORNERSTONE
2-2
(continued)**

Calculation:

Step 1—Find the high and low points: The high number of machine hours is in March, and the low number of machine hours is in June. (*Hint:* Did you notice that the high cost of $4,200 was for August? Yet, August is not the high point because its number of machine hours is not the highest activity level. Remember, the high point is associated with the highest activity level; the low point is associated with the lowest activity level.)

Step 2—Calculate the variable rate:

Variable rate = (High cost − Low cost)/(High machine hours − Low machine hours)
        = ($4,100 − $2,575)/(600 − 350) = $1,525/250
        = $6.10 per machine hour

Step 3—Calculate the fixed cost:

Fixed cost = Total cost − (Variable rate × Machine hours)

Let's choose the high point with cost of $4,100 and machine hours of 600.

Fixed cost = $4,100 − ($6.10 × 600) = $4,100 − $3,660
        = $440

(*Hint:* Check your work by computing fixed cost using the low point.)

Step 4—Construct a cost formula: If the variable rate is $6.10 per machine hour and fixed cost is $440 per month, then the formula for monthly electricity cost is:

Total electricity cost = $440 + ($6.10 × Machine hours)

**CORNERSTONE
2-3**

HOW TO Use the High-Low Method to Calculate Predicted Total Variable Cost and Total Cost for Budgeted Output

Information: Recall that BlueDenim Company constructed the following formula for monthly electricity cost. (Refer to Cornerstone 2-2 to see how the fixed cost per month and the variable rate were computed.)

Total electricity cost = $440 + ($6.10 × Machine hours)

Required: Assume that 550 machine hours are budgeted for the month of September. Use the above cost formula for the following calculations:

1. Calculate total variable electricity cost for October.
2. Calculate total electricity cost for October.

Calculation:
1. Total variable electricity cost = Variable rate × Machine hours
                = $6.10 × 550
                = $3,355

2. Total electricity cost = Fixed cost + (Variable rate × Machine hours)
                = $440 + ($6.10 × 550)
                = $440 + $3,355
                = $3,795

intercept, or fixed cost must be adjusted. To convert monthly fixed cost to yearly fixed cost, simply multiply the monthly fixed cost by 12 (because there are 12 months in a year). If weekly data were used to calculate the fixed and variable costs, one would multiply the weekly fixed cost by 52 to convert it to yearly fixed cost, and so on. Cornerstone 2-4 shows how to use the high-low method to calculate predicted total variable cost and total cost for budgeted output in which the time period differs from the data period.

The high-low method has several important advantage. One advantage is its objectivity. That is, any two people using the high-low method on a particular data set will arrive at the same answer. Also the high-low method allows a manager to get a quick fix on a cost relationship by using only two data points. For example, a manager may have only two months of data. Sometimes, this will be enough to get a crude approximation of the cost relationship. In addition, the high-low method is simple, inexpensive, and easily communicated to other individuals, even those who are not comfortable with numerical analyses. For these reasons, the high-low method is frequently used in reality.

However the high-low method also has several important disadvantages that lead some managers to believe that it often is usually not as good as the other methods of separating mixed costs into fixed and variable components. Why? First, the high and low points often can be what are known as outliers. They may represent atypical cost-activity relationships. For example, in the Anderson Company example, if the high output had been 1,000 moves (rather than 500) due to some extremely unusual business activity during a given month, then this high point likely would have fallen outside of the company's relevant range of operations and, therefore, represented an outlier. In the

---

HOW TO Use the High-Low Method to Calculate Predicted Total Variable Cost and Total Cost for a Time Period That Differs from the Data Period

CORNERSTONE 2-4

Information: Recall that BlueDenim Company constructed the following formula for *monthly* electricity cost. (Refer to Cornerstone 2-2 to see how the fixed cost per month and variable rate were computed.)

Total electricity cost = $440 + ($6.10 × Machine hours)

Required: Assume that 6,500 machine hours are budgeted for the coming year. Use the above cost formula to make the following calculations:

1. Calculate total variable electricity cost for the year.
2. Calculate total fixed electricity cost for the year.
3. Calculate total electricity cost for the coming year.

Calculation:

1. Total variable electricity cost = Variable rate × Machine hours
   = $6.10 × 6,500
   = $39,650

2. There's a trick here; the cost formula is for the month, but we are being asked to budget electricity for the year. So, we will need to multiply the fixed cost for the month by 12 (the number of months in a year).

   Total fixed electricity cost = Fixed cost × 12 months in a year
   = $440 × 12
   = $5,280

3. Total electricity cost = 12($440) + ($6.10 × 6,500)
   = $5,280 + $39,650
   = $44,930

case of outliers the cost formula computed using these two points will not represent what usually takes place. The scattergraph method can help a manager avoid this trap by selecting two points that appear to be representative of the general cost-activity pattern. Second, even if the high and low points are not outliers, other pairs of points may clearly be more representative. To stress the likelihood of this possibility, a high-low analysis of 50 weeks of data would ignore 96 percent (i.e., 48 out of the 50 weeks) of the data! Again, the scattergraph method allows the choice of more representative points.

Scattergraph Method

The **scattergraph method** is a way to see the cost relationship by plotting the data points on a graph. The first step in applying the scattergraph method is to plot the data points so that the relationship between materials handling costs and activity output can be seen. This plot is referred to as a scattergraph and is shown in Exhibit 2-6A. The vertical axis is total cost (materials handling cost), and the horizontal axis is the driver or output measure (number of moves). Looking at Exhibit 2-6A, we see that the relationship between materials handling costs and number of moves is reasonably linear; cost goes up as the number of moves goes up and vice versa.

Now let's examine Exhibit 2-6B to see if the line determined by the high and low points is representative of the overall relationship. Notice that three points lie above the high-low line and four lie below it. This realization does not give us confidence in the high-low results for fixed and variable costs. In particular, we might wonder if the variable cost (slope) is somewhat higher than it should be and the fixed cost is somewhat lower than it should be.

Thus, one purpose of a scattergraph is to see whether or not a straight line reasonably describes the cost relationship. Additionally, inspecting the scattergraph may reveal one or more points that do not seem to fit the general pattern of behavior. Upon investigation, it may be discovered that these points (the outliers) were due to some irregular occurrences that are not expected to happen again. This knowledge might justify their elimination and perhaps lead to a better estimate of the underlying cost function.

We can use the scattergraph to visually fit a line to the data points on the graph. Of course, the manager or cost analyst will choose the line that appears to fit the points the

---

Exhibit 2-6A

Anderson Company's Materials Handling Cost

Scattergraph Showing Data Points

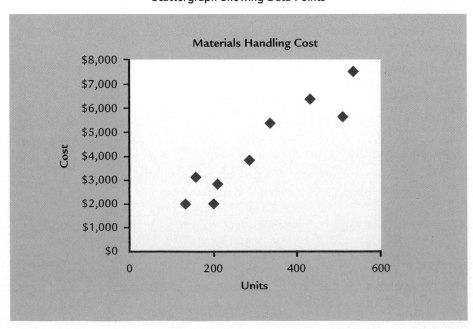

Exhibit 2-6B

Scattergraph with the High-Low Cost Line

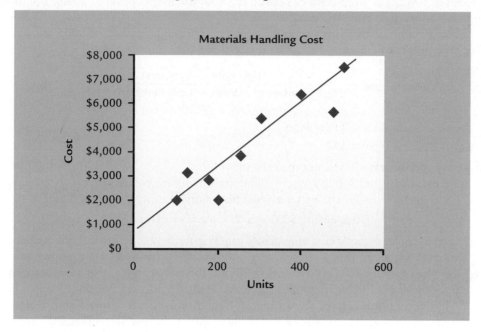

Exhibit 2-6C

Scattergraph with the Cost Line Fitted by Visual Inspection

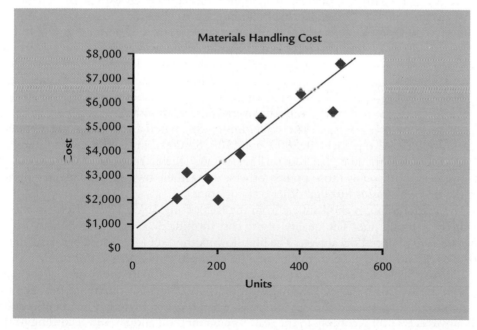

best, and perhaps that choice will take into account past experience with the behavior of the cost item. Experience may provide a good intuitive sense of how materials handling costs behave; the scattergraph then becomes a useful tool to quantify this intuition. Fitting a line to the points in this way is how the scattergraph method works. Keep in mind that the scattergraph and other statistical aids are tools that can help managers improve their judgment. Using the tools does not restrict the manager from using judgment to alter any of the estimates produced by formal methods.

Examine Exhibit 2-6A carefully. Based only on the information contained in the graph, how would you fit a line to the points in it? Of course, an infinite number of lines might go through the data, but let's choose one that goes through the point for January (100, $2,000) and intersects the y-axis at $800. Now, we have the straight line shown in Exhibit 2-6C. The fixed cost, of course, is $800, the intercept. We can use the high-low method to determine the variable rate.

First, remember that our two points are (100, $2,000) and (0, $800). Next, use these two points to compute the variable rate (the slope):

$$\text{Variable rate} = \frac{\text{High cost} - \text{Low cost}}{\text{High number of moves} - \text{Low number of moves}}$$

$$= (\$2,000 - \$800)/(100 - 0)$$
$$= \$1,200/100$$
$$= \$12$$

Thus, the variable rate is $12 per material move.

The fixed cost and variable rate for materials handling cost have now been identified. The cost formula for the materials handling activity can be expressed as:

$$\text{Total cost} = \$800 + \$12 \times \text{Number of moves}$$

Using this formula, the total cost of materials handling for between 100 and 500 moves can be predicted and then broken down into fixed and variable components. For example, assume that 350 moves are planned for November. Using the cost formula, the predicted cost is $5,000 [$800 + ($12 × 350)]. Of this total cost, $800 is fixed, and $4,200 is variable.

A significant advantage of the scattergraph method is that it allows a cost analyst to inspect the data visually. Exhibit 2-7 illustrates cost behavior situations that are not appropriate for the simple application of the high-low method. Exhibit 2-7A shows a nonlinear relationship between cost and output. An example of this type of relationship is a volume discount given on direct materials or evidence of learning by workers (e.g., as more hours are worked, the total cost increases at a decreasing rate due to the increased efficiency of the workers). Exhibit 2-7B shows an upward shift in cost if more than X_1 units are made—perhaps because an additional supervisor must be hired or a second shift run. Exhibit 2-7C shows outliers that do not represent the overall cost relationship.

The cost formula for materials handling was obtained by fitting a line to two points [(0, $800) and (100, $2,000)] in Exhibit 2-6C. Judgment was used to select the line. Whereas one person may decide that the best-fitting line is the one passing through those points, others, using their own judgment, may decide that the best line passes through other pairs of points.

The scattergraph method suffers from the lack of any objective criterion for choosing the best-fitting line. The quality of the cost formula depends on the quality of the subjective judgment of the analyst. The high-low method removes the subjectivity in the choice of the line. Regardless of who uses the method, the same line will result.

Looking again at Exhibits 2-6B and 2-6C, we can compare the results of the scattergraph method with those of the high-low method. There is a difference between the fixed cost components and the variable rates. The predicted materials handling cost for 350 moves is $5,000 according to the scattergraph method and $5,438 according to the high-low method. Which is correct? Since the two methods can produce significantly different cost formulas, the question of which method is the best naturally arises. Ideally, a method that is objective and, at the same time, produces the best-fitting line is needed. Let's take a look at the method of least squares.

Concept Q&A

Draw a straight line through the high and low points on each graph in Exhibit 2-7. Can you see that these lines, the high-low lines, could give misleading information on fixed and variable costs?

Yes, it is quite important to consider the relevant range.

Answer:

The Method of Least Squares

The **method of least squares (regression)** is a statistical way to find the *best-fitting* line through a set of data points. One advantage of the method of least squares is that for a given set of data, it will always produce the same cost formula. Basically, the best-fitting line is the

Exhibit 2-7

Scattergraphs with Nonlinear Cost

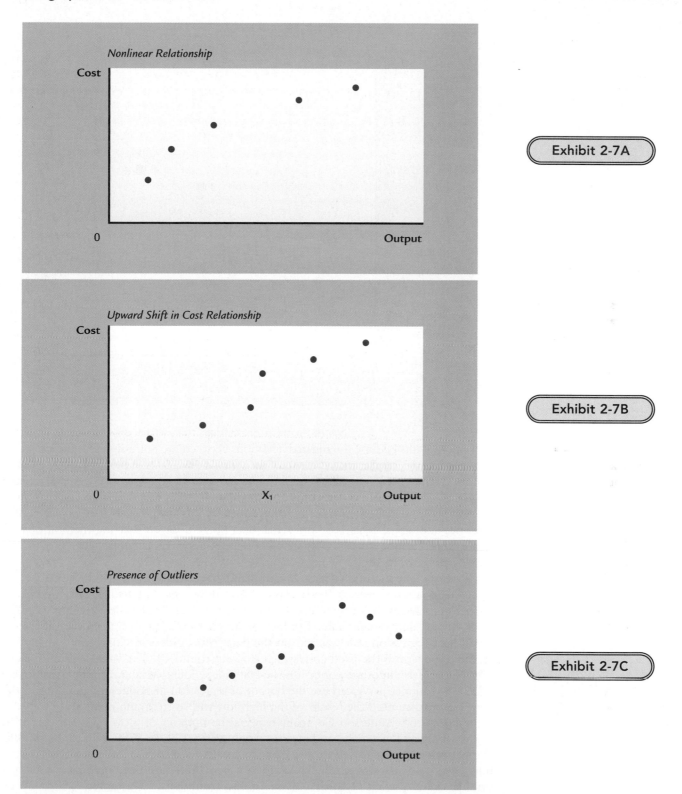

Nonlinear Relationship

Exhibit 2-7A

Upward Shift in Cost Relationship

Exhibit 2-7B

Presence of Outliers

Exhibit 2-7C

one in which the data points are closer to the line than to any other line. What do we mean by closest? Let's take a look at Exhibit 2-8 on page 72. Notice that there are a series of data points and a line—we'll assume that it is the regression line calculated by the method of least squares. The data points do not all lie directly on the line; this is typical. However, the

Exhibit 2-8

Line Deviations

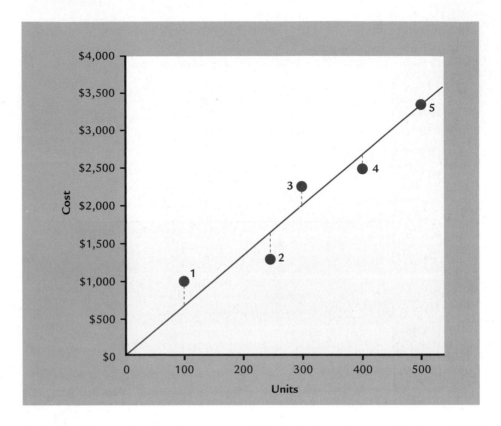

regression line better describes the pattern of the data than other possible lines. This best description results because the squared deviations between the regression line and each data point are, in total, smaller than the sum of the squared deviations of the data points and any other line. The least squares statistical formulas can find the one line with the smallest sum of squared deviations. In other words, this method identifies the regression line that minimizes the cost prediction errors or differences between predicted costs (i.e., on the regression line) and actual costs (i.e., the actual data points). Given that the method of least squares generates the smallest possible cost prediction errors, many managers refer to it as the most accurate method.

Formerly, the method of least squares had to be calculated by hand. It was a complicated and lengthy process. Today, spreadsheet programs for personal computers have regression packages. It is easy to use them to input data and to let the programs calculate the fixed cost and variable rate. Exhibit 2-9 shows a printout from a Microsoft Excel® spreadsheet regression that was run on the data from Anderson Company. Notice that the intercept term is the fixed cost, which is $789 (rounded). The variable rate is shown as "X Variable 1"; in other words, it is the first independent variable. So, the variable rate is $12.38 (rounded). We can use the output of regression in budgeting and control the same way that we used the results of the high-low and scattergraph methods.

Suppose that Anderson Company expects the number of moves for November to be 350. Budgeted materials handling cost would be $5,122, or $789 + ($12.38 × 350). Alternatively, suppose the controller wondered whether or not October's materials handling cost of $6,240 was reasonably close to what would have been predicted. Our cost formula would predict October cost of $6,051 (rounded). (This amount is found by multiplying $12.38 times the 425 actual moves and then adding the fixed cost of $789.) The actual cost is just $189 different from the predicted cost and probably would be judged to be reasonably close to the budgeted cost. Cornerstone 2-5 shows how to use results of regression to construct a cost formula.

Exhibit 2-9

A Portion of the Summary Output from Excel for Anderson Company

	A	B	C	D	E	F	G	H
	Anderson Company.xls							
1	Coefficients:							
2	Intercept	788.7806						
3	X Variable 1	12.38058						
4								
5								
6								
7								
8								
9								
10								
11								
12								
13								
14								
15								
16								

Sheet1 / Sheet2 / Sheet3 /

HOW TO Use the Regression Method to Calculate Fixed Cost and the Variable Rate and to Construct a Cost Formula and to Determine Budgeted Cost

**CORNERSTONE
2-5**

Information: BlueDenim Company makes blue jeans. The company controller wanted to calculate the fixed and variable costs associated with electricity used in the factory. Data for the past eight months were collected:

Month	Electricity Cost ($)	Machine Hours
January	3,255	460
February	3,485	500
March	4,100	600
April	3,300	470
May	3,312	470
June	2,575	350
July	3,910	570
August	4,200	590

Coefficients shown by a regression program are:

Intercept   321
X Variable 1   6.38

Required: Using the results of regression, calculate the fixed cost of electricity and the variable rate per machine hour. Construct the cost formula for total electricity cost. Calculate the budgeted cost for next month, assuming that 550 machine hours are budgeted.

Calculation:
1. The fixed cost and the variable rate are given directly by regression.

$$\text{Fixed cost} = \$ 321$$
$$\text{Variable rate} = \$6.38$$

2. The cost formula is:

Total electricity cost = $321 + ($6.38 × Machine hours)

3. Budgeted electricity cost = $321 + ($6.38 × 550) = $3,830

Managerial Judgment

Managerial judgment is critically important in determining cost behavior and is by far the most widely used method in practice. Many managers simply use their experience and past observation of cost relationships to determine fixed and variable costs. This method, however, may take a number of forms. Some managers simply assign some costs to the fixed category and others to the variable category. They ignore the possibility of mixed costs. Thus, a chemical firm may regard materials and utilities as strictly variable, with respect to pounds of chemical produced, and all other costs as fixed. Even labor, the textbook example of a strictly variable cost, may be fixed for this firm. The appeal of this method is simplicity. Before opting for this method, management would do well to make sure that each cost is predominantly fixed or variable and that the decisions being made are not highly sensitive to errors in classifying costs as fixed or variable.

To illustrate the use of judgment in assessing cost behavior, consider **Elgin Sweeper Company**, a leading manufacturer of motorized street sweepers. Using production volume as the measure of activity output, Elgin revised its chart of accounts to organize costs into fixed and variable components. Elgin's accountants used their knowledge of the company to assign expenses to either a fixed or variable category, using a decision rule that categorized an expense as fixed if it were fixed 75 percent of the time and as variable if it were variable 75 percent of the time.[3]

Management may instead identify mixed costs and divide these costs into fixed and variable components by deciding what the fixed and variable parts are; that is, they may use experience to say that a certain amount of a cost is fixed and that the rest therefore must be variable. Suppose that a small business had a photocopier with a fixed cost of $3,000 per year. The variable component could be computed by using one or more cost/volume data points. This has the advantage of accounting for mixed costs but is subject to a similar type of error as the strict fixed/variable dichotomy. That is, management may be wrong in its assessment.

Finally, management may use experience and judgment to refine statistical estimation results. Perhaps the experienced manager might "eyeball" the data and throw out several points as being highly unusual or revise results of estimation to take account of projected changes in cost structure or technology. For example, **Tecnol Medical Products Inc.** radically changed its method of manufacturing medical face masks. Traditionally, facemask production was labor intensive, requiring hand stitching. Tecnol developed its own highly automated equipment and became the industry's low cost supplier—besting both **Johnson & Johnson** and **3M**. Tecnol's rapid expansion into new product lines and European markets means that historical data on costs and revenues are for the most part irrelevant. Tecnol's management must look forward, not back, to predict the impact of changes on profit.[4] Statistical techniques are highly accurate in depicting the past, but they cannot foresee the future, which of course is what management really wants.

The advantage of using managerial judgment to separate fixed and variable costs is its simplicity. In situations in which the manager has a deep understanding of the firm and its cost patterns, this method can give good results. However, if the manager does not have good judgment, errors will occur. Therefore, it is important to consider the experience of the manager, the potential for error, and the effect that error could have on related decisions.

Concept Q&A

Suppose that you own a small business with a photocopier that neighboring businesses ask to use occasionally. What is the average cost of copying one page? What cost items would you include? Now consider Kinko's: What cost items do you think that they would include?

Answer:

If a neighboring business owner only needed a copy rarely, you might consider it a favor and not charge at all. If it happened several times a month, you might charge the variable cost of paper and toner. Finally, if the neighboring business owner used your copier frequently, you might charge 10¢ to 20¢ per page—a price similar to that of an outside photocopying shop. Alternatively, the neighbor might buy you a ream a paper from time to time. Kinko's must include all costs in determining the cost of copies—including paper, toner, depreciation on equipment, cost of electricity and utilities, wages of staff, and so on.

[3]John P. Callan, Wesley N. Tredup, and Randy S. Wissinger, "Elgin Sweeper Company's Journey Toward Cost Management," *Management Accounting* (July 1991): 24–27.
[4]Stephanie Anderson Forest, "Who's Afraid of J&J and 3M," *Business Week* (December 5, 1994): 66, 68.

Ethics There are ethical implications to the use of managerial judgment. Managers use their knowledge of fixed and variable costs to make important decisions, such as whether to switch suppliers, expand or contract production, or lay off workers. These decisions affect the lives of workers, suppliers, and customers. The ethical manager will make sure that he or she has the best information possible when making these decisions. In addition, the manager will not let personal factors affect the use of cost information. For example, suppose that the purchase department manager has a good friend who wants to supply some materials for production. The price of the materials is slightly lower than that of the current supplier; however, the friend's company will not ensure 100% quality control—and that will lead to additional costs for rework and warranty repair. The ethical manager will include these additional costs along with the purchase price to calculate the full cost of purchasing from the friend's company.◆

Summary of Learning Objectives

1. Explain the meaning of cost behavior, and define and describe fixed and variable costs.
   - Cost behavior is the way a cost changes in relation to changes in activity output.
   - Time horizon is important because costs can change from fixed to variable depending on whether the decision takes place over the short run or the long run.
   - Variable costs change *in total* as the driver, or output measure, changes. Usually, we assume that variable costs increase in direct proportion to increases in activity output.
   - Fixed costs do not change *in total* as activity output changes.
2. Define and describe mixed and step costs.
   - Mixed costs have both a variable and a fixed component.
   - Step costs remain at a constant level of cost for a range of output and then jump to a higher level of cost at some point, where it remains for a similar range of output.
   - Cost objects that display a step cost behavior must be purchased in chunks.
   - The width of the step defines the range of output for which a particular amount of the resource applies.
3. Separate mixed costs into their fixed and variable components using the high-low method, the scattergraph method, and the method of least squares.
   - In the high-low method, only two data points are used—the high point and the low point, with respect to activity level. These two points then are used to compute the intercept and the slope of the line on which they lie.
   - The high-low method is objective and easy, but a nonrepresentative high or low point will lead to an incorrectly estimated cost relationship.
   - The scattergraph method involves inspecting a graph showing total mixed cost at various output levels and selecting two points that seem to best represent the relationship between cost and output, and drawing a straight line. The intercept gives an estimate of the fixed cost component and the slope an estimate of the variable cost per unit of activity.
   - The scattergraph method is a good way to identify nonlinearity, the presence of outliers, and the presence of a shift in the cost relationship. Its disadvantage is that it is subjective.
   - The method of least squares uses all of the data points (except outliers) on the scattergraph and produces a line that best fits all of the points.
   - This method of least squares offers ways to assess the reliability of cost equations.
   - Managers use their experience and knowledge of cost and activity-level relationships to identify outliers, understand structural shifts, and adjust parameters due to anticipated changing conditions.

Summary of Important Equations

1. Cost formula: Total cost = Total fixed cost + (Variable rate × Units of output)
2. Total variable cost = Variable rate × Units of output

Cornerstone 2-1   How to create and use a cost formula, page 63

Cornerstone 2-2   How to use the high-low method to calculate fixed cost and the variable rate and to construct a cost formula, page 65

Cornerstone 2-3   How to use the high-low method to calculate predicted total variable cost and total cost for budgeted output, page 66

Cornerstone 2-4   How to use the high-low method to calculate predicted total variable cost and total cost for a time period that differs from the data period, page 67

Cornerstone 2-5   How to use the regression method to calculate fixed cost and the variable rate and to construct a cost formula and to determine budgeted cost, page 73

CORNERSTONES FOR CHAPTER 2

Key Terms

OBJECTIVE ④
Use a personal computer spreadsheet program to perform the method of least squares.

Appendix: Using the Regression Programs

Computing the regression formula manually is tedious, even with only a few data points. As the number of data points increases, manual computation becomes impractical. Fortunately, spreadsheet packages such as Lotus 1-2-3®, Quattro Pro®, and Microsoft Excel have regression routines that will perform the computations. All you need to do is input the data. The spreadsheet regression program supplies more than the estimates of the coefficients. It also provides information that can be used to see how reliable the cost equation is—a feature that is not available for the scattergraph and high-low methods.

The first step in using the computer to calculate regression coefficients is to enter the data. Exhibit 2-10 shows the computer screen that you would see if you entered the Anderson Company data on setups into a spreadsheet. It is a good idea to label your variables as is done in the exhibit. That is, the months are labeled, as are column B for setup costs and column C for number of setup hours. The next step is to run the regression. In Excel, the regression routine is located under the tools menu (located toward the top right of the screen). When you pull down the tools menu, you will see other menu possibilities. Choose add in, and then add the data analysis tools. When the data analysis tools have been added, data analysis will appear at the bottom of the tools menu; click on data analysis and then on regression.

When the regression screen pops up, you can tell the program where the dependent and independent variables are located. Simply place the cursor at the beginning of the

Exhibit 2-10

Spreadsheet Data for Anderson Company

	A	B	C	D	E	F	G	H
	Spreadsheet Data for Anderson Company.xls							
1	Month	Cost	# Moves					
2	January	$2,000	100					
3	February	3,090	125					
4	March	2,780	175					
5	April	1,990	200					
6	May	7,500	500					
7	June	5,300	300					
8	July	3,800	250					
9	August	6,300	400					
10	September	5,600	475					
11								
12								
13								
14								

independent rectangle and then (again using the cursor) block the values under the independent variable column—in this case, cells c2 through c10. Then, move the cursor to the beginning of the dependent rectangle, and block the values in cells b2 through b10. Finally, you need to tell the computer where to place the output. Block a nice-size rectangle, say cells a13 through f20, and click on OK. In less than the blink of an eye, the regression output is complete. The regression output is shown in Exhibit 2-11.

Now, let's take a look at the output in Exhibit 2-11. First, let's locate the fixed cost and variable rate coefficients. At the bottom of the exhibit, the intercept and X Variable 1 are shown, and the next column gives their coefficients. Rounding, the fixed cost is 789, and the variable rate is 12.38. Now, we can construct the cost formula for materials handling cost. It is:

Materials handling cost = $789 + ($12.38 × Number of moves)

We can use this formula to predict the materials handling cost for future months as we did with the formulas for the high-low and scattergraph methods.

Since the regression cost formula is the best-fitting line, it should produce better predictions of materials handling costs. For 350 moves, the total materials handling cost predicted by the least squares line is $5,122 [$789 + ($12.38 × 350)], with a fixed component of $789 plus a variable component of $4,333. Using this prediction as a standard, the scattergraph line most closely approximates the least squares line.

Exhibit 2-11

Regression Output for Anderson Company

	A	B	C	D	E	F	G	H
	Regression Output for Anderson Company.xls							
1	SUMMARY OUTPUT							
2								
3	Regression Statistics							
4	Multiple R	0.92436						
5	R Square	0.854442						
6	Standard Error	810.1969						
7	Observations	9						
8								
9								
10		Coefficients						
11	Intercept	788.7806						
12	X Variable 1	12.38058						
13								
14								
15								

While the computer output in Exhibit 2-11 can give us the fixed and variable cost coefficients, its major usefulness lies in its ability to provide information about reliability of the estimated cost formula. This is a feature not provided by either the scattergraph or high-low methods.

Goodness of Fit

Regression routines provide information on goodness of fit. Goodness of fit tells us how well the independent variable predicts the dependent variable. This information can be used to assess reliability of the estimated cost formula, a feature not provided by either the scattergraph or high-low methods. The printout in Exhibit 2-11 provides a wealth of statistical information. However, we will look at just one more feature—the coefficient of determination or R^2. (The remaining information is discussed in statistics classes and higher-level accounting classes.)

The Anderson Company example suggests that the number of moves can explain changes in materials handling costs. The scattergraph shown in Exhibit 2-6A confirms this belief because it reveals that materials handling costs and activity output (as measured by number of moves) seem to move together. It is quite likely that a significant percentage of the total variability in cost is explained by our output variable. We can determine statistically just how much variability is explained by looking at the coefficient of determination. The percentage of variability in the dependent variable explained by an independent variable (in this case, a measure of activity output) is called the **coefficient of determination (R^2)**. The higher the percentage of cost variability explained, the better job the independent variable does of explaining the dependent variable. Since R^2 is the percentage of variability explained, it always has a value between 0 and 1.00. In the printout in Exhibit 2-11, the coefficient of determination is labeled R Square (R^2). The value given is 0.85 (rounded), which means that 85 percent of the variability in the materials handling cost is explained by the number of moves. How good is this result? There is no cut-off point for a good versus bad coefficient of determination. Clearly, the closer R^2 is to 1.00, the better. Is 85 percent good enough? How about 73 percent? Or even 46 percent? The answer is that it depends. If your cost equation yields a coefficient of determination of 75 percent, you know that your independent variable explains three-fourths of the variability in cost. You also know that some other factor or combination of factors explains the remaining one-fourth. Depending on your tolerance for error, you may want to improve the equation by trying different independent variables (e.g., materials handling hours worked rather than number of moves) or by trying multiple regression. (Multiple regression uses two or more independent variables. This topic is saved for later courses.)

We note from the computer output in Exhibit 2-11 that the R^2 for materials handling cost is 0.85. In other words, material moves explain about 85 percent of the variability in the materials handling cost. This is not bad. However, something else explains the remaining 15 percent. Anderson Company's controller may want to keep this in mind when using the regression results.

Review Problem

Kim Wilson, controller for Max Enterprises, has decided to estimate the fixed and variable components associated with the company's shipping activity. She has collected the following data for the past six months:

Packages Shipped	Total Shipping Costs ($)
10	800
20	1,100
15	900
12	900
18	1,050
25	1,250

Required:
1. Estimate the fixed and variable components for the shipping costs using the high-low method. Using the cost formula, predict the total cost of shipping if 14 packages are shipped.
2. (APPENDIX) Estimate the fixed and variable components using the method of least squares. Using the cost formula, predict the total cost of shipping if 14 packages are shipped.
3. (APPENDIX) For the method of least squares, explain what the coefficient of determination tells us.

Solution:
1. The estimate of fixed and variable costs using the high-low method is as follows:

$$\text{Variable rate} = (\$1{,}250 - \$800)/(25 - 10)$$
$$= \$450/15$$
$$= \$30 \text{ per package}$$
$$\text{Fixed amount} = \$1{,}250 - \$30(25) = \$500$$

$$\text{Total cost} = \$500 + \$30X$$
$$= \$500 + \$30(14)$$
$$= \$920$$

2. The output of a spreadsheet regression routine is as follows:
    Regression output:

Constant	509.911894273125
Std Err of Y Est	32.1965672507378
R Squared	0.96928536465981
4	
No. of Observations	6
Degrees of Freedom	4
X Coefficient(s)	29.4052863436125
Std Err of Coef	2.61723229918858

$Y = \$509.91 + \$29.41(14) = \$921.65$

3. The coefficient of determination (R^2) tells us that about 96.9 percent of total shipping cost is explained by the number of packages shipped.

Discussion Questions

1. Why is knowledge of cost behavior important for managerial decision making? Give an example to illustrate your answer.
2. What is a driver? Give an example of a cost and its corresponding output measure or driver.
3. Suppose a company finds that shipping cost is $3,560 each month plus $6.70 per package shipped. What is the cost formula for monthly shipping cost? Identify the independent variable, the dependent variable, the fixed cost per month, and the variable rate.
4. Some firms assign mixed costs to either the fixed or variable cost categories without using any formal methodology to separate them. Explain how this practice can be defended.
5. Explain the difference between committed and discretionary fixed costs. Give examples of each.
6. Explain why the concept of relevant range is important when dealing with step costs.
7. Why do mixed costs pose a problem when it comes to classifying costs into fixed and variable categories?

8. Describe the cost formula for a strictly fixed cost such as depreciation of $15,000 per year.

9. Describe the cost formula for a strictly variable cost such as electrical power cost of $1.15 per machine hour (i.e., every hour the machinery is run, electrical power cost goes up by $1.15).

10. What is the scattergraph method, and why is it used? Why is a scattergraph a good first step in separating mixed costs into their fixed and variable components?

11. Describe how the scattergraph method breaks out the fixed and variable costs from a mixed cost. Now describe how the high-low method works. How do the two methods differ?

12. What are the advantages of the scattergraph method over the high-low method? The high-low method over the scattergraph method?

13. Describe the method of least squares. Why is this method better than either the high-low method or the scattergraph method?

14. What is meant by the best-fitting line?

15. Explain the meaning of the coefficient of determination.

Multiple-Choice Exercises

2-1 A factor that causes or leads to a change in a cost or activity is a(n)

a.   driver.
b.   intercept.
c.   slope.
d.   variable term.
e.   ratchet.

2-2 Which of the following would probably be a variable cost in a soda bottling plant?

a.   Direct labor
b.   Bottles
c.   Carbonated water
d.   Power to run the bottling machine
e.   All of the above

2-3 Which of the following would probably be a fixed cost in an automobile insurance company?

a.   Application forms
b.   Time spent by adjusters to evaluate accidents
c.   The salary of customer service representatives
d.   All of the above

2-4 The following cost formula was developed by using monthly data for a hospital.

Total cost = $41,670 + ($350 × Number of patient days)

The term "$41,670"

a.   is the independent variable.
b.   is the dependent variable.
c.   is the intercept.
d.   is the variable rate.
e.   cannot be determined from the above formula.

2-5 The following cost formula was developed using monthly data for a hospital.

Total cost = $41,670 + ($350 × Number of patient days)

The term "$350"

a. is the independent variable.
b. is the dependent variable.
c. is the intercept.
d. is the variable rate.
e. cannot be determined from the above formula.

2-6 The following cost formula was developed using monthly data for a hospital.

Total cost = $41,670 + ($350 × Number of patient days)

The term "Number of patient days"

a. is the independent variable.
b. is the dependent variable.
c. is the intercept.
d. is the variable rate.
e. cannot be determined from the above formula.

2-7 The following cost formula was developed using monthly data for a hospital.

Total cost = $41,670 + ($350 × Number of patient days)

The term "Total cost"

a. is the independent variable.
b. is the dependent variable.
c. is the intercept.
d. is the variable rate.
e. cannot be determined from the above formula.

2-8 The following cost formula for total purchasing cost in a factory was developed using monthly data.

Purchasing cost = $56,000 + ($2 × Number of purchase orders)

Next month, 800 purchase orders are predicted. The total cost predicted for the purchasing department next month

a. is $56,000.
b. is $1,600.
c. is $57,600.
d. is $800.
e. cannot be determined from the above formula.

2-9 An advantage of the high-low method is that it
a. is objective.
b. is subjective.
c. is the most accurate method.
d. removes outliers.
e. is descriptive of nonlinear data.

2-10 The following six months of data were collected on maintenance cost and the number of machine hours in a factory:

Month	Maintenance Cost ($)	Machine Hours
January	16,900	5,600
February	13,900	4,500
March	10,900	3,800
April	11,450	3,700
May	13,050	4,215
June	16,990	4,980

Select the independent and dependent variables.

	Independent Variable	Dependent Variable
a.	Maintenance cost	Machine hours
b.	Machine hours	Maintenance cost
c.	Maintenance cost	Month
d.	Machine hours	Month
e.	Month	Maintenance cost

2-11 The following six months of data were collected on maintenance cost and the number of machine hours in a factory:

Month	Maintenance Cost ($)	Machine Hours
January	16,900	5,600
February	13,900	4,500
March	10,900	3,800
April	11,450	3,700
May	13,050	4,215
June	16,990	4,980

Select the correct set of high and low months.

	High	Low
a.	January	April
b.	January	March
c.	June	March
d.	June	April

2-12 An advantage of the scattergraph method is that it
a.   is objective.
b.   is easier to use than the high-low method.
c.   is the most accurate method.
d.   removes outliers.
e.   is descriptive of nonlinear data.

2-13 The cost formula for monthly supervisory cost in a factory is:

Total cost = $4,500

This cost

a.   is strictly variable.
b.   is strictly fixed.
c.   is a mixed cost.
d.   is a step cost.
e.   cannot be determined from this information.

2-14 (Appendix) In the method of least squares, the coefficient that tells the percentage of variation in the dependent variable that is explained by the independent variable is

a.   the intercept term.
b.   the x-coefficient.
c.   the coefficient of correlation.
d.   the coefficient of determination.
e.   none of the above.

Exercises

Exercise 2-15 Variable and Fixed Costs   OBJECTIVE ①

What follows are a number of resources that are used by a manufacturer of futons. Assume that the output measure or cost driver is the number of futons produced. All direct labor is paid on an hourly basis, and hours worked can be easily changed by management. All other factory workers are salaried.

a.   Power to operate a drill (to drill holes in the wooden frames of the futons)
b.   Cloth to cover the futon mattress
c.   Salary of the factory receptionist
d.   Cost of food and decorations for the annual Fourth of July party for all factory
      employees
e.   Fuel for a forklift used to move materials in a factory
f.   Depreciation on the factory
g.   Depreciation on a forklift used to move partially completed goods
h.   Wages paid to workers who assemble the futon frame
i.   Wages paid to workers who maintain the factory equipment
j.   Cloth rags used to wipe the excess stain off the wooden frames

Required:
Classify the resource costs as variable or fixed.

Exercise 2-16 Cost Behavior, Classification   OBJECTIVE ①

Smith Concrete Company owns enough ready-mix trucks to deliver up to 100,000 cubic yards of concrete per year (considering each truck's capacity, weather, and distance to each job). Total truck depreciation is $200,000 per year. Raw materials (cement, gravel, and so on) cost about $25 per cubic yard of cement.

Required:
1.   Prepare a graph for truck depreciation. Use the vertical axis for cost and the horizontal axis for cubic yards of cement.
2.   Prepare a graph for raw materials. Use the vertical axis for cost and the horizontal axis for cubic yards of cement.
3.   Assume that the normal operating range for the company is 90,000 to 96,000 cubic yards per year. Classify truck depreciation and raw materials as variable or fixed costs.

Exercise 2-17 Classifying Costs as Fixed and Variable in a Service   OBJECTIVE ①
Organization

Alva Community Hospital has five laboratory technicians who are responsible for doing a series of standard blood tests. Each technician is paid a salary of $30,000. The lab facility represents a recent addition to the hospital and cost $300,000. It is expected to last 20 years. Equipment used for the testing cost $10,000 and has a life expectancy of five years. In addition to the salaries, facility, and equipment, Alva expects to spend $200,000 for chemicals, forms, power, and other supplies. This $200,000 is enough for 200,000 blood tests.

Required:
Assuming that the driver (measure of output) for each type of cost is the number of blood tests run, classify the costs by completing the following table. Put a check mark in the appropriate box for variable cost, discretionary fixed cost, or committed fixed cost.

Cost Category	Variable Cost	Discretionary Fixed Cost	Committed Fixed Cost
Technician salaries			
Laboratory facility			
Laboratory equipment			
Chemicals and other supplies			

OBJECTIVE ①
CORNERSTONE 2-1

Exercise 2-18 Cost Behavior

Carson Company manufactures digital thermometers. Based on past experience, Carson has found that its total maintenance costs can be represented by the following formula: Maintenance cost = $24,000 + $0.30X, where X = Number of digital thermometers. Last year, Carson produced 200,000 thermometers. Actual maintenance costs for the year were as expected.

Required:
1. What is the total maintenance cost incurred by Carson last year?
2. What is the total fixed maintenance cost incurred by Carson last year?
3. What is the total variable maintenance cost incurred by Carson last year?
4. What is the maintenance cost per unit produced?
5. What is the fixed maintenance cost per unit?
6. What is the variable maintenance cost per unit?

OBJECTIVE ①
CORNERSTONE 2-1

Exercise 2-19 Cost Behavior

Refer to Exercise 2-18. Now assume that Carson Company produced *100,000* thermometers.

Required:
1. What is the total maintenance cost incurred by Carson last year?
2. What is the total fixed maintenance cost incurred by Carson last year?
3. What is the total variable maintenance cost incurred by Carson last year?
4. What is the maintenance cost per unit produced?
5. What is the fixed maintenance cost per unit?
6. What is the variable maintenance cost per unit?

OBJECTIVE ②

Exercise 2-20 Step Costs, Relevant Range

Bellati Inc. produces large industrial machinery. Bellati has a machining department and a group of direct laborers called machinists. Each machinist is paid $50,000 and can machine up to 500 units per year. Bellati also hires supervisors to develop machine specification plans and to oversee production within the machining department. Given the planning and supervisory work, a supervisor can oversee, at most, three machinists. Bellati's accounting and production history shows the following relationships between number of units produced and the costs of materials handling and supervision (measured on an annual basis):

Units Produced	Direct Labor ($)	Supervision ($)
0–500	36,000	40,000
501–1,000	72,000	40,000
1,001–1,500	108,000	40,000
1,501–2,000	144,000	80,000
2,001–2,500	180,000	80,000
2,501–3,000	216,000	80,000
3,001–3,500	252,000	120,000
3,501–4,000	288,000	120,000

Required:

1. Prepare a graph that illustrates the relationship between direct labor cost and number of units produced in the machining department. (Let cost be the vertical axis and number of units produced the horizontal axis.) Would you classify this cost as a strictly variable cost, a fixed cost, or a step cost?
2. Prepare a graph that illustrates the relationship between the cost of supervision and the number of units produced. (Let cost be the vertical axis and number of units produced the horizontal axis.) Would you classify this cost as a strictly variable cost, a fixed cost, or a step cost?
3. Suppose that the normal range of activity is between 1,400 and 1,500 units and that the exact number of machinists are currently hired to support this level of activity. Further suppose that production for the next year is expected to increase by an additional 500 units. By how much will the cost of direct labor increase? Cost of supervision?

Exercise 2-21 Mixed Costs

OBJECTIVE ②

Ben Palman owns an art gallery. He accepts paintings and sculpture on consignment and then receives 20 percent of the price of each piece as his fee. Space is limited, and there are costs involved, so Ben is careful about accepting artists. When he does accept one, he arranges for an opening show (usually for three hrs. on a weekend night) and sends out invitations to his customer list. At the opening, he serves wine, soft drinks, and casual munchies to create a comfortable environment for prospective customers to view the new works and to chat with the artist. On average, each opening costs $500. Ben has given as many as 20 opening shows in a year. The total cost of running the gallery, including rent, furniture and fixtures, utilities, and a part-time assistant, amounts to $80,000 per year.

Required:

1. Prepare a graph that illustrates the relationship between the cost of giving opening shows and the number of opening shows given. (Let opening show cost be the vertical axis and number of opening shows given the horizontal axis.) Would you classify this cost as a strictly variable cost, a fixed cost, or a mixed cost?
2. Prepare a graph that illustrates the relationship between the cost of running the gallery and the number of opening shows given. (Let gallery cost be the vertical axis and number of opening shows given the horizontal axis.) Would you classify this cost as a strictly variable cost, a fixed cost, or a mixed cost?
3. Prepare a graph that illustrates the relationship between Ben's total costs (the sum of the costs of giving opening shows and running the gallery) and the number of opening shows given. Let the cost be the vertical axis and number of opening shows given the horizontal axis. Would you classify this cost as a strictly variable cost, a fixed cost, or a mixed cost?

OBJECTIVE ③
CORNERSTONE 2-3

Exercise 2-22 Mixed Costs and Cost Formula

Refer to **Exercise 2-21**.

Required:

1. Assume that the cost driver is number of opening shows. Develop the cost formula for the gallery's costs for a year.
2. Using the formula developed in Requirement 1, what is the total cost for Ben in a year with 12 opening shows? With 14 opening shows?

OBJECTIVE ③
CORNERSTONE 2-2
CORNERSTONE 2-3

Exercise 2-23 High-Low Method

Luisa Crimini has been operating a beauty shop in a college town for the past 10 years. Recently, Luisa rented space next to her shop and opened a tanning salon. She anticipated that the costs for the tanning service would primarily be fixed but found that tanning salon costs increased with the number of appointments. Costs for this service over the past eight months are as follows:

Month	Tanning Appointments	Total Cost ($)
January	700	1,758
February	2,000	2,140
March	3,100	2,790
April	2,500	2,400
May	1,500	1,800
June	2,300	2,275
July	2,150	2,200
August	3,000	2,640

Required:

1. Which month represents the high point? The low point?
2. Using the high-low method, compute the variable rate for tanning. Compute the fixed cost per month.
3. Using your answers to Requirement 2, write the cost formula for tanning services.
4. Calculate the total predicted cost of tanning services for September for 2,500 appointments using the formula found in Requirement 3. Of that total cost, how much is the total fixed cost for September? How much is the total predicted variable cost for September?

OBJECTIVE ③

Exercise 2-24 Scattergraph Method

Refer to **Exercise 2-23** for data on Luisa Crimini's tanning salon.

Required:
Prepare a scattergraph based on Luisa's data. Use cost for the vertical axis and number of tanning appointments for the horizontal. Based on an examination of the scattergraph, does there appear to be a linear relationship between the cost of tanning services and the number of appointments?

OBJECTIVE ③
CORNERSTONE 2-5

Exercise 2-25 Method of Least Squares

Refer to **Exercise 2-23** for data on Luisa Crimini's tanning salon. Now assume that Luisa's accountant collected data on costs for this service over the past eight months and used an Excel spreadsheet program to run ordinary least squares on the data. The following results were produced.

Intercept	1,290
X Variable	0.45

Required:

1. Compute the cost formula for tanning services using the results from the method of least squares.
2. Using the formula computed in Requirement 1, what is the predicted cost of tanning services for September for 2,500 appointments?

Exercise 2-26 High-Low Method, Cost Formulas

During the past year, the high and low use of three different resources in a factory occurred in May and November. The resources are machine depreciation, power, and maintenance. The number of machine hours is the driver. The total costs of the three resources and the related number of machine hours are as follows:

OBJECTIVE ③
CORNERSTONE 2-2
CORNERSTONE 2-3

spreadsheet

Resource	Machine Hours	Total Cost ($)
Machine depreciation:		
High	75,000	165,000
Low	20,000	165,000
Power:		
High	75,000	4,500
Low	20,000	1,200
Maintenance:		
High	75,000	53,800
Low	20,000	19,700

Required:

Use the high-low method to answer the following questions.

1. What is the variable rate for machine depreciation? The fixed cost?
2. What is the cost formula for machine depreciation?
3. What is the variable rate for power? The fixed cost?
4. What is the cost formula for power?
5. What is the variable rate for maintenance? The fixed cost?
6. What is the cost formula for maintenance?
7. Using the three cost formulas that you developed, predict the cost of each resource in a month with 40,000 machine hours.

Exercise 2-27 Changing the Cost Formula for a Month to the Cost Formula for a Year

Refer to the data provided in **Exercise 2-26**.

OBJECTIVE ③
CORNERSTONE 2-4

Required:

1. Develop annual cost formulas for machine depreciation, power, and maintenance.
2. Using the three annual cost formulas that you developed, predict the cost of each resource in a year with 630,000 machine hours.

Exercise 2-28 Method of Least Squares, Developing and Using the Cost Formula

The method of least squares was used to develop a cost equation to predict the cost of receiving. Eighty data points from monthly data were used for the regression. The following computer output was received:

OBJECTIVE ③
CORNERSTONE 2-5

Intercept	17,350
Slope	16

The driver used was number of receiving orders.

Required:

1. What is the cost formula?
2. Using the cost formula from Requirement 1, identify each of the following: independent variable, dependent variable, variable rate, and fixed cost per month.
3. Using the cost formula, predict the cost of receiving for a month in which 1,000 orders are processed.

OBJECTIVE ③
CORNERSTONE 2-4

Exercise 2-29 Method of Least Squares, Budgeted Time Period Is Different from Time Period Used to Generate Results

Refer to **Exercise 2-28**.

Required:

1. What is the cost formula for a year?
2. Using the cost formula from Requirement 1, predict the cost of receiving for a year in which 12,500 orders are processed.

OBJECTIVE ③
CORNERSTONE 2-1

Exercise 2-30 Identifying the Parts of the Cost Formula, Calculating Monthly, Quarterly, and Yearly Costs Using a Cost Formula Based on Monthly Data

Landring Company's controller estimated the following formula, based on monthly data, for overhead cost:

Overhead cost = \$7,344 + (\$10.50 × Machine hours)

Required:

1. Link each term in column A to the corresponding term in column B.

Column A	Column B
Overhead cost	Variable rate (slope)
\$7,344	Independent variable
\$10.50	Fixed cost (intercept)
Machine hours	Dependent variable

2. If next month's budgeted machine hours equal 10,000, what is the budgeted overhead cost?
3. If next quarter's budgeted machine hours equal 31,000, what is the budgeted overhead cost?
4. If next year's budgeted machine hours equal 125,000, what is the budgeted overhead cost?

OBJECTIVE ④
CORNERSTONE 2-5

spreadsheet

Exercise 2-31 (Appendix) Method of Least Squares Using Computer Spreadsheet Program

The controller for Beckham Company believes that the number of direct labor hours is associated with overhead cost. He collected the following data on the number of direct labor hours and associated factory overhead cost for the months of January through August.

Month	Number of Direct Labor Hours	Overhead Cost (\$)
January	689	5,550
February	700	5,590
March	720	5,650
April	690	5,570
May	680	5,570
June	590	5,410
July	750	5,720
August	675	5,608

Required:

1. Using a computer spreadsheet program such as Excel, run a regression on these data. Print out your results.
2. Using your results from Requirement 1, write the cost formula for overhead cost. (You may round the fixed cost to the nearest dollar and the variable rate to the nearest cent.)
3. What is R^2 based on your results? Do you think that the number of direct labor hours is a good predictor of factory overhead cost?
4. Assuming that expected September direct labor hours are 700, what is expected factory overhead cost using the cost formula in Requirement 2?

Exercise 2-32 (Appendix) Method of Least Squares Using Computer Spreadsheet Program

OBJECTIVE ④

CORNERSTONE 2-5

Susan Lewis, owner of a florist shop, is interested in predicting the cost of delivering floral arrangements. She collected monthly data on the number of deliveries and the total monthly delivery cost (depreciation on the van, wages of the driver, and fuel) for the past year.

Month	Number of Deliveries	Delivery Cost ($)
January	100	1,200
February	550	1,800
March	85	1,100
April	115	1,050
May	160	1,190
June	590	1,980
July	500	1,800
August	520	1,700
September	100	1,100
October	200	1,275
November	260	1,400
December	450	2,200

Required:

1. Using a computer spreadsheet program such as Excel, run a regression on these data. Print out your results.
2. Using your results from Requirement 1, write the cost formula for delivery cost. (You may round the fixed cost to the nearest dollar and the variable rate to the nearest cent.)
3. What is R^2 based on your results? Do you think that the number of direct labor hours is a good predictor of delivery cost?
4. Using the cost formula in Requirement 2, what would predicted delivery cost be for a month with 300 deliveries?

Problems

Problem 2-33 Identifying Fixed, Variable, Mixed, and Step Costs

OBJECTIVES ① ②

Consider each of the following independent situations:

a. A computer service agreement in which a company pays $150 per month and $15 per hour of technical time.
b. Fuel cost of the company's fleet of motor vehicles.
c. The cost of beer for a bar.
d. The cost of computer of computer printers and copiers in your college.
e. Rent for a dental office.
f. The salary of a receptionist in a law firm.
g. The wages of counter help in a fast-food restaurant.

h. The salaries of dental hygienists in a three-dentist office. One hygienist can take care of 120 cleanings per month.

i. Electricity cost, which includes a $15 per month billing charge and an additional amount depending on the number of kilowatt-hours used.

Required:

1. For each situation, describe the cost as one of the following: fixed cost, variable cost, mixed cost, or step cost. (*Hint:* First, consider what the driver or output measure is. If additional assumptions are necessary to support your cost type decision, be sure to write them down.)

    Example: Raw materials used in production—Variable cost

2. Change your assumption(s) for each situation so that the cost type changes to a different cost type. List the new cost type and the changed assumption(s) that gave rise to it.

    Example: Raw materials used in production. Changed assumption—the materials are difficult to obtain, and a year's worth must be contracted for in advance. Now, this is a fixed cost. (This is the case with diamond sales by DeBeers Inc. to its sightholders. See the following website for information: http://www.keyguide.net/sightholders/.)

OBJECTIVE ③

Problem 2-34 Identifying Use of the High-Low, Scattergraph, and Least Squares Methods

Consider each of the following independent situations:

a. Shaniqua Boyer just started her new job as controller for St. Matthias General Hospital. She wants to get a feel for the cost behavior of various departments of the hospital. Shaniqua first looks at the radiology department. She has annual data on total cost and the number of procedures that have been run for the past 15 years. However, she knows that the department upgraded its equipment substantially two years ago and is doing a wider variety of tests. So, Shaniqua decides to use just the past two years.

b. Francis Hidalgo is a summer intern in the accounting department of a manufacturing firm. His boss assigned him a special project to determine the cost of manufacturing a special order. Francis needs information on variable and fixed overhead, so he gathers monthly data on overhead cost and machine hours for the past 60 months and enters them into his personal computer. A few keystrokes later, he has information on fixed and variable overhead costs.

c. Ron Wickstead sighed and studied his computer printout again. The results made no sense to him. He seemed to recall that sometimes it helped to visualize the cost relationships. He reached for some graph paper and a pencil.

d. Lois March had hoped that she could find information on the actual cost of promoting new products. Unfortunately, she had spent the weekend going through the files and was only able to find data on the total cost of the sales department by month for the past three years. She was also able to figure out the number of new product launches by month for the same time period. Now, she had just 15 minutes before a staff meeting in which she needed to give the vice president of sales an expected cost of the average new product launch. A light bulb went off in her head, and she reached for paper, pencil, and a calculator.

Required:

Determine which of the following cost separation methods is being used: the high-low method, the scattergraph method, or the method of least squares.

Problem 2-35 Identifying Variable Costs, Committed Fixed Costs, and Discretionary Fixed Costs

OBJECTIVE ①

Required:
Classify each of the following costs for a jeans manufacturing company as a variable cost, committed fixed cost, or discretionary fixed cost.

a.   The cost of buttons.
b.   The cost to lease warehouse space for completed jeans. The lease contract runs for two years at $5,000 per year.
c.   The salary of a summer intern.
d.   The cost of landscaping and mowing the grass. The contract with a local mowing company runs from month to month.
e.   Advertising in a national magazine for teenage girls.
f.   Electricity to run the sewing machines.
g.   Oil and spare needles for the sewing machines.
h.   Quality training for employees—typically given for four hours at a time, every six months.
i.   Food and beverages for the company Fourth of July picnic.
j.   Natural gas to heat the factory during the winter.

Problem 2-36 Scattergraph, High-Low Method, and Predicting Cost for a Different Time Period from the One Used to Develop a Cost Formula

OBJECTIVE ③

spreadsheet

Farnsworth Company has gathered data on its overhead activities and associated costs for the past 10 months. Tracy Heppler, a member of the controller's department, has convinced management that overhead costs can be better estimated and controlled if the fixed and variable components of each overhead activity are known. One such activity is receiving raw materials (unloading incoming goods, counting goods, and inspecting goods), which she believes is driven by the number of receiving orders. Ten months of data have been gathered for the receiving activity and are as follows:

Month	Receiving Orders	Receiving Cost ($)
1	1,000	18,000
2	700	15,000
3	1,500	28,000
4	1,200	17,000
5	1,300	25,000
6	1,100	21,000
7	1,600	29,000
8	1,400	24,000
9	1,700	27,000
10	900	16,000

Required:
1.   Prepare a scattergraph based on the 10 months of data. Does the relationship appear to be linear?
2.   Using the high-low method, prepare a cost formula for the receiving activity. Using this formula, what is the predicted cost of receiving for a month in which 1,450 receiving orders are processed?
3.   Prepare a cost formula for the receiving activity for a quarter. Based on this formula, what is the predicted cost of receiving for a quarter in which 4,650 receiving orders are anticipated? Prepare a cost formula for the receiving activity for a year. Based on this formula, what is the predicted cost of receiving for a year in which 18,000 receiving orders are anticipated?

OBJECTIVE ③

Problem 2-37 Method of Least Squares, Predicting Cost for Different Time Periods from the One Used to Develop a Cost Formula

Refer to **Problem 2-36**. Now assume that Tracy has used the method of least squares on the receiving data and has gotten the following results:

Intercept	3,212
Slope	15.15

Required:

1. Using the results from the method of least squares, prepare a cost formula for the receiving activity.
2. Using the formula from Requirement 1, what is the predicted cost of receiving for a month in which 1,450 receiving orders are processed? (Round your answer to the nearest dollar.)
3. Prepare a cost formula for the receiving activity for a quarter. Based on this formula, what is the predicted cost of receiving for a quarter in which 4,650 receiving orders are anticipated? Prepare a cost formula for the receiving activity for a year. Based on this formula, what is the predicted cost of receiving for a year in which 18,000 receiving orders are anticipated?

OBJECTIVE ④

spreadsheet

Problem 2-38 (Appendix) Method of Least Squares

Refer to **Problem 2-36** for the first 10 months of data on receiving orders and receiving cost. Now suppose that Tracy has gathered two more months of data:

Month	Receiving Orders	Receiving Cost ($)
11	1,200	$28,000
12	950	17,500

For the following requirements, round the intercept terms to the nearest dollar; round the variable rates to the nearest cent.

Required:

1. Run two regressions using a computer spreadsheet program such as Excel. First, use the method of least squares on the first 10 months of data. Then, use the method of least squares on all 12 months of data. Write down the results for the intercept, slope, and R^2 for each regression. Compare the results.
2. Prepare a scattergraph using all 12 months of data. Do any points appear to be outliers? Suppose Tracy has learned that the factory suffered severe storm damage during month 11 that required extensive repairs to the receiving area—including major repairs on a forklift. These expenses, included in month 11 receiving costs, are not expected to recur. What step might Tracy, using her judgment, take to amend the results from the method of least squares?
3. Rerun the method of least squares, using all the data except for month 11. (You should now have 11 months of data.) Prepare a cost formula for receiving based on these results, and calculate the predicted receiving cost for a month with 1,450 receiving orders. Discuss the results from this regression versus those from the regression for 12 months of data.

OBJECTIVES ③④

Problem 2-39 (Appendix) Scattergraph, High-Low Method, Method of Least Squares, Use of Judgment

The management of Wheeler Company has decided to develop cost formulas for its major overhead activities. Wheeler uses a highly automated manufacturing process, and power costs are a significant manufacturing cost. Cost analysts have decided that power costs are mixed; thus, they must be broken into their fixed and variable elements so that the cost behavior of the power usage activity can be properly described. Machine hours have been selected as the activity driver for power costs. The following data for the past eight quarters have been collected:

Quarter	Machine Hours	Power Cost ($)
1	20,000	26,000
2	25,000	38,000
3	30,000	42,500
4	22,000	37,000
5	21,000	34,000
6	18,000	29,000
7	24,000	36,000
8	28,000	40,000

For the following requirements, round the fixed cost to the nearest dollar; round the variable rates to the nearest cent.

Required:
1. Prepare a scattergraph by plotting power costs against machine hours. Does the scattergraph show a linear relationship between machine hours and power cost?
2. Using the high and low points, compute a power cost formula.
3. Use the method of least squares to compute a power cost formula. Evaluate the coefficient of determination.
4. Rerun the regression, and drop the point (20,000, $26,000) as an outlier. Compare the results from this regression to those for the regression in Requirement 3. Which is better?

Problem 2-40 Cost Behavior, High-Low Method, Pricing Decision   OBJECTIVES ① ② ③

Fonseca, Ruiz and Dunn is a large, local accounting firm located in a southwestern city. Carlos Ruiz, one of the firm's founders, appreciates the success his firm has enjoyed and wants to give something back to his community. He believes that an inexpensive accounting services clinic could provide basic accounting services for small businesses located in the barrio. He wants to price the services at cost.

Since the clinic is brand new, it has no experience to go on. Carlos decided to operate the clinic for two months before determining how much to charge per hour on an ongoing basis. As a temporary measure, the clinic adopted an hourly charge of $25, half the amount charged by Fonseca, Ruiz and Dunn for professional services.

The accounting services clinic opened on January 1. During January, the clinic had 120 hours of professional service. During February, the activity was 150 hours. Costs for these two levels of activity usage are as follows:

	120 Professional Hours ($)	150 Professional Hours ($)
Salaries:		
Senior accountant	2,500	2,500
Office assistant	1,200	1,200
Internet and software subscriptions	700	850
Consulting by senior partner	1,200	1,500
Depreciation (equipment)	2,400	2,400
Supplies	905	1,100
Administration	500	500
Rent (offices)	2,000	2,000
Utilities	332	365

Required:

1. Classify each cost as fixed, variable, or mixed, using hours of professional service as the activity driver.
2. Use the high-low method to separate the mixed costs into their fixed and variable components.
3. Luz Mondragon, the chief paraprofessional of the clinic, has estimated that the clinic will average 140 professional hours per month. If the clinic is to be operated as a nonprofit organization, how much will it need to charge per professional hour? How much of this charge is variable? How much is fixed?
4. Suppose the accounting center averages 170 professional hours per month. How much would need to be charged per hour for the center to cover its costs? Explain why the per-hour charge decreased as the activity output increased.

OBJECTIVES ③ ④   **Problem 2-41 Separating Fixed and Variable Costs, Service Setting**

Louise McDermott, controller for the Galvin plant of Veromar Inc. wanted to determine the cost behavior of moving materials throughout the plant. She accumulated the following data on the number of moves (from 100 to 800 in increments of 100) and the total cost of moving materials at those levels of moves:

Number of Moves	Total Cost ($)
100	3,000
200	4,650
300	3,400
400	8,500
500	10,000
600	12,600
700	13,600
800	14,560

Required:

1. Prepare a scattergraph based on these data. Use cost for the vertical axis and number of moves for the horizontal. Based on an examination of the scattergraph, does there appear to be a linear relationship between the total cost of moving materials and the number of moves?
2. Compute the cost formula for moving materials by using the high-low method. Calculate the predicted cost for a month with 550 moves by using the high-low formula.
3. Compute the cost formula for moving materials using the method of least squares. Using the regression cost formula, what is the predicted cost for a month with 550 moves? What does the coefficient of determination tell you about the cost formula computed by regression?
4. Evaluate the cost formula using the least squares coefficients. Could it be improved? Try dropping the third data point (300, $3,400), and rerun the regression.

OBJECTIVES ① ② ③   **Problem 2-42 Flexible and Committed Resources, Capacity Usage for a Service**

Jana Morgan is about to sign up for cellular telephone service. She is primarily interested in the safety aspect of the phone; that is, she wants to have one available for emergencies. She does not want to use it as her primary phone. Jana has narrowed her options down to two plans:

	Plan 1	Plan 2
Monthly fee	$20	$ 30
Free local minutes	60	120
Additional charges per minute:		
Airtime	$ 0.40	$ 0.30
Long distance	0.15	—
Regional roaming	0.60	—
National roaming	0.60	0.60

Both plans are subject to a $25 activation fee and a $120 cancellation fee if the service is cancelled before one year. Jana's brother will give her a cell phone that he no longer needs. It is not the latest version (and is not Internet capable) but will work well with both plans.

Required:

1. Classify the charges associated with the cellular phone service as (a) committed resources or (b) flexible resources.
2. Assume that Jana will use, on average, 45 minutes per month in local calling. For each plan, split her minute allotment into used and unused capacity. Which plan will be most cost effective? Why?
3. Assume that Jana loves her cell phone and ends up talking frequently with friends while traveling within her region. On average, she uses 60 local minutes a month and 30 regional minutes. For each plan, split her minute allotment into used and unused capacity. Which plan will be most cost effective? Why?
4. Analyze your own cellular phone plan by comparing it with other possible options.

Problem 2-43 Variable and Fixed Costs, Cost Formula, High-Low Method

OBJECTIVES ① ③

Li Ming Yuan and Tiffany Shaden are the department heads for the accounting department and human resources department, respectively, at a large textile firm in the southern United States. They have just returned from an executive meeting at which the necessity of cutting costs and gaining efficiency has been stressed. After talking with Tiffany and some of her staff members, as well as his own staff members, Li Ming discovered that there were a number of costs associated with the claims processing activity. These costs included the salaries of the two paralegals who worked full-time on claims processing; the salary of the accountant who cut the checks; the cost of claims forms, checks, envelopes, and postage; and depreciation on the office equipment dedicated to the processing. Some of the paralegals' time is spent in the routine processing of uncontested claims, but much time is spent on the claims that have incomplete documentation or are contested. The accountant's time appears to vary with the number of claims processed.

Li Ming was able to separate the costs of processing claims from the costs of running the departments of accounting and human resources. He gathered the data on claims processing cost and the number of claims processed per month for the past six months. These data are as follows:

Month	Claims Processing Cost ($)	Number of Claims Processed
February	34,907	5,700
March	31,260	4,900
April	37,950	6,100
May	38,250	6,500
June	44,895	7,930
July	44,055	7,514

Required:

1. Classify the claims processing costs that Li Ming identified as variable and fixed.
2. What is the independent variable? The dependent variable?
3. Use the high-low method to find the fixed cost per month and the variable rate. What is the cost formula?
4. Suppose that an outside company bids on the claims processing business. The bid price is $4.60 per claim. If Tiffany expects 75,600 claims next year, should she outsource the claims processing or continue to do it in house?

OBJECTIVES ① ②   **Problem 2-44 Cost Separation**

About eight years ago, Kicker faced the problem of rapidly increasing costs associated with workplace accidents. The costs included the following:

State unemployment insurance premiums	$100,000
Average cost per injury	$1,500
Number of injuries per year	15
Number of serious injuries	4
Number of workdays lost	30

A safety program was implemented with the following features: hiring a safety director, new employee orientation, stretching required four times a day, and systematic monitoring of adherence to the program by directors and supervisors. A year later, the indicators were as follows:

State unemployment insurance premiums	$50,000
Average cost per injury	$50
Number of injuries per year	10
Number of serious injuries	0
Number of workdays lost	0
Safety director's starting salary	$60,000

Required:

1. Discuss the safety-related costs listed. Are they variable or fixed with respect to speakers sold? With respect to other independent variables (describe)?
2. Did the safety program pay for itself? Discuss your reasoning.

Cases

OBJECTIVES ① ② ③ ④   **Case 2-45 Cost Formulas, Single and Multiple Cost Drivers**

For the past five years, Garner Company has had a policy of producing to meet customer demand. As a result, finished goods inventory is minimal, and for the most part, units produced equal units sold.

Recently, Garner's industry entered a recession, and the company is producing well below capacity (and expects to continue doing so for the coming year). The president is willing to accept orders that at least cover their variable costs so that the company can keep its employees and avoid layoffs. Also, any orders above variable costs will increase overall profitability of the company. Toward that end, the president of Garner Company implemented a policy that any special orders will be accepted if they cover the costs that the orders cause.

To help implement the policy, Garner's controller developed the following cost formulas:

Direct material usage = $94X,	$R^2 = 0.90$
Direct labor usage = $16X,	$R^2 = 0.92$
Overhead = $350,000 + $80X,	$R^2 = 0.56$
Selling costs = $50,000 + $7X,	$R^2 = 0.86$

where X = direct labor hours

Required:

1. Compute the total unit variable cost. Suppose that Garner has an opportunity to accept an order for 20,000 units at $212 per unit. Each unit uses one direct labor hour for production. Should Garner accept the order? (The order would not displace any of Garner's regular orders.)

2. (Appendix) Explain the significance of the coefficient of determination measures for the cost formulas. Did these measures have a bearing on your answer in Requirement 1? Should they have a bearing? Why?

3. (Appendix) Suppose that a multiple regression equation is developed for overhead costs: $Y = \$100{,}000 + \$85X1 + \$5{,}000X2 + \$300X3$, where X1 = Direct labor hours, X2 = Number of setups, and X3 = Engineering hours. The coefficient of determination for the equation is 0.89. Assume that the order of 20,000 units requires 12 setups and 600 engineering hours. Given this new information, should the company accept the special order referred to in Requirement 1? Is there any other information about cost behavior that you would like to have? Explain.

Case 2-46 Suspicious Acquisition of Data, Ethical Issues

OBJECTIVE ①

Bill Lewis, manager of the Thomas Electronics Division, called a meeting with his controller, Brindon Peterson, and his marketing manager, Patty Fritz. The following is a transcript of the conversation that took place during the meeting:

Bill: Brindon, the variable costing system that you developed has proved to be a big plus for our division. Our success in winning bids has increased, and as a result, our revenues have increased by 25 percent. However, if we intend to meet this year's profit targets, we are going to need something extra—am I not right, Patty?

Patty: Absolutely. While we have been able to win more bids, we still are losing too many, particularly to our major competitor, Kilborn Electronics. If we knew more about their bidding strategy, we could be more successful at competing with them.

Brindon: Would knowing their variable costs help?

Patty: Certainly. It would give me their minimum price. With that knowledge, I'm sure that we could find a way to beat them on several jobs, particularly on those jobs where we are at least as efficient. It would also help us to identify where we are not cost competitive. With this information, we might be able to find ways to increase our efficiency.

Brindon: Well, I have good news. I've been talking with Carl Penobscot, Kilborn's assistant controller. Carl doesn't feel appreciated by Kilborn and wants to make a change. He could easily fit into our team here. Plus, Carl has been preparing for a job switch by quietly copying Kilborn's accounting files and records. He's already given me some data that reveal bids that Kilborn made on several jobs. If we can come to a satisfactory agreement with Carl, he'll bring the rest of the information with him. We'll easily be able to figure out Kilborn's prospective bids and find ways to beat them. Besides, I could use another accountant on my staff. Bill, would you authorize my immediate hiring of Carl with a favorable compensation package?

Bill: I know that you need more staff, Brindon, but is this the right thing to do? It sounds like Carl is stealing those files, and surely Kilborn considers this information confidential. I have real ethical and legal concerns about this. Why don't we meet with Laurie, our attorney, and determine any legal problems?

Required:

1. Is Carl's behavior ethical? What would Kilborn think?
2. Is Bill correct in supposing that there are ethical and/or legal problems involved with the hiring of Carl? (Reread the section on corporate codes of conduct in Chapter 1.) What would you do if you were Bill? Explain.

3

Cost-Volume-Profit Analysis: A Managerial Planning Tool

After studying Chapter 3, you should be able to:

① Determine the break-even point in number of units and in total sales dollars.

② Determine the number of units that must be sold, and the amount of revenue required, to earn a targeted profit.

③ Prepare a profit-volume graph and a cost-volume-profit graph and explain the meaning of each.

④ Apply cost-volume-profit analysis in a multiple-product setting.

⑤ Explain the impact of risk, uncertainty, and changing variables on cost-volume-profit analysis.

© BOYNE RESORTS USA

**E**xperience Managerial Decisions
with Boyne Resorts

Boyne USA Resorts owns and operates ski resorts in British Columbia, Washington, Montana, and Michigan, including Boyne Highlands. Established in 1947, Boyne Highlands is located in Michigan's northern Lower Peninsula near the picturesque village of Petoskey. Naturally, Boyne earns a large portion of its revenue from winter skiing. However, winter ski volume is heavily dependent on natural snowfall, which varies significantly from year to year. The business risk associated with such large snow-fall variation has led Boyne to develop numerous other profitable activities that are not dependent on snowfall. For example, consider the ski lifts that Boyne uses to transport skiers to the mountain top. What other revenue-generating activities can you think of that Boyne might develop that revolve around such ski lifts? What additional variable and fixed costs might be involved with your activities, as well as the profit implications?

Boyne develops numerous lift ticket packages to try and accommodate as many snow skiers and snowboarders as possible. For example, lift tickets are interchangeable between multiple Boyne properties and can be used during night skiing in certain areas. Like many ski resorts, Boyne also markets spring, summer, and fall activities as well. Other ski resorts, such as in Aspen, Colorado, build elaborate children's playgrounds and bungee trampolines at the top of ski areas to generate additional summer business in ski areas that otherwise would be dormant during the off-season. Using cost-volume-profit equations and contribution margin formulas, as well as cost-volume-profit and profit volume graphs, Boyne spends considerable effort analyzing the revenue, cost, volume, and profit implications of the various types of activities mentioned above. With careful cost-volume-profit analysis and sound judgment, Boyne attempts to make the best decisions possible to continue its profitability and reputation for fun.

OBJECTIVE ①
Determine the break-even point in number of units and in total sales dollars.

Break-Even Point in Units and in Sales Dollars

Cost-volume-profit (CVP) analysis estimates how changes in costs (both variable and fixed), sales volume, and price affect a company's profit. CVP is a powerful tool for planning and decision making. In fact, CVP is one of the most versatile and widely applicable tools used by managerial accountants to help managers make better decisions.

You might have read of companies using CVP analyses to reach important benchmarks, such as their break even point. The **break-even** point is the point where total revenue equals total cost (i.e., the point of zero profit). New start-up companies typically experience losses (negative operating income) initially and view their first break-even period as a significant milestone. For example, on-line retail pioneer **Amazon.com** was founded in 1994 but did not break even for the first time until the fourth quarter of 2001! Also, managers become very interested in CVP analysis during times of economic trouble. For example, to the dismay of many of its shareholders, **Sirius Radio** signed shock jock Howard Stern to a five-year, $500 million employment contract for joining the young company. As a result of Stern's monstrous contract cost, some analysts estimated that Sirius would need to sign on 2.4 million additional subscribers (i.e., customers) to reach break-even. Therefore, CVP analysis helps managers pinpoint problems and find solutions.

CVP analysis can address many other issues as well, such as the number of units that must be sold to break even, the impact of a given reduction in fixed costs on the break-even point, and the impact of an increase in price on profit. Additionally, CVP analysis allows managers to do sensitivity analysis by examining the impact of various price or cost levels on profit.

Since CVP analysis shows how revenues, expenses, and profits behave as volume changes, it is natural to begin by finding the firm's break-even point in units sold.

Here's The Real Kicker

Kicker separates cost into fixed and variable components by using judgment. Because the bulk of manufacturing is outsourced, the cost of a set of speakers starts with the purchase price from the manufacturer. This is a strictly variable cost. Also variable are the cost of duty (ranging from 9–30 percent—electronics are at the high end) and freight, as all units are shipped to Stillwater, Oklahoma, for distribution to customers. In-house labor may be needed at Kicker's Stillwater facilities, and that cost has both fixed (salaried workers) and variable (temporary workers) components.

The entire salaried staff in Stillwater, research and development, depreciation on property, plant and equipment, utilities, and so on, are all fixed.

These fixed and variable costs are used in CVP analusis (done monthly) and in management decision making. For example, the monthly CVP figures can be used to monitor the effect of changing volume on profit and spotlight increases in fixed and variable costs. If costs are going up, management finds out about the problem early and can make adjustments.

Using Operating Income in Cost-Volume-Profit Analysis

Remember from Chapter 1 that operating income is total revenue minus total expense. For the income statement, expenses were classified according to function, that is, the manufacturing (or service provision) function, the selling function, and the administrative function. For CVP analysis, however, it is much more useful to organize costs into fixed and variable components. The focus is on the firm as a whole. Therefore, the costs refer to all costs of the company—production, selling, and administration. So variable costs are all costs that increase as more units are sold, including direct materials, direct labor, variable overhead, and variable selling and administrative costs. Similarly, fixed costs include fixed overhead and fixed selling and administrative expenses. The income statement format that is based on the separation of costs into fixed and variable components is called the **contribution margin income statement.** Exhibit 3-1 shows the format for the contribution margin income statement.

Exhibit 3-1

The Contribution Margin Income Statement

Sales	$XXX
Less: Total variable expense	(XXX)
Total contribution margin	$XXX
Less: Total fixed expense	(XXX)
Operating income	$XXX

The contribution margin income statement in Exhibit 3-1 contains a new term, *contribution margin*. **Contribution margin** is the difference between sales and variable expense. It is the amount of sales revenue that is left over after all the variable expenses are covered that can be used to contribute to fixed expense and operating income. The contribution margin can be calculated in total (as it was in Exhibit 3-1) or per unit.

Let's use Whittier Company, a manufacturer of mulching lawn mowers, for an example. Whittier's controller has budgeted the following production costs for the coming year:

Direct materials per mower	$ 180
Direct labor per mower	100
Variable factory overhead per mower	25
Total fixed factory overhead	15,000

Whittier also has $30,000 in fixed selling and administrative expense, as well as a $20 sales commission on each mower sold. In the coming year, Whittier Company plans to produce and sell 1,000 mowers at a price of $400 each.

The total variable cost per mower includes direct materials, direct labor, variable overhead per unit, and the sales commission. Thus, variable cost per unit is $325 ($180 + $100 + $25 + $20). The total fixed expense includes fixed factory overhead and fixed selling and administrative expense; the total fixed expense is $45,000 ($15,000 + $30,000). Notice that both the variable cost per mower and the total fixed expense include all types of cost—both product and selling cost across the value chain.

The contribution margin income statement for Whittier Company for the coming year is shown in Cornerstone 3-1 (see page 102).

Notice that the contribution margin income statement shown in Cornerstone 3-1 shows a total contribution margin of $75,000. The per-unit contribution margin is $75($400 – $325). That is, every mower sold contributes $75 toward fixed expense and operating income.

What does Whittier's contribution margin income statement show? First, of course, we notice that Whittier will more than break even at sales of 1,000 mowers. In fact, it expects an operating income of $30,000. Clearly, Whittier would just break even if total contribution margin equaled the total fixed cost. Let's see how to calculate the break-even point.

Break-Even Point in Units

If the contribution margin income statement is recast as an equation, it becomes more useful for solving CVP problems. The operating income equation is:

Operating income = Sales – Total variable expenses – Total fixed expenses

Notice that all we have done is remove the total contribution margin line, since it is identical to sales minus total variable expense. This equation is the basis of all our coming work on CVP. We can think of it as the basic CVP equation.

We can expand the operating income equation by expressing sales revenues and variable expenses in terms of unit dollar amounts and the number of units sold. Specifically, sales revenue is equal to the unit selling price times the number of units

**CORNERSTONE
3-1**

HOW TO Prepare a Contribution Margin Income Statement

Information: Whittier Company plans to sell 1,000 mowers at $400 each in the coming year. Product costs include:

Direct materials per mower	$180
Direct labor per mower	100
Variable factory overhead per mower	25
Total fixed factory overhead	15,000

Variable selling expense is a commission of $20 per mower; fixed selling and administrative expense totals $30,000.

Required:
1. Calculate the total variable cost per unit.
2. Calculate the total fixed expense for the year.
3. Prepare a contribution margin income statement for Whittier Company for the coming year.

Calculation:
1. Variable cost per unit
   = Direct materials + Direct labor + Variable factory + Variable selling expense
                                                     overhead
   = $180   + $100   + $25   + $20
   = $325
2. Total fixed expense = $15,000 + $30,000 = $45,000
3.

Whittier Company
Contribution Margin Income Statement
For the Coming Year

	Total	Per Unit
Sales ($400 × 1,000 mowers)	$400,000	$400
Total variable expense ($325 × 1,000)	325,000	325
Total contribution margin	$ 75,000	$ 75
Total fixed expense	45,000	
Operating income	$ 30,000	

sold, and total variable costs are the unit variable cost times the number of units sold. With these expressions, the operating income equation becomes:

**Operating income = (Price × Number of units sold) − (Variable cost per unit
× Number of units sold) − Total fixed cost**

At the break-even point, of course, operating income equals $0. Let's see how we can use the operating income equation to find the break-even point in units for Whittier Company. Recall that Whittier Company sells mowers at $400 each, and variable cost per mower is $325. Total fixed cost equals $45,000.

$$(\$400 \times \text{Break-even units}) - (\$325 \times \text{Break-even units}) - \$45,000 = \$0$$
$$(\$75 \times \text{Break-even units}) - \$45,000 = \$0$$
$$\text{Break-even units} = \frac{\$45,000}{\$75}$$
$$\text{Break-even units} = 600$$

It is easy to see that a contribution margin income statement for Whittier Company, with sales of 600 mowers, does result in zero operating income.

Sales ($400 × 600 mowers)	$240,000
Total variable expense ($325 × 600)	195,000
Total contribution margin	$ 45,000
Total fixed expense	45,000
Operating income	$ 0

When Whittier breaks even, total contribution margin is just equal to the total fixed cost. Exhibit 3-2 illustrates this point.

The operating income equation can be rearranged as follows to show the number of units at break-even:

$$\text{Break-even units} = \frac{\text{Total fixed cost}}{\text{Price} - \text{Variable cost per unit}}$$

In other words, the break-even units are equal to the fixed cost divided by the contribution margin per unit. So, if a company sells enough units for the contribution margin to just cover fixed costs, it will earn zero operating income. In other words, it will break even. It is quicker to solve break-even problems using this break-even version of the operating income equation than it is using the original operating income equation. Cornerstone 3-2 on page 104 shows how to use the break-even units equation to solve for the break-even point for Whittier Company.

Break-Even Point in Sales Dollars

In some cases when using CVP analysis, managers may prefer to use sales revenue as the measure of sales activity instead of units sold. A units sold measure can be converted to a sales revenue measure by multiplying the unit selling price by the units sold. For example, the break-even point for Whittier Company is 600 mulching mowers. Since the selling price for each lawn mower is $400, the break-even volume in sales revenue is $240,000 ($400 × 600).

Any answer expressed in units sold can be easily converted to one expressed in sales revenues, but the answer can be computed more directly by developing a separate formula for the sales revenue case. In this case, the important variable is sales dollars, so both the revenue and the variable costs must be expressed in dollars instead of units. Since sales

Exhibit 3-2

Contribution Margin and Fixed Cost at Break-Even for Whittier Company

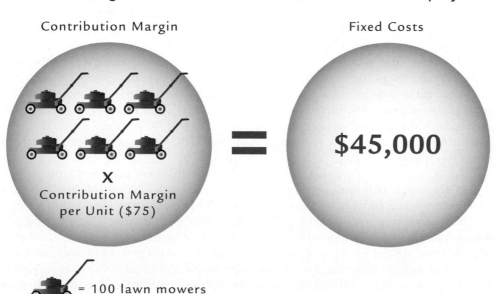

= 100 lawn mowers

**CORNERSTONE
3-2**

HOW TO Solve for the Break-Even Point in Units

Information: Whittier Company plans to sell 1,000 mowers at $400 each in the coming year. Product costs include:

Direct materials per mower	$ 180
Direct labor per mower	100
Variable factory overhead per mower	25
Total fixed factory overhead	15,000

Variable selling expense is a commission of $20 per mower; fixed selling and administrative expense totals $30,000.

Required:
1. Calculate the total variable cost per unit.
2. Calculate the total fixed expense for the year.
3. Calculate the number of mowers that Whittier Company must sell to break even.
4. Check your answer by preparing a contribution margin income statement based on the break-even point.

Calculation:
1. Variable cost per unit = $180 + $100 + $25 + $20 = $325
2. Total fixed expense = $15,000 + $30,000 = $45,000
3. Break-even number of mowers = $45,000/($400 − $325) = 600
4. Contribution margin income statement based on 600 mowers.

Sales ($400 × 600 mowers)	$240,000
Total variable expense ($325 × 600)	195,000
Total contribution margin	$ 45,000
Total fixed expense	45,000
Operating income	$ 0

Indeed, selling 600 units does yield a zero profit.

revenue is always expressed in dollars, measuring that variable is no problem. Let's look more closely at variable costs and see how they can be expressed in terms of sales dollars.

To calculate the break-even point in sales dollars, total variable costs are defined as a percentage of sales rather than as an amount per unit sold. For example, suppose that a company sells a product for $10 per unit and incurs a variable cost of $6 per unit. Of course, the remainder is contribution margin of $4 ($10 − $6). If 10 units are sold, total variable costs are $60 ($6 × 10 units). Alternatively, since each unit sold earns $10 of revenue and has $6 of variable cost, one could say that 60 percent of each dollar of revenue earned is attributable to variable cost ($6/$10). Thus, sales revenues of $100 would result in total variable costs of $60 (0.60 × $100).

This 60 percent is the variable cost ratio. The **variable cost ratio** is the proportion of each sales dollar that must be used to cover variable costs. The variable cost ratio can be computed using either total data or unit data. The percentage of sales dollars remaining after variable costs are covered is the contribution margin ratio. The **contribution margin ratio** is the proportion of each sales dollar available to cover fixed costs and provide for profit. In this example, if the variable cost ratio is 60 percent of sales, then the contribution margin ratio must be the remaining 40 percent of sales. It makes sense that the complement of the variable cost ratio is the contribution margin ratio. After all, total variable costs and total contribution margin sum to sales revenue.

Just as the variable cost ratio can be computed using total or unit figures, the contribution margin ratio, 40 percent in our example, also can be computed in these two ways. That is, one can divide the total contribution margin by total sales ($40/$100), or one can divide the unit contribution margin by price ($4/$10). Naturally, if the variable cost ratio is known, it can be subtracted from 1 to yield the contribution margin ratio (1 – 0.60 = 0.40). Cornerstone 3-3 shows how the income statement can be expanded to yield the variable cost ratio and the contribution margin ratio.

Notice in Cornerstone 3-3, Requirement 3, that sales revenue, variable costs, and contribution margin have been expressed as a percent of sales. The variable cost ratio is 0.8125 ($325,000/$400,000); the contribution margin ratio is 0.1875 (computed either as 1 – 0.8125, or $75,000/$400,000).

How do fixed costs relate to the variable cost ratio and contribution margin ratio? Since the total contribution margin is the revenue remaining after total variable costs are covered, it must be the revenue available to cover fixed costs and contribute to profit. How does the relationship of fixed cost to contribution margin affect operating income? There are three possibilities: Fixed cost can equal contribution margin; fixed cost can be less than contribution margin; or fixed cost can be greater than contribution margin. If fixed cost equals contribution margin, then operating income is $0 (the company is at break-even). If fixed cost is less than contribution margin, the company earns a positive operating income. Finally, if fixed cost is greater than contribution margin, then the company faces an operating loss.

Concept Q&A

1. If the contribution margin ratio is 30 percent, what is the variable cost ratio?
2. If the variable cost ratio is 77 percent, what is the contribution margin ratio?
3. Explain why the contribution margin ratio and the variable cost ratio always total 100 percent.

Answers:
1. Variable cost ratio = 1.00 – 0.30 = 0.70, or 70 percent.
2. Contribution margin ratio = 1.00 – 0.77 = 0.23, or 23 percent.
3. The contribution margin ratio and the variable cost ratio always equal 100 percent of sales revenue. By definition, total variable cost and total contribution margin sum to sales revenue.

HOW TO Calculate the Variable Cost Ratio and the Contribution Margin Ratio

Information: Whittier Company plans to sell 1,000 mowers at $400 each in the coming year. Variable cost per unit is $325. Total fixed cost is $45,000.

Required:
1. Calculate the variable cost ratio.
2. Calculate the contribution margin ratio using unit figures.
3. Prepare a contribution margin income statement based on the budgeted figures for next year. In a column next to the income statement, show the percentages based on sales for sales, total variable costs, and total contribution margin.

**CORNERSTONE
3-3**

Calculation:
1. Variable cost ratio = $325/$400 = 0.8125, or 81.25%
2. Contribution margin per unit = $400 – $325 = $75
   Contribution margin ratio = $75/$400 = 0.1875, or 18.75%
3. Contribution margin income statement based on budgeted figures:

		Percent of Sales
Sales ($400 × 1,000 mowers)	$400,000	100.00
Total variable expense (0.8125 × $400,000)	325,000	81.25
Total contribution margin	$ 75,000	18.75
Total fixed expense	45,000	
Operating income	$ 30,000	

Now, let's turn to the equation for calculating the break-even point in sales dollars. One way of calculating break-even sales revenue is to multiply the break-even units by the price. However, often the company is a multiple-product firm, and it can be difficult to figure the break-even point for each product sold. The operating income equation can be used to solve for break-even sales for Whittier as follows:

Operating income = Sales − Total variable expenses − Total fixed expenses

Break-even sales − 0.8125 × Break-even sales − $45,000 = $0

Break-even sales = $45,000/(1.00 − 0.8125)

Break-even sales = $240,000

So, Whittier Company has sales of $240,000 at the break-even point.

Just as it was quicker to use an equation to calculate the break-even units directly, it is helpful to have an equation to figure the break-even sales dollars. This equation is:

Break-even sales = Total fixed expenses/Contribution margin ratio

Cornerstone 3-4 shows how to obtain the break-even point in sales dollars for Whittier Company.

**CORNERSTONE
3-4**

HOW TO Solve for the Break-Even Point in Sales Dollars

Information: Whittier Company plans to sell 1,000 mowers at $400 each in the coming year. Total variable expense per unit is $325. Total fixed expense is $45,000.

Required:
1. Calculate the contribution margin ratio.
2. Calculate the sales revenue that Whittier Company must make to break even by using the break-even point in sales equation.
3. Check your answer by preparing a contribution margin income statement based on the break-even point in sales dollars.

Calculation:
1. Contribution margin per unit = $400 − $325 = $75
   Contribution margin ratio = Contribution margin per unit/Price
   $\qquad\qquad\qquad\qquad\quad$ = $75/$400 = 0.1875, or 18.75%
   [*Hint:* The contribution margin ratio comes out cleanly to four decimal places. Don't round it, and your break-even point in sales dollars will yield an operating income of $0 (rather than being a few dollars off due to rounding).]
   $\qquad$ Notice that the variable cost ratio equals 0.8125, or the difference between 1.0000 and the contribution margin ratio.
2. Calculate the break-even point in sales dollars:

   Break-even sales dollars = $45,000/0.1875 = $240,000

3. Contribution margin income statement based on sales of $240,000:

Sales	$240,000
Total variable expense (0.8125 × $240,000)	195,000
Total contribution margin	$ 45,000
Total fixed expense	45,000
Operating income	$ 0

Indeed, sales equal to $240,000 does yield a zero profit.

Units and Sales Dollars Needed to Achieve a Target Income

While the break-even point is useful information and an important benchmark for relatively young companies, most companies would like to earn operating income greater than $0. CVP analysis gives us a way to determine how many units must be sold, or how much sales revenue must be earned, to earn a particular target income. Let's look first at the number of units that must be sold to earn a targeted operating income.

Units to Be Sold to Achieve a Target Income

Remember that at the break-even point, operating income is $0. How can the equations used in our earlier break-even analyses be adjusted to find the number of units that must be sold to earn a target income? The answer is that we add the target income amount to the fixed costs. Let's try it two different ways—with the operating income equation and with the basic break-even equation.

Remember that the equation for the operating income is:

Operating income = (Price × Units sold) − (Unit variable cost × Units sold) − Fixed cost

To solve for positive operating income, replace the operating income term with the target income. Recall that Whittier Company sells mowers at $400 each, incurs variable cost per unit of $325, and has total fixed expense of $45,000. Suppose that Whittier wants to make a target operating income of $37,500. The number of units that must be sold to achieve that target income is calculated as follows:

$37,500 = ($400 × Number of units) − ($325 × Number of units) − $45,000

Number of units = ($37,500 + $45,000)/($400 − $325) = 1,100

Does the sale of 1,100 units really result in operating income of $37,500? The contribution margin income statement provides a good check.

Sales ($400 × 1,100)	$440,000
Total variable expense ($325 × 1,100)	357,500
Total contribution margin	$ 82,500
Total fixed expense	45,000
Operating income	$ 37,500

Indeed, selling 1,100 units does yield operating income of $37,500.

The operating income equation can be used to find the number of units to sell to earn a targeted income. However, it is quicker to adjust the break-even units equation by adding target income to the fixed cost. This adjustment results in the following equation:

Number of units to earn target income = $\dfrac{\text{Fixed cost + Target income}}{\text{Price − Variable cost per unit}}$

This equation was used when calculating the 1,100 units needed to earn operating income of $37,500. Cornerstone 3-5 shows how Whittier Company can use this approach.

Another way to check the number of units to be sold to yield a target operating income is to use the break-even point. As shown in Cornerstone 3-5 on page 108 Whittier must sell 1,100 lawn mowers, or 500 more than the break-even volume of 600 units, to earn a profit of $37,500. The contribution margin per lawn mower is $75. Multiplying $75 by the 500 lawn mowers above break-even produces the operating income of $37,500 ($75 × 500). This outcome demonstrates that contribution margin per unit for each unit above break-even is equivalent to operating income per unit. Since the break-even point had already been computed, the number of lawn mowers to be

**CORNERSTONE
3-5**

HOW TO Solve for the Number of Units to Be Sold to Earn a Target Operating Income

Information: Whittier Company sells mulching mowers at $400 each. Variable cost per unit is $325, and total fixed costs are $45,000.

Required:
1. Calculate the number of units that Whittier Company must sell to earn operating income of $37,500.
2. Check your answer by preparing a contribution margin income statement based on the number of units calculated.

Calculation:
1. Number of units = ($45,000 + $37,500)/($400 − $325) = 1,100
2. Contribution margin income statement based on sales of 1,100 units:

Sales ($400 × 1,100)	$440,000
Total variable expense ($325 × 1,100)	357,500
Total contribution margin	$ 82,500
Total fixed expense	45,000
Operating income	$ 37,500

Indeed, selling 1,100 units does yield operating income of $37,500.

sold to yield a $37,500 operating income could have been calculated by dividing the unit contribution margin into the target income and adding the resulting amount to the break-even volume.

In general, assuming that fixed costs remain the same, the impact on a firm's income resulting from a change in the number of units sold can be assessed by multiplying the unit contribution margin by the change in units sold. For example, if 1,400 lawn mowers instead of 1,100 are sold, how much more operating income will be earned? The change in units sold is an increase of 300 lawn mowers, and the unit contribution margin is $75. Thus, operating income will increase by $22,500 ($75 × 300) over the $37,500 initially calculated, and total operating income will be $60,000.

Sales Revenue to Achieve a Target Income

Consider the following question: How much sales revenue must Whittier generate to earn an operating income of $37,500? This question is similar to the one we asked earlier in terms of units but phrases the question directly in terms of sales revenue. To answer the question, add the targeted operating income of $37,500 to the $45,000 of fixed cost and divide by the contribution margin ratio. Then, the equation is the following:

$$\text{Sales dollars to earn target income} = \frac{\textbf{Fixed cost + Target income}}{\textbf{Contribution margin ratio}}$$

Cornerstone 3-6 shows how to calculate the sales revenue needed to earn a target operating income of $37,500.

Whittier must earn revenues equal to $440,000 to achieve a profit target of $37,500. Since break-even sales equals $240,000, additional sales of $200,000 ($440,000 − $240,000) must be earned above break-even. Notice that multiplying the contribution margin ratio by revenues above break-even yields the profit of $37,500 (0.1875 × $200,000).

**CORNERSTONE
3-6**

HOW TO Solve for the Sales Needed to Earn a Target Operating Income

Information: Whittier Company sells mulching mowers at $400 each. Variable cost per unit is $325, and total fixed costs are $45,000.

Required:
1. Calculate the contribution margin ratio.
2. Calculate the sales that Whittier Company must make to earn an operating income of $37,500.
3. Check your answer by preparing a contribution margin income statement based on the sales dollars calculated.

Calculation:
1. Contribution margin ratio = ($400 − $325)/$400 = 0.1875
2. Sales dollars = ($45,000 + $37,500)/0.1875 = $440,000
3. Contribution margin income statement based on sales revenue of $440,000:

Sales	$440,000
Total variable expense (0.8125 × $440,000)	357,500
Total contribution margin	$ 82,500
Total fixed expense	45,000
Operating income	$ 37,500

Indeed, sales revenue of $440,000 does yield operating income of $37,500.

Above break-even, the contribution margin ratio is a profit ratio; therefore, it represents the proportion of each sales dollar attributable to profit. For Whittier Company, every sales dollar earned above break-even increases profits by $0.1875.

In general, assuming that fixed costs remain unchanged, the contribution margin ratio can be used to find the profit impact of a change in sales revenue. To obtain the total change in profits from a change in revenues, multiply the contribution margin ratio times the change in sales. For example, if sales revenues are $400,000 instead of $440,000, how will the expected profits be affected? A decrease in sales revenues of $40,000 will cause a decrease in profits of $7,500 (0.1875 × $40,000).

Concept Q&A

Lorna makes and sells decorative candles through gift shops. She knows she must sell 200 candles a month to break even. Every candle has a contribution margin of $1.50. So far this month, Lorna has sold 320 candles. How much has Lorna earned so far this month in operating income? If she sells 10 more candles, by how much will income increase?

_____

Answer:
320 candles sold − 200 candles at break-even = 120 candles above break-even, 120 × $1.50 = $180. Lorna has earned operating income of $180 so far during the month. An additional 10 candles contribute $15 to operating income ($1.50 × 10).

Graphs of Cost-Volume-Profit Relationships

It may be helpful in understanding CVP relationships to see them portrayed visually. A graphical representation can help managers see the difference between variable cost and revenue. It may also help them understand quickly what impact an increase or decrease in sales will have on the break-even point. Two basic graphs, the profit-volume graph and the CVP graph, are presented here.

OBJECTIVE ③
Prepare a profit-volume graph and a cost-volume-profit graph, and explain the meaning of each.

The Profit-Volume Graph

A **profit-volume graph** visually portrays the relationship between profits (operating income) and units sold. The profit-volume graph is the graph of the operating income equation [Operating income = (Price × Units) – (Unit variable cost × Units) – Total fixed cost]. In this graph, operating income is the dependent variable, and units is the independent variable. Usually, values of the independent variable are measured along the horizontal axis, and values of the dependent variable are measured along the vertical axis.

To make this discussion more concrete, a simple set of data will be used. Assume that Tyson Company produces a single product with the following cost and price data:

Total fixed costs	$100
Variable costs per unit	5
Selling price per unit	10

Using these data, operating income can be expressed as:

$$\text{Operating income} = (\$10 \times \text{Units}) - (\$5 \times \text{Units}) - \$100$$
$$= (\$5 \times \text{Units}) - \$100$$

This relationship can be graphed by plotting units along the horizontal axis and operating income (or loss) along the vertical axis. Two points are needed to graph a linear equation. While any two points will do, the two points often chosen are those that correspond to zero units sold and zero profits. When units sold are 0, Tyson experiences an operating loss of $100 (or an operating income of –$100). The point corresponding to zero sales volume, therefore, is (0, –$100). When no sales take place, the company suffers a loss equal to its total fixed costs. When operating income is $0, the units sold are equal to 20. The point corresponding to zero profits (break-even) is (20, $0). These two points, plotted in Exhibit 3-3, define the profit graph.

The graph in Exhibit 3-3 can be used to assess Tyson's profit (or loss) at any level of sales activity. For example, the profit associated with the sale of 40 units can be read from the graph by (1) drawing a vertical line from the horizontal axis to the profit line and (2) drawing a horizontal line from the profit line to the vertical axis. As illustrated in Exhibit 3-3, the profit associated with sales of 40 units is $100. The profit-volume graph, while easy to interpret, fails to reveal how costs change as sales volume changes. An alternative approach to graphing can provide this detail.

The Cost-Volume-Profit Graph

The **cost-volume-profit graph** depicts the relationships among cost, volume, and profits (operating income) by plotting the total revenue line and the total cost line on a graph. To obtain the more detailed relationships, it is necessary to graph two separate lines: the total revenue line and the total cost line. These two lines are represented by the following two equations:

Revenue = Price × Units
Total cost = (Unit variable cost × Units) + Fixed cost

Using the Tyson Company example, the revenue and cost equations are:

$$\text{Revenue} = \$10 \times \text{Units}$$
$$\text{Total cost} = (\$5 \times \text{Units}) + \$100$$

To portray both equations in the same graph, the vertical axis is measured in dollars, and the horizontal axis is measured in units sold.

Again, two points are needed to graph each equation. For the revenue equation, setting number of units equal to 0 results in revenue of $0; setting number of units equal to 20 results in revenue of $200. Therefore, the two points for the revenue equation are

Exhibit 3-3

Profit-Volume Graph

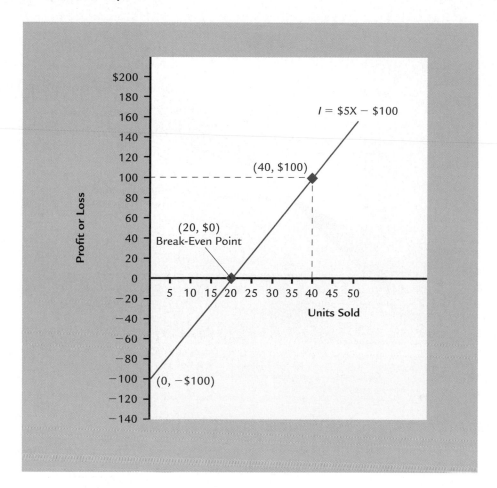

(0, \$0) and (20, \$200). For the cost equation, units sold of 0 and units sold of 20 produce the points (0, \$100) and (20, \$200). The graph of each equation appears in Exhibit 3-4.

Notice that the total revenue line begins at the origin and rises with a slope equal to the selling price per unit (a slope of 10). The total cost line intercepts the vertical axis at a point equal to total fixed costs and rises with a slope equal to the variable cost per unit (a slope of 5). When the total revenue line lies below the total cost line, a loss region is defined. Similarly, when the total revenue line lies above the total cost line, a profit region is defined. The point where the total revenue line and the total cost line intersect is the break-even point. To break even, Tyson Company must sell 20 units and, thus, receive \$200 in total revenues.

Now, let's compare the information available from the CVP graph with that available from the profit-volume graph. To do so, consider the sale of 40 units. Recall that the profit-volume graph revealed that 40 units produced profits of \$100. Examine Exhibit 3-4 again. The CVP graph also shows profits of \$100, but it reveals more as well. The CVP graph discloses that total revenues of \$400 and total costs of \$300 are associated with the sale of 40 units. Furthermore, the total costs can be broken down into fixed costs of \$100 and variable costs of \$200. The CVP graph provides revenue and cost information not provided by the profit-volume graph. Unlike the profit-volume graph, some computation is needed to determine the profit associated with a given sales volume. Nonetheless, because of the greater information content, managers are likely to find the CVP graph a more useful tool.

Exhibit 3-4

Cost-Volume-Profit Graph

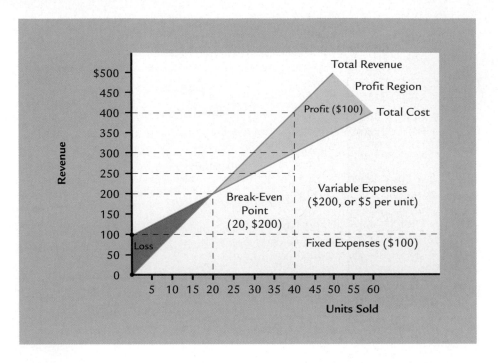

Assumptions of Cost-Volume-Profit Analysis

The profit-volume and CVP graphs just shown rely on some important assumptions. Some of these assumptions are as follows:

- There are linear revenue and linear cost functions.
- Price, total fixed costs, and unit variable costs can be identified and remain constant over the relevant range.
- Selling prices and costs are known with certainty.
- Units produced are sold—there are no finished goods inventories.
- Sales mix is known with certainty for multiple-product break-even settings (explained later in this chapter).

Linear Cost and Revenue Functions   CVP assumes that cost and revenue functions are linear; that is, they are straight lines. But, as was discussed in Chapter 2 on cost behavior, these functions often are not linear. They may be curved or step functions. Fortunately, it is not necessary to consider all possible ranges of production and sales for a firm. Remember that CVP analysis is a short-run decision-making tool. (We know that it is short run in orientation because some costs are fixed.) It is only necessary for us to determine the current operating range, or relevant range, for which the linear cost and revenue relationships are valid. Once a relevant range has been identified, then the cost and price relationships are assumed to be known and constant.

Concept Q&A

Suppose that the revenue line in Exhibit 3-4 had a steeper slope due to a higher price. What would that imply for the break-even point? For the amount of operating income (profit) for units sold above break-even?

Now suppose that the revenue line remains unchanged but that variable cost per unit increases. How would this increase affect the total cost line? What would this increase imply for the break-even point? What would this increase imply for the amount of operating income (profit) for units sold above break-even?

Answer:

A steeper revenue line would intersect the total cost line sooner. Thus, the break-even point would be lower; operating income above break-even would be higher. (Hint: Draw a steeper total revenue line on Exhibit 3-4 to check this reasoning. Remember, revenue still starts at the origin; zero units sold means zero total revenue.) Increased variable cost per unit means a steep slope for the total cost line. Thus, the break-even point would be higher, and the operating income above break-even would be lower.

Prices and Costs Known with Certainty   In actuality, firms seldom know prices, variable costs, and fixed costs with certainty. A change in one variable usually affects the value of others. Often, there is a probability distribution to consider. Furthermore, there are formal ways of explicitly building uncertainty into the CVP model. These issues are explored in the section on incorporating risk and uncertainty into CVP analysis.

Production Equal to Sales   CVP assumes all units produced also are sold. There is no change in inventory over the period. The idea that inventory has no impact on break-even analysis makes sense. Break-even analysis is a short-run decision-making technique; so, we are looking to cover all costs of a particular period of time. Inventory embodies costs of a previous period and is not considered in CVP analyses.

Constant Sales Mix   In single-product analysis, the sales mix is obviously constant—the one product accounts for 100 percent of sales. Multiple-product break-even analysis requires a constant sales mix. However, it is virtually impossible to predict with certainty the sales mix. Typically, this constraint is handled in practice through sensitivity analysis. By using the capabilities of spreadsheet analysis, the sensitivity of variables to a variety of sales mixes can be readily assessed.

Multiple-Product Analysis

OBJECTIVE ④
Apply cost-volume-profit analysis in a multiple-product setting.

CVP analysis is fairly simple in the single-product setting. However, most firms produce and sell a number of products or services. Even though CVP analysis becomes more complex with multiple products, the operation is reasonably straightforward. Let's see how we can adapt the formulas used in a single-product setting to a multiple-product setting by expanding the Whittier Company example.

Whittier Company has decided to offer two models of lawn mowers: a mulching mower that sells for $400 and a riding mower that sells for $800. The marketing department is convinced that 1,200 mulching mowers and 800 riding mowers can be sold during the coming year. The controller has prepared the following projected income statement based on the sales forecast:

	Mulching Mower	Riding Mower	Total
Sales	$480,000	$640,000	$1,120,000
Less: Variable expenses	390,000	480,000	870,000
Contribution margin	$ 90,000	$160,000	$ 250,000
Less: Direct fixed expenses	30,000	40,000	70,000
Product margin	$ 60,000	$120,000	$ 180,000
Less: Common fixed expenses			26,250
Operating income			$ 153,750

Note that the controller has separated *direct fixed expenses* from *common fixed expenses*. The **direct fixed expenses** are those fixed costs that can be traced to each segment and would be avoided if the segment did not exist. The **common fixed expenses** are the fixed costs that are not traceable to the segments and would remain even if one of the segments was eliminated.

Break-Even Point in Units

The owner of Whittier is somewhat apprehensive about adding a new product line and wants to know how many of each model must be sold to break even. If you were given the responsibility of answering this question, how would you respond? One possible response is to use the equation developed earlier in which fixed costs were divided by the contribution margin. This equation presents a problem, however; it was developed for single-product analysis. For two products, there are two prices and two variable costs per unit. The variable cost per unit is derived from the income statement. For the mulching mower, total variable costs are $390,000 based on sales of 1,200 units, yielding a per-unit variable cost of $325 ($390,000/1,200). For the riding mower, total variable costs are $480,000 based on sales of 800 units, yielding a per-unit variable cost of $600 ($480,000/800). Then, the mulching mower has a contribution margin per unit of $75 ($400 − $325); the riding mower has a contribution margin per unit of $200 ($800 − $600).

One possible solution is to apply the analysis separately to each product line. It is possible to obtain individual break-even points when income is defined as product margin. Break-even for the mulching mower is as follows:

Mulching mower break-even units = Fixed cost/(Price − Unit variable cost)
= $30,000/$75
= 400 units

Break-even for the riding mower can be computed as well:

Riding mower break-even units = Fixed cost/(Price − Unit variable cost)
= $40,000/$200
= 200 units

Thus, 400 mulching mowers and 200 riding mowers must be sold to achieve a break-even product margin. But a break-even product margin covers only direct fixed costs; the common fixed costs remain to be covered. Selling these numbers of lawn mowers would result in a loss equal to the common fixed costs. This level of sales is not the break-even point for the firm as a whole; somehow the common fixed costs must be factored into the analysis.

Allocating the common fixed costs to each product line before computing a break-even point may resolve this difficulty. The problem with this approach is that allocation of the common fixed costs is arbitrary. Thus, no meaningful break-even volume is readily apparent.

Another possible solution is to convert the multiple-product problem into a single-product problem. If this conversion can be accomplished, then all of the single-product CVP methodology can be applied directly. The key to this conversion is to identify the expected sales mix, in units, of the multiple products being marketed. **Sales mix** is the relative combination of products being sold by a firm.

Determining the Sales Mix

The sales mix is measured in units sold. For example, if Whittier plans on selling 1,200 mulching mowers and 800 riding mowers, then the sales mix in units is 1,200:800. Usually, the sales mix is reduced to the smallest possible whole numbers. Thus, the relative mix, 1,200:800, can be reduced to 12:8, and further reduced to 3:2. That is, Whittier expects that for every three mulching mowers sold, two riding mowers will be sold.

An endless number of different sales mixes can be used to define the break-even volume in a multiple-product setting. For example, a sales mix of 2:1 will define a break-even point of 550 mulching mowers and 275 riding mowers. The total contribution margin produced by this mix is $96,250 [($75 × 550) + ($200 × 275)]. Similarly, if 350 mulching mowers and 350 riding mowers are sold (corresponding to a 1:1 sales mix), then the total contribution margin is also $96,250 [($75 × 350) + ($200 × 350)]. Since total fixed costs are $96,250, both sales mixes define break-even points. Fortunately, every sales mix need not be considered. Can Whittier really expect a sales mix of 2:1 or 1:1? For every two mulching mowers sold, does Whittier expect to sell a riding mower? Or, for every mulching mower, can Whittier really sell one riding mower?

According to Whittier's marketing study, a sales mix of 3:2 can be expected. This is the ratio that should be used; all others can be ignored. The sales mix that is expected to prevail should be used for CVP analysis.

Sales Mix and Cost-Volume-Profit Analysis   Defining a particular sales mix allows the conversion of a multiple-product problem into a single-product CVP format. Since Whittier expects to sell three mulching mowers for every two riding mowers, it can define the single product it sells as a package containing three mulching mowers and two riding mowers. By defining the product as a package, the multiple-product problem is converted into a single-product one. To use the approach of break-even point in units, the package selling price and the variable cost per package must be known. To compute these package values, the sales mix, individual product prices, and individual variable costs are needed. Cornerstone 3-7 shows how the overall break-even point for each product can be determined.

HOW TO Calculate the Break-Even Units for a Multiple-Product Firm

**CORNERSTONE
3-7**

Information: Recall that Whittier Company sells two products: mulching mowers priced at $400 and riding mowers priced at $800. The variable costs per unit are $325 per mulching mower and $600 per riding mower. Total fixed expense is $96,250. Whittier's expected sales mix is three mulching mowers to two riding mowers.

Required:
1. Form a package of mulching and riding mowers based on the sales mix, and calculate the package contribution margin. (*Hint:* each package consists of three mulching mowers and two riding mowers.)
2. Calculate the break-even point in units for mulching mowers and for riding mowers.
3. Check your answers by preparing a contribution margin income statement.

Calculation:

1.

Product	Price	Unit Variable Cost	Unit Contribution Margin	Sales Mix	Package Unit Contribution Margin
Mulching	$400	$325	$ 75	3	$225
Riding	800	600	200	2	400
Package total					$625

The three mulching mowers in the package yield $225 (3 × $75) in contribution margin. The two riding mowers in the package yield $400 (2 × $200) in contribution margin. Thus, a package of five mowers (three mulching and two riding) has a total contribution margin of $625.

2. Break-even packages = Fixed cost/Package contribution margin
    $$= \$96,250/\$625$$
    $$= 154 \text{ packages}$$
    Mulching mower break-even units = 154 × 3 = 462
    Riding mower break-even units = 154 × 2 = 308
3. Income statement—break-even solution:

	Mulching Mower	Riding Mower	Total
Sales	$184,800	$246,400	$431,200
Less: Variable expenses	150,150	184,800	334,950
Contribution margin	$ 34,650	$ 61,600	$ 96,250
Less: Total fixed expenses			96,250
Operating income			$ 0

Concept Q&A

Suppose a men's clothing store sells two brands of suits: designer suits with a contribution margin of $600 each and regular suits with a contribution margin of $500 each. At break-even, the store must sell a total of 100 suits a month. Last month, the store sold 100 suits in total but incurred an operating loss. There was no change in fixed cost, variable cost, or price. What happened?

Answer:

Probably, the sales mix shifted toward the relatively lower contribution margin suits. For example, suppose that the break-even point for regular suits was 80, and the break-even point for designer suits was 20. If the mix shifted to 90 regular and 10 designer, it is easy to see that less total contribution margin (and, hence, operating income) would be realized.

The complexity of the approach of break-even point in units increases dramatically as the number of products increases. Imagine performing this analysis for a firm with several hundred products. This observation seems more overwhelming than it is in reality. Computers can easily handle a problem with so much data. Furthermore, many firms simplify the problem by analyzing product groups rather than individual products. Another way to handle the increased complexity is to switch from the units sold to the sales revenue approach. This approach can accomplish a multiple-product CVP analysis using only the summary data found in an organization's income statement. The computational requirements are much simpler.

Break-Even Point in Sales Dollars

To illustrate the break-even point in sales dollars, the same examples will be used. However, the only information needed is the projected income statement for Whittier Company as a whole.

Sales	$1,120,000
Less: Variable costs	870,000
Contribution margin	$ 250,000
Less: Fixed costs	96,250
Operating income	$ 153,750

**CORNERSTONE
3-8**

HOW TO Calculate the Break-Even Sales Dollars for a Multiple-Product Firm

Information: Recall that Whittier Company sells two products that are expected to produce total revenue next year of $1,120,000 and total variable costs of $870,000. Total fixed costs are expected to equal $96,250.

Required:
1. Calculate the break-even point in sales dollars for Whittier Company.
2. Check your answer by preparing a contribution margin income statement.

Calculation:
1. The contribution margin ratio = $250,000/$1,120,000 = 0.22
    Break-even sales = Fixed cost/Contribution margin ratio
    = $96,250/0.22
    = $437,500
    [*Note:* Total break-even sales differ slightly between Cornerstones 3-7 and 3-8 ($431,200 vs. $437,500) due to the rounding of the contribution margin ratio to only two decimal places (.22).]
2. Income statement—break-even solution:

Sales	$437,500
Less: Variable costs (0.78 × $437,500)	341,250
Contribution margin	$ 96,250
Less: Fixed costs	96,250
Operating income	$ 0

Notice that this income statement corresponds to the total column of the more detailed income statement examined previously. The projected income statement rests on the assumption that 1,200 mulching mowers and 800 riding mowers will be sold (a 3:2 sales mix). The break-even point in sales revenue also rests on the expected sales mix. (As with the units sold approach, different sales mixes will produce different results.)

With the income statement, the usual CVP questions can be addressed. For example, how much sales revenue must be earned to break even? Cornerstone 3-8 shows how to calculate the break-even point in sales dollars for a multiple-product firm.

The break-even point in sales dollars implicitly uses the assumed sales mix but avoids the requirement of building a package contribution margin. No knowledge of individual product data is needed. The computational effort is similar to that used in the single-product setting. Moreover, the answer is still expressed in sales revenue. Unlike the break-even point in units, the answer to CVP questions using sales dollars is still expressed in a single summary measure. The sales revenue approach, however, does sacrifice information concerning individual product performance.

Cost-Volume-Profit Analysis and Risk and Uncertainty

OBJECTIVE ⑤
Explain the impact of risk, uncertainty, and changing variables on cost-volume-profit analysis.

Because firms operate in a dynamic world, they must be aware of changes in prices, variable costs, and fixed costs. They must also account for the effect of risk and uncertainty. The break-even point can be affected by changes in price, unit contribution margin, and fixed cost. Managers can use CVP analysis to handle risk and uncertainty. For example, France-based **Airbus** reported in 2006 its first ever loss, which resulted from a decreased sales volume and major costly production delays involving a redesign of its "extra wide–body" passenger jet to compete with **Boeing**'s 787 Dreamliner. In response to this loss, Airbus used CVP analysis to estimate how a $2.6 billion reduction in its annual variable and fixed costs, as well as various reductions in its $144 million unit jet price, would affect its annual profit.[1]

For a given sales mix, CVP analysis can be used as if the firm were selling a single product. However, when the prices of individual products change, the sales mix can be affected because consumers may buy relatively more or less of the product. Keep in mind that a new sales mix will affect the units of each product that need to be sold in order to achieve a desired profit target. If the sales mix for the coming period is uncertain, it may be necessary to look at several different mixes. In this way, a manager gains insight into the possible outcomes facing the firm.

Suppose that Whittier Company recently conducted a market study of the mulching lawn mower that revealed three different alternatives:

1. *Alternative 1:* If advertising expenditures increase by $8,000, then sales will increase from 1,600 units to 1,725 units.
2. *Alternative 2:* A price decrease from $400 to $375 per lawn mower will increase sales from 1,600 units to 1,900 units.
3. *Alternative 3:* Decreasing price to $375 *and* increasing advertising expenditures by $8,000 will increase sales from 1,600 units to 2,600 units.

Should Whittier maintain its current price and advertising policies, or should it select one of the three alternatives described by the marketing study?

The first alternative, increasing advertising costs by $8,000 with a resulting sales increase of 125 units, is summarized in Exhibit 3-5. This alternative can be analyzed by using the contribution margin per unit of $75. Since units sold increase by 125, the increase in total contribution margin is $9,375 ($75 × 125 units). However, since fixed

---

[1]"Planemaker Airbus to report its first annual loss," *USA Today* (January 18, 2007): 3B.

costs increase by $8,000, profits only increase by $1,375 ($9,375 − $8,000). Notice that we need to look only at the incremental increase in total contribution margin and fixed expenses to compute the increase in total operating income.

For the second alternative, the price is dropped to $375 (from $400), and the units sold increase to 1,900 (from 1,600). The effects of this alternative are summarized in Exhibit 3-6. Here, fixed expenses do not change, so only the change in total contribution margin is relevant. For the current price of $400, the contribution margin per unit is $75 ($400 − $325), and the total contribution margin is $120,000 ($75 × 1,600). For the new price, the contribution margin drops to $50 per unit ($375 − $325). If 1,900 units are sold at the new price, then the new total contribution margin is $95,000 ($50 × 1,900). Dropping the price results in a profit decline of $25,000 ($120,000 − $95,000).

Exhibit 3-5

Summary of the Effects of Alternative 1

	Before the Increased Advertising	With the Increased Advertising
Units sold	1,600	1,725
Unit contribution margin	× $75	× $75
Total contribution margin	$120,000	$129,375
Less: Fixed expenses	45,000	53,000
Operating income	$ 75,000	$ 76,375

	Difference in Profit
Change in sales volume	125
Unit contribution margin	× $75
Change in contribution margin	$9,375
Less: Change in fixed expenses	8,000
Increase in operating income	$1,375

Exhibit 3-6

Summary of the Effects of Alternative 2

	Before the Proposed Price Decrease	With the Proposed Price Decrease
Units sold	1,600	1,900
Unit contribution margin	× $75	× $50
Total contribution margin	$120,000	$95,000
Less: Fixed expenses	45,000	45,000
Operating income	$ 75,000	$50,000

	Difference in Profit
Change in contribution margin ($95,000 − $120,000)	$(25,000)
Less: Change in fixed expenses	—
Decrease in operating income	$(25,000)

The third alternative calls for a decrease in the unit selling price and an increase in advertising costs. Like the first alternative, the profit impact can be assessed by looking at the incremental effects on contribution margin and fixed expenses. The incremental profit change can be found by (1) computing the incremental change in total contribution margin, (2) computing the incremental change in fixed expenses, and (3) adding the two results. As shown in Exhibit 3-7, the current total contribution margin (for 1,600 units sold) is $120,000. Since the new unit contribution margin is $50, the new total contribution margin is $130,000 ($50 × 2,600 units). Thus, the incremental increase in total contribution margin is $10,000 ($130,000 – $120,000). However, to achieve this incremental increase in contribution margin, an incremental increase of $8,000 in fixed costs is needed. The net effect is an incremental increase in operating income of $2,000.

Of the three alternatives identified by the marketing study, the third alternative promises the most benefit. It increases total operating income by $2,000. The first alternative increases operating income by only $1,375, and the second *decreases* operating income by $25,000.

These examples are all based on a units sold approach. However, we could just as easily have applied a sales revenue approach. The answers would be the same.

Introducing Risk and Uncertainty

An important assumption of CVP analysis is that prices and costs are known with certainty. This assumption is seldom accurate. Risk and uncertainty are a part of business decision making and must be dealt with somehow. Formally, risk differs from uncertainty in that under risk, the probability distributions of the variables are known; under uncertainty, the probability distributions are not known. For purposes of CVP analysis, however, the terms will be used interchangeably.

How do managers deal with risk and uncertainty? There are a variety of methods. First, of course, is that management must realize the uncertain nature of future prices, costs, and quantities. Next, managers move from consideration of a break-even point to what might be called a "break-even band." In other words, given the uncertain nature of the data, perhaps a firm might break even when 1,800 to 2,000 units are sold instead of at the point estimate of 1,900 units. Further, managers may engage in sensitivity or

---

Exhibit 3-7

Summary of the Effects of Alternative 3

	Before the Proposed Price and Advertising Changes	With the Proposed Price Decrease and Advertising Increase
Units sold	1,600	2,600
Unit contribution margin	× $75	× $50
Total contribution margin	$120,000	$130,000
Less: Fixed expenses	45,000	53,000
Profit	$ 75,000	$ 77,000

	Difference in Profit
Change in contribution margin ($130,000 − $120,000)	$10,000
Less: Change in fixed expenses ($53,000 − $45,000)	8,000
Increase in profit	$ 2,000

what-if analysis. In this instance, a computer spreadsheet is helpful, as managers set up the break-even (or targeted profit) relationships and then check to see the impact that varying costs and prices have on quantity sold. Two concepts useful to management are margin of safety and operating leverage. Both of these concepts may be considered measures of risk. Each concept requires knowledge of fixed and variable costs.

Margin of Safety

The **margin of safety** is the units sold or the revenue earned above the break-even volume. For example, if the break-even volume for a company is 200 units and the company is currently selling 500 units, then the margin of safety is 300 units (500 − 200). The margin of safety can be expressed in sales revenue as well. If the break-even volume is $200,000 and current revenues are $500,000, then the margin of safety is $300,000. ($500,000 − $200,000). In addition, margin of safety sales revenue can be expressed as a percentage of total sales dollars, which some managers refer to as the margin of safety ratio. In this example, the margin of safety ratio would be 60% ($300,000/$500,000). Exhibit 3-8 shows the calculation of margin of safety in units and in sales revenue. Cornerstone 3-9 shows the expected margin of safety for Whittier Company.

The margin of safety can be viewed as a crude measure of risk. There are always events, unknown when plans are made, that can lower sales below the original expected level. In the event that sales take a downward turn, the risk of suffering losses is less if a firm's expected margin of safety is large than if the margin of safety is small. Managers who face a low margin of safety may wish to consider actions to increase sales or decrease costs. These steps will increase the margin of safety and lower the risk of incurring losses.

Operating Leverage

In physics, a lever is a simple machine used to multiply force. Basically, the lever multiplies the effort applied to create more work. The larger the load moved by a given amount of effort, the greater is the mechanical advantage. In financial terms, operating leverage is concerned with the relative mix of fixed costs and variable costs in an organization. It is sometimes possible to trade off fixed costs for variable costs. As variable costs

Concept Q&A

Two companies have identical sales revenue of $15 million. Is it true that both have the same operating income and the same margin of safety? Is it possible that one company has a higher margin of safety?

Answer:

It is not necessarily true that the two companies make the same operating income. If one company has lower variable costs per unit and/or a lower total fixed cost, then its operating income would be higher. The differences in variable cost per unit and total fixed cost would lead to different break-even revenues. Of course, the company with the lower break-even sales would have a higher margin of safety.

Exhibit 3-8

The Margin of Safety

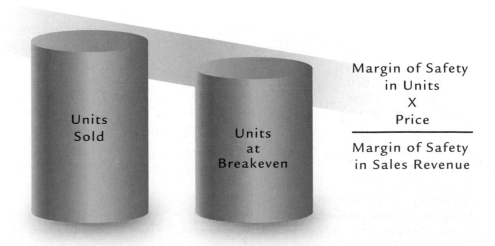

Units Sold

Units at Breakeven

Margin of Safety
in Units
X
Price
—————
Margin of Safety
in Sales Revenue

HOW TO Compute the Margin of Safety

Information: Recall that Whittier Company plans to sell 1,000 mowers at $400 each in the coming year. Whittier has variable costs of $325 and fixed costs of $45,000. Break-even units were previously calculated as 600.

Required:
1. Calculate the margin of safety for Whittier Company in terms of the number of units.
2. Calculate the margin of safety for Whittier Company in terms of sales revenue.

Calculation:
1. Margin of safety in units = 1,000 – 600 = 400
2. Margin of safety in sales revenue = $400(1,000) – $400(600) = $160,000

**CORNERSTONE
3-9**

decrease, the unit contribution margin increases, making the contribution of each unit sold that much greater. In such a case, fluctuations in sales have an increased effect on profitability. Thus, firms that have realized lower variable costs by increasing the proportion of fixed costs will benefit with greater increases in profits as sales increase than will firms with a lower proportion of fixed costs. Fixed costs are being used as leverage to increase profits. Unfortunately, it is also true that firms with a higher operating leverage will experience greater reductions in profits as sales decrease. **Operating leverage** is the use of fixed costs to extract higher percentage changes in profits as sales activity changes.

The **degree of operating leverage (DOL)** can be measured for a given level of sales by taking the ratio of contribution margin to operating income, as follows:

Degree of operating leverage = Contribution margin/Operating income

If fixed costs are used to lower variable costs such that contribution margin increases and operating income decreases, then the degree of operating leverage increases—signaling an increase in risk. Cornerstone 3-10 shows how to compute the degree of operating leverage for Whittier Company.

The greater the degree of operating leverage, the more that changes in sales will affect operating income. Because of this phenomenon, the mix of costs that an organization chooses can have a considerable influence on its operating risk and profit level. A company's mix of fixed costs relative to variable costs is referred to as its **cost structure**. Often, a company changes its cost structure by taking on more of one type of cost in exchange for reducing its amount of the other type of cost. For example, as U.S. companies try to

HOW TO Compute the Degree of Operating Leverage

Information: Recall that Whittier Company plans to sell 1,000 mowers at $400 each in the coming year. Whittier has variable costs of $325 and fixed costs of $45,000. Operating income at that level of sales was previously computed as $30,000.

Required: Calculate the degree of operating leverage for Whittier Company.

Calculation:
Degree of operating leverage = Total contribution margin/Operating income
= ($400 − $325)(1,000 units)/$30,000
= 2.5

**CORNERSTONE
3-10**

compete more effectively with foreign competitors' significantly lower hourly labor costs (i.e., a variable cost), many are altering their cost structures by taking on more plant machine automation (i.e., a fixed cost) in exchange for using less labor.

To illustrate the impact of these concepts on decision making, consider a firm that is planning to add a new product line. In adding the line, the firm can choose to rely heavily on automation or on labor. If the firm chooses to emphasize automation rather than labor, fixed costs will be higher, and unit variable costs will be lower. Relevant data for a sales level of 10,000 units follow:

	Automated System	Manual System
Sales	$1,000,000	$1,000,000
Less: Variable costs	500,000	800,000
Contribution margin	$ 500,000	$ 200,000
Less: Fixed costs	375,000	100,000
Operating income	$ 125,000	$ 100,000
Unit selling price	$100	$100
Unit variable cost	50	80
Unit contribution margin	50	20

The degree of operating leverage for the automated system is 4.0 ($500,000/ $125,000). The degree of operating leverage for the manual system is 2.0 ($200,000/ $100,000). What happens to profit in each system if sales increase by 40 percent? We can generate the following income statements to see the following:

	Automated System	Manual System
Sales	$1,400,000	$1,400,000
Less: Variable costs	700,000	1,120,000
Contribution margin	$ 700,000	$ 280,000
Less: Fixed costs	375,000	100,000
Operating income	$ 325,000	$ 180,000

Profits for the automated system would increase by $200,000 ($325,000 − $125,000) for a 160-percent increase. In the manual system, profits increase by only $80,000 ($180,000 − $100,000) for an 80-percent increase. The automated system has a greater percentage increase because it has a higher degree of operating leverage.

The degree of operating leverage can be used directly to calculate the change in operating income that would result from a given percentage change in sales.

Percentage change in operating income = DOL × Percent change in sales

Since sales are predicted to increase by 40 percent, and the DOL for the automated system is 4.0, operating income increases by 160 percent. Since operating income based on the original sales level is $125,000, the operating income based on the increased sales level would be $325,000 [$125,000 + ($125,000 × 1.6)]. Similarly, for the manual system, increased sales of 40 percent and DOL of 2.0 imply increased operating income of 80 percent. Therefore, operating income based on the increased sales level would be $180,000 [$100,000 + ($100,000 × 0.8)]. Cornerstone 3-11 illustrates the impact of increased sales on operating income using the degree of operating leverage.

In choosing between the two systems, the effect of operating leverage is a valuable piece of information. Higher operating leverage multiplies the impact of increased sales on income. However, the effect is a two-edged sword. As sales decrease, the automated system will also show much higher percentage decreases. Moreover, the increased operating leverage is available under the automated system because of the presence of increased fixed costs. The break-even point for the automated system is 7,500 units

HOW TO Compute the Impact of Increased Sales on Operating Income Using the Degree of Operating Leverage

CORNERSTONE 3-11

Information: Recall that Whittier Company had expected to sell 1,000 mowers and earn operating income equal to $30,000 next year. Whittier's degree of operating leverage is equal to 2.5. Now, the company plans to increase sales by 20 percent next year.

Required:
1. Calculate the percent change in operating income expected by Whittier Company for next year using the degree of operating leverage.
2. Calculate the operating income expected by Whittier Company next year using the percent change in operating income calculated in Requirement 1.

Calculation:
1. Percent change in operating income = DOL × % change in sales
$$= 2.5 \times 20\% = 50\%$$
2. Expected operating income = $30,000 + (0.5 \times \$30,000) = \$45,000$

($375,000/$50), whereas the break-even point for the manual system is 5,000 units ($100,000/$20). Thus, the automated system has greater operating risk. The increased risk, of course, provides a potentially higher profit level as long as units sold exceed 9,167. Why 9,167? Because that is the quantity for which the operating income for the automated system equals the operating income for the manual system. The quantity at which two systems produce the same operating income is referred to as the **indifference point**. This number of units is computed by setting the operating income equations of the two systems equal and solving for number of units as follows:

$$\$50 \text{ (Units)} - \$375,000 = \$20 \text{ (Units)} - \$100,000$$
$$\text{Units} = \$9,167$$

In choosing between the automated and manual systems, the manager must consider the likelihood that sales will exceed 9,167 units. If after careful study there is a strong belief that sales will easily exceed this level, then the choice is obviously the automated system. On the other hand, if sales are unlikely to exceed 9,167 units, then the manual system is preferable. Exhibit 3–9 summarizes the relative differences between the manual and automated systems in terms of some of the CVP concepts.

Exhibit 3-9

Differences between a Manual and an Automated System

	Manual System	Automated System
Price	Same	Same
Variable cost	Relatively higher	Relatively lower
Fixed cost	Relatively lower	Relatively higher
Contribution margin	Relatively lower	Relatively higher
Break-even point	Relatively lower	Relatively higher
Margin of safety	Relatively higher	Relatively lower
Degree of operating leverage	Relatively lower	Relatively higher
Down-side risk	Relatively lower	Relatively higher
Up-side potential	Relatively lower	Relatively higher

CORNERSTONES FOR CHAPTER 3

Key Terms

Break-even point, 100
Common fixed expenses, 113
Contribution margin, 101
Contribution margin income
   statement, 100
Contribution margin ratio, 104
Cost structure, 121
Cost-volume-profit graph, 110
Degree of operating leverage (DOL), 121

Direct fixed expenses, 113
Indifference point, 123
Margin of safety, 120
Operating leverage, 121
Profit-volume graph, 110
Sales mix, 114
Sensitivity analysis, 124
Variable cost ratio, 104

Review Problem

I.   Single Product Cost-Volume-Profit Analysis

Cutlass Company's projected profit for the coming year is as follows:

	Total	Per Unit
Sales	$200,000	$20
Less: Variable expenses	120,000	12
Contribution margin	$ 80,000	$ 8
Less: Fixed expenses	64,000	
Operating income	$ 16,000	

Required:
1. Compute the variable cost ratio. Compute the contribution margin ratio.
2. Compute the break-even point in units.
3. Compute the break-even point in sales dollars.
4. How many units must be sold to earn a profit of $30,000?
5. Compute the contribution margin ratio. Using that ratio, compute the additional profit that Cutlass would earn if sales were $25,000 more than expected.
6. For the projected level of sales, compute the margin of safety in units and in sales dollars.
7. Calculate the degree of operating leverage. Now suppose that Cutlass revises the forecast to show a 30% increase in sales over the original forecast. What is the percent change in operating income expected for the revised forecast? What is the total operating income expected by Cutlass after revising the sales forecast?

Solution:
1. Variable cost ratio = Total variable cost/Sales
    $$= \$120,000/\$200,000$$
    $$= 0.60 \text{ or } 60\%$$
    Contribution margin ratio = Contribution margin/Sales
    $$= \$80,000/\$200,000$$
    $$= 0.40 \text{ or } 40\%$$
2. The break-even point is computed as follows:
    Units = Fixed cost/(Price − Unit variable cost)
    $$= \$64,000/(\$20 - \$12)$$
    $$= \$64,000/\$8$$
    $$= 8,000 \text{ units}$$
3. The break-even point in sales dollars is computed as follows:
    Break-even sales dollars = Fixed cost/Contribution margin ratio
    $$= \$64,000/0.40$$
    $$= \$160,000$$
4. The number of units that must be sold to earn a profit of $30,000 is calculated as follows:
    Units = ($64,000 + $30,000)/$8
    $$= \$94,000/\$8$$
    $$= 11,750 \text{ units}$$
5. The additional contribution margin on additional sales of $25,000 would be 0.40 × $25,000 = $10,000.
6. Margin of safety in units = Projected units − Breakeven units
    $$= 10,000 - 8,000$$
    $$= 2,000 \text{ units}$$
    Margin of safety in sales dollars = $200,000 − or $40,000 in sales revenues.
7. Degree of operating leverage = Contribution margin/Operating income
    $$= \$80,000/\$16,000$$
    $$= 5.0$$
    Percent change in operating income = Degree of operating leverage
    $$\times \% \text{ change in sales}$$
    $$= 5.0 \times 30\%$$
    $$= 150\%$$
    Expected operating income = $16,000 + (1.5 × $16,000)
    $$= \$40,000$$

II.   Multiple-Product Cost-Volume-Profit Analysis

Alpha Company produces and sells two products: Alpha-Basic and Alpha-Deluxe. In the coming year, Alpha expects to sell 3,000 units of Alpha-Basic and 1,500 units of Alpha-Deluxe. Information on the two products is as follows:

	Alpha-Basic	Alpha-Deluxe
Price	$120	$200
Variable cost per unit	40	80

Total fixed costs are $140,000.

Required:
1. What is the sales mix of Alpha-Basic to Alpha-Deluxe?
2. Compute the break-even quantity of each product.

Solution:
1. The sales mix of Alpha-Basic to Alpha-Deluxe is 3,000:1,500 or 2:1.
2. Each package consists of two Alpha-Basic and one Alpha-Deluxe:

Product	Price	Unit Variable Cost	Unit Contribution Margin	Sales Mix	Package Unit Contribution Margin
Alpha-Basic	$120	$40	$ 80	2	$160
Alpha-Deluxe	200	80	120	1	120
Package total					$280

Break-even packages = Total fixed cost/Package contribution margin
= $140,000/$280
= 500 packages
Alpha-Basic break-even units = 500 × 2 = 1,000
Alpha-Deluxe break-even units = 500 × 1 = 500

Discussion Questions

1. Explain how CVP analysis can be used for managerial planning.
2. Describe the difference between the units sold approach to CVP analysis and the sales revenue approach.
3. Define the term *break-even point*.
4. Explain why contribution margin per unit becomes profit per unit above the break-even point.
5. What is the variable cost ratio? The contribution margin ratio? How are the two ratios related?
6. Suppose a firm with a contribution margin ratio of 0.3 increased its advertising expenses by $10,000 and found that sales increased by $30,000. Was it a good decision to increase advertising expenses? Suppose that the contribution margin ratio is now 0.4. Would it be a good decision to increase advertising expenses?
7. Define the term *sales mix*, and give an example to support your definition.
8. Explain how CVP analysis developed for single products can be used in a multiple-product setting.
9. Since break-even analysis focuses on making zero profit, it is of no value in determining the units a firm must sell to earn a targeted profit. Do you agree or disagree with this statement? Why?
10. How does target profit enter into the break-even units equation?
11. Explain how a change in sales mix can change a company's break-even point.
12. Define the term *margin of safety*. Explain how it can be used as a crude measure of operating risk.
13. Explain what is meant by the term *operating leverage*. What impact does increased leverage have on risk?
14. How can sensitivity analysis be used in conjunction with CVP analysis?
15. Why is a declining margin of safety over a period of time an issue of concern to managers?

Multiple-Choice Exercises

3-1 If the variable cost per unit goes up,

	Contribution margin	Break-even point
a.	increases	increases.
b.	increases	decreases.
c.	decreases	decreases.
d.	decreases	increases.
e.	decreases	remains unchanged.

3-2 The amount of revenue required to earn a targeted profit is equal to

a. fixed cost divided by contribution margin.
b. fixed cost divided by contribution margin ratio.
c. fixed cost plus targeted profit divided by contribution margin ratio.
d. targeted profit divided by contribution margin ratio.
e. targeted profit divided by variable cost ratio.

3-3 Break-even revenue for the multiple-product firm can

a. be calculated by dividing total fixed cost by the overall contribution margin ratio.
b. be calculated by dividing segment fixed cost by the overall contribution margin ratio.
c. be calculated by dividing total fixed cost by the package contribution margin.
d. be calculated by multiplying total fixed cost by the contribution margin ratio.
e. not be calculated; break-even revenue can only be computed for a single-product firm.

3-4 In the cost-volume-profit graph,

a. the break-even point is found where the total revenue curve crosses the x-axis.
b. the area of profit is to the left of the break-even point.
c. the area of loss cannot be determined from this graph.
d. both the total revenue curve and the total cost curve appear on this graph.
e. neither the total revenue curve nor the total cost curve appear on this graph.

3-5 An important assumption of cost-volume-profit analysis is that

a. both costs and revenues are linear functions.
b. all cost and revenue relationships are analyzed within the relevant range.
c. there is no change in inventories.
d. sales mix remains constant.
e. All of the above are assumptions of CVP analysis.

3-6 The use of fixed costs to extract higher percentage changes in profits as sales activity changes involves

a. margin of safety.
b. operating leverage.
c. degree of operating leverage.
d. sensitivity analysis.
e. variable cost reduction.

3-7 If the margin of safety is 0, then

a. the company is operating at a loss.
b. the company is precisely breaking even.
c. the company is earning a small profit.
d. the margin of safety cannot be less than or equal to 0; it must be positive.
e. None of the above is true.

3-8 The contribution margin is the

a.   amount by which sales exceed fixed cost.
b.   difference between sales and total expenses.
c.   difference between sales and operating income.
d.   difference between sales and total variable expense.
e.   difference between variable expense and fixed expense.

Use the following information for 3-9 and 3-10.
Corleone Company produces a single product with a price of $15, variable costs per unit of $12, and fixed costs of $9,000.

3-9 Corleone's break-even point in units

a.   is 600.
b.   is 750.
c.   is 9,000.
d.   is 3,000.
e.   cannot be determined from the information given.

3-10 The variable cost ratio and the contribution margin ratio for Corleone are

	Variable cost ratio	Contribution margin ratio
a.	80%	80%.
b.	20%	80%.
c.	20%	20%.
d.	80%	20%.
e.	The contribution margin ratio cannot be determined from the information given.	

3-11 If a company's fixed costs rise by $10,000, which of the following will be true?

a.   The break-even point will decrease.
b.   The variable cost ratio will increase.
c.   The break-even point will be unchanged.
d.   The variable cost ratio will decrease.
e.   The contribution margin ratio will be unchanged.

3-12 Solemon Company has fixed costs of $15,000, variable cost per unit of $5, and a price of $8. If Solemon wants to earn a targeted profit of $3,600, how many units must be sold?

a.   6,200
b.   5,000
c.   1,200
d.   3,720
e.   1,875

Exercises

OBJECTIVE ①
CORNERSTONE 3-1
CORNERSTONE 3-2
CORNERSTONE 3-3

Exercise 3-13 Basic Break-Even Calculations

Suppose that Adams Company sells a product for $16. Unit costs are as follows:

Direct materials	$3.90
Direct labor	1.40
Variable overhead	2.10
Variable selling and administrative expense	1.60

Total fixed overhead is $52,000 per year, and total fixed selling and administrative expense is $37,950.

Required:
1. Calculate the variable cost per unit and the contribution margin per unit.
2. Prepare a contribution margin income statement assuming that 13,000 units are sold.
3. Calculate the contribution margin ratio and the variable cost ratio.
4. Calculate the break-even units.

Exercise 3-14 Break-Even in Units

OBJECTIVE ①

The controller of Greenbrough Company prepared the following projected income statement:

CORNERSTONE 3-1
CORNERSTONE 3-2

Sales (5,000 units @ $12)	$60,000
Less: Variable costs	45,000
Contribution margin	$15,000
Less: Fixed costs	6,900
Operating income	$ 8,100

Required:
1. Calculate the unit variable cost. Calculate the break-even number of units.
2. Prepare an income statement for Greenbrough at break-even.

Exercise 3-15 Contribution Margin Ratio, Variable Cost Ratio, Break-Even in Sales Revenue

OBJECTIVE ①

CORNERSTONE 3-3
CORNERSTONE 3-4

Refer to **Exercise 3-14** for data.

Required:
1. What is the contribution margin per unit for Greenbrough Company? What is the contribution margin ratio?
2. What is the variable cost ratio for Greenbrough Company?
3. Calculate the break-even revenue.

Exercise 3-16 Units Needed to Earn Target Income

OBJECTIVE ②

CORNERSTONE 3-5
CORNERSTONE 3-6

Refer to **Exercise 3-14** for data.

Required:
1. How many units must Greenbrough sell to earn income equal to $9,900?
2. How much sales revenue must Greenbrough make to earn income equal to $9,900?
3. Prepare an income statement based on the number of units you calculated in Requirement 1 (or the revenue you calculated in Requirement 2) to prove your answer.

Exercise 3-17 Units Sold to Break Even, Unit Variable Cost, Unit Manufacturing Cost

OBJECTIVE ①

Prachi Company produces and sells disposable foil baking pans to retailers for $2.45 per pan. The variable costs per pan are as follows:

Direct materials	$0.27
Direct labor	0.58
Variable overhead	0.63
Variable selling	0.17

Fixed manufacturing costs total $131,650 per year. Administrative costs (all fixed) total $18,350.

Required:
1. Compute the number of pans that must be sold for Prachi to break even.
2. What is the unit variable cost? What is the unit variable manufacturing cost? Which is used in CVP analysis and why?

OBJECTIVE ②
CORNERSTONE 3-6

Exercise 3-18 Units and Sales to Earn Target Income

Refer to **Exercise 3-17** for data.

Required:
1. How many pans must be sold for Prachi to earn operating income of $12,600?
2. How much sales revenue must Prachi have to earn operating income of $12,600?

OBJECTIVE ⑤
CORNERSTONE 3-9

Exercise 3-19 Margin of Safety

Refer to **Exercise 3-17** for data, and suppose that Prachi expects to sell 215,000 pans.

Required:
1. What is the margin of safety in pans?
2. What is the margin of safety in dollars?

OBJECTIVE ①

spreadsheet

Exercise 3-20 Contribution Margin, Unit Amounts, Break-Even Units

Information on four independent companies follows. Calculate the correct amount for each question mark.

	A	B	C	D
Sales	$5,000	$?	$?	$9,000
Total variable costs	4,000	11,700	9,750	?
Total contribution margin	$1,000	$ 3,900	$?	$?
Total fixed costs	?	4,000	?	750
Operating income (loss)	$ 500	$?	$ 400	$2,850
Units sold	?	1,300	125	90
Price per unit	$ 5	?	$ 130	?
Variable cost per unit	?	$ 9	?	?
Contribution margin per unit	?	$ 3	?	?
Contribution margin ratio	?	?	40%	?
Break-even in units	?	?	?	?

OBJECTIVES ① ②

Exercise 3-21 Sales Revenue Approach, Variable Cost Ratio, Contribution Margin Ratio

Rezler Company's controller prepared the following budgeted income statement for the coming year:

Sales	$315,000
Less: Variable expenses	141,750
Contribution margin	$173,250
Less: Fixed expenses	63,000
Profit before taxes	$110,250
Less: Taxes	33,075
Profit after taxes	$ 77,175

Required:
1. What is Rezler's variable cost ratio? What is its contribution margin ratio?
2. Suppose Rezler's actual revenues are $30,000 more than budgeted. By how much will operating income increase? Give the answer without preparing a new income statement.
3. How much sales revenue must Rezler earn to break even? Prepare a contribution margin income statement to verify the accuracy of your answer.

Exercise 3-22 Margin of Safety

OBJECTIVE ⑤
CORNERSTONE 3-9

Refer to **Exercise 3-21** for data.

Required:
1. What is Rezler's expected margin of safety?
2. What is Rezler's margin of safety if sales revenue is $280,000?

Exercise 3-23 Multiple-Product Break-Even

OBJECTIVE ④
CORNERSTONE 3-7

Switzer Company produces and sells yoga-training products: how-to videotapes and a basic equipment set (blocks, strap, and small pillows). Last year, Switzer sold 10,000 videotapes and 5,000 equipment sets. Information on the two products is as follows:

	Videotapes	Equipment Sets
Price	$12	$15
Variable cost per unit	4	6

Total fixed costs are $70,000.

Required:
1. What is the sales mix of videotapes and equipment sets?
2. Compute the break-even quantity of each product.

Exercise 3-24 Contribution Margin Ratio, Break-Even Sales Revenue, and Margin of Safety for Multiple-Product Firm

OBJECTIVES ① ⑤
CORNERSTONE 3-8
CORNERSTONE 3-9

Refer to **Exercise 3-23** for data.

Required:
1. Prepare an income statement for Switzer for last year. What is the overall contribution margin ratio? The overall break-even sales revenue?
2. Compute the margin of safety for last year.

Exercise 3-25 Multiple-Product Break-Even, Break-Even Sales Revenue

OBJECTIVES ④ ⑤
spreadsheet

Refer to **Exercise 3-23**. Suppose that in the coming year, Switzer plans to produce an extra-thick yoga mat for sale to health clubs. The company estimates that 20,000 mats can be sold at a price of $18 and a variable cost per unit of $13. Fixed costs must be increased by $48,350 (making total fixed costs of $118,350). Assume that anticipated sales of the other products, as well as their prices and variable costs, remain the same.

Required:
1. What is the sales mix of videotapes, equipment sets, and yoga mats?
2. Compute the break-even quantity of each product.
3. Prepare an income statement for Switzer for the coming year. What is the overall contribution margin ratio? The overall break-even sales revenue?
4. Compute the margin of safety for the coming year in sales dollars. (Round the contribution margin ratio to three significant digits; round the break-even sales revenue to the nearest dollar.)

Exercise 3-26 Cost-Volume-Profit Graphs

OBJECTIVE ③
spreadsheet

Lotts Company produces and sells one product. The selling price is $10, and the unit variable cost is $6. Total fixed costs are $10,000.

Required:

1. Prepare a CVP graph with "Units Sold" as the horizontal axis and "$ Profit" as the vertical axis. Label the break-even point on the horizontal axis.
2. Prepare CVP graphs for each of the following independent scenarios:
   a. Fixed costs increase by $5,000.
   b. Unit variable cost increases to $7.
   c. Unit selling price increases to $12.
   d. Assume that fixed costs increase by $5,000 and unit variable cost is $7.

OBJECTIVE ①   Exercise 3-27 Basic Cost-Volume-Profit Concepts

Berry Company produces a single product. The projected income statement for the coming year is as follows:

Sales (50,000 units @ $45)	$2,250,000
Less: Variable costs	1,305,000
Contribution margin	$ 945,000
Less: Fixed costs	812,700
Operating income	$ 132,300

Required:

1. Compute the unit contribution margin and the units that must be sold to break even.
2. Suppose 30,000 units are sold above break-even. What is the operating income?
3. Compute the contribution margin ratio and the break-even point in dollars. Suppose that revenues are $200,000 more than expected. What would the total operating income be?

OBJECTIVE ⑤   Exercise 3-28 Margin of Safety and Operating Leverage

CORNERSTONE 3-9
CORNERSTONE 3-10
CORNERSTONE 3-11

Refer to **Exercise 3-27** for data.

Required:

1. Compute the margin of safety in sales dollars.
2. Compute the degree of operating leverage (rounded to two decimal places).
3. Compute the new profit level if sales are 20 percent higher than expected.

OBJECTIVE ④   Exercise 3-29 Multiple-Product Break-Even

Parker Pottery produces a line of vases and a line of ceramic figurines. Each line uses the same equipment and labor; hence, there are no traceable fixed costs. Common fixed costs equal $30,000. Parker's accountant has begun to assess the profitability of the two lines and has gathered the following data for last year:

	Vases	Figurines
Price	$ 40	$ 70
Variable cost	30	42
Contribution margin	$ 10	$ 28
Number of units	1,000	500

Required:

1. Compute the number of vases and the number of figurines that must be sold for the company to break even.
2. Parker Pottery is considering upgrading its factory to improve the quality of its products. The upgrade will add $5,260 per year to total fixed costs. If the upgrade is successful, the projected sales of vases will be 1,500, and figurine sales will increase to 1,000 units. What is the new break-even point in units for each of the products?

Problems

Problem 3-30 Break-Even Units, Contribution Margin Ratio, Margin of Safety

OBJECTIVES ① ② ⑤

Cutlass Company's projected profit for the coming year is as follows:

	Total	Per Unit
Sales	$200,000	$20
Less: Variable expenses	120,000	12
Contribution margin	$ 80,000	$ 8
Less: Fixed expenses	64,000	
Operating income	$ 16,000	

Required:
1. Compute the break-even point in units.
2. How many units must be sold to earn a profit of $30,000?
3. Compute the contribution margin ratio. Using that ratio, compute the additional profit that Cutlass would earn if sales were $25,000 more than expected.
4. For the projected level of sales, compute the margin of safety in units.

Problem 3-31 Break-Even Units, Operating Income, Margin of Safety

OBJECTIVES ① ⑤

Dory Manufacturing Company produces T-shirts screen-printed with the logos of various sports teams. Each shirt is priced at $10 and has a unit variable cost of $5. Total fixed costs are $96,000.

Required:
1. Compute the break-even point in units.
2. Suppose that Dory could reduce its fixed costs by $13,500 by reducing the amount of setup and engineering time needed. How many units must be sold to break even in this case?
3. How does the reduction in fixed costs affect the break-even point? Operating income? The margin of safety?

Problem 3-32 Contribution Margin, Break-Even Units, Break-Even Sales, Margin of Safety, Degree of Operating Leverage

OBJECTIVES ① ② ⑤

Sohrwide Company produces a variety of chemicals. One division makes reagents for laboratories. The division's projected income statement for the coming year is:

Sales (128,000 units @ $50)	$6,400,000
Less: Variable expenses	4,480,000
Contribution margin	$1,920,000
Less: Fixed expenses	1,000,000
Operating income	$ 920,000

Required:
1. Compute the contribution margin per unit, and calculate the break-even point in units (round to the nearest unit). Calculate the contribution margin ratio and the break-even sales revenue.
2. The divisional manager has decided to increase the advertising budget by $100,000. This will increase sales revenues by $1 million. By how much will operating income increase or decrease as a result of this action?
3. Suppose sales revenues exceed the estimated amount on the income statement by $315,000. Without preparing a new income statement, by how much are profits underestimated?
4. Compute the margin of safety based on the original income statement.
5. Compute the degree of operating leverage based on the original income statement. If sales revenues are 20 percent greater than expected, what is the percentage increase in profits?

OBJECTIVE ④

Problem 3-33 Multiple-Product Analysis, Changes in Sales Mix, Sales to Earn Target Operating Income

Gosnell Company produces two products: squares and circles. The projected income for the coming year, segmented by product line, follows:

	Squares	Circles	Total
Sales	$300,000	$2,500,000	$2,800,000
Less: Variable expenses	100,000	500,000	600,000
Contribution margin	$200,000	$2,000,000	$2,200,000
Less: Direct fixed expenses	28,000	1,500,000	1,528,000
Product margin	$172,000	$ 500,000	$ 672,000
Less: Common fixed expenses			100,000
Operating income			$ 572,000

The selling prices are $30 for squares and $50 for circles.

Required:

1. Compute the number of units of each product that must be sold for Gosnell Company to break even.
2. Assume that the marketing manager changes the sales mix of the two products so that the ratio is three squares to five circles. Repeat Requirement 1.
3. Refer to the original data. Suppose that Gosnell can increase the sales of squares with increased advertising. The extra advertising would cost an additional $245,000, and some of the potential purchasers of circles would switch to squares. In total, sales of squares would increase by 25,000 units, and sales of circles would decrease by 5,000 units. Would Gosnell be better off with this strategy?

OBJECTIVES ① ② ③

Problem 3-34 Cost-Volume-Profit Equation, Basic Concepts, Solving for Unknowns

Tressa Company produces combination shampoos and conditioners in individual-use bottles for hotels. Each bottle sells for $0.36. The variable costs for each bottle (materials, labor, and overhead) total $0.27. The total fixed costs are $54,000. During the most recent year, 830,000 bottles were sold.

Required:

1. What is the break-even point in units for Tressa? What is the margin of safety in units for the most recent year?
2. Prepare an income statement for Tressa's most recent year.
3. How many units must be sold for Tressa to earn a profit of $36,000?

OBJECTIVES ① ⑤

Problem 3-35 Contribution Margin Ratio, Break-Even Sales, Operating Leverage

Doerhing Company produces plastic mailboxes. The projected income statement for the coming year follows:

Sales	$560,400
Less: Variable costs	257,784
Contribution margin	$302,616
Less: Fixed costs	150,000
Operating income	$152,616

Required:
1. Compute the contribution margin ratio for the mailboxes.
2. How much revenue must Doerhing earn in order to break even?
3. What is the effect on the contribution margin ratio if the unit selling price and unit variable cost each increase by 10 percent?
4. Suppose that management has decided to give a 3-percent commission on all sales. The projected income statement does not reflect this commission. Recompute the contribution margin ratio, assuming that the commission will be paid. What effect does this have on the break-even point?
5. If the commission is paid as described in Requirement 4, management expects sales revenues to increase by $80,000. How will this affect operating leverage? Is it a sound decision to implement the commission? Support your answer with appropriate computations.

Problem 3-36 Multiple Products, Break-Even Analysis, Operating Leverage

OBJECTIVES ④ ⑤

Carlyle Lighting Products produces two different types of lamps: a floor lamp and a desk lamp. Floor lamps sell for $30, and desk lamps sell for $20. The projected income statement for the coming year follows:

Sales	$600,000
Less: Variable costs	400,000
Contribution margin	$200,000
Less: Fixed costs	150,000
Operating income	$ 50,000

The owner of Carlyle estimates that 60 percent of the sales revenues will be produced by floor lamps and the remaining 40 percent by desk lamps. Floor lamps are also responsible for 60 percent of the variable expenses. Of the fixed expenses, one-third are common to both products, and one-half are directly traceable to the floor lamp product line.

Required:
1. Compute the sales revenue that must be earned for Carlyle to break even.
2. Compute the number of floor lamps and desk lamps that must be sold for Carlyle to break even.
3. Compute the degree of operating leverage for Carlyle Lighting Products. Now assume that the actual revenues will be 40 percent higher than the projected revenues. By what percentage will profits increase with this change in sales volume?

Problem 3-37 Multiple-Product Break-Even

OBJECTIVES ① ④

Polaris Inc. manufactures two types of metal stampings for the automobile industry: door handles and trim kits. Fixed costs equal $146,000. Each door handle sells for $12 and has variable costs of $9; each trim kit sells for $8 and has variable costs of $5.

Required:
1. What are the contribution margin per unit and the contribution margin ratio for door handles and for trim kits?
2. If Polaris sells 20,000 door handles and 40,000 trim kits, what is the operating income?
3. How many door handles and how many trim kits must be sold for Polaris to break even?
4. Assume that Polaris has the opportunity to rearrange its plant to produce only trim kits. If this is done, fixed costs will decrease by $35,000, and 70,000 trim kits can be produced and sold. Is this a good idea? Explain.

OBJECTIVES ① ⑤ **Problem 3-38 Cost-Volume-Profit, Margin of Safety**

Victoria Company produces a single product. Last year's income statement is as follows:

Sales (29,000 units)	$1,218,000
Less: Variable costs	812,000
Contribution margin	$ 406,000
Less: Fixed costs	300,000
Operating income	$ 106,000

Required:
1. Compute the break-even point in units and sales dollars.
2. What was the margin of safety for Victoria Company last year?
3. Suppose that Victoria Company is considering an investment in new technology that will increase fixed costs by $250,000 per year but will lower variable costs to 45 percent of sales. Units sold will remain unchanged. Prepare a budgeted income statement assuming that Victoria makes this investment. What is the new break-even point in units and sales dollars, assuming that the investment is made?

OBJECTIVES ① ⑤ **Problem 3-39 Cost-Volume-Profit, Margin of Safety**

Isaac Company had revenues of $930,000 last year with total variable costs of $353,400 and fixed costs of $310,000.

Required:
1. What is the variable cost ratio for Isaac? What is the contribution margin ratio?
2. What is the break-even point in sales revenue?
3. What was the margin of safety for Isaac last year?
4. Isaac is considering starting a multimedia advertising campaign that is supposed to increase sales by $7,500 per year. The campaign will cost $5,000. Is the advertising campaign a good idea? Explain.

OBJECTIVE ① **Problem 3-40 Using the Break-Even Equations to Solve for Price and Variable Cost per Unit**

Solve the following independent problems.

Required:
1. Sarah Company's break-even point is 1,500 units. Variable cost per unit is $300; total fixed costs are $120,000 per year. What price does Sarah charge?
2. Jesper Company charges a price of $3.50; total fixed costs are $160,000 per year, and the break-even point is 128,000 units. What is the variable cost per unit?

OBJECTIVES ① ② ⑤ **Problem 3-41 Contribution Margin, Cost-Volume-Profit, Margin of Safety**

Candyland Inc. produces a particularly rich praline fudge. Each 10-ounce box sells for $5.60. Variable unit costs are as follows:

Pecans	$0.70
Sugar	0.35
Butter	1.85
Other ingredients	0.34
Box, packing material	0.76
Selling commission	0.20

Fixed overhead cost is $32,300 per year. Fixed selling and administrative costs are $12,500 per year. Candyland sold 35,000 boxes last year.

Required:
1. What is the contribution margin per unit for a box of praline fudge? What is the contribution margin ratio?
2. How many boxes must be sold to break even? What is the break-even sales revenue?
3. What was Candyland's operating income last year?
4. What was the margin of safety?
5. Suppose that Candyland Inc. raises the price to $6.20 per box but anticipates a sales drop to 31,500 boxes. What will the new break-even point in units be? Should Candyland raise the price? Explain.

Problem 3-42 Break-Even Sales, Operating Leverage, Change in Income

OBJECTIVE ⑤

Income statements for two different companies in the same industry are as follows:

	Company A	Company B
Sales	$500,000	$500,000
Less: Variable costs	400,000	200,000
Contribution margin	$100,000	$300,000
Less: Fixed costs	50,000	250,000
Operating income	$ 50,000	$ 50,000

Required:
1. Compute the degree of operating leverage for each company.
2. Compute the break-even point for each company. Explain why the break-even point for Company B is higher.
3. Suppose that both companies experience a 50-percent increase in revenues. Compute the percentage change in profits for each company. Explain why the percentage increase in Company B's profits is so much larger than that of Company A.

Problem 3-43 Contribution Margin, Break-Even Sales, Margin of Safety

OBJECTIVES ①⑤

spreadsheet

Suppose that Kicker had the following sales and cost experience (in thousands of dollars) for May of the current year and for May of the prior year:

	May, Current Year	May, Prior Year
Total sales	$43,560	$41,700
Less:		
Purchase price paid	(17,000)	(16,000)
Additional labor and supplies	(1,400)	(1,200)
Commissions	(1,250)	(1,100)
Contribution margin	$23,910	$23,400
Less:		
Fixed warehouse cost	(680)	(500)
Fixed administrative cost	(4,300)	(4,300)
Fixed selling cost	(5,600)	(5,000)
Research and development	(9,750)	(4,000)
Operating income	$ 3,580	$ 9,600

In August of the prior year, Kicker started an intensive quality program designed to enable it to build original equipment manufacture (OEM) speaker systems for a major automobile company. The program was housed in research and development. In the beginning of the current year, Kicker's accounting department exercised tighter control over sales commissions, ensuring that no dubious (e.g., double) payments were made. The increased sales in the current year required additional warehouse space that Kicker rented in town.

Integrative Multi-Chapter Exercise

Cost Behavior and Cost-Volume-Profit Analysis for Many Glacier Hotel

CHAPTERS 1-3
OBJECTIVES 1-4, 2-3, 3-1, 3-2, 3-4, 3-5
CORNERSTONES 2-2, 3-2, 3-5, 3-7, 3-9

The purpose of this integrated exercise is to demonstrate the interrelationship between cost estimation techniques and subsequent uses of cost information. In particular, this exercise illustrates how the variable and fixed cost information estimated from a high-low analysis can be used in a single- and multiple-product CVP analysis.

Using the High-Low Method to Estimate Variable and Fixed Costs

Located on Swiftcurrent Lake in Glacier National Park, Many Glacier Hotel was built in 1915 by the Great Northern Railway. In an effort to supplement its lodging revenue, the hotel decided in 1998 to begin manufacturing and selling small wooden canoes decorated with symbols hand painted by Native Americans living near the park. Due to the great success of the canoes, the hotel began manufacturing and selling paddles as well in 2001. Many hotel guests purchase a canoe and paddles for use in self-guided tours of Swiftcurrent Lake. Because production of the two products began in different years, the canoes and paddles are produced in separate production facilities and employ different laborers. Each canoe sells for $500, and each paddle sells for $50. A 2001 fire destroyed the hotel's accounting records. However, a new system put into place before the 2002 season provides the following aggregated data for the hotel's canoe and paddle manufacturing and marketing activities:

Manufacturing Data:

Year	Number of Canoes Manufactured	Total Canoe Manufacturing Costs	Year	Number of Paddles Manufactured	Total Paddle Manufacturing Costs
2007	250	106,000	2007	900	38,500
2006	275	115,000	2006	1,200	49,000
2005	240	108,000	2005	1,000	42,000
2004	310	122,000	2004	1,100	45,500
2003	350	130,000	2003	1,400	56,000
2002	400	140,000	2002	1,700	66,500

Marketing Data:

Year	Number of Canoes Sold	Total Canoe Marketing Costs	Year	Number of Paddles Sold	Total Paddle Marketing Costs
2007	250	45,000	2007	900	7,500
2006	275	47,500	2006	1,200	9,000
2005	240	44,000	2005	1,000	8,000
2004	310	51,000	2004	1,100	8,500
2003	350	55,000	2003	1,400	10,000
2002	400	60,000	2002	1,700	11,500

Required:

1. High-Low Cost Estimation Method

   a. Use the high-low method to estimate the per-unit variable costs and total fixed costs for the *canoe* product line.
   b. Use the high-low method to estimate the per-unit variable costs and total fixed costs for the *paddle* product line.

2. Cost-Volume-Profit Analysis, Single-Product Setting
   Use CVP analysis to calculate the break-even point in units for:

   a. The *canoe* product line *only* (i.e., single-product setting)
   b. The *paddle* product line *only* (i.e., single-product setting)

3. Cost-Volume-Profit Analysis, Multiple-Product Setting
   The hotel's accounting system data show an average sales mix of approximately 300 canoes and 1,200 paddles each season. Significantly more paddles are sold relative to canoes because some inexperienced canoe guests accidentally break one or more paddles, while other guests purchase additional paddles as presents for friends and relatives. In addition, for this multiple-product CVP analysis, assume the existence of an additional $30,000 of common fixed costs for a customer service hotline used for both canoe and paddle customers. Use CVP analysis to calculate the break-even point in units for both the canoe and paddle product lines combined (i.e., the multiple-product setting).

4. Cost Classification

   a. Classify the manufacturing costs, marketing costs, and customer service hotline costs either as production expenses or period expenses.
   b. For the period expenses, further classify them into either selling expenses or general and administrative expenses.

5. Sensitivity Cost-Volume-Profit Analysis and Production Versus Period Expenses, Multiple-Product Setting
   If both the variable and fixed *production* expenses (refer to your answer to part 1) associated with the canoe product line increased by 5% (beyond the estimate from the high-low analysis), how many canoes and paddles would need to be sold in order to earn a target income of $96,000? Assume the same sales mix and additional fixed costs as in part 4.

6. Margin of Safety
   Calculate the hotel's margin of safety (both in units and in sales dollars) for Many Glacier Hotel, assuming it sells 700 canoes and 2,500 paddles next year.

4

Job-Order Costing

Disturbed Dan Donegan plays a
Chicago **Washburn Maya** guitar.
www.washburn.com/donegan

© WASHBURN GUITARS

Washburn.

After studying Chapter 4, you should be able to:

① Describe the differences between job-order costing and process costing, and identify the types of firms that would use each method.

② Compute the predetermined overhead rate, and use the rate to assign overhead to units or services produced.

③ Identify and set up the source documents used in job-order costing.

④ Describe the cost flows associated with job-order costing.

⑤ (Appendix) Prepare the journal entries associated with job-order costing.

Experience Managerial Decisions
with Washburn Guitars

Founded in 1883 just north of Chicago, Washburn Guitars manufactures high-quality acoustic and electric guitars for musicians ranging from garage bands to some of the world's most famous bands (see www.washburn.com/artists/index.aspx for a listing of artists who play Washburn guitars). Washburn produces numerous guitar series, each of which has many different models that require the use of varied resources. For example, one of Washburn's recent offerings is the Damen Idol, which retails for $2,249. As an example of the complexity and individuality of Washburn's guitars, the Damen model features a mahogany body, flame maple top, mahogany neck with cream binding, rosewood fingerboard, Seymour Duncan Custom pickups in the bridge and a Seymour Duncan '59 in the neck, a Tone Pros Bridge and Tailpiece, and numerous other options regarding frets, scaling, finishing, and tuning. Currently playing the Damen Idol are Joe Trohman from Fall Out Boy, Aaron Dugan of Matisyahu, Mike Kennerty from The All American Rejects, Shaun Glass from Soil, and Marty Casey from the Lovehammers and INXS.

Many guitar buyers, including most professionals, request various product customizations. While customization can create great publicity for Washburn, it also creates significant design and production variability (or differences) between guitars, even those within the same model line of a given series. Design and production variability results in resource consumption differences, which necessitate that Washburn estimates the cost of each guitar job according to how the customer desires to customize the order. Washburn managers rely heavily on their effective job-order costing system to help them understand the costs associated with such product alterations to ensure that Washburn continues to be profitable well into its third century of operations!

The Importance of Cost Systems

The cost estimation methods, such as high-low, scattergraph, and regression studied in Chapter 2, are useful for estimating total costs. However, for many decisions, managers often need to understand how total costs relate to specific cost objects on an individual unit level. Cost systems are useful for estimating these unit costs. Therefore, the next several chapters focus on how different cost systems (e.g., job-order vs. process) can be used in different business environments to accurately estimate unit costs.

Characteristics of the Job-Order Environment

OBJECTIVE ①
Describe the differences between job-order costing and process costing, and identify the types of firms that would use each method.

Companies can be divided into two major types, depending on whether or not their products/services are unique. Manufacturing and service firms producing unique products or services require a job-order accounting system. Washburn Guitars falls into this category. On the other hand, those firms producing similar products or services can use a process-costing accounting system. **BP**, one of the world's largest oil producers, falls into this latter category, as its barrels of oil are indistinguishable from one another. The characteristics of a company's actual production process give rise to whether it needs a job-order or a process-costing accounting system.

Here's The Real Kicker

In the 1970s, Kicker began operations in Steve Irby's garage. Steve was an engineering student at Oklahoma State University and also a keyboard player with a local band. The band needed speakers but couldn't afford new ones. Steve and his father built wooden boxes and fitted them with second-hand components. Word spread, and other bands asked for speakers. Steve partnered with a friend to fill the orders. Then, one friend who worked in the oil fields asked if Steve could rig up speakers for his pickup truck. Long days bouncing over rough fields went more smoothly with music, but the built-in "audio" systems at the time were awful. Steve designed and built a speaker to fit behind the driver's seat, and Kicker was born.

At first, each job was made to order to fit a particular truck or car. The price Steve charged depended heavily on the cost of the job. Since each job was different, the various costs had to be computed individually. Clearly, the costs of wood, fabric, glue, and components were traceable to the each job. Steve could also trace labor time. But the other costs of design time, use of power tools, and space were lumped together to create an overhead rate. To the extent that the price of a job was greater than its costs, Steve earned a profit.

Job-Order Production and Costing

Firms operating in job-order industries produce a wide variety of services or products that are quite distinct from each other. Customized or built-to-order products fit into this category, as do services that vary from customer to customer. A **job**, then, is one distinct unit or set of units. For example, it may be a remodeling job for the Ruiz family, or a set of 12 tables for the children's reading room of the local library. Common job-order processes include printing, construction, furniture making, medical and dental services, automobile repair, and beautician services. Often, a job is associated with a particular customer order. The key feature of job-order costing is that the cost of one job differs from that of another and must be kept track of separately.

For job-order production systems, costs are accumulated by job. This approach to assigning costs is called a **job-order costing system**. In a job-order firm, collecting costs

Exhibit 4-1

Comparison of Job-Order and Process Costing

Job-Order Costing	Process Costing
1. Wide variety of distinct products	1. Homogeneous products
2. Costs accumulated by job	2. Costs accumulated by process or department
3. Unit cost computed by dividing total job costs by units produced on that job	3. Unit cost computed by dividing process costs of the period by the units produced in the period

by job provides vital information for management. For example, frequently, prices are based on costs in a job-order environment.

Process Production and Costing

Firms in process industries mass-produce large quantities of similar or homogeneous products. Examples of process manufacturers include food, cement, petroleum, and chemical firms. One gallon of paint is the same as another gallon; one bottle of aspirin is the same as another bottle. The important point here is that the cost of one unit of a product is identical to the cost of another. Service firms can also use a process-costing approach. For example, check-clearing departments of banks incur a uniform cost to clear a check, no matter the size of the check or the name of the payee.

Process firms accumulate production costs by process or by department for a given period of time. The output for the process for that period of time is measured. Unit costs are computed by dividing the process costs for the given period by the output of the period. This approach to cost accumulation is known as a **process-costing system** and is examined in detail in Chapter 5. A comparison of job-order costing and process costing is given in Exhibit 4-1.

Production Costs in Job-Order Costing

While the variety of product-costing definitions discussed in Chapter 1 applies to both job-order and process costing, we will use the traditional definition to illustrate job-order costing procedures. That is, production costs consist of direct materials, direct labor, and overhead. Direct materials and direct labor are typically fairly easy to trace to individual jobs. In fact, this tracing will be considered later in this chapter in the section on source documents. It is overhead that presents the problem. By definition, overhead is all production costs other than direct materials and direct labor. Some of these might be easily traced to jobs, but most cannot be. The solution is to apply overhead to production. The next section examines in detail the way overhead is treated.

Concept Q&A

Give an example of a business in your community that would use job-order costing, and tell why it would be appropriate. Give an example of a business in your community that would use process costing and why it would be appropriate.

Possible Answer:

A tax accounting firm would keep track of costs by job because some tax returns are relatively simple, while others are complex and require time to fill out additional forms and to do necessary research. A "while you wait" oil change shop would use process costing (but cost the oil required separately) since each car would take about the same amount of time and supplies to perform the oil change.

Normal Costing and Overhead Application

Unit costs are very important because managers need accurate cost information on materials, labor, and overhead when making decisions. For example, **Bechtel Construction**, whose notable projects include the Channel Tunnel connecting England

OBJECTIVE ②
Compute the predetermined overhead rate, and use the rate to assign overhead to units or services produced.

overhead is simply the firm's best estimate of the amount of overhead (utilities, indirect labor, depreciation, etc.) to be incurred in the coming year. The estimate is often based on last year's figures and is adjusted for anticipated changes in the coming year.

The associated activity level depends on which activity is best associated with overhead. Often, the activity chosen is the number of direct labor hours or the direct labor cost. This choice makes sense when much of overhead cost is associated with direct labor (e.g., fringe benefits, worker safety training programs, the cost of running the personnel department). The number of machine hours could be a good choice for a company with automated production. Then, much of the overhead cost might consist of equipment maintenance, depreciation on machinery, electricity to run the machinery, and so on. The estimated activity level is simply the number of direct labor hours, or machine hours, expected for that activity in the coming year.

The predetermined overhead rate is calculated using the following formula:

Overhead rate = Estimated annual overhead/Estimated annual activity level

Notice that the predetermined overhead rate includes estimated amounts in *both* the numerator and the denominator. This estimation is necessary is because the predetermined overhead rate is calculated in advance, usually at the beginning of the year. It is impossible to use actual overhead or actual activity level for the year because at that time, the company does not know what the actual levels will be. Therefore, only estimated or budgeted amounts are used in calculating the predetermined overhead rate.

Applying Overhead to Production

Once the overhead rate has been computed, the company can begin to apply overhead to production. **Applied overhead** is found by multiplying the predetermined overhead rate by the actual use of the associated activity for the period. Suppose that a company has an overhead rate of $5 per machine hour. In the first week of January, the company used 9,000 hours of machine time. The overhead applied to the week's production is $45,000 ($5 × 9,000). The total cost of product for that first week is the actual direct materials and direct labor, plus the applied overhead. The concept is the same for any time period. So, if the company runs its machines for 50,000 hours in the month of January, applied overhead for January would be $250,000 ($5 × 50,000). Cornerstone 4-1 shows

**CORNERSTONE
4 - 1**

HOW TO Calculate the Predetermined Overhead Rate and Apply Overhead to Production

Information: At the beginning of the year, Argus Company estimated the following costs:

Overhead	$360,000
Direct labor cost	720,000

Argus uses normal costing and applies overhead on the basis of direct labor cost. (Direct labor cost is equal to total direct labor hours worked multiplied by the wage rate.) For the month of February, direct labor cost was $56,000.

Required:
1. Calculate the predetermined overhead rate for the year.
2. Calculate the overhead applied to production in February.

Calculation:
1. Predetermined overhead rate = $360,000/$720,000
   = 0.50, or 50 percent of direct labor cost
2. Overhead applied to February production = 0.50 × $56,000 = $28,000

how to calculate the predetermined overhead rate and how to use that rate to apply overhead to production.

Reconciling Applied Overhead with Actual Overhead

Recall that two types of overhead must be taken into consideration. One is actual overhead, and those costs are tracked throughout the year in the overhead account. The second type is applied overhead. Overhead applied to production is computed throughout the year and is added to actual direct materials and actual direct labor to get total product cost. At the end of the year, however, it is time to reconcile any difference between actual and applied overhead and to correct the cost of goods sold account to reflect actual overhead spending.

Suppose that Proto Company had actual overhead of $400,000 for the year but had applied $390,000 to production. Notice that the amount of overhead applied to production ($390,000) differs from the actual overhead ($400,000). Since the predetermined overhead rate is based on estimated data, applied overhead will rarely equal actual overhead. Since only $390,000 was applied in our example, the firm has *underapplied* overhead by $10,000. If applied overhead had been $410,000, then too much overhead would have been applied to production. The firm would have *overapplied* overhead by $10,000. The difference between actual overhead and applied overhead is called an **overhead variance**. If actual overhead is greater than applied overhead, then the variance is called **underapplied overhead**. If actual overhead is less than applied overhead, then the variance is called **overapplied overhead**. If overhead has been underapplied, then product cost has been understated; in this case, the cost appears lower than it really is. Conversely, if overhead has been overapplied, then product cost has been overstated; in this case, the cost appears higher than it really is. Exhibit 4-2 illustrates the concepts of over- and underapplied overhead.

Overhead variances occur because it is impossible to perfectly estimate future overhead costs and production activity. The presence of overhead variances is virtually inevitable. A problem arises if the overhead variances are not corrected. At year-end, costs reported on the financial statements must be actual, not estimated, amounts. Thus, something must be done with the overhead variance. Most often, the entire overhead variance is assigned to cost of goods sold. This practice is justified on the basis of materiality, the same principle used to justify expensing the entire cost of a pencil sharpener in the period acquired rather than depreciating its cost over the life of the sharpener. Since the overhead variance is usually relatively small, the method of disposition is not a critical matter. All production costs should appear in cost of goods sold eventually. Thus, the overhead

(Exhibit 4-2)

Actual and Applied Overhead

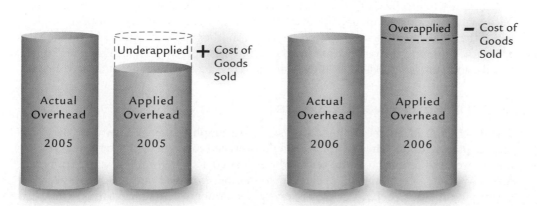

**CORNERSTONE
4-2**

HOW TO Reconcile Actual Overhead with Applied Overhead

Information: At the beginning of the year, Argus Company estimated the following:

Overhead	$360,000
Direct labor cost	720,000

By the end of the year, actual data are:

Overhead	$375,400
Direct labor cost	750,000

Argus uses normal costing and applies overhead on the basis of direct labor cost. At the end of the year, Cost of Goods Sold (before adjusting for any overhead variance) is $632,000.

Required:
1. Calculate the overhead variance for the year.
2. Dispose of the overhead variance by adjusting Cost of Goods Sold.

Calculation:
1. Predetermined overhead rate = $360,000/$720,000 = 0.50 of direct labor cost
   Overhead applied for the year = 0.50 × $750,000 = $375,000
2.

Actual overhead	$375,400
Applied overhead	375,000
Overhead variance—underapplied	$ 400
Unadjusted COGS	$632,000
Add: Overhead variance—underapplied	400
Adjusted COGS	$632,400

variance is added to the cost of goods sold, if underapplied, and subtracted from cost of goods sold, if overapplied. For example, assume that Proto Company has an ending balance in its cost of goods sold account equal to $607,000. The underapplied overhead variance of $10,000 would be added to produce a new, adjusted balance of $617,000. (Since applied overhead was $390,000, and actual overhead was $400,000, production costs were *understated* by $10,000. Cost of goods sold must be increased to correct the problem.) If the variance had been overapplied, it would have been subtracted from cost of goods sold to produce a new balance of $597,000. Cornerstone 4-2 shows how to reconcile actual overhead with applied overhead for the Argus Company example.

If the overhead variance is material, or large, another approach would be taken. That approach, allocating the variance among the ending balances of Work in Process, Finished Goods, and Cost of Goods Sold, is discussed in more detail in later accounting courses.

Departmental Overhead Rates

The description of overhead application so far has emphasized the plantwide overhead rate. A **plantwide overhead rate** is a single overhead rate calculated by using all estimated overhead for a factory divided by the estimated activity level across the entire factory. However, some companies believe that multiple overhead rates give more accurate costing information. Service firms, or service departments of manufacturing firms, can also use separate overhead rates to charge out their services.

Departmental overhead rates are a widely used type of multiple overhead rate. A **departmental overhead rate** is simply estimated overhead for a department divided by the estimated activity level for that same department. The steps involved in calculating and applying overhead are the same as those involved for one plantwide overhead rate. The company has as many overhead rates as it has departments. Cornerstone 4-3 shows how to calculate and apply departmental overhead rates.

It is important to realize that departmental overhead rates simply carve total overhead into two or more parts. The departments can be added back to get plantwide overhead. Cornerstone 4-4 on page 154 shows how this is done.

HOW TO Calculate Predetermined Departmental Overhead Rates and Apply Overhead to Production

CORNERSTONE 4-3

Information: At the beginning of the year, Sorrel Company estimated the following:

	Machining Department	Assembly Department	Total
Overhead	$240,000	$360,000	$600,000
Direct labor hours	135,000	240,000	375,000
Machine hours	200,000	—	200,000

Sorrel uses departmental overhead rates. In the machining department, overhead is applied on the basis of machine hours. In the assembly department, overhead is applied on the basis of direct labor hours. Actual data for the month of June are as follows:

	Machining Department	Assembly Department	Total
Overhead	$22,500	$30,750	$53,250
Direct labor hours	11,000	20,000	31,000
Machine hours	17,000	—	17,000

Required:
1. Calculate the predetermined overhead rates for the machining and assembly departments.
2. Calculate the overhead applied to production in each department for the month of June.
3. By how much has each department's overhead been overapplied? Underapplied?

Calculation:
1. Machining department overhead rate = $240,000/200,000
$$= \$1.20 \text{ per machine hour}$$
   Assembly department overhead rate = $360,000/240,000
$$= \$1.50 \text{ per direct labor hour}$$
2. Overhead applied to machining in June = $1.20 × 17,000 = $20,400
   Overhead applied to assembly in June = $1.50 × 20,000 = $30,000
3.

	Machining Department	Assembly Department
Actual overhead	$22,500	$30,750
Applied overhead	20,400	30,000
Underapplied overhead	$ 2,100	$ 750

**CORNERSTONE
4 - 4**

HOW TO Convert Departmental Data to Plantwide Data to Calculate the Overhead Rate and Apply Overhead to Production

Information: At the beginning of the year, Sorrel Company estimated the following:

	Machining Department	Assembly Department	Total
Overhead	$240,000	$360,000	$600,000
Direct labor hours	135,000	240,000	375,000
Machine hours	200,000	—	200,000

Sorrel has decided to use a plantwide overhead rate based on direct labor hours. Actual data for the month of June are as follows:

	Machining Department	Assembly Department	Total
Overhead	$22,500	$30,750	$53,250
Direct labor hours	11,000	20,000	31,000
Machine hours	17,000	—	17,000

Required:
1. Calculate the predetermined plantwide overhead rate.
2. Calculate the overhead applied to production for the month of June.
3. Calculate the overhead variance for the month of June.

Calculation:
1. Predetermined plantwide overhead rate = $600,000/375,000
   = $1.60 per direct labor hour
2. Overhead applied in June = $1.60 × 31,000 = $49,600
3. Overhead variance = Actual overhead − Applied overhead
   = $53,250 − $49,600
   = $3,650 underapplied

Considerable emphasis has been placed on describing how overhead costs are treated because this is the key to normal costing. Now, it is time to see how normal costing is used to develop unit costs in the job-order costing system.

Unit Costs in the Job-Order System

In a job-order environment, predetermined overhead rates are always used because the completion of a job rarely coincides with the completion of a fiscal year. Therefore, in the remainder of this chapter, normal costing is used.

The unit cost of a job is simply the total cost of materials used on the job, labor worked on the job, and applied overhead. Although the concept is simple, the practical reality of the computation can be somewhat more complex because of the record keeping involved. Let's look at a simple example.

Suppose that Stan Johnson forms a new company, Johnson Leathergoods, which specializes in the production of custom leather products. Stan believes that there is a market for one-of-a-kind leather purses, briefcases, and backpacks. In January, its first month of operation, he obtains two orders: the first is for 20 leather backpacks for a local sporting goods store; the second is for 10 distinctively tooled briefcases for the coaches of a local college. Stan agrees to provide these orders at a price of cost plus 50 percent. The first order, the backpacks, will require direct materials (leather, thread, buckles), direct labor (cutting, sewing, assembling), and overhead. Assume that overhead is applied using direct labor hours. Suppose that the materials cost $1,000 and the direct labor costs

$1,080 (120 hrs at $9 per hr). If the predetermined overhead rate is $2 per direct labor hour, then the overhead applied to this job is $240 (120 hrs at $2 per hr). The total cost of the backpacks is $2,320, and the unit cost is $116, computed as follows:

Direct materials	$1,000
Direct labor	1,080
Overhead	240
Total cost	$2,320
÷ Number of units	÷ 20
Unit cost	$ 116

Since cost is so closely linked to price in this case, it is easy to see that Stan will charge the sporting goods store $3,480 (cost of $2,320 plus 50 percent of $2,320), or $174 per backpack.

This is a simplified example of how Stan will arrive at the total cost of a single job. But how does he know that actual materials will cost $1,000 or that actual direct labor for this particular job will come to $1,080? In order to determine those figures, Stan will need to keep track of costs using a variety of source documents. These documents are described in the next section.

Keeping Track of Job Costs with Source Documents

OBJECTIVE ③
Identify and set up the source documents used in job-order costing.

Accounting for job-order production begins by preparing the source documents that are used to keep track of the costs of jobs. In a job-order firm, where price is so often based on cost, it is critically important to keep careful track of the costs of a job. Ethical issues arise when a firm adds costs from one job to the job-order sheet of another job. The first job is undercosted and underpriced while the second job is overcosted and overpriced. Customers rely on the professionalism and honesty of the job-order firm in record keeping.

Job-Order Cost Sheet

Every time a new job is started, a job-order cost sheet is prepared. The earlier computation for Stan's backpack job, which lists the total cost of materials, labor, and overhead for a single job, is the simplest example of a job-order cost sheet. The **job-order cost sheet** is prepared for every job; it is subsidiary to the work-in-process account and is the primary document for accumulating all costs related to a particular job. Exhibit 4-3 illustrates a simple job-order cost sheet.

Exhibit 4-3

Job-Order Cost Sheet

Johnson Leathergoods
Job-Order Cost Sheet

Job Name: <u>Backpacks</u>   Date Started: <u>Jan. 3, 2009</u>   Date Completed: <u>Jan. 29, 2009</u>

Direct materials	$1,000
Direct labor	1,080
Applied overhead	240
Total cost	$2,320
÷ Number of units	÷ 20
Unit cost	$ 116

Concept Q&A

Suppose that Johnson Leathergoods created an automated tooling department and decides to track the number of machine hours used on each job. Design a source document for this purpose.

The form might be similar to the time ticket shown in Exhibit 4-5. However, the hourly rate and amount columns could be deleted and a column added for the initials of the worker entering the information.

Possible Answer:

All completed job-order cost sheets of a firm can serve as a subsidiary ledger for the finished goods inventory. Then, the work-in-process account consists of all of the job-order cost sheets for the unfinished jobs. The finished goods inventory account consists of all the job-order cost sheets for jobs that are complete but not yet sold. As finished goods are sold and shipped, the cost records will be pulled (or deleted) from the finished goods inventory file. These records then form the basis for calculating a period's cost of goods sold. We will examine the flow of costs through these accounts next.

OBJECTIVE ④
Describe the cost flows associated with job-order costing.

The Flow of Costs through the Accounts

Cost flow describes the way costs are accounted for from the point at which they are incurred to the point at which they are recognized as an expense on the income statement. The principal interest in a job-order costing system is the flow of manufacturing costs. Accordingly, we begin with a description of exactly how the three manufacturing cost elements—direct materials, direct labor, and overhead—flow through the work-in-process account, into Finished Goods, and, finally, into Cost of Goods Sold.

The simplified job-shop environment provided by Johnson Leathergoods will continue to serve as an example. To start the business, Stan leased a small building and bought the necessary production equipment. Recall that he finalized two orders for January: one for 20 backpacks for a local sporting goods store and a second for 10 briefcases for the coaches of a local college. Both orders will be sold for manufacturing costs plus 50 percent. Stan expects to average two orders per month for the first year of operation.

Stan created two job-order cost sheets, one for each order. The first job-order cost sheet is for the backpacks; the second is for the briefcases.

Accounting for Materials

Since the company is just starting business, it has no beginning inventories. To produce the backpacks and briefcases in January and to have a supply of materials on hand at the beginning of February, Stan purchases, on account, $2,500 of raw materials (leather, webbing for backpack straps, heavy-duty thread, buckles). Physically, the materials are put in a materials storeroom. In the accounting records, the raw materials and the accounts payable accounts are each increased by $2,500. Raw Materials is an inventory account (it appears on the balance sheet under current assets). It also is the controlling account for all raw materials. Any purchase increases the raw materials account.

When the production supervisor needs materials for a job, materials are removed from the storeroom. The cost of the materials is removed from the raw materials account and added to the work-in-process account. Of course, in a job-order environment, the materials moved from the storeroom to work stations on the factory floor must be "tagged" with the appropriate job name. Suppose that Stan needs $1,000 of materials for the backpacks and $500 for the briefcases. Then, the job-order cost sheet for the backpacks would show $1,000 for direct materials, and the job-order cost sheet for the briefcases would show $500 for direct materials. Exhibit 4-6 summarizes the raw materials cost flow into these two jobs.

The raw materials account increased by $2,500 due to purchases and decreased by $1,500 as materials were withdrawn for use in production. So, what is the balance in the raw materials account after these two transactions? It is $1,000. This is calculated by taking the beginning balance in the raw materials account of $0, adding $2,500 of purchases, and subtracting $1,500 of materials used in production.

Exhibit 4-6

Summary of Materials Cost Flows

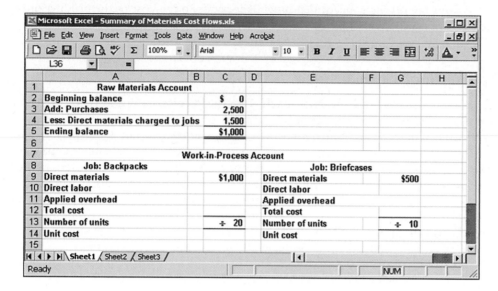

Summary of Direct Labor Cost Flows

Exhibit 4-7

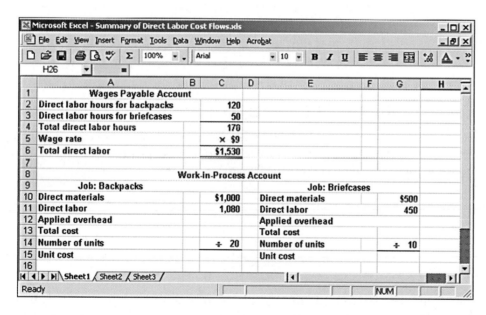

Accounting for Direct Labor Cost

Since two jobs were in progress during January, Stan must determine not only the total number of direct labor hours worked but also the time worked on each job. The backpacks required 120 hours at an average wage rate of $9 per hour, for a total direct labor cost of $1,080. For the briefcases, the total was $450, based on 50 hours at an average hourly wage of $9. These amounts are posted to each job's cost sheet. The summary of the labor cost flows is given in Exhibit 4-7. Notice that the direct labor costs assigned to the two jobs exactly equal the total labor costs assigned to Work in Process. Remember that the labor cost flows reflect only direct labor cost. Indirect labor is assigned as part of overhead.

More accounts are involved in this transaction than meets the eye in Exhibit 4-7. Accounting for labor cost is a complex process because the company must keep track of FICA, Medicare, federal and state unemployment taxes, vacation time, and so on. We will concentrate on the concept that direct labor adds to the cost of the product or service and not on the details of the various labor-related accounts.

Accounting for Overhead

The use of normal costing means that actual overhead costs are not assigned directly to jobs. Overhead is applied to each job by using a predetermined rate. Actual overhead costs incurred must be accounted for as well, but on an overall (not a job-specific) basis.

Overhead costs can be assigned using a single plantwide overhead rate or departmental rates. Typically, direct labor hours is the measure used to calculate a plantwide overhead rate, and departmental rates are based on drivers such as direct labor hours, machine hours, or direct materials dollars. The use of a plantwide rate has the virtue of being simple and reduces data collection requirements. To illustrate these two features, assume that total estimated overhead cost for Johnson Leathergoods is $9,600, and the estimated direct labor hours total 4,800 hours. Accordingly, the predetermined overhead rate is:

$$\text{Overhead rate} = \$9,600/4,800 = \$2 \text{ per direct labor hour}$$

For the backpacks, with a total of 120 hours worked, the amount of applied overhead cost posted to the job-order cost sheet is $240 ($2 × 120). For the briefcases, the applied overhead cost is $100 ($2 × 50). Note also that assigning overhead to jobs only requires a rate and the direct labor hours used by the job. Since direct labor hours are already being collected to assign direct labor costs to jobs, overhead assignment will not demand any additional data collection.

Accounting for Actual Overhead Costs

Overhead has been applied to the jobs, but what about the actual overhead incurred? To illustrate how actual overhead costs are recorded, assume that Johnson Leathergoods incurred the following indirect costs for January:

Lease payment	$200
Utilities	50
Equipment depreciation	100
Indirect labor	65
Total overhead costs	$415

It is important to understand that the actual overhead costs never enter the work-in-process account. The usual procedure is to record actual overhead to the overhead control account. Then, at the end of a period (typically a year), actual overhead is reconciled with applied overhead, and, if the variance is immaterial, it is closed to the cost of goods sold account.

For Johnson Leathergoods at the end of January, actual overhead incurred is $415, while applied overhead is $340. Therefore, the overhead variance of $75 ($415 − $340) means that overhead is underapplied for the month of January.

The flow of overhead costs is summarized in Exhibit 4-8. Notice that the total overhead applied from all jobs is entered in the work-in-process account.

Let's take a moment to recap. The cost of a job includes direct materials, direct labor, and applied overhead. These costs are entered on the job-order cost sheet. Work in Process, at any point in time, is the total of the costs on all open job-order cost sheets. When the job is complete, it must leave Work in Process and be entered into Finished Goods or Cost of Goods Sold.

Exhibit 4-8

Summary of Overhead Cost Flows

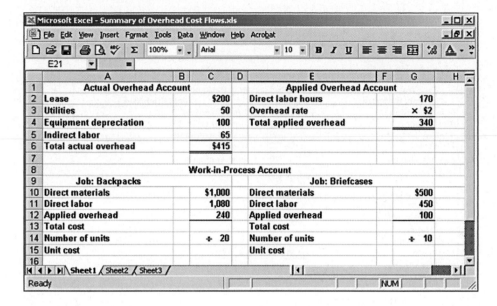

Accounting for Finished Goods

When a job is complete, direct materials, direct labor, and applied overhead amounts are totaled to yield the manufacturing cost of the job. Simultaneously, the costs of the completed job are transferred from the work-in-process account to the finished goods account.

For example, assume that the backpacks were finished in January with the completed cost sheet shown in Exhibit 4-8. Since the backpacks are finished, the total manufacturing costs of $2,320 must be transferred from the work-in-process account to the finished goods account. A summary of the cost flows occurring when a job is finished is shown in Exhibit 4-9.

The completion of a job is an important step in the flow of manufacturing costs. The cost of the finished job must be removed from Work in Process, added to Finished Goods, and, eventually, added to cost of goods sold expense on the income statement. To ensure accuracy in computing these costs, a cost of goods manufactured statement is prepared. The schedule of the cost of goods manufactured presented in Exhibit 4-10 summarizes the production activity of Johnson Leathergoods for January. It is important to note that applied overhead is used to arrive at the cost of goods manufactured. Both work-in-process and finished goods inventories are carried at normal cost rather than actual cost.

Notice that ending work in process is $1,050. Where did this figure come from? Of the two jobs, the backpacks were finished and transferred to finished goods. The briefcases are still in process, however, and the manufacturing costs assigned thus far are direct materials, $500; direct labor, $450; and overhead applied, $100. The total of these costs gives the cost of ending work in process. You may want to check these figures against the job-order cost sheet for briefcases shown at the top right of Exhibit 4-9.

Accounting for Cost of Goods Sold

In a job-order firm, units can be produced for a particular customer, or they can be produced with the expectation of selling the units later. If a job is produced especially for a customer (as with the backpacks) and then shipped to the customer, then the cost of the finished job becomes the cost of goods sold. When the backpacks are finished, Cost of Goods Sold increases by $2,320, while Work in Process decreases by the same amount

Exhibit 4-9

Summary of Cost Flows from Work in Process to Finished Goods

	A	B	C	D	E	F	G	H
1	Work-in-Process Account BEFORE Transfer of Backpacks to Finished Goods							
2	Job: Backpacks				Job: Briefcases			
3	Direct materials		$1,000		Direct materials		$ 500	
4	Direct labor		1,080		Direct labor		450	
5	Applied overhead		240		Applied overhead		100	
6	Total cost		$2,320		Total cost		$1,050	
7	Number of units		÷ 20		Number of units			
8	Unit cost*		$ 116		Unit cost*			
9								
10	Work-in-Process Account AFTER Transfer of Backpacks to Finished Goods							
11	Job: Briefcases							
12	Direct materials		$ 500					
13	Direct labor		450					
14	Applied overhead		100					
15	Total cost		$1,050					
16	Number of units							
17	Unit cost							
18								
19	Finished Goods Account							
20	Beginning balance		$ 0					
21	Add: Completed backpacks		2,320					
22	Less: Jobs sold		0					
23	Ending balance		$2,320					
24								

*Unit cost information is included for backpacks because they are finished. The briefcases are still in process, so no unit cost is calculated.

(the job is no longer incomplete, so its costs cannot stay in Work in Process). Then, the sale is recognized by increasing both Sales Revenue and Accounts Receivable by $3,480 (cost plus 50 percent of cost or $2,320 + $1,160).

A schedule of cost of goods sold usually is prepared at the end of each reporting period (e.g., monthly and quarterly). Exhibit 4-11 presents such a schedule for Johnson Leathergoods for January. Typically, the overhead variance is not material and, therefore, is closed to the cost of goods sold account. The cost of goods sold before an adjustment for an overhead variance is called **normal cost of goods sold**. After the adjustment for the period's overhead variance takes place, the result is called the **adjusted cost of goods sold**. It is this latter figure that appears as an expense on the income statement.

However, closing the overhead variance to the cost of goods sold account is not done until the end of the year. Variances are expected each month because of nonuniform production and nonuniform actual overhead costs. As the year unfolds, these monthly variances should, by and large, offset each other so that the year-end variance is small. Nonetheless, to illustrate how the year-end overhead variance would be treated, we will close out the overhead variance experienced by Johnson Leathergoods in January.

Notice that there are two cost of goods sold figures in Exhibit 4-11. The first is normal cost of goods sold and is equal to actual direct materials, actual direct labor, and applied overhead for the jobs that were sold. The second figure is adjusted cost of goods sold. The adjusted cost of goods sold is equal to normal cost of goods sold plus or minus the overhead variance. In this case, overhead has been underapplied (actual overhead of $415 is $75 higher than the applied overhead of $340), so this amount is added to normal cost of goods sold. If the overhead variance shows overapplied overhead, then that amount will be subtracted from normal cost of goods sold.

Exhibit 4-10

Schedule of Cost of Goods Manufactured

Johnson Leathergoods Schedule of Cost of Goods Manufactured For the Month of January		
Direct materials:		
Beginning raw materials inventory	$ 0	
Purchases of raw materials	2,500	
Total raw materials available	$2,500	
Ending raw materials	1,000	
Total raw materials used		$1,500
Direct labor		1,530
Overhead:		
Lease	$ 200	
Utilities	50	
Depreciation	100	
Indirect labor	65	
	$ 415	
Less: Underapplied overhead	75	
Overhead applied		340
Current manufacturing costs		$3,370
Add: Beginning work in process		0
Total manufacturing costs		$3,370
Less: Ending work in process		1,050
Cost of goods manufactured		$2,320

Exhibit 4-11

Statement of Cost of Goods Sold

Statement of Cost of Goods Sold	
Beginning finished goods inventory	$ 0
Cost of goods manufactured	2,320
Goods available for sale	$2,320
Less: Ending finished goods inventory	0
Normal cost of goods sold	$2,320
Add: Underapplied overhead	75
Adjusted cost of goods sold	$2,395

Suppose that the backpacks had not been ordered by a customer but had been produced with the expectation that they could be sold through a subsequent marketing effort. Then, all 20 units might not be sold at the same time. Assume that on January 31, there were 15 backpacks sold. In this case, the cost of goods sold figure is the unit cost times the number of units sold ($116 × 15, or $1,740). The unit cost figure is found on the cost sheet in Exhibit 4-9.

Sometimes, it is simpler to use a briefer version of the job-order cost sheet in order to calculate ending Work in Process, Finished Goods, and Cost of Good Sold. (This is particularly true when working homework and test questions.) Cornerstone 4-5 shows how to set up such a version to calculate account balances.

**CORNERSTONE
4-5**

HOW TO Prepare Brief Job-Order Cost Sheets

Information: At the beginning of June, Galway Company had two jobs in process, Job 78 and Job 79, with the following accumulated cost information:

	Job 78	Job 79
Direct materials	$1,000	$ 800
Direct labor	600	1,000
Applied overhead	750	1,250
Balance, June 1	$2,350	$3,050

During June, two more jobs (80 and 81) were started. The following direct materials and direct labor costs were added to the four jobs during the month of June:

	Job 78	Job 79	Job 80	Job 81
Direct materials	$500	$1,110	$ 900	$100
Direct labor	400	1,400	2,000	320

At the end of June, Jobs 78, 79, and 80 were completed. Only Job 79 was sold. On June 1, the balance in Finished Goods was zero.

Required:
1. Calculate the overhead rate based on direct labor cost.
2. Prepare a brief job-order cost sheet for the four jobs. Show the balance as of June 1 as well as direct materials and direct labor added in June. Apply overhead to the four jobs for the month of June, and show the ending balances.
3. Calculate the ending balances of Work in Process and Finished Goods as of June 30.
4. Calculate the Cost of Goods Sold for June.

Calculation:
1. Ordinarily, the predetermined overhead rate is calculated using estimated overhead and, in this case, estimated direct labor cost. Those figures were not given. However, it is possible to work backward from the applied overhead by the beginning of June for Jobs 78 and 79.

   Applied overhead = Predetermined overhead rate × Actual activity level

   For Job 78,

   $750 = Predetermined overhead rate × $600

   Predetermined overhead rate = $750/$600
   = 1.25, or 125 percent of direct labor cost

   (The predetermined overhead rate using Job 79 is identical.)

2.

	Job 78	Job 79	Job 80	Job 81
Beginning balance, June 1	$2,350	$3,050	$ 0	$ 0
Direct materials	500	1,110	900	100
Direct labor	400	1,400	2,000	320
Applied overhead	500	1,750	2,500	400
Total, June 30	$3,750	$7,310	$5,400	$820

**CORNERSTONE
4 - 5
(continued)**

3. By the end of June, Jobs 78, 79, and 80 have been transferred out of Work in Process. Therefore, the ending balance in Work in Process consists only of Job 81.

Work in process, June 30	$820

While three jobs (78, 79, and 80) were transferred out of Work in Process and into Finished Goods during June, only two jobs remain (Jobs 78 and 80).

Finished goods, June 1	$ 0
Job 78	3,750
Job 80	5,400
Finished goods, June 30	$9,150

4. One job, Job 79, was sold during June.

Cost of goods sold	$7,310

Accounting for Nonmanufacturing Costs

Manufacturing costs, however, are not the only costs experienced by a firm. Non-manufacturing costs are also incurred. Recall that costs associated with selling and general administrative activities are period costs. Selling and administrative costs are never assigned to the product; they are not part of the manufacturing cost flows.

To illustrate how these costs are accounted for, assume Johnson Leathergoods had the following additional transactions in January:

Advertising circulars	$ 75
Sales commission	125
Office salaries	500
Depreciation, office equipment	50

The first two transactions fall in the category of selling expense and the last two into the category of administrative expense. So, the selling expense account would increase by $200 ($75 + $125), and the administrative expense account would increase by $550 ($500 + $50).

Controlling accounts accumulate all of the selling and administrative expenses for a period. At the end of the period, all of these costs flow to the period's income statement. An income statement for Johnson Leathergoods is shown in Exhibit 4-12.

Exhibit 4-12

Income Statement

Johnson Leathergoods
Income Statement
For the Month Ended January 31, 2009

Sales		$3,480
Less: Cost of goods sold		2,395
Gross margin		$1,085
Less selling and administrative expenses:		
Selling expenses	$200	
Administrative expenses	550	750
Net operating income		$ 335

With the preparation of the income statement, the flow of costs through the manufacturing, selling, and administrative expense accounts is complete. A more detailed look at the actual accounting for these cost flows is undertaken in the appendix to this chapter.

Summary of Learning Objectives

1. Describe the differences between job-order costing and process costing, and identify the types of firms that would use each method.
    *   Job-order firms collect costs by job.
    *   Job-order firms produce heterogeneous products/services—each unit or batch has a different total cost.
    *   Job-order firms include construction, custom cabinetry, dentistry, medical services, and automotive repair.
    *   Process firms produce homogeneous products.
    *   In process firms, the cost of one batch or unit is the same as another batch or unit.
    *   Process firms include paint manufacturing, check clearing, and toy manufacturing.
2. Compute the predetermined overhead rate, and use the rate to assign overhead to units or services produced.
    *   Predetermined overhead is total budgeted overhead divided by total budgeted activity level.
    *   Overhead is applied by multiplying the rate by the actual activity usage.
    *   Applied overhead is added to total product cost, which is divided by number of units to yield unit cost.
3. Identify and set up the source documents used in job-order costing.
    *   Job-order cost sheets summarize all costs associated with a job.
    *   Materials requisition forms are used to request direct materials for a job.
    *   Labor time tickets show the number of labor hours worked on a job.
4. Describe the cost flows associated with job-order costing.
    *   The job-order cost sheet is subsidiary to the work in process account.
    *   The Balance in Work in Process consists of the balances of all incomplete jobs.
    *   The cost of a finished job is transferred out of Work in Process and into Finished Goods.
    *   The cost of jobs sold is transferred out of Finished Goods and into Cost of Goods Sold.

Summary of Important Equations

1. Predetermined overhead rate = Estimated annual overhead/Estimated annual activity level
2. Applied overhead = Predetermined overhead rate × Actual activity usage
3. Overhead variance = Applied overhead − Actual overhead
4. Adjusted COGS = Unadjusted COGS ± Overhead variance
    (*Note*: Applied overhead > Actual overhead **means** Overapplied overhead
       Applied overhead < Actual overhead **means** Underapplied overhead)
5. Departmental overhead rate = Estimated departmental overhead/Estimated departmental activity level
6. Total product cost = Total direct materials + Total direct labor + Applied overhead
7. Unit product cost = Total product cost/Number of units

Cornerstone 4-1	How to calculate the predetermined overhead rate and apply overhead to production, page 150
Cornerstone 4-2	How to reconcile actual overhead with applied overhead, page 152
Cornerstone 4-3	How to calculate predetermined departmental overhead rates and apply overhead to production, page 153
Cornerstone 4-4	How to convert departmental data to plantwide data to calculate the overhead rate and apply overhead to production, page 154
Cornerstone 4-5	How to prepare brief job-order cost sheets, page 164

CORNERSTONES FOR CHAPTER 4

Key Terms

Actual cost system, 148	Normal cost system, 148
Adjusted cost of goods sold, 162	Overapplied overhead, 151
Applied overhead, 150	Overhead variance, 151
Departmental overhead rate, 153	Plantwide overhead rate, 152
Job, 146	Predetermined overhead rate, 149
Job-order cost sheet, 155	Process-costing system, 147
Job-order costing system, 146	Time ticket, 157
Materials requisition form, 156	Underapplied overhead, 151
Normal cost of goods sold, 162	

Appendix: Journal Entries Associated with Job-Order Costing

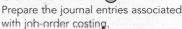

OBJECTIVE ⑤
Prepare the journal entries associated with job-order costing.

The transactions that flow through the accounts in job-order costing are entered into the accounting system by making journal entries and posting them to the accounts.

Let's summarize the various transactions that occurred during the month of January for Johnson Leathergoods.

1.   Purchased raw materials costing $2,500 on account.
2.   Requisitioned materials costing $1,500 for use in production.
3.   Recognized direct labor costing $1,530 (that is, it was not paid in cash but was shown as a liability in the wages payable account).
4.   Applied overhead to production at the rate of $2 per direct labor hour. A total of 170 direct labor hours were worked.
5.   Incurred actual overhead costs of $415.
6.   Completed the backpack job and transferred it to Finished Goods.
7.   Sold the backpack job at cost plus 50 percent.
8.   Closed underapplied overhead to Cost of Goods Sold.

The journal entries for each of the above transactions are as follows:

1.	Raw Materials	2,500	
	Accounts Payable		2,500
2.	Work in Process	1,500	
	Raw Materials		1,500
3.	Work in Process	1,530	
	Wages Payable		1,530

During the year, several jobs were completed. Data pertaining to one such job, Job #330, follow:

Direct materials	$730,000
Direct labor cost:	
Assembly (5,000 hrs. @ $12 per hr.)	$ 60,000
Finishing (400 hrs. @ $12 per hr.)	$ 4,800
Machine hours used:	
Assembly	100
Finishing	1,200
Units produced	10,000

Lindberg Company uses a plantwide predetermined overhead rate based on direct labor hours to assign overhead to jobs.

Required:

1. Compute the predetermined overhead rate.
2. Using the predetermined rate, compute the per-unit manufacturing cost for Job #330. (Round the unit cost to the nearest cent.)
3. Recalculate the unit manufacturing cost for Job #330 using departmental overhead rates. Use direct labor hours (DLH) for Assembly and machine hours (MH) for Finishing.

Solution:

1. Predetermined overhead rate = $1,330,000/175,000 = $7.60 per DLH.
   Add the budgeted overhead for the two departments, and divide by the total expected direct labor hours (DLH = 150,000 + 25,000).

2.

Direct materials	$730,000
Direct labor ($12 × 5,400)	64,800
Overhead ($7.60 × 5,400 DLH)	$ 41,040
Total manufacturing costs	$835,840

   Unit cost ($835,830/10,000) $83.58

3. Predetermined rate for Assembly = $330,000/150,000 = $2.20 per DLH.
   Predetermined rate for Finishing = $1,000,000/125,000 = $8 per MH.

Direct materials	$730,000
Direct labor	64,800
Overhead:	
Assembly ($2.20 × 5,000)	11,000
Finishing ($8 × 1,200)	9,600
Total manufacturing costs	$815,400

   Unit cost ($815,400/10,000) $81.54

II. Calculation of Work in Process and Cost of Goods Sold with Multiple Jobs

KKB (Kennedy Kitchen and Bath) Company designs and installs upscale kitchens and bathrooms. On May 1, there were three jobs in process, Jobs #77, #78, and #79. During May, two more jobs were started, Jobs #80 and #81. By May 31, Jobs #77, #78, and #80 were completed. The following data were gathered:

	Job #77	Job #78	Job #79	Job #80	Job #81
5/1 Balance	$875	$1,140	$410	$ 0	$ 0
Direct materials	690	320	500	3,500	2,750
Direct labor	450	420	80	1,800	1,300

Overhead is applied at the rate of 150 percent of direct labor cost. Jobs are sold at cost plus 30 percent. Operating expenses for May totaled $2,700.

Required:
1. Prepare job-order cost sheets for each job as of May 31.
2. Calculate the ending balance in Work in Process (as of May 31) and Cost of Goods Sold for May.
3. Construct an income statement for KKB Company for the month of May.

Solution:
1.

	Job #77	Job #78	Job #79	Job #80	Job #81
5/1 Balance	$ 875	$1,140	$ 410	$ 0	$ 0
Direct materials	690	320	500	3,500	2,750
Direct labor	450	420	80	1,800	1,300
Applied overhead	675	630	120	2,700	1,950
Totals	$2,690	$2,510	$1,110	$8,000	$6,000

2. Ending balance in Work in Process = Job #79 + Job #81
$$= \$1,110 + \$6,000$$
$$= \$7,110$$

Cost of Goods Sold for May = Job #77 + Job #78 + Job #80
$$= \$2,690 + \$2,510 + \$8,000$$
$$= \$13,200$$

3.

KKB Company
Income Statement
For the Month Ended May 31, 20XX

Sales*	$17,160
Cost of goods sold	13,200
Gross margin	$ 3,960
Less: Operating expenses	2,700
Operating income	$ 1,260

*Sales = $13,200 + 0.30($13,200) = $17,160

Discussion Questions

1. What are job-order costing and process costing? What types of firms use job-order costing? Process costing?
2. Give some examples of service firms that might use job-order costing, and explain why it is used in those firms.
3. What is normal costing? How does it differ from actual costing?
4. Why are actual overhead rates seldom used in practice?
5. Explain how overhead is assigned to production when a predetermined overhead rate is used.
6. What is underapplied overhead? When Cost of Goods Sold is adjusted for underapplied overhead, will the cost increase or decrease? Why?
7. What is overapplied overhead? When Cost of Goods Sold is adjusted for overapplied overhead, will the cost increase or decrease? Why?
8. Suppose that you and a friend decide to set up a lawn mowing service next summer. Describe the source documents that you would need to account for your activities.
9. Why might a company decide to use departmental overhead rates instead of a plantwide overhead rate?
10. What is the role of materials requisition forms in a job-order costing system? Time tickets? Predetermined overhead rates?
11. Carver Company uses a plantwide overhead rate based on direct labor cost. Suppose that during the year, Carver raises its wage rate for direct labor. How would that affect overhead applied? The total cost of jobs?

12. What is an overhead variance? How is it accounted for typically?
13. Is the cost of a job related to the price charged? Explain.
14. If a company decides to increase advertising expense by $25,000, how will that affect the predetermined overhead rate? Eventual cost of goods sold?
15. How can a departmental overhead system be converted to a plantwide overhead system?

Multiple-Choice Exercises

4-1 Which of the following statements is true?

a.   Job-order costing is used only in manufacturing firms.
b.   The job cost sheet is subsidiary to the work-in process account.
c.   Job-order costing is simpler to use than process costing because the record-keeping requirements are less.
d.   Process costing is used only for services.
e.   All of the above are true.

4-2 The ending balance of which of the following accounts is calculated by summing the totals of the open (unfinished) job-order cost sheets?

a.   Raw Materials
b.   Work in Process
c.   Finished Goods
d.   Cost of Goods Sold
e.   Overhead Control

4-3 In a normal costing system, the cost of a job includes

a.   actual direct materials, actual direct labor, and actual overhead.
b.   estimated direct materials, estimated direct labor, and estimated overhead.
c.   actual direct materials, actual direct labor, actual overhead, and actual selling cost.
d.   actual direct materials, actual direct labor, and estimated (applied) overhead.
e.   None of the above. Job-order costing requires the use of actual, not normal, costing.

4-4 The predetermined overhead rate is

a.   calculated at the end of each month.
b.   calculated at the end of the year.
c.   equal to actual overhead divided by actual activity level for a period.
d.   equal to estimated overhead divided by actual activity level for a period.
e.   calculated at the beginning of the year.

4-5 The predetermined overhead rate equals

a.   actual overhead divided by actual activity level for a period.
b.   estimated overhead divided by estimated activity level for a period.
c.   actual overhead minus estimated overhead.
d.   actual overhead multiplied by actual activity level for a period.
e.   one-twelfth of estimated overhead.

4-6 Applied overhead is

a.   an important part of normal costing.
b.   never used in normal costing.
c.   an important part of actual costing.
d.   the predetermined overhead rate multiplied by estimated activity level.
e.   the predetermined overhead rate multiplied by estimated activity level for the month.

4-7 The overhead is overapplied if

a.   actual overhead is less than applied overhead.
b.   actual overhead is more than applied overhead.
c.   applied overhead is less than actual overhead.
d.   estimated overhead is less than applied overhead.
e.   estimated overhead is more than applied overhead.

4-8 Which of the following is typically a job-order costing firm?

a.   Paint manufacturer
b.   Pharmaceutical manufacturer
c.   A large regional medical center
d.   Cement manufacturer
e.   Cleaning products' manufacturer

4-9 Which of the following is typically a process-costing firm?

a.   Paint manufacturer
b.   Custom cabinetmaker
c.   A large regional medical center
d.   A law office
e.   Custom framing shop

4-10 When materials are requisitioned for use in production in a job-order costing firm, the cost of materials is added to the

a.   raw materials account.
b.   work-in-process account.
c.   finished goods account.
d.   accounts payable account.
e.   cost of goods sold account.

4-11 When a job is completed, the total cost of the job is

a.   subtracted from the raw materials account.
b.   subtracted from the work-in-process account.
c.   subtracted from the finished goods account.
d.   added to the accounts payable account.
e.   subtracted from the cost of goods sold account.

4-12 The costs of a job are accounted for on the

a.   materials requisition sheet.
b.   time ticket.
c.   requisition for overhead application.
d.   job-order cost sheet.
e.   sales invoice.

4-13 Wilson Company has a predetermined overhead rate of $5 per direct labor hour. The job-order cost sheet for Job 145 shows 1,000 direct labor hours costing $10,000 and materials requisitions totaling $7,500. Job 145 had 500 units completed and transferred to Finished Goods. What is the cost per unit for Job 145?

a. $35
b. $135
c. $30
d. $45
e. $22,500

4-14 (Appendix) When a job costing $2,000 is finished, the following journal entry is made:

a.	Cost of Goods Sold	2,000	
	Finished Goods		2,000
b.	Finished Goods	2,000	
	Cost of Goods Sold		2,000
c.	Finished Goods	2,000	
	Work in Process		2,000
d.	Work in Process	2,000	
	Finished Goods		2,000
e.	Cost of Goods Sold	2,000	
	Sales		2,000

Exercises

OBJECTIVE ①   **Exercise 4-15 Job-Order Costing versus Process Costing**

- a.   Paint manufacturing
- b.   Auto manufacturing
- c.   Toy manufacturing
- d.   Custom cabinet making
- e.   Airplane manufacturing (e.g., 767s)
- f.   Personal computer assembly
- g.   Furniture making
- h.   Custom furniture making
- i.   Dental services
- j.   Hospital services
- k.   Paper manufacturing
- l.   Auto repair
- m.   Architectural services
- n.   Landscape design services
- o.   Light bulb manufacturing

Required:
Identify each of these types of businesses as either job-order or process costing.

OBJECTIVE ①   **Exercise 4-16 Job-Order versus Process**

- a.   Auto manufacturing
- b.   Dental services
- c.   Auto repair
- d.   Costume making

Required:
For each of the given types of industries, give an example of a firm that would use job-order costing. Then, give an example of a firm that would use process costing.

OBJECTIVE ②
CORNERSTONE 4-1   **Exercise 4-17 Calculating the Predetermined Overhead Rate, Applying Overhead to Production**

At the beginning of the year, Jeffords Company estimated the following:

Overhead	$450,000
Direct labor hours	90,000

Jeffords uses normal costing and applies overhead on the basis of direct labor hours. For the month of March, direct labor hours equaled 7,300.

Required:
1. Calculate the predetermined overhead rate for Jeffords.
2. Calculate the overhead applied to production in March.

Exercise 4-18 Calculating the Predetermined Overhead Rate, Applying Overhead to Production

OBJECTIVE ②

CORNERSTONE 4-1

At the beginning of the year, Badiyan Company estimated the following:

Overhead	$270,000
Direct labor hours	90,000

Badiyan uses normal costing and applies overhead on the basis of direct labor hours. For the month of January, direct labor hours equaled 8,150.

Required:
1. Calculate the predetermined overhead rate for Badiyan.
2. Calculate the overhead applied to production in January.

Exercise 4-19 Reconciling Overhead at the End of the Year, Adjusting Cost of Goods Sold for Under- and Overapplied Overhead

OBJECTIVE ②

CORNERSTONE 4-2

spreadsheet

Refer to **Exercise 4-18**. By the end of the year, Badiyan showed the following actual amounts:

Overhead	$308,000
Direct labor hours	102,600

Assume that unadjusted Cost of Goods Sold for Badiyan was $235,670.

Required:
1. Calculate the total overhead applied for the year. Was overhead over- or underapplied? By how much?
2. Calculated adjusted Cost of Goods Sold after adjusting for the overhead variance.

Exercise 4-20 Calculating Departmental Overhead Rates and Applying Overhead to Production

OBJECTIVE ②

CORNERSTONE 4-3

At the beginning of the year, Videosym Company estimated the following:

	Assembly Department	Testing Department	Total
Overhead	$620,000	$180,000	$800,000
Direct labor hours	155,000	20,000	175,000
Machine hours	80,000	120,000	200,000

Videosym uses departmental overhead rates. In the assembly department, overhead is applied on the basis of direct labor hours. In the testing department, overhead is applied on the basis of machine hours. Actual data for the month of March are as follows:

	Assembly Department	Testing Department	Total
Overhead	$53,000	$15,500	$68,500
Direct labor hours	13,000	1,680	14,680
Machine hours	6,800	13,050	19,850

Required:
1. Calculate the predetermined overhead rates for the assembly and testing departments.
2. Calculate the overhead applied to production in each department for the month of March.
3. By how much has each department's overhead been overapplied? Underapplied?

OBJECTIVE ③
CORNERSTONE 4-5

Exercise 4-21 Job-Order Cost Sheet

On June 1, Job 17 had a beginning balance of $100. During June, direct materials of $250 and direct labor of $300 were added to the job. Overhead is applied to production at the rate of 70 percent of direct labor cost.

Required:
1. Set up a simple job-order cost sheet for Job 17. What is the total cost of Job 17?
2. If Job 17 consisted of five units, what is the unit cost?

OBJECTIVE ③

Exercise 4-22 Source Documents

Required:
For each of the following independent situations, give the source document that would be referred to for the necessary information.
1. Direct materials costing $460 are requisitioned for use on a job.
2. Greiner's Garage uses a job-order costing system. Overhead is applied to jobs based on direct labor hours. Which source document gives the number of direct labor hours worked on Job 2004-276?
3. Pasilla Investigative Services bills clients on a monthly basis for costs to date. Job 3-48 involved an investigator following the client's business partner for a week by automobile. Mileage is billed at number of miles times $0.75.
4. The foreman on the Jackson job wonders what the actual direct materials cost was for that job.

OBJECTIVE ④

Exercise 4-23 Applying Overhead to Jobs, Costing Jobs

LaSalle Inc. designs and builds sheds and outbuildings for individual customers. On August 1, there were two jobs in process: Job 214 with a beginning balance of $13,400, and Job 215 with a beginning balance of $9,670. LaSalle applies overhead at the rate of $16 per direct labor hour. Direct labor wages average $10 per hour.

During August, Jobs 216 and 217 were started. Data on August costs for all jobs are as follows:

	Job 214	Job 215	Job 216	Job 217
Direct materials	$2,200	$9,000	$1,500	$3,450
Direct labor cost	1,800	4,000	150	800

Required:
1. Calculate the number of direct labor hours that were worked on each job in August.
2. Calculate the overhead applied to each job during the month of August.
3. Prepare job-order cost sheets for each job as of the end of August.

OBJECTIVE ④

Exercise 4-24 Work in Process Balance, Job Cost

Refer to **Exercise 4-23**. Job 214 was completed on August 22, and the client was billed at cost plus 30 percent. All other jobs remained in process.

Required:
1. Calculate the balance in Work in Process on August 31.
2. What is the price of Job 214?

OBJECTIVE ④

Exercise 4-25 Applying Overhead to Jobs, Costing Jobs

Perrine Company builds internal conveyor equipment to client specifications. On October 1, Job 877 was in process with a cost of $20,520 to date.

During October, Jobs 878, 879, and 880 were started. Data on costs added during October for all jobs are as follows:

	Job 877	Job 878	Job 879	Job 880
Direct materials	$13,960	$ 7,000	$ 350	$4,800
Direct labor	13,800	10,000	1,500	4,000

Overhead is applied to production at the rate of 85 percent of direct labor cost. Job 878 was completed on October 28, and the client was billed at cost plus 50 percent. All other jobs remained in process.

Required:
1. Prepare a brief job-order cost sheet showing the October 1 balances of all four jobs, plus the direct materials and direct labor costs during October. (There is no need to calculate applied overhead at this point or to total the costs.)
2. Calculate the overhead applied during October, and complete the job-order cost sheet for each job as of the end of October.
3. Calculate the balance in Work in Process on October 31.
4. What is the price of Job 878?

Exercise 4-26 Balance of Work in Process and Finished Goods, Cost of Goods Sold

OBJECTIVE ④

Grenelin Company uses job-order costing. At the end of the month, the following information was gathered:

Job #	Total Cost	Complete?	Sold?
301	$450	Yes	No
302	300	Yes	Yes
303	500	No	No
304	670	Yes	No
305	800	Yes	No
306	230	No	No
307	150	Yes	Yes
308	700	No	No
309	915	No	No
310	103	No	No

The beginning balance of Finished Goods was zero.

Required:
1. Calculate the balance in Work in Process at the end of the month.
2. Calculate the balance in Finished Goods at the end of the month.
3. Calculate Cost of Goods Sold for the month.

Exercise 4-27 Job-Order Cost Sheets, Balance in Work in Process and Finished Goods

OBJECTIVE ④

Geneva Company, a job-order costing firm, worked on three jobs in July. Data are as follows:

	Job 37	Job 38	Job 39
Balance, 7/1	$12,450	$ 0	$ 0
Direct materials	$ 6,900	$7,900	$15,350
Direct labor	$10,000	$8,500	$23,000
Machine hours	200	150	1,000

Overhead is applied to jobs at the rate of $20 per machine hour. By July 31, Jobs 37 and 39 were completed. Jobs 35 and 37 were sold. Job 38 remained in process. On July 1, the balance in Finished Goods was $49,000 (consisting of Job 35 for $19,000 and Job 36 for $30,000).

Required:

1. Prepare job-order cost sheets for all jobs in process during July, showing all costs through July 31.
2. Calculate the balance in Work in Process on July 31.
3. Calculate the balance in Finished Goods on July 31.
4. Calculate Cost of Goods Sold for July.

OBJECTIVE ④ **Exercise 4-28 Income Statement for the Job-Order Costing Firm**

Refer to **Exercise 4-27**. Geneva prices its jobs at cost plus 40 percent. During July, variable marketing expenses were 10 percent of sales, and fixed marketing expenses were $2,000; administrative expenses were $3,500.

Required:
Prepare an income statement for Geneva Company for the month of July.

OBJECTIVE ④ **Exercise 4-29 Cost Flows**

Consider the following independent jobs. Overhead is applied in Department 1 at the rate of $6 per direct labor hour. Overhead is applied in Department 2 at the rate of $8 per machine hour. Direct labor wages average $10 per hour in each department.

	Job 213	Job 214	Job 217	Job 225
Total sales revenue	$?	$4,375	$5,600	$1,150
Price per unit	$ 12	$?	$ 14	$ 5
Materials used in production	$ 365	$?	$ 488	$ 207
Department 1, Direct labor cost	$?	$ 700	$2,000	$ 230
Department 1, Machine hours	15	35	50	12
Department 2, Direct labor cost	$ 50	$ 100	$?	$ 0
Department 2, Machine hours	25	50	?	?
Department 1, Overhead applied	$ 90	$?	$1,200	$ 138
Department 2, Overhead applied	$?	$ 400	$ 160	$ 0
Total manufacturing cost	$ 855	$3,073	$?	$ 575
Number of units	?	350	400	?
Unit cost	$8.55	$?	$ 9.87	$?

Required:
Fill in the missing data for each job.

OBJECTIVE ④ **Exercise 4-30 Job Cost Flows**

Timter Company uses a normal job-order costing system. The company has two departments through which most jobs pass. Overhead is applied using a plantwide overhead rate of $10 per direct labor hour. During the year, several jobs were completed. Data pertaining to one such job, Job 10, follow:

Direct materials	$20,000
Direct labor cost:	
Department A (5,000 hrs. @ $6)	$30,000
Department B (1,000 hrs. @ $6)	$ 6,000
Machine hours used:	
Department A	100
Department B	1,200
Units produced	10,000

Required:

1. Compute the total cost of Job 10.
2. Compute the per-unit manufacturing cost for Job 10.

Exercise 4-31 Departmental Overhead Rates and Job Cost

OBJECTIVE ④

Refer to **Exercise 4-30**. Suppose that Timter no longer used a plantwide overhead rate. Instead, an overhead rate is calculated for each department. In Department A, overhead is applied at the rate of $2 per direct labor hour. In Department B, overhead is applied at the rate of $10 per machine hour.

Required:
1. Compute the total cost of Job 10.
2. Compute the per-unit manufacturing cost for Job 10.

Exercise 4-32 Calculation of Work in Process and Cost of Goods Sold with Multiple Jobs

OBJECTIVE ④

Greenthumb Landscape Design designs landscape plans and plants the material for clients. On April 1, there were three jobs in process, Jobs 68, 69, and 70. During April, two more jobs were started, Jobs 71 and 72. By April 30, Jobs 69, 70, and 72 were completed and sold. The following data were gathered:

	Job 68	Job 69	Job 70	Job 71	Job 72
Balance, April 1	$540	$1,230	$990	—	—
Direct materials	700	560	75	$3,500	$2,750
Direct labor	500	600	90	2,500	2,000

Overhead is applied at the rate of 120 percent of direct labor cost. Jobs are sold at cost plus 40 percent. Selling and administrative expenses for April totaled $3,670.

Required:
1. Prepare job-order cost sheets for each job as of April 30.
2. Calculate the ending balance in Work in Process (as of April 30) and Cost of Goods Sold for April.
3. Construct an income statement for Greenthumb Landscape Design for the month of April.

Exercise 4-33 (Appendix) Journal Entries

OBJECTIVE ⑤

Kaycee Inc. uses a job-order costing system. During the month of May, the following transactions occurred:

a. Purchased materials on account for $23,175.
b. Requisitioned materials totaling $19,000 for use in production. Of the total, $8,200 was for Job 62, $7,100 for Job 63, and the remainder for Job 64.
c. Incurred direct labor for the month of $22,500, with an average wage of $15 per hour. Job 62 used 700 hours; Job 63, 500 hours; Job 64, 300 hours.
d. Incurred and paid actual overhead of $15,500 (credit various payables).
e. Charged overhead to production at the rate of $8 per direct labor hour.
f. Completed and transferred Jobs 62 and 63 to Finished Goods.
g. Sold Job 58 (see beginning balance of Finished Goods) and Job 62 to their respective clients on account for a price of cost plus 30 percent.

Beginning balances as of May 1 were:

Materials	$ 5,170
Work in Process	0
Finished Goods (Job 58)	23,000

Required:
1. Prepare the journal entries for events (a) through (g).
2. Prepare brief job-order cost sheets for Jobs 62, 63, and 64.
3. Calculate the ending balance of Raw Materials.
4. Calculate the ending balance of Work in Process.
5. Calculate the ending balance of Finished Goods.

Problems

OBJECTIVES ② ④ ## Problem 4-34 Overhead Application and Job-Order Costing

Zavner Company is a job-order costing firm that uses a plantwide overhead rate based on direct labor hours. Estimated information for the year is as follows:

Overhead	$450,000
Direct labor hours	40,000

Zavner worked on five jobs in July. Data are as follows:

	Job 60	Job 61	Job 62	Job 63	Job 64
Balance, July 1	$32,450	$40,770	$29,090	$0	$0
Direct materials	$26,000	$37,900	$25,350	$11,000	$13,560
Direct labor cost	$40,000	$38,500	$43,000	$20,900	$18,000
Direct labor hours	2,500	2,400	2,600	1,200	1,100

By July 31, Jobs 60 and 62 were completed and sold. The remaining jobs were in process.

Required:
1. Calculate the plantwide overhead rate for Zavner Company.
2. Prepare job-order cost sheets for each job showing all costs through July 31.
3. Calculate the balance in Work in Process on July 31.
4. Calculate Cost of Goods Sold for July.

OBJECTIVES ① ③ ## Problem 4-35 Job Cost, Source Documents

Spade Millhone Detective Agency performs investigative work for a variety of clients. Recently, Reliance Insurance Company asked Spade Millhone to investigate a series of suspicious claims for whiplash. In each case, the claimant was driving on a freeway and was suddenly rear-ended by a Reliance-insured client. The claimants were all driving old, uninsured automobiles. The Reliance clients reported that the claimants suddenly changed lanes in front of them, and the accidents were unavoidable. Reliance suspected that these "accidents" were the result of insurance fraud. Basically, the claimants cruised the freeways in virtually worthless cars, attempting to cut in front of expensive late-model cars that would surely be insured. Reliance believed that the injuries were faked.

Scott Spade spent 40 hours shadowing the claimants and taking pictures as necessary. His surveillance methods located the office of a doctor used by all claimants. He also took pictures of claimants performing tasks that they had sworn were now impossible to perform, due to whiplash injuries. Kris Millhone spent 25 hours using the Internet to research court records in surrounding states to locate the names of the claimants and their doctor. She found a pattern of similar insurance claims for each of the claimants.

Spade Millhone Detective Agency bills clients for detective time at $100 per hour. Mileage is charged at $0.40 per mile. The agency logged in 430 miles on the Reliance job. The film and developing amounted to $80.

Required:
1. Prepare a job-order cost sheet for the Reliance job.
2. Why is overhead not specified in the charges? How does Spade Millhone charge clients for the use of overhead (e.g., the ongoing costs of their office—supplies, paper for notes and reports, telephone, utilities)?
3. The mileage is tallied from a source document. Design a source document for this use, and make up data for it that would total the 430 miles driven on the Reliance job.

Problem 4-36 Calculating Ending Work in Process, Income Statement

OBJECTIVE ④

Brandt Company produces unique metal sculptures. On January 1, three jobs were in process with the following costs:

	Job 35	Job 36	Job 37
Direct materials	$100	$ 340	$ 780
Direct labor	350	700	1,050
Applied overhead	420	840	1,260
Total	$870	$1,880	$3,090

During the month of January, two more jobs were started, Jobs 38 and 39. Materials and labor costs incurred by each job in January are as follows:

	Materials	Direct Labor
Job 35	$400	$300
Job 36	150	200
Job 37	260	150
Job 38	800	650
Job 39	760	700

Jobs 37 and 38 were completed and sold by January 31.

Required:

1. If overhead is applied on the basis of direct labor dollars, what is the overhead rate?
2. Prepare simple job-order cost sheets for each of the five jobs in process during January.
3. What is the ending balance of Work in Process on January 31? What is the Cost of Goods Sold in January?
4. Suppose that Brandt Company prices its jobs at cost plus 50 percent. In addition, during January, marketing and administrative costs of $1,200 were incurred. Prepare an income statement for the month of January.

Problem 4-37 Overhead Applied to Jobs, Departmental Overhead Rates

OBJECTIVE ②

Watson Products Inc. uses a normal job-order costing system. Currently, a plantwide overhead rate based on machine hours is used. Marlon Burke, the plant manager, has heard that departmental overhead rates can offer significantly better cost assignments than a plantwide rate can offer. Watson has the following data for its two departments for the coming year:

	Department A	Department B
Overhead costs (expected)	$50,000	$22,000
Normal activity (machine hours)	20,000	16,000

Required:

1. Compute a predetermined overhead rate for the plant as a whole based on machine hours.
2. Compute predetermined overhead rates for each department using machine hours. (Carry your calculations out to three decimal places.)
3. Job 73 used 20 machine hours from Department A and 50 machine hours from Department B. Job 74 used 50 machine hours from Department A and 20 machine hours from Department B. Compute the overhead cost assigned to each job using the plantwide rate computed in Requirement 1. Repeat the computation using the departmental rates found in Requirement 2. Which of the two approaches gives the fairer assignment? Why?
4. Repeat Requirement 3, assuming the expected overhead cost for Department B is $40,000 (not $22,000). For this company, would you recommend departmental rates over a plantwide rate?

OBJECTIVE ②

spreadsheet

Problem 4-38 Overhead Rates, Unit Costs

Lacy Company manufactures specialty tools to customer order. There are three producing departments. Departmental information on budgeted overhead and various activity measures for the coming year is as follows:

	Department 1	Department 2	Department 3
Estimated overhead	$ 40,000	$25,000	$ 25,000
Direct labor hours	9,000	5,000	15,000
Direct labor cost	$180,000	$20,000	$200,000
Machine hours	5,000	3,000	2,000

Currently, overhead is applied on the basis of machine hours using a plantwide rate. However, Jennifer, the controller, has been wondering whether it might be worthwhile to use departmental overhead rates. She has analyzed the overhead costs and drivers for the various departments and decided that Departments 1 and 3 should base their overhead rates on machine hours and that Department 2 should base its overhead rate on direct labor hours.

Jennifer has been asked to prepare bids for two jobs with the following information:

	Job 1	Job 2
Direct materials	$4,500	$8,600
Direct labor cost	$1,000	$2,000
Direct labor hours:		
Department 1	10	20
Department 2	60	20
Department 3	30	80
Number of machine hours:		
Department 1	50	30
Department 2	40	5
Department 3	110	165

The typical bid price includes a 30-percent markup over full manufacturing cost.

Required:

1.   Calculate a plantwide rate for Lacy Company based on machine hours. What is the bid price of each job using this rate?
2.   Calculate departmental overhead rates for the departments. What is the bid price of each job using these rates? (Round all answers to the nearest dollar.)

OBJECTIVES ④ ⑤

Problem 4-39 (Appendix) Unit Cost, Ending Work in Process, Journal Entries

During August, Pamell Inc. worked on two jobs. Data relating to these two jobs follow:

	Job 64	Job 65
Units in each order	50	100
Units sold	50	—
Materials requisitioned	$1,240	$ 985
Direct labor hours	410	583
Direct labor cost	$6,150	$8,745

Overhead is assigned on the basis of direct labor hours at a rate of $12. During August, Job 64 was completed and transferred to Finished Goods. Job 65 was the only unfinished job at the end of the month.

Required:

1.   Calculate the per-unit cost of Job 64.
2.   Compute the ending balance in the work-in-process account.
3.   Prepare the journal entries reflecting the completion and sale on account of Job 64. The selling price is 160 percent of cost.

Problem 4-40 (Appendix) Journal Entries, Job Costs

OBJECTIVES ④ ⑤

The following transactions occurred during the month of April for Kearney Company.

a. Purchased materials costing $3,000 on account.
b. Requisitioned materials totaling $1,700 for use in production, $500 for Job 443 and the remainder for Job 444.
c. Recorded 50 hours of direct labor on Job 443 and 100 hours on Job 444 for the month. Direct laborers are paid at the rate of $8 per hour.
d. Applied overhead using a plantwide rate of $7.50 per direct labor hour.
e. Incurred and paid in cash actual overhead for the month of $1,230.
f. Completed and transferred Job 443 to Finished Goods.
g. Sold on account Job 442, which had been completed and transferred to Finished Goods in March, for cost ($2,000) plus 25 percent.

Required:

1. Prepare journal entries for transactions (a) through (e).
2. Prepare job-order cost sheets for Jobs 443 and 444. Prepare journal entries for transactions (f) and (g).
3. Prepare a statement of cost of goods manufactured for April. Assume that the beginning balance in the raw materials account was $1,400 and that the beginning balance in the work-in-process account was zero.

Problem 4-41 (Appendix) Predetermined Overhead Rates, Variances, Cost Flows

OBJECTIVES ② ④ ⑤

Barrymore Costume Company, located in New York City, sews costumes for plays and musicals. Barrymore considers itself primarily a service firm, as it never produces costumes without a pre-existing order and only purchases materials to the specifications of the particular job. Any finished goods ending inventory is temporary and is zeroed out as soon as the show producer pays for the order. Overhead is applied on the basis of direct labor cost. During the first quarter of the year, the following activity took place in each of the accounts listed:

Work in Process			
Bal.	17,000	DM	245,000
DL	80,000		
OH	140,000		
DM	40,000		
Bal.	32,000		

Finished Goods			
Bal.	40,000		210,000
	245,000		
Bal.	75,000		

Overhead			
	138,500		140,000
		Bal.	1,500

Cost of Goods Sold	
210,000	

Job 32 was the only job in process at the end of the first quarter. A total of 1,000 direct labor hours at $10 per hour were charged to Job 32.

Required:

1. Assuming that overhead is applied on the basis of direct labor cost, what was the overhead rate used during the first quarter of the year?
2. What was the applied overhead for the first quarter? The actual overhead? The under- or overapplied overhead?
3. What was the cost of the goods manufactured for the quarter?
4. Assume that the overhead variance is closed to the cost of goods sold account. Prepare the journal entry to close out the overhead control account. What is the adjusted balance in Cost of Goods Sold?
5. For Job 32, identify the costs incurred for direct materials, direct labor, and overhead.

OBJECTIVES ② ④ ⑤

spreadsheet

Problem 4-42 (Appendix) Overhead Application, Journal Entries, Job Cost

At the beginning of the year, Paxton Company budgeted overhead of $180,000 as well as 15,000 direct labor hours. During the year, Job K456 was completed with the following information: direct materials cost, $2,340; direct labor cost, $3,600. The average wage for Paxton Company employees is $10 per hour.

By the end of the year, 15,400 direct labor hours had actually been worked, and Paxton Company incurred the following actual overhead costs for the year:

Equipment lease	$ 5,000
Depreciation on building	20,000
Indirect labor	100,000
Utilities	15,000
Other overhead	45,000

Required:
1. Calculate the overhead rate for the year.
2. Calculate the total cost of Job K456.
3. Prepare the journal entries to record actual overhead and to apply overhead to production for the year.
4. Is overhead overapplied or underapplied? By how much?
5. Assuming that the normal cost of goods sold for the year is $700,000, what is the adjusted cost of goods sold?

OBJECTIVES ① ④ ⑤

Problem 4-43 (Appendix) Journal Entries, T-Accounts

Lowder Inc. builds custom conveyor systems for warehouses and distribution centers. During the month of July, the following occurred:

a. Purchased materials on account for $42,630.
b. Requisitioned materials totaling $27,000 for use in production: $12,500 for Job 703 and the remainder for Job 704.
c. Recorded direct labor payroll for the month of $26,320 with an average wage of $14 per hour. Job 703 required 780 direct labor hours; Job 704 required 1,100 direct labor hours.
d. Incurred and paid actual overhead of $19,950.
e. Charged overhead to production at the rate of $10 per direct labor hour.
f. Completed Job 703 and transferred it to finished goods.
g. Kept Job 704, which was started during July, in process at the end of the month.
h. Sold Job 700, which had been completed in May, on account for cost plus 30 percent.

Beginning balances as of July 1 were:

Raw Materials	$ 6,070
Work in Process (for Job 703)	10,000
Finished Goods (for Job 700)	6,240

Required:
1. Prepare the journal entries for events (a) through (e).
2. Prepare simple job-order cost sheets for Jobs 703 and 704.
3. Prepare the journal entries for events (f) and (h).
4. Calculate the ending balances of the following:
   a. Raw Materials
   b. Work in Process
   c. Finished Goods

Problem 4-44 Calculate Job Cost and Use It to Calculate Price

Suppose that back in the 1970s, Steve was asked to build speakers for two friends. The first friend, Jan, needed a speaker for her band. The second friend, Ed, needed a speaker built into the back of his hatchback automobile. Steve figured the following costs for each:

	Jan's Job	Ed's Job
Materials	$50	$75
Labor hours	10	20

Steve knew that Jan's job would be easier, since he had experience in building the type of speaker she needed. Her job would not require any special equipment or specialized fitting. Ed's job, on the other hand, required specialized design and precise fitting. Steve thought he might need to build a mock-up of the speaker first, to fit it into the space. In addition, he might have to add to his tool collection to complete the job. Normally, Steve figured a wage rate of $6 per hour and charged 20 percent of labor and materials as an overhead rate.

Required:
1. Prepare job order cost sheets for the two jobs, showing total cost.
2. Which cost do you think is more likely to be accurate? How might Steve build in some of the uncertainty of Ed's job into a budgeted cost?

Cases

Case 4-45 Overhead Assignment: Actual and Normal Activity Compared

Reynolds Printing Company specializes in wedding announcements. Reynolds uses an actual job-order costing system. An actual overhead rate is calculated at the end of each month using actual direct labor hours and overhead for the month. Once the actual cost of a job is determined, the customer is billed at actual cost plus 50 percent.

During April, Mrs. Lucky, a good friend of owner Jane Reynolds, ordered three sets of wedding announcements to be delivered May 10, June 10, and July 10, respectively. Reynolds scheduled production for each order on May 7, June 7, and July 7, respectively. The orders were assigned job numbers 115, 116, and 117, respectively.

Reynolds assured Mrs. Lucky that she would attend each of her daughters' weddings. Out of sympathy and friendship, she also offered a lower price. Instead of cost plus 50 percent, she gave her a special price of cost plus 25 percent. Additionally, she agreed to wait until the final wedding to bill for the three jobs.

On August 15, Reynolds asked her accountant to bring her the completed job-order cost sheets for Jobs 115, 116, and 117. She also gave instructions to lower the price as had been agreed upon. The cost sheets revealed the following information:

	Job 115	Job 116	Job 117
Cost of direct materials	$250.00	$250.00	$250.00
Cost of direct labor (5 hrs.)	25.00	25.00	25.00
Cost of overhead	200.00	400.00	400.00
Total cost	$475.00	$675.00	$675.00
Total price	$593.75	$843.75	$843.75
Number of announcements	500	500	500

Reynolds could not understand why the overhead costs assigned to Jobs 116 and 117 were so much higher than those for Job 115. She asked for an overhead cost summary sheet for the months of May, June, and July, which showed that actual overhead costs were $20,000 each month. She also discovered that direct labor hours worked on all jobs were 500 hours in May and 250 hours each in June and July.

Required:

1. How do you think Mrs. Lucky will feel when she receives the bill for the three sets of wedding announcements?
2. Explain how the overhead costs were assigned to each job.
3. Assume that Reynolds's average activity is 500 hours per month and that the company usually experiences overhead costs of $240,000 each year. Can you recommend a better way to assign overhead costs to jobs? Recompute the cost of each job and its price given your method of overhead cost assignment. Which method do you think is best? Why?

OBJECTIVES ② ⑤   Case 4-46 Assigning Overhead to Jobs—Ethical Issues

Tonya Martin, CMA and controller of the Parts Division of Gunderson Inc. was meeting with Doug Adams, manager of the division. The topic of discussion was the assignment of overhead costs to jobs and their impact on the division's pricing decisions. Their conversation was as follows:

Tonya: Doug, as you know, about 25 percent of our business is based on government contracts, with the other 75 percent based on jobs from private sources won through bidding. During the last several years, our private business has declined. We have been losing more bids than usual. After some careful investigation, I have concluded that we are overpricing some jobs because of improper assignment of overhead costs. Some jobs are also being underpriced. Unfortunately, the jobs being overpriced are coming from our higher-volume, labor-intensive products; thus, we are losing business.

Doug: I think I understand. Jobs associated with our high-volume products are being assigned more overhead than they should be receiving. Then, when we add our standard 40-percent markup, we end up with a higher price than our competitors, who assign costs more accurately.

Tonya: Exactly. We have two producing departments, one labor-intensive and the other machine-intensive. The labor-intensive department generates much less overhead than the machine-intensive department. Furthermore, virtually all of our high-volume jobs are labor-intensive. We have been using a plantwide rate based on direct labor hours to assign overhead to all jobs. As a result, the high-volume, labor-intensive jobs receive a greater share of the machine-intensive department's overhead than they deserve. This problem can be greatly alleviated by switching to departmental overhead rates. For example, an average high-volume job would be assigned $100,000 of overhead using a plantwide rate and only $70,000 using departmental rates. The change would lower our bidding price on high-volume jobs by an average of $42,000 per job. By increasing the accuracy of our product costing, we can make better pricing decisions and win back much of our private-sector business.

Doug: Sounds good. When can you implement the change in overhead rates?

Tonya: It won't take long. I can have the new system working within four to six weeks—certainly by the start of the new fiscal year.

Doug: Hold it. I just thought of a possible complication. As I recall, most of our government contract work is done in the labor-intensive department. This new overhead assignment scheme will push down the cost on the government jobs, and we will lose revenues. They pay us full cost plus our standard markup. This business is not threatened by our current costing procedures, but we can't switch our rates for only the private business. Government auditors would question the lack of consistency in our costing procedures.

Tonya: You do have a point. I thought of this issue also. According to my estimates, we will gain more revenues from the private sector than we will lose from our government contracts. Besides, the costs of our government jobs are distorted; in effect, we are overcharging the government.

Doug: They don't know that and never will unless we switch our overhead assignment procedures. I think I have the solution. Officially, let's keep our plantwide overhead rate. All of the official records will reflect this overhead costing approach for both our private and government business. Unofficially, I want you to develop a separate set of books that can be used to generate the information we need to prepare competitive bids for our private-sector business.

Required:
1. Do you believe that the solution proposed by Doug is ethical? Explain.
2. Suppose that Tonya decides that Doug's solution is not right and objects strongly. Further suppose that, despite Tonya's objections, Doug insists strongly on implementing the action. What should Tonya do?

5

Process Costing

© BP, INC.

After studying Chapter 5, you should be able to:

① Describe the basic characteristics and cost flows associated with process manufacturing.

② Define *equivalent units* and explain their role in process costing. Explain the differences between the weighted average method and the first-in, first-out (FIFO) method of accounting for process costs.

③ Prepare a departmental production report using the weighted average method.

④ Explain how nonuniform inputs and multiple processing departments affect process costing.

⑤ (Appendix) Prepare a departmental production report using the FIFO method.

Experience Managerial Decisions
with BP

The only consideration that most people give to gasoline is the price charged at the local pump. However, BP, one of the largest energy companies in the world, has been thinking about this issue and a lot more for quite a long time. BP was founded in 1901 after William D'Arcy obtained permission from the shah of Persia to dig for oil in what is now the Iranian desert. BP drastically expanded its reach as it built a new refinery in Australia in 1924 and then established new exploration and excavation sites in places such as Canada, South America, Africa, and Europe, in addition to its Middle Eastern sites. As of the early 21st century, BP had active excavation and production occurring in 22 countries. BP runs its processes nonstop—24 hours a day, 365 days a year—to produce to full capacity, which represents 2.6 million barrels of oil each day or approximately 30 barrels every second! Producing that much of anything is a bit mind-boggling, which hints at the importance of BP's effective process-costing system in determining the costs associated with its numerous products, which include gasoline, heating fuel, greases, and asphalt.

In order to determine costs for a particular process, BP needs to know the total costs of the raw materials and the total number of units processed in a specified period of time. The costs include raw crude oil, which varies widely from sweet West Texas crude to heavier Canadian crude, plus labor and management overhead. Other costs include catalysts, which enhance the reactivity to make a molecule actually turn into something else, and chemicals, which become part of the final product. BP goes to a lot of trouble to combine its process-costing system outputs, current market prices, and a linear programming model in order to calculate the most profitable mix of products to produce from a given mix of raw crude materials. Determining the costs associated with running a refinery with a continuous production process is complex. However, by calculating process costs and carefully setting production levels and product mixes, BP is able to manage this complex process at its facilities around the globe, thereby providing continued big profits for use in future energy discovery and distribution efforts.

OBJECTIVE ①
Describe the basic characteristics and cost flows associated with process manufacturing.

Characteristics of Process Manufacturing

A company's production process helps to determine the best way of accounting for its costs. Let's assume that a large number of similar products pass through an identical set of processes. Since each product within a product line passing through the three processes would receive similar "doses" of materials, labor, and overhead, the company's accountant would see no need to accumulate costs by batches (a job-order costing system). Instead, the accountant should recommend accumulating costs by process.

Process costing works well whenever relatively homogeneous products pass through a series of processes and they receive similar amounts of manufacturing costs. Large manufacturing plants, such as for chemical, tire manufacturers, and food, use process costing. For example, Americans purchase about 100 million bags of chocolate chips every year, many of which are made by Nestle. **Nestle** accounts for the costs of its vast chocolate chip production by using a process-costing system.

Let's consider the process-costing environment of **Healthblend Nutritional Supplements**, which manufactures various products including minerals, herbs, and vitamins. Healthblend uses three processes, each centered in a producing department: picking, encapsulation, and bottling. In the picking department, direct labor selects the appropriate herbs, vitamins, minerals, and inert materials (typically some binder such as cornstarch) for the product to be manufactured. Then, the materials are measured and combined in a mixer to blend them thoroughly. When the mix is complete, the resulting mixture is sent to the encapsulation department. In encapsulating, the vitamin, mineral, or herb blend is loaded into a machine that fills one-half of a gelatin capsule. The filled half is matched to another half of the capsule, and a safety seal is applied. This process is entirely mechanized. Overhead in this department consists of depreciation on machinery, maintenance of machinery, supervision, fringe benefits, lights, and power. The final department is bottling. Filled capsules are transferred to this department, loaded into a hopper, and automatically counted into bottles. Filled bottles are mechanically capped, and direct labor then manually packs the correct number of bottles into boxes to ship to retail outlets.

Types of Processes

Production at Healthblend Nutritional Supplements is an example of sequential processing. **Sequential processing** requires that units pass through one process before they can be worked on in later processes. Exhibit 5-1 shows the sequential pattern of the manufacture of Healthblend's minerals, herbs, and vitamins.

To summarize, in a process firm, units typically pass through a series of manufacturing or producing departments; in each department or process is an operation that

| Exhibit 5-1 |

Sequential Processing Illustrated

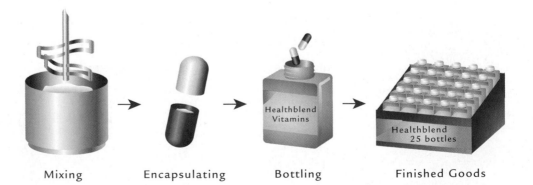

Mixing   Encapsulating   Bottling   Finished Goods

brings a product one step closer to completion. As well, in each department, materials, labor, and overhead may be needed. Upon completion of a particular process, the partially completed goods are transferred to the next department. After passing through the final department, the goods are completed and transferred to the warehouse.

Parallel processing is another processing pattern that requires two or more sequential processes to produce a finished good. Partially completed units (e.g., two subcomponents) can be worked on simultaneously in different processes and then brought together in a final process for completion. Consider, for example, the manufacture of hard disk drives for personal computers. In one series of processes, write-heads and cartridge disk drives are produced, assembled, and tested. In a second series of processes, printed circuit boards are produced and tested. These two major subcomponents then come together for assembly in the final process. Exhibit 5-2 portrays this type of process pattern. Notice that processes 1 and 2 can occur independently of (or parallel to) processes 3 and 4.

Other forms of parallel processes also exist. However, regardless of which processing pattern exists within a firm, all units produced share a common property. Since units are homogeneous and subjected to the same operations for a given process, each unit produced in a period should receive the same unit cost. Understanding how unit costs are computed requires an understanding of the manufacturing cost flows that take place in a process-costing firm.

How Costs Flow through the Accounts in Process Costing

The manufacturing cost flows for a process-costing system are generally the same as those for a job-order system. As raw materials are purchased, the cost of these materials flows into a raw materials inventory account. Similarly, raw materials, direct labor, and applied overhead costs flow into a work-in-process (WIP) account. When goods are completed, the cost of the completed goods is transferred from WIP to the finished goods account. Finally, as goods are sold, the cost of the finished goods is transferred to the cost of goods sold account. The journal entries generally parallel those described in a job-order costing system.

Although job-order and process cost flows are generally similar, some differences exist. In process costing, each producing department has its own WIP account. As goods are completed in one department, they are transferred to the next department. Exhibit 5-3 on page 192 illustrates this process for Healthblend. Notice that a product (let's say multivitamins) starts out in the picking department, where the proper amounts of vitamin, mineral, and inert materials are mixed. Picking direct labor and applied overhead are recognized and

Exhibit 5-3 on page 192 illustrates this process for Healthblend.

Parallel Processing Illustrated

Exhibit 5-2

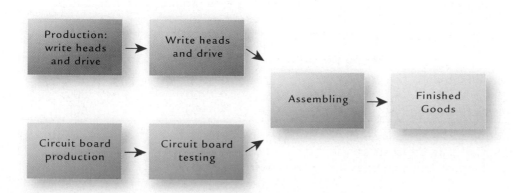

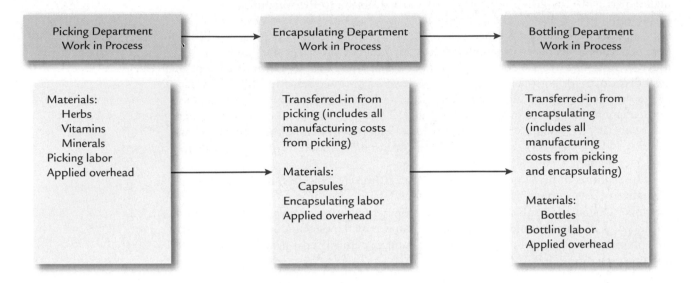

Exhibit 5-3

Flow of Manufacturing Costs through the Accounts of a Process-Costing Firm

Concept Q&A

Will process costing be the same for sequential and parallel processing systems?

Answer:

Yes. Process-costing procedures are the same for both process settings. Costs are collected by process and are assigned to units produced by the process. Each process undergoes this costing action regardless of whether it is a member of a sequential or a parallel process system. Once goods are costed, they are transferred out to the next process.

added to the picking WIP account. When the mixture is properly blended, it is transferred to the encapsulating department, where capsules are filled. The filled capsules are transferred out to the bottling department. In bottling, the capsules are bottled, and the bottles are packaged. The important point is that as the product is transferred from one department to another, so are all of the costs attached to the product. By the end of the process, all manufacturing costs end up in the final department (here, bottling) with the final product. Let's attach some costs to the various departments and follow them through the accounts. Cornerstone 5-1 shows how cost flows are computed when there are no WIP inventories.

Cornerstone 5-1 shows that when the multivitamin mixture is transferred from the picking department to the encapsulating department, it takes $2,200 of cost along with it. **Transferred-in costs** are costs transferred from a prior process to a subsequent process. From the viewpoint of the

---

CORNERSTONE 5-1

HOW TO Calculate Cost Flows without Work in Process

Information: Suppose that Healthblend decides to produce 2,000 bottles of multivitamins with the following costs:

	Picking Department	Encapsulating Department	Bottling Department
Direct materials	$1,700	$1,000	$800
Direct labor	50	60	300
Applied overhead	450	500	600

Required:
1. Calculate the costs transferred out of each department.
2. Prepare journal entries that reflect these cost transfers.

Calculation:
1.

	Picking Department	Encapsulating Department	Bottling Department
Direct materials	$1,700	$1,000	$ 800
Direct labor	50	60	300
Applied overhead	450	500	600
Costs added	$2,200	$1,560	$ 1,700
Costs transferred in	0	2,200	3,760
Costs transferred out	$2,200	$3,760	$ 5,460

2. Journal entries:

Work in Process (Encapsulating)	2,200	
Work in Process (Picking)		2,200
Work in Process (Bottling)	3,760	
Work in Process (Encapsulating)		3,760
Finished Goods	5,460	
Work in Process (Bottling)		5,460

**CORNERSTONE
5-1
(continued)**

subsequent process, transferred in costs are a type of raw material cost. The same relationship exists between the encapsulating and bottling departments. The completed bottles of multivitamins are transferred to the finished goods warehouse at a total cost of $5,460.

Accumulating Costs in the Production Report

In process costing, costs are accumulated by department for a period of time. The **production report** is the document that summarizes the manufacturing activity that takes place in a process department for a given period of time. A production report contains information on costs transferred in from prior departments as well as costs added in the department such as direct materials, direct labor, and overhead; it is subsidiary to the WIP account, just as the job-order cost sheet is subsidiary to the WIP account in a job-order costing system.

A production report provides information about the physical units processed in a department and also about the manufacturing costs associated with them. Thus, a production report is divided into a unit information section and a cost information section. The unit information section has two major subdivisions: (1) units to account for and (2) units accounted for. Similarly, the cost information section has two major subdivisions: (1) costs to account for and (2) costs accounted for. A production report traces the flow of units through a department, identifies the costs charged to the department, shows the computation of unit costs, and reveals the disposition of the department's costs for the reporting period.

Service and Manufacturing Firms

Any product or service that is basically homogeneous and repetitively produced can take advantage of a process-costing approach. Let's look at three possibilities: services, manufacturing firms with a just-in-time (JIT) orientation, and traditional manufacturing firms.

Analytical Q&A

Encapsulating transferred $5,000 of partially completed goods to bottling. Bottling added $3,000 of manufacturing cost and then transferred the completed goods to the finished goods warehouse. What two journal entries would be made for these transactions?

Work in Process (Bottling)		8,000
Finished Goods	8,000	
Work in Process (Encapsulating)		5,000
Work in Process (Bottling)	5,000	

Answer:

Check processing in a bank, teeth cleaning by a hygienist, air travel between Dallas and Los Angeles, sorting mail by zip code, and laundering and pressing shirts are examples of homogeneous services that are repetitively produced. Although services cannot be stored, it is possible for firms engaged in service production to have WIP inventories. For example, a batch of tax returns can be partially completed at the end of a period. However, many services are provided so quickly that there are no WIP inventories. Teeth cleaning, funerals, surgical operations, sonograms, and carpet cleaning are a few examples where WIP inventories virtually would be nonexistent. Therefore, process costing for services is relatively simple. The total costs for the period are divided by the number of services provided to compute unit cost.

Manufacturing firms may also operate without significant WIP inventories. Specifically, firms that have adopted a JIT approach to manufacturing view the carrying of unnecessary inventories as wasteful. These firms try to reduce WIP inventories to very low levels. Furthermore, JIT firms usually structure their manufacturing so that process costing can be used to determine product costs.

In many JIT firms, work cells are created that produce a product or subassembly from start to finish. Costs are collected by cell for a period of time, and output for the cell is measured for the same period. Unit costs are computed by dividing the costs of the period by output of the period. There is no ambiguity concerning what costs belong to the period and how output is measured. One of the objectives of JIT manufacturing is simplification. Keep this in mind as you study the process-costing requirements of manufacturing firms that carry WIP inventories. The difference between the two settings is impressive and illustrates one of the significant benefits of JIT.

Finally, traditional manufacturing firms may have significant beginning and ending WIP inventories. It is the presence of these inventories that leads to much of the complication surrounding process costing. These complications are due to several factors such as the presence of beginning and ending WIP inventories and different approaches to the treatment of beginning inventory cost. These complicating factors are discussed in the following sections.

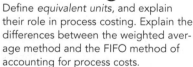

OBJECTIVE ②
Define *equivalent units*, and explain their role in process costing. Explain the differences between the weighted average method and the FIFO method of accounting for process costs.

The Impact of Work-in-Process Inventories on Process Costing

The computation of unit cost for the work performed during a period is a key part of the production report. This unit cost is needed both to compute the cost of goods transferred out of a department and to value ending work-in-process (EWIP) inventory. Conceptually, calculating the unit cost is easy—just divide total cost by the number of units produced. However, the presence of WIP inventories causes two problems. First, defining the units produced can be difficult, given that some units produced during a period are complete, while those in ending inventory are not. This is handled through the concept of equivalent units of production. Second, how should the costs and work of beginning work-in-process (BWIP) be treated? Should they be counted with the current period work and costs or treated separately? Two methods have been developed to solve this problem: the weighted average method and the FIFO method.

Equivalent Units of Production

By definition, EWIP is not complete. Thus, a unit completed and transferred out during the period is not identical (or equivalent) to one in EWIP inventory, and the cost attached to the two units should not be the same. In computing the unit cost, the output of the period must be defined. A major problem of process costing is making this definition.

To illustrate the output problem of process costing, assume that Department A had the following data for October:

Units in BWIP	—
Units completed	1,000
Units in EWIP (25 percent complete)	600
Total manufacturing costs	$11,500

What is the output in October for this department? 1,000? 1,600? If the answer is 1,000 units, the effort expended on the units in EWIP is ignored. Furthermore, the manufacturing costs incurred in October belong to both the units completed and to the partially completed units in EWIP. On the other hand, if the answer is 1,600 units, the fact that the 600 units in EWIP are only partially completed is ignored. Somehow, output must be measured so that it reflects the effort expended on both completed and partially completed units.

The solution is to calculate equivalent units of output. **Equivalent units of output** are the complete units that could have been produced given the total amount of manufacturing effort expended for the period under consideration. Determining equivalent units of output for transferred out units is easy; a unit would not be transferred out unless it were complete. Thus, every transferred-out unit is an equivalent unit. Units remaining in EWIP inventory, however, are not complete. Thus, someone in production must "eyeball" EWIP to estimate its degree of completion. Estimating the degree of completion is an act that requires judgment and, at the same time, ethical behavior. For example, overestimating the degree of completion will increase the equivalent units of output and decrease per unit costs. This outcome, in turn, would cause an increase in both income (cost of goods sold will be less) and in assets (WIP cost will increase). Deliberating overestimating the degree of completion would clearly be in violation of ethical professional practice. Cornerstone 5-2 illustrates how to calculate equivalent units of production, with the assumption that the degree of completion has been fairly assessed and stated.

Analytical Q&A

In March, a company completed 8,000 tons of aluminum ingots and had 2,500 tons of ingots in EWIP, 60 percent complete. Calculate the equivalent units for March.

Answer:

$Equivalent\ units = 8,000 + (0.6 \times 2,500) = 9,500.$

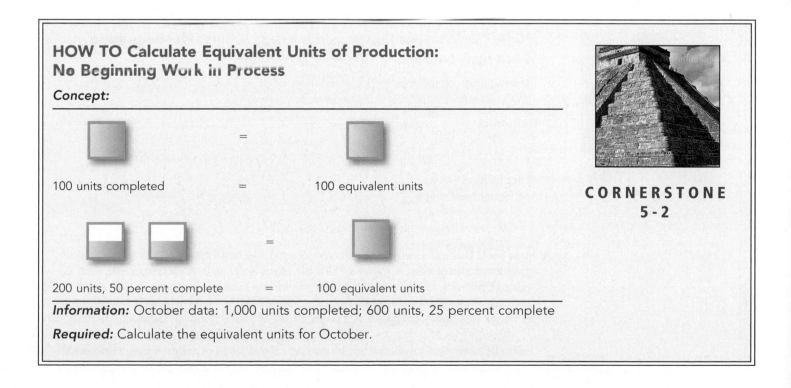

HOW TO Calculate Equivalent Units of Production: No Beginning Work in Process

Concept:

100 units completed = 100 equivalent units

200 units, 50 percent complete = 100 equivalent units

CORNERSTONE 5-2

Information: October data: 1,000 units completed; 600 units, 25 percent complete

Required: Calculate the equivalent units for October.

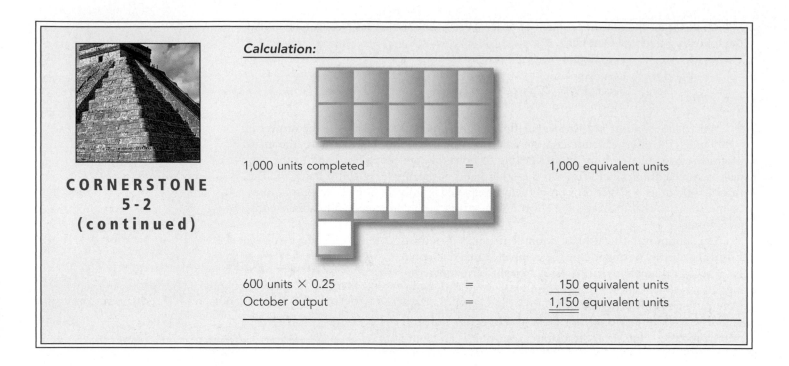

CORNERSTONE 5-2 (continued)

Calculation:

1,000 units completed   =   1,000 equivalent units

600 units × 0.25   =   150 equivalent units
October output   =   1,150 equivalent units

Knowing the output for a period and the manufacturing costs for the department for that period, a unit cost can be calculated. The unit cost can then be used to determine the cost of units transferred out and the cost of the units in EWIP. Cornerstone 5-3 shows how the calculations are done when there is no BWIP. The unit cost of $10 is used to assign a cost of $10,000 ($10 × 1,000) to the 1,000 units transferred out and a cost of $1,500 ($10 × 150) to the 600 units in EWIP. Notice that the cost of the EWIP is obtained by multiplying the unit cost by the equivalent units, not the actual number of partially completed units.

CORNERSTONE 5-3

HOW TO Measure Output and Assign Costs: No Beginning Work in Process

Information: Manufacturing costs of the period, $11,500; units transferred out, 1,000; units in EWIP, 600 (25 percent complete).

Required:
1. Calculate the unit cost.
2. Calculate the cost of goods transferred out and the cost of EWIP.

Calculation:
1. Equivalent units:

Units completed	1,000
Units in EWIP × 25 percent (600 × 0.25)	150
Equivalent units	1,150

Cost assignment:
Cost per equivalent unit = $11,500/1,150
                         = $10

2. Cost of goods transferred out = $10 per unit × 1,000 equivalent units = $10,000
   Cost of EWIP = $10 per unit × 150 equivalent units = $1,500

Two Methods of Treating Beginning Work-in-Process Inventory

The calculations illustrated by Cornerstones 5-2 and 5-3 become more complicated when there are BWIP inventories. The work done on these partially completed units represents prior-period work, and the costs assigned to them are prior-period costs. In computing a current-period unit cost for a department, two approaches have evolved for dealing with the prior-period output and prior-period costs found in BWIP: the weighted average method and the FIFO method.

The **weighted average costing method** combines beginning inventory costs and work done with current-period costs and work to calculate this period's unit cost. In essence, the costs and work carried over from the prior period are counted as if they belong to the current period. Thus, beginning inventory work and costs are pooled with current work and costs, and an average unit cost is computed and applied to both units transferred out and units remaining in ending inventory.

The **FIFO costing method**, on the other hand, separates work and costs of the equivalent units in beginning inventory from work and costs of the equivalent units produced during the current period. Only current work and costs are used to calculate this period's unit cost. It is assumed that units from beginning inventory are completed first and transferred out. The costs of these units include the costs of the work done in the prior period as well as the current-period costs necessary to complete the units. Units started in the current period are divided into two categories: units started and completed and units started but not finished (EWIP). Units in both of these categories are valued using the current period's cost per equivalent unit.

If product costs do not change from period to period, or if there is no BWIP inventory, the FIFO and weighted average methods yield the same results. The weighted average method is discussed in more detail in the next section. Further discussion of the FIFO method is found in the chapter appendix.

Analytical Q&A

During March, a molding process transferred out 9,000 equivalent units to grinding and had 1,250 equivalent units in EWIP. The cost per equivalent unit for March was $8.00. Calculate the cost of goods transferred out and the cost of the EWIP.

Answer:

Cost of goods transferred out: $8.00 × 9,000 = $72,000; EWIP = $8.00 × 1,250 = $10,000.

Weighted Average Costing

OBJECTIVE ③
Prepare a departmental production report using the weighted average method.

The weighted average costing method treats beginning inventory costs and the accompanying equivalent output as if they belong to the current period. This is done for costs by adding the manufacturing costs in BWIP to the manufacturing costs incurred during the current period. The total cost is treated as if it were the current period's total manufacturing cost. Similarly, beginning inventory output and current-period output are merged in the calculation of equivalent units. Under the weighted average method, equivalent units of output are computed by adding units completed to equivalent units in EWIP. Notice that the equivalent units in BWIP are included in the computation. Consequently, these units are counted as part of the current period's equivalent units of output.

Concept Q&A

What is the key difference between FIFO and the weighted average costing methods?

Answer:

FIFO treats work and costs in BWIP separately from the work and costs of the current period. Weighted average rolls back and picks up the work and costs of BWIP and counts them as if they belong to the current period's work and costs.

Overview of the Weighted Average Method

The essential conceptual and computational features of the weighted average method are illustrated by Cornerstone 5-4. The example uses production data for Healthblend's picking department for July. The objective is to calculate a unit cost for July and to use this unit cost to value goods transferred out and EWIP. Unit cost equals costs of the period divided by output of the period. Thus, output needs to be calculated and costs defined for July to value goods transferred out and EWIP.

Cornerstone 5-4 illustrates that costs from BWIP are pooled with costs added to production during July. These total pooled costs ($13,650) are averaged and assigned to units transferred out and to units in EWIP. On the output side, it is necessary to concentrate on the degree of completion of all units at the end of the period. There is no need to be concerned with the percentage of completion of BWIP inventory. The only issue is whether these units are complete or not by the end of July. Thus, equivalent units are computed by pooling manufacturing efforts from June and July.

CORNERSTONE
5-4

HOW TO Measure Output and Assign Costs: Weighted Average Method

Information:
Production:

Units in process, July 1, 75 percent complete	20,000 gallons
Units completed and transferred out	50,000 gallons
Units in process, July 31, 25 percent complete	10,000 gallons

Costs:

Work in process, July 1	$ 3,525
Costs added during July	10,125

Required:
1. Calculate an output measure for July.
2. Assign costs to units transferred out and EWIP using the weighted average method.

Calculation:
1. Equivalent units:

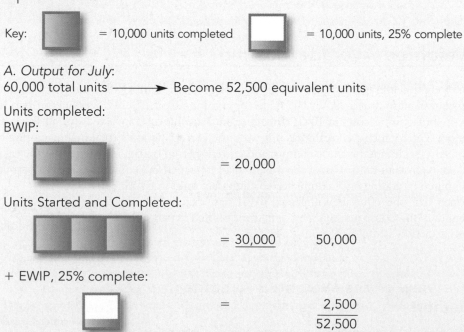

Key: ⬜ = 10,000 units completed   ⬜ = 10,000 units, 25% complete

A. *Output for July:*
60,000 total units ⟶ Become 52,500 equivalent units

Units completed:
BWIP:

= 20,000

Units Started and Completed:

= 30,000   50,000

+ EWIP, 25% complete:

=   2,500
     52,500

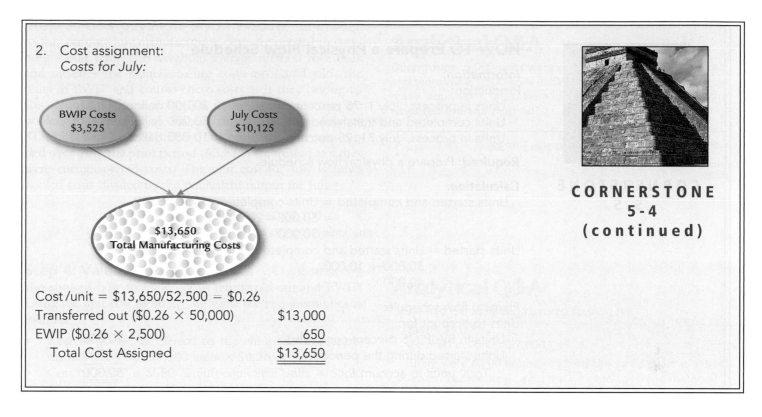

2. Cost assignment:
    Costs for July:

BWIP Costs
$3,525

July Costs
$10,125

$13,650
Total Manufacturing Costs

CORNERSTONE
5-4
(continued)

Cost/unit = $13,650/52,500 = $0.26

Transferred out ($0.26 × 50,000)	$13,000
EWIP ($0.26 × 2,500)	650
Total Cost Assigned	$13,650

Five Steps in Preparing a Production Report

The elements of Cornerstone 5-4 are used to prepare a production report. Recall that the production report summarizes cost and manufacturing activity for a producing department for a given period of time. The production report is subsidiary to the WIP account for a department. The following five steps describe the general pattern of a process-costing production report:

1. Physical flow analysis.
2. Calculation of equivalent units.
3. Computation of unit cost.
4. Valuation of inventories (goods transferred out and EWIP).
5. Cost reconciliation.

These five steps provide structure to the method of accounting for process costs.

Analytical Q&A

The weighted average cost per equivalent unit for April is $10. There were 3,800 units completed and transferred out during April and 750 units in EWIP, 40 percent complete. Calculate the cost of goods transferred out and the cost assigned to EWIP.

Answer:

Cost of goods transferred out: $10 × 3,800 = $38,000; EWIP = $10 × 0.4 × 750 = $3,000.

Step 1: Physical Flow Analysis   The purpose of step 1 is to trace the physical units of production. Physical units are not equivalent units; they are units that may be in any stage of completion. The **physical flow schedule**, like the one shown by Cornerstone 5-5 for Healthblend's picking department, provides an analysis of the physical flow of units. To construct the schedule from the information given in the example, two calculations are needed.

*   Units started and completed in this period are obtained by subtracting the units in BWIP from the total units completed.
*   The units started are obtained by adding the units started and completed to the units in EWIP.

Notice that the "Total units to account for" must equal the "Total units accounted for." The physical flow schedule is important because it contains the information needed to calculate equivalent units (step 2).

Analytical Q&A

A mixing process produced 200 equivalent units of material and 500 equivalent units of conversion activity during the month. If the materials cost was $400 and the conversion cost was $1,000, what is the cost per equivalent unit for the month?

Answer:

Unit cost = Unit materials cost + Unit conversion cost = ($400/200) + ($1,000/500) = $2 + $2 = $4

department correspond to the units transferred out from the prior department (assuming that there is a one-to-one relationship between the output measures of both departments). Cornerstone 5-8 shows how to calculate the first three process-costing steps when there are transferred-in goods, where steps 2 and 3 are restricted to the transferred-in category.

The only additional complication introduced in the analysis for a subsequent department is the presence of the transferred-in category. As has just been shown, dealing

---

**CORNERSTONE
5-8**

HOW TO Calculate the Physical Flow Schedule, Equivalent Units, and Unit Costs with Transferred-In Goods

Information: For September, Heathblend's encapsulating department had 15,000 units in beginning inventory (with transferred-in costs of $3,000) and completed 70,000 units during the month. Further, the picking department completed and transferred out 60,000 units at a cost of $13,200 in September.

Required:
1. Prepare a physical flow schedule with transferred-in goods.
2. Calculate equivalent units for the transferred-in category.
3. Calculate unit cost for the transferred-in category.

Calculation:
1. In constructing a physical flow schedule for the encapsulating department, its dependence on the picking department must be considered:

Units to account for:

Units in BWIP	15,000
Units transferred in during September	60,000
Total units to account for	75,000

Units accounted for:

Units completed and transferred out:	
Started and completed	55,000
From BWIP	15,000
Units in EWIP	5,000
Total units accounted for	75,000

2. Equivalent units for the transferred-in category only:

Transferred in:	
Units completed	70,000
Add: Units in EWIP ×	
Fraction complete (5,000 × 100 percent)*	5,000
Equivalent units of output	75,000

*Remember that the EWIP is 100 percent complete with respect to transferred-in costs, not to all costs of the encapsulating department.

3. To find the unit cost for the transferred-in category, we add the cost of the units transferred in from picking in September to the transferred-in costs in BWIP and divide by transferred-in equivalent units:

Unit cost (transferred-in category) = ($13,200 + $3,000)/75,000
= $16,200/75,000
= $0.216

with this category is similar to handling any other category. However, it must be remembered that the current cost of this special type of raw material is the cost of the units transferred in from the prior process and that the units transferred in are the units started.

Concept Q&A

How are transferred-in goods viewed and treated by the department receiving them?

Transferred-in goods are viewed as materials added at the beginning of the process. They are treated as a separate input category, and equivalent units and a unit cost are calculated for transferred-in materials.

Answer:

Summary of Learning Objectives

1. Describe the basic characteristics and cost flows associated with process manufacturing.
   - Cost flows under process costing are similar to those under job-order costing.
   - Raw materials are purchased and debited to the raw materials account.
   - Direct materials used in production, direct labor, and applied overhead are charged to the WIP account.
   - In a production process with several processes, there is a WIP account for each department or process. Goods completed in one department are transferred out to the next department.
   - When units are completed in the final department or process, their cost is credited to Work in Process and is debited to Finished Goods.
2. Define _equivalent units_, and explain their role in process costing. Explain the differences between the weighted average method and the FIFO method of accounting for process costs.
   - Equivalent units of production are the complete units that could have been produced given the total amount of manufacturing effort expended during the period.
   - The number of physical units is multiplied by the percentage of completion to calculate equivalent units.
   - The weighted average costing method combines beginning inventory costs to compute unit costs.
   - The FIFO costing method separates units in beginning inventory from those produced during the current period.
3. Prepare a departmental production report using the weighted average method.
   - The production report summarizes the manufacturing activity occurring in a department for a given period.
   - It discloses information concerning the physical flow of units, equivalent units, unit costs, and the disposition of the manufacturing costs associated with the period.
4. Explain how nonuniform inputs and multiple processing departments affect process costing.
   - Nonuniform inputs and multiple departments are easily handled by process-costing methods.
   - When inputs are added nonuniformly, equivalent units and unit cost are calculated for each separate input category.
   - The adjustment for multiple departments is also relatively simple.
   - The goods transferred from a prior department to a subsequent department are treated as a material added at the beginning of the process. Thus, there is a separate transferred-in materials category, where the equivalent units and unit cost are calculated.

CORNERSTONES FOR CHAPTER 5

CORNERSTONES FOR CHAPTER 5

Key Terms

OBJECTIVE ⑤
Prepare a departmental production report using the FIFO method.

Appendix: Production Report—First-In, First-Out Costing

Under the FIFO costing method, the equivalent units and manufacturing costs in BWIP are excluded from the current-period unit cost calculation. This method recognizes that the work and costs carried over from the prior period legitimately belong to that period.

Differences between the First-In, First-Out and Weighted Average Methods

If changes occur in the prices of the manufacturing inputs from one period to the next, then FIFO produces a more accurate (i.e., more current) unit cost than does the weighted average method. A more accurate unit cost means better cost control, better pricing decisions, and so on. Keep in mind that if the period is as short as a week or a month, however, the unit costs calculated under the two methods are not likely to differ much. In that case, the FIFO method has little, if anything, to offer over the weighted average method. Perhaps for this reason, many firms use the weighted average method.

Since FIFO excludes prior-period work and costs, it is necessary to create two categories of completed units. FIFO assumes that units in BWIP are completed first, before any new units are started. Thus, one category of completed units is BWIP units. The second category is for those units started and completed during the current period.

For example, assume that a department had 20,000 units in BWIP and completed and transferred out a total of 50,000 units. Of the 50,000 completed units, 20,000 are the units initially found in WIP. The remaining 30,000 were started and completed during the current period.

These two categories of completed units are needed in the FIFO method so that each category can be costed correctly. For the units started and completed, the unit cost is obtained by dividing total current manufacturing costs by the current-period equivalent output. However, for the BWIP units, the total associated manufacturing costs are the sum of the prior-period costs plus the costs incurred in the current period to finish the units.

Example of the First-In, First-Out Method

Cornerstone 5-9 shows how FIFO handles output and cost calculations. The computations of Cornerstone 5-9 are based on the same Healthblend data used for the weighted average method (Cornerstone 5-4). Using the same data highlights the differences between the two methods. Cornerstone 5-9 shows that the equivalent unit calculation measures only the output for the current period. Cornerstone 5-9 also reveals that costs from the current period and costs carried over from June (beginning inventory costs) are not pooled to calculate July's unit cost. The unit cost calculation uses only July (current-period) costs. The five steps to cost out production follow.

Step 1: Physical Flow Analysis The purpose of step 1 is to trace the physical units of production. As with the weighted average method, in the FIFO method, a

---

HOW TO Calculate Output and Cost Assignments: First-In, First-Out Method

CORNERSTONE 5-9

Information:
Production:

Units in process, July 1, 75 percent complete	20,000 gallons
Units completed and transferred out	50,000 gallons
Units in process, July 31, 25 percent complete	10,000 gallons

Costs:

Work in process, July 1	$ 3,525
Costs added during July	10,125

Required:
1. Calculate the output measure for July.
2. Assign costs to units transferred out and EWIP using the FIFO method.

Calculation:
1. Equivalent units:

Key: ▦ = 10,000 units completed

☐ = 10,000 units, 25% complete

Output for July:
60,000 total units ⟶ Become 37,500 equivalent units
BWIP: To be completed (20,000 × 25%):

**CORNERSTONE
5-9
(continued)**

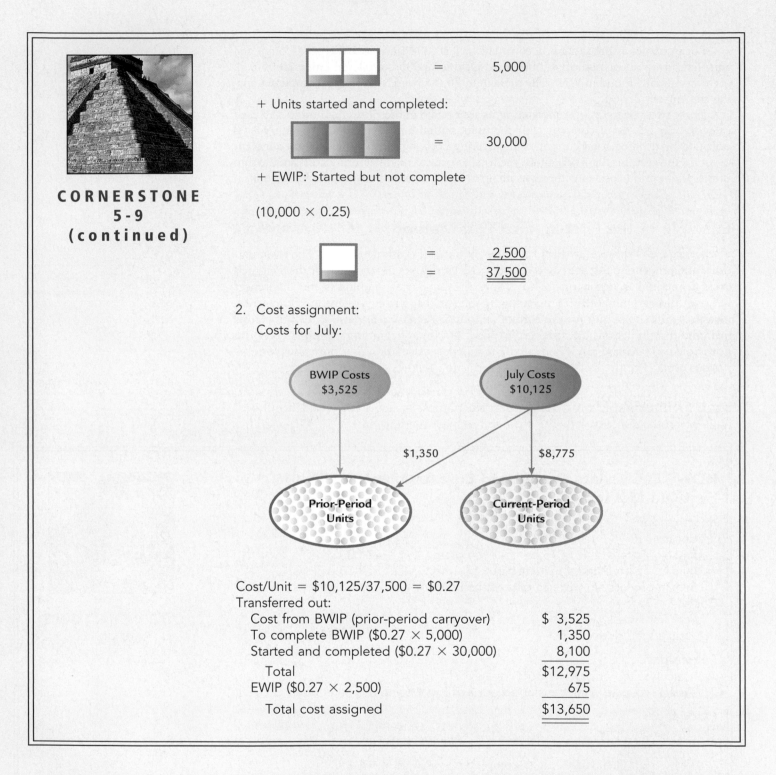

= 5,000

+ Units started and completed:

= 30,000

+ EWIP: Started but not complete

(10,000 × 0.25)

= $\underline{2,500}$
= $\underline{37,500}$

2. Cost assignment:
    Costs for July:

BWIP Costs
$3,525

July Costs
$10,125

$1,350

$8,775

**Prior-Period
Units**

**Current-Period
Units**

Cost/Unit = $10,125/37,500 = $0.27
Transferred out:

Cost from BWIP (prior-period carryover)	$ 3,525
To complete BWIP ($0.27 × 5,000)	1,350
Started and completed ($0.27 × 30,000)	8,100
Total	$12,975
EWIP ($0.27 × 2,500)	675
Total cost assigned	$13,650

physical flow schedule is prepared, as shown in Exhibit 5-5. This schedule is identical for both methods. (See Cornerstone 5-5 for details on how to prepare this schedule.)

Step 2: Calculation of Equivalent Units Cornerstone 5-9 illustrates the calculation of equivalent units under the FIFO method and is summarized following without the graphic detail:

Units started and completed	30,000
Add: Units in BWIP × Fraction to be completed (20,000 × 25 percent)	5,000
Add: Units in EWIP × Fraction complete (10,000 × 25 percent)	2,500
Equivalent units of output	37,500

Exhibit 5-5

Physical Flow Schedule

Units to account for:		
Units in beginning work in process (75 percent complete)		20,000
Units started during the period		40,000
Total units to account for		60,000
Units accounted for:		
Units completed:		
Started and completed	30,000	
From beginning work in process	20,000	50,000
Units in ending work in process (25 percent complete)		10,000
Total units accounted for		60,000

From the equivalent unit computation, one difference between weighted average and FIFO becomes immediately apparent. Under FIFO, the equivalent units in BWIP (work done in the prior period) are not counted as part of the total equivalent work. Only the equivalent work to be completed this period is counted. The equivalent work to be completed for the units from the prior period is computed by multiplying the number of units in BWIP by the percentage of work remaining. Since in this example the percentage of work done in the prior period is 75 percent, the percentage left to be completed this period is 25 percent, or an equivalent of 5,000 additional units of work.

The effect of excluding prior-period effort is to produce the current-period equivalent output. Recall that under the weighted average method, 52,500 equivalent units were computed for this month. Under FIFO, only 37,500 units are calculated for the same month. These 37,500 units represent current-period output. The difference, of course, is explained by the fact that the weighted average method rolls back and counts the 15,000 equivalent units of prior-period work (20,000 units BWIP × 75 percent) as belonging to this period.

Step 3: Computation of Unit Cost   The additional manufacturing costs incurred in the current period are $10,125. Thus, the current-period unit manufacturing cost is $10,125/37,500, or $0.27. Notice that the costs of beginning inventory are excluded from this calculation. Only current-period manufacturing costs are used.

Step 4: Valuation of Inventories   Cornerstone 5-9 shows FIFO values for EWIP and goods transferred out. Since all equivalent units in ending work in process are current-period units, the cost of EWIP is $0.27 × 2,500, or $675, the same value that the weighted average method would produce. However, when it comes to valuing goods transferred out, a significant difference emerges between the weighted average method and FIFO.

Under weighted average, the cost of goods transferred out is the unit cost multiplied by the units completed. Under FIFO, however, there are two sources of completed units: 20,000 units from beginning inventory and 30,000 units started and completed. The cost of the 30,000 units that were started and completed in the current period and transferred

Analytical Q&A

For August, there are 40,000 units in BWIP that are 30 percent complete and 20,000 units in EWIP that are 60 percent complete. There were 80,000 units started and completed. How many equivalent units were produced in August using the FIFO method?

Answer:

$Equivalent\ units = 80,000 + (0.70 \times 40,000) + (0.60 \times 20,000) = 120,000$

Concept Q&A

The FIFO cost per equivalent unit for July was $12. The BWIP had 25,000 units, 20 percent complete, with $50,000 of costs carried over from June. What is the total cost that these 25,000 units will contribute to the cost of goods transferred out?

Answer:

$($50,000) + ($12 \times 25,000 \times 0.8) = $290,000.$

out is $8,100 ($0.27 × 30,000). For these units, the use of the current-period unit cost is entirely appropriate. However, the cost of the BWIP units that were transferred out is another matter. These units started the period with $3,525 of manufacturing costs already incurred and 15,000 units of equivalent output already completed. To finish these units, the equivalent of 5,000 units were needed. The cost of finishing the units in BWIP is $1,350 ($0.27 × 5,000). Adding this $1,350 to the $3,525 in cost carried over from the prior period gives a total manufacturing cost for these units of $4,875. The unit cost of these 20,000 units, then, is about $0.244 ($4,875/20,000).

Step 5: Cost Reconciliation   The total costs assigned to production are as follows:

Goods transferred out:	
Units in BWIP	$ 4,875
Units started and completed	8,100
Goods in EWIP	675
Total costs accounted for	$13,650

The total manufacturing costs to account for during the period are:

BWIP	$ 3,525
Incurred during the period	10,125
Total costs to account for	$13,650

The costs assigned, thus, equal the costs to account for. With the completion of step 5, the production report can be prepared. Cornerstone 5-10 shows how to prepare this report for FIFO.

**CORNERSTONE
5-10**

HOW TO Prepare a Production Report: First-In, First-Out Method

Information: The five steps for the Healthblend Company.
Required: Prepare a production report for July 2008 (FIFO method).
Calculation:

**Healthblend Company
Picking Department
Production Report for July 2008
(FIFO Method)**

UNIT INFORMATION

Units to account for:		
Units in beginning work in process	20,000	
Units started during the period	40,000	
Total units to account for	60,000	

	Physical Flow	Equivalent Units
Units accounted for:		
Units started and completed	30,000	30,000
Units completed from beginning work in process	20,000	5,000
Units in ending work in process	10,000	2,500
Total units accounted for	60,000	37,500

COST INFORMATION			
Costs to account for:			
Beginning work in process	$ 3,525		
Incurred during the period	10,125		
Total costs to account for	$13,650		
Cost per equivalent unit	$ 0.27		

**CORNERSTONE
5-10
(continued)**

	Transferred Out	Ending Work in Process	Total
Costs accounted for:			
Units in beginning work in process:			
From prior period	$ 3,525	—	$ 3,525
From current period ($0.27 × 5,000)	1,350	—	1,350
Units started and completed			
($0.27 × 30,000)	8,100	—	8,100
Goods in ending work in process			
($0.27 × 2,500)	—	$675	675
Total costs accounted for	$12,975	$675	$13,650

Appendix: Summary of Learning Objective

- **(Appendix) Prepare a departmental production report using the FIFO method.** A production report prepared according to the FIFO method separates the cost of BWIP from the cost of the current period. BWIP is assumed to be completed and transferred out first. Costs from BWIP are not pooled with the current period costs in computing unit cost. Additionally, equivalent units of production exclude work done in the prior period. When calculating the cost of goods transferred out, the prior period costs are added to the costs of completing the units in BWIP, and then these costs are added to the costs of units started and completed.

Cornerstone 5-9   How to calculate output and cost assignments: First-in, first-out method, page 209

Cornerstone 5-10   How to prepare a production report: First-in, first-out method, page 212

**CORNERSTONES
FOR APPENDIX TO
CHAPTER 5**

Review Problems

I. Process Costing

Springville Company, which uses the weighted average method, produces a product that passes through two departments: blending and cooking. In the blending department, all materials are added at the beginning of the process. All other manufacturing inputs are added uniformly. The following information pertains to the mixing department for February:

a.   BWIP, May 1: 100,000 pounds, 40 percent complete with respect to conversion costs. The costs assigned to this work are as follows:

Materials	$20,000
Labor	10,000
Overhead	30,000

b.   EWIP, May 31: 50,000 pounds, 60 percent complete with respect to conversion costs.
c.   Units completed and transferred out: 370,000 pounds. The following costs were added during the month:

Materials	$211,000
Labor	100,000
Overhead	270,000

Required:
1.   Prepare a physical flow schedule.
2.   Prepare a schedule of equivalent units.
3.   Compute the cost per equivalent unit.
4.   Compute the cost of goods transferred out and the cost of EWIP.
5.   Prepare a cost reconciliation.

Solution:
1.   Physical flow schedule:

Units to account for:		
Units in BWIP	100,000	
Units started	320,000	
Total units to account for	420,000	
Units accounted for:		
Units completed and transferred out:		
Started and completed	270,000	
From BWIP	100,000	370,000
Units in EWIP		50,000

2.   Schedule of equivalent units:

	Materials	Conversion
Units completed	370,000	370,000
Units in EWIP × Fraction complete:		
Materials (50,000 × 100%)	50,000	—
Conversion (50,000 × 60%)	—	30,000
Equivalent units of output	420,000	400,000

3.   Cost per equivalent unit:

Materials unit cost = ($20,000 + $211,000)/420,000 = $0.550
Conversion unit cost = ($40,000 + $370,000)/400,000 = $1.025
Total unit cost = $1.575 per equivalent unit

4.   Cost of goods transferred out and cost of EWIP:

Cost of goods transferred out = $1.575 × 370,000
                            = $582,750

Cost of EWIP = ($0.550 × 50,000) + ($1.025 × 30,000)
            = $58,250

5. Cost reconciliation:

Costs to account for:		
BWIP		$ 60,000
Incurred during the period		581,000
Total costs to account for		$641,000
Costs accounted for:		
Goods transferred out		$582,750
WIP		58,250
Total costs accounted for		$641,000

II.   Process Costing

Now suppose that Springville Company uses the FIFO method for inventory valuations. Springville produces a product that passes through two departments: blending and cooking. In the blending department, all materials are added at the beginning of the process. All other manufacturing inputs are added uniformly. The following information pertains to the mixing department for February:

a.   BWIP, February 1: 100,000 pounds, 40 percent complete with respect to conversion costs. The costs assigned to this work are as follows:

Materials	$20,000
Labor	10,000
Overhead	30,000

b.   EWIP, February 28: 50,000 pounds, 60 percent complete with respect to conversion costs.

c.   Units completed and transferred out: 370,000 pounds. The following costs were added during the month:

Materials	$211,000
Labor	100,000
Overhead	270,000

Required:
1. Prepare a physical flow schedule.
2. Prepare a schedule of equivalent units.
3. Compute the cost per equivalent unit.
4. Compute the cost of goods transferred out and the cost of EWIP.

Solution:
1. Physical flow schedule:

Units to account for:		
Units in BWIP	100,000	
Units started	320,000	
Total units to account for	420,000	
Units accounted for:		
Units completed and transferred out:		
Started and completed	270,000	
From BWIP	100,000	370,000
Units in EWIP		50,000

2. Schedule of equivalent units:

	Direct Materials	Conversion Costs
Units started and completed	270,000	270,000
Units, BWIP × Percentage complete:	—	60,000
Units, EWIP × Percentage complete:		
Direct materials (50,000 × 100%)	50,000	—
Conversion costs (50,000 × 60%)	—	30,000
Equivalent units of output	320,000	360,000

OBJECTIVE ③
CORNERSTONE 5-4

Exercise 5-27 Weighted Average Method, Unit Costs, Valuing Inventories

Orley Inc. produces a product that passes through two processes. During February, equivalent units were calculated using the weighted average method:

Units completed	60,000
Add: Units in EWIP × Fraction complete: 20,000 × 40 percent	8,000
Equivalent units of output (weighted average)	68,000
Less: Units in BWIP × Fraction complete: 10,000 × 70 percent	7,000
Equivalent units of output (FIFO)	61,000

The costs that Orley had to account for during the month of February were as follows:

BWIP	$ 42,000
Costs added	397,200
Total	$439,200

Required:

1. Using the weighted average method, calculate unit cost. Round to two decimal places.
2. Under the weighted average method, what is the total cost of units transferred out? What is the cost assigned to units in ending inventory?

OBJECTIVE ③
CORNERSTONE 5-5

spreadsheet

Exercise 5-28 Physical Flow Schedule

The following information was obtained for the first department of LPZ Company for April:

a. BWIP had 30,500 units, 30 percent complete with respect to manufacturing costs.
b. EWIP had 8,400 units, 25 percent complete with respect to manufacturing costs.
c. LPZ started 33,000 units in April.

Required:
Prepare a physical flow schedule.

OBJECTIVE ③
CORNERSTONE 5-5

Exercise 5-29 Physical Flow, Weighted Average Method

Nelrok Company manufactures fertilizer. Department 1 mixes the chemicals required for the fertilizer. The following data are for the year:

BWIP (40 percent complete)	25,000
Units started	142,500
Units in EWIP (60 percent complete)	35,000

Required:
Prepare a physical flow schedule.

OBJECTIVE ③
CORNERSTONE 5-6

Exercise 5-30 Production Report, Weighted Average

Mino Inc. manufactures chocolate syrup in three departments: cooking, mixing, and bottling. Mino uses the weighted average method. The following are cost and production data for the cooking department for April (assume that units are measured in gallons):

Production:	
Units in process, April 1, 60 percent complete	20,000
Units completed and transferred out	50,000
Units in process, April 30, 20 percent complete	10,000
Costs:	
WIP, April 1	$ 93,600
Costs added during April	314,600

Required:
Prepare a production report for the cooking department.

Exercise 5-31 Nonuniform Inputs, Equivalent Units

OBJECTIVE ④

CORNERSTONE 5-7

Terry Linens Inc. manufactures bed and bath linens. The bath linens department sews terry cloth into towels of various sizes. Terry uses the weighted average method. All materials are added at the beginning of the process. The following data are for the bath linens department for August:

Production:
Units in process, August 1, 25 percent complete*   10,000
Units completed and transferred out   60,000
Units in process, August 31, 60 percent complete*   20,000
*With respect to conversion costs.

Required:
Calculate equivalent units of production for the bath linens department for August.

Exercise 5-32 Unit Cost and Cost Assignment, Nonuniform Inputs

OBJECTIVE ④

CORNERSTONE 5-7

Millard Inc. had the following equivalent units schedule and cost for its fabrication department during the month of September:

	Materials	Conversion
Units completed	120,000	120,000
Add: Units in ending WIP × Fraction complete (40,000 × 60%)	40,000	24,000
Equivalent units of output	160,000	144,000
Costs:		
Work in process, September 1:		
Materials	$ 98,000	
Conversion costs	5,250	
Total	$103,250	
Current costs:		
Materials	$702,000	
Conversion costs	157,470	
Total	$859,470	

Required:
1. Calculate the unit cost for materials, for conversion, and in total for the fabrication department for September.
2. Calculate the cost of units transferred out and the cost of EWIP.

Exercise 5-33 Nonuniform Inputs, Transferred-In Cost

OBJECTIVE ④

CORNERSTONE 5-8

Drysdale Dairy produces a variety of dairy products. In Department 12, cream (transferred in from Department 6) and other materials (sugar and flavorings) are mixed and churned to make ice cream. The following data are for Department 12 for August:

Production:
Units in process, August 1, 25 percent complete*   40,000
Units completed and transferred out   120,000
Units in process, August 31, 60 percent complete*   30,000
*With respect to conversion costs.

Required:
1. Prepare a physical flow schedule for the month.
2. Calculate equivalent units for the following categories: transferred-in, materials, and conversion.

OBJECTIVE ④

CORNERSTONE 5-8

Exercise 5-34 Transferred-In Cost

Golding's finishing department had the following data for the month of July:

	Transferred-In	Materials	Conversion
Units transferred out	60,000	60,000	60,000
Units in EWIP	15,000	15,000	9,000
Equivalent units	75,000	75,000	69,000

Costs:	
Work in process, July 1:	
Transferred-in from fabricating	$2,100
Materials	1,500
Conversion costs	3,000
Total	$6,600

Current costs:	
Transferred-in from fabricating	$30,900
Materials	22,500
Conversion costs	45,300
Total	$98,700

Required:
1. Calculate unit costs for the following categories: transferred-in, materials, and conversion.
2. Calculate total unit cost.

OBJECTIVE ⑤

CORNERSTONE 5-9

Exercise 5-35 (Appendix) First-In, First-Out Method; Equivalent Units

Lawson Company produces a product where all manufacturing inputs are applied uniformly. The company produced the following physical flow schedule for March:

Units to account for:	
Units in BWIP (40 percent complete)	15,000
Units started	35,000
Total units to account for	50,000

Units accounted for:	
Units completed:	
From BWIP	10,000
Started and completed	32,000
	42,000
Units, EWIP (75 percent complete)	8,000
Total units accounted for	50,000

Required:
Prepare a schedule of equivalent units using the FIFO method.

OBJECTIVE ⑤

CORNERSTONE 5-9

Exercise 5-36 (Appendix) First-In, First-Out Method; Unit Cost; Valuing Inventories

Loren Inc. manufactures products that pass through two or more processes. During April, equivalent units were computed using the FIFO method:

Units started and completed	4,600
Units in BWIP × Fraction to complete (60 percent)	840
Units in EWIP × Fraction complete:	
4,000 × 60 percent	2,400
Equivalent units of output (FIFO)	7,840

April's costs to account for are as follows:	
BWIP (40 percent complete)	$ 1,120
Materials	10,000
Conversion cost	4,000
Total	$15,120

Required:

1. Calculate the unit cost for April using the FIFO method. Round to two decimal places.
2. Using the FIFO method, determine the cost of EWIP and the cost of the goods transferred out.

Problems

Problem 5-37 Basic Flows, Equivalent Units

OBJECTIVES ① ②

Lapp Company produces a pain medication that passes through two departments: mixing and tableting. Lapp uses the weighted average method. Data for November for mixing is as follows: BWIP was zero; EWIP had 600 units, 50 percent complete; and 7,000 units were started.

Tableting's data for November is as follows: BWIP was 400 units, 20 percent complete; and 200 units were in EWIP, 40 percent complete.

Required:

1. For mixing, calculate the following:
    a. Number of units transferred to tableting.
    b. Equivalent units of production.
2. For tableting, calculate the number of units transferred out to Finished Goods.
3. Suppose that the units in the mixing department are measured in ounces, while the units in tableting are measured in bottles of 100 tablets, with a total weight of eight ounces (excluding the bottle). Decide how you would treat units that are measured differently, and then repeat Requirement 2 using this approach.

Problem 5-38 Steps in Preparing a Cost of Production Report

OBJECTIVES ① ② ③ ④

Stillwater Designs is expanding its market by becoming an original equipment supplier to DaimlerChrysler. DaimlerChrysler will offer a higher-end Kicker audio package for its Dodge Neon SRT4 line. As part of this effort, Stillwater Designs will produce the plastic cabinet prototypes that will house the Kicker speakers and amplifiers. After producing the prototype cabinets, their production will be outsourced. However, assembly will remain in-house. Stillwater Designs will assemble the product by placing the speakers and amplifiers (produced according to specifications by outside manufacturers) in the plastic cabinets. Plastic cabinets and Kicker speaker and amplifier components are added at the beginning of the assembly process.

Assume that Stillwater Designs uses the weighted average method to cost out the audio package. The following are cost and production data for the assembly process for April:

Production:	
Units in process, April 1, 60 percent complete	40,000
Units completed and transferred out	100,000
Units in process, April 30, 20 percent complete	20,000
Costs:	
WIP, April 1:	
Plastic cabinets	$ 800,000
Kicker components	8,400,000
Conversion costs	3,600,000
Costs added during April:	
Plastic cabinets	$ 1,600,000
Kicker components	16,800,000
Conversion costs	5,760,000

Required:

1. Prepare a physical flow analysis for the assembly department for the month of April.
2. Calculate equivalent units of production for the assembly department for the month of April.
3. Calculate unit cost for the assembly department for the month of April.
4. Calculate the cost of units transferred out and the cost of EWIP inventory.
5. Prepare a cost reconciliation for the assembly department for the month of April.

OBJECTIVES ① ③   **Problem 5-39 Steps for a Cost of Production Report**

The owner of Stillwater Designs was pleased with the prospect of becoming an original equipment supplier to DaimlerChrysler. Stillwater designs will provide an audio package for the Dodge Neon SRT4 line. Assembling the plastic cabinets, speakers, and amplifiers for this audio package will be done in-house.

Assume that Stillwater Designs uses the weighted average method to cost out the audio package. The following are cost and production data for the assembly process for April:

Production:	
Units in process, April 1, 60 percent complete	40,000
Units completed and transferred out	100,000
Units in process, April 30, 20 percent complete	20,000

Costs:	
WIP, April 1:	
Plastic cabinets	$ 800,000
Kicker components	8,400,000
Conversion costs	3,600,000
Costs added during April:	
Plastic cabinets	$ 1,600,000
Kicker components	16,800,000
Conversion costs	5,760,000

Required:

1. Prepare a cost of production report for the assembly department for the month of April.
2. Write a one-page report that compares the purpose and content of the cost of production report with the job-order cost sheet.

OBJECTIVES ① ② ③ ④   **Problem 5-40 Equivalent Units, Unit Cost, Weighted Average**

Fino Linens Inc. manufactures bed and bath linens. The bath linens department sews terry cloth into towels of various sizes. Fino uses the weighted average method. All materials are added at the beginning of the process. The following data are for the bath linens department for August:

Production:	
Units in process, August 1, 60 percent complete	20,000
Units completed and transferred out	60,000
Units in process, August 31, 60 percent complete	20,000

Costs:	
WIP, August 1	$11,520
Current costs	72,000
Total	$83,520

Required:

1. Prepare a physical flow analysis for the bath linens department for August.
2. Calculate equivalent units of production for the bath linens department for August.
3. Calculate the unit cost for the bath linens department for August.

4. Show that the cost per unit calculated in Requirement 3 is a weighted average of the cost per equivalent unit in BWIP and the current (FIFO) cost per equivalent unit. (*Hint:* The weights are in proportion to the number of units from each source.)

Problem 5-41 Cost of Production Report

OBJECTIVE ③

spreadsheet

The owner of Fino Linens Inc., a manufacturer of bed and bath linens, insisted on a formal report that provided all the details of the weighted average method. In the manufacturing process, all materials are added at the beginning. The following data are for the bath linens department for August:

Production:
Units in process, August 1, 60 percent complete	20,000
Units completed and transferred out	60,000
Units in process, August 31, 60 percent complete	20,000

Costs:
WIP, August 1	$11,520
Current costs	72,000
Total	$83,520

Required:
Prepare a cost of production report for the bath linens department for August using the weighted average method.

Problem 5-42 Weighted Average Method, Physical Flow, Equivalent Units, Unit Costs, Cost Assignment

OBJECTIVES ① ② ③

Yomasca Inc. manufactures various Halloween masks. Each mask is shaped from a piece of rubber in the molding department. The masks are then transferred to the finishing department, where they are painted and have elastic bands attached. Yomasca uses the weighted average method. In April, the molding department reported the following data:

a. BWIP consisted of 6,000 units, 20 percent complete. Cost in beginning inventory totaled $552.
b. Costs added to production during the month were $8,698.
c. At the end of the month, 18,000 units were transferred out to finishing. Then, 2,000 units remained in EWIP, 25 percent complete.

Required:
1. Prepare a physical flow schedule.
2. Calculate equivalent units of production.
3. Compute unit cost.
4. Calculate the cost of goods transferred to finishing at the end of the month. Calculate the cost of ending inventory.
5. Assume that the masks are inspected at the end of the molding process. Of the 18,000 units inspected, 1,000 are rejected as faulty and are discarded. Thus, only 17,000 units are transferred to the finishing department. The manager of Yomasca considers all such spoilage as abnormal and does not want to assign any of this cost to the 17,000 good units produced and transferred to finishing. Your task is to determine the cost of this spoilage of 1,000 units and then to discuss how you would account for this spoilage cost. Now suppose that the manager feels that this spoilage cost is just part of the cost of producing the good units transferred out. Therefore, he wants to assign this cost to the good production. Explain how this would be handled. (*Hint:* Spoiled units are a type of output, and equivalent units of spoilage can be calculated.)

6

Activity-Based Costing and Management

© COLD STONE CREAMERY

After studying Chapter 6, you should be able to:

1. Explain why functional (or volume)-based costing approaches may produce distorted costs.

2. Explain how an activity-based costing system works for product costing.

3. Describe activity-based customer costing and activity-based supplier costing.

4. Explain how activity-based management can be used for cost reduction.

Experience Managerial Decisions
with Cold Stone Creamery

Experts believe that ice cream as we currently know it was invented in the 1600s and was popularized in part by Charles I of England as he made it a staple of the royal table. Ice cream remains as popular as ever today. However, trips to the local ice cream parlor have changed dramatically over the past quarter century. Cold Stone Creamery, founded in 1988 in Tempe, Arizona, has helped to lead this change with its innovative new business model focused on making the ice cream trip an entertainment experience for the entire family. Cold Stone operates 1,400 stores worldwide, with another 1,000 franchises in the works. Cold Stone executives must understand and control the company's complex cost structure in order to profitably manage its ice cream empire. For example, its most popular product line-ice cream with "mix in" ingredients-boasts 16 basic ice cream flavors with 30 different ingredients and three sizes, which represents a total of over 1,400 possible ice cream product options! These impressively numerous selection opportunities are great for customers with varied tastes but are quite challenging for Cold Stone to manage given the different types of activities associated with different types of product orders. Therefore, Cold Stone adopted ABC first to identify the activity drivers associated with each type of ice cream order and then to estimate the costs of these activities.

Two important drivers of costs for Cold Stone include ingredients and time, both of which vary significantly across different ice cream product orders. With the insights gained from its ABC analysis, Cold Stone understands the cost of various orders' preparation time, which is measured in seconds. In addition to labor, Cold Stone's ABC system considers the costs associated with training, uniforms, and employee benefits when estimating the cost of each second required in making each product. When combined with other costs, the ABC analysis provides an estimate of profit margin by product type. If a particular product is not making its expected margin, Cold Stone managers know to look at the activities involved in creating the product and to fine-tune that activity. Understanding its complex cost structure provides Cold Stone managers with a significant challenge. However, it is the mastery of this costing challenge that has provided Cold Stone with a valuable competitive advantage to become one of the most profitable and fastest-growing franchises in America.

OBJECTIVE ①
Explain why functional-based costing approaches may produce distorted costs.

Limitations of Functional-Based Cost Accounting Systems

Plantwide and departmental rates based on direct labor hours, machine hours, or other volume-based measures have been used for decades to assign overhead costs to products and continue to be used successfully by many organizations. However, for many settings, this approach to costing is equivalent to an averaging approach and may produce distorted or inaccurate costs. Distorted costs can be a real problem in extremely competitive environments like the automobile industry, where, in 2007, **General Motors** for the first time in 76 years lost its spot as the world's largest automaker as a result of unrelenting competition from an increasing number of competitors like **Toyota**. To understand why average costing can cause difficulties, consider the case where two individuals go out for dinner. One orders steak and lobster, costing $40, and the other orders a chef salad, costing $10. Thus, the total cost of the food is $50. If the bill is split evenly between the two, each individual would pay $25. The $25 would be the average cost of the meals, but it doesn't represent well the actual cost of each meal. One meal is overstated by $15, and the other is understated by $15. If it is important to know the cost of each meal (e.g., so that the one ordering steak and lobster can be reimbursed by his company), then the averaging approach will not be suitable.

In the same way, plantwide and departmental rates can produce average costs that severely under- or overstate individual product costs. Product cost distortions can be damaging, particularly for those firms whose business environment is characterized by intense or increasing competitive pressures (often on a worldwide level), small profit margins, continuous improvement, total quality management, total customer satisfaction, and sophisticated technology. Firms operating in theses types of business environments in particular need accurate cost information in order to make effective decisions. In order for accurate cost information to be produced, it is important that the firm's cost system accurately reflects the firm's underlying business, or economic, reality. However, as firms operating in an intensely competitive environment (or the other environments mentioned above) adopt new strategies to achieve competitive excellence, their cost accounting systems often must change to keep pace. Unfortunately, due to the time commitment and costs required to change cost systems, some firms do not change their systems when their business environment changes. Cost distortions subsequently result due to the poor matching between the firm's actual business reality and the cost system's representation of that reality. Thus, it is important that the managerial accountant continually asks the following question, "How well does the cost system's *representation* of my business match the economic *reality* of my business?" If the answer is, "not very well," then it is likely that the cost system needs to be changed. Therefore, in much the same way that financial statements must be transparent for external users, the cost system must be transparent in its assignment of costs for internal users.

The need for more accurate product costs has forced many companies to take a serious look at their costing procedures. At least two major factors impair the ability of unit-based plantwide and departmental rates to assign overhead costs accurately: (1) the proportion of nonunit-related overhead costs to total overhead costs is large, and (2) the degree of product diversity is great.

Nonunit-Related Overhead Costs

The use of either plantwide rates or departmental rates assumes that a product's consumption of overhead resources is related strictly to the units produced. For **unit-level activities**—activities that are performed each time a unit is produced—this assumption makes sense. Traditional, volume-based cost systems label the costs associated with these activities as variable in nature, because they increase or decrease in direct proportion to increases or decreases in the levels of these unit-level activities.

All other costs (i.e., ones that are not unit-level) are considered fixed by volume-based cost systems.

But what if there are *nonunit-level activities*—activities that are not performed each time a unit of product is produced? The costs associated with these nonunit-level activities are unlikely to vary (i.e., increase or decrease) with units produced. However, sometimes these costs vary with some other factor(s), besides units, and identifying such factor(s) is very helpful in predicting and managing these costs. Proponents of **activity-based costing (ABC)** refer to the ABC cost hierarchy that categorizes costs either as *unit-level* (i.e., vary with output volume), *batch-level* (i.e., vary with the number of groups or batches that are run), *product-sustaining* (i.e., vary with the diversity of the product or service line), or *facility-sustaining* (i.e., do not vary with any factor but are necessary in operating the plant).[1] Exhibit 6-1 shows the ABC hierarchy. ABC is discussed in detail later in this chapter, but the ABC cost hierarchy is identified at this point to illustrate its usefulness in helping managers realize that certain costs associated with nonunit-level activities are driven by other factors.

Consider the following two examples of nonunit-level activities: setting up equipment and reengineering products. Often, the same equipment is used to produce different products. Setting up equipment means to prepare it for the particular type of product being made. For example, a vat may be used to dye T-shirts. After completing a batch of 1,000 red T-shirts, the vat must be carefully cleaned before a batch of 3,000 green T-shirts is produced. Thus, setup costs are incurred each time a batch of products is produced. A batch may consist of 1,000 or 3,000 units, and the cost of setup is the same. Yet, as more setups are done, setup costs increase. The number of setups (a batch-level cost), not the number of units produced (a unit-level cost), is a much better measure of the consumption of the setup activity.

At times, based on customer feedback, firms face the necessity of redesigning their products. This product reengineering activity is authorized by a document called an *engineering work order*. For example, **Rio Novo**, a Brazilian appliance manufacturer, may issue engineering work orders to correct design flaws of its refrigerators, freezers, and washers. Product reengineering costs may depend on the number of different engineering work

---

Exhibit 6-1

ABC Heirarchy

Type of Cost	Description of Cost Driver	Example
Unit level	Varies with output volume (eg., unites); traditional variable costs	Cost of indirect materials for labeling each bottle of **Victoria's Secret** perfume
Batch-level	Varies with the number of batches produced	Cost of setting up laser engraving equipment for each batch of **Epilog** key chains
product-sustaining	Varies with the number of product lines	Cost of inventory handling and warranty servicing of different brands carried by **Best Buy** electronics store
Facility-sustaining	Necessary to operate the plant facility but does not vary with units, batches, or product lines	Cost of General Motors plant manager salary

---

[1]Robin Cooper, Cost Classification in Unit-Based and Activity-Based Manufacturing Cost Systems, *Journal of Cost Management*, 1990.

orders (a product-sustaining cost) rather than the units produced of any given product. Thus, *nonunit-level drivers* such as setups and engineering orders are needed for accurate cost assignment of nonunit-level activities. Also, **JetBlue**'s decision to add a second type of jet, the Embraer 190, to its existing fleet of Airbus A320s caused it to incur significant additional product-sustaining costs that it would not have incurred had it stayed with only one type of jet. These additional product-sustaining costs included the costs for doubling the spare parts inventory, maintenance programs, and separate pilot-training tracks.[2] Therefore, **nonunit-level activity drivers** (i.e., batch, product-sustaining, and facility-sustaining) are factors that measure the consumption of non-unit-level activities by products and other cost objects, whereas **unit-level activity drivers** measure the consumption of unit-level activities. **Activity drivers**, then, are factors that measure the consumption of activities by products and other cost objects and can be classified as either *unit-level* or *nonunit-level*.

Using only unit-based activity drivers to assign nonunit-related overhead costs can create distorted product costs. The severity of this distortion depends on what proportion of total overhead costs these nonunit-based costs represent. For many companies, this percentage can be significant. This possibility suggests that some care should be exercised in assigning nonunit-based overhead costs. If nonunit-based overhead costs are only a small percentage of total overhead costs, then the distortion of product costs will be quite small. In such a case, using unit-based activity drivers to assign overhead costs is acceptable.

Concept Q&A

One department inspects each product produced. A second department inspects a small sample of each batch of products produced. Which inspection activity is unit-level, and which is nonunit-level?

Answer:

A unit-level activity is performed each time a unit is produced, whereas a nonunit-level activity is performed at times that do not correspond to individual unit production. Thus, inspection is unit-level for the first department and nonunit-level for the second department.

Product Diversity

The presence of significant nonunit overhead costs is a necessary but not sufficient condition for plantwide and departmental rate failure (i.e., distorted costs). For example, if products consume the nonunit-level overhead activities in the same proportion as the unit-level overhead activities, then no product-costing distortion will occur (with the use of traditional overhead assignment methods). The presence of product diversity is also necessary for product cost distortion to occur. **Product diversity** means that products consume overhead activities in systematically different proportions, and this may occur for several reasons. For example, differences in product size, product complexity, setup time, and size of batches all can cause products to consume overhead at different rates. Regardless of the nature of the product diversity, product cost will be distorted whenever the quantity of unit-based overhead that a product consumes does not vary in direct proportion to the quantity consumed of nonunit-based overhead. The proportion of each activity consumed by a product is defined as the **consumption ratio**. How nonunit-level overhead costs and product diversity can produce distorted product costs is discussed next.

Illustrating the Failure of Unit-Based Overhead Rates

To illustrate how traditional unit-based overhead rates can distort product costs, we will provide detailed information for Rio Novo's Porto Belho plant. The Porto Belho plant produces two models of washers: a deluxe and a regular model. The detailed data are provided in Exhibit 6-2 (assume that the measures are expected and actual outcomes). Because the quantity of regular models produced is 10 times greater than that of the deluxe, we can label the regular model a high-volume product and the deluxe model a low-volume product. The models are produced in batches.

[2]S. Carey, "Balancing Act: Amid JetBlue's Rapid Ascent, CEO Adopts Big Rivals' Traits," *The Wall Street Journal* (August 25, 2005): A1-A6.

> **Exhibit 6-2**

Product-Costing Data

	Deluxe	Regular	Total
		Activity Usage Measures	
Units produced	10	100	110
Prime costs	$800	$8,000	$8,800
Direct labor hours	20	80	100
Machine hours	10	40	50
Setup hours	3	1	4
Number of moves	6	4	10

Activity Cost Data (Overhead Activities)	
Activity	**Activity Cost**
Setting up equipment	$1,200
Moving goods	800
Machining	1,500
Assembly	500
Total	$4,000

Remember that prime costs represent direct materials and direct labor. Given that these costs are direct in nature, they can be traced to each product line cost object. It is the indirect, or overhead, costs that typically are treated differently by different types of cost systems. Usually, activity-based cost systems generate more accurate cost data than unit-based cost systems because of their more appropriate treatment of overhead costs. For simplicity, only four types of overhead activities, performed by four distinct support departments, are assumed: setting up the equipment for each batch (different configurations are needed for the electronic components associated with each model), moving a batch, machining, and assembly. Assembly is performed after each department's operations.

Problems with Costing Accuracy   The activity usage data in Exhibit 6-2 reveal some serious problems with either plantwide or departmental rates for assigning overhead costs. The main problem with either procedure is the assumption that unit-level drivers such as machine hours or direct labor hours drive or cause all overhead costs.

From Exhibit 6-2, it can be seen that regular models, the high-volume product, use four times as many direct labor hours as deluxe models, the low-volume product (80 hours vs. 20 hours). Thus, if a plantwide rate is used, the regular models will be assigned four times more overhead cost than the deluxe models. But is this reasonable? Do unit-based drivers explain the consumption of all overhead activities? In particular, is it reasonable to assume that each product's consumption of overhead increases in direct proportion to the direct labor hours used? Now consider the four overhead activities to see if the unit-level drivers accurately reflect the demands of regular and deluxe model production.

Examination of the data in Exhibit 6-2 suggests that a significant portion of overhead costs is not driven or caused by direct labor hours. Each product's demands for setup and

Analytical Q&A

The activity driver for the receiving activity is number of orders processed. Product A uses 10 orders, and Product B uses 30 orders. Calculate the consumption ratios for Product A and Product B.

Answer:
Product A = 10/40 = 0.25; Product B = 30/40 = 0.75.

material-moving activities are more logically related to the setup hours and the number of moves, respectively. These nonunit activities represent 50 percent ($2,000/ $4,000) of the total overhead costs—a significant percentage. Notice that the low-volume product, deluxe models, uses three times more setup hours than the regular models (3/1) and one and a half as many moves (6/4). However, using a plantwide rate based on direct labor hours, a unit-based activity driver, assigns four times more setup and material-moving costs to the regular models than to the deluxe. Thus, product diversity exists, and we should expect product cost distortion because the quantity of unit-based overhead that each product consumes does not vary in direct proportion to the quantity of nonunit-based overhead that each product consumes.

Cornerstone 6-1 illustrates how to calculate the consumption ratios for the two products. Consumption ratios represent the proportion of each activity consumed by a product. The consumption ratios suggest that a plantwide rate based on direct labor hours will overcost the regular models and undercost the deluxe models.

Solving the Problem of Cost Distortion   The cost distortion just described can be solved by the use of activity rates. That is, rather than assigning the overhead costs by using a single, plantwide rate, why not calculate a rate for each overhead activity and then use these activity rates to assign overhead costs? Cornerstone 6-2 shows how to calculate these rates.

To assign overhead costs, the amount of activity consumed by each product is needed along with the activity rates. Cornerstone 6-3 shows how to calculate the unit cost for each product by using activity rates. A visual summary is provided in Exhibit 6-3 on page 244.

Analytical Q&A

Inspecting provides 4,000 inspection hours and costs $80,000 per year. What is the activity rate for inspecting?

Answer:

Rate = $80,000/4,000 inspection hours = $20 per inspection hour.

Comparison of Functional-Based and Activity-Based Product Costs

A plantwide rate based on direct labor hours is calculated by dividing the total overhead costs by the total direct labor hours: $4,000/100 = $40 per direct labor hour. The

CORNERSTONE
6 - 1

HOW TO Calculate Consumption Ratios

Information: Activity usage information, Exhibit 6-2.

Required: Calculate the consumption ratios for each product.

Calculation: First, we must identify the activity driver for each activity. Next, divide the amount of driver used for each product by the total driver quantity. We obtain the following:

	Consumption Ratios		
Overhead Activity	**Deluxe Model**	**Regular Model**	**Activity Driver**
Setting up equipment	0.75[a]	0.25[a]	Setup hours
Moving goods	0.60[b]	0.40[b]	Number of moves
Machining	0.20[c]	0.80[c]	Machine hours
Assembly	0.20[d]	0.80[d]	Direct labor hours

[a]3/4 (deluxe) and 1/4 (regular).
[b]6/10 (deluxe) and 4/10 (regular).
[c]10/50 (deluxe) and 40/50 (regular).
[d]20/100 (deluxe) and 80/100 (regular).

HOW TO Calculate Activity Rates

Information: (from Exhibit 6-2)

Activity	Activity Cost ($)	Driver	Driver Quantity
Setting up equipment	1,200	Setup hours	4
Moving goods	800	Number of moves	10
Machining	1,500	Machine hours	50
Assembly	500	Direct labor hours	100

Required: Calculate activity rates.

Calculation: The rates are obtained by dividing the activity cost by the total driver quantity:

Setup rate	$1,200/4 setup hours = $300 per setup hour
Materials handling rate	$800/10 moves = $80 per move
Machining rate	$1,500/50 machine hours = $30 per machine hour
Assembly rate	$500/100 direct labor hours = $5.00 per direct labor hour

CORNERSTONE 6-2

HOW TO Calculate Activity-Based Unit Costs

Information:

	Deluxe	Regular	Activity Rate ($)
Units produced per year	10	100	
Prime costs	$800	$8,000	
Setup hours	3	1	300
Number of moves	6	4	80
Machine hours	10	40	30
Direct labor hours	20	80	5

Required: Calculate the unit cost for deluxe and regular models.

Calculation:

	Deluxe	Regular
Prime costs	$ 800	$ 8,000
Overhead costs:		
Setups:		
$300 × 3	900	
$300 × 1		300
Moving materials:		
$80 × 6	480	
$80 × 4		320
Machining:		
$30 × 10	300	
$30 × 40		1,200
Assembly:		
$5 × 20	100	
$5 × 80	—	400
Total manufacturing costs	$2,580	$10,220
Units produced	÷ 10	÷ 100
Unit cost (Total costs/Units)	$ 258	$102.20

CORNERSTONE 6-3

Exhibit 6-3

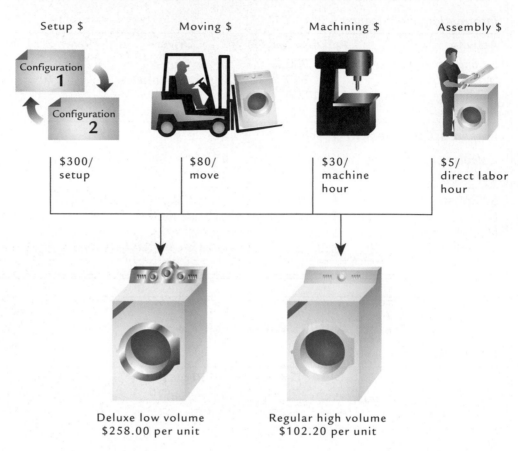

Visual Summary of Cornerstones 6-2 and 6-3

Setup $	Moving $	Machining $	Assembly $
$300/ setup	$80/ move	$30/ machine hour	$5/ direct labor hour

Deluxe low volume
$258.00 per unit

Regular high volume
$102.20 per unit

product cost for each product using this single unit-level overhead rate is calculated as follows:

	Deluxe	Regular
Prime costs	$ 800	$ 8,000
Overhead costs:		
$40 × 20	800	
$40 × 80		3,200
Total cost	$1,600	$11,200
Units produced	÷ 10	÷ 100
Unit cost	$ 160	$ 112

Now compare these product costs with the activity-based cost of Cornerstone 6-3. This comparison clearly illustrates the effects of using only unit-based activity drivers to assign overhead costs. The activity-based cost assignment reflects the pattern of overhead consumption and is, therefore, the most accurate. Activity-based product costing reveals that functional-based costing undercosts the low-volume deluxe models and overcosts the high-volume regular models. In fact, the ABC assignment increases the reported cost of the deluxe models by $98 per unit and decreases the reported cost of the regular models by almost $10 per unit—a movement in the right direction given the pattern of overhead consumption. In a diverse

Analytical Q&A

Producing 5,000 units of a DVD player requires $150,000 of prime costs, uses 1,000 machine hours, and takes 600 setup hours. The activity rates are $20 per machine hour and $50 per setup hour. What is the unit cost of a DVD player?

Answer:
Unit cost = [$150,000 + ($20 × 1,000) + ($50 × 600)]/5,000 = $40.

product environment, ABC promises greater accuracy, and given the importance of making decisions based on accurate facts, a detailed look at ABC is certainly merited.

Ethics One of the ethical standards of the Institute of Management Accountants (IMA) requires that its members maintain professional expertise by continually developing knowledge and skills. An interesting issue is whether accounting professionals who resist learning different cost management methods are exhibiting ethical behavior. At the very least, cost accounting professionals should learn about different approaches and assess whether the benefit-cost trade-offs justify their use.◆

Activity-Based Product Costing: Detailed Description

OBJECTIVE ②
Explain how an activity-based costing system works for product costing.

Functional-based overhead costing involves two major stages: first, overhead costs are assigned to an organizational unit (plant or department), and second, overhead costs are then assigned to products. As Exhibit 6-4 illustrates, an activity-based costing (ABC) system first traces costs to activities and then to products. The underlying assumption is that activities consume resources, and products, in turn, consume activities. Thus, ABC also is a two-stage process. An ABC system, however, emphasizes direct tracing and driver tracing (exploiting cause-and-effect relationships), while a volume-based costing system tends to be allocation-intensive (largely ignoring cause-and-effect relationships). As the Exhibit 6-4 model reveals, the focus of ABC is activities. Thus, identifying activities must be the first step in designing an ABC system.

Identifying Activities and Their Attributes

Since an activity is action taken or work performed by equipment or people for other people, identifying activities usually is accomplished by interviewing managers or representatives of functional work areas (departments). A set of key questions is asked in which answers provide much of the data needed for an ABC system. These interview-derived data are used to prepare an *activity dictionary*. An **activity dictionary** lists the activities in an organization along with some critical activity attributes. **Activity attributes** are financial and nonfinancial information items that describe individual activities. What attributes are used depends on the purpose. Examples of activity attributes associated with a costing objective include types of resources consumed, amount (percentage) of time spent on an activity by workers, cost objects that consume the activity output (reason for performing the activity), a measure of the activity output (activity driver), and the activity name. To prevent the number of activities from becoming unmanageably large, a common rule of thumb employed by the interviewer is to tell the interviewee to ignore activities that require less than 5 percent of an individual's time.

Concept Q&A

What are some key differences between ABC and volume-based costing?

Answer:
ABC uses cause-and-effect relationships to assign overhead costs. Volume-based costing uses unit-based drivers such as direct labor hours, which often have nothing to do with the actual overhead resources consumed by a product.

Set of Key Questions   Interview questions can be used to identify activities and activity attributes needed for costing purposes. The information derived from these questions serves as the basis for constructing an activity dictionary as well as providing data helpful for assigning resource costs to individual activities. The list is not exhaustive but serves to illustrate the nature of the information gathering process.

1. How many employees are in your department? (Activities consume labor.)
2. What do they do (please describe)? (Activities are people doing things for other people.)
3. Do customers outside your department use any equipment? (Activities also can be equipment working for other people.)

Exhibit 6-4

Activity-Based Costing: Two-Stage Assignment

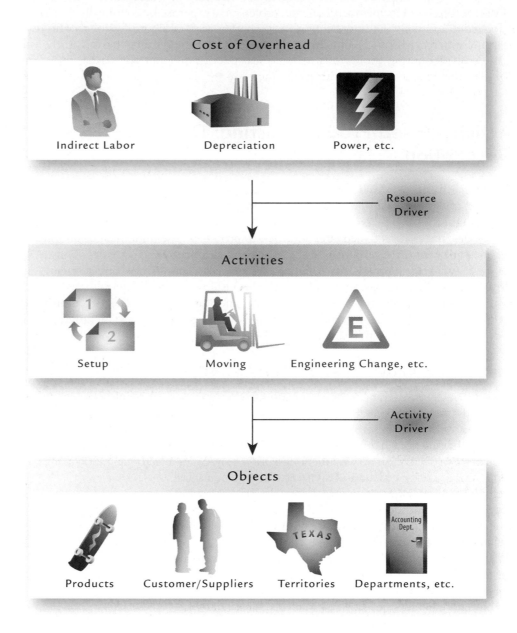

4. What resources are used by each activity (equipment, materials, energy)? (Activities consume resources in addition to labor.)
5. What are the outputs of each activity? (Helps to identify activity drivers.)
6. Who or what uses the activity output? (Identifies the cost object: products, other activities, customers, etc.)
7. How much time do workers spend on each activity? Time on each activity by equipment? (Information needed to assign the cost of labor and equipment to activities.)

Illustrative Example: Service Firm   Suppose that a manager of a bank's credit card department is interviewed and presented with the seven questions just listed. Consider the purpose and response to each question in the order indicated.

• *Question 1 (labor resource):* There are five employees.

- *Question 2 (activity identification):* There are three major activities: processing credit card transactions, issuing customer statements, and answering customer questions.
- *Question 3 (activity identification):* Yes. Automatic bank tellers service customers who require cash advances.
- *Question 4 (resource identification):* Each employee has his or her own computer, printer, and desk. Paper and other supplies are needed to operate the printers. Of course, each employee has a telephone as well.
- *Question 5 (potential activity drivers):* Processing transactions produces a posting for each transaction in our computer system and serves as a source for preparing the monthly statements. The number of monthly customer statements has to be the product for the issuing activity, and I suppose that customers served is the output for the answering activity. The number of cash advances measures the product of the automatic teller activity, although the teller really generates more transactions for other products such as checking accounts. So, perhaps the number of teller transactions is the real output.
- *Question 6 (potential cost objects identified):* We have three products: classic, gold, and platinum credit cards. Transactions are processed for these three types of cards, and statements are sent to clients holding these cards. Similarly, answers to questions are all directed to clients who hold these cards.
- *Question 7 (identifying resource drivers):* I just completed a work survey and have the percentage of time calculated for each worker. All five clerks work on each of the three departmental activities. About 40 percent of their time is spent processing transactions, with the rest of their time split evenly between preparing statements and answering questions. Phone time is used only for answering client questions, and computer time is 70 percent transaction processing, 20 percent statement preparation, and 10 percent answering questions. Furthermore, my own time and that of my computer are 100 percent administrative.

Concept Q&A

What is the purpose of the interview questions?

Answer:
The purpose is to identify activities, drivers, and other important attributes essential for ABC.

Activity Dictionary   Based on the answers to the survey, an activity dictionary can now be prepared. Exhibit 6-5 illustrates the dictionary for the credit card department. The activity dictionary names the activity (usually by using an action verb and an object that receives the action), describes the tasks that make up the activity, lists the users (cost objects), and identifies a measure of activity output (activity driver). The three products, classic, gold, and platinum credit cards, in turn, consume the activities. It is not unusual for a typical organization to produce an activity dictionary containing 200 to 300 activities.

> **Exhibit 6-5**

Activity Dictionary: Credit Card Department

Activity Name	Activity Description	Cost Object(s)	Activity Driver
Processing	Sorting, keying, and transactions verifying	Credit cards	Number of transactions
Preparing statements	Reviewing, printing, stuffing, and mailing	Credit cards	Number of statements
Answering questions	Answering, logging, reviewing database, and making call backs	Credit cards	Number of calls
Providing automatic tellers	Accessing accounts, withdrawing funds	Credit cards, checking and savings accounts	Number of teller transactions

Assigning Costs to Activities

Once activities are identified and described, the next task is to determine how much it costs to perform each activity. This determination requires identification of the resources being consumed by each activity. Some cost system experts consider this task to be the most difficult one in creating an accurate cost system. Activities consume resources such as labor, materials, energy, and capital. The cost of these resources is found in the general ledger, but the money spent on each activity is not revealed. Thus, it becomes necessary to assign the resource costs to activities by using direct and driver tracing. For labor resources, a *work distribution matrix* often is used. A work distribution matrix identifies the amount of labor consumed by each activity and is derived from the interview process (or a written survey). Exhibit 6-6 provides an example of a work distribution matrix supplied by the manager of the credit card department for individual activities (refer to Question 7).

The time spent on each activity is the basis for assigning the labor costs to the activity. If the time is 100 percent, then labor is exclusive to the activity, and the assignment method is direct tracing. If the resource is shared by several activities (as is the case of the clerical resource), then the assignment is driver tracing, and the drivers are called *resource drivers*. **Resource drivers** are factors that measure the consumption of resources by activities. Once resource drivers are identified, then the costs of the resource can be assigned to the activity. Cornerstone 6-4 shows how resource drivers and direct tracing are used to assign labor cost to the credit department activities.

Labor, of course, is not the only resource consumed by activities. Activities also consume materials, capital, and energy. The interview, for example, reveals that the activities within the credit card department use computers (capital), phones (capital), desks (capital), and paper (materials). The automatic teller activity uses the automatic teller (capital) and energy. The cost of these other resources must also be assigned to the various activities. They are assigned in the same way as was described for labor (using direct tracing and resource drivers). The cost of computers could be assigned

Concept Q&A

How are resource costs assigned to activities?

Answer:

Resource costs are assigned by using both direct tracing (for exclusive—direct—resources) and driver tracing (for shared—indirect—resources).

Exhibit 6-6

Work Distribution Matrix

Activity	Percentage of Time on Each Activity
Processing transactions	40%
Preparing statements	30%
Answering questions	30%

HOW TO Assign Resource Costs to Activities by Using Direct Tracing and Resource Drivers

Information: Assume that each clerk is paid a salary of $30,000 ($150,000 total clerical cost for five clerks). Refer also to the work distribution matrix of Exhibit 6-5.

Required: Assign the cost of labor to each of the activities in the credit department.

Calculation: The amount of labor cost assigned to each activity is given below. The percentages come from the work distribution matrix.

Processing transactions	$60,000 (0.4 × $150,000)
Preparing statements	$45,000 (0.3 × $150,000)
Answering questions	$45,000 (0.3 × $150,000)

CORNERSTONE
6-4

by using direct tracing (for the supervising activity) and hours of usage for the remaining activities. From the interview, we know the relative usage of computers by each activity. The general ledger reveals that the cost per computer is $1,200 per year. Thus, an additional $6,000 (5 × $1,200) would be assigned to three activities based on relative usage: 70 percent to processing transactions ($4,200), 20 percent to preparing statements ($1,200), and 10 percent to answering questions ($600). Repeating this process for all resources, the total cost of each activity can be calculated. Exhibit 6-7 gives the cost of the activities associated with the credit card department under the assumption that all resource costs have been assigned (these numbers are assumed because all resource data are not given for their calculation).

Analytical Q&A

A company has three inspectors, each earning a salary of $50,000. One inspector works exclusively on inspecting parts received from outside suppliers, while the other two spend 30 percent of their time inspecting parts and 70 percent of their time inspecting final products. How much labor cost should be assigned to the activity of inspecting parts?

Cost assigned = $50,000 + (0.30 × $50,000) + (0.30 × $50,000) = $80,000.

Answer:

Assigning Costs to Products

From Cornerstone 6-3, we know that activity costs are assigned to products by multiplying a predetermined activity rate by the usage of the activity, as measured by activity drivers. Exhibit 6-5 identified the activity drivers for each of the four credit card activities: number of transactions for processing transactions, number of statements for preparing statements, number of calls for answering questions, and number of teller transactions for the activity of providing automatic tellers. To calculate an activity rate, the practical capacity of each activity must be determined. To assign costs, the amount of each activity consumed by each product must also be known. Assuming that the practical activity capacity is equal to the total activity usage by all products, the following actual data have been collected for the credit card example:

	Classic Card	Gold Card	Platinum Card	Total
Number of cards	5,000	3,000	2,000	10,000
Transactions processed	600,000	300,000	100,000	1,000,000
Number of statements	60,000	36,000	24,000	120,000
Number of calls	10,000	12,000	8,000	30,000
Number of teller Transactions*	15,000	3,000	2,000	20,000

*The number of teller transactions for the cards is 10 percent of the total transactions from all sources. Thus, teller transactions total 20,000 (0.10 × 200,000).

Applying Cornerstone 6-2 by using the data and costs from Exhibit 6-7, the activity rates are calculated as follows:

Rate calculations:

Processing transactions	$130,000/1,000,000 = $0.13 per transaction
Preparing statements	$102,000/120,000 = $0.85 per statement
Answering questions	$92,400/30,000 = $3.08 per call
Providing automatic tellers	$250,000/200,000 = $1.25 per transaction

These rates provide the cost of each activity usage. Using these rates, costs are assigned as shown in Exhibit 6-8 on p. 250. However, we now know the whole story behind the development of the activity rates and usage measures. Furthermore, the banking setting emphasizes the utility of ABC in service organizations.

Exhibit 6-7

Activity Costs, First Stage: Credit Card Department

Processing transactions	$130,000
Preparing statements	102,000
Answering questions	92,400
Providing automatic tellers	250,000

**CORNERSTONE
6-6
(continued)**

| | Murray Inc. | | Plata Associates | |
	Part A1	Part B2	Part A1	Part B2
Repairing products:				
$400 × 1,600	640,000			
$400 × 380		152,000		
$400 × 10			4,000	
$400 × 10				4,000
Expediting products:				
$2,000 × 60	120,000			
$2,000 × 40		80,000		
Total costs	$2,360,000	$2,312,000	$244,000	$564,000
Units	÷ 80,000	÷ 40,000	÷ 10,000	÷ 10,000
Total unit cost	$ 29.50	$ 57.80	$ 24.40	$ 56.40

Concept Q&A

How are costs assigned to suppliers by using the ABC approach?

Answer:

Costs are traced to activities and are then assigned to suppliers based on a cause-and-effect relationship.

The example in Cornerstone 6-6 shows that Murray, the "low-cost" supplier (as measured by the purchase price of the two parts), actually costs more when the supplier-related activities of repairing and expediting are considered. If all costs are considered, then the choice becomes clear: Plata Associates is the better supplier with a higher-quality product, more on-time deliveries, and, consequently, a lower overall cost per unit.

OBJECTIVE ④
Explain how activity-based management can be used for cost reduction.

Process-Value Analysis

Process-value analysis is fundamental to **activity-based management**, focuses on cost reduction instead of cost assignment, and emphasizes the maximization of systemwide performance. As the model in Exhibit 6-10 illustrates, process-value analysis is concerned with (1) *driver analysis*, (2) *activity analysis*, and (3) *performance measurement*.

Driver Analysis: The Search for Root Causes

Managing activities requires an understanding of what causes activity costs. Every activity has inputs and outputs. **Activity inputs** are the resources consumed by the activity in producing its output. **Activity output** is the result or product of an activity. For example, if the activity is moving materials, the inputs would be such things as a forklift, a forklift driver, fuel (for the forklift), and crates. The output would be moved goods and materials. An **activity output measure** is the number of times the activity is performed. It is the quantifiable measure of the output. For example, the number of moves or distance moved are possible output measures for the material moving activity.

Exhibit 6-10

Process-Value Analysis Model

The output measure effectively is a measure of the demands placed on an activity and is what we have been calling an *activity driver*. As the demands for an activity change, the cost of the activity can change. For example, as the number of programs written increases, the activity of writing programs may need to consume more inputs (labor, disks, paper, and so on). However, output measures, such as the number of programs, may not (and usually do not) correspond to the root causes of activity costs; rather, they are the consequences of the activity being performed. The purpose of driver analysis is to reveal root causes. Thus, **driver analysis** is the effort expended to identify those factors that are the root causes of activity costs. For example, an analysis may reveal that the root cause of the cost of moving materials is plant layout. Once the root cause is known, then action can be taken to improve the activity. Specifically, reorganizing plant layout can reduce the cost of moving materials.

Often, the root cause of the cost of an activity is also the root cause of other related activities. For example, the costs of inspecting purchased parts and reordering may both be caused by poor supplier quality. By working with suppliers to reduce the number of defective components supplied (or choosing suppliers that have fewer defects), the demand for both activities may then decrease, allowing the company to save money.

Activity Analysis: Identifying and Assessing Value Content

The heart of process-value analysis is activity analysis. **Activity analysis** is the process of identifying, describing, and evaluating the activities that an organization performs. Activity analysis should produce four outcomes: (1) what activities are done; (2) how many people perform the activities; (3) the time and resources required to perform the activities; and (4) an assessment of the value of the activities to the organization, including a recommendation to select and keep only those that add value. Steps 1 to 3 have been described earlier and are common to the information needed for determining and assigning activity costs. Knowing how much an activity costs is clearly an important part of activity-based management. Step 4, determining the value-added content of activities, is concerned with cost reduction rather than cost assignment. Thus, some managerial accountants feel that this is the most important part of activity analysis. Activities can be classified as *value-added* or *nonvalue-added*.

Concept Q&A

What is the purpose of driver analysis?

Answer:
The objective of driver analysis is to find the root causes of activity costs. By knowing root causes, costs can be managed effectively.

Value-Added Activities

Those activities necessary to remain in business are called **value-added activities**. Some activities—required activities—are necessary to comply with legal mandates. Activities needed to comply with the reporting requirements of the Securities Exchange Commission (SEC) and the filing requirements of the Internal Revenue Service (IRS) are examples. These activities are value-added by *mandate*. The remaining activities in the firm are *discretionary*. A discretionary activity is classified as value-added provided it simultaneously satisfies three conditions: (1) the activity produces a change of state, (2) the change of state was not achievable by preceding activities, and (3) the activity enables other activities to be performed.

For example, consider the production of rods used in hydraulic cylinders. The first activity, cutting rods, cuts long rods into the correct lengths for the cylinders. Next, the cut rods are welded to cut plates. The cutting rod activity is value-added because (1) it causes a change of state—uncut rods become cut rods, (2) no prior activity was supposed to create this change of state, and (3) it enables the welding activity to be performed. Though the value-added properties are easy to see for an operational activity like cutting rods, what about a more general activity like supervising production workers? A managerial activity is specifically designed to manage other value-added activities—to ensure that they are

Concept Q&A

What is a value-added activity?

Answer:
A value-added activity is one that must be performed for the firm to remain in business.

performed in an efficient and timely manner. Supervision certainly satisfies the enabling condition. Is there a change in state? There are two ways of answering in the affirmative. First, supervising can be viewed as an enabling resource that is consumed by the operational activities that do produce a change of state. Thus, supervising is a secondary activity that serves as an input that is needed to help bring about the change of state expected for value-added primary activities. Second, it could be argued that the supervision brings order by changing the state from uncoordinated activities to coordinated activities. Once value-added activities are identified, we can define value-added costs. **Value-added costs** are the costs to perform value-added activities with perfect efficiency.

Nonvalue-Added Activities   All activities other than those that are absolutely essential to remain in business, and therefore considered unnecessary, are referred to as **nonvalue-added activities**. A nonvalue-added activity can be identified by its failure to satisfy any one of the three previous defining conditions. Violation of the first two is the usual case for nonvalue-added activities. Inspecting cut rods (for correct length), for example, is a nonvalue-added activity. Inspection is a state-detection activity, not a state-changing activity (it tells us the state of the cut rod—whether it is the right length or not). Thus, it fails the first condition. Consider the activity of reworking goods or subassemblies. Rework is designed to bring a good from a nonconforming state to a conforming state. Thus, a change of state occurs. Yet, the activity is nonvalue-added because it repeats work; it is doing something that should have been done by preceding activities (Condition 2 is violated).

Nonvalue-added costs are costs that are caused either by nonvalue-added activities or the inefficient performance of valued-added activities. For nonvalue-added activities, the nonvalue-added cost is the cost of the activity itself. For inefficient value-added activities, the activity cost must be broken into its value-added and nonvalue-added components. For example, if receiving should use 10,000 receiving orders but uses 20,000, then half the cost of receiving is value-added and half is nonvalue-added. The value-added component is the wastefree component of the value-added activity and is, therefore, the *value-added standard*. Due to increased competition, many firms are attempting to eliminate nonvalue-added activities because they add unnecessary cost and impede performance; firms are also striving to optimize value-added activities. Thus, activity analysis identifies and eventually eliminates all unnecessary activities and, simultaneously, increases the efficiency of necessary activities.

The theme of activity analysis is waste elimination. As waste is eliminated, costs are reduced. The cost reduction *follows* the elimination of waste. Note the value of managing the causes of the costs rather than the costs themselves. Though managing costs may increase the efficiency of an activity, if the activity is unnecessary, what does it matter if it's performed efficiently? An unnecessary activity is wasteful and should be eliminated. For example, moving raw materials and partially finished goods is often cited as a nonvalue-added activity. Installing an automated materials handling system may increase the efficiency of this activity, but changing to cellular manufacturing with on-site, just-in-time delivery of raw materials could virtually eliminate the activity. It's easy to see which is preferable.

Examples of Nonvalue-Added Activities   Reordering parts, expediting production, and rework because of defective parts are all examples of nonvalue-added activities. Other examples include warranty work, handling customer complaints, and reporting defects. Nonvalue-added activities can exist anywhere in the organization. In the manufacturing operation, five major activities are often cited as wasteful and unnecessary:

1. *Scheduling*. An activity that uses time and resources to determine when different products have access to processes (or when and how many setups must be done) and how much will be produced.

Concept Q&A

How can a value-added activity have nonvalue-added costs?

Answer:

If a value-added activity is performed inefficiently, the inefficient component is waste and is the nonvalue-added cost.

2. *Moving.* An activity that uses time and resources to move raw materials, work in process, and finished goods from one department to another.
3. *Waiting.* An activity in which raw materials or work in process use time and resources by waiting on the next process.
4. *Inspecting.* An activity in which time and resources are spent ensuring that the product meets specifications.
5. *Storing.* An activity that uses time and resources while a good or raw material is held in inventory.

None of these activities adds any value for the customer. (Note that inspection would not be necessary if the product were produced correctly the first time and, therefore, adds no value for the customer.) The challenge of activity analysis is to find ways to produce the good without using any of these activities.

Here's The Real Kicker

For Stillwater Designs, warranty work is a significant cost. Warranty work associated with defective products is typically labeled a nonvalue-added cost. Stillwater Designs recognizes the nonvalue-added nature of this activity and takes measures to eliminate the causes of the defective units. The company tracks return failures (over time) and provides this information to its research and development (R&D) department. R&D then uses this information to make design improvements on existing models (running changes) as well to change the design on future models. The objective of the design changes is to reduce the demand for the warranty activity, thus reducing warranty cost.

However, not all Kicker warranty costs can be classified as nonvalue-added. When products are returned, customer service decides whether or not the problem is covered under warranty. Sometimes, problems are covered even though they are not attributable to a defective product. When the company decides to replace a nondefective product, it is making a conscious decision to increase customer satisfaction and brand loyalty. This part of the warranty cost is a "marketing warranty cost" and could be classified as a value-added cost. For example, customers sometimes buy amplifiers that are more powerful than the subwoofers can handle, resulting in burnt voice coils. By replacing the product (even though technically it's the customer's fault), the customer will be more likely to buy again and to provide good word-of-mouth advertising for Kicker products.

Cost Reduction   Activity management carries with it the objective of cost reduction. Competitive conditions dictate that companies must deliver customer-desired products on time and at the lowest possible cost. These conditions mean that an organization must continually strive for cost improvement. Activity management can reduce costs in four ways:[4]

1. Activity elimination
2. Activity selection
3. Activity reduction
4. Activity sharing

Activity elimination focuses on nonvalue-added activities. Once activities that fail to add value are identified, measures must be taken to rid the organization of these activities. For example, the activity of inspecting incoming parts seems necessary to ensure that the product using the parts functions according to specifications. Use of a bad part can produce a bad final product. Yet, this activity is necessary only because of the poor-quality performance of the supplying firms. Selecting suppliers who are able to supply high-quality parts or who are willing to improve their quality performance to achieve this

---

[4]Peter B. B. Turney, "How Activity-Based Costing Helps Reduce Cost," *Journal of Cost Management* (Winter 1991): 29–35.

objective will eventually allow the elimination of incoming inspection. Cost reduction then follows.

Activity selection involves choosing among different sets of activities that are caused by competing strategies. Different strategies cause different activities. Different product design strategies, for example, can require significantly different activities. Activities, in turn, cause costs. Each product design strategy has its own set of activities and associated costs. All other things being equal, the lowest-cost design strategy should be chosen. In a kaizen cost framework, redesign of existing products and processes can lead to a different, cheaper set of activities. Thus, activity selection can have a significant effect on cost reduction.

Activity reduction decreases the time and resources required by an activity. This approach to cost reduction should be primarily aimed at improving the efficiency of necessary activities or a short-term strategy for improving nonvalue-added activities until they can be eliminated. Setup activity is a necessary activity that is often cited as an example for which less time and fewer resources need to be used. Finding ways to reduce setup time—and thus lower the cost of setups—is another example of the concept of gradual reductions in activity costs.

Activity sharing increases the efficiency of necessary activities by using economies of scale. Specifically, the quantity of the cost driver is increased without increasing the total cost of the activity itself. This lowers the per-unit cost of the cost driver and the amount of cost traceable to the products that consume the activity. For example, a new product can be designed to use components already being used by other products. By using existing components, the activities associated with these components already exist, and the company avoids the creation of a whole new set of activities.

Cornerstone 6-7 shows how to determine the nonvalue-added cost of activities. Determining the cost is followed by a root-cause analysis and then by the selection of an approach to reduce the waste found in the activity. For example, defective products cause warranty work. Defective products, in turn, are caused by such factors as defective internal processes, poor product design, and defective supplier components. Correcting the causes will lead to the elimination of the warranty activity. Inefficient purchasing could be attributable to such root causes as poor product design (too many components), orders that are incorrectly filled out, and defective supplier components (producing additional orders). Correcting the causes will reduce the demand for the purchasing activity, and as the activity is reduced, cost reduction will follow.

CORNERSTONE 6-7

HOW TO Assess Nonvalue-Added Costs

Information: Consider the following two activities: (1) Performing warranty work, cost: $120,000. The warranty cost of the most efficient competitor is $20,000. (2) Purchasing components, cost: $200,000 (10,000 purchase orders). A benchmarking study reveals that the most efficient level will use 5,000 purchase orders and entail a cost of $110,000.

Required: Determine the nonvalue-added cost of each activity.

Calculation: Determine the value content of each activity: Is the activity nonvalue-added or value-added? Performing warranty work is nonvalue-added; it is done to correct something that wasn't done right the first time. Thus, the nonvalue-added cost of performing warranty work is $120,000. The cost of the competitor is also nonvalue-added and has no bearing on the analysis. Root causes for warranty work are defective products. Purchasing components is necessary so that materials are available to produce products and, thus, is value-added. However, the activity is not performed efficiently, as revealed by the benchmarking study. The nonvalue-added cost is $90,000 ($200,000 − $110,000).

Activity Performance Measurement

Assessing how well activities (and processes) are performed is fundamental to management's efforts to improve profitability. Activity performance measures exist in both financial and nonfinancial forms. These measures are designed to assess how well an activity was performed and the results achieved. They are also designed to reveal if constant improvement is being realized. Measures of activity performance center on three major dimensions: (1) efficiency, (2) quality, and (3) time.

Efficiency focuses on the relationship of activity inputs to activity outputs. For example, one way to improve activity efficiency is to produce the same activity output with lower cost for the inputs used. Thus, cost and trends in cost become important measures of efficiency. *Quality* is concerned with doing the activity right the first time it is performed. If the activity output is defective, then the activity may need to be repeated, causing unnecessary cost and reduction in efficiency. Quality cost management is a major topical area and is treated in detail in the appendix to this chapter. The *time* required to perform an activity is also critical. Longer times usually mean more resource consumption and less ability to respond to customer demands. Time measures of performance tend to be nonfinancial, whereas efficiency and quality measures are both financial and nonfinancial.

Cycle time and *velocity* are two operational measures of time-based performance. Cycle time can be applied to any activity or process that produces an output, and it measures how long it takes to produce an output from start to finish. Consider the manufacturing process. In this case, **cycle time** is the length of time that it takes to produce a unit of output from the time raw materials are received (starting point of the cycle) until the good is delivered to finished goods inventory (finishing point of the cycle). Thus, cycle time is the time required to produce one unit of a product (time/units produced). **Velocity** is the number of units of output that can be produced in a given period of time (units produced/time). Notice that velocity is the reciprocal of cycle time. For the cycle time example, the velocity is two units per hour. Cornerstone 6-8 demonstrates how to compute cycle time and velocity.

Concept Q&A

What are the three dimensions of performance for activities? Explain why they are important.

Answer:
Efficiency, quality, and time are the three performance dimensions. All three relate to the ability of a manager to reduce activity cost.

Quality Cost Management

Activity-based management also is useful for understanding how quality costs can be managed. Quality costs can be substantial in size and a source of considerable savings if managed effectively. Improving quality can produce significant improvements in profitability and overall efficiency. Quality improvement can increase profitability in

---

HOW TO Calculate Cycle Time and Velocity

Information: Assume that a company takes 10,000 hours to produce 20,000 units of a product.

Required: What is the velocity? Cycle time?

Calculation: Velocity = 20,000/10,000 = 2 units per hour; Cycle time = 10,000/20,000 = 1/2 hour.

**CORNERSTONE
6-8**

7

Profit Planning

After studying Chapter 7, you should be able to:

1. Define budgeting, and discuss its role in planning, control, and decision making.

2. Define and prepare the operating budget, identify its major components, and explain the interrelationships of its various components.

3. Define and prepare the financial budget, identify its major components, and explain the interrelationships of its various components.

4. Describe the behavioral dimension of budgeting.

© HIGH SIERRA

Experience Managerial Decisions
with High Sierra

Have you ever wondered where that huge backpack you use to lug 50 pounds of books and educational "gear" all over campus originated? If so, you might be surprised by the history behind one of its first manufacturers. After World War II, an abundance of Army and Navy Surplus stores supplied tents, canteens, and canvas bags to consumers. Among these stores was Seaway Importing, a company run by Harry Bernbaum. When his son Hank joined the business a year later in 1979, they recognized the need to develop more durable products and founded the High Sierra Sport Company.

Budgeting plays an important role in High Sierra's decision-making process. Throughout the 1980s, High Sierra developed its brand reputation as a manufacturer and supplier of numerous types of quality outdoor and foul weather gear, including backpacks, duffel bags, book bags, and hydration gear. Then, during the mid-1990s, budgeting played a key role in helping High Sierra realize that it would need to streamline its brand identity in order to keep its competitive edge in quality and price. Along these lines, High Sierra's management used its budgeting process to eliminate poor-performing products and to analyze new products, such as a winter sports product line that focused more directly on the company's brand and target market (e.g., alliances with the U.S. Ski and Snowboard Association). During the early 2000s, High Sierra's budgeting process showed management that it needed to expand operations by outsourcing some of its production overseas in order to remain cost competitive. To ensure that its budgeting process continues to provide useful insights, High Sierra often adopts new techniques, such as participative budgeting and continuous budgeting, where each month management prepares the next month's budget in a rolling fashion so that the firm is never without a budget plan. In summary, High Sierra uses budgeting as an effective planning and control tool to promote successful new product development that creates value for the company and keeps students buying those huge backpacks every year!

Description of Budgeting

All businesses should prepare budgets; all large businesses do. Business entities come in a variety of forms: sole proprietorships (single-owner businesses), partnerships, and corporations. Even small, professional corporations like dental practices can benefit from the planning and control provided by budgeting.

Budgeting and Planning and Control

Planning and control are tied together in an important and vital way. *Planning* is looking ahead to see what actions should be taken to realize particular goals. *Control* is looking backward, determining what actually happened and comparing it with the previously planned outcomes. This comparison can then be used to adjust the budget, looking forward once more. Exhibit 7-1 illustrates the cycle of planning, control, and budgets.

Budgets are financial plans for the future and are a key component of planning. They identify objectives and the actions needed to achieve them. Before a budget is prepared, an organization should develop a strategic plan. The **strategic plan** identifies strategies for future activities and operations, generally covering at least five years. The organization can translate the overall strategy into long- and short-term objectives. These objectives form the basis of the budget. The budget and the strategic plan should be tightly linked. Budgets, especially one-year period plans, are short run in nature, and therefore, this linkage is important because it helps management to ensure that not all attention is not focused on the short run. For example, on May 14, 2007, private-equity firm **Cerberus Capital Management** announced it would buy an 80.1 percent stake in Chrysler from its German parent **DaimlerChrysler** for $7.41 billion! Managers at Cerberus undoubtedly performed detailed budgetary analyses of Chrysler's expected

Exhibit 7-1

Planning, Control, and Budgets

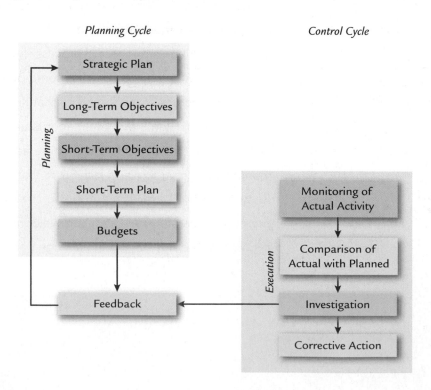

future cash inflows and outflows, as well as earnings. Short-run analyses were especially important to Cerberus, as auto analysts speculated that Cerberus would attempt to make Chrysler leaner through cost cutting before turning around and selling it to another company for a profit relatively soon thereafter. However, Cerberus's analyses also needed to demonstrate sufficient cash flows and earnings for Chrysler over the long term as well, in case its anticipated plan to unload the company in the near term did not materialize.

Advantages of Budgeting

A budgetary system gives an organization several advantages.

1. It forces managers to plan.
2. It provides information that can be used to improve decision making.
3. It provides a standard for performance evaluation.
4. It improves communication and coordination.

Budgeting forces management to plan for the future. It encourages managers to develop an overall direction for the organization, foresee problems, and develop future policies.

Budgets improve decision making. For example, the budgeting process reveals to a dentist, Dr. Jones, the amount of expected revenues and the costs of supplies, lab fees, utilities, salaries, and so on. This budgeting information will improve the dentist's decision making by affecting decisions involving, the rate of salary increases for his staff, whether or not to borrow money and the amount of nonessential equipment to purchase for the office. These better decisions, in turn, might prevent problems from arising and result in a better financial status for the dental office.

Budgets set standards that can control the use of a company's resources and motivate employees. A vital part of the budgetary system, **control** is achieved by comparing actual results with budgeted results on a periodic basis (e.g., monthly). A large difference between actual and planned results is feedback revealing that the system is out of control. Steps should be taken to find out why and then to correct the situation. For example, if Dr. Jones knows how much amalgam should be used in a filling and what the cost should be, he can evaluate his use of this resource. If more amalgam is being used than expected, Dr. Jones may discover that he is often careless in its use and that extra care will produce savings. The same principle applies to other resources used by the corporation. In total, the savings could be significant.

Budgets also serve to communicate and coordinate. Budgets formally communicate the plans of the organization to each employee. Accordingly, all employees can be aware of their particular role in achieving those objectives. Since budgets for the various areas and activities of the organization must all work together to achieve organizational objectives, coordination is promoted. Managers can see the needs of other areas and are encouraged to subordinate their individual interests to those of the organization. The role of communication and coordination becomes more significant as an organization increases in size.

Concept Q&A

How can a budget help in planning and control?

Answer:
A budget requires a plan. It also sets benchmarks that can be used to evaluate performance.

The Master Budget

The **master budget** is the comprehensive financial plan for the organization as a whole. Typically, the master budget is for a one-year period, corresponding to the fiscal year of the company. Yearly budgets are broken down into quarterly and monthly budgets. The use of smaller time periods allows managers to compare actual data with budgeted data more frequently, so problems may be noticed and resolved sooner.

Some organizations have developed a continuous budgeting philosophy. A **continuous budget** is a moving 12-month budget. As a month expires in the budget, an additional month in the future is added so that the company always has a 12-month plan on hand. Proponents of continuous budgeting maintain that it forces managers to plan ahead constantly.

Directing and Coordinating

Most organizations prepare the master budget for the coming year during the last four or five months of the current year. The **budget committee** reviews the budget, provides policy guidelines and budgetary goals, resolves differences that arise as the budget is prepared, approves the final budget, and monitors the actual performance of the organization as the year unfolds. The president of the organization appoints the members of the committee, who are usually the president, vice president for marketing, vice president for manufacturing, other vice presidents, and the controller. The controller usually serves as the **budget director**, the person responsible for directing and coordinating the organization's overall budgeting process.

Major Components of the Master Budget

A master budget can be divided into operating and financial budgets. **Operating budgets** describe the income-generating activities of a firm: sales, production, and finished goods inventories. The ultimate outcome of the operating budgets is a pro forma or budgeted income statement. **Financial budgets** detail the inflows and outflows of cash and the overall financial position. Planned cash inflows and outflows appear in the cash budget. The expected financial position at the end of the budget period is shown in a budgeted, or pro forma, balance sheet. Since many of the financing activities are not known until the operating budgets are known, the operating budget is prepared first. Describing and illustrating the individual budgets that make up the master budget will make apparent the interdependencies of the component budgets. A diagram displaying these interrelationships is shown in Exhibit 7-2. Details of the capital budget are covered in a separate chapter.

Concept Q&A

What is the main objective of continuous budgeting?

Answer:

It forces managers to plan ahead constantly—something especially needed when firms operate in rapidly changing environments.

OBJECTIVE ②
Define and prepare the operating budget, identify its major components, and explain the interrelationships of its various components.

Preparing the Operating Budget

The operating budget consists of a budgeted income statement accompanied by the following supporting schedules:

1. Sales budget
2. Production budget
3. Direct materials purchases budget
4. Direct labor budget
5. Overhead budget
6. Selling and administrative expenses budget
7. Ending finished goods inventory budget
8. Cost of goods sold budget

To illustrate the master budgeting process, we will use an example based on the activities of **Texas Rex Inc.**, a trendy restaurant in the Southwest that sells T-shirts with the Texas Rex logo (a dinosaur that engages in a variety of adventures while eating the Mexican food for which the restaurant is known). The example focuses on the Texas Rex clothing manufacturing plant.

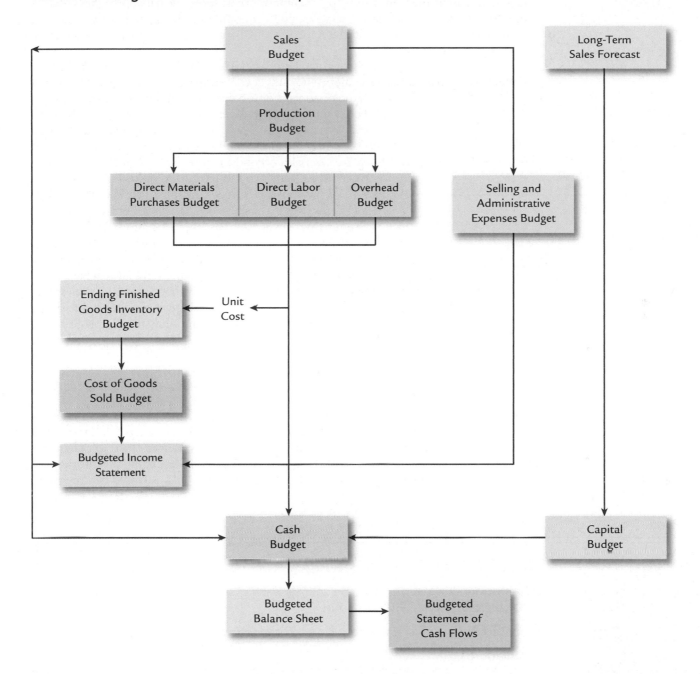

Exhibit 7-2

The Master Budget and Its Interrelationships

Sales Budget

The **sales budget** is the projection approved by the budget committee that describes expected sales in units and dollars. Because the sales budget is the basis for all of the other operating budgets and most of the financial budgets, it is important that the sales budget be as accurate as possible.

The first step in creating a sales budget is to develop the sales forecast. This is usually the responsibility of the marketing department. One approach to forecasting sales is the *bottom-up approach*, which requires individual salespeople to submit sales predictions. These predictions are aggregated to form a total sales forecast. The accuracy of this sales forecast may be improved by considering other factors such as the general economic climate, competition, advertising, pricing policies, and so on. Some companies supplement the bottom-up approach with other, more formal approaches, such as time-series analysis, correlation analysis, and econometric modeling. For example, the regression technique studied in the Appendix of Chapter 2 can be applied to forecasting sales, in addition to costs.

The sales forecast is merely the initial estimate. The sales forecast is presented to the budget committee for consideration. The budget committee may decide that the forecast is too pessimistic or too optimistic and revise it appropriately. For example, if the budget committee decides that the forecast is too pessimistic and not in harmony with the strategic plan of the organization, it may recommend specific actions to increase sales beyond the forecast level, such as increasing promotional activities and hiring additional salespeople.

Cornerstone 7-1 shows how to prepare the sales budget for Texas Rex's standard T-shirt line. For simplicity, we assume that Texas Rex has only one product: a standard short-sleeved T-shirt with the Texas Rex logo screen printed on the back. (For a multiple-product firm, the sales budget reflects sales for each product in units and sales dollars.)

Notice that the sales budget in Cornerstone 7-1 reveals that Texas Rex's sales fluctuate seasonally. Most sales take place in the summer and fall quarters. This is due to the popularity of the T-shirts in the summer and the sales promotions that Texas Rex puts on for "back to school" and Christmas.

Concept Q&A

Why is the sales budget not necessarily the same as the sales forecast?

Answer:

The sales forecast is a starting point and an important input to the budgetary process; however, it is usually adjusted up or down, depending on the strategic objectives and plans of management.

Production Budget

The **production budget** describes how many units must be produced in order to meet sales needs and satisfy ending inventory requirements. For example, a production budget for Texas Rex would reveal how many T-shirts are needed to satisfy sales demand for each quarter and for the year. If there were no beginning or ending inventories, the T-shirts to be produced would exactly equal the units to be sold as would be the case in

**CORNERSTONE
7-1**

HOW TO Prepare a Sales Budget

Information: Budgeted units to be sold for each quarter: 1,000, 1,200, 1,500, and 2,000. Selling price is $10 per T-shirt.

Required: Prepare a sales budget for each quarter and for the year.

Calculation:

Texas Rex Inc.
Sales Budget
For the Year Ended December 31, 2009

| | Quarter | | | | |
	1	2	3	4	Year
Units	1,000	1,200	1,500	2,000	5,700
Unit selling price	× $10	× $10	× $10	× $10	× $10
Budgeted sales	$10,000	$12,000	$15,000	$20,000	$57,000

Here's The Real Kicker

Stillwater Designs has 14 departments. Each department is given a budget for the coming fiscal year. The budgeting process begins with a sales forecast prepared by the president and vice presidents. The fiscal year for the company is October 1 through September 30. The budget is prepared during August and September, the last two months of the fiscal year. The fiscal year is driven by the seasonal nature of the business. In January of each year, there is a consumer electronics show in Las Vegas, Nevada. New products are introduced, and initial orders from distributors are taken. The sales season starts earnestly in March, reaches its peak in June or July, and drops to its lowest level in the fall. The sales season is driven by the anticipation of warm weather. The young men buying the Kicker speakers and amplifiers want to drive with windows down—with the apparent hope of impressing the girls!

Each department is given a percentage of sales as its budget. The amount ultimately decided upon is not simply a top-down decision. Department managers submit a request for their desired budget. Negotiation takes place between the department managers and their associated vice president (each departmental manager is answerable to a specific vice president). Whether or not the desired levels are provided depends on how well the departmental manager can justify the expenditures. An important criterion is the notion that resources are expended to make profits.

The budget is reviewed monthly. Any large deviations from the budget are investigated (usually more than a 10-percent deviation is required for an investigation). However, no formal incentive system is tied to budgetary performance. The budget is viewed as a guideline. If more resources are needed, then they can be obtained provided the request is backed up with a good idea and a promising payout.

a just-in-time (JIT) firm. However, many manufacturing firms use inventories as a buffer against uncertainties in demand or production. Thus, they need to plan for inventory levels as well as sales.

To compute the units to be produced, both unit sales and units of beginning and ending finished goods inventory are needed:

**Units to be produced = Expected unit sales + Units in ending inventory (DEI)
− Units in beginning inventory (BI)**

Cornerstone 7-2 illustrates how to prepare a production budget using this formula. Consider the first column (quarter 1) of the budget in Cornerstone 7-2 found on page 298. Texas Rex anticipates sales of 1,000 T-shirts. In addition, the company wants 240 T-shirts in ending inventory at the end of the first quarter (0.20 × 1,200). Thus, 1,240 T-shirts are needed during the first quarter. Where will these 1,240 T-shirts come from? Beginning inventory can provide 180 of them, leaving 1,060 tee shirts to be produced during the quarter. Notice that the production budget is expressed in terms of units.

Two important points should be emphasized. First, the beginning inventory for one quarter is always equal to the ending inventory of the previous quarter. For quarter 2, the beginning inventory is 240 T-shirts, which is identical to the desired ending inventory of quarter 1. Second, the column for the year is not simply the addition of the amounts for the four quarters. Notice that the desired ending inventory for the year is 200 T-shirts, which is, of course, equal to the desired ending inventory for the fourth quarter.

Analytical Q&A

Assume that the expected sales for January and February are 2,000 units and 2,500 units, respectively. The desired ending inventory is 20 percent of the next month's expected sales. If the inventory on hand at the beginning of January is 150 units, how many units should be budgeted for production?

Answer:

$Budgeted\ units = Sales + DEI − BI = 2,000 + (0.20 × 2,500) − 150 = 2,350.$

Direct Materials Purchases Budget

After the production budget is completed, the budgets for direct materials, direct labor, and overhead can be prepared. The **direct materials purchases budget** tells the amount and cost of raw materials to be purchased in each time period; it depends on

**CORNERSTONE
7-2**

HOW TO Prepare the Production Budget

Information: Refer to Cornerstone 7-1 for the sales budget. Assume that company policy requires 20 percent of the next quarter's sales in ending inventory and that beginning inventory of T-shirts for the first quarter of the year was 180. Assume also that sales for the first quarter of 2010 are estimated at 1,000 units.

Required: Prepare a production budget for each quarter and for the year.

Calculation:

**Texas Rex Inc.
Production Budget
For the Year Ended December 31, 2009**

	Quarter				
	1	2	3	4	Year
Sales (Cornerstone 7-1)	1,000	1,200	1,500	2,000	5,700
Desired ending inventory	240	300	400	200	200
Total needs	1,240	1,500	1,900	2,200	5,900
Less: Beginning inventory	(180)	(240)	(300)	(400)	(180)
Units to be produced	1,060	1,260	1,600	1,800	5,720

*0.20 × 1,000.

the expected use of materials in production and the raw materials inventory needs of the firm. The company needs to prepare a separate direct materials purchases budget for every type of raw material used. The formula used for calculating purchases is as follows:

**Purchases = Direct materials needed for production
            + Desired direct materials in ending inventory
            − Direct materials in beginning inventory**

The quantity of direct materials in inventory is determined by the firm's inventory policy.

Texas Rex uses two types of raw materials: plain T-shirts and ink. The direct materials purchases budgets for these two materials are presented in Cornerstone 7-3. Notice how similar the direct materials purchases budget is to the production budget. Consider the first quarter, starting with the plain T-shirts. It takes one plain T-shirt for every logo tee, so the 1,060 logo T-shirts to be produced are multiplied by one to obtain the number of plain T-shirts needed for production. Next, the desired ending inventory of 126 (10 percent of the next quarter's production needs) is added. Thus, 1,186 plain T-shirts are needed during the first quarter. Of this total, 58 are already in beginning inventory, meaning that the remaining 1,128 must be purchased. Multiplying the 1,128 plain T-shirts by the cost of $3 each gives Texas Rex the $3,384 expected cost of plain T-shirt purchases for the first quarter of the year.

The second section of the direct materials purchases budget is for ink. Again, the first quarter will be used for illustration. It takes five ounces of ink for every logo tee, so the 1,060 logo T-shirts to be produced are multiplied by five to obtain the 5,300 ounces of ink needed for production. Next, the desired ending inventory of 630 ounces (10 percent of the next quarter's production needs) is added, yielding a requirement of 5,930 ounces of ink for the first quarter. Of this total, 390 ounces are already in beginning inventory, meaning that the remaining 5,540 ounces must be purchased.

HOW TO Prepare a Direct Materials Purchases Budget

Information: Refer to Cornerstone 7-2 for the production budget. Plain T-shirts cost $3 each, and ink (for the screen printing) costs $0.20 per ounce. On a per-unit basis, the factory needs one plain T-shirt and five ounces of ink for each logo T-shirt that it produces. Texas Rex's policy is to have 10 percent of the following quarter's production needs in ending inventory. The factory has 58 plain T-shirts and 390 ounces of ink on hand on January 1. At the end of the year, the desired ending inventory is 106 plain T-shirts and 530 ounces of ink.

Required: Prepare a direct materials purchases budget for plain T-shirts and one for ink.

**CORNERSTONE
7-3**

Calculation:

Texas Rex Inc.
Direct Materials Purchases Budget
For the Year Ended December 31, 2009

Plain T-Shirts	Quarter				
	1	2	3	4	Year
Units to be produced (Cornerstone 7-2)	1,060	1,260	1,600	1,800	5,720
Direct materials per unit	× 1	× 1	× 1	× 1	× 1
Production needs	1,060	1,260	1,600	1,800	5,720
Desired ending inventory (DEI)	126	160	180	106	106
Total needs	1,186	1,420	1,780	1,906	5,826
Less: Beginning inventory (BI)	(58)	(126)	(160)	(180)	(58)
Direct materials to be purchased	1,128	1,294	1,620	1,726	5,768
Cost per unit	× $3	× $3	× $3	× $3	× $3
Total purchase cost plain T-shirts	$3,384	$3,882	$4,860	$5,178	$17,304

Ink	Quarter				
	1	2	3	4	Year
Units to be produced (Cornerstone 7-2)	1,060	1,260	1,600	1,800	5,720
Direct materials per unit	× 5	× 5	× 5	× 5	× 5
Production needs	5,300	6,300	8,000	9,000	28,600
Desired ending inventory (DEI)	630	800	900	530	530
Total needs	5,930	7,100	8,900	9,530	29,130
Less: Beginning inventory (BI)	(390)	(630)	(800)	(900)	(390)
Direct materials to be purchased	5,540	6,470	8,100	8,630	28,740
Cost per ounce	×$0.20	×$0.20	×$0.20	×$0.20	×$0.20
Total purchase cost of ink	$1,108	$1,294	$1,620	$1,726	$ 5,748
Total direct materials purchase cost	$4,492	$5,176	$6,480	$6,904	$23,052

Multiplying the 5,540 ounces of ink by the cost of $0.20 per ounce gives Texas Rex the $1,108 expected cost of ink purchases for the first quarter of the year.

The total direct materials purchases of $4,492 for the first quarter are the sum of the $3,384 plain T-shirt purchases and the $1,108 ink purchases. As you can see, there is a separate direct materials purchases budget for each type of raw material in a firm.

Direct Labor Budget

The **direct labor budget** shows the total direct labor hours needed and the associated cost for the number of units in the production budget. As with direct materials, the budgeted hours of direct labor are determined by the relationship between labor and output. For example, if a batch of 100 logo T-shirts requires 12 direct labor hours, then the direct labor time per logo T-shirt is 0.12 hour.

Given the direct labor used per unit of output and the units to be produced from the production budget, the way to prepare the direct labor budget is shown by Cornerstone 7-4. In the direct labor budget, the wage rate ($10 per hour in this example) is the average wage paid the direct laborers associated with the production of the T-shirts. Since it is an average, it allows for the possibility of differing wage rates paid to individual laborers.

Analytical Q&A

Assume that a product uses 10 pounds of plastic per unit. Expected production for the year is 1,250 units, and the desired ending inventory is 500 pounds. If the inventory on hand at the beginning of the year is 250 pounds, how many pounds of plastic should be budgeted for purchase?

Answer:

$Purchases = Needs + DEI - BI = (10 \times 1,250) + 500 - 250 = 12,750.$

Overhead Budget

The **overhead budget** shows the expected cost of all production costs other than direct materials and direct labor. Unlike direct materials and direct labor, there is no readily identifiable input-output relationship for overhead items. Instead, there are a series of activities and related drivers. These drivers are used to separate overhead costs into fixed

---

CORNERSTONE 7-4

HOW TO Prepare a Direct Labor Budget

Information: Refer to Cornerstone 7-2 for the production budget. It takes 0.12 hour to produce one T-shirt. The average wage cost per hour is $10.

Required: Prepare a direct labor budget.

Calculation:

Texas Rex Inc.
Direct Labor Budget
For the Year Ended December 31, 2009

| | Quarter | | | | |
	1	2	3	4	Year
Units to be produced (Cornerstone 7-2)	1,060	1,260	1,600	1,800	5,720
Direct labor time per unit (hr.)	×0.12	×0.12	×0.12	×0.12	×0.12
Total hours needed	127.2	151.2	192.0	216.0	686.4
Average wage per hour	×$10	×$10	×$10	×$10	×$10
Total direct labor cost	$1,272	$1,512	$1,920	$2,160	$6,864

HOW TO Prepare an Overhead Budget

Information: Refer to Cornerstone 7-4 for the direct labor budget. The variable overhead rate is $5 per direct labor hour; fixed overhead is budgeted at $1,645 per quarter.

Required: Prepare an overhead budget.

Calculation:

**CORNERSTONE
7-5**

Texas Rex Inc.
Overhead Budget
For the Year Ended December 31, 2009

	Quarter				
	1	2	3	4	Year
Budgeted direct labor hours	127.2	151.2	192.0	216.0	686.4
Variable overhead rate	× $5	× $5	× $5	× $5	× $5
Budgeted variable overhead	$ 636	$ 756	$ 960	$1,080	$ 3,432
Budgeted fixed overhead*	1,645	1,645	1,645	1,645	6,580
Total overhead	$2,281	$2,401	$2,605	$2,725	$10,012

*Includes $540 of depreciation in each quarter.

and variable components. Past experience can be used as a guide to determine how these overhead activities vary with their drivers. Although multiple drivers may be used, many companies use only one driver (direct labor hours being the most common). Individual items that vary with the selected driver(s) are identified. These items are pooled, and a variable overhead rate is calculated. For example, the rate may be $5 per direct labor hour. Those items whose costs do not vary with direct labor hours are collected into one pool. For our example, assume that two overhead cost pools are created, one for overhead activities that vary with direct labor hours and one for all other activities, which are fixed. The method for preparing an overhead budget using this approach to cost behavior is shown in Cornerstone 7-5.

Ending Finished Goods Inventory Budget

The **ending finished goods inventory budget** supplies information needed for the balance sheet and also serves as an important input for the preparation of the cost of goods sold budget. To prepare this budget, the unit cost of producing each T-shirt must be calculated by using information from the direct materials, direct labor, and overhead budgets. The way to calculate the unit cost of a T-shirt and the cost of the planned ending inventory is shown in Cornerstone 7-6 on the following page.

Analytical Q&A

Assume that a product uses two hours of direct labor per unit. Expected production for the year is 1,250 units. The average wage cost per hour is $8. What is the budget for direct labor cost?

Answer:

$Budget = (2 \times 1,250) \times \$8 = \$20,000.$

Analytical Q&A

Assume that the budget formula for overhead costs (OH) is OH = $2,000 + $3X, where X = total direct labor hours. If the company expects to work 5,000 direct labor hours, what is the budgeted variable overhead? Budgeted fixed overhead? Budgeted total overhead?

Answer:

$Variable\ overhead = \$3 \times 5,000 = \$15,000; Fixed\ overhead = \$2,000.$
$Total\ budgeted\ overhead = \$15,000 + \$2,000 = \$17,000.$

**CORNERSTONE
7-6**

HOW TO Prepare the Ending Finished Goods Inventory Budget

Information: Refer to Cornerstones 7-3, 7-4, and 7-5 for the direct materials, direct labor, and overhead budgets.

Required: Prepare an ending finished goods inventory budget.

Calculation:

Texas Rex Inc.
Ending Finished Goods Inventory Budget
For the Year Ended December 31, 2009

Unit cost computation:	
Direct materials ($3 + $1)	$4.00
Direct labor (0.12 hr. @ $10)	1.20
Overhead:	
Variable (0.12 hr. @ $5)	0.60
Fixed (0.12 hr. @ $9.59*)	1.15
Total unit cost	$6.95

*Budgeted fixed overhead/Budgeted direct labor hours = $6,580/686.4 = $9.59.

	Units	Unit Cost ($)	Total ($)
Finished goods: Logo T-shirts	200	6.95	1,390

Concept Q&A

What operating budgets are needed to calculate a budgeted unit cost?

Answer:

Materials, labor, and overhead budgets. It could be argued that sales and production budgets are needed also because the three budgets listed cannot be developed until the sales and production budgets are known.

Analytical Q&A

Assume that the budgeted cost of goods sold is $700. There is no beginning finished goods inventory. Budgeted manufacturing costs are $1,000. What is the budgeted finished goods inventory?

Answer:

Ending finished goods = Goods available for sale − Cost of goods sold = $1,000 − $700 = $300.

Cost of Goods Sold Budget

Assuming that the beginning finished goods inventory is valued at $1,251, the budgeted cost of goods sold schedule can be prepared using information from Cornerstones 7-3 to 7-6. The **cost of goods sold budget** reveals the expected cost of the goods to be sold and is shown in Cornerstone 7-7.

Selling and Administrative Expenses Budget

The next budget to be prepared, the **selling and administrative expenses budget**, outlines planned expenditures for non-manufacturing activities. As with overhead, selling and administrative expenses can be broken down into fixed and variable components. Such items as sales commissions, freight, and supplies vary with sales activity. The selling and administrative expenses budget is illustrated in Cornerstone 7-8.

Budgeted Income Statement

With the completion of the budgeted cost of goods sold schedule and the budgeted selling and administrative expenses budget, Texas Rex has all the operating budgets needed to prepare an estimate of *operating* income. The way to prepare this budgeted income

HOW TO Prepare a Cost of Goods Sold Budget

Information: Refer to Cornerstones 7-3 to 7-6 for the direct materials, direct labor, overhead, and ending finished goods budgets.

Required: Prepare a cost of goods sold budget.

Calculation:

**CORNERSTONE
7-7**

**Texas Rex Inc.
Cost of Goods Sold Budget
For the Year Ended December 31, 2009**

Direct materials used (Cornerstone 7-3)*	$22,880
Direct labor used (Cornerstone 7-4)	6,864
Overhead (Cornerstone 7-5)	10,012
Budgeted manufacturing costs	$39,756
Beginning finished goods	1,251
Goods available for sale	$41,007
Less: Ending finished goods (Cornerstone 7-6)	(1,390)
Budgeted cost of goods sold	$39,617

*Production needs = (5,720 plain T-shirts × $3) + (28,600 oz. ink × $0.20).

HOW TO Prepare a Selling and Administrative Expenses Budget

Information: Refer to Cornerstone 7-1 for the sales budget. Variable expenses are $0.10 per unit sold. Salaries average $1,420 per quarter; utilities, $50 per quarter; and depreciation, $150 per quarter. Advertising for quarters 1 through 4 is $100, $200, $300, and $500, respectively. Insurance is $500 and is paid in the third quarter.

Required: Prepare a selling and administrative expenses budget.

Calculation:

**CORNERSTONE
7-8**

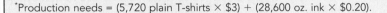

**Texas Rex Inc.
Selling and Administrative Expenses Budget
For the Year Ended December 31, 2009**

	Quarter				
	1	2	3	4	Year
Planned sales in units (Cornerstone 7-1)	1,000	1,200	1,500	2,000	5,700
Variable selling and administrative expenses per unit	×$0.10	×$0.10	×$0.10	×$0.10	×$0.10
Total variable expenses	$ 100	$ 120	$ 150	$ 200	$ 570
Fixed selling and administrative expenses:					
Salaries	$1,420	$1,420	$1,420	$1,420	$5,680
Utilities	50	50	50	50	200

**CORNERSTONE
7-8
(continued)**

| | Quarter | | | | |
	1	2	3	4	Year
Advertising	100	200	300	500	1,100
Depreciation	150	150	150	150	600
Insurance	—	—	500	—	500
Total fixed expenses	$1,720	$1,820	$2,420	$2,120	$8,080
Total selling and administrative expenses	$1,820	$1,940	$2,570	$2,320	$8,650

Concept Q&A

Assume that sales agents are paid a commission of 2 percent of sales revenue. Further, the only fixed selling expense is advertising, which is expected to be $10,000. If sales revenue is budgeted at $500,000, what is the budgeted selling expense?

Answer:

Budgeted selling expense = $10,000 + (0.02 × $500,000) = $20,000.

statement is shown in Cornerstone 7-9. The eight budgets already prepared, along with the budgeted operating income statement, define the operating budget for Texas Rex.

Operating income is *not* equivalent to the net income of a firm. To yield net income, interest expense and taxes must be subtracted from operating income. The interest expense deduction is taken from the cash budget for Texas Rex (Cornerstone 7-10), a budget discussed in the section on financial budgets. The taxes owed depend on the current federal and state tax laws. For simplicity, a combined rate of 40 percent is assumed.

**CORNERSTONE
7-9**

HOW TO Prepare a Budgeted Income Statement

Information: Refer to Cornerstones 7-1, 7-7, 7-8, and 7-10 for the sales budget, the cost of goods sold budget, the selling and administrative expenses budget, and the cash budget. Assume that the tax rate is 40 percent.

Required: Prepare a budgeted income statement.

Calculation:

**Texas Rex Inc.
Budgeted Income Statement
For the Year Ended December 31, 2009**

Sales (Cornerstone 7-1)	$57,000
Less: Cost of goods sold (Cornerstone 7-7)	(39,617)
Gross margin	$17,383
Less: Selling and administrative expenses (Cornerstone 7-8)	(8,650)
Operating income	$ 8,733
Less: Interest expense (Cornerstone 7-10)	(60)
Income before taxes	$ 8,673
Less: Income taxes (0.40 × $8,673)	(3,469)
Net income	$ 5,204

Preparing the Financial Budget

OBJECTIVE ③

Define and prepare the financial budget, identify its major components, and explain the interrelationships of its various components.

The remaining budgets found in the master budget are the financial budgets. The usual financial budgets prepared are:

1. The cash budget
2. The budgeted balance sheet
3. The budget for capital expenditures

The master budget also contains a plan for acquiring long-term assets—assets that have a time horizon that extends beyond the one-year operating period. Some of these assets may be purchased during the coming year; plans to purchase others may be detailed for future periods. This part of the master budget is typically referred to as the *capital budget*. Decision making for capital expenditures is considered in Chapter 12. Accordingly, only the cash budget and the budgeted balance sheet will be illustrated here.

Concept Q&A

Why is it not possible to prepare a budgeted income statement by using only operating budgets?

Interest expense comes from the financial budgets. Only operating income can be computed by using operating budgets.

Answer:

Cash Budget

Knowledge of cash flows is critical to managing a business. Often, a business is successful in producing and selling a product but fails because of timing problems associated with cash inflows and outflows. By knowing when cash deficiencies and surpluses are likely to occur, a manager can plan to borrow cash when needed and to repay the loans during periods of excess cash. Bank loan officers use a company's **cash budget** to document the need for cash as well as to determine the ability to repay. Because cash flow is the lifeblood of an organization, the cash budget is one of the most important budgets in the master budget. The basic structure of a cash budget is illustrated in Exhibit 7-3.

Cash available consists of the beginning cash balance and the expected cash receipts. Expected cash receipts include all sources of cash for the period being considered. The principal source of cash is from sales. Because a significant proportion of sales is usually on account, a major task of an organization is to determine the pattern of collection for its accounts receivable. If a company has been in business for a while, it can use past experience in creating an accounts receivable aging schedule. In other words, the company can determine, on average, what percentages of its accounts receivable are paid in

Exhibit 7-3

The Cash Budget

Beginning cash balance	$ 1,000
Add: Cash receipts	10,000
Cash available	$11,000
Less: Cash disbursements	9,000
Less: Minimum cash balance	1,000
Cash surplus (deficiency)	$ 1,000
Add: Cash from loans	0
Less: Loan repayments	500
Add: Minimum cash balance	1,000
Ending cash balance	$ 1,500

the months following sales. For example, assume that a company, Patton Hardware, has the following accounts receivable payment experience:

Percent paid in the month of sale	30
Percent paid in the month after the sale	60
Percent paid in the second month after the sale	10

If Patton sells $100,000 worth of goods on account in the month of May, then it would expect to receive $30,000 cash from May credit sales in the month of May, $60,000 cash from May credit sales in June, and $10,000 from May credit sales in July. (Notice that Patton expects to receive all of its accounts receivable. This is not typical. If a company experiences, let's say, 3 percent uncollectible accounts, then this 3 percent of sales is ignored for the purpose of cash budgeting—because no cash is received from customers who default.)

The cash disbursements section lists all planned cash outlays for the period. All expenses not resulting in a cash outlay are excluded from the list (e.g., depreciation is never included in the disbursements section). A disbursement that is typically not included in this section is interest on short-term borrowing. This interest expenditure is reserved for the section on loan repayments.

The cash excess or deficiency line compares the cash available with the cash needed. Cash needed is the total cash disbursements plus the minimum cash balance required by company policy. The minimum cash balance is the lowest amount of cash on hand that the firm finds acceptable. Consider your own checking account. You probably try to keep at least some cash in the account, perhaps because by having a minimum balance you avoid service charges, or because a minimum balance allows you to make an unplanned purchase. Similarly, companies also require minimum cash balances. The amount varies from firm to firm and is determined by each company's particular needs and policies. If the total cash available is less than the cash needed, a deficiency exists. In such a case, a short-term loan will be needed. On the other hand, with a cash excess (cash available is greater than the firm's cash needs), the firm has the ability to repay loans and perhaps to make some temporary investments.

The final section of the cash budget consists of borrowings and repayments. If there is a deficiency, this section shows the necessary amount to be borrowed. When excess cash is available, this section shows planned repayments, including interest expense.

The last line of the cash budget is the planned ending cash balance. Remember that the minimum cash balance was subtracted to find the cash excess or deficiency. However, the minimum cash balance is not a disbursement, so it must be added back to yield the planned ending balance. The way to prepare a cash budget is illustrated in Cornerstone 7-10.

Cornerstone 7-10 reveals that much of the information needed to prepare the cash budget comes from the operating budgets. However, these operating budgets by themselves do not supply all of the needed information. The collection pattern for revenues and the payment pattern for materials must be known before the cash flow for sales and purchases on credit can be budgeted. Exhibit 7-4 on page 308 displays the specific pattern of cash inflows from both cash and credit sales. For example, cash sales for the first quarter are budgeted for $2,500 (0.25 × $10,000; Cornerstone 7-1). Collections on account for the first quarter relate to credit sales made during the last quarter of the previous year and the first quarter of 2009. Quarter 4, 2008, credit sales equaled $13,500 (0.75 × $18,000), and $1,350 of those sales (0.10 × $13,500) remain to be

Concept Q&A

Why would a company want a minimum cash balance? Suppose that the minimum cash balance is $1,000 and that the projected cash surplus is $500. What would a company have to do to achieve the desired minimum?

Answer:
A minimum cash balance is needed to reduce the risk of insufficient funds and satisfy account agreements with the banks. In the event of a shortage, it is necessary to borrow the difference.

Concept Q&A

Sales for a month totaled $10,000. Cash receipts for the same month were $15,000. How is it possible for cash receipts to be more than sales?

Answer:
Money can be collected from credit sales of prior month(s).

HOW TO Prepare a Cash Budget

**CORNERSTONE
7-10**

Information: Refer to Cornerstones 7-1, 7-3, 7-4, 7-5, 7-8, and 7-9 as well as the following details:

a. A $1,000 minimum cash balance is required for the end of each quarter. Money can be borrowed and repaid in multiples of $1,000. Interest is 12 percent per year. Interest payments are made only for the amount of the principal being repaid. All borrowing takes place at the beginning of a quarter, and all repayment takes place at the end of a quarter.

b. Twenty-five percent of all sales are for cash, 90 percent of credit sales are collected in the quarter of sale, and the remaining 10 percent are collected in the following quarter. The sales for the fourth quarter of 2008 were $18,000.

c. Purchases of raw materials are made on account; 80 percent of purchases are paid for in the quarter of purchase. The remaining 20 percent are paid for in the following quarter. The purchases for the fourth quarter of 2008 were $5,000.

d. Budgeted depreciation is $540 per quarter for overhead and $150 per quarter for selling and administrative expenses (Cornerstones 7-5 and 7-8).

e. The capital budget for 2009 revealed plans to purchase additional screen printing equipment. The cash outlay for the equipment, $6,500, will take place in the first quarter. The company plans to finance the acquisition of the equipment with operating cash, supplementing it with short-term loans as necessary.

f. Corporate income taxes are approximately $3,469 and will be paid at the end of the fourth quarter (Cornerstone 7-9).

g. Beginning cash balance equals $5,200.

h. All amounts in the budget are rounded to the nearest dollar.

Required: Prepare a cash budget for Texas Rex.

Calculation:

Texas Rex Inc.
Cash Budget
For the Year Ended December 31, 2009

	Quarter				Year	Source[a]
	1	2	3	4		
Beginning cash balance	$ 5,200	$ 1,023	$ 1,611	$ 3,762	$ 5,200	g
Collections:						
Cash sales	2,500	3,000	3,750	5,000	14,250	b,1
Credit sales:						
Current quarter	6,750	8,100	10,125	13,500	38,475	b,1
Prior quarter	1,350	750	900	1,125	4,125	b,1
Total cash available	$ 15,800	$ 12,873	$ 16,386	$ 23,387	$ 62,050	
Less disbursements:						
Raw materials:						
Current quarter	$ (3,594)	$ (4,141)	$ (5,184)	$ (5,523)	$(18,442)	c,3
Prior quarter	(1,000)	(898)	(1,035)	(1,296)	(4,229)	c,3

CORNERSTONE 7-10 (continued)

| | Quarter | | | | | |
	1	2	3	4	Year	Source[a]
Direct labor	(1,272)	(1,512)	(1,920)	(2,160)	(6,864)	4
Overhead	(1,741)	(1,861)	(2,065)	(2,185)	(7,852)	d,5
Selling and Administrative	(1,670)	(1,790)	(2,420)	(2,170)	(8,050)	d,8
Income taxes	—	—	—	(3,469)	(3,469)	f,9
Equipment	(6,500)	—	—	—	(6,500)	e
Total disbursements	$(15,777)	$(10,202)	$(12,624)	$(16,803)	$(55,406)	
Minimum cash balance	(1,000)	(1,000)	(1,000)	(1,000)	(1,000)	a
Total cash needs	$(16,777)	$(11,202)	$(13,624)	$(17,803)	$(56,406)	
Excess (deficiency) of cash available over needs	$ (977)	$ 1,671	$ 2,762	$ 5,584	$ 5,644	
Financing:						
Borrowings	1,000	—	—	—	1,000	
Repayments	—	(1,000)	—	—	(1,000)	a
Interest[b]	—	(60)	—	—	(60)	a
Total financing	$ 1,000	$ (1,060)		—	$ (1,060)	
Ending cash balance[c]	$ 1,023	$ 1,611	$ 3,762	$ 6,584	$ 6,584	

[a]Letters refer to the detailed information above. Numbers refer to Cornerstone schedules.
[b]Interest payment is 6/12 × 0.12 × $1,000. Since borrowings occur at the beginning of the quarter and repayments at the end of the quarter, the principal repayment takes place after six months.
[c]Total cash available minus total disbursements plus (or minus) total financing.

Exhibit 7-4

Texas Rex's Cash Receipts Pattern for 2009

Source	Quarter 1	Quarter 2	Quarter 3	Quarter 4
Cash sales	$ 2,500	$ 3,000	$ 3,750	$ 5,000
Received on account from:				
Quarter 4, 2008	1,350			
Quarter 1, 2009	6,750	750		
Quarter 2, 2009		8,100	900	
Quarter 3, 2009			10,125	1,125
Quarter 4, 2009	—	—	—	13,500
Total cash receipts	$10,600	$11,850	$14,775	$19,625

collected in quarter 1, 2009. Quarter 1, 2009, credit sales are budgeted at $7,500, and 90 percent will be collected in that quarter. Therefore, $6,750 will be collected on account for credit sales made in that quarter. Similar computations are made for the remaining quarters.

As well, similar computations are done for purchases. In both cases, patterns of collection and payment are needed in addition to the information supplied by the operating budgets. Additionally, all noncash expenses, such as depreciation, need to be removed from the total amounts reported in the expense budgets. Thus, the budgeted expenses in Cornerstones 7-5 and 7-8 were reduced by the budgeted depreciation for each quarter. Overhead expenses in Cornerstone 7-5 were reduced by depreciation of $540 per quarter. Selling and administrative expenses in Cornerstone 7-8 were reduced by $150 per quarter. The net amounts are what appear in the cash budget.

The cash budget underscores the importance of breaking down the annual budget into smaller time periods. The cash budget for the year gives the impression that sufficient operating cash will be available to finance the acquisition of the new equipment. Quarterly information, however, shows the need for short-term borrowing ($1,000) because of both the acquisition of the new equipment and the timing of the firm's cash flows. Most firms prepare monthly cash budgets, and some even prepare weekly and daily budgets.

Another significant piece of information emerges from Texas Rex's cash budget. By the end of the third quarter, the firm has more cash ($3,762) than necessary to meet operating needs. The management of Texas Rex should consider investing the excess cash in an interest-bearing account. Once plans are finalized for use of the excess cash, the cash budget should be revised to reflect those plans. Budgeting is a dynamic process. As the budget is developed, new information becomes available, and better plans can be formulated.

Budgeted Balance Sheet

The budgeted balance sheet depends on information contained in the current balance sheet and in the other budgets in the master budget. Cornerstone 7-11 shows how the budgeted balance sheet for December 31, 2009, is prepared. Explanations for the budgeted figures are provided in the footnotes.

HOW TO Prepare the Budgeted Balance Sheet

Information:

1. Last year's balance sheet:

**CORNERSTONE
7-11**

Texas Rex Inc.
Balance Sheet
December 31, 2008

Assets

Current assets:		
Cash	$ 5,200	
Accounts receivable	1,350	
Raw materials inventory	252	
Finished goods inventory	1,251	
Total current assets		$ 8,053
Property, plant, and equipment (PP&E):		
Land	$ 1,100	
Building and equipment	30,000	
Accumulated depreciation	(5,000)	
Total PP&E		26,100
Total assets		$34,153

**CORNERSTONE
7-11
(continued)**

Liabilities and Owner's Equity

Current liabilities:

Accounts payable		$ 1,000
Owner's equity:		
Retained earnings	33,153	
Total owner's equity		33,153
Total liabilities and owner's equity		$34,153

2. Cornerstones 7-1, 7-3, 7-5, 7-6, 7-8, 7-9, and 7-10.

Required: Prepare a budgeted balance sheet for 2009.

Calculation:

Texas Rex Inc.
Budgeted Balance Sheet
December 31, 2009

Assets

Current assets:

Cash	$ 6,584[a]	
Accounts receivable	1,500[b]	
Raw materials inventory	424[c]	
Finished goods inventory	1,390[d]	
Total current assets		$ 9,898
Property, plant, and equipment (PP&E):		
Land	$ 1,100[e]	
Building and equipment	36,500[f]	
Accumulated depreciation	(7,760)[g]	
Total PP&E		29,840
Total assets		$39,738

Liabilities and Owner's Equity

Current liabilities:

Accounts payable		$ 1,381[h]
Owner's equity:		
Retained earnings	$38,557[i]	
Total owner's equity		38,357
Total liabilities and owner's equity		$39,738

[a]Ending balance from Cornerstone 7-10.
[b]Ten percent of fourth-quarter credit sales (0.75 × $20,000)—see Cornerstones 7-1 and 7-10.
[c]From Cornerstone 7-3 [(106 × $3) + (530 × $0.20)].
[d]From Cornerstone 7-6.
[e]From the December 31, 2008, balance sheet.
[f]December 31, 2008, balance ($30,000) plus new equipment acquisition of $6,500 (see the 2008 ending balance sheet and Cornerstone 7-10).
[g]From the December 31, 2008, balance sheet, Cornerstone 7-5, and Cornerstone 7-8 ($5,000 + $2,160 + $600).
[h]Twenty percent of fourth-quarter purchases (0.20 × $6,904)—see Cornerstones 7-3 and 7-10.
[i]$33,153 + $5,204 (December 31, 2008, balance plus net income from Cornerstone 7-9).

Using Budgets for Performance Evaluation

Budgets often are used to judge the performance of managers. Bonuses, salary increases, and promotions all are affected by a manager's ability to achieve or beat budgeted goals. Since a manager's financial status and career can be affected, budgets can have a significant effect on their behavior. Whether that effect is positive or negative depends in large part on how budgets are used.

Positive behavior occurs when the goals of each manager are aligned with the goals of the organization and each manager has the drive to achieve them. The alignment of managerial and organizational goals is often referred to as **goal congruence**. If the budget is improperly administered, subordinate managers may subvert the organization's goals (i.e., use the organization's money for purposes other than what is in the organization's best interest). **Dysfunctional behavior** is individual behavior that is in basic conflict with the goals of the organization.

An ideal budgetary system is one that achieves complete goal congruence and, simultaneously, creates a drive in managers to achieve the organization's goals in an ethical manner. While an ideal budgetary system probably does not exist, research and practice have identified some key features that promote a reasonable degree of positive behavior. These features include frequent feedback on performance, monetary and nonmonetary incentives, participative budgeting, realistic standards, controllability of costs, and multiple measures of performance.

Concept Q&A

In the last quarter of the fiscal year, a divisional manager chose to delay budgeted preventive maintenance expenditures so that the budgeted income goals could be achieved. Is this an example of goal congruent behavior or dysfunctional behavior?

Answer:
Assuming that the budgeted maintenance expenditures were well specified, the manager is sacrificing the long-run well-being of the division to achieve a short-run benefit (dysfunctional behavior).

Frequent Feedback on Performance

Managers need to know how they are doing as the year unfolds. Providing them with frequent, timely performance reports allows them to know how successful their efforts have been, to take corrective actions, and to change plans as necessary.

Monetary and Nonmonetary Incentives

A sound budgetary system encourages goal-congruent behavior. The means an organization uses to influence a manager to exert effort to achieve an organization's goal are called **incentives**. Traditional organizational theory assumes that employees are primarily motivated by monetary rewards, they resist work, and they are inefficient and wasteful. Thus, **monetary incentives** are used to control a manager's tendency to shirk and waste resources by relating budgetary performance to salary increases, bonuses, and promotions. The threat of dismissal is the ultimate economic sanction for poor performance. In reality, employees are motivated by more than economic factors. Employees are also motivated by intrinsic psychological and social factors, such as the satisfaction of a job well done, recognition, responsibility, self-esteem, and the nature of the work itself. Thus, **nonmonetary incentives**, including job enrichment, increased responsibility and autonomy, recognition programs, and so on, can be used to enhance a budgetary control system.

Participative Budgeting

Rather than imposing budgets on subordinate managers, **participative budgeting** allows subordinate managers considerable say in how the budgets are established. Typically, overall objectives are communicated to the manager, who helps develop a budget that will accomplish these objectives. Participative budgeting communicates a sense of responsibility to subordinate managers and fosters creativity. Since the subordinate manager creates the budget, the budget's goals will more likely become the manager's personal goals, resulting in greater goal congruence. The increased responsibility and challenge inherent in the process provide nonmonetary incentives that lead to a higher level of performance performance than when participative budgeting is not used.

Participative budgeting has three potential problems:

1. Setting standards that either are too high or too low
2. Building slack into the budget (often referred to as padding the budget)
3. Pseudoparticipation

Some managers may tend to set the budget either too loose or too tight. Since budgeted goals tend to become the manager's goals when participation is allowed, making this mistake in setting the budget can result in decreased performance levels. If goals are too easily achieved, a manager may lose interest, and performance may drop. Feeling challenged is important to aggressive and creative individuals. Similarly, setting the budget too tight ensures failure to achieve the standards and frustrates the manager. This frustration, too, can lead to poorer performance. The trick is to get managers in a participative setting to set high but achievable goals.

The second problem with participative budgeting is the opportunity for managers to build slack into the budget. **Budgetary slack** (or *padding the budget*) exists when a manager deliberately underestimates revenues or overestimates costs in an effort to make the future period appear less attractive in the budget than he or she thinks it will be in reality. Either approach increases the likelihood that the manager will achieve the budget and consequently reduces the risk that the manager faces. Top management should carefully review budgets proposed by subordinate managers and provide input, where needed, in order to decrease the effects of building slack into the budget (Exhibit 7-5). Furthermore, the act of padding the budget is questionable when considering what is viewed as ethical professional practice. Padding the budget is certainly not communicating information fairly and objectively and constitutes a violation of the credibility standard. In addition, the motive for such behavior is inconsistent with the professional responsibility to exhibit integrity.

The third problem with participation occurs when top management assumes total control of the budgeting process, seeking only superficial participation from lower-level managers. This practice is termed **pseudoparticipation**. Top management is merely obtaining formal acceptance of the budget from subordinate managers, not seeking real input. Accordingly, none of the behavioral benefits of participation will be realized.

Concept Q&A

Assume that a company evaluates and rewards its managers based on their ability to achieve budgeted goals. Why would the same company ask its managers to participate in setting their budgeted standards?

Answer:
Participation encourages managers to internalize the goals and make them their own, leading to improved performance.

Exhibit 7-5

The Art of Standard Setting

Standard Set Too Loose
Goals Too Easily Achieved

Standard Set Too Tight
Frustration

Realistic Standards

Budgeted objectives are used to gauge performance; accordingly, they should be based on realistic conditions and expectations. Budgets should reflect operating realities such as actual levels of activity, seasonal variations, efficiencies, and general economic trends. Flexible budgets, which are studied in Chapter 9, are used to ensure that budgeted costs can be realistically compared with costs for actual levels of activity. Interim budgets should reflect seasonal effects. **Toys "R" Us**, for example, would expect much higher sales in the quarter that includes Christmas than in other quarters. Budgetary cuts should be based on *planned* increases in efficiency and not arbitrary across-the-board reductions. Across-the-board cuts without any formal evaluation may impair the ability of some units to carry out their missions. General economic conditions also need to be considered. Budgeting for a significant increase in sales when a recession is projected is not only foolish but also is potentially dangerous.

Controllability of Costs

Ideally, managers are held accountable only for costs that they can control. **Controllable costs** are costs whose level a manager can influence. For example, divisional managers have no power to authorize such corporate-level costs as research and development and salaries of top managers. Therefore, they should not be held accountable for the incurrence of those costs. If noncontrollable costs are put in the budgets of subordinate managers to help them understand that these costs also need to be covered, then they should be separated from controllable costs and labeled as *noncontrollable*.

Multiple Measures of Performance

Often, organizations make the mistake of using budgets as their only measure of managerial performance. While financial measures of performance are important, overemphasis can lead to a form of dysfunctional behavior called *milking the firm* or *myopia*. **Myopic behavior** occurs when a manager takes actions that improve budgetary performance in the short run but bring long-run harm to the firm. For example, to meet budgeted cost objectives or profits, managers can fail to promote deserving employees or to reduce expenditures for preventive maintenance, advertising, and new product development. Using measures that are both financial and nonfinancial and that are long term and short term in nature can alleviate this problem. For example, **Starwood Hotels** incurs considerable costs every year to research consumer trends and to train its hotel staff members to help ensure sustainable growth in room revenue for its luxury St. Regis brand. Budgetary measures by themselves are inadequate to prevent myopic behavior.

Summary of Learning Objectives

1. Define budgeting, and discuss its role in planning, control, and decision making.
   - Budgeting is the creation of a plan of action expressed in financial terms.
   - Budgeting plays a key role in planning, control, and decision making.
   - Budgets also serve to improve communication and coordination, a role that becomes increasingly important as organizations grow in size.
   - The master budget, which is the comprehensive financial plan of an organization, is made up of the operating and financial budgets.

2. Define and prepare the operating budget, identify its major components, and explain the interrelationships of its various components.
   - The operating budget is the budgeted income statement and all supporting budgets.
   - The sales budget consists of the anticipated quantity and price of all products to be sold.
   - The production budget gives the expected production in units to meet forecasted sales and desired ending inventory goals; expected production is supplemented by beginning inventory.
   - The direct materials purchases budget gives the necessary purchases during the year for every type of raw material to meet production and desired ending inventory goals.
   - The direct labor budget and overhead budget give the amounts of these resources necessary for the coming year's production.
   - The overhead budget may be broken down into fixed and variable components to facilitate preparation of the budget.
   - The selling and administrative expenses budget gives the forecasted costs for these functions.
   - The finished goods inventory budget and the cost of goods sold budget detail production costs for the expected ending inventory and the units sold, respectively.
   - The budgeted income statement outlines the net income to be realized if budgeted plans come to fruition.

3. Define and prepare the financial budget, identify its major components, and explain the interrelationships of its various components.
   - The financial budget includes the cash budget, the capital expenditures budget, and the budgeted balance sheet.
   - The cash budget is the beginning balance in the cash account, plus anticipated receipts, minus anticipated disbursements, plus or minus any necessary borrowing.
   - The budgeted (or pro forma) balance sheet gives the anticipated ending balances of the asset, liability, and equity accounts if budgeted plans hold.

4. Describe the behavioral dimension of budgeting.
   - The success of a budgetary system depends on how seriously human factors are considered.
   - To discourage dysfunctional behavior, organizations should avoid overemphasizing budgets as a control mechanism.
   - Budgets can be improved as performance measures by using participative budgeting and other nonmonetary incentives, providing frequent feedback on performance, using flexible budgeting, ensuring that the budgetary objectives reflect reality, and holding managers accountable for only controllable costs.

Summary of Important Equations

1. Units to be produced = Expected unit sales + Units in ending inventory (DEI)
   − Units in beginning inventory (BI)
2. Purchases = Direct materials needed for production
   + Desired direct materials in ending inventory
   − Direct materials in beginning inventory

CORNERSTONES FOR CHAPTER 7

Key Terms

Budget committee, 294
Budget director, 294
Budgetary slack, 312
Budgets, 292
Cash budget, 305
Continuous budget, 294
Control, 293
Controllable costs, 313
Cost of goods sold budget, 302
Direct labor budget, 300
Direct materials purchases budget, 297
Dysfunctional behavior, 311
Ending finished goods inventory budget, 301
Financial budgets, 294

Goal congruence, 311
Incentives, 311
Master budget, 293
Monetary incentives, 311
Myopic behavior, 313
Nonmonetary incentives, 311
Operating budgets, 294
Overhead budget, 300
Participative budgeting, 311
Production budget, 296
Pseudoparticipation, 312
Sales budget, 295
Selling and administrative expenses budget, 302
Strategic plan, 292

Review Problems

I. Selected Operational Budgets

Joven Products produces coat racks. The projected sales for the first quarter of the coming year and the beginning and ending inventory data are as follows:

Unit sales	100,000
Unit price	$15
Units in beginning inventory	8,000
Units in targeted ending inventory	12,000

The coat racks are molded and then painted. Each rack requires four pounds of metal, which costs $2.50 per pound. The beginning inventory of materials is 4,000 pounds. Young Products wants to have 6,000 pounds of metal in inventory at the end of the quarter. Each rack produced requires 30 minutes of direct labor time, which is billed at $9 per hour.

Required:

1. Prepare a sales budget for the first quarter.
2. Prepare a production budget for the first quarter.
3. Prepare a direct materials purchases budget for the first quarter.
4. Prepare a direct labor budget for the first quarter.

Solution:

1.

Joven Products
Sales Budget
For the First Quarter

Units	100,000
Unit price	× $15
Sales	$1,500,000

2.

Joven Products
Production Budget
For the First Quarter

Sales (in units)	100,000
Desired ending inventory	12,000
Total needs	112,000
Less: Beginning inventory	8,000
Units to be produced	104,000

3.

Joven Products
Direct Materials Purchases Budget
For the First Quarter

Units to be produced	104,000
Direct materials per unit (lb.)	× 4
Production needs (lb.)	416,000
Desired ending inventory (lb.)	6,000
Total needs (lb.)	422,000
Less: Beginning inventory (lb.)	4,000
Materials to be purchased (lb.)	418,000
Cost per pound	× $2.50
Total purchase cost	$1,045,000

4.

Joven Products
Direct Labor Budget
For the First Quarter

Units to be produced	104,000
Labor: Hours per unit	× 0.5
Total hours needed	52,000
Cost per hour	× $9
Total direct labor cost	$468,000

II. Cash Budgeting

Kylles Inc. expects to receive cash from sales of $45,000 in March. In addition, Kylles expects to sell property worth $3,500. Payments for materials and supplies are expected to total $10,000, direct labor payroll will be $12,500, and other expenditures are budgeted at $14,900. On March 1, the cash account balance is $1,230.

Required:

1. Prepare a cash budget for Kylles Inc. for the month of March.
2. Assume that Kylles Inc. wanted a minimum cash balance of $15,000 and that it could borrow from the bank in multiples of $1,000 at an interest rate of 12 percent per year. What would the adjusted ending balance for March be for Kylles? How

much interest would Kylles owe in April, assuming that the entire amount borrowed in March would be paid back?

Solution:

1.

Kylles Inc.
Cash Budget for the Month of March

Beginning cash balance	$ 1,230
Cash sales	45,000
Sale of property	3,500
Total cash available	$49,730
Less disbursements:	
Materials and supplies	$10,000
Direct labor payroll	12,500
Other expenditures	14,900
Total disbursements	$37,400
Ending cash balance	$12,330

2.

Unadjusted ending balance	$12,330
Plus borrowing	3,000
Adjusted ending balance	$15,330

In April, interest owed would be $(1/12 \times 0.12 \times \$3,000) = \$30$.

Discussion Questions

1. Define the term *budget*. How are budgets used in planning?
2. Define *control*. How are budgets used to control?
3. Explain how both small and large organizations can benefit from budgeting.
4. Discuss some reasons for budgeting.
5. What is a master budget? An operating budget? A financial budget?
6. Explain the role of a sales forecast in budgeting. What is the difference between a sales forecast and a sales budget?
7. All budgets depend on the sales budget. Is this true? Explain.
8. Why is goal congruence important?
9. Why is it important for a manager to receive frequent feedback on his or her performance?
10. Discuss the roles of monetary and nonmonetary incentives. Do you believe that nonmonetary incentives are needed? Why?
11. What is participative budgeting? Discuss some of its advantages.
12. A budget too easily achieved will lead to diminished performance. Do you agree? Explain.
13. What is the role of top management in participative budgeting?
14. Explain why a manager has an incentive to build slack into the budget.
15. Explain how a manager can milk the firm to improve budgetary performance.

Multiple-Choice Exercises

7-1 A budget

a. is a long-term plan.
b. covers at least two years.
c. is only a control tool.
d. is necessary only for large firms.
e. is a short-term financial plan.

7-2 Which of the following is *not* part of the control process?

a.   Monitoring of actual activity
b.   Comparison of actual with planned activity
c.   Investigating
d.   Developing a strategic plan
e.   Taking corrective action

7-3 Which of the following is *not* an advantage of budgeting?

a.   It forces managers to plan.
b.   It provides information for decision making.
c.   It guarantees an improvement in organizational efficiency.
d.   It provides a standard for performance evaluation.
e.   It improves communication and coordination.

7-4 The budget committee

a.   reviews the budget.
b.   resolves differences that arise as the budget is prepared.
c.   approves the final budget.
d.   is directed (typically) by the controller.
e.   does all of the above.

7-5 A moving, 12-month budget that is updated monthly is

a.   a waste of time and effort.
b.   a continuous budget.
c.   a master budget.
d.   not used by industrial firms.
e.   always used by firms that prepare a master budget.

7-6 Which of the following is *not* part of the operating budget?

a.   The capital budget
b.   The cost of goods sold budget
c.   The production budget
d.   The direct labor budget
e.   The selling and administrative expenses budget

7-7 Before a direct materials purchases budget can be prepared, you should first

a.   prepare a sales budget.
b.   prepare a production budget.
c.   decide on the desired ending inventory of materials.
d.   obtain the expected price of each type of material.
e.   do all of the above.

7-8 The first step in preparing the sales budget is to

a.   talk with past customers.
b.   review the production budget carefully.
c.   assess the desired ending inventory of finished goods.
d.   prepare a sales forecast.
e.   increase sales beyond the forecast level.

7-9 Which of the following is needed to prepare the production budget?

a. Direct materials needed for production
b. Expected unit sales
c. Direct labor needed for production
d. Units of materials in ending inventory
e. None of the above

7-10 A company requires 100 pounds of plastic to meet the production needs of a small toy. It currently has 10 pounds of plastic inventory. The desired ending inventory of plastic is 30 pounds. How many pounds of plastic should be budgeted for purchasing during the coming period?

a. 100 pounds
b. 120 pounds
c. 130 pounds
d. 140 pounds
e. None of the above

7-11 A company plans on selling 200 units. The selling price per unit is $12. There are 20 units in beginning inventory, and the company would like to have 50 units in ending inventory. How many units should be produced for the coming period?

a. 250
b. 200
c. 230
d. 220
e. None of the above

7-12 Which of the following is needed to prepare a budgeted income statement?

a. The production budget
b. The budgeted balance sheet
c. Budgeted selling and administrative expenses
d. The capital expenditures budget
e. None of the above

7-13 Select the one budget below that is not a financial budget.

a. The cost of goods sold budget
b. The cash budget
c. The budgeted balance sheet
d. The capital expenditures budget
e. None of the above

7-14 The cash budget serves which of the following purposes?

a. Documents the need for liberal inventory policies
b. Provides information about the ability to repay loans
c. Reveals the amount lost due to uncollectible accounts
d. Reveals the amount of depreciation expense
e. None of the above

7-15 Assume that a company has the following accounts receivable collection pattern:

Month of sale	40%
Month following sale	60%

All sales are on credit. If credit sales for January and February are $100,000 and $200,000, respectively, the cash collections for February are

a. $140,000.
b. $300,000.
c. $120,000.
d. $160,000.
e. $80,000.

7-16 The percentage of accounts receivable uncollectible can be ignored for cash budgeting because

a.   for most companies, it is not a material amount.
b.   it is included in cash sales.
c.   it appears on the budgeted income statement.
d.   no cash is received from an account that defaults.
e.   none of the above.

7-17 An ideal budgetary system is one that

a.   encourages dysfunctional behavior.
b.   encourages myopic behavior.
c.   encourages goal-congruent behavior.
d.   encourages subversion of an organization's goals.
e.   does none of the above.

7-18 Some key budgetary features that tend to promote positive managerial behavior are

a.   frequent feedback on performance.
b.   participative budgeting.
c.   realistic standards.
d.   well-designed monetary and nonmonetary incentives.
e.   all of the above.

7-19 Which of the following is *not* an advantage of participative budgeting?

a.   It fosters a sense of creativity in managers.
b.   It encourages budgetary slack.
c.   It fosters a sense of responsibility.
d.   It encourages greater goal congruence.
e.   It tends to lead to a higher level of performance.

7-20 Which of the following items is *not* a possible example of myopic behavior?

a.   Promotion of deserving employees
b.   Reducing expenditures on preventive maintenance
c.   Cutting back on new product development
d.   Laying off top sales personnel so that budgeted income can be achieved
e.   Buying cheaper, lower-quality materials so that the company does not exceed the materials purchases budget

Exercises

Exercise 7-21 Planning and Control

OBJECTIVE ①

a. Dr. Jones, a dentist, wants to increase the size and profitability of his business by building a reputation for quality and timely service.

b. To achieve this, he plans on adding a dental laboratory to his building so that crowns, bridges, and dentures can be made in-house.

c. To add the laboratory, he needs additional money, which he decides must be obtained by increasing revenues. After some careful calculation, Dr. Jones concludes that annual revenues must be increased by 10 percent.

d. Dr. Jones finds that his fees for fillings and crowns are below the average in his community and decides that the 10-percent increase can be achieved by increasing these fees.

e. He then identifies the quantity of fillings and crowns expected for the coming year, the new per-unit fee, and the total fees expected.

f. As the year unfolds (on a month-by-month basis), Dr. Jones compares the actual revenues received with the budgeted revenues. For the first three months, actual revenues were less than planned.

g. Upon investigating, he discovered that he had some reduction in the number of patients because he had also changed his available hours of operation.

h. He returned to his old schedule and found out that the number of patients was restored to the original expected levels.

i. However, to make up the shortfall, he also increased the price of some of his other services.

Required:

Match each statement with the following planning and control elements (a letter may be matched to more than one item):

1. Corrective action
2. Budgets
3. Feedback
4. Investigation
5. Short-term plan
6. Comparison of actual with planned
7. Monitoring of actual activity
8. Strategic plan
9. Short-term objectives
10. Long-term objectives

Exercise 7-22 Sales Budget

OBJECTIVES ① ②

CORNERSTONE 7-1

Assume that Stillwater Designs produces two automotive subwoofers: S12L7 and S12L5. The S12L7 sells for $500, and the S12L5 sells for $300. Projected sales (number of speakers) for the coming five quarters are as follows:

	S12L7	S12L5
First quarter, 2007	1,000	500
Second quarter, 2007	2,000	1,000
Third quarter, 2007	8,000	4,000
Fourth quarter, 2007	4,000	2,000
First quarter, 2008	1,200	700

The vice president of sales believes that the projected sales are realistic and can be achieved by the company.

Required:
1. Prepare a sales budget for each quarter of 2007 and for the year in total. Show sales by product and in total for each time period.
2. How will Stillwater Designs use this sales budget?

Exercise 7-23 Production Budget

Refer to **Exercise 7-22**. Stillwater Designs needs a production budget for each product (representing the amount that must be outsourced to manufacturers located in Asia). Beginning inventory of S12L7 for the first quarter, 2007, was 500 boxes. The company's policy is to have 50 percent of the next quarter's sales of S12L7 in ending inventory. Beginning inventory of S12L5 was 200 boxes. The company's policy is to have 40 percent of the next quarter's sales of S12L5 in ending inventory.

Required:
Prepare a production budget for each quarter for 2007 and for the year in total.

Exercise 7-24 Production Budget

Seafood Inc. produces shrimp in cans. The sales budget for the first four months of the year is as follows:

	Unit Sales	Dollar Sales ($)
January	200,000	150,000
February	240,000	180,000
March	220,000	165,000
April	200,000	150,000

Company policy requires that ending inventories for each month be 35 percent of next month's sales. At the beginning of January, the inventory of shrimp is 36,000 cans.

Required:
Prepare a production budget for the first quarter of the year. Show the number of cans that should be produced each month as well as for the quarter in total.

Exercise 7-25 Direct Materials Purchases Budget

Seafood Inc. produces shrimp in cans. The two raw materials needed are shrimp and cans. Each can of shrimp requires one can and four ounces of shrimp. Company policy requires that ending inventories of raw materials for each month be 20 percent of the next month's production needs. That policy was met on January 1.

The units budgeted for production for the first three months of the year are as follows:

	Budgeted Units to Produce
January	248,000
February	233,000
March	213,000

Company policy requires that ending inventories for each month be 35 percent of next month's sales. At the beginning of January, the inventory of shrimp is 36,000 cans.

Required:
Prepare separate direct materials purchases budgets for cans and for shrimp for the months of January and February.

Exercise 7-26 Production Budget

OBJECTIVE ②
CORNERSTONE 7-2

Carson Inc. produces office supplies, including pencils. Pencils are bundled in packages of four and are sold for $0.50. The sales budget for the first four months of the year for this product is as follows:

	Unit Sales	Dollar Sales ($)
January	200,000	100,000
February	240,000	120,000
March	220,000	110,000
April	200,000	100,000

Company policy requires that ending inventories for each month be 15 percent of next month's sales. However, at the beginning of January, due to greater sales in December than anticipated, the beginning inventory of pencils is only 18,000 packages.

Required:
Prepare a production budget for the first quarter of the year. Show the number of units that should be produced each month as well as for the quarter in total.

Exercise 7-27 Direct Materials Purchases Budget

OBJECTIVE ②
CORNERSTONE 7-3

spreadsheet

Lester Company produces a variety of labels, including iron-on name labels, which are sold to parents of camp-bound children. (The camps require campers to have their name on each article of clothing.) The labels are sold in a roll of 1,000, which requires about 25 yards of paper strip. Each yard of paper strip costs $0.17. Lester has budgeted production of the label rolls for the next four months as follows:

	Units
March	5,000
April	25,000
May	35,000
June	6,000

Inventory policy requires that sufficient paper strip be in ending monthly inventory to satisfy 20 percent of the following month's production needs. The inventory of paper strip at the beginning of March equals exactly the amount needed to satisfy the inventory policy.

Required:
Prepare a direct materials purchases budget for March, April, and May, showing purchases in units and in dollars for each month and in total.

Exercise 7-28 Direct Labor Budget

OBJECTIVE ②
CORNERSTONE 7-4

Refer to the production budget in **Exercise 7-27**. Each roll of labels produced requires (on average) 0.03 direct labor per hour. The average cost of direct labor is $8 per hour.

Required:
Prepare a direct labor budget for March, April, and May, showing the hours needed and the direct labor cost for each month and in total.

Exercise 7-29 Sales Budget

OBJECTIVE ②
CORNERSTONE 7-5

Norton Inc. manufactures six models of leaf blowers and weed eaters. Norton's budgeting team is finalizing the sales budget for the coming year. Sales in units and dollars for last year follow:

financial stability, Dr. Jones has made available the financial information describing a typical month in the following table.

Revenues

	Average Fee ($)	Quantity
Fillings	50	90
Crowns	300	19
Root canals	170	8
Bridges	500	7
Extractions	45	30
Cleaning	25	108
X-rays	15	150

Costs

Salaries:		
Two dental assistants	$1,900	
Receptionist/bookkeeper	1,500	
Hygienist	1,800	
Public relations (Mrs. Jones)	1,000	
Personal salary	6,500	
Total salaries		$12,700
Benefits		1,344
Building lease		1,500
Dental supplies		1,200
Janitorial		300
Utilities		400
Phone		150
Office supplies		100
Lab fees		5,000
Loan payments		570
Interest payments		500
Miscellaneous		500
Depreciation		700
Total costs		$24,964

Benefits include Dr. Jones's share of social security and a health insurance premium for all employees. Although all revenues billed in a month are not collected, the cash flowing into the business is approximately equal to the month's billings because of collections from prior months. The dental office is open Monday through Thursday from 8:30 A.M. to 4:00 P.M. and on Friday from 8:30 A.M. to 12:30 P.M. A total of 32 hours are worked each week. Additional hours could be worked, but Dr. Jones is reluctant to do so because of other personal endeavors that he enjoys.

Dr. Jones has noted that the two dental assistants and receptionist are not fully utilized. He estimates that they are busy about 65 to 70 percent of the time. Dr. Jones's wife spends about five hours each week on a monthly newsletter that is sent to all patients; she also maintains a birthday list and sends cards to patients on their birthdays.

Dr. Jones spends about $2,400 yearly on informational seminars. These seminars, targeted especially for dentists, teach them how to increase their revenues. It is from one of these seminars that Dr. Jones decided to invest in promotion and public relations (the newsletter and the birthday list).

Required:

1. Prepare a monthly cash budget for Dr. Jones. Does Dr. Jones have a significant cash flow problem? How would you use the budget to show Dr. Jones why he is having financial difficulties?

2. Using the cash budget prepared in Requirement 1 and the information given in the case, recommend actions to solve Dr. Jones's financial problems. Prepare a cash budget that reflects these recommendations and demonstrates to Dr. Jones that the

problems can be corrected. Do you think that Dr. Jones will accept your recommendations? Do any of the behavioral principles discussed in the chapter have a role in this type of setting? Explain.

Case 7-46 Budgetary Performance, Rewards, Ethical Behavior

OBJECTIVES ① ④

Linda Ellis, division manager, is evaluated and rewarded on the basis of budgetary performance. Linda, her assistants, and the plant managers are all eligible to receive a bonus if actual divisional profits are between budgeted profits and 120 percent of budgeted profits. The bonuses are based on a fixed percentage of actual profits. Profits above 120 percent of budgeted profits earn a bonus at the 120-percent level (in other words, there is an upper limit on possible bonus payments). If the actual profits are less than budgeted profits, no bonuses are awarded. Consider the following actions taken by Linda:

a. Linda tends to overestimate expenses and underestimate revenues. This approach facilitates the ability of the division to attain budgeted profits. Linda believes that the action is justified because it increases the likelihood of receiving bonuses and helps to keep the morale of the managers high.

b. Suppose that toward the end of the fiscal year, Linda saw that the division would not achieve budgeted profits. Accordingly, she instructed the sales department to defer the closing of a number of sales agreements to the following fiscal year. She also decided to write off some inventory that was nearly worthless. Deferring revenues to next year and writing off the inventory in a no-bonus year increased the chances of a bonus for next year.

c. Assume that toward the end of the year, Linda saw that actual profits would likely exceed the 120-percent limit and that she took actions similar to those described in item b.

Required:

1. Comment on the ethics of Linda's behavior. Are her actions right or wrong? What role does the company play in encouraging her actions?
2. Suppose that you are the marketing manager for the division, and you receive instructions to defer the closing of sales until the next fiscal year. What would you do?
3. Suppose that you are a plant manager, and you know that your budget has been padded by the division manager. Further, suppose that the padding is common knowledge among the plant managers, who support it because it increases the ability to achieve the budget and receive a bonus. What would you do?
4. Suppose that you are the division controller, and you receive instructions from the division manager to accelerate the recognition of some expenses that legitimately belong to a future period. What would you do?

Standard Costing: A Managerial Control Tool

© NAVISTAR

After studying Chapter 8, you should be able to:

① Explain how unit standards are set and why standard cost systems are adopted.

② Explain the purpose of a standard cost sheet.

③ Describe the basic concepts underlying variance analysis, and explain when variances should be investigated.

④ Compute the materials variances, and explain how they are used for control.

⑤ Compute the labor variances, and explain how they are used for control.

⑥ (Appendix) Prepare journal entries for materials and labor variances.

Experience Managerial Decisions
with Navistar

Understanding an income statement is a relatively easy task. However, understanding the causes underlying net income represents a far more challenging task, especially for Fortune 300 companies like Navistar International Truck and Engine Corporation, whose annual net income typically falls in the neighborhood of several hundred million dollars! Navistar uses variance analysis as an important tool for understanding the many causes of its net income. This type of analysis helps managers at Navistar to learn which parts of the company are contributing to net income as expected and which are not and, as such, will require careful attention to improve in the future. For example, Navistar recently reported that its monthly production cost was $48 million to manufacture 1,228 actual units—considerably higher than its budgeted production cost of only $41 million to produce 883 expected units. If you were the manager in charge of Navistar's production, what would you do after receiving the news that actual costs were $7 million greater (or approximately 17 percent more than the budgeted total production cost) than expected?

Before Navistar's management took any rash actions, it performed an in-depth variance analysis on all of its key production factors to try and understand what had caused the unfavorable static budget variance between its actual costs at month-end and its budgeted costs at the beginning of the month. These key production factors included direct and indirect materials, direct and indirect labor, benefits, utilities, depreciation, and information technology expense. As you might expect, variance analysis revealed that the $7 million unfavorable static budget variance was comprised of numerous smaller variances, some favorable and others unfavorable, involving many of Navistar's key production factors. Most importantly, Navistar's managers were happy to learn that when adjusting the total budgeted costs for the higher production volume, total production costs should have increased by over $11 million, much less than the actual cost increase of $7 million. In fact, effective management of labor and materials purchasing—both of which had large favorable flexible budget variances—actually helped Navistar to save $4 million. Without variance analysis, Navistar would have a much harder time understanding the causes of its net income and taking the appropriate action when components of income are different than expected.

OBJECTIVE ①
Explain how unit standards are set and why standard cost systems are adopted.

Unit Standards

Most operating managers recognize the need to control costs. Cost control often means the difference between success and failure or between above-average profits and lesser profits. For example, as healthcare costs skyrocket due to the large and aging baby boomer generation, the growing complexity of medical treatments, the growing number of uninsured patients, and so on, most healthcare facilities are desperately trying to budget and control costs more effectively. Usually, cost control means that managers must be cost conscious, and assume responsibility for this important objective.

In Chapter 7, we learned that budgets set standards that are used to control and evaluate managerial performance. However, budgets are aggregate measures of performance; they identify the revenues and costs in total that an organization should experience if plans are executed as expected. By comparing the actual costs and actual revenues with the corresponding budgeted amounts at the same level of activity, a measure of managerial efficiency emerges.

Although the process just described provides significant information for control, developing standards for unit amounts as well as for total amounts can enhance control. To determine the unit standard cost for a particular input, two decisions must be made: (1) the amount of input that *should* be *used* per unit of output (the quantity decision) and (2) the amount that *should* be *paid* for the quantity of the input to be used (the pricing decision). The quantity decision produces **quantity standards**, and the pricing decision produces **price standards**. The unit standard cost can be computed by multiplying these two standards: Quantity standard × Price standard.

For example, a soft-drink bottling company may decide that five ounces of fructose should be used for every 16-ounce bottle of cola (the quantity standard), and the price of the fructose should be $0.05 per ounce (the price standard). The standard cost of the fructose per bottle of cola is then $0.25 (5 × $0.05). The standard cost per unit of fructose can be used to predict what the total cost of fructose should be as the activity level varies; thus, it becomes a flexible budget formula. If 10,000 bottles of cola are produced, then the total expected cost of fructose is $2,500 ($0.25 × 10,000); if 15,000 bottles are produced, then the total expected cost of fructose is $3,750 ($0.25 × 15,000).

Analytical Q&A

If the unit quantity standard for a raw material is 10 pounds per unit, and the cost per pound of this material is $8, what is the standard cost per unit of product for the material?

Answer:
Standard cost = 10 × $8 = $80.

How Standards Are Developed

Historical experience, engineering studies, and input from operating personnel are three potential sources of quantitative standards. Although historical experience may provide an initial guideline for setting standards, it should be used with caution. Often, processes are operating inefficiently; adopting input–output relationships from the past thus perpetuates these inefficiencies. Engineering studies can determine the most efficient way to operate and can provide rigorous guidelines; however, engineered standards often are too rigorous. They may not be achievable by operating personnel. Since operating personnel are accountable for meeting standards, they should have significant input in setting standards. The same principles governing participative budgeting pertain to setting unit standards.

Price standards are the joint responsibility of operations, purchasing, personnel, and accounting. Operating personnel determine the quality of the inputs required; personnel and purchasing have the responsibility of acquiring the labor and materials quality requested at the lowest price. Market forces, trade unions, and other external forces limit the range of choices for price standards. In setting price standards, purchasing must consider discounts, freight, and quality; personnel, on the other hand, must consider payroll taxes, fringe benefits, and qualifications. Accounting is responsible for recording the price standards as well as for preparing reports that compare actual performance with the standard.

Types of Standards

Standards are generally classified as either *ideal* or *currently attainable*. **Ideal standards** demand maximum efficiency and can be achieved only if everything operates perfectly. No machine breakdowns, slack, or lack of skill (even momentarily) are allowed. **Currently attainable standards** can be achieved under efficient operating conditions. Allowance is made for normal breakdowns, interruptions, less than perfect skill, and so on. These standards are demanding but achievable. Exhibit 8-1 provides a visual and conceptual portrayal of the two standards.

Of the two types, currently attainable standards offer the most behavioral benefits. If standards are too tight and never achievable, workers become frustrated and performance levels decline. However, challenging but achievable standards tend to extract higher performance levels—particularly when the individuals subject to the standards have participated in their creation.

Concept Q&A

What is the difference between an ideal standard and a currently attainable standard?

Answer:

An ideal standard is a standard of perfection—absolute efficiency is required. A currently attainable standard is rigorous but achievable and reflects a reasonable level of efficiency.

Why Standard Cost Systems Are Adopted

Two reasons for adopting a standard cost system are frequently mentioned: to improve planning and control and to facilitate product costing.

Planning and Control   Standard costing systems enhance planning and control and improve performance measurement. Unit standards are a fundamental requirement for a flexible budgeting system, which is a key feature of a meaningful planning and control system. Budgetary control systems compare actual costs with budgeted costs by computing *variances*, the difference between the actual and planned costs for the actual level of activity. By developing unit price and quantity standards, an overall variance can be decomposed into a price variance and a usage or efficiency variance.

Exhibit 8-1

Types of Standards

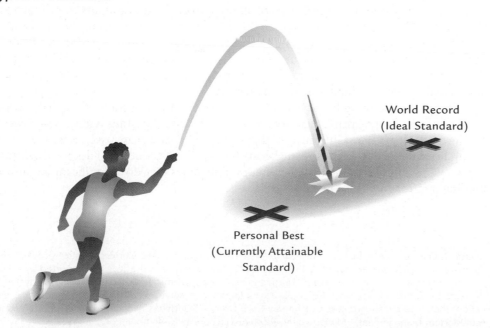

World Record
(Ideal Standard)

Personal Best
(Currently Attainable
Standard)

Performing this decomposition provides a manager with additional information beyond that of the overall variance. For example, if the variance is unfavorable, this decomposition can inform a manager whether it is attributable to discrepancies between planned prices and actual prices, to discrepancies between planned usage and actual usage, or to both. Since managers have more control over the usage of inputs than over their prices, efficiency variances provide specific signals regarding the need for corrective action and where that action should be focused. Thus, in principle, the use of efficiency variances enhances operational control. Additionally, by breaking out the price variance, over which managers potentially have less control, the system provides an improved measure of managerial efficiency.

The benefits of operational control, however, may not extend to the manufacturing environments that are emphasizing continuous improvement and just-in-time (JIT) purchasing and manufacturing. The use of a standard cost system for operational control in these settings can produce dysfunctional behavior. For example, materials price variance reporting may encourage the purchasing department to buy in large quantities in order to take advantage of discounts. Yet, this practice might lead to holding significant inventories, something not desired by JIT firms. Therefore, the detailed computation of variances—at least at the operational level—is discouraged in this new environment. Nonetheless, standards in this newer manufacturing environment are still useful for planning, such as in the creation of bids. Also, variances may still be computed and presented in reports to higher-level managers so that the financial dimension can be monitored. In addition, other incentives, such as a fee charged to managers for holding excessive inventories, can be created to discourage managers from allowing inventories to grow beyond the level desired by JIT systems.

Finally, it should be mentioned that many firms operate with conventional manufacturing systems. Standard cost systems are widely used. According to one survey, 87 percent of the firms responding used a standard cost system.[1] Furthermore, the survey revealed that significant numbers of respondents were calculating variances at the operational level. For example, about 40 percent of the firms using a standard costing system reported labor variances for small work crews or individual workers.

Product Costing   In a *standard* costing system, costs are assigned to products using quantity and price standards for all three manufacturing costs: direct materials, direct labor, and overhead. At the other end of the cost assignment spectrum, an *actual* costing system assigns the actual costs of all three manufacturing inputs to products. In the middle of this spectrum is a *normal* costing system, which predetermines overhead costs for the purpose of product costing but assigns direct materials and direct labor to products by using actual costs. Thus, a normal costing system assigns actual direct costs to products but allocates budgeted indirect costs to products by using a budgeted rate and actual activity. Exhibit 8-2 summarizes these three cost assignment approaches. Standard product costing has several advantages over normal costing and actual costing. One, of course, is the greater capacity for control. Standard costing systems also provide readily available unit cost information that can be used for pricing decisions at any time throughout the period because actual costs (either direct or indirect) do not need to be known. This ability is particularly helpful for companies that do a significant amount of bidding and that are paid on a cost-plus basis.

[1]Bruce R. Gaumnitz, and Felix P. Kollaritsch, "Manufacturing Variances: Current Practice and Trends," *Journal of Cost Management* (Spring 1991): 59–64. Similar widespread usage is also reported by Carole B. Cheatham and Leo R. Cheatham, "Redesigning Cost Systems: Is Standard Costing Obsolete?" *Accounting Horizons* (December 1996): 23–31. Furthermore, a survey of UK firms revealed that 76 percent of them use a standard cost system; see Colin Drury, "Standard Costing: A Technique at Variance with Modern Management," *Management Accounting* (London, November 1999): 56–58.

Cost Assignment Approaches

Exhibit 8-2

| | Manufacturing Costs | | |
	Direct Materials	Direct Labor	Overhead
Actual costing system	Actual	Actual	Actual
Normal costing system	Actual	Actual	Budgeted
Standard costing system	Standard	Standard	Standard

Other simplifications also are possible. For example, if a process-costing system uses standard costing to assign product costs, there is no need to compute a unit cost for each equivalent unit cost category. A standard unit cost would exist for each category. Additionally, there is no need to distinguish between the first-in, first-out (FIFO) and weighted average methods of accounting for beginning inventory costs. Usually, a standard process-costing system will follow the equivalent unit calculation of the FIFO approach. That is, current equivalent units of work are calculated. By calculating current equivalent work, current actual production costs can be compared with standard costs for control purposes.

Concept Q&A

Why would a firm adopt a standard costing system?

Standard costing enhances planning and control and improves performance evaluation. It also simplifies product costing. Having a readily available product cost facilitates pricing decisions.

Answer:

Standard Product Costs

In manufacturing firms, standard costs are developed for direct materials, direct labor, and overhead. Using these costs, the **standard cost per unit** is computed. The **standard cost sheet** provides the production data needed to calculate the standard unit cost. To illustrate, a standard cost sheet will be developed for a 16-ounce bag of corn chips produced by Crunchy Chips Inc. The production of corn chips begins by steaming and soaking corn kernels overnight in a lime solution. This process softens the kernels so that they can be shaped into a sheet of dough. The dough is then cut into small triangular chips. Next, the chips are toasted in an oven and are dropped into a deep fryer. After cooking, the chips pass under a salting device and are inspected for quality. Substandard chips are sorted and discarded; the chips that pass inspection are bagged by a packaging machine. The bagged chips are manually packed into boxes for shipping.

Four materials are used to process corn chips: yellow corn, cooking oil, salt, and lime. The package in which the chips are placed is also classified as a direct material. Crunchy Chips has two types of direct laborers: machine operators and inspectors (or sorters). Variable overhead is made up of three costs: gas, electricity, and water. Both variable and fixed overhead are applied by using direct labor hours. The standard cost sheet is given in Exhibit 8-3 on page 342. Note that it should cost $0.88 to produce a 16-ounce package of corn chips. Also, notice that the company should use 18 ounces of corn to produce a 16-ounce package of chips. There are two reasons for this two-ounce difference. First, some chips are discarded during the inspection process. The company plans on a normal amount of waste. Second, the company wants to have more than 16 ounces in each package to increase customer satisfaction with its product and to avoid any problems with fair packaging laws.

Exhibit 8-3 also reveals other important insights. The standard usage for variable and fixed overhead is tied to the direct labor standards. For variable overhead, the rate is

OBJECTIVE ②
Explain the purpose of a standard cost sheet.

Exhibit 8-3

Standard Cost Sheet for Corn Chips

Description	Standard Price	Standard Usage	Standard Cost*	Subtotal
Direct materials:				
Yellow corn	$ 0.01	18 oz.	$0.18	
Cooking oil	0.03	2 oz.	0.06	
Salt	0.01	1 oz.	0.01	
Lime	0.50	0.04 oz.	0.02	
Bags	0.05	1 bag	0.05	
Total direct materials				$0.32
Direct labor:				
Inspection	8.00	0.01 hr.	$0.08	
Machine operators	10.00	0.01 hr.	0.10	
Total direct labor				0.18
Overhead:				
Variable overhead	4.00	0.02 hr.	$0.08	
Fixed overhead	15.00	0.02 hr.	0.30	
Total overhead				0.38
Total standard unit cost				$0.88

*Calculated by multiplying price times usage.

Analytical Q&A

A product is allowed three ounces of silver per unit and 0.5 hour of labor. If 3,000 units are produced, what is the standard quantity of silver allowed? Standard quantity of labor?

Answer:

$SQ = 3 \times 3,000 = 9,000$ ounces; $SH = 0.5 \times 3,000 = 1,500$ direct labor hours

$4.00 per direct labor hour. Since one package of corn chips should use 0.02 hours of direct labor per unit, the variable overhead cost assigned to a package of corn chips is $0.08 ($4.00 $\times$ 0.02). For fixed overhead, the rate is $15.00 per direct labor hour, making the fixed overhead cost per package of corn chips $0.30 ($15.00 $\times$ 0.02). About one-third of the cost of production is fixed, indicating a capital-intensive production effort. Indeed, much of the operation is mechanized.

The standard cost sheet also reveals the quantity of each input that should be used to produce one unit of output. The unit quantity standards can be used to compute the total amount of inputs allowed for the actual output. This computation is an essential component in computing efficiency variances. A manager should be able to compute the **standard quantity of materials allowed** (*SQ*) and the **standard hours allowed** (*SH*) for the actual output. This computation must be done for every class of direct material and every class of direct labor. Cornerstone 8-1 shows how to compute these quantities by using one type of material and one class of labor.

OBJECTIVE 3
Describe the basic concepts underlying variance analysis, and explain when variances should be investigated.

Variance Analysis: General Description

It is possible to calculate the costs that should have been incurred for the actual level of activity. This figure is obtained by multiplying the amount of input allowed (either materials or labor) for the actual output by the standard price of the input. Letting *SP* be the standard unit price of an input and *SQ* the standard quantity of input allowed for

Here's The Real Kicker

About 15 percent of the defective Kicker speakers returned to Stillwater Designs can be rebuilt. The other 85 percent are sold as metal scrap. Speakers are candidates for rebuilding if the cost of direct materials and labor is less than the sum of the speaker's purchase cost, shipping cost, and duty (the production of Kicker speakers is outsourced to mostly Asian producers). This is true, for example, of the square S12L7 speakers.

To rebuild a square S12L7, the returned speaker is torn down to its basic structures, chemical and glue residues are removed, and the speaker is demagnetized so that it is possible to get rid of metal shavings and pieces. After this preparatory work, recone kits are used to replace the stripped-out components. The rebuilt woofer is then placed in a cabinet and sealed. The completed unit undergoes two tests—one to ensure that the power is hooked up correctly and a second that checks for air leaks.

Every two years, standard costs for materials and labor are set. Time studies are used to determine the time required for rebuilding, and, thus, the labor content. The cost of the recone kit is the major material cost. These standard costs are used for two purposes: (1) to determine if rebuilding is feasible for a given model and (2) to assign costs to the rebuilt product on an ongoing basis if rebuilding is the decision.

HOW TO Compute Standard Quantities Allowed (*SQ* and *SH*)

CORNERSTONE 8-1

Information: Assume that 100,000 packages of corn chips are produced during the first week of March. The unit quantity standard is 18 ounces of yellow corn per package (Exhibit 8-2). The unit quantity standard for machine operators is 0.01 hour per package produced (Exhibit 8-2).

Required: How much yellow corn and how many operator hours should be used for the actual output of 100,000 packages?

Calculation:
Corn allowed:
SQ = Unit quantity standard × Actual output
    = 18 × 100,000
    = 1,800,000 ounces
Operator hours allowed:
SH = Unit labor standard × Actual output
    = 0.01 × 100,000
    = 1,000 direct labor hours

the actual output, the planned or budgeted input cost is $SP \times SQ$. The actual input cost is $AP \times AQ$, where AP is the actual price per unit of the input and AQ is the actual quantity of input used. The **total budget variance** is the difference between the actual cost of the input and its planned cost. As will be explained in Chapter 9, this budget is formally called the *static budget variance*. However, for now, the total budget variance will simply be called the *total variance*:

$$\text{Total variance} = \text{Actual cost} - \text{Planned cost}$$
$$= (AP \times AQ) - (SP \times SQ)$$

Because responsibility for deviations from planned prices tends to be located in the purchasing or personnel department and responsibility for deviations from planned usage of inputs tends to be located in the production department, it is important to separate the total variance into price and usage (quantity) variances.

Concept Q&A

Refer to the control chart in Cornerstone 8-2. What action would you take for an actual value of $89,750?

Answer:

This would produce a value below the lower control limit, so there should be an investigation to find the cause or causes of the deviation. Corrective action could then be taken.

management determines the allowable deviation from standard.[4] The actual deviations from standard often are plotted over time against the upper and lower limits to allow managers to see the significance of the variance. Cornerstone 8-2 shows how control limits are used to trigger an investigation. The control chart graphically illustrates the concept of control limits. The assumed standard is $100,000, and the allowable deviation is plus or minus $10,000. The upper limit is $110,000, and the lower limit is $90,000. Investigation occurs whenever an observation falls outside of these limits (as would be the case for the sixth observation). Trends can also be important.

The control limits often are expressed both as a percentage of the standard and as an absolute dollar amount. For example, the allowable deviation may be expressed as the lesser of 10 percent of the standard amount, or $10,000.

In other words, management will not accept a deviation of more than $10,000 even if that deviation is less than 10 percent of the standard. Alternatively, even if the dollar

---

CORNERSTONE 8-2

HOW TO Use Control Limits to Trigger a Variance Investigation

Information: Standard cost: $100,000; allowable deviation: ±10,000; actual costs for six months:

June	$ 97,500	September	$102,500
July	105,000	October	107,500
August	95,000	November	112,500

Required: Plot the actual costs over time against the upper and lower control limits. Determine when a variance should be investigated.

Calculation:

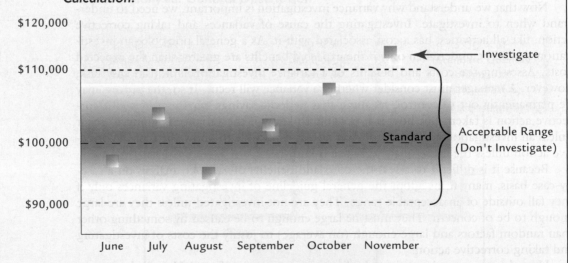

The control chart reveals that the last variance should be investigated. The chart also reveals a short-term increasing trend that suggests the process is moving out of control. A nongraphical approach is to calculate the difference between the actual cost and the upper or lower limit and see if it exceeds $10,000.

---

[4]Bruce Gaumnitz and Felix Kollaritsch, "Manufacturing Variances: Current Practices and Trends," reports that about 45 to 47 percent of the firms use dollar or percentage control limits. Most of the remaining firms use judgment rather than any formal identification of limits.

amount is less than $10,000, an investigation is required if the deviation is more than 10 percent of the standard amount.

Variance Analysis: Materials

The total variance for materials measures the difference between the actual costs of materials and their budgeted costs for the actual level of activity. Cornerstone 8-3 illustrates how to calculate the total variance for materials by using selected data from Crunchy Chips for the first week of March. To keep the example simple, only one material (corn) is illustrated.

OBJECTIVE ④
Compute the materials variances, and explain how they are used for control.

Direct Materials Variances

To help control the cost of materials, price and usage variances are calculated. However, the sum of the price and usage variances will add up to the total materials variance calculated in Cornerstone 8-3 *only if the materials purchased equal the materials used.* The materials price variance is computed by using the actual quantity of materials purchased, and the materials usage variances is computed by using the actual quantity of materials used.

Since it is better to have information on variances earlier rather than later, the materials price variance uses the actual quantity of materials purchased rather than the actual quantity of materials used. The more timely the information, the more likely that proper managerial action can be taken. Old information often is useless information. Materials may sit in inventory for weeks or months before they are needed in production. By the time the materials price variance is computed, signaling a problem, it may be too late to take corrective action. Or, even if corrective action is still possible, the delay may cost the company thousands of dollars. For example, suppose a new purchasing agent is unaware of the availability of a quantity discount on a raw material. If the materials price variance that ignores the discount is computed when a new purchase is made, the resulting unfavorable signal would lead to quick corrective action. (In this case, the action would be to use the discount for future purchases.) If the materials price variance is not computed

---

HOW TO Calculate the Total Variance for Materials

Information: Unit standards from Exhibit 8-3; the actual results for the first week in March:

Actual production	48,500 bags of corn chips
Actual cost of corn	780,000 ounces at $0.015 = $11,700
Actual cost of inspection labor	360 hours at $8.35 = $3,006

Required: Calculate the total variance for corn for the first week in March.

Calculation:

CORNERSTONE 8-3

	Actual Costs	Budgeted Costs*	Total Variance
	AQ × AP	SQ × SP	(AQ × AP) − (SQ × SP)
Corn	$11,700	$8,730	$2,970 U

*The standard quantities for materials and labor are computed as unit quantity standards from Exhibit 8-3:

Corn: SQ = 18 × 48,500 × 873,000 ounces

Multiplying these standard quantities by the unit standard prices given in Exhibit 8-3 produces the budgeted amounts appearing in this column:

Corn: $0.01 × 873,000 = $8,730

Concept Q&A

When is the total materials variance the sum of the price variance and the usage variance?

When the materials purchased equal the materials used.

Answer:

until the material is issued to production, it may be several weeks or even months before the problem is discovered.

Materials price and usage variances normally should be calculated using variance formulas. However, the three-pronged (columnar) approach is used when the materials purchased equal the materials used. Cornerstone 8-4 shows how to use the materials variance formulas, which we now specifically state and define.

**CORNERSTONE
8-4**

HOW TO Calculate Materials Variances: Formula and Columnar Approaches

Information: Unit standards from Exhibit 8-3; the actual results for the first week in March:

Actual production	48,500 bags of corn chips
Actual cost of corn	780,000 ounces @ $0.015

Required: Calculate the materials price and usage variances by using the three-pronged (columnar) and formula approaches.

Calculation:

1. Formulas (recommended approach for materials variances because materials purchased may differ from materials used):

$$MPV = (AP - SP)AQ$$
$$= (\$0.015 - \$0.01)780,000$$
$$= \$3,900 \text{ U}$$
$$MUV = (AQ - SQ)SP$$
$$= (780,000 - 873,000)(\$0.01)$$
$$= \$930 \text{ F}$$

2. Columnar (this approach is possible only if the materials purchased five materials used):

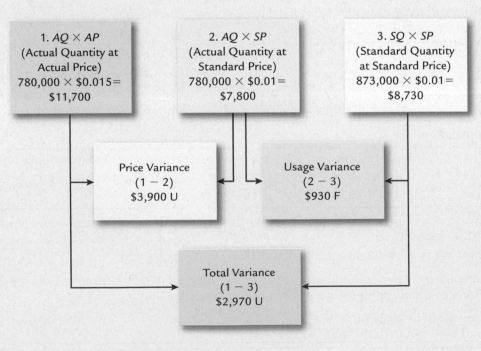

| 1. $AQ \times AP$ (Actual Quantity at Actual Price) $780,000 \times \$0.015 = \$11,700$ | 2. $AQ \times SP$ (Actual Quantity at Standard Price) $780,000 \times \$0.01 = \$7,800$ | 3. $SQ \times SP$ (Standard Quantity at Standard Price) $873,000 \times \$0.01 = \$8,730$ |

Price Variance
(1 − 2)
$3,900 U

Usage Variance
(2 − 3)
$930 F

Total Variance
(1 − 3)
$2,970 U

The **materials price variance** (*MPV*) measures the difference between what should have been paid for raw materials and what was actually paid. The formula for computing this variance is:

$$MPV = (AP \times AQ) - (SP \times AQ)$$

or, factoring, we have:

$$MPV = (AP - SP) AQ$$

where

> **AP = The actual price per unit**
> **SP = The standard price per unit**
> **AQ = The actual quantity of material *purchased***

It should be noted that the MPV formula uses the *actual* quantity purchased, rather than the standard amount that should have been purchased, because purchasing managers typically influence the amount of materials actually purchased. Likewise, the MPV uses material *purchased*, rather than used, because purchasing managers typically do not control the amount of material actually used in production. Thus, the MPV contains items over which purchasing managers likely have control, which is helpful given that their bonuses often are affected by the MPV.

The **materials usage variance** (*MUV*) measures the difference between the direct materials actually used and the direct materials that should have been used for the actual output. The formula for computing this variance is:

$$MUV = (SP \times AQ) - (SP \times SQ)$$

or, factoring:

$$MUV = (AQ - SQ) SP$$

where

> **AQ = The actual quantity of materials used**
> **SQ = The standard quantity of materials allowed for the actual output**
> **SP = The standard price per unit**

It should be noted that the MUV formula uses the *standard* price that should have been paid, rather than the actual price that was paid, because production managers typically do not influence the actual price paid for materials. Using the standard price in the MUV—a variance for which production managers typically are held accountable—prevents them from unfairly being affected by the actual price. Cornerstone 8-4 shows how to calculate the materials price and usage variances by using either a columnar approach or a formula approach for the Crunchy Chips example (for corn only).

Analytical Q&A

Assume that *SP* = $3 and *AP* — $2. If 100 units are purchased, what is the materials price variance?

Answer:
$MPV = (\$2.00 - \$3.00)100 = \$100$ F.

Using Materials Variance Information

Calculating materials variances is only the first step. Using the variance information to exercise control is fundamental to a standard cost system. Responsibility must be assigned, variance significance must be assessed, and the variances must be accounted for and disposed of at the end of the year.

Responsibility for the Materials Price Variance

The responsibility for controlling the materials price variance usually belongs to the purchasing agent. Admittedly, the price of materials is largely beyond his or her control; however, the price variance can be influenced by such factors as quality, quantity discounts, distance of the source from the plant, and so on. These factors often are under the control of the agent.

Using the price variance to evaluate the performance of purchasing has some limitations. Emphasis on meeting or beating the standard can produce some undesirable outcomes. For example, if the purchasing agent feels pressured to produce favorable variances, materials of lower quality than desired may be purchased or too much inventory may be acquired to take advantage of quantity discounts.

Analysis of the Materials Price Variance

The first step in variance analysis is deciding whether or not the variance is significant. If it is judged insignificant, no further steps are needed. The materials price variance is $3,900 unfavorable, which is about 45 percent of standard cost ($3,900/$8,730). Most managers would judge this variance to be significant. The next step is to find out why it occurred.

For the Crunchy Chips example, the investigation revealed that a higher-quality corn was purchased because of a shortage of the usual grade in the market. Once the reason is known, corrective action can be taken if necessary—and if possible. In this case, no corrective action is needed. The firm has no control over the supply shortage; it will simply have to wait until market conditions improve.

Responsibility for the Materials Usage Variance

The production manager is generally responsible for materials usage. Minimizing scrap, waste, and rework are all ways in which the manager can ensure that the standard is met. However, at times, the cause of the variance is attributable to others outside of the production area, as the next section shows.

As with the price variance, using the usage variance to evaluate performance can lead to undesirable behavior. For example, a production manager feeling pressure to produce a favorable variance might allow a defective unit to be transferred to finished goods. While this transfer avoids the problem of wasted materials, it may create customer-relation problems.

Analysis of the Materials Usage Variance

The materials usage variance is approximately 11 percent of standard cost ($930/$8,730). A deviation greater than 10 percent likely is to be judged significant. Thus, investigation is needed. Investigation revealed that the favorable materials usage variance was the result of the higher-quality corn acquired by the purchasing department. In this case, the favorable variance is essentially assignable to purchasing. Since the materials usage variance is favorable—but smaller than the unfavorable price variance—the overall result of the change in purchasing is unfavorable. In the future, management should try to resume purchasing of the normal-quality corn.

If the overall variance had been favorable, a different response would be expected. If the favorable variance were expected to persist, the higher-quality corn should be purchased regularly and the price and quantity standards revised to reflect it. As this possibility reveals, standards are not static. As improvements in production take place and conditions change, standards may need to be revised to reflect the new operating environment. The importance of evaluating current business conditions and updating standards to reflect any changes in these conditions cannot be overemphasized.

Accounting and Disposition of Materials Variances

Recognizing the price variance for materials at the point of purchase also means that the raw materials inventory is carried at standard cost. In general, materials variances are not inventoried. Typically, materials variances are added to cost of goods sold if unfavorable and are subtracted from cost of goods sold if favorable. The journal entries associated with the purchase and usage of raw materials for a standard cost system are illustrated in the Appendix.

Variance Analysis: Direct Labor

OBJECTIVE ⑤
Compute the labor variances, and explain how they are used for control.

The total labor variance measures the difference between the actual costs of labor and their budgeted costs for the actual level of activity. Cornerstone 8-5 illustrates how to calculate the total variance for labor by using selected data from Crunchy Chips for the first week of March. To keep the example simple, only inspection labor is illustrated.

Direct Labor Variances

Labor hours cannot be purchased and stored for future use as can be done with materials (i.e., there can be no difference between the amount of labor purchased and the amount of labor used). Therefore, unlike the total materials variance, the labor rate and labor efficiency variances always will add up to the total labor variance, as calculated in Cornerstone 8-5. Thus, the rate (price) and efficiency (usage) variances for labor can be calculated by using either the columnar approach or the associated formulas. Which technique to use is a matter of preference. The formulas are adapted to reflect the specific terms used for labor prices (rates) and usage (efficiency).

The **labor rate variance (LRV)** computes the difference between what was paid to direct laborers and what should have been paid:

$$\textbf{LRV = (AR} \times \textbf{AH)} - \textbf{(SR} \times \textbf{AH)}$$

or, factoring:

$$\textbf{LRV = (AR} - \textbf{SR) AH}$$

where

$$\textbf{AR} = \textbf{The actual hourly wage rate}$$
$$\textbf{SR} = \textbf{The standard hourly wage rate}$$
$$\textbf{AH} = \textbf{The actual direct labor hours used}$$

HOW TO Calculate the Total Variance for Labor

Information: Unit standards from Exhibit 8-3; the actual results for the first week in March:

Actual production	48,500 bags of corn chips
Actual cost of inspection labor	360 hours @ $8.35 = $ 3,006

Required: Calculate the total variance for inspection labor for the first week in March.

Calculation:

	Actual Costs	Budgeted Costs*	Total Variance
	AQ × AP	SQ × SP	(AQ × AP) − (SQ × SP)
Inspection labor	$3,006	$3,880	$874 *F*

*The standard quantities for inspection labor are computed as unit quantity standards from Exhibit 8-3:

Labor: SH = 0.01 × 48,500 = 485 hours

Multiplying these standard quantities by the unit standard prices given in Exhibit 8-3 produces the budgeted amounts appearing in this column:

Labor: $8.00 × 485 = $3,880

**CORNERSTONE
8 - 5**

The **labor efficiency variance (*LEV*)** measures the difference between the labor hours that were actually used and the labor hours that should have been used:

$$LEV = (AH \times SR) - (SH \times SR)$$

or, factoring:

$$LEV = (AH - SH)\ SR$$

where

AH = The actual direct labor hours used
SH = The standard direct labor hours that should have been used
SR = The standard hourly wage rate

Cornerstone 8-6 shows how to calculate the labor rate and efficiency variances for the Crunchy Chips example (for inspection labor only) by using either a columnar approach or a formula approach.

**CORNERSTONE
8-6**

HOW TO Calculate Labor Variances: Formula and Columnar Approaches

Information: Unit standards from Exhibit 8-3; the actual results for the first week in March:

Actual production	48,500 bags of corn chips
Actual cost of inspection labor	360 hours @ $8.35

Required: Calculate the labor rate and efficiency variances by using the three-pronged (columnar) and formula approaches.

Calculation:
Formulas:

LRV = (AR − SR)AH   LEV = (AH − SH)SR
   = ($8.35 − $8.00)360   = (360 − 485)($8.00)
   = $126 U   = $1,000 F

Columnar:

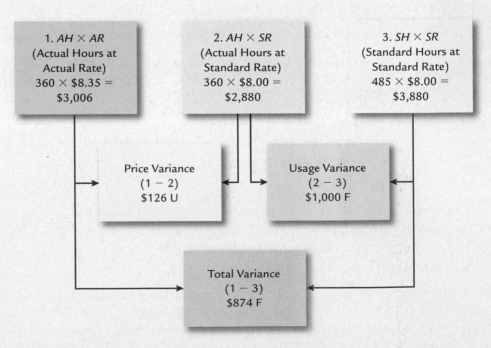

Using Labor Variance Information

As with materials variances, calculating labor variances initiates the feedback process. Using the labor variance information to exercise control is fundamental. Responsibility must be assigned, variance significance must be assessed, and the variances must be accounted for and disposed of at the end of the year.

Responsibility for the Labor Rate Variance

Labor rates are largely determined by such external forces as labor markets and union contracts. The actual wage rate rarely departs from the standard rate. When labor rate variances do occur, they usually do so because an average wage rate is used for the rate standard and because more skilled and more highly paid laborers are used for less skilled tasks. Unexpected overtime also can be the cause of a labor rate variance.

Wage rates for a particular labor activity often differ among workers because of differing levels of seniority. Rather than selecting labor rate standards reflecting those different levels, an average wage rate often is chosen. As the seniority mix of workers changes, the average rate changes. This rate change will give rise to a labor rate variance; it also calls for a new standard to reflect the new seniority mix. Controllability is not assignable for this cause of a labor rate variance.

However, the use of labor is controllable by the production manager. The use of more skilled workers to perform less skilled tasks (or vice versa) is a decision that a production manager consciously makes. For this reason, responsibility for the labor rate variance generally is assigned to the individuals who decide how labor will be used.

Analytical Q&A

Assume that AH = 100 hours and SH = 80 hours, with SR = $10. What is the labor efficiency variance?

Answer:

$$LEV = (AH - SH)SR = (100 - 80)\$10 = \$200\ U.$$

Analysis of the Labor Rate Variance

The labor rate variance is only 3 percent of the standard cost ($126/$3,880). Although a 3-percent variance is not likely to be judged significant, for illustrative purposes, assume that an investigation is conducted. The cause of the variance is found to be the use of more highly paid and skilled machine operators as inspectors, which occurred because two inspectors quit without formal notice. The corrective action is to hire and train two new inspectors.

Responsibility for the Labor Efficiency Variance

Generally speaking, production managers are responsible for the productive use of direct labor. However, as is true of all variances, once the cause is discovered, responsibility may be assigned elsewhere. For example, frequent breakdowns of machinery may cause interruptions and nonproductive use of labor. But the responsibility for these breakdowns may be faulty maintenance. If so, the maintenance manager should be charged with the unfavorable labor efficiency variance.

Production managers may be tempted to engage in dysfunctional behavior if too much emphasis is placed on the labor efficiency variance. For example, to avoid losing hours or using additional hours because of possible rework, a production manager could deliberately transfer defective units to finished goods.

Analysis of the Labor Efficiency Variance

The labor efficiency variance is 26 percent of standard cost ($1,000/$3,880). This favorable variance is judged to be significant, and an investigation is undertaken. Investigation revealed that inspections flowed more smoothly because of the higher quality of materials. This additional benefit of the higher-quality materials should be factored into whether Crunchy should return to purchasing the normal-quality corn when it becomes available or whether the higher-quality material should again be purchased. In this case, even with this additional benefit, the materials price variance is so large that the correct action is to acquire the normal-quality material when it again becomes available.

Additional Cost Management Practices: Kaizen Costing and Target Costing

In addition to standard costing, some companies choose to employ other cost management practices, such as kaizen costing and target costing. **Kaizen costing** focuses on the continuous reduction of the *manufacturing* costs of existing products and processes. *Kaizen* is a Japanese word meaning continuous improvement. The philosophy in a standard costing system is that the budgeted expectation, or standard, should be met each period. However, as the phrase "continuous improvement" suggests, the philosophy in a kaizen costing system is that the budgeted expectation, or kaizen standard, of the current period should exceed the improvement accomplished the previous period. Using this philosophy, each period's kaizen standard is set based on prior periods' improvements, thereby locking in these improvements to push for even greater improvements in the future. Typically, continuous cost improvements are achieved by identifying a large number of relatively small cost-reducing opportunities (e.g., repositioning factory work space, placing or transporting work-in-process inventory in such a way that the next worker can immediately access the inventory and begin working on it, etc.). For example, **Honda** uses kaizen costing practices to help its engineers implement the product design improvements identified by its shop floor workers.

Target costing focuses on the reduction of the *design* costs of existing and future products and processes. Increasingly, companies such as **Toyota**, **Boeing**, and **Olympus** are emphasizing cost management in the design stage as they begin to recognize that an astonishingly large percentage (somewhere between 75 and 90 percent) of a product's total costs are "locked in" or "committed to" by the time it finishes the design stage and moves into the manufacturing stage (see "Why product development teams need management accountants" by Hertenstein and Platt in *Management Accounting*, 1998)! A target cost is the difference between the sales price needed to capture a predetermined market share and the desired per-unit profit (i.e., target cost per unit = expected sales price per unit – desired profit per unit). The sales price reflects the product specifications or functions valued by the customer. If the target cost is *less* than the current actual cost, then management must find cost reductions that decrease the actual cost to the target cost. Some managers refer to this process as closing the cost gap, which is the difference between current actual cost and the necessary target cost. Closing this cost gap is the principal challenge of target costing and usually requires the participation of suppliers and other business partners outside of the company over a period of several years. If this cost gap is not closed to zero (i.e., the actual cost is not reduced to the target cost) by the date that the new product is planned to launch, then most target costing proponents will follow the cardinal rule of target costing and delay the product launch date until the gap is closed. The reason for the delay is that many managers feel that once the product launches, the incentive to reduce the actual cost falls significantly, and, thus, the likelihood of the actual cost eventually decreasing to the target cost level necessary to generate the desired profit margin becomes unacceptably small. **Caterpillar** is famous for adhering to this rule even though the launch delay means that the company must forego significant sales revenues during the delay period.

As you might have noticed, target costing is more than just cost control, because it includes expected sales revenues and desired profit margins in the calculation of the target cost. For this reason, target costing often is referred to as a profit planning technique. In addition, target costing is more of a long-term approach to cost reduction, whereas kaizen costing is more of a continuous, short-term approach to cost reduction. Finally, given that target and kaizen costing practices focus on different segments of the value chain, they can serve as effective complements as an organization strives to reduce its costs along the entire value chain.

Summary of Learning Objectives

1. Explain how unit standards are set and why standard cost systems are adopted.
    *   A standard cost system budgets quantities and costs on a unit basis. These unit budgets are for labor, materials, and overhead. Standard costs, therefore, are the amount that should be expended to produce a product or service.
    *   Standards are set by using historical experience, engineering studies, and input from operating personnel, marketing, and accounting.
    *   Currently attainable standards are those that can be achieved under efficient operating conditions.
    *   Ideal standards are those achievable under maximum efficiency, or ideal operating conditions.
    *   Standard cost systems are adopted to improve planning and control and to facilitate product costing. By comparing actual outcomes with standards and breaking the variance into price and quantity components, detailed feedback is provided to managers. This information allows managers to exercise a greater degree of cost control than that found in a normal or actual cost system.

2. Explain the purpose of a standard cost sheet.
    *   The standard cost sheet provides the details for computing the standard cost per unit. It shows the standard costs for materials, labor, and variable and fixed overhead.
    *   The standard cost sheet also reveals the quantity of each input that should be used to produce one unit of output. By using these unit quantity standards, the standard quantity of materials allowed and the standard hours allowed can be computed for the actual output.

3. Describe the basic concepts underlying variance analysis, and explain when variances should be investigated.
    *   The total variance is the difference between actual costs and planned costs.
    *   In a standard costing system, the total variance is broken down into price and usage variances. By breaking the total variance into price and usage variances, managers are better able to analyze and control the total variance.
    *   Variances should be investigated if they are material (i.e., significant) and if the benefits of corrective action are greater than the costs of investigation. Because of the difficulty of assessing cost and benefits on a case-by-case basis, many firms set up formal control limits—either a dollar amount, a percentage, or both. Other firms use judgment to assess the need to investigate.

4   Compute the materials variances, and explain how they are used for control.
    *   The materials price and usage variances are computed by using either a three-pronged (columnar) approach or formulas.
    *   The materials price variance is the difference between what was actually paid for materials (generally associated with the purchasing activity) and what should have been paid.
    *   The materials usage variance is the difference between the actual amount of materials used (generally associated with the production activity) and the amount of materials that should have been used.
    *   When a significant variance is signaled, an investigation is undertaken to find the cause. Corrective action is taken, if possible, to put the system back in control.

5. Compute the labor variances and explain how they are used for control.
    *   The labor variances are computed by using either a three-pronged approach or formulas.
    *   The labor rate variance is caused by the actual wage rate differing from the standard wage rate. It is the difference between the wages that were paid and those that should have been paid.
    *   The labor efficiency variance is the difference between the actual amount of labor that was used and the amount of labor that should have been used. When

9

Flexible Budgets and Overhead Analysis

© Brand X Pictures/Jupiter Images

After studying Chapter 9, you should be able to:

① Prepare a flexible budget and use it for performance reporting.

② Calculate the variable overhead variances and explain their meaning.

③ Calculate the fixed overhead variances and explain their meaning.

④ Prepare an activity-based flexible budget.

Experience Managerial Decisions
with Second City

If you ask someone from Chicago about its most popular local businesses, you likely will receive answers such as Billy Goat Tavern (founded in 1934 and made famous in the 1970s in Saturday Night Live skits featuring Bill Murray and John Belushi), Ed Debevick's (a series of 1950s-style diners), and Second City. **Second City** has been North America's premiere live improvisational and sketch comedy theater company for the past 50 years. Many famous stars began their careers at Second City, including John Candy, Tina Fey, Mike Myers, Eugene Levy, and Bill Murray. More than just Second City Television (i.e., SCTV), Second City also includes training centers, national touring companies, media and entertainment offshoots, and a corporate communication division. As you might imagine, Second City is an entrepreneurial organization, as evidenced most recently by its decision to provide a comedy theater aboard Norwegian Cruise Line ships.

Given the nature of its businesses, Second City is extremely dependent on overhead costs. These overhead costs must be allocated to each business to create accurate budgets, which is followed by variance analyses when actual overhead costs are very different from budgeted overhead costs. Its fixed overhead costs are associated with capacity and, as such, relate more to its home and resident stages in Chicago, Toronto, Las Vegas, Denver, and Detroit, rather than to its traveling shows business. Examples of Second City's fixed overhead costs include salaries, stage and other facilities rent, facilities maintenance, depreciation, taxes, and insurance. These overhead costs then are assigned to individual business budgets by using allocation bases such as square footage, number of employees, and percentage of earnings. Second City then uses overhead cost variances to "red flag" potential problems that might not be self-correcting and need managerial attention.

For example, Second City Theatricals might have a slow year because the producers are too busy with other ventures to mount a new production, while at the same time, the Second City Training Center might have a surge in enrollment. Such a scenario likely would lead Second City financial executives to shift some assigned overhead costs from the theatrical business to the training center business. Also, Second City uses flexible budgeting to adjust budgets for its businesses that experience sporadic volumes, such as the seasonality present in some of its traveling and cruise activities. While the managerial accountants likely do not intentionally provide too many jokes, they do provide the critical function of budgeting and examining variances for overhead costs, which allows the comic talent of Second City to continue to do what it does best—make us laugh!

OBJECTIVE ①
Prepare a flexible budget, and use it for performance reporting.

Using Budgets for Performance Evaluation

Budgets are useful for both planning and control. They also are used as benchmarks for performance evaluation, as budget variances frequently appear in managerial incentive systems. Thus, determining how budgeted amounts should be compared with actual results is a major consideration that must be addressed to improve performance reporting and decision making.

Static Budgets versus Flexible Budgets

In Chapter 7, we learned how companies prepare a master budget based on their best estimate of the level of sales and production activity for the coming period (the best estimate is the budgeted level for the period). We also discussed some behavioral issues associated with performance reporting. However, no detailed discussion was provided on how to prepare budgetary *performance reports*. A **performance report** compares actual costs with budgeted costs. Two possibilities exist for making this comparison: (1) comparison of actual costs (at the actual level of activity) with the budgeted costs for the *budgeted* level of activity and (2) comparison of actual costs (at the actual level of activity) with the budgeted costs for the *actual* level of activity. The first choice is a report based on *static budgets*, whereas the second choice is for a report based on *flexible budgets*. The two approaches for variance calculation are illustrated in Exhibit 9-1.

Static Budgets and Performance Reports   A **static budget** is a budget for a particular level of activity. Master budgets are generally created for a particular level of activity. Thus, one way to prepare a performance report is to compare the actual costs with the budgeted costs from the master budget. As an example, the production of Texas Rex T-shirts from Chapter 7 will again be considered. Cornerstone 9-1 shows how to prepare a performance report based on a static budget for the Texas Rex clothing manufacturing plant for its first quarter of operations. For simplicity, the report only considers production costs.

According to the report, there were unfavorable variances for direct materials, direct labor, maintenance, and power. However, there is something fundamentally wrong with the report. Actual costs for production of 1,200 T-shirts are being compared with planned costs for production of 1,060. Because direct materials, direct labor, and variable overhead are variable costs, one would expect them to be greater at a higher level of production. Thus, even if cost control were perfect for the production of 1,200 units, unfavorable

---

Exhibit 9-1

Static and Flexible Budget Variances

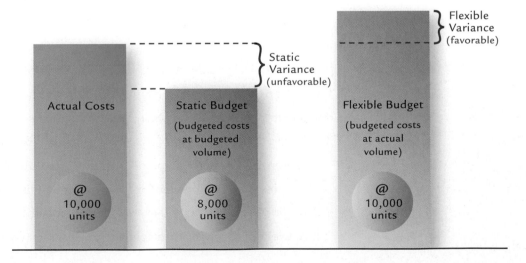

HOW TO Prepare a Performance Report Based on a Static Budget (Using Budgeted Production)

**CORNERSTONE
9-1**

Information:

Relationships from the Master Budget	Actual Data for Quarter 1
Budgeted production for Quarter 1: 1,060	Production: 1,200 units
Materials:	
1 plain T-shirt @ $3.00	Materials cost: $4,380
5 ounces of ink @ $0.20	
Labor:	
0.12 hour @ $10.00	Labor cost: $1,500
Variable overhead:	
Maintenance:	
0.12 hour @ $3.75	Maintenance cost: $535
Power:	
0.12 hour @ $1.25	Power cost: $170
Fixed overhead:	
Grounds keeping: $1,200 per quarter	Grounds keeping: $1,050
Depreciation: $600 per quarter	Depreciation: $600

Required: Prepare a performance report using a budget based on expected production.

Calculation:

	Actual	Budgeted	Variance
Units produced	1,200	1,060	140 F[a]
Direct materials cost	$4,830	$4,240[b]	$590 U[c]
Direct labor cost	1,500	1,272[d]	228 U
Variable overhead:			
Maintenance	535	477[e]	58 U
Power	170	159[f]	11 U
Fixed overhead:			
Grounds keeping	1,050	1,200	(150) F
Depreciation	600	600	0
Total	$8,685	$7,948	$737 U

[a]F means the variance is favorable.
[b][(1,060 × $3) + (1,060 × 5 × $0.20)].
[c]U means the variance is unfavorable.
[d]0.12 × 1,060 × $10.00.
[e]0.12 × 1,060 × $3.75.
[f]0.12 × 1,060 × $1.25.

variances likely would be produced for at least some of the variable costs. To create a meaningful performance report, actual costs and expected costs must be compared at the *same* level of activity. Since actual output often differs from planned output, a method is needed to compute what the costs should have been for the actual output level.

Ethics If a company were to insist on using the budget for planned output as the benchmark for performance evaluation, it would invite potential abuse by managers subject to this approach. Although unethical, a manager could manipulate the performance report by deliberately producing less than the planned output—producing, for example, 1,000 T-shirts instead of the planned 1,060. By producing less, the costs likely will be less than the budgeted amounts, creating a favorable performance outcome. Using flexible budgeting allows the benchmark to be adjusted to reflect the expected costs for the actual level of output.◆

Flexible Budgets A **flexible budget** enables a firm to compute expected costs for a range of activity levels. The key to flexible budgeting is knowledge of fixed and variable costs. The two types of flexible budgets are:

1. *Before-the-fact.* This type of flexible budget helps managers deal with uncertainty by allowing them to see the expected outcomes for a range of activity levels. It can be used to generate financial results for a number of plausible scenarios.

2. *After-the-fact.* This flexible budget is the budget for the actual level of activity. This type of budget is used to compute what costs should have been for the actual level of activity. Those expected costs then are compared with the actual costs in order to assess performance.

Flexible budgeting is the key to providing the frequent feedback that managers need to exercise control and effectively carry out the plans of an organization.

To illustrate the before-the-fact capability of flexible budgeting, suppose that the management of Texas Rex wants to know the cost of producing 1,000 T-shirts, 1,200 T-shirts, and 1,400 T-shirts. To compute the expected cost for these different levels of output, the cost behavior pattern of each item in the budget needs to be known. Knowing the variable cost per unit and the total fixed costs allows the calculation of the expected costs for various levels of activity. Cornerstone 9-2 shows how budgets can be prepared for different levels of activity, using cost formulas for each item.

Notice in Cornerstone 9-2 that total budgeted production costs increase as the production level increases. Budgeted costs change because total variable costs go up as output increases. Because of this typical cost behavior and budgeted costs, flexible budgets are sometimes referred to as **variable budgets**. Since Texas Rex has a mix of variable and fixed costs, the unit cost of producing one T-shirt goes *down* as production goes *up*. This observation makes sense. As production increases, there are more units over which to spread the fixed production costs.

It should also be pointed out that the flexible budget formulas often are based on direct labor hours instead of units. This practice is easy to do because direct labor hours

Concept Q&A

Why are static budgets usually not a good choice for benchmarks in preparing a performance report?

Answer:

The actual output may differ from the budgeted output, thus causing significant differences in cost. Comparing planned costs for one level of activity with the actual costs of a different level of activity does not provide good control information.

Here's The Real Kicker

Stillwater Designs has a Product Steering Committee whose charge is to decide on the timing for upgrades and redesigns for its various Kicker speaker models. About every four years, a complete redesign is done for a Kicker speaker. A complete redesign takes about 16 to 18 months. A specification workshop is held that identifies features, benefits, customers, and competitors. Additionally, the costs of the new model, including the design costs (research and development), acquisition costs, freight, and duties, are estimated for various sales volumes. During this phase, the company will work closely with the manufacturers to control the design so that manufacturing costs are carefully set. A financial analysis is run over the expected life cycle of the new product (two to three years) to see what the profit potential is. Thus, both expected revenues and costs for various levels of activity are assessed. This before-the-fact flexible budgeting analysis is especially done for those products with which the company has less experience. At times, a new product may be produced even if at the most likely volume the product is not expected to be profitable. The reason? The new product may complete a line or may enhance the overall image of the Kicker speakers.

HOW TO Prepare a Flexible Production Budget

CORNERSTONE 9 – 2

Information:

Levels of output: 1,000, 1,200, and 1,400.

Materials:

  1 plain T-shirt @ $3.00

  5 ounces of ink @ $0.20

Labor:

  0.12 hour @ $10.00

Variable overhead:

  Maintenance: 0.12 hour @ $3.75

  Power: 0.12 hour @ $1.25

Fixed overhead:

  Grounds keeping: $1,200 per quarter

  Depreciation: $600 per quarter

Required: Prepare a budget for three levels of output: 1,000, 1,200, and 1,400 units.

Calculation:

Production Costs	Variable Cost per Unit	Range of Production (units) 1,000	1,200	1,400
Variable:				
Direct materials	$4.00[a]	$4,000	$4,800	$5,600
Direct labor	1.20[b]	1,200	1,440	1,680
Variable overhead:				
Maintenance	0.45[c]	450	540	630
Power	0.15[d]	150	180	210
Total variable costs	$5.80	$5,800	$6,960	$8,120
Fixed overhead:				
Grounds keeping		$1,200	$1,200	$1,200
Depreciation		600	600	600
Total fixed costs		$1,800	$1,800	$1,800
Total production costs		$7,600	$8,760	$9,920

[a][($3.00 × 1) × ($0.20 × 5)].

[b]($10.00 × 0.12).

[c]($3.75 × 0.12).

[d]($1.25 × 0.12).

are correlated with units produced. For example, the variable cost formulas for variable overhead are $3.75 and $1.25 per direct labor hour ($5.00 per direct labor hour in total) for maintenance and power, respectively. However, two choices are available for hours: standard hours allowed for the units produced and actual hours used for the units produced. The output levels for hours allowed would be 120 (0.12 × 1,000), 144 (0.12 × 1,200), and 168 (0.12 × 1,400).

Flexible budgets are powerful control tools because they allow management to compute what the costs should be for the level of output that actually occurred. Cornerstone 9-2 also reveals what the costs should have been for the actual level of activity (1,200 units). It is now possible to provide management with a

Analytical Q&A

What is the budgeted cost of maintenance if 2,000 T-shirts are produced?

Answer:
$0.45 × 2,000=$900.

CORNERSTONE 9–3

HOW TO Prepare a Performance Report using a Flexible Budget

Information: Budgeted costs for the actual level of activity (Cornerstone 9-2); actual costs (Cornerstone 9-1).

Required: Prepare a performance report using budgeted costs for the actual level of activity.

Calculation:

	Actual	Budget	Variance
Units produced	1,200	1,200	—
Production costs:			
Direct materials	$4,830	$4,800	$ 30 U
Direct labor	1,500	1,440	60 U
Variable overhead:			
Maintenance	535	540	(5) F
Power	170	180	(10) F
Total variable costs	$7,035	$6,960	$ 75 U
Fixed overhead:			
Grounds keeping	$1,050	$1,200	$(150) F
Depreciation	600	600	(0)
Total fixed costs	$1,650	$1,800	$(150) F
Total production costs	$8,685	$8,760	$ (75) F

useful performance report, one that compares actual and budgeted costs for the actual level of activity. This is the second type of flexible budget and preparation of this report is shown by Cornerstone 9-3. The revised performance report in Cornerstone 9-3 paints a much different picture from the one in Cornerstone 9-1. All of the variances are fairly small. Had they been larger, management would have searched for the cause and tried to correct the problems.

A difference between the actual (cost) amount and the flexible budget (cost) amount is the **flexible budget variance**. The flexible budget provides a measure of the efficiency of a manager. In other words, given the level of production achieved, how well did the manager control costs? To measure whether or not a manager accomplishes his or her goals, the static budget is used. The static budget represents certain goals that the firm wants to achieve. A manager is effective if the goals described by the static budget are achieved or exceeded. In the Texas Rex example, production volume was 140 units greater than the original budgeted amount; the manager exceeded the original budgeted production goal. Therefore, the effectiveness of the manager is not in question, assuming that exceeding the production volume budgeted at the beginning of the year is good for the organization.

OBJECTIVE ②
Calculate the variable overhead variances, and explain their meaning.

Variable Overhead Analysis

In Chapter 8, total variances for direct materials and direct labor were broken down into price and efficiency variances. In a standard cost system, the total overhead variance, which is the difference between applied and actual overhead, also is broken down into component variances. The number of component variances computed depends on the method of variance analysis used. Only one method is described in this chapter. First, overhead is divided into fixed and variable categories. Next, component variances are calculated for each category. The total variable overhead variance is divided into two components: the variable overhead spending variance and the variable overhead efficiency variance. Similarly, the total fixed overhead variance is divided into two components: the fixed overhead spending variance and the fixed overhead volume variance.

Total Variable Overhead Variance

To illustrate the variable overhead variances, the first quarter data for Texas Rex will be used again. The unit prices and quantities used for the flexible budget are assumed to be the standards associated with Texas Rex's standard cost system. Cornerstone 9-4 illustrates how to calculate the total variable overhead variance. The total variable overhead variance is the difference between the total actual variable overhead and applied variable overhead. Variable overhead is applied by using hours allowed in a standard cost system. The total variable overhead variance can be divided into spending and efficiency variances. Variable overhead spending and efficiency variances can be calculated by using either the three-pronged (columnar) approach or formulas. The best approach is a matter of preference. However, the formulas first need to be expressed specifically for variable overhead.

Variable Overhead Spending Variance   The **variable overhead spending variance** measures the aggregate effect of differences between the actual variable overhead rate ($AVOR$) and the standard variable overhead rate ($SVOR$). The actual variable overhead rate is computed by dividing actual variable overhead divided by actual hours. For our example, this rate is $4.70 per hour ($705/150 hours). The formula for computing the variable overhead spending variance is:

$$\text{Variable overhead spending variance} = (AVOR \times AH) - (SVOR \times AH)$$
$$= (AVOR - SVOR)AH$$

Variable Overhead Efficiency Variance   Variable overhead is assumed to vary as the production volume changes. Thus, variable overhead changes in proportion to changes in the direct labor hours used. The **variable overhead efficiency variance** measures the change in variable overhead consumption that occurs because of efficient

---

HOW TO Calculate the Total Variable Overhead Variance

Information:

Standard variable overhead rate (*SVOR*)	$ 5.00 per direct labor hour
Actual variable overhead costs	150 hours (*AH*) @ $4.70 (*AVOR*)
Standard hours (*SH*) allowed per unit	0.12 hour
Actual production	1,200 units

Required: Calculate the total variable overhead variance.

Calculation:

Actual Costs	Applied Costs*	Total Variance
AH × AVOR	SH × SVOR	(AH × AVOR) – (SH × SVOR)
$705	$720	$(15)

*SH × SVOR = 0.12 × 1,200 × $5.

**CORNERSTONE
9 - 4**

(or inefficient) use of direct labor. The efficiency variance is computed by using the following formula:

$$\textbf{Variable overhead efficiency variance =}$$
$$\textbf{(AH − SH)SVOR}$$

CORNERSTONE 9-5

HOW TO Calculate Variable Overhead Variances: Columnar and Formula Approaches

Information:

Standard variable overhead rate (*SVOR*)	$5.00 per direct labor hour
Actual variable overhead rate (*AVOR*)	$4.70
Actual hours worked (*AH*)	150 hours
Number of T-shirts produced	1,200 units
Hours allowed for production (*SH*)	144 hours[a]

[a]0.12 × 1,200.

Required: Calculate the variable overhead spending and efficiency variances.

Calculation:

Columnar:

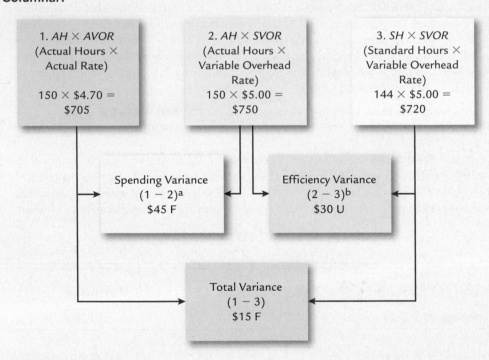

Formulas:

[a]*VOH* spending variance = (*AVOR* − *SVOR*)*AH*
                = ($4.70 − $5.00)150
                = $45 F

[b]*VOH* efficiency variance = (*AH* − *SH*)*SVOR*
                = (150 − 144)($5.00)
                = $30 U

Cornerstone 9-5 shows how to calculate the variable overhead variances for the Texas Rex example by using either a columnar or formula approach.

Analytical Q&A

If *AH* = 100, *SH* = 90, and *SVOR* = $6, what is the variable overhead efficiency variance?

Answer:
Variable overhead efficiency variance = (*AH* − *SH*)*SVOR* = (100 − 90)$6
= $60.

Comparison of the Variable Overhead Spending Variance with the Price Variances of Materials and Labor

Although more complicated, the formula for the variable overhead spending variance is, in essence, the same as the formulas for the materials price variance and labor price variance in Chapter 8. For example, the material price variance is the difference between two prices (the actual price and the standard price) multiplied by the actual quantity purchased. Similarly, the variable overhead spending variance also is the difference between two prices—or rates (the actual variable overhead rate and the standard variable overhead rate—multiplied by the actual amount used of the allocation base.

However, several important conceptual differences exist between the variable overhead spending variance and the price variances of materials and labor. Variable overhead is not a homogeneous input—it is made up of a large number of individual items, such as indirect materials, indirect labor, electricity, maintenance, and so on. The standard variable overhead rate represents the weighted cost per direct labor hour that should be incurred for all variable overhead items. The difference between what should have been spent per hour and what actually was spent per hour is a type of price variance.

A variable overhead spending variance can arise because prices for individual variable overhead items have increased or decreased. Assume, for the moment, that the price changes of individual overhead items are the only cause of the spending variance. If the spending variance is unfavorable, price increases for individual variable overhead items are the cause; if the spending variance is favorable, price decreases dominate and are the cause of the variance.

If the only source of the variable overhead spending variance were price changes, then it would be completely analogous to the price variances of materials and labor. Complicating the issue, however, is the fact that the spending variance also is affected by how efficiently overhead is used. Waste or inefficiency in the use of variable overhead increases the actual variable overhead cost. This increased cost, in turn, is reflected in an increased actual variable overhead rate. Thus, even if the actual prices of the individual overhead items were equal to the budgeted or standard prices, an unfavorable variable overhead spending variance could still take place. For example, more kilowatt-hours of power may be used than should be—yet, this is not captured by any change in direct labor hours. However, the effect is reflected by an increase in the total cost of power and, thus, the total cost of variable overhead. Similarly, efficiency (i.e., using fewer kilowatt-hours than should be used) can decrease the actual variable overhead cost and decrease the actual variable overhead rate. Efficient use of variable overhead items contributes to a favorable spending variance. If the waste effect dominates, then the net contribution will be unfavorable; if efficiency dominates, then the net contribution is favorable. Therefore, the variable overhead spending variance is the result of both price and efficiency.

Concept Q&A

How does the variable overhead spending variance differ from the materials and labor price variances?

Answer:
The variable overhead spending variance is affected by price changes of individual items as well as efficiency issues.

Responsibility for the Variable Overhead Spending Variance

Many variable overhead items, such as utilities, are affected by several responsibility centers. To the extent that consumption of variable overhead can be traced to a responsibility center, responsibility can be assigned. Consumption of indirect materials is an example of a traceable variable overhead cost.

Controllability is a prerequisite for assigning responsibility. Price changes of variable overhead items are essentially beyond the control of supervisors. If price changes are small (as they often are), then the spending variance is primarily a matter of the efficient use of overhead in production, which is controllable by production supervisors. Accordingly, responsibility for the variable overhead spending variance is generally assigned to production departments.

Responsibility for the Variable Overhead Efficiency Variance

The variable overhead efficiency variance is directly related to the direct labor efficiency or usage variance. If variable overhead is truly proportional to direct labor consumption, then like the labor usage variance, the variable overhead efficiency variance is caused by efficient or inefficient use of direct labor. If more (or fewer) direct labor hours are used than the standard calls for, then the total variable overhead cost will increase (or decrease). The validity of the measure depends on the validity of the relationship between variable overhead costs and direct labor hours. In other words, do variable overhead costs really change in proportion to changes in direct labor hours? If so, responsibility for the variable overhead efficiency variance should be assigned to the individual who has responsibility for the use of direct labor: the production manager.

A Performance Report for the Variable Overhead Spending and Efficiency Variances

Cornerstone 9-5 showed a favorable $45 spending variance and an unfavorable $30 efficiency variance. The $45 F spending variance means that overall Texas Rex spent less than expected on variable overhead. The reasons for the $30 unfavorable variable overhead efficiency variance are the same as those offered for an unfavorable labor usage variance. An unfavorable variance means that more hours were used than called for by the standard. Because these variances are aggregate measures, they reveal nothing about how individual variable overhead items were controlled. Even if the variances are insignificant, they reveal nothing about how well costs of *individual* variable overhead items were controlled. It is possible for two large variances of opposite sign to cancel each other out. Control of variable overhead requires line-by-line analysis for each item. Cornerstone 9-6 shows how to prepare a performance report that supplies the line-by-line information essential for detailed analysis of the variable overhead variances.

The analysis on a line-by-line basis reveals no unusual problems such as two large individual item variances with opposite signs. No individual item variance is greater than 10 percent of its budgeted amount. Thus, no variance at the individual item level appears to be of a large enough magnitude to be of concern.

Concept Q&A

Why are the labor efficiency and variable overhead efficiency variances similar in nature?

Answer:
Both variances depend on the difference between actual and standard direct labor hours.

$$SFOR = \$1,800/180$$
$$= \$10 \text{ per direct labor hour}$$

HOW TO Prepare a Performance Report for the Variable Overhead Variances

Information:

Standard variable overhead rate (SVOR)	$5.00 per direct labor hour
Actual costs:	
Maintenance	$ 535
Power	$ 170
Actual hours worked (AH)	150 hours
Number of T-shirts produced	1,200 units
Hours allowed for production (SH)	144 hours[a]
Variable overhead:	
Maintenance	0.12 hour @ $3.75
Power	0.12 hour @ $1.25

**CORNERSTONE
9-6**

[a]$0.12 \times 1,200$.

Required: Prepare a performance report that shows the variances on an item-by-item basis.

Calculation:

Performance Report
For the Quarter Ended March 31, 2007

Cost	Cost Formula[a]	Actual Costs	Budget for Actual Hours[b]	Spending Variance[c]	Budget for Standard Hours[d]	Efficiency Variance[e]
Maintenance	$3.75	$535	$562.50	$27.50 F	$540	$22.50 U
Power	1.25	170	187.50	17.50 F	180	7.50 U
Total	$5.00	$705	$750.00	$45.00 F	$720	$30.00 U

[a]Per direct labor hour.
[b]Computed using the cost formula and 150 actual hours.
[c]Spending variance = Actual costs − Budget for actual hours.
[d]Computed using the cost formula and an activity level of 144 standard hours.
[e]Efficiency variance = Budget for actual hours − Budget for standard hours.

Fixed Overhead Analysis

OBJECTIVE ③
Calculate the fixed overhead variances, and explain their meaning.

Fixed overhead costs are capacity costs. They represent manufacturing activity capacity acquired in advance of usage. The standard fixed overhead rate is calculated as follows:

SFOR = Budgeted fixed overhead costs/Practical capacity

For example, if Texas Rex can produce 1,500 T-shirts per quarter under efficient operating conditions, then practical capacity measured in standard hours (SH_p) is calculated by the following formula:

$$SH_p = \text{Unit standard} \times \text{Units of practical capacity}$$
$$= 0.12 \times 1,500$$
$$= 180 \text{ hours}$$

Analytical Q&A

If the budgeted fixed overhead is $10,000 and the standard fixed overhead rate is $100 per direct labor hour (calculated using practical capacity), what is the practical capacity, measured in direct labor hours?

Answer:

Practical capacity = $10,000/$100 = 100 direct labor hours.

Using Texas Rex's budgeted fixed overhead costs (from Cornerstone 9-2), the standard fixed overhead rate is calculated as follows:

$$SFOR = \$1,800/180$$
$$= \$10 \text{ per direct labor hour}$$

From the calculation for *SFOR*, it is easy to see how the budgeted fixed overhead (*BFOH*) can be expressed as the product of the rate and practical capacity as follows:

$$BFOH = SFOR \times SH_p$$
$$= \$10 \times 180$$
$$= \$1,800$$

Some firms use average or expected capacity instead of practical capacity to calculate fixed overhead rates. In this case, the standard hours used to calculate the fixed overhead rate will typically be less than SH_p.

Total Fixed Overhead Variances

The total fixed overhead variance is the difference between actual fixed overhead and applied fixed overhead, when applied fixed overhead is obtained by multiplying the standard fixed overhead rate times the standard hours allowed for the actual output. Thus, the applied fixed overhead (A_pFOH) is:

$$A_pFOH = SFOR \times SH$$

The total fixed overhead variance is the difference between the actual fixed overhead (*AFOH*) and the applied fixed overhead:

Total variance = Actual fixed overhead − Applied fixed overhead
$$= AFOH - A_pFOH$$

Cornerstone 9-7 illustrates how to calculate the total fixed overhead variance, using the Texas Rex example. The total fixed overhead variance can be divided into spending and volume variances. Spending and volume variances can be calculated by using either the three-pronged (columnar) approach or formulas. The best approach to use is a matter of preference. However, the formulas first need to be expressed specifically for fixed overhead.

**CORNERSTONE
9-7**

HOW TO Calculate the Total Fixed Overhead Variance

Information:

Standard fixed overhead rate (*SFOR*)	$10.00 per direct labor hour
Actual fixed overhead costs	$1,650
Standard hours allowed per unit	0.12 hour
Actual production	1,200 units

Required: Calculate the total fixed overhead variance.

Calculation:

Actual Costs	Applied Fixed Overhead*	Total Variance
AFOH	SH × SFOR	AFOH – ApFOH
$1,650	$1,440	$210 U

*SH × SFOR = 0.12 × 1,200 × $10.

Fixed Overhead Spending Variance

Fixed Overhead Spending Variance   The **fixed overhead spending variance** is defined as the difference between the actual fixed overhead and the budgeted fixed overhead (*BFOH*):

$$\text{FOH spending variance} = \text{AFOH} - \text{BFOH}$$

Fixed Overhead Volume Variance   The **fixed overhead volume variance** is the difference between budgeted fixed overhead and applied fixed overhead:

$$\text{Volume variance} = \text{Budgeted fixed overhead} - \text{Applied fixed overhead}$$
$$= \text{BFOH} - \text{ApFOH}$$
$$= (\text{SH}_p \times \text{SFOR}) - (\text{SH} \times \text{SFOR})$$
$$= (\text{SH}_p - \text{SH})\text{SFOR}$$

The volume variance measures the effect of the actual output differing from the output used at the beginning of the year to compute the predetermined standard fixed overhead rate. If you think of the output used to calculate the fixed overhead rate as the activity capacity acquired (practical capacity) and the actual output as the activity capacity used, then the volume variance is the cost of unused activity capacity. Cornerstone 9-8 illustrates how to calculate the fixed overhead variances using either a columnar or a formula approach.

Responsibility for the Fixed Overhead Spending Variance

Fixed overhead is made up of a number of items such as salaries, depreciation, taxes, and insurance. Many fixed overhead items—long-run investments, for instance—are not subject to change in the short run; consequently, fixed overhead costs often are beyond the immediate control of management. Since many fixed overhead costs are affected primarily by long-run decisions, and not by changes in production levels, the budget variance usually is small. For example, depreciation, salaries, taxes, and insurance costs are not likely to be much different from planned costs.

Analysis of the Fixed Overhead Spending Variance

Because fixed overhead is made up of many individual items, a line-by-line comparison of budgeted costs with actual costs provides more information concerning the causes of the spending variance. The fixed overhead section of Cornerstone 9-3 provides such a report. The report reveals that the fixed overhead spending variance is out of line with expectations. Less was spent on grounds keeping than expected. In fact, the entire spending variance is attributable to this one item. Since the amount is more than

---

HOW TO Calculate Fixed Overhead Variances: Columnar and Formula Approaches

Information:

Standard fixed overhead rate (*SFOR*)	$10.00 per direct labor hour
Budgeted fixed overhead (*BFOH*)	$1,800
Number of T-shirts produced	1,200 units
Hours allowed for production (*SH*)	144 hours[a]

[a]0.12 × 1,200.

CORNERSTONE 9-8

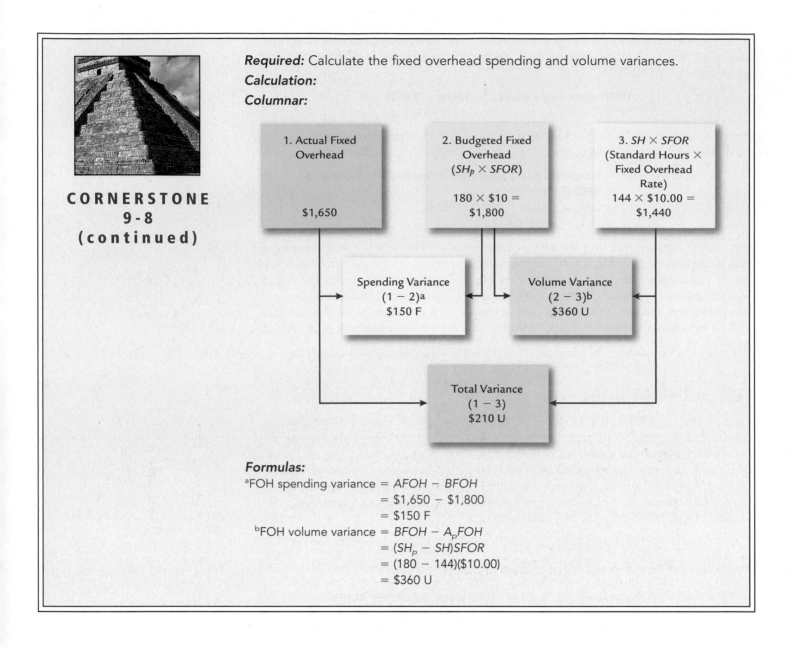

CORNERSTONE 9-8 (continued)

Required: Calculate the fixed overhead spending and volume variances.

Calculation:

Columnar:

Formulas:

[a]FOH spending variance $= AFOH - BFOH$
$= \$1,650 - \$1,800$
$= \$150$ F

[b]FOH volume variance $= BFOH - A_pFOH$
$= (SH_p - SH)SFOR$
$= (180 - 144)(\$10.00)$
$= \$360$ U

10 percent of budget, it merits an investigation. An investigation, for example, might reveal that the weather was especially wet and thus reduced the cost of watering for the period involved. In this case, no action is needed, as a natural correction would be forthcoming.

Responsibility for the Fixed Overhead Volume Variance

Assuming that volume variance measures capacity utilization implies that the general responsibility for this variance should be assigned to the production department. At times, however, investigation into the reasons for a significant volume variance may reveal the cause to be factors beyond the control of production. In this instance, specific responsibility may be assigned elsewhere. For example, if the purchasing department acquires a raw material of lower quality than usual, significant rework time may result, causing lower production and an unfavorable volume variance. In this case, responsibility for the variance rests with purchasing, not production.

Exhibit 9–2

Graphical Analysis of the Volume Variance

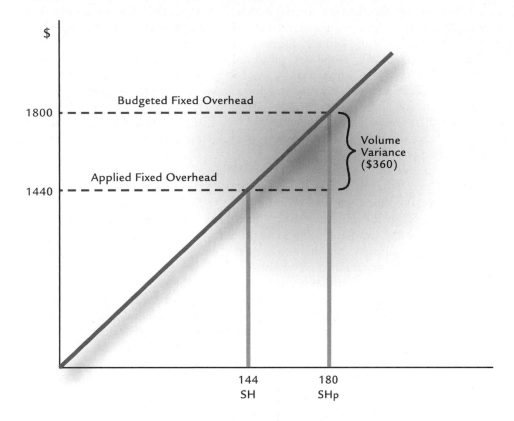

Analysis of the Volume Variance

The $360 U variance (Cornerstone 9-8) occurs because the production capacity is 180 hours and only 144 hours should have been used. Why the company failed to use all of its capacity is not specifically revealed. Given that unutilized capacity is about 20 percent of the total, investigation seems merited. Exhibit 9-2 graphically illustrates the volume variance. Notice that the volume variance occurs because fixed overhead is treated as if it were a variable cost. In reality, fixed costs do not change as activity changes as a predetermined fixed overhead rate allows.

Activity-Based Budgeting

OBJECTIVE ④
Prepare an activity-based flexible budget.

In Chapter 7, the budgetary process used a traditional approach, especially with respect to the overhead and selling and administrative expenses budgets. Traditional, functional-based budgeting is concerned with budgeting the costs of resources associated with organizational units, such as departments and plants. Companies that have implemented an activity-based costing (ABC) system may also wish to install an *activity-based budgeting system*. A budgetary system at the activity level can be a useful approach to support continuous improvement and process management. Furthermore, because activities are what consume resources and, thus, are the causes of costs, activity-based budgeting may prove to be a much more powerful planning and control tool than the traditional, functional-based budgeting approach. An activity-based budgetary approach can be used to emphasize cost reduction through the elimination of wasteful activities and improving the efficiency of necessary activities.

Static Activity Budgets

Activities cause costs by consuming resources; however, the amount of resources consumed depends on the demand for the activity's output. Building an **activity-based budgeting (ABB) system** requires three steps: (1) the activities within an organization must be identified, (2) the demand for each activity's output must be estimated, and (3) the cost of resources required to produce each activity's output must be assessed. If an organization has implemented an ABC or activity-based management (ABM) system, then step 1 will already have been accomplished. Assuming that ABC has been implemented, the major emphasis for ABB is estimating the workload (demand) for each activity and then budgeting the resources required to sustain this workload. The workload for each activity must be set to support the sales and production activities expected for the coming period.

As with traditional, functional-based budgeting, ABB begins with sales and production budgets. Direct materials and direct labor budgets also are compatible with an ABC framework because these production inputs are directly traceable to the individual products. The major differences between functional and activity-based budgeting are found within the overhead and selling and administration categories. In a functional-based approach, budgets within these categories typically are detailed by cost elements. These cost elements are classified as variable or fixed, using production or sales output measures as the basis for determining cost behavior. Furthermore, these budgets usually are constructed by budgeting for a cost item within a department (function) and then rolling these items up into the master overhead budget. For example, the cost of supervision in an overhead budget is the sum of all the supervision costs of the various departments. ABB, on the other hand, identifies the overhead, selling, and administrative *activities* and then builds a budget for each activity, based on the resources needed to provide the required activity output levels. Costs are classified as variable or fixed with respect to the *activity* output measure.

Consider, for example, the activity of purchasing materials. The demand for this activity is a function of the materials requirements for the various products and services produced. An activity driver, such as number of purchase orders, measures the activity output demand. Cornerstone 9-9 illustrates how to prepare a budget at the activity level for the purchasing activity.

**CORNERSTONE
9-9**

HOW TO Prepare a Static Budget for an Activity

Information:
1. Demand for purchase orders based on materials requirements: 15,000 purchase orders.
2. Resources needed:
    a. Five purchasing agents, each capable of processing 3,000 orders per year; salary, $40,000 each.
    b. Supplies (forms, paper, stamps, envelopes, etc.), projected to cost $1.00 per purchase order.
    c. Desks and computers: depreciation, $5,000 per year.
    d. Office space, rent, and utilities, $6,000.

Required: Prepare a budget for the purchasing activity.

Calculation: Purchasing budget:

Salaries	Depreciation	Supplies	Occupancy	Total
$200,000	$5,000	$15,000	$6,000	$226,000

Of the resources consumed by the purchasing activity in Cornerstone 9-9, supplies is a flexible resource and, therefore, a variable cost, whereas the other resources consumed are committed resources and display a fixed cost behavior (a step-fixed cost behavior in the case of salaries and depreciation). However, one important difference should be mentioned: Fixed and variable purchasing costs are defined with respect *to the number of purchase orders* and not direct labor hours or units produced or other measures of production output. In budgeting at the activity level, the cost behavior of each activity is defined with respect to its output measure (which often is different from the production-based drivers used in functional-based budgeting).

Knowing the output measure provides significant insights for controlling activity costs. In an activity framework, controlling costs translates into managing activities. For example, by redesigning products so that they use more common components, the number of purchase orders can be decreased. By decreasing the number of purchase orders demanded, flexible resource demand is reduced; furthermore, decreasing the number of purchase orders demanded also reduces the activity capacity needed. Thus, activity costs will decrease.

Concept Q&A

What are the main differences between ABB and traditional budgeting?

Answer:
ABB differs primarily with overhead and selling and administrative budgets. ABB builds a budget for each activity based on the demands of the activity for resources, whereas traditional budgeting focuses on cost items required by organizational units such as departments.

Activity Flexible Budgeting

The ability to identify changes in activity costs as activity output changes allows managers to more carefully plan and monitor activity improvements. **Activity flexible budgeting** is the prediction of what activity costs will be as activity output changes. Variance analysis within an activity framework makes it possible to improve traditional budgetary performance reporting. It also enhances the ability to manage activities.

In a functional-based approach, budgeted costs for the actual level of activity are obtained by assuming that a single unit-based driver (units of product or direct labor hours) drives all costs. A cost formula is developed for each cost item as a function of units produced or direct labor hours. Exhibit 9-3 illustrates a traditional flexible budget based on direct labor hours. If, however, costs vary with respect to more than one driver, and the drivers are not highly correlated with direct labor hours, then the predicted costs can be misleading.

Exhibit 9–3

Flexible Budget: Direct Labor Hours

	Cost Formula		Direct Labor Hours	
	Fixed	Variable	10,000	20,000
Direct materials	—	$10	$100,000	$200,000
Direct labor	—	8	80,000	160,000
Maintenance	$ 20,000	3	50,000	80,000
Machining	15,000	1	25,000	35,000
Inspections	120,000	—	120,000	120,000
Setups	50,000	—	50,000	50,000
Purchasing	220,000	—	220,000	220,000
Total	$425,000	$22	$645,000	$865,000

The solution, of course, is to build flexible budget formulas for more than one driver. Cost estimation procedures (high-low method, the method of least squares, and so on) can be used to estimate and validate the cost formulas for each activity. In principle, the variable cost component for each activity should correspond to resources acquired as needed (flexible resources) and the fixed cost component should correspond to resources acquired in advance of usage (committed resources). This multiple-formula approach allows managers to predict more accurately what costs should be for different levels of activity usage, as measured by the activity output measure. These costs can then be compared with the actual costs to help assess budgetary performance. Cornerstone 9-10 illustrates how to prepare an activity flexible budget. The approach

**CORNERSTONE
9-10**

HOW TO Prepare an Activity Flexible Budget

Information: For simplicity, the full set of information is not listed, but the individual activities, drivers, their cost formulas, and the output levels are the inputs needed to prepare the budget. To illustrate, the maintenance activity would require the following information for its role in the budget:

Activity: Maintenance
Driver: Machine hours
Fixed activity cost: $20,000
Variable activity rate: $5.50 per machine hour

Required: Prepare an activity-based flexible budget.

Calculation:

	Formula		Level of Activity	
Driver: Direct Labor Hours				
	Fixed	**Variable**	**10,000**	**20,000**
Direct materials	$ —	$ 10	$100,000	$200,000
Direct labor	—	8	80,000	160,000
Subtotal	$ 0	$ 18	$180,000	$360,000
Driver: Machine Hours				
	Fixed	**Variable**	**8,000**	**16,000**
Maintenance	$ 20,000	$ 5.50	$ 64,000	$108,000
Machining	15,000	2.00	31,000	47,000
Subtotal	$ 35,000	$ 7.50	$ 95,000	$155,000
Driver: Number of Setups				
	Fixed	**Variable**	**25**	**30**
Setups	$ —	$ 1,800	$ 45,000	$ 54,000
Inspections	80,000	2,100	132,500	143,000
Subtotal	$ 80,000	$ 3,900	$177,500	$197,000
Driver: Number of Orders				
	Fixed	**Variable**	**15,000**	**25,000**
Purchasing	$211,000	$ 1	$226,000	$236,000

for calculating this budget follows that illustrated earlier in Cornerstone 9-2. The principal difference is that flexible budgets are computed for *each driver*. Notice that the budgeted amounts for materials and labor are the same as those reported in Exhibit 9-3; they use the same activity output measure. The budgeted amounts for the other items differ significantly from the traditional amounts because the activity output measures differ by driver.

Assume that the first activity level for each driver in Cornerstone 9-10 corresponds to the actual activity usage levels. Cornerstone 9-11 illustrates how to prepare a performance report by using activity-based flexible budgeting. Notice that the report compares the budgeted costs for the actual activity usage levels with the actual costs. One item is on target, and the other six items are mixed. The net outcome is a favorable variance of $21,500. The performance report in Cornerstone 9-11 compares total budgeted costs for the actual level of activity with the total actual costs for each activity. The preparation of the performance report follows the pattern and approach used in Cornerstone 9-3. The difference is that the comparison is for each activity. It is also possible to compare the actual fixed activity costs with the budgeted fixed activity costs and the actual variable activity costs with the budgeted variable costs. For example, assume that the actual fixed inspection costs are $82,000 (due to a midyear salary adjustment, reflecting a more favorable union agree-

Concept Q&A

Why does activity-based flexible budgeting provide a more accurate prediction of costs?

Answer:
Activity-based flexible budgeting is more accurate if costs vary with more than one driver and the drivers are not highly correlated with direct labor hours (which is often the case).

HOW TO Prepare an Activity-Based Performance Report

Information: Actual activity level is the first one for each activity listed in Cornerstone 9-10.

Actual costs:

Direct materials	$101,000
Direct labor	80,000
Maintenance	55,000
Machining	29,000
Inspections	125,500
Setups	46,500
Purchases	220,000

**CORNERSTONE
9-11**

Required: Prepare an activity-based performance report.
Calculation:

	Actual Costs	Budgeted Costs	Budget Variance
Direct materials	$101,000	$100,000	$ 1,000 U
Direct labor	80,000	80,000	—
Maintenance	55,000	64,000	9,000 F
Machining	29,000	31,000	2,000 F
Inspections	125,500	132,500	7,000 F
Setups	46,500	45,000	1,500 U
Purchases	220,000	226,000	6,000 F
Total	$657,000	$678,500	$21,500 F

ment than anticipated) and that the actual variable inspection costs are $43,500. The variable and fixed budget variances for the inspection activity are computed as follows:

Activity	Actual Cost	Budgeted Cost	Variance
Inspection			
Fixed	$ 82,000	$ 80,000	$2,000 U
Variable	43,500	52,500	9,000 F
Total	$125,500	$132,500	$7,000 F

Breaking each variance into fixed and variable components provides more insight into the source of the variation in planned and actual expenditures.

Summary of Learning Objectives

1. Prepare a flexible budget and use it for performance reporting.
    * Static budgets provide expected cost for a given level of activity, usually prepared at the beginning of the period. If the actual level of activity differs from the level associated with the static budget level, then comparing actual costs with budgeted costs does not make any sense. The solution is flexible budgeting.
    * Flexible budgets divide costs into those that vary with units of production (or direct labor hours) and those that are fixed with respect to these unit-level drivers. These relationships allow the identification of a cost formula for each item in the budget.
    * Cost formulas are the means for calculating expected costs for various levels of activity. There are two applications of flexible budgets: before-the-fact and after-the-fact.
    * Before-the-fact applications allow managers to see what costs will be for different levels of activity, thus helping in planning.
    * After-the-fact applications allow managers to see what the cost should have been for the actual level of activity. Knowing these after-the-fact expected or budgeted costs then provides the opportunity to evaluate efficiency by comparing actual costs with budgeted costs.
2. Calculate the variable overhead variances, and explain their meaning.
    * Overhead costs are often a significant proportion of costs in a budget.
    * Comparing actual variable and fixed overhead costs with applied overhead costs yields a total overhead variance.
    * In a standard cost system, it is possible to break down these overhead variances into component variances.
    * For variable overhead, the two component variances are the spending variance and the efficiency variance.
    * The spending variance is the result of comparing the actual costs with budgeted costs.
    * The variable overhead efficiency variance is the result of efficient or inefficient use of labor because variable overhead is assumed to vary with direct labor hours.
3. Calculate the fixed overhead variances, and explain their meaning.
    * For fixed overhead, the two component variances are the spending variance and the volume variance.
    * The spending variance is the result of comparing the actual costs with budgeted costs.
    * The fixed overhead volume variance is the result of producing a level of output that is different than that used to calculate the predetermined fixed overhead rate. It can be interpreted as a measure of capacity utilization.

4. Prepare an activity-based flexible budget.
   - ABB is performed at the activity level.
   - First, the activities associated with production are identified.
   - Next, the level of activity output needed to support the expected production level is estimated.
   - Finally, the cost of resources needed to support the required activity output are estimated. This then becomes the activity budget.
   - It is also possible to define activity flexible budgets. These budgets differ from traditional flexible budgeting because the cost formulas are based on the activity drivers for the respective activities rather than being based only on direct labor hours.

Summary of Important Equations

1. Variable overhead spending variance $= (AVOR \times AH) - (SVOR \times AH)$
$$= (AVOR - SVOR)AH$$
2. Variable overhead efficiency variance $= (AH - SH)SVOR$
3. $SFOR =$ Budgeted fixed overhead costs/Practical capacity
4. $ApFOH = SFOR \times SH$
5. FOH spending variance $= AFOH - BFOH$
6. Volume variance $=$ Budgeted fixed overhead $-$ Applied fixed overhead
$$= BFOH - ApFOH = (SH_p \times SFOR) - (SH \times SFOR)$$
$$= (SH_p - SH)SFOR$$

CORNERSTONES FOR CHAPTER 9

Cornerstone 9-1	How to prepare a performance report based on a static budget (using budgeted production), page 381
Cornerstone 9-2	How to prepare a flexible production budget, page 383
Cornerstone 9-3	How to prepare a performance report using a flexible budget, page 384
Cornerstone 9-4	How to calculate the total variable overhead variance, page 385
Cornerstone 9-5	How to calculate variable overhead variances: columnar and formula approaches, page 386
Cornerstone 9-6	How to prepare a performance report for the variable overhead variances, page 389
Cornerstone 9-7	How to calculate the total fixed overhead variance, page 390
Cornerstone 9-8	How to calculate fixed overhead variances: columnar and formula approaches, page 391
Cornerstone 9-9	How to prepare a static budget for an activity, page 394
Cornerstone 9-10	How to prepare an activity flexible budget, page 396
Cornerstone 9-11	How to prepare an activity-based performance report, page 397

Key Terms

Activity flexible budgeting, 395
Activity-based budget (ABB) system, 394
Fixed overhead spending variance, 391
Fixed overhead volume variance, 391
Flexible budget, 382
Flexible budget variance, 384

Performance report, 380
Static budget, 380
Variable budgets, 382
Variable overhead efficiency variance, 385
Variable overhead spending variance, 385

7. What is the difference between an activity flexible budget and a functional-based (traditional) flexible budget?
8. Why would an activity-based performance report be more accurate than a report based on a traditional flexible budget?
9. Explain why the variable overhead spending variance is not a pure price variance.
10. The variable overhead efficiency variance has nothing to do with efficient use of variable overhead. Do you agree or disagree? Why?
11. Describe the difference between the variable overhead efficiency variance and the labor efficiency variance.
12. Explain why the fixed overhead spending variance is usually very small.
13. What is the cause of an unfavorable volume variance?
14. Does the volume variance convey any meaningful information to managers?
15. Which do you think is more important for control of fixed overhead costs: the spending variance or the volume variance? Explain.

Multiple-Choice Exercises

9-1 For performance reporting, it is best to compare actual costs with budgeted costs using

a. flexible budgets.
b. static budgets.
c. master budgets.
d. short-term budgets.
e. None of the above.

9-2 To create a meaningful performance report, actual costs and expected costs should be compared

a. at the budgeted level of activity.
b. weekly.
c. at the actual level of activity.
d. at the average level of activity.
e. hourly.

9-3 To help deal with uncertainty, managers should use

a. a static budget.
b. a master budget.
c. an after-the-fact flexible budget.
d. a before-the-fact flexible budget.
e. None of the above.

9-4 To help assess performance, managers should use

a. a static budget.
b. a master budget.
c. an after-the-fact flexible budget.
d. a before-the-fact flexible budget.
e. None of the above.

9-5 A firm comparing the actual variable costs of producing 10,000 units with the total variable costs of a static budget based on 9,000 units would probably see

a. no variances.
b. small favorable variances.
c. small unfavorable variances.
d. large favorable variances.
e. large unfavorable variances.

9-6 The total variable overhead variance is the difference between

a. the budgeted variable overhead and the actual variable overhead.
b. the actual variable overhead and the applied variable overhead.
c. the budgeted variable overhead and the applied variable overhead.
d. the applied variable overhead and the budgeted total overhead.
e. None of the above.

9-7 A variable overhead spending variance can occur because

a. prices for individual overhead items have increased.
b. prices for individual overhead items have decreased.
c. more of an individual overhead item was used than expected.
d. less of an individual overhead item was used than expected.
e. All of the above.

9-8 Because the calculation of both variances is based on direct labor hours, an unfavorable labor efficiency variance implies that

a. the variable overhead efficiency variance will also be unfavorable.
b. the variable overhead efficiency variance will be favorable.
c. there will be no variable overhead efficiency variance.
d. the variable overhead spending variance will be unfavorable.
e. the variable overhead is overapplied.

9-9 The total variable overhead variance can be expressed as the sum of

a. the underapplied variable overhead and the spending variance.
b. the efficiency variance and the overapplied variable overhead.
c. the spending and efficiency variances.
d. the spending, efficiency, and volume variances.
e. None of the above.

9-10 In a performance report that details the spending and efficiency variances, which of the following columns will be found?

a. A cost formula for each item
b. A budget for actual hours for each item
c. A budget of standard hours for each item
d. All of the above.
e. Only a and b.

9-11 The total fixed overhead variance is

a. the difference between actual and budgeted fixed overhead costs.
b. the difference between budgeted and applied fixed overhead costs.
c. the difference between budgeted fixed and variable overhead costs.
d. the difference between actual and applied fixed overhead costs.
e. None of the above.

9-12 The total fixed overhead variance can be expressed as the sum of

a. the spending and efficiency variances.
b. the spending and volume variances.
c. the efficiency and volume variances.
d. the flexible budget and the volume variances.
e. None of the above.

9-13 Because of the nature of fixed overhead items, the difference between the actual fixed overhead cost and the budgeted fixed overhead is

a.   likely to be small.
b.   likely to be large.
c.   usually a major concern.
d.   often attributable to labor inefficiency.
e.   None of the above.

9-14 An unfavorable volume variance can occur because

a.   too much finished goods inventory was held.
b.   the company overproduced.
c.   the actual output was less than expected or practical capacity.
d.   the actual output was greater than expected or practical capacity.
e.   All of the above.

9-15 Responsibility for the volume variance usually is assigned to

a.   the purchasing department.
b.   the receiving department.
c.   the shipping department.
d.   the manufacturing department.
e.   None of the above.

9-16 If ABC has been implemented, then activity-based budgeting must

a.   estimate the demand for each activity's output.
b.   estimate the resources required to support the activity output demanded.
c.   assign activity costs to individual suppliers.
d.   Only a and b.
e.   None of the above.

9-17 In activity-based budgeting, costs are classified as variable or fixed with respect to

a.   the activity driver.
b.   only the units produced.
c.   only the units sold.
d.   only the direct labor hours.
e.   None of the above.

9-18 Activity flexible budgeting makes it possible to

a.   predict what activity costs will be as activity output changes.
b.   improve traditional budgetary performance reporting.
c.   enhance the ability to manage activities.
d.   All of the above.
e.   Only a and c.

9-19 In activity-based budgeting, flexible budget formulas are created

a.   using only unit-level drivers.
b.   using only nonunit-level drivers.
c.   using both unit-level and nonunit-level drivers.
d.   using only direct labor hours.
e.   All of the above.

9-20 For activity-based budgeting, the variable component in a flexible budget cost formula corresponds to

a.   resources acquired as needed and used (flexible resources).
b.   resources acquired in advance of usage (committed resources).
c.   the cost of capital resources.
d.   the cost of depreciation.
e.   All of the above.

Exercises

Exercise 9-21 Performance Report

OBJECTIVE ①
CORNERSTONE 9-2

Master Budget	Actual Data
Budgeted production: 1,000	Actual production: 1,100 units
Materials:	
2 leather strips @ $5.00	Materials cost: $11,200
Labor:	
0.5 hours @ $8.00	Labor cost: $4,400

Required:
1.   Prepare a performance report using a budget based on expected production.
2.   Comment on the limitations of this report.

Exercise 9-22 Overhead Budget for a Particular Level of Activity

OBJECTIVE ①
CORNERSTONE 9-2

spreadsheet

Regina Johnson, controller for Pet-Care Company, has been instructed to develop a flexible budget for overhead costs. The company produces two types of dog food. One, BasicDiet, is a standard mixture for healthy dogs. The second, SpecDiet, is a reduced protein formulation for older dogs with health problems. The two dog foods use common raw materials in different proportions. The company expects to produce 100,000 50-pound bags of each product during the coming year. BasicDiet requires 0.25 direct labor hour per bag, and SpecDiet requires 0.30. Regina has developed the following fixed and variable costs for each of the four overhead items:

Overhead Item	Fixed Cost ($)	Variable Rate $ per direct labor hour
Maintenance	17,000	0.40
Power		0.50
Indirect labor	26,500	1.60
Rent	18,000	

Required:
Prepare an overhead budget for the expected activity level for the coming year.

Exercise 9-23 Flexible Budget

OBJECTIVE ①
CORNERSTONE 9-2

Refer to the information in **Exercise 9-22**.

Required:
Prepare an overhead budget that reflects production that is 10 percent higher than expected (for both products) and one for production that is 20 percent lower than expected.

Exercise 9-24 Performance Report

OBJECTIVE ①
CORNERSTONE 9-3

Refer to the information given in **Exercise 9-22**. Assume that Pet-Care actually produced 120,000 bags of BasicDiet and 100,000 bags of SpecDiet. The actual overhead costs incurred were as follows:

Maintenance	$40,500	Indirect labor	$119,000
Power	31,700	Rent	18,000

Required:
1. Prepare a performance report for the period.
2. Based on the report, would you judge any of the variances to be significant? Can you think of some possible reasons for the variances?

OBJECTIVE ④

CORNERSTONE 9-9

Exercise 9-25 Activity-Based Budgeting: Static

Jamison Inc. uses three forklifts to move materials from receiving to stores. The forklifts are also used to move materials from stores to the production area. The forklifts are obtained through an operating lease that costs $8,000 per year per forklift. Each move requires the use of a crate (costing $1 per unit). The crates are used to store the parts and are only emptied when used in production. Crates are disposed of after one cycle (two moves), where a cycle is defined as moving from receiving to stores to production. Forklifts can make three moves per hour and are used for 280 days per year, 24 hours per day (the remaining time is downtime for various reasons).

Required:
Prepare an annual budget for the activity moving materials, assuming that all of the capacity of the activity is used. Identify which resources you would treat as fixed costs and which would be viewed as variable costs.

OBJECTIVE ④

CORNERSTONE 9-10
CORNERSTONE 9-11

Exercise 9-26 Activity-Based Flexible Budgeting

Refer to the information in **Exercise 9-25**. Assume that the company uses only 90 percent of the activity capacity. The actual costs incurred at this level were as follows:

Lease	$24,000
Crates	50,000

Required:
1. What is the budget for this level of activity?
2. Prepare a performance report.

OBJECTIVE ④

CORNERSTONE 9-10

Exercise 9-27 Performance Report and Activity-Based Budgeting

Refer to the information in **Exercise 9-25**. Suppose that a redesign of the plant layout reduces the demand for moving materials by 75 percent.

Required:
What would be the budget for this new activity level?

OBJECTIVE ①

CORNERSTONE 9-6

Exercise 9-28 Performance Report for Variable Overhead Variances

Larsen Company had the data below for its most recent year, ending December 2007:

Actual costs:		Variable overhead standards:	
Indirect labor	$3,000	Indirect labor	0.10 hour @ $8.00
Supplies	$ 700	Supplies	0.10 hour @ $2.00
Actual hours worked	400 hours	Standard variable	
Number of units produced	5,000 units	overhead rate	$10.00 per direct labor hour
Hours allowed for production	500 hours		

Required:
Prepare a performance report that shows the variances on an item-by-item basis.

Exercise 9-29 Variable Overhead Variances, Service Company

Joven Inc, operates a delivery service for over 70 restaurants. The corporation has a fleet of vehicles and has invested in a sophisticated computerized communications system to coordinate its deliveries. Joven has gathered the following data on last year's operations:

> Deliveries made: 42,000
> Direct labor: 30,000 delivery hours @ $7.00
> Actual variable overhead: $138,000

Joven employs a standard costing system. During the year, a variable overhead rate of $4.05 per hour was used. The labor standard requires 0.75 hour per delivery.

Required:
Compute the variable overhead spending and efficiency variances.

OBJECTIVE ②
CORNERSTONE 9-4
CORNERSTONE 9-5

Exercise 9-30 Fixed Overhead Variances

Refer to **Exercise 9-29**. Assume that the actual fixed overhead was $420,000 and that the standard fixed overhead rate is $12 per delivery hour. The fixed overhead rate was calculated using practical capacity of 33,750 delivery hours.

Required:
Compute the fixed overhead spending and volume variances.

OBJECTIVE ③
CORNERSTONE 9-7
CORNERSTONE 9-8

Exercise 9-31 Fixed Overhead Application, Variances

Tules Company is planning to produce 2,400,000 power drills for the coming year. Each drill requires 0.5 standard hour of labor for completion. The company uses direct labor hours to assign overhead to products. The total fixed overhead budgeted for the coming year is $1,320,000. Predetermined overhead rates are calculated using expected production, measured in direct labor hours. Actual results for the year are:

> Actual production (units)   2,360,000
> Actual direct labor hours   1,190,000
> Actual fixed overhead $1,260,000

Required:
1. Compute the applied fixed overhead.
2. Compute the fixed overhead spending and volume variances.

OBJECTIVE ③
CORNERSTONE 9-7
CORNERSTONE 9-8

Exercise 9-32 Variable Overhead Application, Variances

Refer to the information in **Exercise 9-31**. The total budgeted overhead was $2,700,000. Actual variable overhead incurred was $1,410,000.

Required:
1. Compute the applied variable overhead.
2. Compute the variable overhead spending and efficiency variances.

OBJECTIVE ②
CORNERSTONE 9-4
CORNERSTONE 9-5

Exercise 9-33 Overhead Variances

At the beginning of the year, Raydom Company had the following standard cost sheet for one of its chemical products:

> Direct materials (5 lbs. @ $6.40) $32.00
> Direct labor (2 hrs. @ $18.00)   36.00
> Fixed overhead (2 hrs. @ $4.00)   8.00
> Variable overhead (2 hrs. @ $1.50)   3.00
> Standard cost per unit $79.00

OBJECTIVES ① ②
CORNERSTONE 9-5
CORNERSTONE 9-8

spreadsheet

Raydom computes its overhead rates using practical volume, which is 144,000 units. The actual results for the year are as follows:

a. Units produced: 140,000
b. Direct labor: 290,000 hours at $9.05
c. Fixed overhead: $1,160,000
d. Variable overhead: $436,000

Required:
1. Compute the fixed overhead spending and volume variances.
2. Compute the variable overhead spending and efficiency variances.

OBJECTIVE ① **Problem 9-34 Overhead Budget, Flexible Budget**

Torino Inc. manufactures machine parts in its Alva plant. Torino has developed the following flexible budget for overhead for the coming year. Activity level is measured in direct labor hours.

	Variable Cost Formula	Activity Level (hours)		
		10,000	20,000	30,000
Variable costs:				
Maintenance	$1.20	$12,000	$24,000	$36,000
Supplies	0.80	8,000	16,000	24,000
Power	0.10	1,000	2,000	3,000
Total variable costs	$2.10	$21,000	$ 42,000	$ 63,000
Fixed costs:				
Depreciation		$7,800	$7,800	$7,800
Salaries		66,000	66,000	66,000
Total fixed costs		$73,800	$73,800	$73,800
Total overhead costs		$94,800	$115,800	$136,800

The Alva plant produces two different types of parts. The production budget for November is 40,000 units for Part A23 and 20,000 units for Part B14. Part A23 requires 15 minutes of direct labor time, and Part B14 requires 24 minutes. Fixed overhead costs are incurred uniformly throughout the year.

Required:
1. Calculate the number of direct labor hours needed in November to produce Part A23 and the number of direct labor hours needed in November to produce Part B14. What are the total direct labor hours budgeted for November?
2. Prepare an overhead budget for November.

OBJECTIVE ① **Problem 9-35 Kicker Speakers, Before-the-Fact Flexible Budgeting, Flexible Budgeting for the New Solo X18 Model**

Stillwater Designs is considering a new Kicker speaker model: Solo X18, which is a large and expensive subwoofer (projected price is $760 to distributors). The company controls the design specifications of the model and contracts with manufacturers in mainland China to produce the model. Stillwater Designs pays the freight and custom duties. The product is shipped to Stillwater and then sold to distributors throughout the United States.

The market for this type of subwoofer is small and competitive. It is expected to have a three-year life cycle. Market test reviews were encouraging. One potential customer noted that the speaker could make a deaf person hear again. Another remarked that the bass could be heard two miles away. Another customer was simply impressed by the size and watts of the subwoofer (a maximum of 10,000 watts capability). Encouraged by the results of market tests, the Product Steering Committee also wanted to review the financial analysis. The projected revenues and costs at three levels of sales volume are as follows (for the three-year life cycle):

	Pessimistic	Most Likely	Optimistic
Sales volume (units)	72,000	150,000	250,000
Variable costs (total):			
Acquisition cost	$43,200,000	$ 90,000,000	$150,000,000
Freight	4,320,000	9,000,000	15,000,000
Duties	1,800,000	3,750,000	6,250,000
Total	$49,320,000	$102,750,000	$171,250,000
Fixed costs (total):			
Engineering (R&D)	$10,000,000	$ 10,000,000	$ 10,000,000
Overhead	3,000,000	3,000,000	3,000,000
Total	$13,000,000	$ 13,000,000	$ 13,000,000

Required:
1. Prepare flexible budget formulas for the cost items listed for the Solo X18 model. Also, provide a flexible budget formula for total costs.
2. Prepare an income statement for each of the three levels of sales volume. Discuss the value of before-the-fact flexible budgeting and relate this to the current example.
3. Form a group with two to four other students. Assume that the group is acting as a Product Steering Committee. Evaluate the feasibility of producing the Solo X18 model (using the given financial data and the results of Requirements 1 and 2.) If the financial performance of the model is questionable, discuss possible courses of action that the company might take to improve the financial performance of the product. Also, discuss some reasons why the company might wish to produce the model even if it does not promise a good financial return.

Problem 9-36 Flexible Budgeting

OBJECTIVE ①

Quarterly budgeted overhead costs for two different levels of activity follow. The 2,000 level was the expected level from the master budget.

	Cost Formula ($)		Direct Labor Hours	
	Fixed	Variable	1,000 Hours	2,000 Hours
Maintenance	4,000	6.00	$10,000	$16,000
Depreciation	5,000	—	5,000	5,000
Supervision	15,000	—	15,000	15,000
Supplies	—	1.40	1,400	2,800
Power	—	0.75	750	1,500
Other	8,000	0.10	8,100	8,200

The actual activity level was 1,650 hours.

Required:
1. Prepare a flexible budget for an activity level of 1,650 direct labor hours.
2. Suppose that all of the formulas for each item are missing. You only have the budgeted costs for each level of activity. Show how you can obtain the formulas for each item by using the information given for the budgeted costs for the two levels.

OBJECTIVE ①

Problem 9-37 Flexible Budgeting

Fruta Inc. purchases fruit from numerous growers and packs fruit boxes and fruit baskets for sale. Fruta has developed the following flexible budget for overhead for the coming year. Activity level is measured in direct labor hours.

		Activity Level (hours)		
		2,000	2,500	3,000
Variable costs:				
Maintenance	$0.80	$ 1,600	$ 2,000	$ 2,400
Supplies	0.20	400	500	600
Power	0.40	800	1,000	1,200
Total variable costs	$1.40	$ 2,800	$ 3,500	$ 4,200
Fixed costs:				
Depreciation		$ 4,800	$ 4,800	$ 4,800
Salaries		18,000	18,000	18,000
Total fixed costs		$22,800	$22,800	$22,800
Total overhead costs		$25,600	$26,300	$27,000

Required:
1. Prepare an overhead budget for May.
2. The Cushing High School Parent–Teacher Organization ordered 200 gift baskets from Fruta to be given to high school teachers and support staff as a thank you for a successful school year. These gift baskets must be ready by May 31 and were not included in the original production budget for May. Without preparing a new overhead budget, what is Fruta's new total budgeted overhead for May?

OBJECTIVE ①

Problem 9-38 Performance Reporting

Fernando's is a hole-in-the-wall sandwich shop just off the State University campus. Customers enter off the street into a small counter area to order one of 10 varieties of sandwiches and a soft drink. All orders must be taken out because there is no space for dining in.

The owner of Fernando's is Luis Azaria, son of Fernando Azaria who founded the shop. Luis is attempting to construct a series of budgets. He has accumulated the following information:

a. The average sandwich (which sells for $4.50) requires 1 roll, 4 ounces of meat, 2 ounces of cheese, 0.05 head of lettuce, 0.25 of a tomato, and a healthy squirt (1 oz.) of secret sauce. (We can't reveal the recipe here, but it includes Serrano pepper and hoisin sauce.)
b. Each customer typically orders one soft drink (average price $1.50) consisting of a cup and 12 ounces of soda. Refills on the soda are free, but this offer is seldom taken advantage of because the typical customer carries his/her sandwich and soda back to the office or common area.
c. Use of paper supplies (napkins, bag, sandwich wrap, cups) varies somewhat from customer to customer but averages $1,650 per month.
d. Fernando's is open for two 4-hour shifts. The noon shift on Monday through Friday requires two workers earning $10 per hour. The evening shift is only worked on Friday, Saturday, and Sunday nights. The two evening shift employees also earn $10 per hour. There are 4.3 weeks in a month.
e. Rent is $575 per month. Other monthly cash expenses average $1,800.
f. Food costs are:

Meat	$7.00/pound
Cheese	$6.00/pound
Rolls	$28.80/gross
Lettuce (a box contains 24 heads)	$12.00/box
Tomatoes (a box contains about 20 tomatoes)	$4/box
Secret sauce	$6.40/gallon
Soda (syrup and carbonated water)	$2.56/gallon

In a normal month when school is in session, Fernando's sells 5,000 sandwiches and 5,000 sodas. In October, State U holds its homecoming celebration. Therefore, Luis figured that if he added a noon shift on Saturday and Sunday of homecoming weekend, October sales would be 30 percent higher than normal. To advertise his noon shifts during homecoming weekend, Luis bought cups emblazoned with the State U Homecoming schedule. This added $200 to paper costs for the month. Last year, he did add the two additional shifts, and his sales goal was realized.

Required:
1.   Prepare a flexible budget for a normal school month.
2.   Prepare a flexible budget for October.
3.   Do you think it was worthwhile for Luis to add the additional shifts for homecoming weekend last October?

Problem 9-39 Functional versus Activity Flexible Budgeting

OBJECTIVES ① ④

Amy Bunker, production manager, was upset with the latest performance report, which indicated that she was $100,000 over budget. Given the efforts that she and her workers had made, she was confident that they had met or beat the budget. Now she was not only upset but also genuinely puzzled over the results. Three items—direct labor, power, and setups—were over budget. The actual costs for these three items follow:

Direct labor	$ 210,000
Power	135,000
Setups	140,000
Total	$ 485,000

Amy knew that her operation had produced more units than originally had been budgeted so more power and labor had naturally been used. She also knew that the uncertainty in scheduling had led to more setups than planned. When she pointed this out to Gary Grant, the controller, he assured her that the budgeted costs had been adjusted for the increase in productive activity. Curious, Amy questioned Gary about the methods used to make the adjustment.

Gary: If the actual level of activity differs from the original planned level, we adjust the budget by using budget formulas—formulas that allow us to predict the costs for different levels of activity.

Amy: The approach sounds reasonable. However, I'm sure something is wrong here. Tell me exactly how you adjusted the costs of direct labor, power, and setups.

Gary: First, we obtain formulas for the individual items in the budget by using the method of least squares. We assume that cost variations can be explained by variations in productive activity where activity is measured by direct labor hours. Here is a list of the cost formulas for the three items you mentioned. The variable X is the number of direct labor hours.

Direct labor cost = $10X
Power cost = $5,000 + $4X
Setup cost = $100,000

Amy: I think I see the problem. Power costs don't have a lot to do with direct labor hours. They have more to do with machine hours. As production increases, machine hours increase more rapidly than direct labor hours. Also, . . .

Gary: You know, you have a point. The coefficient of determination for power cost is only about 50 percent. That leaves a lot of unexplained cost variation. The coefficient for labor, however, is much better—it explains about 96 percent of the cost variation. Setup costs, of course, are fixed.

Amy: Well, as I was about to say, setup costs also have little to do with direct labor hours. And I might add that they certainly are not fixed—at least not all of them. We had to do more setups than our original plan called for because of the scheduling changes. And we have to pay our people when they work extra hours. It seems like we are always paying overtime. I wonder if we simply do not have enough people for the setup activity. Also, there are supplies that are used for each setup, and these are not cheap. Did you build these extra costs of increased setup activity into your budget?

Gary: No, we assumed that setup costs were fixed. I see now that some of them could vary as the number of setups increases. Amy, let me see if I can develop some cost formulas based on better explanatory variables. I'll get back to you in a few days.

Assume that after a few days' work, Gary developed the following cost formulas, all with a coefficient of determination greater than 90 percent:

Direct labor cost = $10X, where X = Direct labor hours
Power cost = $68,000 + 0.9Y, where Y = Machine hours
Setup cost = $98,000 + $400Z, where Z = Number of setups

The actual measure of each activity driver is as follows:

Direct labor hours	20,000
Machine hours	90,000
Number of setups	110

Required:

1. Prepare a performance report for direct labor, power, and setups using the direct labor-based formulas.
2. Prepare a performance report for direct labor, power, and setups using the multiple cost driver formulas that Gary developed.
3. Of the two approaches, which provides the more accurate picture of Amy's performance? Why?

OBJECTIVE ④   **Problem 9-40 Activity Flexible Budgeting**

Billy Adams, controller for Westcott, Inc., prepared the following budget for manufacturing costs at two different levels of activity for 2007:

DIRECT LABOR HOURS

	Level of Activity	
	50,000	100,000
Direct materials	$300,000	$ 600,000
Direct labor	200,000	400,000
Depreciation (plant)	100,000	100,000
Subtotal	$600,000	$1,100,000

MACHINE HOURS

	Level of Activity	
	200,000	300,000
Maintaining equipment	$360,000	$510,000
Machining	112,000	162,000
Subtotal	$472,000	$672,000

MATERIAL MOVES

	Level of Activity	
	20,000	40,000
Materials handling	$165,000	$290,000

NUMBER OF BATCHES INSPECTED

	Level of Activity	
	100	200
Inspecting products	$ 125,000	$ 225,000
Total	$ 1,362,000	$ 2,287,000

During 2007, Westcott employees worked a total of 80,000 direct labor hours, used 250,000 machine hours, made 32,000 moves, and performed 120 batch inspections. The following actual costs were incurred:

Direct materials	$440,000
Direct labor	355,000
Depreciation	100,000
Maintenance	425,000
Machining	142,000
Materials handling	232,500
Inspecting products	160,000

Westcott applies overhead using rates based on direct labor hours, machine hours, number of moves, and number of batches. The second level of activity (the far right column in the preceding table) is the practical level of activity (the available activity for resources acquired in advance of usage) and is used to compute predetermined overhead pool rates.

Required:

1. Prepare a performance report for Westcott's manufacturing costs in 2007.
2. Assume that one of the products produced by Westcott is budgeted to use 10,000 direct labor hours, 15,000 machine hours, and 500 moves and will be produced in five batches. A total of 10,000 units will be produced during the year. Calculate the budgeted unit manufacturing cost.
3. One of Westcott's managers said the following: "Budgeting at the activity level makes a lot of sense. It really helps us manage costs better. But the above budget really needs to provide more detailed information. For example, I know that the materials handling activity involves the usage of forklifts and operators, and this information is lost with simply reporting the total cost of the activity for various levels of output. We have four forklifts, each capable of providing 10,000 moves per year. We lease these forklifts for five years, at $10,000 per year. Furthermore, for our two shifts, we need up to eight operators if we run all four forklifts. Each operator is paid a salary of $30,000 per year. Also, I know that fuel costs us about $0.25 per move."

Based on these comments, explain how this additional information may help Westcott to better manage its costs. Also, assuming that these are the only three items, expand the detail of the flexible budget for materials handling to reveal the cost of these three resource items for 20,000 moves and 40,000 moves, respectively. You may wish to review the concepts of flexible, committed, and discretionary resources found in Chapter 2.

Problem 9-41 Flexible Budgeting

OBJECTIVE ①

At the beginning of last year, Jean Bingham, controller for Thorpe Inc., prepared the following budget for conversion costs at two levels of activity for the coming year:

	Direct Labor Hours	
	100,000	120,000
Direct labor	$1,000,000	$1,200,000
Supervision	180,000	180,000
Utilities	18,000	21,000
Depreciation	225,000	225,000
Supplies	25,000	30,000
Maintenance	240,000	284,000
Rent	120,000	120,000
Other	60,000	70,000
Total manufacturing cost	$1,868,000	$2,130,000

During the year, the company worked a total of 112,000 direct labor hours and incurred the following actual costs:

Direct labor	$963,200
Supervision	190,000
Utilities	20,500
Depreciation	225,000
Supplies	24,640
Maintenance	237,000
Rent	120,000
Other	60,500

Thorpe applied overhead on the basis of direct labor hours. Normal volume of 120,000 direct labor hours is the activity level to be used to compute the predetermined overhead rate.

Required:
1. Determine the cost formula for each of Thorpe's conversion costs. (*Hint:* Use the high-low method.)
2. Prepare a performance report for Thorpe's conversion costs for last year. Should any cost item be given special attention? Explain.

OBJECTIVES ② ③   **Problem 9-42 Overhead Application, Overhead Variances**

Tavera Company uses a standard cost system. The direct labor standard indicates that six direct labor hours should be used for every unit produced. Tavera produces one product. The normal production volume is 120,000 units of this product. The budgeted overhead for the coming year is as follows:

Fixed overhead	$2,160,000*
Variable overhead	1,440,000

*At normal volume.

Tavera applies overhead on the basis of direct labor hours. During the year, Tavera produced 119,000 units, worked 731,850 direct labor hours, and incurred actual fixed overhead costs of $2.25 million and actual variable overhead costs of $1.425 million.

Required:
1. Calculate the standard fixed overhead rate and the standard variable overhead rate.
2. Compute the applied fixed overhead and the applied variable overhead. What is the total fixed overhead variance? Total variable overhead variance?
3. Break down the total fixed overhead variance into a spending variance and a volume variance. Discuss the significance of each.
4. Compute the variable overhead spending and efficiency variances. Discuss the significance of each.
5. Journal entries for overhead variances were not discussed in this chapter. Typically, the overhead variance entries happen at the end of the year. Assume that applied fixed (variable) overhead is accumulated on the credit side of the fixed (variable overhead) control account. Actual fixed (variable) overhead costs are accumulated on the debit side of the respective control accounts. At the end of the year, the balance in each control account is the total (fixed) variable variance. Create accounts for each of the four overhead variances and close out the total variances to each of these four variance accounts. These four variance accounts are then usually disposed of by closing them to Cost of Goods Sold.

    Form a group with two to four other students, and prepare the journal entries that isolate the four variances. Finally, prepare the journal entries that close these variances to Cost of Goods Sold.

Problem 9-43 Overhead Variance Analysis

OBJECTIVES ② ③

spreadsheet

The Lubbock plant of Morril's Small Motor Division produces a major subassembly for a 6.0 horsepower motor for lawn mowers. The plant uses a standard costing system for production costing and control. The standard cost sheet for the subassembly follows:

Direct materials (6.0 lbs. @ $5.00)	$30.00
Direct labor (1.6 hrs. @ $12.00)	19.20
Variable overhead (1.6 hrs. @ $10.00)	16.00
Fixed overhead (1.6 hrs. @ $6.00)	9.60
Standard unit cost	$74.80

During the year, the Lubbock plant had the following actual production activity:

a. Production of motors totaled 50,000 units.
b. The company used 82,000 direct labor hours at a total cost of $1,066,000.
c. Actual fixed overhead totaled $556,000.
d. Actual variable overhead totaled $860,000.

The Lubbock plant's practical activity is 60,000 units per year. Standard overhead rates are computed based on practical activity measured in standard direct labor hours.

Required:
1. Compute the variable overhead spending and efficiency variances.
2. Compute the fixed overhead spending and volume variances. Interpret the volume variance. What can be done to reduce this variance?

Problem 9-44 Overhead Variances

OBJECTIVES ② ③

Extrim Company produces monitors. Extrim's plant in San Antonio uses a standard costing system. The standard costing system relies on direct labor hours to assign overhead costs to production. The direct labor standard indicates that four direct labor hours should be used for every microwave unit produced. (The San Antonio plant produces only one model.) The normal production volume is 120,000 units. The budgeted overhead for the coming year is given below.

Fixed overhead	$1,286,400
Variable overhead	888,000*
*At normal volume.	

Extrim applies overhead on the basis of direct labor hours.

During the year, Extrim produced 119,000 units, worked 487,900 direct labor hours, and incurred actual fixed overhead costs of $1.3 million and actual variable overhead costs of $927,010.

Required:
1. Calculate the standard fixed overhead rate and the standard variable overhead rate.
2. Compute the applied fixed overhead and the applied variable overhead. What is the total fixed overhead variance? Total variable overhead variance?
3. Break down the total fixed overhead variance into a spending variance and a volume variance. Discuss the significance of each.
4. Compute the variable overhead spending and efficiency variances. Discuss the significance of each.

Problem 9-45 Incomplete Data, Overhead Analysis

OBJECTIVES ② ③

Lynwood Company produces surge protectors. To help control costs, Lynwood employs a standard costing system and uses a flexible budget to predict overhead costs at various levels of activity. For the most recent year, Lynwood used a standard overhead rate of $18 per direct labor hour. The rate was computed using practical activity. Budgeted overhead costs are $396,000 for 18,000 direct labor hours and $540,000 for

30,000 direct labor hours. During the past year, Lynwood generated the following data:

a. Actual production: 100,000 units
b. Fixed overhead volume variance: $20,000 U
c. Variable overhead efficiency variance: $18,000 F
d. Actual fixed overhead costs: $200,000
e. Actual variable overhead costs: $310,000

Required:

1. Calculate the fixed overhead rate.
2. Determine the fixed overhead spending variance.
3. Determine the variable overhead spending variance.
4. Determine the standard hours allowed per unit of product.

OBJECTIVES ① ② ③   Problem 9-46 Flexible Budget, Overhead Variances

Shumaker Company manufactures a line of high-top basketball shoes. At the beginning of the year, the following plans for production and costs were revealed:

Pairs of shoes to be produced and sold	55,000
Standard cost per unit:	
Direct materials	$ 15
Direct labor	12
Variable overhead	6
Fixed overhead	3
Total unit cost	$ 36

During the year, a total of 50,000 units were produced and sold. The following actual costs were incurred:

Direct materials	$ 775,000
Direct labor	590,000
Variable overhead	310,000
Fixed overhead	180,000

There were no beginning or ending inventories of raw materials. In producing the 50,000 units, 63,000 hours were worked, 5 percent more hours than the standard allowed for the actual output. Overhead costs are applied to production using direct labor hours.

Required:

1. Using a flexible budget, prepare a performance report comparing expected costs for the actual production with actual costs.
2. Determine the following:
    a. Fixed overhead spending and volume variances.
    b. Variable overhead spending and efficiency variances.

Cases

OBJECTIVE ③   Case 9-47 Fixed Overhead Spending and Volume Variances, Capacity Management

Lorale Company, a producer of recreational vehicles, recently decided to begin producing a major subassembly for jet skis. The subassembly would be used by Lorale's jet ski plants and also would be sold to other producers. The decision was made to lease two large buildings in two different locations: Little Rock, Arkansas, and Athens, Georgia. The company agreed to a 9-year, renewable lease contract. The plants were of the same size, and each had 10 production lines. New equipment was purchased for each line and workers were hired to operate the equipment. The company also hired production line supervisors for each plant. A supervisor is capable of directing up to two production lines per shift. Two shifts are run for each plant. The practical production capacity of each plant is 300,000 subassemblies per year. Two standard direct labor hours are allowed for each subassembly. The costs for leasing, equipment depreciation, and supervision for a single plant are as follows (the costs are assumed to be the same for each plant):

Supervision (10 supervisors @ $50,000)	$ 500,000
Building lease (annual payment)	800,000
Equipment depreciation (annual)	1,100,000
Total fixed overhead costs*	$2,400,000

*For simplicity, assume these are the only fixed overhead costs.

After beginning operations, Lorale discovered that demand for the product in the region covered by the Little Rock plant was less than anticipated. At the end of the first year, only 240,000 units were sold. The Athens plant sold 300,000 units as expected. The actual fixed overhead costs at the end of the first year were $2,500,000 (for each plant).

Required:
1. Calculate a fixed overhead rate based on standard direct labor hours.
2. Calculate the fixed overhead spending and volume variances for the Little Rock and Athens plants. What is the most likely cause of the spending variance? Why are the volume variances different for the two plants?
3. Suppose that from now on the sales for the Little Rock plant are expected to be no more than 240,000 units. What actions would you take to manage the capacity costs (fixed overhead costs)?
4. Calculate the fixed overhead cost per subassembly for each plant. Do they differ? Should they differ? Explain. Do ABC concepts help in analyzing this issue?

Case 9-48 Ethical Considerations; Flexible Budgeting and the Environment

Harry Johnson, the chief financial officer of Ur Thrift, Inc, a large retailer, had just finished a meeting with the Roger Swasey, the chief financial officer of the large retailer, and Connie Baker, its environmental officer. Over the years, Harry had overseen the development of a number of cost formulas that allowed Ur Thrift to budget the variable costs of a variety of items. For example, packaging for one of its private line of dolls had a cost formula of Y = $2.20X, where X represented the number of dolls sold. The formula was used to calculate the expected packaging costs which were then compared with the actual packaging costs. Over the last several years, the actual costs and budgeted costs were virtually on target, prompting Harry to claim that packaging costs were well controlled.

Connie Baker, however, argued that the packaging costs were not well controlled. In fact, she was adamant in her view that the packaging was excessive and that by reducing the packaging, costs could be reduced and the environmental impacts reduced as well. She argued that the company had an ethical obligation to reduce environmental impacts and that cost savings would also be captured, improving the profitability of the company. As another example, Connie discussed the fleet of trucks used by Ur Thrift to move goods from its warehouses to retail outlets. The fuel cost formula was $3X, where X represented gallons of fuel consumed. She pointed out that the performance data also revealed that fuel costs were in control. Yet, her office had recently recommended the installation of an auxiliary power unit to heat and cool the cabs of the trucks could during the mandatory ten-hour breaks required of its drivers, thus avoiding the need to have the engine idle during this rest period. She claimed that this would significantly reduce fuel costs and easily pay for the new auxiliary units in a short period of time.

Connie had also made some comments that caused Harry to pause and do some soul searching. She noted that the financial officers of the company should be more concerned about reducing costs than simply predicting what they should be. Thus, (according to her view), cost formulas are useful only to tell us where we currently are so that they can be used to assess how to reduce costs. The so-called flexible budgets are simply a means of enforcing static standards. She also said that the company's managers had an ethical obligation to not overconsume the resources of the planet. She urged both Harry and Roger to help position the company so that it could reduce its environmental impacts.

Required:

1. Do financial officers have an ethical obligation to help in reducing negative environmental impacts? Identify and discuss which of the Institute of Management Accountant's ethical standards might be used to sustain this point of view. Also, describe the role that flexible budgeting may play in reducing environmental impacts.

2. Suppose that Harry and Connie embark on a cooperative effort to eliminate any excessive packaging. The projected results are impressive. The expected reductions will save $3 million in shipping costs ($0.50 per package), $1.5 million in packaging materials ($0.40 per package), 5,000 trees, and 1.25 million barrels of oil. Are there any ethical issues associated with these actions? What standards might apply?

3. Identify two potential ethical dilemmas that might surface in the use of flexible budgeting for performance evaluation (the dilemmas do not need to be connected with environmental activities).

10

Performance Evaluation, Variable Costing, and Decentralization

After studying Chapter 10, you should be able to:

① Explain how and why firms choose to decentralize.

② Explain the difference between absorption and variable costing, and prepare segmented income statements.

③ Compute and explain return on investment.

④ Compute and explain residual income and economic value added.

⑤ Explain the uses of the Balanced Scorecard and the role of transfer pricing in a decentralized firm.

© Herman Miller, Inc.

Experience Managerial Decisions

with Herman Miller

The goal of performance evaluation is to provide information useful for assessing the effectiveness of past decisions so that future decisions can be improved. As you might guess, this goal is a difficult one to achieve because of the sheer quantity of information present in organizations and the complexity of the business environment in which most decisions are made. However, **Herman Miller Inc.**, a large furniture manufacturer headquartered in western Michigan with business activities in over 40 countries, uses an increasingly popular performance evaluation technique—economic value added (EVA)—to help it make better decisions. For example, the entire office furniture market experienced a devastating slump in the early 2000s as a result of the dot com bust and the 9/11 disaster. EVA measures provided Herman Miller with information beyond traditional accounting performance metrics that was critical to its dramatic and quick recovery from the negative operating margins it experienced during the slump to the near double-digit positive margins it enjoyed only a few years later. EVA identifies the return generated by the company's assets and then subtracts the cost of all capital, both debt (e.g., money raised from loans, leases, and bonds) and equity (e.g., money raised from investors), used by the company to finance those assets in order to determine whether value is being created or destroyed. More specifically, EVA helps Herman Miller to quantify the long-term financial benefits of carrying less inventory and employing fewer fixed assets in its business. As a result of such EVA analyses, Herman Miller makes fundamentally different strategic and operating decisions involving its furniture production processes than it would if it relied solely on traditional accounting metrics. The ability to impact decisions in such a positive fashion has catapulted EVA into a position of prominence in Herman Miller's successful performance evaluation system.

OBJECTIVE ①
Explain how and why firms choose to decentralize.

Decentralization and Responsibility Centers

In general, a company is organized along lines of responsibility. The traditional organizational chart, with its pyramid shape, illustrates the lines of responsibility flowing from the chief executive officer down through the vice presidents to middle- and lower-level managers. As organizations grow larger, these lines of responsibility become longer and more numerous. The structure becomes cumbersome. Contemporary practice is moving toward a flattened hierarchy. This structure—emphasizing teams—is consistent with decentralization. **GE Capital**, for example, is essentially a group of smaller businesses. A strong link exists between the structure of an organization and its responsibility accounting system. Ideally, the responsibility accounting system mirrors and supports the structure of an organization.

Firms with multiple responsibility centers usually choose one of two decision-making approaches to manage their diverse and complex activities: *centralized* or *decentralized*. In centralized decision making, decisions are made at the very top level, and lower-level managers are charged with implementing these decisions. On the other hand, decentralized decision making allows managers at lower levels to make and implement key decisions pertaining to their areas of responsibility. **Decentralization** is the practice of delegating decision-making authority to the lower levels of management in a company. Exhibit 10-1 illustrates the difference between centralized and decentralized companies.

Organizations range from highly centralized to strongly decentralized. Most firms fall somewhere in between, with the majority tending toward decentralization. The reasons for the popularity of decentralization and the ways in which a company may choose to decentralize are discussed next.

Reasons for Decentralization

Firms decide to decentralize for several reasons, including (1) ease of gathering and using local information; (2) focusing of central management; (3) training and motivating of segment managers; and (4) enhanced competition, exposing segments to market forces.

Exhibit 10-1

Centralization and Decentralization

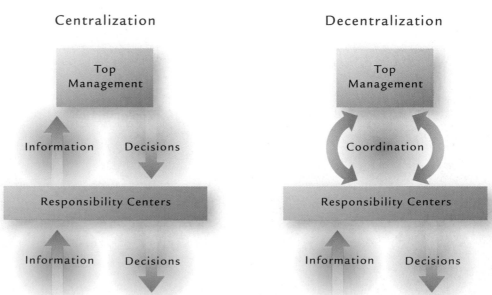

Gathering and Using Local Information   The quality of decisions is affected by the quality of information available. As a firm grows in size and operates in different markets and regions, central management may not understand local conditions. Lower-level managers, however, are in contact with immediate operating conditions (such as the strength and nature of local competition, the nature of the local labor force, and so on). As a result, they often are better positioned to make local decisions. For example, **McDonald's** has restaurants around the world. The tastes of people in China or France differ from those of people in the United States. So, McDonald's tailors its menu to different countries. The result is that the McDonald's in each country can differentiate to meet the needs of its local market.

Focusing of Central Management   By decentralizing the operating decisions, central management is free to engage in strategic planning and decision making. The long-run survival of the organization should be of more importance to central management than day-to-day operations.

Training and Motivating of Managers   Organizations always need well-trained managers to replace higher-level managers who leave to take advantage of other opportunities. What better way to prepare a future generation of higher-level managers than by providing them the opportunity to make significant decisions? These opportunities also enable top managers to evaluate local managers' capabilities. Those who make the best decisions are the ones who can be promoted.

Enhanced Competition   In a highly centralized company, overall profit margins can mask inefficiencies within the various subdivisions. Large companies now find that they cannot afford to keep a noncompetitive division. One of the best ways to improve performance of a division or factory is to expose it more fully to market forces. At **Koch Industries Inc.**, each unit is expected to act as an autonomous business unit and to set prices both externally and internally. Units whose services are not required by other Koch units may face possible elimination.

Divisions in the Decentralized Firm

Decentralization involves a cost-benefit trade-off. As a firm decentralizes, it passes more decision authority down the managerial hierarchy to lower-level managers. As a result, managers in a decentralized firm make and implement more decisions than do managers in a centralized firm. The benefit of decentralization is that decisions are more likely to be made by managers who possess the specific local knowledge—not possessed by high-level managers-to use the firm's resources in the best way possible to maximize firm value (e.g., stock price). However, the cost of decentralization is that lower-level managers who have the knowledge to make the best decisions with the firm's resources are less likely to possess the same incentive as high-level managers to maximize firm value. Stated differently, as compared with high-level managers, lower-level managers are more likely to use the firm's resources for personal gain than for increasing the firm's stock price. Therefore, decentralization requires the use of costly incentives, such as profit-sharing and stock options, to try and motivate lower-level managers to make decisions that maximize firm value. **Starbucks**, for example, is famous for offering incentives, such as healthcare benefits and stock options, even to its part-time employees. Successful decentralized firms manage this trade-off in an effective fashion.

Decentralization usually is achieved by creating units called *divisions*. One way in which divisions are differentiated is by the types of goods or services produced. For example, divisions of **PepsiCo** include the Snack Ventures Europe Division (a joint venture with **General Mills**), **Frito-Lay Inc.**, and **Tropicana**, as well as its flagship soft-drink division. Exhibit 10-2 shows decentralized divisions of PepsiCo. These divisions are organized on the basis of product lines. Notice that some divisions depend on other divisions.

Exhibit 10-2

Decentralized Divisions

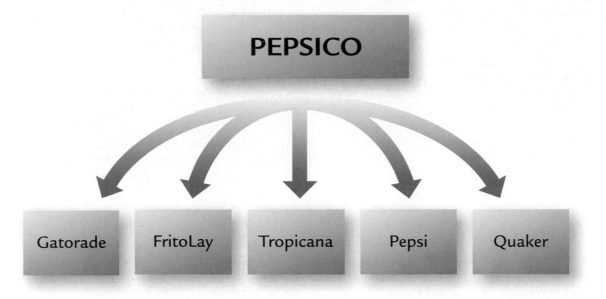

For example, PepsiCo spun off its restaurant divisions to **YUM**. As a result, the cola you drink at **Pizza Hut**, **Taco Bell**, and **KFC** will be Pepsi—not Coke. In a decentralized setting, some interdependencies usually exist; otherwise, a company would merely be a collection of totally separate entities.

Divisions may also be created along geographic lines. For example, **UAL Inc.** (parent of **United Airlines**) has a number of regional divisions: Asian/Pacific, Caribbean, European, Latin American, and North American. The presence of divisions spanning one or more regions creates the need for performance evaluation that can take into account differences in divisional environments.

A third way divisions differ is by the type of responsibility given to the divisional manager. As a firm grows, top management typically creates areas of responsibility, known as responsibility centers, and assigns subordinate managers to those areas. A **responsibility center** is a segment of the business whose manager is accountable for specified sets of activities. The results of each responsibility center can be measured according to the information that managers need to operate their centers. The four major types of responsibility centers are as follows:

1. **Cost center:** A responsibility center in which a manager is responsible only for costs.
2. **Revenue center:** A responsibility center in which a manager is responsible only for sales.
3. **Profit center:** A responsibility center in which a manager is responsible for both revenues and costs.
4. **Investment center:** A responsibility center in which a manager is responsible for revenues, costs, and investments.

The choice of responsibility center typically mirrors the actual situation and the type of information available to the manager. Information is the key to appropriately holding managers responsible for outcomes. For example, a production department manager is held responsible for departmental costs but not for sales. This responsibility choice occurs because the production department manager understands and directly controls

Concept Q&A

Think about summer jobs that you and your friends have held. To what extent did you or your friends work in a centralized or decentralized decision-making environment?

Answer:

If you worked at a Taco Bell or Pizza Hut, you were working for a decentralized company, YUM. This company owns many Taco Bells and Pizza Huts. Some decision making is pushed down to lower-level managers. On the other hand, suppose you worked for a small local law or accounting firm that has only the local office. Then you were working for a centralized company, and the owner probably made all important operating and strategic decisions.

Exhibit 10-3

Types of Responsibility Centers and Accounting Information
Used to Measure Performance

	Cost	Sales	Capital Investment	Other
Cost center	X			
Revenue center		X		
Profit center	X	X		
Investment center	X	X	X	X

some production costs but does not set prices. Any difference between actual and expected costs can best be explained at this level.

The marketing department manager sets the price and projected sales. Therefore, the marketing department may be evaluated as a revenue center. Direct costs of the marketing department and overall sales are the responsibility of the sales manager.

In some companies, plant managers are given the responsibility for manufacturing and marketing their products. These plant managers control both costs and revenues, putting them in control of a profit center. Operating income is an important performance measure for profit-center managers.

Finally, divisions often are cited as examples of investment centers. In addition to having control over cost and pricing decisions, divisional managers have the power to make investment decisions such as plant closings and openings and decisions to keep or drop a product line. As a result, both operating income and some type of ROI are important performance measures for investment center managers. Exhibit 10-3 displays these centers along with the type of information that managers need to manage their operations. As the exhibit shows, investment centers represent the greatest degree of decentralization (followed by profit centers and finally by cost and revenue centers) because their managers have the freedom to make the greatest variety of decisions.

It is important to realize that while the responsibility center manager has responsibility only for the activities of that center, decisions made by that manager can affect other responsibility centers. For example, the sales force at a floor care products firm routinely offers customers price discounts at the end of the month. Sales increase dramatically, which is good for revenue and the sales force. However, the factory is forced to institute overtime shifts to keep up with demand. These overtime shifts increase the costs of the factory, as well as the cost per unit of product.

Organizing divisions as responsibility centers creates the opportunity to control the divisions through the use of responsibility accounting. Revenue-center control is achieved by evaluating the efficiency and the effectiveness of divisional managers on the basis of sales revenue. Cost-center control is based on control of costs and frequently employs variance analysis, as described in Chapters 8 and 9. This chapter will focus on the evaluation of profit centers and investment centers.

Measuring the Performance of Profit Centers by Using Variable and Absorption Income Statements

OBJECTIVE
Explain the difference between absorption and variable costing, and prepare segmented income statements.

Profit centers are evaluated based on income statements. However, the overall income statement for the company would be of little use for this purpose. Instead, it is important to develop a segmented income statement for each profit center. Two common methods of computing income on a segmented basis include one based on variable costing and another based on full or absorption costing. These are costing methods because they refer to the way in which product costs are determined. Recall from Chapter 1 that *product costs* are inventoried; they include direct materials, direct labor, and overhead. As discussed in Chapter 1, product costs are included in inventory (an asset on the balance sheet) until the product is sold, at which time these costs are expensed in the form of cost of goods sold on the income statement. *Period costs*, such as selling and administrative expense, are expensed in the period incurred. The difference between variable and absorption costing hinges on the treatment of one particular aspect of product cost: fixed factory (i.e., manufacturing or plant) overhead.

Variable costing stresses the difference between fixed and variable manufacturing costs. **Variable costing** assigns only variable manufacturing costs to the product; these costs include direct materials, direct labor, and variable overhead. Fixed overhead is treated as a period expense and is excluded from the product cost. The rationale for this treatment is that fixed overhead is a cost of capacity, or staying in business. Once the period is over, any benefits provided by capacity have expired and should not be inventoried. Under variable costing, fixed overhead of a period is seen as expiring that period and is charged in total against the revenues of the period.

Absorption costing assigns *all* manufacturing costs to the product. Direct materials, direct labor, variable overhead, and fixed overhead define the cost of a product. Thus, under absorption costing, fixed overhead is viewed as a product cost, not a period cost. Under this method, fixed overhead is assigned to the product through the use of a predetermined fixed overhead rate and is not expensed until the product is sold. In other words, fixed overhead is an inventoriable cost. Exhibit 10-4 illustrates the classification of costs as product or period costs under absorption and variable costing.

Generally accepted accounting principles (GAAP) require absorption costing for external reporting. The Financial Accounting Standards Board (FASB), the Internal Revenue Service (IRS), and other regulatory bodies do not accept variable costing as a product-costing method for external reporting. Yet, variable costing can supply vital cost information for decision making and control that is not supplied by absorption costing, such as the performance of profit-center managers in many situations. For *internal* application, variable costing is an invaluable managerial tool.

Inventory Valuation

Inventory is valued at product (or manufacturing cost). Under absorption costing, that product cost includes direct materials, direct labor, variable overhead, and fixed overhead. Under variable costing, the product cost includes only direct materials, direct labor, and variable overhead. Cornerstone 10-1 on page 427 shows how to compute inventory cost under both methods.

Exhibit 10-4

Classification of Costs as Product or Period Costs under Absorption and Variable Costing

	Absorption Costing	Variable Costing
Product costs	Direct materials	Direct materials
	Direct labor	Direct labor
	Variable overhead	Variable overhead
	Fixed overhead	
Period costs	Selling expenses	Fixed overhead
	Administrative expenses	Selling expenses
		Administrative expenses

HOW TO Compute Inventory Cost under Absorption and Variable Costing

Information: During the most recent year, Fairchild Company had the following data associated with the product it makes:

Units in beginning inventory	—
Units produced	10,000
Units sold ($300 per unit)	8,000
Variable costs per unit:	
Direct materials	$ 50
Direct labor	100
Variable overhead	50
Fixed costs:	
Fixed overhead per unit produced	25
Fixed selling and administrative	100,000

CORNERSTONE
10-1

Required:
1. How many units are in ending inventory?
2. Using absorption costing, calculate the per-unit product cost. What is the value of ending inventory?
3. Using variable costing, calculate the per-unit product cost. What is the value of ending inventory?

Calculation:
1. Units ending inventory = Units beginning inventory + Units produced − Units sold
$$= 0 + 10,000 - 8,000$$
$$= 2,000$$

2. Absorption costing:

Direct materials	$ 50
Direct labor	100
Variable overhead	50
Fixed overhead	25
Unit product cost	$225

Value of ending inventory = 2,000 × $225 = $450,000

3. Variable costing:

Direct materials	$ 50
Direct labor	100
Variable overhead	50
Unit product cost	$200

Value of ending inventory = 2,000 × $200 = $400,000

Notice that the only difference between the two approaches is the treatment of fixed factory overhead. Thus, the unit product cost under absorption costing is always greater than the unit product cost under variable costing.

Income Statements Using Variable and Absorption Costing

Because unit product costs are the basis for cost of goods sold, the variable- and absorption-costing methods can lead to different operating income figures. The difference arises because of the amount of fixed overhead recognized as an expense under the two methods. Cornerstone 10-2 shows how to develop cost of goods sold and income statements for both variable and absorption costing.

Cornerstone 10-2 demonstrates that absorption-costing income is $50,000 higher than variable-costing income. This difference is due to some of the period's fixed

**CORNERSTONE
10-2**

HOW TO Prepare Income Statements under Absorption and Variable Costing

Information: During the most recent year, Fairchild Company had the following data associated with the product it makes:

Units in beginning inventory	—
Units produced	10,000
Units sold ($300 per unit)	8,000
Variable costs per unit:	
Direct materials	$ 50
Direct labor	100
Variable overhead	50
Fixed costs:	
Fixed overhead per unit produced	25
Fixed selling and administrative	100,000

Required:
1. Calculate the cost of goods sold under absorption costing.
2. Calculate the cost of goods sold under variable costing.
3. Prepare an income statement using absorption costing.
4. Prepare an income statement using variable costing.

Calculation:
1. Cost of goods sold = Absorption unit product cost × Units sold
$$= \$225 \times 8,000 = \$1,800,000$$
2. Cost of goods sold = Variable unit product cost × Units sold
$$= \$200 \times 8,000 = \$1,600,000$$
3.

Fairchild Company
Absorption-Costing Income Statement

Sales ($300 × 8,000)	$2,400,000
Less: Cost of goods sold	1,800,000
Gross margin	$ 600,000
Less: Selling and administrative expenses	100,000
Net income	$ 500,000

4.

Fairchild Company
Variable-Costing Income Statement

Sales ($300 × 8,000)		$2,400,000
Less variable expenses:		
Variable cost of goods sold		1,600,000
Contribution margin		$ 800,000
Less fixed expenses:		
Fixed overhead	$250,000	
Fixed selling and administrative	100,000	350,000
Net income		$ 450,000

overhead flowing into inventory when absorption costing is used. As a result, less fixed overhead cost flowed into the absorption-costing cost of goods sold, thereby increasing net income by $50,000 relative to variable costing net income. In fact, only $200,000 ($25 × 8,000) of fixed overhead was included in cost of goods sold for absorption costing; the remaining $50,000 ($25 × 2,000) was added to inventory. Under variable costing, however, all of the $250,000 of fixed overhead cost for the period was added to expense on the income statement.

Notice that selling and administrative expenses are never included in product cost. They always are expensed on the income statement and never appear on the balance sheet.

Production, Sales, and Income Relationships

The relationship between variable-costing income and absorption-costing income changes as the relationship between production and sales changes. If more units are sold than were produced, variable-costing income is greater than absorption-costing income. This situation is just the opposite of that for the Fairchild example. Selling more than was produced means that beginning inventory units and units produced in the current period are being sold. Under absorption costing, units coming out of inventory have attached to them fixed overhead from a prior period. In addition, units produced and sold have all of the current period's fixed overhead attached. Thus, the amount of fixed overhead expensed by absorption costing is greater than the current period's fixed overhead by the amount of fixed overhead flowing out of inventory. Therefore, when the number of units sold exceeds the number of units produced in the period, variable-costing income is greater than absorption costing income by the amount of fixed overhead flowing out of beginning inventory and into cost of goods sold.

If production and sales are equal, of course, no difference exists between the two reported incomes. Since the units produced are all sold, absorption costing, like variable costing, will recognize the total fixed overhead of the period as an expense. No fixed overhead flows into or out of inventory.

The relationships between production, sales, and the two reported incomes are summarized in Exhibit 10-5. Note that if production is greater than sales, then inventory has increased. If production is less than sales, then inventory must have decreased. If production is equal to sales, then beginning inventory is equal to ending inventory.

The difference between absorption and variable costing centers on the recognition of expense associated with fixed factory overhead. Under absorption costing, fixed factory overhead must be assigned to units produced. This assignment presents two problems that we have not explicitly considered. First, how do we convert factory overhead applied on the basis of direct labor hours or machine hours into factory overhead applied to units produced? Second, what is done when actual factory overhead does not equal applied factory overhead? The solution to these problems is reserved for a more advanced accounting course.

Evaluating Profit-Center Managers

While cost-center managers are evaluated based on costs and revenue-center managers are evaluated based on revenues, the evaluation of profit-center managers often is tied to the profitability of the units that they control. How income changes from one period

Exhibit 10-5

Production, Sales, and Income Relationships

	If	Then
1.	Production > Sales	Absorption income > Variable income
2.	Production < Sales	Absorption income < Variable income
3.	Production = Sales	Absorption income = Variable income

to the next and how actual income compares with planned income are frequently used as signals of managerial ability. To be meaningful signals, however, income should reflect managerial effort. For example, if a manager has worked hard and increased sales while holding costs in check, income should increase over the prior period, signaling success. In general terms, if income performance is expected to reflect managerial performance, then managers have the right to expect the following:

1. As sales revenue increases from one period to the next, all other things being equal, income should increase.
2. As sales revenue decreases from one period to the next, all other things being equal, income should decrease.
3. As sales revenue remains unchanged from one period to the next, all other things being equal, income should remain unchanged.

Variable costing does ensure that the above relationships hold, however, absorption costing may not.

Segmented Income Statements Using Variable Costing

Variable costing is useful in preparing segmented income statements because it gives useful information on variable and fixed expenses. A **segment** is a subunit of a company of sufficient importance to warrant the production of performance reports. Segments can be divisions, departments, product lines, customer classes, and so on. In segmented income statements, however, fixed expenses are broken down into two categories: *direct fixed expenses* and *common fixed expenses*. This additional subdivision highlights controllable versus noncontrollable costs and enhances the manager's ability to evaluate each segment's contribution to overall firm performance.

Direct fixed expenses are fixed expenses that are directly traceable to a segment. These are sometimes referred to as *avoidable fixed expenses* or *traceable fixed expenses* because they vanish if the segment is eliminated. For example, if the segments were sales regions, a direct fixed expense for each region would be the rent for the sales office, salary of the sales manager of each region, and so on. If one region were to be eliminated, then those fixed expenses would disappear. For instance, if **United Airlines** were to vacate the $515 million, 85-acre "Terminal for Tomorrow" at Chicago's O'Hare International Airport, it would avoid the substantial costs it incurs each year to operate and maintain the terminal.

Common fixed expenses are jointly caused by two or more segments. These expenses persist even if one of the segments to which they are common is eliminated. For example, depreciation on the corporate headquarters building, the salary of the CEO, and the cost of printing and distributing the annual report to shareholders are common fixed expenses for the **Walt Disney Company**. If Disney were to sell a theme park or open a new one, then those common expenses would not be affected.

Cornerstone 10-3 on page 431 shows how to prepare a segmented income statement where the segments are product lines. In the example, Audiomatronics produces both MP3 players and DVD players.

Notice that Cornerstone 10-3 shows that both MP3 players and DVD players have large positive contribution margins ($180,000 for MP3 players and $125,500 for DVD players). Both products are providing revenue above variable costs that can be used to help cover the firm's fixed costs. However, some of the firm's fixed costs are caused by the segments themselves. Thus, the real measure of the profit contribution of each segment is what is left over after these direct fixed costs are covered.

The profit contribution each segment makes toward covering a firm's common fixed costs is called the **segment margin**. A segment should at least be able to cover both its own variable costs and direct fixed costs. Ignoring any effect a segment may have on the sales of other segments, the segment margin measures the change in a firm's profits that would occur if the segment were eliminated. A negative segment margin drags down the firm's total profit, making it time to consider dropping the product. In other words, a negative segment margin suggests that the firm would be more profitable as a whole without the segment than with the segment.

HOW TO Prepare a Segmented Income Statement

Information: Audiomatronics Inc. produces MP3 players and DVD players in a single factory. The following information was provided for the coming year.

	MP3 Players	DVD Players
Sales	$400,000	$290,000
Variable cost of goods sold	200,000	150,000
Direct fixed overhead	30,000	20,000

A sales commission of 5 percent of sales is paid for each of the two product lines. Direct fixed selling and administrative expense was estimated to be $10,000 for the MP3 line and $15,000 for the DVD line.

   Common fixed overhead for the factory was estimated to be $100,000; common selling and administrative expense was estimated to be $20,000.

Required: Prepare a segmented income statement for Audiomatronics Inc. for the coming year, using variable costing.

Calculation:

CORNERSTONE 10-3

Audiomatronics Inc.
Segmented Income Statement
For the Coming Year

	MP3 Players	DVD Players	Total
Sales	$400,000	$290,000	$690,000
Variable cost of goods sold	(200,000)	(150,000)	(350,000)
Variable selling expense	(20,000)	(14,500)	(34,500)
Contribution margin	$180,000	$125,500	$305,500
Less direct fixed expenses:			
Direct fixed overhead	(30,000)	(20,000)	(50,000)
Direct selling and administrative	(10,000)	(15,000)	(25,000)
Segment margin	$140,000	$ 90,500	$230,500
Less common fixed expenses:			
Common fixed overhead			(100,000)
Common selling and administrative			(20,000)
Operating income			$110,500

Measuring the Performance of Investment Centers by Using Return on Investment

OBJECTIVE ③
Compute and explain return on investment.

Typically, investment centers are evaluated on the basis of **return on investment (ROI)**, which is the profit earned per dollar of investment. Other measures, such as residual income and economic value added, are discussed in the following section.

Return on Investment

Divisions that are investment centers will have an income statement and a balance sheet. So, could those divisions be ranked on the basis of income? Suppose, for example, that a company has two divisions—Alpha and Beta. Alpha's income is $100,000, and Beta's income is $200,000. Did Beta perform better than Alpha? What if Alpha used an investment of

$500,000 to produce the contribution of $100,000, while Beta used an investment of $2 million to produce the $200,000 contribution? Does your response change? Clearly, relating the reported operating profits to the assets used to produce them is a more meaningful measure of performance.

One way to relate operating profits to assets employed is to compute the ROI. ROI is the most common measure of performance for an investment center. It can be defined as follows:

$$\text{ROI} = \text{Operating income/Average operating assets}$$

Operating income refers to earnings before interest and taxes. **Operating assets** are all assets acquired to generate operating income, including cash, receivables, inventories, land, buildings, and equipment. The figure for average operating assets is computed as follows:

$$\text{Average operating assets} = \text{(Beginning assets + Ending assets)/2}$$

Opinions vary regarding how long-term assets (plant and equipment) should be valued (e.g., gross book value vs. net book value or historical cost vs. current cost). Most firms use historical cost and net book value.[1]

Going back to our example, Alpha's ROI is 0.20 ($100,000/$500,000), while Beta's ROI is only 0.10 ($200,000/$2,000,000). The formula for ROI is quick and easy to use. However, the decomposition of ROI into margin and turnover ratios gives additional information. Cornerstone 10-4 on page 433 shows how to calculate these ratios.

Margin and Turnover

A second way to calculate ROI is to separate the formula (Operating income/Average operating assets) into margin and turnover.

$$\text{ROI} = \underbrace{\frac{\text{Operating income}}{\text{Sales}}}_{\text{Margin}} \times \underbrace{\frac{\text{Sales}}{\text{Average operating assets}}}_{\text{Turnover}}$$

Notice that "Sales" in the above formula can be cancelled out to yield the original ROI formula of Operating income/Average operating assets.

Margin is the ratio of operating income to sales. It tells how many cents of operating income result from each dollar of sales; it expresses the portion of sales that is available for interest, taxes, and profit. Some managers also refer to margin as return on sales. **Turnover** is a different measure; it is found by dividing sales by average operating assets. Turnover tells how many dollars of sales result from every dollar invested in operating assets; it shows how productively assets are being used to generate sales.

Suppose, for example, that Alpha had sales of $400,000. Then, margin would be 0.25 ($100,000/$400,000), and turnover would be 0.80 ($400,000/$500,000). Alpha's ROI would still be 0.20 (0.25 × 0.80).

While both approaches yield the same ROI, the calculation of margin and turnover gives a manager valuable information. To illustrate this additional information, consider the data presented in Exhibit 10-6 on page 434. The Electronics Division improved its ROI from 18 percent in year 1 to 20 percent in year 2. The Medical Supplies Division's

[1]There is no one correct way to calculate ROI. The important thing is to be sure that one method is applied consistently, which allows the company to compare the ROIs among divisions and over time.

HOW TO Calculate Average Operating Assets, Margin, Turnover, and Return on Investment

CORNERSTONE 10-4

Information: Celimar Company's Western Division earned operating income last year as shown in the following income statement:

Sales	$480,000
Cost of goods sold	222,000
Gross margin	$258,000
Selling and administrative expense	210,000
Operating income	$ 48,000

At the beginning of the year, the value of operating assets was $277,000. At the end of the year, the value of operating assets was $323,000.

Required: For the Western Division, calculate:
1. Average operating assets
2. Margin
3. Turnover
4. Return on investment

Calculation:
1. Average operating assets = (Beginning assets + Ending assets)/2
   = ($277,000 + $323,000)/2
   = $300,000
2. Margin = Operating income/Sales = $48,000/$480,000 = 0.10, or 10 percent
3. Turnover = Sales/Average operating assets = $480,000/$300,000 = 1.6
4. ROI = Margin × Turnover = 0.10 × 1.6 = 0.16, or 16 percent

Alternatively,

ROI = Operating income/Average operating assets
   = $48,000/$300,000
   = 0.16, or 16 percent

ROI, however, dropped from 18 to 15 percent. Computing the margin and turnover ratios for each division gives a better picture of what caused the change in rates. As with variance analysis, understanding the causes of managerial accounting measures (i.e., variances, margins, turnover, etc.) helps managers take actions to improve these measures. These ratios also are presented in Exhibit 10-6.

Notice that the margins for both divisions dropped from year 1 to year 2. In fact, the divisions experienced the *same* percentage of decline (16.67 percent). A declining margin could be explained by increasing expenses, by competitive pressures (forcing a decrease in selling prices), or both.

Despite the declining margin, the Electronics Division was able to increase its rate of return. The reason is that the increase in turnover more than compensated for the decline in margin. One explanation for the increased turnover could be a deliberate policy to reduce inventories. (Notice that the average assets employed remained the same for the Electronics Division even though sales increased by $10 million.)

Concept Q&A

Think about some stores in your town, such as a jewelry store, fast-food outlet, and grocery store. How do you suppose their margins and turnover ratios compare with each other? Explain your thinking.

Answer:
Fast-food outlets and grocery stores probably have low margins and high turnover. These financial characteristics exist because they deal in perishables and must have continual turnover or the food will go bad. A jewelry store, on the other hand, has high margin and relatively low turnover. These financial characteristics exist because the goods are not perishable and there is relatively less competition in this market. (The existence of competition, of course, changes as more jewelry stores enter a market and as consumers become more confident about buying jewelry online.)

Exhibit 10-6

Comparison of Divisional Performance

	Comparison of ROI	
	Electronics Division	Medical Supplies Division
Year 1:		
Sales	$30,000,000	$117,000,000
Operating income	1,800,000	3,510,000
Average operating assets	10,000,000	19,510,000
ROI[a]	18%	18%
Year 2:		
Sales	$40,000,000	$117,000,000
Operating income	2,000,000	2,925,000
Average operating assets	10,000,000	19,500,000
ROI[a]	20%	15%

	Margin and Turnover Comparisons			
	Electronics Division		Medical Supplies Division	
	Year 1	Year 2	Year 1	Year 2
Margin[b]	6.0%	5.0%	3.0%	2.5%
Turnover[c]	× 3.0	× 4.0	× 6.0	× 6.0
ROI	18.0%	20.0%	18.0%	15.0%

[a]Operating income divided by average operating assets.
[b]Operating income divided by sales.
[c]Sales divided by average operating assets.

The experience of the Medical Supplies Division was less favorable. Because its turnover rate remained unchanged, its ROI dropped. This division, unlike the Electronics Division, could not overcome the decline in margin.

Advantages of Return on Investment

At least three positive results stem from the use of ROI:

1. It encourages managers to focus on the relationship among sales, expenses, and investment, as should be the case for a manager of an investment center.
2. It encourages managers to focus on cost efficiency.
3. It encourages managers to focus on operating asset efficiency.

These advantages are illustrated by the following three scenarios.

Focus on Return on Investment Relationships   Della Barnes, manager of the

Plastics Division, is mulling over a suggestion from her marketing vice president to increase the advertising budget by $100,000. The marketing vice president is confident that this increase will boost sales by $200,000. Della realizes that the increased sales will also raise expenses. She finds that the increased variable cost will be $80,000. The division also will need to purchase additional machinery to handle the increased production. The equipment will cost $50,000 and will add $10,000 of depreciation expense. As a result, the proposal will add $10,000 ($200,000 − $80,000 − $10,000 − $100,000) to operating income. Currently, the division has sales of $2 million, total expenses of $1,850,000, and operating income of $150,000. Operating assets equal $1 million.

	Without Increased Advertising	With Increased Advertising
Sales	$2,000,000	$2,200,000
Less: Expenses	1,850,000	2,040,000
Operating income	$ 150,000	$ 160,000
Average operating assets	$1,000,000	$1,050,000

ROI:

$150,000/$1,000,000 = 0.15, or 15 percent
$160,000/$1,050,000 = 0.1524, or 15.24 percent

The ROI without the additional advertising is 15 percent; the ROI with the additional advertising and $50,000 investment in assets is 15.24 percent. Since ROI is increased by the proposal, Della decides to authorize the increased advertising. In effect, the current ROI, without the proposal, is the *hurdle rate*. This term is frequently used to indicate the minimum ROI necessary to accept an investment.

Focus on Cost Efficiency

Kyle Chugg, manager of Turner's Battery Division, groaned as he reviewed the projections for the last half of the current fiscal year. The recession was hurting his division's performance. Adding the projected operating income of $200,000 to the actual operating income of the first half produced expected annual earnings of $425,000. Kyle then divided the expected operating income by the division's average operating assets to obtain an expected ROI of 12.15 percent. "This is awful," muttered Kyle. "Last year our ROI was 16 percent. And I'm looking at a couple more bad years before business returns to normal. Something has to be done to improve our performance."

Kyle directed all operating managers to identify and eliminate nonvalue-added activities. As a result, lower-level managers found ways to reduce costs by $150,000 for the remaining half of the year. This reduction increased the annual operating income from $425,000 to $575,000, increasing ROI from 12.15 percent to 16.43 percent as a result. Interestingly, Kyle found that some of the reductions could be maintained after business returned to normal.

Focus on Operating Asset Efficiency

The Electronic Storage Division prospered during its early years. In the beginning, the division developed portable external disk drives for storing data; sales and ROI were extraordinarily high. However, during the past several years, competitors had developed competing technology, and the division's ROI had plunged from 30 to 15 percent. Cost cutting had helped initially, but all of the fat had been removed, making further improvements from cost reductions impossible. Moreover, any increase in sales was unlikely—competition was too stiff. The divisional manager searched for some way to increase the ROI by at least 3 to 5 percent. Only by raising the ROI so that it compared favorably with that of the other divisions could the division expect to receive additional capital for research and development (R&D).

The divisional manager initiated an intensive program to reduce operating assets. Most of the gains were made in the area of inventory reductions; however, one plant was closed because of a long-term reduction in market share. By installing a just-in-time purchasing and manufacturing system, the division was able to reduce its asset base without threatening its remaining market share. Finally, the reduction in operating assets meant that operating costs could be decreased still further. The end result was a 50-percent increase in the division's ROI, from 15 percent to more than 22 percent.

Disadvantages of the Return on Investment Measure

Overemphasis on ROI can produce myopic behavior. Two negative aspects associated with ROI frequently are mentioned:

1. It can produce a narrow focus on divisional profitability at the expense of profitability for the overall firm.
2. It encourages managers to focus on the short run at the expense of the long run.

These disadvantages are illustrated by the following two scenarios:

Narrow Focus on Divisional Profitability
A Cleaning Products Division has the opportunity to invest in two projects for the coming year. The outlay required for each investment, the dollar returns, and the ROI are as follows:

	Project I	Project II
Investment	$10,000,000	$4,000,000
Operating income	1,300,000	640,000
ROI	13%	16%

The division currently earns ROI of 15 percent, with operating assets of $50 million and operating income on current investments of $7.5 million. The division has approval to request up to $15 million in new investment capital. Corporate headquarters requires that all investments earn at least 10 percent (this rate represents the corporation's cost of acquiring the capital). Any capital not used by a division is invested by headquarters, and it earns exactly 10 percent.

The divisional manager has four alternatives: (1) invest in Project I, (2) invest in Project II, (3) invest in both Projects I and II, or (4) invest in neither project. The divisional ROI was computed for each alternative.

	Alternatives			
	Select Project I	Select Project II	Select Both Projects	Select Neither Project
Operating income	$8,800,000	$8,140,000	$9,440,000	$7,500,000
Operating assets	$60,000,000	$54,000,000	$64,000,000	$50,000,000
ROI	14.67%	15.07%	14.75%	15.00%

The divisional manager chose to invest only in Project II, since it would boost ROI from 15.00 percent to 15.07 percent.

While the manager's choice maximized divisional ROI, it did not maximize the profit the company could have earned. If Project I had been selected, the company would have earned $1.3 million profit. By not selecting Project I, the $10 million in capital is invested at 10 percent, earning only $1 million (0.10 × $10,000,000). The single-minded focus on divisional ROI, then, cost the company $300,000 in profits ($1,300,000 − $1,000,000).

Encourages Short-Run Optimization
Ruth Lunsford, manager of a Small Tools Division, was displeased with her division's performance during the first three quarters. Given the expected income for the fourth quarter, the ROI for the year would be 13 percent, at least two percentage points below where she had hoped to be. Such an ROI might not be strong enough to justify the early promotion she wanted. With only three months left, drastic action was needed. Increasing sales for the last quarter was unlikely. Most sales were booked at least two to three months in advance.

Emphasizing extra sales activity would benefit next year's performance. What was needed were some ways to improve this year's performance.

After careful thought, Ruth decided to take the following actions:

1. Lay off five of the highest paid salespeople.
2. Cut the advertising budget for the fourth quarter by 50 percent.
3. Delay all promotions within the division for three months.
4. Reduce the preventive maintenance budget by 75 percent.
5. Use cheaper raw materials for fourth-quarter production.

In the aggregate, these steps would reduce expenses, increase income, and raise the ROI to about 15.2 percent for the current year.

While Ruth's actions increase the profits and ROI in the short run, they have some long-run negative consequences. Laying off the highest paid (and possibly the best) salespeople may harm the division's future sales-generating capabilities. Future sales could also be hurt by cutting back on advertising and using cheaper raw materials. Delaying promotions could hurt employee morale, which could, in turn, lower productivity and future sales. Finally, reducing preventive maintenance will likely increase downtime and decrease the life of the productive equipment.

Ethics Ethical considerations also come into play when managers attempt to "game" ROI. Ruth's five top-earning salespeople probably were her best salespeople. Letting them go meant that sales would probably decrease, an outcome not in the best interests of the firm. Thus, her action is directly contrary to her obligation to take actions in the best interests of the company. The layoffs may also violate the implicit contract a company has with workers that outstanding work will lead to continued employment.◆

Measuring the Performance of Investment Centers by Using Residual Income and Economic Value Added

OBJECTIVE ④
Compute and explain residual income and economic value added.

To compensate for the tendency of ROI to discourage investments that are profitable for the company but that lower a division's ROI, some companies have adopted alternative performance measures such as residual income. Economic value added is an alternate way to calculate residual income that is being used in a number of companies, such as Herman Miller.

Residual Income

Residual income is the difference between operating income and the minimum dollar return required on a company's operating assets:

> **Residual income = Operating income**
> **− (Minimum rate of return × Average operating assets)**

Cornerstone 10-5 shows how to calculate residual income.

The minimum rate of return is set by the company and is the same as the hurdle rate mentioned in the section on ROI. If residual income is greater than zero, then the division is earning more than the minimum required rate of return (or hurdle rate). If residual income is less than zero, then the division is earning less than the minimum required rate of return. Finally, if residual income equals zero, then the division is earning precisely the minimum required rate of return.

Advantage of Residual Income   Recall that the manager of the Cleaning Products Division rejected Project I because it would have reduced divisional ROI; however, that decision cost the company $300,000 in profits. The use of residual income as

**CORNERSTONE
10-5**

HOW TO Calculate Residual Income

Information: Celimar Company's Western Division earned operating income last year as shown in the following income statement:

Sales	$480,000
Cost of goods sold	222,000
Gross margin	$258,000
Selling and administrative expense	210,000
Operating income	$ 48,000

At the beginning of the year, the value of operating assets was $277,000. At the end of the year, the value of operating assets was $323,000. Celimar Company requires a minimum rate of return of 12 percent.

Required: For the Western Division, calculate:
1. Average operating assets
2. Residual income

Calculation:
1. Average operating assets = (Beginning assets + Ending assets)/2
$$= (\$277{,}000 + \$323{,}000)/2$$
$$= \$300{,}000$$
2. Residual income = Operating income − (Minimum rate of return × Average operating assets)
$$= \$48{,}000 - (0.12 \times \$300{,}000)$$
$$= \$48{,}000 - \$36{,}000$$
$$= \$12{,}000$$

the performance measure would have prevented this loss. The residual income for each project is computed as follows:

Project I
Residual income = Operating income − (Minimum rate of return
× Average operating assets)
$$= \$1{,}300{,}000 - (0.10 \times \$10{,}000{,}000)$$
$$= \$1{,}300{,}000 - \$1{,}000{,}000$$
$$= \$300{,}000$$

Project II
Residual income = $640,000 − (0.10 × $4,000,000)
$$= \$640{,}000 - \$400{,}000$$
$$= \$240{,}000$$

Notice that both projects have positive residual income. For comparative purposes, the divisional residual income for each of the four alternatives identified follows:

	Alternatives			
	Select Only Project I	Select Only Project II	Select Both Projects	Select Neither Project
Operating assets	$60,000,000	$54,000,000	$64,000,000	$50,000,000
Operating income	$ 8,800,000	$ 8,140,000	$ 9,440,000	$ 7,500,000
Minimum return[*]	6,000,000	5,400,000	6,400,000	5,000,000
Residual income	$ 2,800,000	$ 2,740,000	$ 3,040,000	$ 2,500,000

[*]0.10 × Operating assets.

As shown on page 438, selecting both projects produces the greatest increase in residual income. The use of residual income encourages managers to accept any project that earns a return that is above the minimum rate.

Disadvantages of Residual Income   Residual income, like ROI, can encourage a short-run orientation. If Ruth Lunsford were being evaluated on the basis of residual income, she could have taken the same actions.

Another problem with residual income is that, unlike ROI, it is an absolute measure of profitability. Thus, direct comparison of the performance of two different investment centers becomes difficult, as the level of investment may differ. For example, consider the residual income computations for Division A and Division B, where the minimum required rate of return is 8 percent.

	Division A	Division B
Average operating assets	$15,000,000	$2,500,000
Operating income	$ 1,500,000	$ 300,000
Minimum return[a]	(1,200,000)	(200,000)
Residual income	$ 300,000	$ 100,000
Residual return[b]	2%	4%

[a]0.08 × Operating assets.
[b]Residual income divided by operating assets.

It is tempting to claim that Division A is outperforming Division B since its residual income is three times higher. Notice, however, that Division A is considerably larger than Division B and has six times as many assets. One possible way to correct this disadvantage is to compute both ROI and residual income and to use both measures for performance evaluation. ROI could then be used for interdivisional comparisons.

Economic Value Added

A specific way of calculating residual income is *economic value added*. **Economic value added (EVA)**[2] is net income (operating income minus taxes) minus the total annual cost of capital. Basically, EVA is residual income with the minimum rate of return equal to the actual cost of capital for the firm (as opposed to some minimum rate of return desired by the company for other reasons). It is said that if EVA is positive, then the company has increased its wealth during the period; if EVA is negative, then the company has decreased its wealth during the period. Consider the old saying, "It takes money to make money." EVA helps the company to determine whether the money it makes is more than the money it takes to make it. Over the long term, only those companies creating capital, or wealth, can survive.

As a form of residual income, EVA is a dollar figure, not a percentage rate of return. However, it does bear a resemblance to rates of return such as ROI because it links net income (return) to capital employed. The key feature of EVA is its emphasis on *after-tax* operating profit and the *actual* cost of capital. Residual income, on the other hand, uses a minimum expected rate of return. Investors like EVA because it relates profit to the amount of resources needed to achieve it. A number of companies have been evaluated on the basis of EVA. In 2003, for example, economic value added for **General Electric** was $5,983 million, for **Wal-Mart** Stores it was $2,928 million, and for **Merck & Co.** it was $3,872 million.[3] Among large companies showing negative EVA were **IBM** at ($8,032) million, **Verizon Communications** at ($5,612) million, and Disney

---

[2]EVA was developed by Stern Stewart & Company in the 1990s. More information can be found on the firm's website, http://www.sternstewart.com/evaabout/whatis.php.
[3]Stephen Taub, "MVPs of MVA," *CFO Magazine* (July 1, 2003). Retrieved December 13, 2006, from http://www.cfo.com/article/1,5309,9854%7C22%7CA%7C14%7C,00.html.

Concept Q&A

What are the differences and similarities between the basic residual income calculation and EVA?

Residual income can use either before-tax income (operating income) or after-tax income. In addition, residual income uses a minimum required rate of return set by upper management. EVA, on the other hand, uses after-tax income and requires the company to compute its actual cost of capital.

Answer:

Company at ($2,072) million. Smaller companies also differed in terms of their economic value added. **Pixar**'s was positive at $31 million while **JetBlue Airways Corp.** came in at $15 million.

Calculating Economic Value Added   EVA is after-tax operating income minus the dollar cost of capital employed. The dollar cost of capital employed is the actual percentage cost of capital[4] multiplied by the total capital employed. The equation for EVA is expressed as follows:

EVA = After-tax operating income
− (Actual percentage cost of capital
× Total capital employed)

Cornerstone 10-6 shows how to calculate EVA.

Behavioral Aspects of Economic Value Added   A number of companies have discovered that EVA helps to encourage the right kind of behavior from their divisions in a way that emphasis on operating income alone cannot. The underlying reason is EVA's reliance on the true cost of capital. In many companies, the responsibility for investment decisions rests with corporate management. As a result, the cost of capital is considered a corporate expense. If a division builds inventories and investment, the cost of financing that investment is passed along to the overall income statement and does not show up as a reduction from the division's operating income. The result is to make investment seem free to the divisions, and of course, they want more.

**CORNERSTONE
10-6**

HOW TO Calculate Economic Value Added

Information: Celimar Company's Western Division earned net income last year as shown in the following income statement:

Sales	$480,000
Cost of goods sold	222,000
Gross margin	$258,000
Selling and administrative expense	210,000
Operating income	$ 48,000
Less: Income taxes (@ 30%)	14,400
Net income	$ 33,600

Total capital employed equaled $300,000. Celimar Company's actual cost of capital is 10 percent.

Required: Calculate EVA for the Western Division.

Calculation:
EVA = After-tax operating income − (Actual percentage cost of capital
 × Total capital employed)
 = $33,600 − (0.10 × $300,000)
 = $33,600 − $30,000
 = $3,600

---

[4]The computation of a company's actual cost of capital is reserved for advanced accounting courses.

The Balanced Scorecard—Basic Concepts

OBJECTIVE ⑤
Explain the uses of the Balanced Scorecard and the role of transfer pricing in a decentralized firm.

Segment income, ROI, residual income, and EVA are important measures of managerial performance. As such, the temptation exists for managers to focus only on dollar figures. This focus may not tell the whole story for the company. In addition, lower-level managers and employees may feel helpless to affect income or investment because such financial measures appear so far removed from their everyday work activities. As a result, many companies develop and manage nonfinancial operating measures as well as financial measures. For example, top management could look at such factors as market share, customer complaints, personnel turnover ratios, and personnel development. By letting lower-level managers know that attention to long-run factors also is vital, the tendency to overemphasize financial measures is reduced.

Managers in an advanced manufacturing environment are especially likely to use multiple measures of performance and to include nonfinancial as well as financial measures. For example, in 2002, Robert Lutz, head of product development at **General Motors**, was evaluated on the basis of 12 criteria. These criteria included how well he used existing parts in new vehicles and how many engineering hours he cut from the development process.[5]

The **Balanced Scorecard** is a strategic management system that defines a strategic-based responsibility accounting system. The Balanced Scorecard *translates* an organization's mission and strategy into operational objectives and performance measures for four different perspectives: the financial perspective, the customer perspective, the internal business process perspective, and the learning and growth (infrastructure) perspective. The **financial perspective** describes the economic consequences of actions taken in the other three perspectives. The **customer perspective** defines the customer and market segments in which the business unit will compete. The **internal business process perspective** describes the internal processes needed to provide value for customers and owners. Finally, the **learning and growth (infrastructure) perspective** defines the capabilities that an organization needs to create long-term growth and improvement. This last perspective is concerned with three major *enabling factors*: employee capabilities, information systems capabilities, and employee attitudes (motivation, empowerment, and alignment). Exhibit 10-7 shows a Balanced Scorecard for a typical hotel based on questionnaire data provided by a research survey of three- and four-star hotels.[6] The scorecard includes the four basic scorecard categories and objectives with key measures for each category.

The Role of Performance Measures The Balanced Scorecard is not simply a collection of critical performance measures. The performance measures are derived from a company's vision, strategy, and objectives. These measures must be *balanced* between outcome measures (i.e., lagged indicators of past financial performance) and performance driver measures (i.e., lead indicators of future financial performance), between objective and subjective measures, between external and internal measures, and between financial and nonfinancial measures. The performance measures must also be carefully *linked* to the organization's strategy. Doing so creates significant advantages for an organization. For example, each quarter, **Analog Devices'** senior managers gather to discuss Balanced Scorecard results for the various divisions. On one occasion, managers noted problems with their new-product ratios—used to measure the effectiveness of R&D spending. They quickly discovered that one division lagged in developing new products. The division's manager focused more on R&D by investing more money and exploring new market segments, new product sales, and marketing strategies. Analog Devices' corporate vice president for marketing, quality, and planning noted that they wouldn't have been able to catch the problem so early if they just looked at financials.[7] Other companies, such as **Hilton Hotels Corporation**, **Verizon Communications**,

---

[5]David Welch, and Kathleen Kerwin, "Rick Wagoner's Game Plan," *Business Week* (February 10, 2003): 52-60.
[6]Nigel Evans, "Assessing the Balanced Scorecard as a Management Tool for Hotels, *International Journal of Contemporary Hospitality Management*, Vol. 17, Issue 4/5 (2005): 376-390.
[7]Joel Kurtzman, "Is Your Company Off Course: Now You Can Find Out Why," *Fortune* (February 17, 1997). Retrieved December 13, 2006, from http://money.cnn.com/magazines/fortune/fortune_archive/1997/02/17/222180/index.htm.

Exhibit 10-7

Balanced Scorecard for Ashley Hotel*

Objective	Measure
Financial Perspective	
Operating Revenues	• Total daily operating revenue • Revenue per available room
Operating Costs	• Operating expenses relative to budget • Cost per occupant
Customer Perspective	
Customer Satisfaction	• Customer satisfaction ratings • Number of monthly complaints
Customer Loyalty	• Number of new reward club members • Percent of returning guests
Internal Perspective	
Employee Turnover	• Employee turnover rate • Number of employee complaints
Response to Customer Complaint	• Percentage of complaints receiving response • Average response time
Learning and Growth	
New Market Identification	• Growth in reward club membership for new demographic segments
Employee Training and Advancement	• Percentage of employees participating in training courses • Survey scores pre- and post-training sessions

* Measures are based on survey data reported from actual hotels—Evans. N. Assessing the Balanced Scorecard as a Management Tool for Hotels, *International Journal of Contemporary Hospitality Management*. Vol. 17 (Issue 4/5): 376–390.

Duke University Children's Hospital, **City of Charlotte**, **NatWest Bancorp**, and **AT&T Canada LDS**, have had similar success. The rapid and widespread adoption of this strategic management system is a strong testimonial of its worth. For example, companies such as General Electric, Verizon, and **Microsoft** have adapted their initial balanced scorecards into risk dashboards that contain key financial and nonfinancial measures pertaining to the important risks that threaten organizational success.[8]

Transfer Pricing

One final issue that affects the performance measurement and evaluation of divisions within a decentralized organization is that of transfer pricing. In many decentralized organizations, the output of one division is used as the input of another. For example, assume that one division of Sony manufactures batteries for its VAIO computers, which in turn sells the

---

[8]Spencer Ante, "Giving the Boss the Big Picture," *Business Week* (February 13, 2006).

batteries to another Sony division that uses them to complete the computer manufacturing process. This internal transfer between two divisions within Sony raises an accounting issue. How is the transferred good valued? When divisions are treated as responsibility centers, they are evaluated on the basis of their contribution to costs, revenues, operating income, ROI, and residual income or EVA depending on the particular center type. As a result, the value of the transferred good is revenue to the selling division and cost to the buying division. This value, or internal price, is called the *transfer price*. In other words, a **transfer price** is the price charged for a component by the selling division to the buying division of the same company. Transfer pricing is a complex issue. The impact of transfer prices on divisions and the company as a whole, as well as methods of setting transfer prices, will be explored briefly in the following section.

Impact of Transfer Pricing on Divisions and the Firm as a Whole

When one division of a company sells to another division, both divisions as well as the company as a whole are affected. The price charged for the transferred good affects the costs of the buying division and the revenues of the selling division. Thus, the profits of both divisions, as well as the evaluation and compensation of their managers, are affected by the transfer price. Since profit-based performance measures of the two divisions are affected (e.g., ROI and residual income), transfer pricing often can be a very emotionally charged issue. Exhibit 10-8 illustrates the effect of the transfer price on two divisions of ABC Inc. Division A produces a component and sells it to another division of the same company, Division C. The $30 transfer price is revenue to Division A; clearly, Division A wants the price to be as high as possible. Conversely, the $30 transfer price is cost to Division C, just like the cost of any raw material. Division C prefers as low a transfer price as possible.

The actual transfer price nets out for the company as a whole in that total *pretax* income for the company is the same regardless of the transfer price. However, transfer pricing can affect the level of *after-tax* profits earned by the multinational company that operates in multiple countries with different corporate tax rates and other legal requirements set by the countries in which the various divisions generate income. For example, if the selling division operates in a low-tax country and the buying division operates in a high-tax country, the transfer price may be set quite high. Then, the high transfer price (a revenue for A) would increase profit in the division in the low-tax country, and the high transfer price (a cost for B) would decrease profit in the division in the high-tax country. This transfer pricing strategy has the result of reducing overall corporate income taxes. The international transfer pricing situation is examined in detail in more advanced courses.

Transfer Pricing Policies

Recall that a decentralized company allows much more authority for decision making at lower management levels. It would be counterproductive for the decentralized company to then decide on the actual transfer prices between two divisions. As a result, top management usually sets the transfer pricing policy.

Exhibit 10-8

Impact of Transfer Price on Transferring Divisions and the Company, ABC Inc., as a Whole

Division A	Division C
Produces component and transfers it to C for transfer price of $30 per unit	Purchases component from A at transfer price of $30 per unit and uses it in production of final product
Transfer price = $30 per unit	Transfer price = $30 per unit
Revenue to A	Cost to C
Increases income	Decreases income
Increases ROI	Decreases ROI

Several transfer pricing policies are used in practice. These transfer pricing policies include market price, cost-based transfer prices, and negotiated transfer prices. If there is a competitive outside market for the transferred product, then the best transfer price is the market price. In such a case, divisional managers' actions will simultaneously optimize divisional profits and firmwide profits. Furthermore, no division can benefit at the expense of another. In this setting, top management will not be tempted to intervene.

Suppose that the Furniture Division of a corporation produces hide-a-beds. The Mattress Division of that same corporation produces mattresses, including a mattress model that fits into the hide-a-bed. If mattresses are transferred from the Mattress division to the Furniture division, a transfer pricing opportunity exists. Suppose that the mattresses can be sold to outside buyers at $50 each; this $50 is the market price and likely would serve as the transfer price.

Frequently, there is no good outside market price. The lack of a market price might occur because the transferred product uses patented designs owned by the parent company. Then, a company might use a cost-based transfer pricing approach. For example, suppose that the mattress company uses a high-density foam padding in the hide-a-bed mattress and that outside companies do not produce this type of mattress in the appropriate size. If the company has set a cost-based transfer pricing policy, then the Mattress Division will charge some measure of cost as the transfer price, such as the $28 mattress production cost.

Finally, top management may allow the selling and buying division managers to negotiate a transfer price. This approach is particularly useful in cases with market imperfections, such as the ability of an in-house division to avoid selling and distribution costs that external market participants would have to incur. Using a negotiated transfer price then allows the two divisions to share any cost savings resulting from avoided costs.

Using the example of the Mattress and Furniture divisions, suppose that the hide-a-bed mattress typically sells for $50 and has product cost of $28. Normally, a sales commission of $5 is paid to the salesperson, but that cost will not be incurred for any internal transfers. Now, a bargaining range exists. That range goes from the minimum transfer price to the maximum. The two divisions will negotiate the transfer price deciding how much of the cost savings will go to each division.

Here's The Real Kicker

Kicker's top management is closely involved in all aspects of the company, from design and development through production, sales, delivery, and after-market activities. Profit performance, as measured by periodic income statements, is an important measure. In addition, Kicker keeps track of a number of other measures of performance.

For example, financial information is very important. Financial statements are presented to the president and vice presidents every month. These are reviewed carefully for trends and are compared with the budgeted amounts. Worrisome increases in expenses or decreases in revenue are analyzed to see what the underlying factors might be. This leads to the next perspective.

Customer satisfaction is also continually measured. Kicker has two major types of customers—dealers who sell Kicker products and end users who have Kicker speakers installed in the car. Each customer type has specific needs. For example, dealers have the exclusive right to sell Kicker products. Theoretically, you must buy from a dealer to get a new set of speakers, amplifier, and so on. Kicker offers a one-year warranty on speakers sold through a dealer.

However, end users want as low a price as possible. Speakers are available on the Internet, which are called "gray market" speakers (that is, the seller is not authorized to sell them). In the past, no warranty was available on nondealer-sold speakers. Problems arose when customers purchased obviously new products through the Internet, something went wrong, and they were not covered under warranty. It was very difficult to explain the no-warranty policy. Finally, Kicker decided to offer a shorter warranty for new products sold by unauthorized sellers. The objective of keeping the customer base happy and increasing satisfaction was achieved.

Kicker focuses on strategic objectives for the long term. For example, engineers in R&D take continuing education to stay current in their fields. When Kicker approached producing and selling original equipment manufacture (OEM) speakers to a major automobile maker, a number of employees had to learn International Organization for Standardization (ISO) quality concepts quickly. They took classes, met with consultants, and traveled to the site of other ISO-qualified firms to learn how to meet quality standards.

Summary of Learning Objectives

1. Explain how and why firms choose to decentralize.
    *   In a decentralized organization, lower-level managers make and implement decisions. In a centralized organization, lower-level managers are responsible only for implementing decisions.
    *   Reasons why companies decentralize:
        *   Local managers can make better decisions using local information.
        *   Local managers can provide a more timely response.
        *   It is impossible for any one central manager to be fully knowledgeable about all products and markets.
    *   Decentralization can train and motivate local managers and free top management from day-to-day operating conditions so that they can spend time on more long-range activities, such as strategic planning.
    *   Four types of responsibility centers are:
        *   Cost centers—manager is responsible for costs.
        *   Revenue centers—manager is responsible for price and quantity sold.
        *   Profit centers—manager is responsible for costs and revenues.
        *   Investment centers—manager is responsible for costs, revenues, and investment.
2. Explain the difference between absorption and variable costing, and prepare segmented income statements.
    *   Absorption costing treats fixed factory overhead as a product cost. Unit product cost consists of direct materials, direct labor, variable factory overhead, and fixed factory overhead.
    *   Absorption-costing income statement groups expenses according to function:
        *   Production cost—cost of goods sold, including variable and fixed product cost.
        *   Selling expense—variable and fixed cost of selling and distributing product.
        *   Administrative expense—variable and fixed cost of administration.
    *   Variable costing treats fixed factory overhead as a period expense. Unit product cost consists of direct materials, direct labor, and variable factory overhead.
    *   Variable-costing income statement groups expenses according to cost behavior:
        *   Variable expenses of manufacturing, selling, and administration.
        *   Fixed expenses of manufacturing (fixed factory overhead), selling, and administration.
    *   Impact of units produced and units sold on absorption-costing income and variable-costing income:
        *   If units produced > units sold, then absorption-costing income > variable-costing income.
        *   If units produced < units sold, then absorption-costing income < variable-costing income.
        *   If units produced = units sold, then absorption-costing income = variable-costing income.
3. Compute and explain return on investment.
    *   ROI is the ratio of operating income to average operating assets.
    *   Margin is operating income divided by sales *or* margin times turnover.
    *   Turnover is sales divided by average operating assets.
    *   Advantage: ROI encourages managers to focus on improving sales, controlling costs, and using assets efficiently.
    *   Disadvantage: ROI can encourage managers to sacrifice long-run benefits for short-run benefits.
4. Compute and explain residual income and economic value added.
    *   Residual income is operating income minus a minimum percentage cost of capital times capital employed.
        *   If residual income > 0, then the division is earning more than the minimum cost of capital.

- If residual income < 0, then the division is earning less than the minimum cost of capital.
- If residual income = 0, then the division is earning just the minimum cost of capital.
- Economic value added is *after-tax* operating profit minus the *actual* total annual cost of capital.
  - If EVA > 0, then the company is creating wealth.
  - If EVA < 0, then the company is destroying capital.
5. Explain the uses of the Balanced Scorecard and the role of transfer pricing in a decentralized firm.
   - Balanced Scorecard is a strategic management system.
   - Objectives and measures are developed for four perspectives:
     - Financial perspective
     - Customer perspective
     - Process perspective
     - Learning and growth perspective
   - Transfer price is charged by the selling division of a company to a buying division of the same company.
     - Increases revenue to the selling division.
     - Increases cost to the buying division.
   - Common transfer pricing policies are:
     - Cost based (e.g., total product cost)
     - Market based (priced charged in the outside market)
     - Negotiated between the buying and selling divisions' managers.

Summary of Important Equations

1. Absorption-costing product cost = Direct materials + Direct labor + Variable overhead + Fixed overhead
2. Variable-costing product cost = Direct materials + Direct labor + Variable overhead
3. ROI = Operating income/Average operating assets
   ROI = Margin × Turnover
4. Average operating assets = (Beginning operating assets + Ending operating assets)/2
5. Margin = Operating income/Sales
6. Turnover = Sales/Average operating assets
7. Residual income = Operating income − (Minimum rate of return × Average operating assets)
8. EVA = After-tax income − (Actual percentage cost of capital × Total capital employed)

CORNERSTONES FOR CHAPTER 10

Cornerstone 10-1 How to compute inventory cost under absorption and variable costing, page 427

Cornerstone 10-2 How to prepare income statements under absorption and variable costing, page 428

Cornerstone 10-3 How to prepare a segmented income statement, page 431

Cornerstone 10-4 How to calculate average operating assets, margin, turnover, and return on investment, page 433

Cornerstone 10-5 How to calculate residual income, page 438

Cornerstone 10-6 How to calculate economic value added, page 440

Key Terms

Absorption costing, 426
Balanced Scorecard, 441
Common fixed expenses, 430
Cost center, 424
Customer perspective, 441
Decentralization, 422
Direct fixed expenses, 430
Economic value added (EVA), 439
Financial perspective, 441
Internal business process perspective, 441
Investment center, 424
Learning and growth (infrastructure)
 perspective, 441

Margin, 432
Operating assets, 432
Operating income, 432
Profit center, 424
Residual income, 437
Responsibility center, 424
Return on investment (ROI), 431
Revenue center, 424
Segment, 430
Segment margin, 430
Transfer price, 443
Turnover, 432
Variable costing, 426

Review Problems

I. Absorption and Variable Costing; Segmented Income Statements

Fine Leathers Company produces a ladies' wallet and a men's wallet. Selected data for the past year follow:

	Ladies' Wallet	Men's Wallet
Production (units)	100,000	200,000
Sales (units)	90,000	210,000
Selling price	$ 5.50	$ 4.50
Direct labor hours	50,000	80,000
Manufacturing costs:		
Direct materials	$ 75,000	$100,000
Direct labor	250,000	400,000
Variable overhead	20,000	24,000

	Ladies' Wallet	Men's Wallet
Fixed overhead:		
Direct	50,000	40,000
Common[a]	20,000	20,000
Nonmanufacturing costs:		
Variable selling	30,000	60,000
Direct fixed selling	35,000	40,000
Common fixed selling[b]	25,000	25,000

[a]Common overhead totals $40,000 and is divided equally between the two products.
[b]Common fixed selling costs total $50,000 and are divided equally between the two products.

Budgeted fixed overhead for the year, $130,000, equaled the actual fixed overhead. Fixed overhead is assigned to products using a plantwide rate based on expected direct labor hours, which were 130,000. The company had 10,000 men's wallets in inventory at the beginning of the year. These wallets had the same unit cost as the men's wallets produced during the year.

Required:

1. Compute the unit cost for the ladies' and men's wallets using the variable-costing method. Compute the unit cost using absorption costing.
2. Prepare an income statement using absorption costing.
3. Prepare an income statement using variable costing.
4. Reconcile the difference between the two income statements.
5. Prepare a segmented income statement using products as segments.

Solution:

1. The unit cost for the ladies' wallet is as follows:

Direct materials ($75,000/100,000)	$0.75
Direct labor ($250,000/100,000)	2.50
Variable overhead ($20,000/100,000)	0.20
Variable cost per unit	$3.45
Fixed overhead [(50,000 × $1.00)/100,000]	0.50
Absorption cost per unit	$3.95

The unit cost for the men's wallet is as follows:

Direct materials ($100,000/200,000)	$0.50
Direct labor ($400,000/200,000)	2.00
Variable overhead ($24,000/200,000)	0.12
Variable cost per unit	$2.62
Fixed overhead [(80,000 × $1.00)/200,000]	0.40
Absorption cost per unit	$3.02

Notice that the only difference between the two unit costs is the assignment of the fixed overhead cost. Notice also that the fixed overhead unit cost is assigned using the predetermined fixed overhead rate ($130,000/130,000 hours = $1 per hour). For example, the ladies' wallets used 50,000 direct labor hours and so receive $1 × 50,000, or $50,000, of fixed overhead. This total, when divided by the units produced, gives the $0.50 per-unit fixed overhead cost. Finally, observe that variable nonmanufacturing costs are not part of the unit cost under variable costing. For both approaches, only manufacturing costs are used to compute the unit costs.

2. The income statement under absorption costing is as follows:

Sales [($5.50 × 90,000) + ($4.50 × 210,000)]	$1,440,000
Less: Cost of goods sold [($3.95 × 90,000) + ($3.02 × 210,000)]	989,700
Gross margin	$ 450,300
Less: Selling expenses*	215,000
Operating income	$ 235,300

*The sum of selling expenses for both products.

3. The income statement under variable costing is as follows:

Sales [($5.50 × 90,000) + ($4.50 × 210,000)]		$1,440,000
Less variable expenses:		
Variable cost of goods sold		
[($3.45 × 90,000) + ($2.62 × 210,000)]	(860,700)	
Variable selling expenses	(90,000)	
Contribution margin		$ 489,300
Less fixed expenses:		
Fixed overhead	(130,000)	
Fixed selling	(125,000)	
Operating income		$ 234,300

4. Reconciliation is as follows:

Absorption costing income − Variable costing income = $235,300 − $234,300 = $1,000

Thus, variable-costing income is $1,000 less than absorption-costing income. This difference can be explained by the net change of fixed overhead found in inventory under absorption costing.

Ladie's wallet:

Units produced	100,000
Units sold	90,000
Increase in inventory	10,000
Unit fixed overhead	× $0.50
Increase in fixed overhead	$5,000

Men's wallets:

Units produced	200,000
Units sold	210,000
Decrease in inventory	(10,000)
Unit fixed overhead	× $0.40
Decrease in fixed overhead	$(4,000)

The net change is a $1,000 ($5,000 − $4,000) increase in fixed overhead in inventories. Thus, under absorption costing, there is a net flow of $1,000 of the current period's fixed overhead into inventory. Since variable costing recognized all of the current period's fixed overhead as an expense, variable-costing income should be $1,000 lower than absorption costing, as it is.

5.   Segmented income statement:

	Ladie's Wallet	Men's Wallet	Total
Sales	$495,000	$945,000	$1,440,000
Less variable expenses:			
Variable cost of goods sold	(310,500)	(550,200)	(860,700)
Variable selling expenses	(30,000)	(60,000)	(90,000)
Contribution margin	$154,500	$334,800	$ 489,300
Less direct fixed expenses:			
Direct fixed overhead	(50,000)	(40,000)	(90,000)
Direct selling expenses	(35,000)	(40,000)	(75,000)
Segment margin	$ 69,500	$254,800	$ 324,300
Less common fixed expenses:			
Common fixed overhead			(40,000)
Common selling expenses			(50,000)
Operating income			$ 234,300

II.   Weighted Average Cost of Capital and Economic Value Added

El Suezo Inc. had after-tax operating income last year of $600,000. Two sources of financing were used by the company: $2.5 million of mortgage bonds paying 8 percent interest and $10 million in common stock, which was considered to be no more or less risky than other stocks. The rate of return on long-term government bonds is 6 percent. El Suezo pays a marginal tax rate of 40 percent. Total capital employed is $5.3 million.

Required:
1.   What is the weighted cost of capital for El Suezo?
2.   Calculate EVA for El Suezo.

Solution:
1.   After-tax cost of the mortgage bonds:
       = [(1 − 0.4)(0.08)] = 0.048
       Cost of the common stock:
       = Return on long-term government bonds + Average premium
       = 6% + 6%
       = 12%

	Amount	Percent	After-Tax Cost =	Weighted Cost
Mortgage bonds	$ 2,500,000	0.20	0.048	0.0096
Common stock	10,000,000	0.80	0.120	0.0960
Total	$12,500,000			
Weighted average cost of capital				0.1056

11

Short-Run Decision Making: Relevant Costing and Inventory Management

After studying Chapter 11, you should be able to:

① Describe the short-run decision-making model and explain how cost behavior affects the information used to make decisions.

② Apply relevant costing and decision-making concepts in a variety of business situations.

③ Choose the optimal product mix when faced with one constrained resource.

④ Explain the impact of cost on pricing decisions.

⑤ Discuss inventory management and just-in-time models.

© NAVISTAR

Experience Managerial Decisions

with Navistar

Relevant decision analysis represents one of the most exciting and widely applicable managerial accounting tools in existence. One big proponent of relevant analysis is **Navistar International Truck and Engine Corporation**, a multi-billion Fortune 300 Company founded in 1902. More than 100 years later, the company has grown to manufacture components and electronics for a wide variety of vehicles, including buses, tractor-trailers, military vehicles, and trucks, to its diverse customers all around the world. Faced with additional important long-term growth issues, Navistar recently used relevant analysis to decide whether to expand axle production at its truck assembly plant in Ontario or to outsource its extra axle production requirements to an outside supplier company. Before the analysis could be conducted, Navistar's managerial accountants first had to identify all relevant factors, both quantitative and qualitative, as well as the short-term and long-term impacts of these factors. Some factors were relatively easy to identify and measure, such as the labor cost that would be required if the additional axles were made in-house or the cost of acquiring the extra factory space needed to produce the additional axles in-house. However, other factors complicated the in-house analysis for Navistar, such as the need to eliminate bottlenecks that would be created from producing the additional axles in-house. In addition, if Navistar decided to make the additional axles in-house, it would require significant capacity-related capital expenditures, which carried a risk associated with the possibility that the current demand for additional axles might not persist in the long-term. In this case, Navistar would be stuck with the cost of the additional capacity without the business to generate additional revenues to cover those costs. On the other hand, if the additional axle production were outsourced, Navistar would have to ensure that its new axle supplier partnered with the Canadian Auto Workers union to minimize the outsourcing effect on Navistar's existing workforce labor agreements. Furthermore, suppliers would have to be trained to deliver parts and subassemblies in sequence with Navistar's demanding schedule. This training represented a considerable outsourcing cost to Navistar. In the end, the relevant costing analysis helped Navistar's executives decide to outsource its additional axle production. As a result, Navistar's Ontario plant has enjoyed annual cost savings of over $3 million! A careful analysis of all relevant factors helped the company make the right decision and avoid being burdened in the long-run by the costs of excess capacity that occur in the always cyclical truck assembly business.

sales per square foot of café floor space, which often is the most important constrained resource. The importance of this metric explains why fast-food restaurants like **McDonald's** push their drive-through service—customers using the drive-through option do not require any internal store floor space. In fact, some restaurants generate more than 80% of sales from this service!

Returning to the Jorgenson Company, the product yielding the highest contribution margin per machine hour should be selected. Gear X earns $12.50 per machine hour ($25/2), but Gear Y earns $20 per machine hour ($10/0.5). Thus, the optimal mix is 80,000 units of Gear Y and none of Gear X. Suppose, however, that there is also a demand constraint. Only 60,000 units of Gear Y can be sold. Cornerstone 11-7 shows how to incorporate this additional constraint.

Multiple Constrained Resources

The presence of only one constrained resource might not be realistic. Organizations face often multiple constraints: limitations of raw materials, limitations of skilled labor,

---

CORNERSTONE 11-7

HOW TO Determine the Optimal Product Mix with One Constrained Resource and a Sales Constraint

Information: Jorgenson Company produces two types of gears, X and Y, with unit contribution margins of $25 and $10, respectively. Each gear must be notched by a special machine. The firm owns eight machines that together provide 40,000 hours of machine time per year. Gear X requires two hours of machine time, and Gear Y requires 0.5 hour of machine time. A maximum of 60,000 units of each gear can be sold.

Required:
1. What is the contribution margin per hour of machine time for each gear?
2. What is the optimal mix of gears?
3. What is the total contribution margin earned for the optimal mix?

Calculation:
1.

	Gear X	Gear Y
Contribution margin per unit	$ 25	$ 10
Four hours of machine time	÷ 2	÷0.5
Contribution margin per hour of machine time	$12.50	$ 20

2. Since Gear Y yields $20 of contribution margin per hour of machine time, the first priority is to produce all of Gear Y that the market will take.

Machine time required for maximum amount of Gear Y = 60,000 × 0.5
= 30,000 hours

Remaining machine time for Gear X = 40,000 − 30,000
= 10,000 hours

Units of Gear X to be produced in 10,000 hours = 10,000/2
= 5,000 units

Now the optimal mix is 60,000 units of Gear Y and 5,000 units of Gear X. This will precisely exhaust the machine time available.

3. Total contribution margin of optimal mix = (60,000 units Gear Y × $10)
+ (5,000 units Gear X × $25)
= $725,000

limited demand for each product, and so on. The solution of the product mix problem in the presence of multiple constraints is considerably more complicated and requires the use of a specialized mathematical technique known as *linear programming*, which is reserved for advanced cost management courses.

The Use of Costs in Pricing Decisions

OBJECTIVE ④
Explain the impact of cost on pricing decisions.

One of the more difficult decisions faced by a company is pricing. This section examines the impact of cost on price and the role of the accountant in gathering the needed information.

Cost-Based Pricing

Demand is one side of the pricing equation; supply is the other side. Since revenue must cover all costs for the firm to make a profit, many companies start with cost to determine price. That is, they calculate product cost and add the desired profit. The mechanics of this approach are straightforward. Usually, there is some cost base and a markup. The **markup** is a percentage applied to the base cost; it includes desired profit and any costs not included in the base cost. Companies that bid for jobs routinely base bid price on cost. Law firms and public accounting firms are service organizations that use cost-plus pricing to bid for clients. Cornerstone 11-8 shows how to apply a markup percentage to cost to obtain price.

Notice in Cornerstone 11-8 that the markup of 20 percent is not pure profit. Instead, it includes other costs not specified, such as overhead (including Elvin's offices and management salaries) as well as any marketing and administrative expenses. The markup percentage can be calculated using a variety of bases.

Retail stores often use markup pricing, and typical markup is 100 percent of cost. Thus, if Graham Department Store purchases a sweater for $24, the retail price marked is $48 [$24 + (1.00 × $24)]. Again, the 100-percent markup is not pure profit—it goes toward the salaries of the clerks, payment for space and equipment (cash registers, furniture, and fixtures), utilities, advertising, and so on. A major advantage of markup pricing is that standard markups are easy to apply. Consider the difficulty of setting a .price for every piece of merchandise in a hardware or department store. It is much

---

HOW TO Calculate Price by Applying a Markup Percentage to Cost

Information: Elvin Company assembles and installs computers to customer specifications. Elvin has decided to price its jobs at the cost of direct materials and direct labor plus 20 percent. The job for a local vocational-technical school included the following costs:

Direct materials	$65,000
Direct labor (assembly and installation)	4,000

Required: Calculate the price charged by Elvin Company to the vocational-technical school.

Calculation:
Price = Cost + Markup percentage × Cost
　　 = $69,000 + 0.20($69,000)
　　 = $69,000 + $13,800
　　 = $82,800

**CORNERSTONE
11-8**

CORNERSTONE 11-9

HOW TO Calculate a Target Cost

Information: Digitime's new wristwatch plus PDA has a target price of $200. Management requires a 15-percent profit on new products.

Required:
1. Calculate the amount of desired profit.
2. Calculate the target cost.

Calculation:
1. Desired profit = 0.15 × Target price
   = 0.15 × $200
   = $30
2. Target cost = Target price − Desired profit
   = $200 − $30
   = $170

Experience Pricing Decisions with Little Guys Home Electronics

A 60-inch, high-definition, big-screen television creates an aura of intense realism for sports aficionados as they watch with unparalleled clarity the fuzz on the tennis ball as it barely catches the line during a night match at the U.S. Open or the insignia on the football as Peyton Manning throws yet another spiral touchdown pass. Using a combination of effective cost-plus pricing and marketplace knowledge, Little Guys Home Electronics has for years helped to bring such exciting sporting events to life for its thousands of customers. Correct pricing decisions are crucial in the home entertainment market, where the profit margin on video products is only 2 to 3 percent!

Little Guys sets prices by marking up full costs and ensuring that the final price falls within a range between the suggested retail price and the minimum advertised price, both of which are affected by the manufacturer and the marketplace. Its managerial accountants must understand cost behavior to be able to predict costs accurately in order for effective markup and pricing decisions to be made. What types of costs does Little Guys consider in its markups? Several examples include product purchases and shipping costs, warehousing costs, labor (including employee healthcare and retirement benefits as well as other labor support costs), store insurance, advertising, delivery truck investments and maintenance, and customer service trips. Also, future demand must be estimated so that Little Guys can figure out how much to charge for each television, receiver, and the like, such that all costs across the value chain are covered and the desired profit is achieved. Armed with an effective pricing strategy involving judgment about costs, markup percentages, and future market trends, Little Guys hopes to continue delivering exciting home electronics products and services to Chicago area families for years to come.

simpler to apply a uniform markup to cost and then to adjust prices as needed if demand is less than anticipated.

Several important observations are in order at this point concerning the relationship between the base cost, the markup percentage, and the firm's cost system. First, when the firm includes relatively few costs in the base cost (rather than a large number of costs), it becomes very important that the firm selects a large enough markup percentage to ensure that the markup covers all of the remaining costs not included in the base cost. Covering more costs with the markup requires significant judgment and cost estimation. Second, on a related note, the effectiveness of cost-plus pricing relies heavily on the accuracy of the cost system and pricing managers' understanding of the firm's cost structure. For example, assume that a firm marks up only its direct manufacturing costs and does not understand well the behavior of its indirect manufacturing costs or its non-manufacturing costs (e.g., research and development costs, distribution costs, customer service costs, etc.). In this case, it is likely that the firm will encounter problems in setting prices either too high—and will be undercut by competitors with more appropriate lower prices—or too low—and will not cover all costs, thereby resulting in a net loss.

Target Costing and Pricing

Many American and European firms set the price of a new product as the sum of the costs and the desired profit. The rationale is that the company must earn sufficient revenues to cover all costs and yield a profit. Peter Drucker writes, "This is true but irrelevant: Customers do not see it as their job to ensure manufacturers a profit. The only sound way to price is to start out with what the market is willing to pay."[3]

Target costing is a method of determining the cost of a product or service based on the price (target price) that customers are willing to pay. The marketing department determines what characteristics and price for a product are most acceptable to consumers; then, it is the job of the company's engineers to design and develop the product such that cost and profit can be covered by that price. Japanese firms have been doing this for years; American companies are beginning to use target costing. For example, **Olympus**, **Toyota**, **Boeing**, **Nissan**, and **Caterpillar** all have used a value-chain perspective to implement target costing. Target costing recognizes that between 75- and 90% percent of a product's cost becomes "committed to" or "locked into" by the time it finishes the design stage.[4] Therefore, it is most effective to make such large changes in the design and development stage of the product life cycle because at this point the features of the product, as well as its costs, still are fairly easy to adjust. Typical target-costing efforts to reduce costs focus on redesigning the product to require fewer or less costly materials, labor and processes during production, delivery, and customer service. **Mercedes**, for instance, used target costing extensively in the design of its popular M-class sports utility vehicle series, which made its public debut in the blockbuster movie *Jurassic Park*.

Consider the target-costing experience used by Digitime Company in developing a wristwatch that incorporates a PDA (personal digital assistant). The "cool factor" on this item is high, but actually inputting data on the watch is difficult. So, the company expects to be able to charge a premium price to a relatively small number of early adopters. The marketing vice president's price estimate is $200. Digitime's management requires a 15-percent profit on new products. Cornerstone 11-9 shows how to calculate a target cost.

Concept Q&A

Consider a situation in which you want to buy something, but it is quite expensive. Suppose the salesperson says that the price of the item is high because the cost to the store is high. (That is, price is related to cost.) Suppose, on the other hand, that the salesperson says the price is high because the demand for the item is strong. (That is, price is not related to cost.) Which explanation would make you happier to buy the item?

Answer:
You would probably be more likely to buy the item when the reason for the high price is high cost to the store. This situation makes the high price seem "fairer" to you, since the store is not gouging you but simply is trying to make a normal profit.

---

[3]Peter Drucker, "The Five Deadly Business Sins," *The Wall Street Journal* (October 21, 1993): A22.

[4]Antonio Davila, and Marc Wouters, "Designing Cost-Competitive Technology Products through Cost Management," *Accounting Horizons*, Vol. 18, No. 1 (2004): 13–26.

At the beginning of the year, a customer from a geographic region outside the area normally served by the company offered to buy 100,000 fixtures for $7 each. The customer also offered to pay all transportation costs. Since there would be no sales commissions involved, this order would not have any variable selling costs.

Required:

1. Based on a quantitative (numerical) analysis, should the company accept the order?
2. What qualitative factors might impact the decision? Assume that no other orders are expected beyond the regular business and the special order.

OBJECTIVES ① ②   **Problem 11-32 Make or Buy, Qualitative Considerations**

Hetrick Dentistry Services operates in a large metropolitan area. Currently, Hetrick has its own dental laboratory to produce porcelain and gold crowns. The unit costs to produce the crowns are as follows:

	Porcelain	Gold
Raw materials	$ 70	$130
Direct labor	27	27
Variable overhead	8	8
Fixed overhead	22	22
Total	$127	$187

Fixed overhead is detailed as follows:

Salary (supervisor)	$26,000
Depreciation	5,000
Rent (lab facility)	32,000

Overhead is applied on the basis of direct labor hours. These rates were computed by using 5,500 direct labor hours.

A local dental laboratory has offered to supply Hetrick all the crowns it needs. Its price is $125 for porcelain crowns and $150 for gold crowns; however, the offer is conditional on supplying both types of crowns—it will not supply just one type for the price indicated. If the offer is accepted, the equipment used by Hetrick's laboratory would be scrapped (it is old and has no market value), and the lab facility would be closed. Hetrick uses 2,000 porcelain crowns and 600 gold crowns per year.

Required:

1. Should Hetrick continue to make its own crowns, or should they be purchased from the external supplier? What is the dollar effect of purchasing?
2. What qualitative factors should Hetrick consider in making this decision?
3. Suppose that the lab facility is owned rather than rented and that the $32,000 is depreciation rather than rent. What effect does this have on the analysis in Requirement 1?
4. Refer to the original data. Assume that the volume of crowns used is 3,400 porcelain and 600 gold. Should Hetrick make or buy the crowns? Explain the outcome.

OBJECTIVES ① ②   **Problem 11-33 Sell or Process Further**

CORNERSTONE 11-2

spreadsheet

Zanda Drug Corporation buys three chemicals that are processed to produce two types of analgesics used as ingredients for popular over-the-counter drugs. The purchased chemicals are blended for two to three hours and then heated for 15 minutes. The results of the process are two separate analgesics, depryl and pencol, which are sent to a drying room until their moisture content is reduced to 6 to 8 percent. For every 1,300 pounds of chemicals used, 600 pounds of depryl and 600 pounds of pencol are produced. After drying, depryl and pencol are sold to companies that process them into their final form.

The selling prices are $12 per pound for depryl and $30 per pound for pencol. The costs to produce 600 pounds of each analgesic are as follows:

Chemicals	$8,500
Direct labor	6,735
Overhead	9,900

The analgesics are packaged in 20-pound bags and shipped. The cost of each bag is $1.30. Shipping costs $0.10 per pound.

Zanda could process depryl further by grinding it into a fine powder and then molding the powder into tablets. The tablets can be sold directly to retail drug stores as a generic brand. If this route were taken, the revenue received per bottle of tablets would be $4.00, with 10 bottles produced by every pound of depryl. The costs of grinding and tableting total $2.50 per pound of depryl. Bottles cost $0.40 each. Bottles are shipped in boxes that hold 25 bottles at a shipping cost of $1.60 per box.

Required:
1. Should Zanda sell depryl at split-off, or should depryl be processed and sold as tablets?
2. If Zanda normally sells 265,000 pounds of depryl per year, what will be the difference in profits if depryl is processed further?

Problem 11-34 Keep or Drop

OBJECTIVES ① ②

AudioMart is a retailer of radios, stereos, and televisions. The store carries two portable sound systems that have radios, tape players, and speakers. System A, of slightly higher quality than System B, costs $20 more. With rare exceptions, the store also sells a headset when a system is sold. The headset can be used with either system. Variable-costing income statements for the three products follow:

	System A	System B	Headset
Sales	$45,000	$ 32,500	$8,000
Less: Variable expenses	20,000	25,500	3,200
Contribution margin	$25,000	$ 7,000	$4,800
Less: Fixed costs*	10,000	18,000	2,700
Operating income	$15,000	$(11,000)	$2,100

*This includes common fixed costs totaling $18,000, allocated to each product in proportion to its revenues.

The owner of the store is concerned about the profit performance of System B and is considering dropping it. If the product is dropped, sales of System A will increase by 30 percent, and sales of headsets will drop by 25 percent.

Required:
1. Prepare segmented income statements for the three products using a better format.
2. Prepare segmented income statements for System A and the headsets assuming that System B is dropped. Should B be dropped?
3. Suppose that a third system, System C, with a similar quality to System B, could be acquired. Assume that with C the sales of A would remain unchanged; however, C would produce only 80 percent of the revenues of B, and sales of the headsets would drop by 10 percent. The contribution margin ratio of C is 50 percent, and its direct fixed costs would be identical to those of B. Should System B be dropped and replaced with System C?

Problem 11-35 Accept or Reject a Special Order

OBJECTIVES ① ②

Steve Murningham, manager of an electronics division, was considering an offer by Pat Sellers, manager of a sister division. Pat's division was operating below capacity and had

OBJECTIVES ①②   **Case 12-45 Internet Research, Group Case**

Often, websites for major airlines contain news of current special fares and flights. A decision to run a brief "fare special" is an example of a tactical decision. Form a group with one to three other students. Have each member of the group choose one or two airlines and check their websites for recent examples of fare specials. Have the group collaborate in preparing a presentation to the class discussing the types of cost and revenue information that would go into making this type of tactical decision.

12

Capital Investment Decisions

After studying Chapter 12, you should be able to:

1. Explain the meaning of *capital investment decisions*, and distinguish between independent and mutually exclusive capital investment decisions.

2. Compute the payback period and accounting rate of return for a proposed investment, and explain their roles in capital investment decisions.

3. Use net present value analysis for capital investment decisions involving independent projects.

4. Use the internal rate of return to assess the acceptability of independent projects.

5. Explain the role and value of postaudits.

6. Explain why net present value is better than internal rate of return for capital investment decisions involving mutually exclusive projects.

© PHOTO COURTESY OF HARD ROCK CAFÉ INTERNATIONAL (USA), INC.

Experience Managerial Decisions
with Hard Rock Cafe

Launched in 1971 in London, England, nearly everyone has visited, or at least seen T-shirts for, one of **Hard Rock International**'s 121 world-famous café restaurants located in 41 different countries. What visitors likely appreciate most is Hard Rock's impressive collection of rock 'n' roll memorabilia and its tasty fare. However, for Hard Rock's managerial accountants and the readers of this textbook, what is most likely to be appreciated is Hard Rock's masterful use of effective capital budgeting techniques to make decisions on a very big scale that are critical to the company's continued success. One of those decisions concerns the opening of new cafés all over the world from Mumbai, India, to Louisville, Kentucky.

New cafés require advanced planning concerning anticipated cash flows, both for future costs and revenues. Future cost-related cash flow projections for the opening of a proposed café include items such as labor and materials from different countries, licensing laws, utilities, kitchen and bar equipment, computers, construction, and audio-visual equipment, which alone total just over $6 million! Future cash flows for food and beverage sales are even more difficult to project than costs because of uncertainties involving demographics, economic conditions, and competition. Another complicating factor is the challenge of estimating local awareness of the Hard Rock brand. Brand awareness is important because it drives Hard Rock's merchandise sales, which account for over 30 percent of its total revenue. Estimates of future cash flows for revenues and expenses are combined to calculate a proposed café's payback period and net present value (NPV). These metrics then are compared with Hard Rock's decision model requirements to help determine whether or not the proposed café is a wise decision. Another capital investment decision for Hard Rock surrounds the buying and selling of its rock 'n' roll memorabilia. Hard Rock uses its memorabilia to generate food and merchandise revenues by attracting more customers into the café. The collection has grown from a single Eric Clapton guitar to more than 60,000 instruments, posters, costumes, photographs, platinum and gold LPs, and music and lyric sheets. Finally, Hard Rock uses capital budgeting techniques for its biggest project ever, a rock 'n' roll theme park requiring a $400 million venture—that represents the equivalent of approximately 70 new cafés! For this monstrous capital investment, Hard Rock relied heavily on input from a management team with experience and expertise in the theme park industry. Without effective capital budgeting practices, Hard Rock would be forced to "shoot from the hip and hope for the best" for its long-term investments. Such a strategy would not likely produce the impressive capital investment successes that Hard Rock has grown to expect in a very competitive market.

OBJECTIVE ①
Explain the meaning of *capital investment decisions*, and distinguish between independent and mutually exclusive capital investment decisions.

Types of Capital Investment Decisions

Organizations often are faced with the opportunity (or need) to invest in assets or projects that represent long-term commitments. New production systems, new plants, new equipment, and new product development are examples of assets and projects that fit this category. Usually, many alternatives are available. For example, an organization may be faced with the decision of whether to invest or not invest in a new plant, or whether to invest in a flexible manufacturing system or to continue with an existing traditional manufacturing system. These long-range decisions are examples of *capital investment decisions*.

Capital investment decisions are concerned with the process of planning, setting goals and priorities, arranging financing, and using certain criteria to select long-term assets. Because capital investment decisions place large amounts of resources at risk for long periods of time and simultaneously affect the future development of the firm, they are among the most important decisions made by managers. Every organization has limited resources, which should be used to maintain or enhance its long-run profitability. Poor capital investment decisions can be disastrous. For example, a failure to invest in automated manufacturing when other competitors do so may result in significant losses in market share because of the inability to compete on the basis of quality, cost, and delivery time. Competitors with more modern facilities may produce more output at lower cost and higher quality. Thus, making the right capital investment decisions is absolutely essential for long-term survival.

The process of making capital investment decisions often is referred to as **capital budgeting**. Two types of capital budgeting projects will be considered: *independent projects* and *mutually exclusive projects*. **Independent projects** are projects that, if accepted or rejected, do not affect the cash flows of other projects. For example, a decision by **General Motors** to build a new plant for production of the Cadillac line is not affected by its decision to build a new plant for the production of its Saturn line. They are independent capital investment decisions. The second type of capital budgeting project requires a firm to choose among competing alternatives that provide the same basic service. Acceptance of one option precludes the acceptance of another. Thus, **mutually exclusive projects** are those projects that, if accepted, preclude the acceptance of all other competing projects. For example, some time ago, **Monsanto's Fibers Division** decided to automate its Pensacola, Florida, plant. Thus, Monsanto was faced with the choice of continuing with its existing manual production operation or replacing it with an automated system. In all likelihood, part of the company's deliberation concerned different types of automated systems. If three different automated systems were being considered, this would produce four alternatives: the current system plus the three potential new systems. Once one system is chosen, the other three are excluded; they are mutually exclusive.

Notice that one of the competing alternatives in the Monsanto example is that of maintaining the status quo (the manual system). This point emphasizes the fact that new investments replacing existing investments must prove to be economically superior. Of course, at times, replacement of the old system is mandatory and not discretionary if the firm wishes to remain in business (e.g., equipment in the old system may be worn out, thereby eliminating the viability of the old system). In such a situation, going out of business could be a viable alternative, especially if none of the new investment alternatives is profitable.

Capital investment decisions often are concerned with investments in long-term capital assets. With the exception of land, these assets depreciate over their lives, and the original investment is used up as the assets are employed. In general terms, a sound capital investment will earn back its original capital outlay over its life and, at the same time, provide a reasonable return on the original investment. Therefore, managers must decide whether or not a capital investment will earn back its original outlay and provide a reasonable return. By making this assessment, a manager can decide on the acceptability of independent projects and compare competing projects on the basis of their economic merits.

But what is meant by reasonable return? It is generally agreed that any new project must cover the opportunity cost of the funds invested. For example, if a company takes money from a money market fund that is earning 6 percent and invests it in a new project, then the project must provide at least a 6-percent return (the return that could have been earned had the money been left in the money market fund). Of course, in reality, funds for investment often come from different sources—each representing a different opportunity cost. The return that must be earned is a blend of the opportunity costs of the different sources. Thus, if a company uses two sources of funds, one with an opportunity cost of 4 percent and the other with an opportunity cost of 6 percent, then the return that must be earned is somewhere between 4 and 6 percent, depending on the relative amounts used from each source. Furthermore, it is usually assumed that managers should select projects that promise to maximize the wealth of the owners of the firm.

To make a capital investment decision, a manager must estimate the quantity and timing of cash flows, assess the risk of the investment, and consider the impact of the project on the firm's profits. One of the most difficult tasks is to estimate the cash flows. Projections must be made years into the future, and forecasting is far from a perfect science. Obviously, as the accuracy of cash flow forecasts increases, the reliability of the decision improves. In making projections, managers must identify and quantify the benefits associated with the proposed project(s). For example, an automated cash deposit system can produce the following benefits (relative to a manual system): bank charge reductions, productivity gains, greater data integrity, lower training costs, and savings in time required to audit and do bank/cash reconciliations. The dollar value of these benefits must be assessed. Although forecasting future cash flows is a critical part of the capital investment process, forecasting methods will not be considered here. Furthermore, the cash flows projected must be *after-tax cash flows*. Taxes have an important role in developing cash flow assessments. However, taxes will not be explicitly considered. Tax effects either are assumed away or the cash flows can be thought of as after-tax cash flows. Forecasting methodologies and tax considerations are issues that are left for more advanced studies. Consequently, after-tax cash flows are assumed to be known; the focus will be on making capital investment decisions *given* these cash flows.

Concept Q&A

What is the difference between independent and mutually exclusive investments?

Answer:
Acceptance or rejection of an independent investment does not affect the cash flows of other investments. Acceptance of a mutually exclusive investment precludes the acceptance of any competing project.

Managers must set goals and priorities for capital investments. They also must identify some basic criteria for the acceptance or rejection of proposed investments. In this chapter, we will study four basic methods to guide managers in accepting or rejecting potential investments. The methods include both nondiscounting and discounting decision approaches (two methods are discussed for each approach). The discounting methods are applied to investment decisions involving both independent and mutually exclusive projects.

Nondiscounting Models

The basic capital investment decision models can be classified into two major categories: *nondiscounting models* and *discounting models*. **Nondiscounting models** ignore the time value of money, whereas **discounting models** explicitly consider it. Although many accounting theorists disparage the nondiscounting models because they ignore the time value of money, many firms continue to use these models in making capital investment decisions. However, the use of discounting models has increased over the years, and few firms use only one model; indeed, most firms seem to use both types.[1]

OBJECTIVE 2
Compute the payback period and accounting rate of return for a proposed investment, and explain their roles in capital investment decisions.

[1]From the mid-1950s to 1988, surveys reveal that the use of discounting models as the primary evaluation method for capital projects went from about 9 to 80 percent. See A. A. Robichek and J. G. McDonald, *Financial Planning in Transition, Long Range Planning Service*, Report No. 268 Menlo Park, CA: Stanford Research Institute, January 1966 and T. Klammer, B. Koch, and N. Wilner, "Capital Budgeting Practices— A Survey of Corporate Use," Working Paper, North Texas State University.

This pattern suggests that both categories—nondiscounted and discounted—supply useful information to managers as they struggle to make a capital investment decision.

Payback Period

One type of nondiscounting model is the *payback period*. The **payback period** is the time required for a firm to recover its original investment. If the cash flows of a project are an equal amount each period, then the following formula can be used to compute its payback period:

Payback period = Original investment/Annual cash flow

If, however, the cash flows are unequal, the payback period is computed by adding the annual cash flows until such time as the original investment is recovered. If a fraction of a year is needed, it is assumed that cash flows occur evenly within each year. Cornerstone 12-1 shows how payback analysis is done for both even and uneven cash flows.

One way to use the payback period is to set a maximum payback period for all projects and to reject any project that exceeds this level. Why would a firm use the payback period in this way? Some analysts suggest that the payback period can be used as a rough measure of risk, with the notion that the longer it takes for a project to pay for itself, the riskier it is. Also, firms with riskier cash flows in general could require a shorter payback period than normal. Additionally, firms with liquidity problems would be more interested in projects

---

**CORNERSTONE
12-1**

HOW TO Calculate Payback

Information: Suppose that a new car wash facility requires an investment of $100,000 and either has:
a. Even cash flows of $50,000 per year or
b. The following expected annual cash flows: $30,000, $40,000, $50,000, $60,000, and $70,000.

Required: Calculate the payback period for each case.

Calculation:
a. Even cash flows:

Payback period = Original investment/Annual cash flow
= $100,000/$50,000 = 2 years

b. Uneven cash flows:

Year	Unrecovered Investment ($) (beginning of year)	Annual Cash Flow ($)	Time Needed for Payback (years)
1	100,000	30,000	1.0
2	70,000	40,000	1.0
3	30,000	50,000	0.6*
4	0	60,000	0.0
5	0	70,000	0.0
			2.6

*At the beginning of year 3, $30,000 is needed to recover the investment. Since a net cash flow of $50,000 is expected, only 0.6 year ($30,000/$50,000) is needed to recover the remaining $30,000, assuming a uniform cash inflow throughout the year.

with quick paybacks. Another critical concern is obsolescence. In some industries, the risk of obsolescence is high; firms within these industries that manufacture computers and MP3 players would be interested in recovering funds rapidly.

Another reason, less beneficial to the firm, may also be involved. Many managers in a position to make capital investment decisions may choose investments with quick payback periods out of self-interest. If a manager's performance is measured using such short-run criteria as annual net income, he or she may choose projects with quick paybacks to show improved net income and cash flow as quickly as possible. Consider that divisional managers often are responsible for making capital investment decisions and are evaluated on divisional profit. The tenure of divisional managers, however, is typically short—three to five years on average. Consequently, the incentive for such managers is to shy away from investments that promise healthy long-run returns but relatively meager returns in the short run. New products and services that require time to develop a consumer following fit this description particularly well. Corporate budgeting policies and a budget review committee can eliminate these problems.

The payback period can be used to choose among competing alternatives. Under this approach, the investment with the shortest payback period is preferred over investments with longer payback periods. However, this use of the payback period is less defensible because this measure suffers from two major deficiencies: (1) it ignores the cash flow performance of the investments beyond the payback period, and (2) it ignores the time value of money.

These two significant deficiencies are easily illustrated. Assume that an engineering firm is considering two different types of computer-aided design (CAD) systems: CAD-A and CAD-B. Each system requires an initial outlay of $150,000, has a five-year life, and displays the following annual cash flows:

Investment	Year 1	Year 2	Year 3	Year 4	Year 5
CAD-A	$90,000	$ 60,000	$50,000	$50,000	$50,000
CAD-B	40,000	110,000	25,000	25,000	25,000

Both investments have payback periods of two years. In other words, if a manager uses the payback period to choose among competing investments, the two investments would be equally desirable. In reality, however, the CAD-A system should be preferred over the CAD-B system for two reasons. First, the CAD-A system provides a much larger dollar return for the years 3, 4, and 5 beyond the payback period ($150,000 vs. $75,000). Second, the CAD-A system returns $90,000 in the first year, while B returns only $40,000. The extra $50,000 that the CAD-A system provides in the first year could be put to productive use, such as investing in another project. It is better to have a dollar now than to have it one year from now, because the dollar on hand can be invested to provide a return one year from now.

In summary, the payback period provides information to managers that can be used as follows:

1. To help control the risks associated with the uncertainty of future cash flows.
2. To help minimize the impact of an investment on a firm's liquidity problems.
3. To help control the risk of obsolescence.
4. To help control the effect of the investment on performance measures.

However, the method suffers significant deficiencies: It ignores a project's total profitability and the time value of money. While the computation of the payback period may be useful to a manager, relying on it solely for a capital investment decision would be foolish.

Analytical Q&A

Suppose that a project requires an investment of $30,000 and produces $8,000 cash per year. What is the payback period?

Answer:
$30,000/$8,000 = 3.75 years

Accounting Rate of Return

The *accounting rate of return* is the second commonly used nondiscounting model. The **accounting rate of return** (ARR) measures the return on a project in terms of income, as opposed to using a project's cash flow. The accounting rate of return is computed by the following formula:

Accounting rate of return = Average income/Initial investment

Income is not equivalent to cash flows because of accruals and deferrals used in its computation. The average income of a project is obtained by summing together the net income for each year of the project and then dividing this total by the number of years. Cornerstone 12-2 shows how to calculate the accounting rate of return.

Unlike the payback period, the accounting rate of return does consider a project's profitability; like the payback period, it ignores the time value of money. Ignoring the time value of money is a critical deficiency in this method as well; it can lead a manager to choose investments that do not maximize profits. The ARR and payback model are referred to as *nondiscounting models* because they ignore the time value of money. Discounting models use **discounted cash flows**, which are future cash flows expressed in terms of their present value. The use of discounting models requires an understanding of the present value concepts. Present value concepts are reviewed in Appendix 12A. You should review these concepts and make sure that you understand them before studying capital investment discount models. Present value tables (Exhibits 12B-1 and 12B-2) are presented in Appendix 12B at the end of this chapter. These tables are referred to and used throughout the rest of this chapter.

In addition to ignoring the time value of money, the ARR also has other potential drawbacks because it is dependent upon net income, which is the financial measure most likely to be manipulated by managers. Some of these reasons for manipulating net income include debt contracts (i.e., debt covenants) and bonuses. Often, debt contracts require that a firm maintain certain financial accounting ratios, which can be affected by the income reported and by the level of long-term assets. Accordingly, the ARR may be used as a screening measure to ensure that any new investment will not adversely affect these ratios. Additionally, because bonuses to managers often are based on accounting income or return on assets, managers may have a personal interest in seeing that any new investment contributes significantly to net income. A manager seeking to maximize personal income is likely to select investments that return the highest net income per dollar invested, even if the selected investments are not the ones that produce the greatest cash flows and return to the firm in the long run.

Concept Q&A

Why would a manager choose only investments that return the highest income per dollar invested?

Answer:

It might be an action that helps the company to comply with debt covenants. It also might have something to do with the manager's incentive compensation.

**CORNERSTONE
12-2**

HOW TO Calculate the Accounting Rate of Return

Information: Assume that an investment requires an initial outlay of $100,000. The life of the investment is five years with the following net income stream: $30,000, $30,000, $40,000, $30,000, and $50,000.

Required: Calculate the accounting rate of return.

Calculation:
Total net income (five yrs.) = $180,000
Average net income = $180,000/5 = $36,000
Accounting rate of return = $36,000/$100,000 = 0.36

Discounting Models: The Net Present Value Method

OBJECTIVE ③
Use net present value analysis for capital investment decisions involving independent projects.

Discounting models explicitly consider the time value of money and, therefore, incorporate the concept of discounting cash inflows and outflows. Two discounting models will be considered: *net present value* (NPV) and *internal rate of return* (IRR). The NPV method will be discussed first; the IRR method is discussed in the following section.

Net Present Value Defined

Net present value is the difference between the present value of the cash inflows and outflows associated with a project:

$$\text{NPV} = [\Sigma CF_t/(1 + i)^t] - I$$
$$= [\Sigma CF_t \, df_t] - I$$
$$= P - I$$

where

I = The present value of the project's cost (usually the initial cash outlay)
CF_t = The cash inflow to be received in period t, with $t = 1 . . . n$
i = The required rate of return
t = The time period
P = The present value of the project's future cash inflows
df_t = $1/(1 + i)^t$, the discount factor

Net present value measures the profitability of an investment. A positive NPV indicates that the investment increases the firm's wealth. To use the NPV method, a *required rate of return* must be defined. The **required rate of return** is the minimum acceptable rate of return. It also is referred to as the *discount rate*, the *hurdle rate*, and the *cost of capital*. In theory, if future cash flows are known with certainty, then the correct required rate of return is the firm's **cost of capital**. In practice, future cash flows are uncertain, and managers often choose a discount rate higher than the cost of capital to deal with the uncertainty. However, if the rate chosen is excessively high, it will bias the selection process toward short-term investments. Because of the risk of being overly conservative, it may be better to use the cost of capital as the discount rate and find other approaches to deal with uncertainty.

If the NPV is positive, it signals that (1) the initial investment has been recovered, (2) the required rate of return has been recovered, and (3) a return in excess of (1) and (2) has been received. Thus, if the NPV is greater than zero, the investment is profitable and, therefore, is acceptable. If the NPV equals zero, the decision maker will find acceptance or rejection of the investment equal. Finally, if the NPV is less than zero, the investment should be rejected. In this case, it is earning less than the required rate of return.

Concept Q&A

Suppose that the NPV of an investment is $2,000. Why does this mean that the investment should be accepted?

NPV greater than zero means that the investment recovers its capital while simultaneously earning a return in excess of the required rate.

Answer:

An Example Illustrating Net Present Value

Brannon Company has developed new earphones for portable MP3 players that it believes are superior to anything on the market. The earphones have a projected product life cycle of five years. Although the marketing manager is excited about the new product's prospects, a decision to manufacture the new product depends on whether it can earn a positive NPV given the company's required rate of return of 12 percent. In order to make a decision regarding the earphones, two steps must be taken: (1) the cash flows for each year must be identified, and (2) the NPV must be computed using the cash flows from step 1. Cornerstone 12-3 shows how to calculate the NPV. Notice that

CORNERSTONE 12-3

HOW TO Assess Cash Flows and Calculate Net Present Value

Information: A detailed market study revealed expected annual revenues of $300,000 for new earphones. Equipment to produce the earphones will cost $320,000. After five years, the equipment can be sold for $40,000. In addition to equipment, working capital is expected to increase by $40,000 because of increases in inventories and receivables. The firm expects to recover the investment in working capital at the end of the project's life. Annual cash operating expenses are estimated at $180,000. The required rate of return is 12 percent.

Required: Estimate the annual cash flows, and calculate the NPV.

STEP 1. CASH FLOW IDENTIFICATION

Year	Item	Cash Flow
0	Equipment	$(320,000)
	Working capital	(40,000)
	Total	$(360,000)
1–4	Revenues	$ 300,000
	Operating expenses	(180,000)
	Total	$ 120,000
5	Revenues	$ 300,000
	Operating expenses	(180,000)
	Salvage	40,000
	Recovery of working capital	40,000
	Total	$ 200,000

STEP 2A. NPV ANALYSIS

Year	Cash Flow[a]	Discount Factor[b]	Present Value
0	$(360,000)	1.000	$(360,000)
1	120,000	0.893	107,160
2	120,000	0.797	95,640
3	120,000	0.712	85,440
4	120,000	0.636	76,320
5	200,000	0.567	113,400
Net present value			$ 117,960

STEP 2B. NPV ANALYSIS

Year	Cash Flow	Discount Factor[c]	Present Value
0	$(360,000)	1.000	$(360,000)
1–4	120,000	3.037	364,440
5	200,000	0.567	113,400
Net present value			$ 117,840[d]

[a]From step 1.
[b]From Exhibit 12B-1, page 531.
[c]Years 1–4 from Exhibit 12B-2, page 532; year 5 from Exhibit 12B-1.
[d]This total differs from the computation in step 2A because of rounding.

step 2 offers two approaches for computing NPV. Step 2A computes NPV by using discount factors from Exhibit 12B-1. Step 2B simplifies the computation by using a single discount factor from Exhibit 12B-2 for the even cash flows occurring in years 1 through 4.

Internal Rate of Return

OBJECTIVE ④
Use the internal rate of return to assess the acceptability of independent projects.

Another discounting model is the *internal rate of return* method. The **internal rate of return** is defined as the interest rate that sets the present value of a project's cash inflows equal to the present value of the project's cost. In other words, it is the interest rate that sets the project's NPV at zero. The following equation can be used to determine a project's IRR:

$$I = \sum CF_t/(1 + i)^t$$

where $t = 1, \ldots, n$

The right-hand side of this equation is the present value of future cash flows, and the left-hand side is the investment. I, CF_t, and t are known. Thus, the IRR (the interest rate, i, in the equation) can be found using trial and error. Once the IRR for a project is computed, it is compared with the firm's required rate of return. If the IRR is greater than the required rate, the project is deemed acceptable; if the IRR is less than the required rate of return, the project is rejected; if the IRR is equal to the required rate of return, the firm is indifferent between accepting or rejecting the investment proposal.

The IRR is the most widely used of the capital investment techniques. One reason for its popularity may be that it is a rate of return, a concept that managers are comfortable with using. Another possibility is that managers may believe (in most cases, incorrectly) that the IRR is the true or actual compounded rate of return being earned by the initial investment. Whatever the reasons for its popularity, a basic understanding of the IRR is necessary.

Example: Multiple-Period Setting with Uniform Cash Flows

Assume initially that the investment produces a series of uniform cash flows. Since the series of cash flows is uniform, a single discount factor from Exhibit 12B-2 can be used to compute the present value of the annuity. Letting *df* be this discount factor and *CF* be the annual cash flow, the IRR equation assumes the following form:

$$I = CF \, (df)$$

Solving for *df*, we obtain:

$$df = I \, / \, CF$$
$$= \text{Investment/Annual cash flow}$$

Assume that the investment (I) is \$100 and that it produces a single-period cash flow of \$110. The discount factor is $I/CF = \$100/\$110 = 0.909$. Looking in Exhibit 12B-2, a discount factor of 0.909 for a single period corresponds to a rate of 10 percent, which is the IRR. In general, once the discount factor is computed, go to Exhibit 12B-2 and find the row corresponding to the life of the project, then move across that row until the computed discount factor is found. The interest rate corresponding to this discount factor is the IRR. Cornerstone 12-4 on the next page illustrates how to calculate the IRR for multiple-period uniform cash flows.

CORNERSTONE
12-4

HOW TO Calculate Internal Rate of Return with Uniform Cash Flows

Information: Assume that a hospital has the opportunity to invest $120,000 in a new ultrasound system that will produce net cash inflows of $49,950 at the end of each year of the next three years.

Required: Calculate the IRR for the ultrasound system.

Calculation:

$df = I/CF$

    $= \$120,000/\$49,950$

    $= 2.402$

Since the life of the investment is three years, find the third row in Exhibit 12B-2 and then move across this row until $df = 2.402$ is found. The interest rate corresponding to 2.402 is 12 percent, which is the IRR.

Exhibit 12B-2 does not provide discount factors for every possible interest rate. To illustrate, assume that the annual cash inflows expected by the hospital (in Cornerstone 12-4) are $51,000 instead of $49,950. The new discount factor is 2.353 ($120,000/$51,000). Going once again to the third row in Exhibit 12B-2, it is clear that the discount factor—and thus the IRR—lies between 12 and 14 percent. Although it is possible to approximate the IRR by interpolation, for simplicity, identify the range for the IRR as indicated by the tabled values. In practice, business calculators or spreadsheet programs like Excel can provide the values of IRR without the use of tables such as Exhibit 12B-2.

Analytical Q&A

Suppose that an investment of $169 produces an annual cash flow of $100 for two years. What is the IRR?

Answer:

$df = 1/CF = \$169/\$100 = 1.69$; from Exhibit 12B-2, the IRR is 12 percent.

Multiple-Period Setting: Uneven Cash Flows

If the cash flows are not uniform, then the IRR equation must be used. For a multiple-period setting, this equation can be solved by trial and error or by using a business calculator or a spreadsheet program. To illustrate solution by trial and error, assume that a $10,000 investment in a PC system produces clerical savings of $6,000 and $7,200 for each of two years. The IRR is the interest rate that sets the present value of these two cash inflows equal to $10,000:

$$P = [\$6,000/(1 + i)] + [\$7,200/(1 + i)^2]$$
$$= \$10,000$$

To solve this equation by trial and error, start by selecting a possible value for i. Given this first guess, the present value of the future cash flows is computed and then compared with the initial investment. If the present value is greater than the initial investment, then the interest rate is too low; if the present value is less than the initial investment, then the interest rate is too high. The next guess is adjusted accordingly.

Assume that the first guess is 18 percent. Using i equal to 0.18, Exhibit 12B-1 yields the following discount factors: 0.847 and 0.718. These discount factors produce the following present value for the two cash inflows:

$$P = (0.847 \times \$6,000) + (0.718 \times \$7,200)$$
$$= \$10,252$$

Since P is greater than \$10,000, the interest rate selected is too low. A higher guess is needed. If the next guess is 20 percent, we obtain the following:

$$P = (0.833 \times \$6,000) + (0.694 \times \$7,200)$$
$$= \$9,995$$

Since this value is reasonably close to \$10,000, we can say that the IRR is 20 percent. (The IRR is, in fact, exactly 20 percent; the present value is slightly less than the investment because of rounding error in the discount factors found in Exhibit 12B-1.)

Postaudit of Capital Projects

OBJECTIVE 5
Explain the role and value of postaudits.

A key element in the capital investment process is a follow-up analysis of a capital project once it is implemented. This analysis is called a *postaudit*. A **postaudit** compares the actual benefits with the estimated benefits and actual operating costs with estimated operating costs; it evaluates the overall outcome of the investment and proposes corrective action if needed. The following real-world case illustrates the usefulness of a postaudit activity.

Honley Medical Company: An Illustrative Application

Allen Manesfield and Jenny Winters were discussing a persistent and irritating problem present in the process of producing intravenous (IV) needles. Both Allen and Jenny are employed by **Honley Medical**, which specializes in the production of medical products and has three divisions: the IV Products Division, the Critical Care Monitoring Division, and the Specialty Products Division. Allen and Jenny both are associated with the IV Products Division—Allen as the senior production engineer and Jenny as the marketing manager.

The IV Products Division produces needles of five different sizes. During one stage of the manufacturing process, the needle itself is inserted into a plastic hub and is bonded by using epoxy glue. According to Jenny, the use of epoxy to bond the needles was causing the division all kinds of problems. In many cases, the epoxy wasn't bonding correctly. The rejects were high, and the division was receiving a large number of complaints from its customers. Corrective action was needed to avoid losing sales. After some discussion and analysis, a recommendation was made to use induction welding in lieu of epoxy bonding. In induction welding, the needles are inserted into the plastic hub, and an RF generator is used to heat the needles. The RF generator works on the same principle as a microwave oven. As the needles get hot, the plastic melts and the needles are bonded.

Switching to induction welding required an investment in RF generators and the associated tooling; the investment was justified by the IV Products Division, based on the savings associated with the new system. Induction welding promised to reduce the cost of direct materials, eliminating the need to buy and use epoxy. Savings of direct labor costs also were predicted because the welding process is much more automated. Adding to these savings were the avoidance of daily clean-up costs and the reduction in rejects. Allen presented a formal NPV analysis showing that the welding system was superior to the epoxy system. Headquarters approved its purchase.

One Year Later

Jenny: Allen, I'm quite pleased with induction welding for bonding needles. In the year since the new process was implemented, we've had virtually no complaints from our customers. The needles are firmly bonded.

Allen: I wish that positive experience were true for all other areas as well. Unfortunately, implementing the process has uncovered some rather sticky and expensive problems that I didn't anticipate. The Internal Audit Department recently completed a postaudit of the project, and now my feet are being held to the fire.

Jenny: That's too bad. What's the problem?

Allen: You mean problems. Let me list a few for you. One is that the RF generators interfered with the operation of other equipment. To eliminate this interference, we had to install filtering equipment. But that's not all. We also discovered that the average maintenance person doesn't know how to maintain the new equipment. Now, we are faced with the need to initiate a training program to upgrade the skills of our maintenance people. Upgrading skills also implies higher wages. Although the RF bonding process is less messy, it also is more complex. The manufacturing people complained to the internal auditors about that. They maintain that a simple process, even if messy, is to be preferred—especially now that demand for the product is increasing by leaps and bounds.

Jenny: What did the internal auditors conclude?

Allen: They concluded that many of the predicted savings did take place but that some significant costs were not foreseen. Because of some of the unforeseen problems, they have recommended that I look carefully at the possibility of moving back to using epoxy. They indicated that NPV analysis using actual data appears to favor that process. With production expanding, the acquisition of additional RF generators and filtering equipment plus the necessary training is simply not as attractive as returning to epoxy bonding. This conclusion is reinforced by the fact that the epoxy process is simpler and by the auditors' conclusion that the mixing of the epoxy can be automated, avoiding the quality problem we had in the first place.

Jenny: Well, Allen, you can't really blame yourself. You had a real problem and took action to solve it. It's difficult to foresee all the problems and hidden costs of a new process.

Allen: Unfortunately, the internal auditors don't totally agree. In fact, neither do I. I probably jumped too quickly. In the future, I intend to think through new projects more carefully.

Benefits of a Postaudit

In the case of the RF bonding decision, some of the estimated capital investment benefits did materialize: complaints from customers decreased, rejects were fewer, and direct labor and materials costs decreased. However, the investment was greater than expected because filtering equipment was needed, and actual operating costs were much higher because of the increased maintenance cost and the increased complexity of the process. Overall, the internal auditors concluded that the investment was a poor decision. The corrective action that they recommended was to abandon the new process and return to epoxy bonding. Based on this recommendation, the firm did abandon inductive welding and returned to epoxy bonding, which was improved by automating the mix.

Firms that perform postaudits of capital projects experience a number of benefits. First, by evaluating profitability, postaudits ensure that resources are used wisely. If the project is doing well, it may call for additional funds and additional attention. If the project is not doing well, corrective action may be needed to improve performance or abandon the project.

A second benefit of the postaudit is its impact on the behavior of managers. If managers are held accountable for the results of a capital investment decision, they are more likely to make such decisions in the best interests of the firm. Additionally, postaudits supply feedback to managers that should help to improve future decision making. Consider Allen's reaction to the postaudit of the RF bonding process. Certainly, we would expect him to be more careful and more thorough in making future investment recommendations. In the future, Allen will probably consider more than one alternative, such as automating the

Concept Q&A

Why do a postaudit?

Answer:

Postaudits allow a company to assess the quality of capital investment decisions and also produce corrective actions where some of the initial assumptions prove to be wrong. They also encourage managerial accountability and provide useful information for improving future capital budgeting decisions.

mixing of the epoxy. Also, for those alternatives being considered, he will probably be especially alert to the possibility of hidden costs, such as increased training requirements for a new process.

The case also reveals that the postaudit was performed by the internal audit staff. Generally, more objective results are obtainable if the postaudit is done by an independent party. Since considerable effort is expended to ensure as much independence as possible for the internal audit staff, that group is usually the best choice for this task.

Postaudits, however, are costly. Moreover, even though they may provide significant benefits, they have other limitations. Most obvious is the fact that the assumptions driving the original analysis may often be invalidated by changes in the actual operating environment. Accountability must be qualified to some extent by the impossibility of foreseeing every possible eventuality.

Mutually Exclusive Projects

OBJECTIVE ⑥
Explain why net present value is better than internal rate of return for capital investment decisions involving mutually exclusive projects.

Up to this point, we have focused on independent projects. Many capital investment decisions deal with mutually exclusive projects. How NPV analysis and IRR are used to choose among competing projects is an interesting question. An even more interesting question to consider is whether NPV and IRR differ in their ability to help managers make wealth-maximizing decisions in the presence of competing alternatives. For example, we already know that the nondiscounting models can produce erroneous choices because they ignore the time value of money. Because of this deficiency, the discounting models are judged to be superior. Similarly, it can be shown that the NPV model is generally preferred to the IRR model when choosing among mutually exclusive alternatives.

Net Present Value Compared with Internal Rate of Return

NPV and IRR both yield the same decision for independent projects. For example, if the NPV is greater than zero, then the IRR is also greater than the required rate of return; both models signal the correct decision. However, for competing projects, the two methods can produce different results. Intuitively, we believe that for mutually exclusive projects, the project with the highest NPV or the highest IRR should be chosen. Since it is possible for the two methods to produce different rankings of mutually exclusive projects, the method that consistently reveals the wealth-maximizing project is preferred.

NPV differs from IRR in two major ways. First, NPV assumes that each cash inflow received is reinvested at the required rate of return, whereas the IRR method assumes that each cash inflow is reinvested at the computed IRR. Reinvesting at the required rate of return is more realistic and produces more reliable results when comparing mutually exclusive projects. Second, the NPV method measures profitability in absolute terms, whereas the IRR method measures it in relative terms. NPV measures the amount by which the value of the firm changes. These differences are summarized in Exhibit 12-1.

Since NPV measures the impact that competing projects have on the value of the firm, choosing the project with the largest NPV is consistent with maximizing the wealth of shareholders. On the other hand, IRR does not consistently result in choices that maximize wealth. IRR, as a relative measure of profitability, has the virtue of measuring accurately the rate of return of funds that remain internally invested. However, maximizing IRR will not necessarily maximize the wealth of firm owners because it cannot, by nature, consider the absolute dollar contributions of projects. In the final analysis, what counts are the total dollars earned—the absolute profits—not the relative profits. Accordingly, NPV, not IRR, should be used for choosing among competing, mutually exclusive projects or competing projects when capital funds are limited.

Exhibit 12-1

Net Present Value Compared with Internal Rate of Return

	NPV	IRR
Type of measure	*Absolute* dollars	*Relative* percentage
Cash flow re-investment assumption	At required rate of return	At internal rate of return

Concept Q&A

Why is NPV better than IRR for choosing among competing projects?

Answer:

NPV uses a more realistic reinvestment assumption, and its signal is consistent with maximizing the wealth of firm owners (IRR does not measure absolute profits).

An independent project is acceptable if its NPV is positive. For mutually exclusive projects, the project with the largest NPV is chosen. There are three steps in selecting the best project from several competing projects: (1) assessing the cash flow pattern for each project, (2) computing the NPV for each project, and (3) identifying the project with the greatest NPV. To illustrate NPV analysis for competing projects, an example is provided.

Example: Mutually Exclusive Projects

Bintley Corporation has committed to improve its environmental performance. One environmental project identified a manufacturing process as being the source of both liquid and gaseous residues. After six months of research activity, the engineering department announced that it is possible to redesign the process to prevent the production of contaminating residues. Two different process designs (A and B) are being considered that prevent the production of contaminants. Both process designs are more expensive to operate than the current process; however, because the designs prevent production of contaminants, significant annual benefits are created. These benefits stem from eliminating the need to operate and maintain expensive pollution control equipment, treat and dispose of toxic liquid wastes, and pay the annual fines for exceeding allowable contaminant releases. Increased sales to environmentally conscious customers also are factored into the benefit estimates. Cornerstone 12-5 shows how NPV and IRR analyses are carried out for this setting.

Based on NPV analysis, Design B is more profitable; it has the larger NPV. Accordingly, the company should select Design B over Design A. Interestingly, Designs A and B have identical internal rates of return. As shown by Cornerstone 12-5, both designs have a discount factor of 3.000. From Exhibit 12B-2, it is easily seen that a discount factor of 3.000 and a life of five years yields an IRR of about 20 percent. Even though both projects have an IRR of 20 percent, the firm should not consider the two designs to be equally desirable. The analysis demonstrates that Design B produces a larger NPV and, therefore, will increase the value of the firm more than Design A. Design B should be chosen. This illustrates the conceptual superiority of NPV over IRR for analysis of competing projects.

HOW TO Calculate Net Present Value and Internal Rate of Return for Mutually Exclusive Projects

**CORNERSTONE
12-5**

Information: Consider two pollution prevention designs: Design A and Design B. Both designs have a project life of five years. Design A requires an initial outlay of $180,000 and has a net annual after-tax cash inflow of $60,000 (revenues of $180,000 minus costs of $120,000). Design B, with an initial outlay of $210,000, has a net annual cash inflow of $70,000 ($240,000 – $170,000). The after-tax cash flows are summarized as follows:

CASH FLOW PATTERN

Year	Design A	Design B
0	$(180,000)	$(210,000)
1	60,000	70,000
2	60,000	70,000
3	60,000	70,000
4	60,000	70,000
5	60,000	70,000

The cost of capital for the company is 12 percent.

Required: Calculate the NPV and the IRR for each project.

Calculation:

DESIGN A: NPV ANALYSIS

Year	Cash Flow	Discount Factor*	Present Value
0	$(180,000)	1.000	$(180,000)
1–5	60,000	3.605	216,300
Net present value			$ 36,300

DESIGN A: IRR ANALYSIS

Discount factor = Initial investment/Annual cash flow
= $180,000/$60,000
= 3.000

From Exhibit 12B-2, *df* = 3.000 for five years implies that IRR = 20 percent.

DESIGN B: NPV ANALYSIS

Year	Cash Flow	Discount Factor*	Present Value
0	$(210,000)	1.000	$(210,000)
1–5	70,000	3.605	252,350
Net present value			$ 42,350

DESIGN B: IRR ANALYSIS

Discount factor = Initial investment/Annual cash flow
= $210,000/$70,000
= 3.000

From Exhibit 12B-2, *df* = 3.000 for five years implies that IRR = 20 percent.

*From Exhibit 12B-2.

Here's The Real Kicker

During the period of 2001–03, Stillwater Designs experienced high sales of their Kicker products. As a consequence, the levels of inventory filled all storage areas to capacity. Consequently, Stillwater Designs began plans to add another building on existing property with 50,000 square feet of capacity. This new facility had an estimated construction cost between $1 and $1.5 million. During this preliminary planning phase, a shipping strike placed extra storage demands on existing facilities, and Stillwater Designs began looking for a warehousing facility that could be leased on a short-term basis.

They identified a large 250,000-square-foot facility, housed on 22 acres, that was owned by Moore Business Forms. This facility not only was an attractive leasing option, but it also quickly became a competing alternative to adding the 50,000-square-foot facility to Stillwater's current complex of buildings. In fact, the company began looking at the possibility of buying and renovating the Moore facility and moving all of its operations into the one facility. Renovation required such actions as installing a new HVAC system, bringing the building up to current fire codes, painting and resealing the floor, and adding a large number of offices. After careful financial analysis, Stillwater Designs decided that the buy-and-renovate option was more profitable than adding the 50,000-square-foot building to its current complex of buildings. Two economic factors affecting the decision were: (1) Selling the current complex of five buildings would help pay for the needed renovations; and (2) The purchase cost of the nonrenovated Moore facility was less than the cost of building the 50,000-square-foot facility.

Special Considerations for the Advanced Manufacturing Environment

How Investment Differs

Investment in automated manufacturing processes is much more complex than investment in the standard manufacturing equipment of the past. For standard equipment, the direct costs of acquisition represent virtually the entire investment. For automated manufacturing, the direct costs can represent as little as 50 or 60 percent of the total investment; software, engineering, training, and implementation are a significant percentage of the total costs. Thus, great care must be exercised to assess the actual cost of an automated system. It is easy to overlook the peripheral costs, which can be substantial.

How Estimates of Operating Cash Flows Differ

Estimates of operating cash flows from investments in standard equipment typically have relied on directly identifiable tangible benefits, such as direct savings from labor, power, and scrap. However, when investing in automated systems, the intangible and indirect benefits can be material and critical to the viability of the project. Greater quality, more reliability, reduced lead time, improved customer satisfaction, and an enhanced ability to maintain market share all are important intangible benefits of an advanced manufacturing system. Reduction of labor in support areas such as production scheduling and stores are indirect benefits. More effort is needed to measure these intangible and indirect benefits in order to assess more accurately the potential value of investments.

An example can be used to illustrate the importance of considering intangible and indirect benefits. Consider a company that is evaluating a potential investment in a flexible manufacturing system (FMS). The choice facing the company is to continue producing with its traditional equipment, expected to last 10 years, or to switch to the new system, which also is expected to have a useful life of 10 years. The company's discount rate is 12 percent. The data pertaining to the investment are presented in Exhibit 12-2. Notice that for this example, the *incremental cash flows* are used to compare the new project with the old. Instead of calculating the NPV for each alternative and comparing, an equivalent approach is to calculate the NPV of the incremental cash flows of the new system (cash flows of new system less cash flows of old system). If the NPV for the incremental cash flows is positive, then the new equipment is preferred to the old.

Using the incremental data in Exhibit 12-2, the NPV of the proposed system can be computed as follows:

Present value ($4,000,000 × 5.650*)	$22,600,000
Investment	18,000,000
NPV	$ 4,600,000

*This number is the discount factor for an interest rate of 12 percent and a life of 10 years (see Exhibit 12B-2).

The NPV is positive and large in magnitude, and it clearly signals the acceptability of the FMS. This outcome, however, is strongly dependent on explicit recognition of both intangible and indirect benefits. If those benefits are eliminated, then the direct savings total $2.2 million, and the NPV is negative:

Present value ($2,200,000 × 5.650)	$12,430,000
Investment	18,000,000
NPV	$ (5,570,000)

The rise of activity-based costing has made identifying indirect benefits easier with the use of cost drivers. Once they are identified, they can be included in the analysis if they are material.

Examination of Exhibit 12-2 reveals the importance of intangible benefits. One of the most important intangible benefits is maintaining or improving a firm's competitive position. A key question is what will happen to the cash flows of the firm if the investment is not made. That is, if the company chooses to forego an investment in technologically advanced equipment, will it be able to continue to compete with other firms on the basis of quality, delivery, and cost? (The question becomes especially relevant if competitors

---

Exhibit 12-2

Investment Data; Direct, Intangible, and Indirect Benefits

	FMS	Status Quo
Investment (current outlay):		
Direct costs	$10,000,000	—
Software, engineering	8,000,000	—
Total current outlay	$18,000,000	$ 0
Net after-tax cash flow	$ 5,000,000	$1,000,000
Less: After-tax cash flows for status quo	1,000,000	n/a
Incremental benefit	$ 4,000,000	n/a
Incremental Benefit Explained		
Direct benefits:		
Direct labor	$ 1,500,000	
Scrap reduction	500,000	
Setups	200,000	$2,200,000
Intangible benefits (quality savings):		
Rework	$ 200,000	
Warranties	400,000	
Maintenance of competitive position	1,000,000	1,600,000
Indirect benefits:		
Production scheduling	$ 110,000	
Payroll	90,000	200,000
Total		$4,000,000

choose to invest in advanced equipment.) If the competitive position deteriorates, the company's current cash flows will decrease.

If cash flows will decrease if the investment is not made, this decrease should show up as an incremental benefit for the advanced technology. In Exhibit 12-2, the company estimates this competitive benefit as $1,000,000. Estimating this benefit requires some serious strategic planning and analysis, but its effect can be critical. If this benefit had been ignored or overlooked, then the NPV would have been negative and the investment alternative rejected:

Present value ($3,000,000 × 5.650)	$ 16,950,000
Investment	18,000,000
NPV	$ (1,050,000)

Summary of Learning Objectives

1. Explain the meaning of *capital investment decisions*, and distinguish between independent and mutually exclusive capital investment decisions.
    *   Capital investment decisions are concerned with the acquisition of long-term assets and usually involve a significant outlay of funds
    *   The two types of capital investment projects are independent and mutually exclusive.
    *   Independent projects are projects that, whether accepted or rejected, do not affect the cash flows of other projects.
    *   Mutually exclusive projects are those projects that, if accepted, preclude the acceptance of all other competing projects.
2. Compute the payback period and accounting rate of return for a proposed investment, and explain their roles in capital investment decisions.
    *   Managers make capital investment decisions by using formal models to decide whether to accept or reject proposed projects.
    *   These decision models are classified as nondiscounting and discounting, depending on whether they address the question of the time value of money.
    *   The two nondiscounting models are the payback period and the ARR.
    *   The payback period is the time required for a firm to recover its initial investment. For even cash flows, it is calculated by dividing the investment by the annual cash flow. For uneven cash flows, the cash flows are summed until the investment is recovered. If only a fraction of a year is needed, then it is assumed that the cash flows occur evenly within each year.
    *   The payback period ignores the time value of money and the profitability of projects because it does not consider the cash inflows available beyond the payback period. However, it does supply some useful information. The payback period is useful for assessing and controlling risk, minimizing the impact of an investment on a firm's liquidity, and controlling the risk of obsolescence.
    *   The ARR is computed by dividing the average income expected from an investment by either the original or average investment.
    *   Unlike the payback period, the ARR does consider the profitability of a project; however, it ignores the time value of money.
    *   The ARR may be useful to managers for screening new investments to ensure that certain accounting ratios are not adversely affected (specifically, accounting ratios that may be monitored to ensure compliance with debt covenants).

3. Use net present value analysis for capital investment decisions involving independent projects.
   - NPV is the difference between the present value of future cash flows and the initial investment outlay.
   - To use the NPV model, a required rate of return must be identified (usually the cost of capital). The NPV method uses the required rate of return to compute the present value of a project's cash inflows and outflows.
   - If the present value of the inflows is greater than the present value of the outflows, then the NPV is greater than zero, and the project is profitable; if the NPV is less than zero, then the project is not profitable and should be rejected.
4. Use the internal rate of return to assess the acceptability of independent projects.
   - The IRR is computed by finding the interest rate that equates the present value of a project's cash inflows with the present value of its cash outflows.
   - If the IRR is greater than the required rate of return (cost of capital), then the project is acceptable; if the IRR is less than the required rate of return, then the project should be rejected.
5. Explain the role and value of postaudits.
   - Postauditing of capital projects is an important step in capital investment.
   - Postaudits evaluate the actual performance of a project in relation to its expected performance.
   - A postaudit may lead to corrective action to improve the performance of the project or to abandon it.
   - Postaudits also serve as an incentive for managers to make capital investment decisions prudently.
6. Explain why net present value is better than internal rate of return for capital investment decisions involving mutually exclusive projects.
   - In evaluating mutually exclusive or competing projects, managers have a choice of using NPV or IRR.
   - When choosing among competing projects, the NPV model correctly identifies the best investment alternative.
   - IRR, at times, may choose an inferior project. Thus, since NPV always provides the correct signal, it should be used.

Summary of Important Equations

1. $NPV = [\sum CF_t/(1 + i)^t] - I$
   $= [\sum CF_t df_t] - I$
   $= P - I$

2. $I = \sum CF_t/(1 + i)^t$

CORNERSTONES FOR CHAPTER 12

Cornerstone 12-1 How to calculate payback, page 512

Cornerstone 12-2 How to calculate the accounting rate of return, page 514

Cornerstone 12-3 How to assess cash flows and calculate net present value, page 516

Cornerstone 12-4 How to calculate internal rate of return with uniform cash flows, page 518

Cornerstone 12-5 How to calculate net present value and internal rate of return for mutually exclusive projects, page 523

Key Terms

Accounting rate of return, 514

Capital budgeting, 510

Capital investment decisions, 510

Cost of capital, 515

Discounted cash flows, 514

Discounting models, 511

Independent projects, 510

Internal rate of return, 517

Mutually exclusive projects, 510

Net present value, 515

Nondiscounting models, 511

Payback period, 512

Postaudit, 519

Required rate of return, 515

Appendix: Present Value Concepts

An important feature of money is that it can be invested and can earn interest. A dollar today is not the same as a dollar tomorrow. This fundamental principle is the backbone of discounting methods. Discounting methods rely on the relationships between current and future dollars. Thus, to use discounting methods, we must understand these relationships.

Future Value

Suppose that a bank advertises a 4-percent annual interest rate. If a customer invests $100, he or she would receive, after one year, the original $100 plus $4 interest [$100 + (0.04)($100)] = (1 + 0.04)$100 = (1.04)($100) = $104. This result can be expressed by the following equation, where F is the future amount, P is the initial or current outlay, and i is the interest rate:

$$F = P(1 + i)$$

For the example, $F = \$100(1 + 0.04) = \$100(1.04) = \$104$.

Now suppose that the same bank offers a 5-percent rate if the customer leaves the original deposit, plus any interest, on deposit for a total of two years. How much will the customer receive at the end of two years? Again assume that a customer invests $100. Using the future value equation, the customer will earn $105 at the end of year 1 [$F = \$100(1 + 0.05) = (\$100 \times 1.05) = \$105$]. If this amount is left in the account for a second year, this equation is used again with P now assumed to be $105. At the end of the second year, then, the total is $110.25 [$F = \$105(1 + 0.05) = (\$105 \times 1.05) = \$110.25$]. In the second year, interest is earned on both the original deposit and the interest earned in the first year. The earning of interest on interest is referred to as **compounding of interest**. The value that will accumulate by the end of an investment's life, assuming a specified compound return, is the **future value**. The future value of the $100 deposit in the second example is $110.25.

A more direct way to compute the future value is possible. Since the first application of the future value equation can be expressed as $F = \$105 = \$100(1.05)$, the second application can be expressed as $F = \$105(1.05) = \$100(1.05)(1.05) = \$100(1.05)^2 = P(1 + i)^2$. This suggests the following compounding interest formula for computing amounts for n periods into the future:

$$F = P(1 + i)^n$$

Present Value

Often, a manager needs to compute not the future value but the amount that must be invested now in order to yield some given future value. The amount that must be invested now to produce the future value is known as the **present value** of the future amount. For example, how much must be invested now in order to yield $363 two years from now, assuming that the interest rate is 10 percent? Or, put another way, what is the present value of $363 to be received two years from now?

In this example, the future value, the years, and the interest rate are all known; we want to know the current outlay that will produce that future amount. In the compounding interest equation, the variable representing the current outlay (the present value of F) is P. Thus, to compute the present value of a future outlay, all we need to do is solve the compounding interest equation for P:

$$P = F/(1 + i)^n$$

Using this present value equation, we can compute the present value of $363:

$$P = \$363/(1 + 0.1)^2$$
$$= \$363/1.21$$
$$= \$300$$

The present value, $300, is what the future amount of $363 is worth today. All other things being equal, having $300 today is the same as having $363 two years from now. Put another way, if a firm requires a 10-percent rate of return, the most the firm would be willing to pay today is $300 for any investment that yields $363 two years from now.

The process of computing the present value of future cash flows is often referred to as **discounting**; thus, we say that we have discounted the future value of $363 to its present value of $300. The interest rate used to discount the future cash flow is the **discount rate**. The expression $1/(1 + i)^n$ in the present value equation is the **discount factor**. By letting the discount factor, called df, equal $1/(1 + i)^n$, the present value equation can be expressed as $P = F(df)$. To simplify the computation of present value, a table of discount factors is given for various combinations of i and n (refer to Exhibit 12B-1 in Appendix 12B). For example, the discount factor for $i = 10$ percent and $n = 2$ is 0.826 (go to the 10-percent column of the table and move down to the second row). With the discount factor, the present value of $363 is computed as follows:

$$P = F(df)$$
$$= \$363 \times 0.826$$
$$= \$300 \text{ (rounded)}$$

Present Value of an Uneven Series of Cash Flows

Exhibit 12B-1 can be used to compute the present value of any future cash flow or series of future cash flows. A series of future cash flows is called an **annuity**. The present value of an annuity is found by computing the present value of each future cash flow and then summing these values. For example, suppose that an investment is expected to produce the following annual cash flows: $110, $121, and $123.10. Assuming a discount rate of 10 percent, the present value of this series of cash flows is computed in Exhibit 12A-1.

Present Value of a Uniform Series of Cash Flows

If the series of cash flows is even, the computation of the annuity's present value is simplified. For example, assume that an investment is expected to return $100 per year for three years. Using Exhibit 12B-1 and assuming a discount rate of 10 percent, the present value of the annuity is computed in Exhibit 12A-2.

Exhibit 12A-1

Present Value of an Uneven Series of Cash Flows

Year	Cash Receipt	Discount Factor	Present Value*
1	$110.00	0.909	$100.00
2	121.00	0.826	100.00
3	133.10	0.751	100.00
			$300.00

*Rounded.

Exhibit 12A-2

Present Value of an Annuity

Year	Cash Receipt*	Discount Factor	Present Value*
1	$100	0.909	$ 90.90
2	100	0.826	82.60
3	100	0.751	75.10
		2.486	$248.60

*The annual cash flow of $100 can be multiplied by the sum of the discount factors (2.486) to obtain the present value of the uniform series ($248.60).

As with the uneven series of cash flows, the present value in Exhibit 12A-2 was computed by calculating the present value of each cash flow separately and then summing them. However, in the case of an annuity displaying uniform cash flows, the computations can be reduced from three to one as described in the footnote to the exhibit. The sum of the individual discount factors can be thought of as a discount factor for an annuity of uniform cash flows. A table of discount factors that can be used for an annuity of uniform cash flows is available in Exhibit 12B-2.

The present value tables are found on pages 531 and 532.

Appendix Key Terms

Annuity, 529
Compounding of interest, 528
Discount factor, 529
Discount rate, 529

Discounting, 529
Future value, 528
Present value, 528

Exhibit 12B-1

Present Value of $1*

Periods	2%	4%	6%	8%	10%	12%	14%	16%	18%	20%	22%	24%	26%	28%	30%	32%	40%
1	0.980	0.962	0.943	0.926	0.909	0.893	0.877	0.862	0.847	0.833	0.820	0.806	0.794	0.781	0.769	0.758	0.714
2	0.961	0.925	0.890	0.857	0.826	0.797	0.769	0.743	0.718	0.694	0.672	0.650	0.630	0.610	0.592	0.574	0.510
3	0.942	0.889	0.840	0.794	0.751	0.712	0.675	0.641	0.609	0.579	0.551	0.524	0.500	0.477	0.455	0.435	0.364
4	0.924	0.855	0.792	0.735	0.683	0.636	0.592	0.552	0.516	0.482	0.451	0.423	0.397	0.373	0.350	0.329	0.260
5	0.906	0.822	0.747	0.681	0.621	0.567	0.519	0.476	0.437	0.402	0.370	0.341	0.315	0.291	0.269	0.250	0.186
6	0.888	0.790	0.705	0.630	0.564	0.507	0.456	0.410	0.370	0.335	0.303	0.275	0.250	0.227	0.207	0.189	0.133
7	0.871	0.760	0.665	0.583	0.513	0.452	0.400	0.354	0.314	0.279	0.249	0.222	0.198	0.178	0.159	0.143	0.095
8	0.853	0.731	0.627	0.540	0.467	0.404	0.351	0.305	0.266	0.233	0.204	0.179	0.157	0.139	0.123	0.108	0.068
9	0.837	0.703	0.592	0.500	0.424	0.361	0.308	0.263	0.225	0.194	0.167	0.144	0.125	0.108	0.094	0.082	0.048
10	0.820	0.676	0.558	0.463	0.386	0.322	0.270	0.227	0.191	0.162	0.137	0.116	0.099	0.085	0.073	0.062	0.035
11	0.804	0.650	0.527	0.429	0.350	0.287	0.237	0.195	0.162	0.135	0.112	0.094	0.079	0.066	0.056	0.047	0.025
12	0.788	0.625	0.497	0.397	0.319	0.257	0.208	0.168	0.137	0.112	0.092	0.076	0.062	0.052	0.043	0.036	0.018
13	0.773	0.601	0.469	0.368	0.290	0.229	0.182	0.145	0.116	0.093	0.075	0.061	0.050	0.040	0.033	0.027	0.013
14	0.758	0.577	0.442	0.340	0.263	0.205	0.160	0.125	0.099	0.078	0.062	0.049	0.039	0.032	0.025	0.021	0.009
15	0.743	0.555	0.417	0.315	0.239	0.183	0.140	0.108	0.084	0.065	0.051	0.040	0.031	0.025	0.020	0.016	0.006
16	0.728	0.534	0.394	0.292	0.218	0.163	0.123	0.093	0.071	0.054	0.042	0.032	0.025	0.019	0.015	0.012	0.005
17	0.714	0.513	0.371	0.270	0.198	0.146	0.108	0.080	0.060	0.045	0.034	0.026	0.020	0.015	0.012	0.009	0.003
18	0.700	0.494	0.350	0.250	0.180	0.130	0.095	0.069	0.051	0.038	0.028	0.021	0.016	0.012	0.009	0.007	0.002
19	0.686	0.475	0.331	0.232	0.164	0.116	0.083	0.060	0.043	0.031	0.023	0.017	0.012	0.009	0.007	0.005	0.002
20	0.673	0.456	0.312	0.215	0.149	0.104	0.073	0.051	0.037	0.026	0.019	0.014	0.010	0.007	0.005	0.004	0.001
21	0.660	0.439	0.294	0.199	0.135	0.093	0.064	0.044	0.031	0.022	0.015	0.011	0.008	0.006	0.004	0.003	0.001
22	0.647	0.422	0.278	0.184	0.123	0.083	0.056	0.038	0.026	0.018	0.013	0.009	0.006	0.004	0.003	0.002	0.001
23	0.634	0.406	0.262	0.170	0.112	0.074	0.049	0.033	0.022	0.015	0.010	0.007	0.005	0.003	0.002	0.002	0.001
24	0.622	0.390	0.247	0.158	0.102	0.066	0.043	0.028	0.019	0.013	0.008	0.006	0.004	0.003	0.002	0.001	0.000
25	0.610	0.375	0.233	0.146	0.092	0.059	0.038	0.024	0.016	0.010	0.007	0.005	0.003	0.002	0.001	0.001	0.000
26	0.598	0.361	0.220	0.135	0.084	0.053	0.033	0.021	0.014	0.009	0.006	0.004	0.002	0.002	0.001	0.001	0.000
27	0.586	0.347	0.207	0.125	0.076	0.047	0.029	0.018	0.011	0.007	0.005	0.003	0.002	0.001	0.001	0.001	0.000
28	0.574	0.333	0.196	0.116	0.069	0.042	0.026	0.016	0.010	0.006	0.004	0.002	0.002	0.001	0.001	0.000	0.000
29	0.563	0.321	0.185	0.107	0.063	0.037	0.022	0.014	0.008	0.005	0.003	0.002	0.001	0.001	0.000	0.000	0.000
30	0.552	0.308	0.174	0.099	0.057	0.033	0.020	0.012	0.007	0.004	0.003	0.002	0.001	0.001	0.000	0.000	0.000

$*P_n = A/(1 + i)^a$

Exhibit 12B-2

Present Value of an Annuity of $1 in Arrears*

Periods	2%	4%	6%	8%	10%	12%	14%	16%	18%	20%	22%	24%	26%	28%	30%	32%	40%
1	0.980	0.962	0.943	0.926	0.909	0.893	0.877	0.862	0.847	0.833	0.820	0.806	0.794	0.781	0.769	0.758	0.714
2	1.942	1.886	1.833	1.783	1.736	1.690	1.647	1.605	1.566	1.528	1.492	1.457	1.424	1.392	1.361	1.331	1.224
3	2.884	2.775	2.673	2.577	2.487	2.402	2.322	2.246	2.174	2.106	2.042	1.981	1.923	1.868	1.816	1.766	1.589
4	3.808	3.630	3.465	3.312	3.170	3.037	2.914	2.798	2.690	2.589	2.494	2.404	2.320	2.241	2.166	2.096	1.849
5	4.713	4.452	4.212	3.993	3.791	3.605	3.433	3.274	3.127	2.991	2.864	2.745	2.635	2.532	2.436	2.345	2.035
6	5.601	5.242	4.917	4.623	4.355	4.111	3.889	3.685	3.498	3.326	3.167	3.020	2.885	2.759	2.643	2.534	2.168
7	6.472	6.002	5.582	5.206	4.868	4.564	4.288	4.039	3.812	3.605	3.416	3.242	3.083	2.937	2.802	2.677	2.263
8	7.325	6.733	6.210	5.747	5.335	4.968	4.639	4.344	4.078	3.837	3.619	3.421	3.241	3.076	2.925	2.786	2.331
9	8.162	7.435	6.802	6.247	5.759	5.328	4.946	4.607	4.303	4.031	3.876	3.566	3.366	3.184	3.019	2.868	2.379
10	8.983	8.111	7.360	6.710	6.145	5.650	5.216	4.833	4.494	4.192	3.923	3.682	3.465	3.269	3.092	2.930	2.414
11	9.787	8.760	7.887	7.139	6.495	5.938	5.453	5.029	4.656	4.327	4.035	3.776	3.543	3.335	3.147	2.978	2.438
12	10.575	9.385	8.384	7.536	6.814	6.194	5.660	5.197	4.793	4.439	4.127	3.851	3.606	3.387	3.190	3.013	2.456
13	11.348	9.986	8.853	7.904	7.103	6.424	5.842	5.342	4.910	4.533	4.203	3.912	3.656	3.427	3.223	3.040	2.469
14	12.106	10.563	9.295	8.244	7.367	6.628	6.002	5.468	5.008	4.611	4.265	3.962	3.695	3.459	3.249	3.061	2.478
15	12.849	11.118	9.712	8.559	7.606	6.811	6.142	5.575	5.092	4.675	4.315	4.001	3.726	3.483	3.268	3.076	2.484
16	13.578	11.652	10.106	8.851	7.824	6.974	6.265	5.668	5.162	4.730	4.357	4.033	3.751	3.503	3.283	3.088	2.489
17	14.292	12.166	10.477	9.122	8.022	7.120	6.373	5.749	5.222	4.775	4.391	4.059	3.771	3.518	3.295	3.097	2.492
18	14.992	12.659	10.828	9.372	8.201	7.250	6.467	5.818	5.273	4.812	4.419	4.080	3.786	3.529	3.304	3.104	2.494
19	15.678	13.134	11.158	9.604	8.365	7.366	6.550	5.877	5.316	4.843	4.442	4.097	3.799	3.539	3.311	3.109	2.496
20	16.351	13.590	11.470	9.818	8.514	7.469	6.623	5.929	5.353	4.870	4.460	4.110	3.808	3.546	3.316	3.113	2.497
21	17.011	14.029	11.764	10.017	8.649	7.562	6.687	5.973	5.384	4.891	4.476	4.121	3.816	3.551	3.320	3.116	2.498
22	17.658	14.451	12.042	10.201	8.772	7.645	6.743	6.011	5.410	4.909	4.488	4.130	3.822	3.556	3.323	3.118	2.498
23	18.292	14.857	12.303	10.371	8.883	7.718	6.792	6.044	5.432	4.925	4.499	4.137	3.827	3.559	3.325	3.120	2.499
24	18.914	15.247	12.550	10.529	8.985	7.784	6.835	6.073	5.451	4.937	4.507	4.143	3.831	3.562	3.327	3.121	2.499
25	19.523	15.622	12.783	10.675	9.077	7.843	6.873	6.097	5.467	4.948	4.514	4.147	3.834	3.564	3.329	3.122	2.499
26	20.121	15.983	13.003	10.810	9.161	7.896	6.906	6.118	5.480	4.956	4.520	4.151	3.837	3.566	3.330	3.123	2.500
27	20.707	16.330	13.211	10.935	9.237	7.943	6.935	6.136	5.492	4.964	4.524	4.154	3.839	3.567	3.331	3.123	2.500
28	21.281	16.663	13.406	11.051	9.307	7.984	6.961	6.152	5.502	4.970	4.528	4.157	3.840	3.568	3.331	3.124	2.500
29	21.844	16.984	13.591	11.158	9.370	8.022	6.983	6.166	5.510	4.975	4.531	4.159	3.841	3.569	3.332	3.124	2.500
30	22.396	17.292	13.765	11.258	9.427	8.055	7.003	6.177	5.517	4.979	4.534	4.160	3.842	3.569	3.332	3.124	2.500

*$P_n = (1/i)[1 - 1/(1 + i)^n]$

Review Problems

I. Basics of Capital Investment

Kenn Day, manager of Day Laboratory, is investigating the possibility of acquiring some new test equipment. To acquire the equipment requires an initial outlay of $300,000. To raise the capital, Kenn will sell stock valued at $200,000 (the stock pays dividends of $24,000 per year) and borrow $100,000. The loan for $100,000 would carry an interest rate of 6 percent. Kenn figures that his weighted average cost of capital is 10 percent $[(2/3 \times 0.12) + (1/3 \times 0.06)]$. This weighted cost of capital is the discount rate that will be used for capital investment decisions.

Kenn estimates that the new test equipment will produce a cash inflow of $50,000 per year. Kenn expects the equipment to last for 20 years.

Required:

1. Compute the payback period.
2. Assuming that depreciation is $14,000 per year, compute the ARR (on total investment).
3. Compute the NPV of the test equipment.
4. Compute the IRR of the test equipment.
5. Should Kenn buy the equipment?

Solution:

1. The payback period is $300,000/$50,000, or six years.
2. The ARR is ($50,000 − $14,000)/$300,000, or 12 percent.
3. From Exhibit 12B-2, the discount factor for an annuity with i at 10 percent and n at 20 years is 8.514. Thus, the NPV is (8.514 × $50,000) − $300,000, or $125,700.
4. The discount factor associated with the IRR is 6.00 ($300,000/$50,000). From Exhibit 12B-2, the IRR is between 14 and 16 percent (using the row corresponding to period 20).
5. Since the NPV is positive and the IRR is greater than Kenn's cost of capital, the test equipment is a sound investment. This, of course, assumes that the cash flow projections are accurate.

II. Capital Investments with Competing Projects.

A hospital is considering the possibility of two new purchases: new x-ray equipment and new biopsy equipment. Each project would require an investment of $750,000. The expected life for each is five years with no expected salvage value. The net cash inflows associated with the two independent projects are as follows:

Year	X-Ray Equipment	Sonogram Equipment
1	$375,000	$ 75,000
2	150,000	75,000
3	300,000	525,000
4	150,000	600,000
5	75,000	675,000

Required:

1. Compute the net present value of each project, assuming a required rate of 12 percent.
2. Compute the payback period for each project. Assume that the manager of the hospital accepts only projects with a payback period of three years or less. Offer some

reasons why this may be a rational strategy even though the NPV computed in Requirement 1 may indicate otherwise.

Solution:

1. X-ray equipment:

Year	Cash Flow	Discount Factor	Present Value
0	$(750,000)	1.000	$ (750,000)
1	375,000	0.893	334,875
2	150,000	0.797	119,550
3	300,000	0.712	213,600
4	150,000	0.636	95,400
5	75,000	0.567	42,525
NPV			$ 55,950

Biopsy equipment:

Year	Cash Flow	Discount Factor	Present Value
0	$(750,000)	1.000	$ (750,000)
1	75,000	0.893	66,975
2	75,000	0.797	59,775
3	525,000	0.712	373,800
4	600,000	0.636	381,600
5	675,000	0.567	382,725
NPV			$ 514,875

2. X-ray equipment:

Payback period =	$ 375,000	1.00 year
	150,000	1.00
	225,000	0.75 ($225,000/$300,000)
	$ 750,000	2.75 years

Biopsy equipment:

Payback period =	$ 75,000	1.00 year
	75,000	1.00
	525,000	1.00
	75,000	0.13 ($75,000/$600,000)
	$ 750,000	3.13 years

This might be a reasonable strategy because payback is a rough measure of risk. The assumption is that the longer it takes a project to pay for itself, the riskier the project is. Other reasons might be that the firm might have liquidity problems, the cash flows might be risky, or there might be a high risk of obsolescence.

Discussion Questions

1. Explain the difference between independent projects and mutually exclusive projects.
2. Explain why the timing and quantity of cash flows are important in capital investment decisions.
3. The time value of money is ignored by the payback period and the ARR. Explain why this is a major deficiency in these two models.
4. What is the payback period? Compute the payback period for an investment requiring an initial outlay of $80,000 with expected annual cash inflows of $30,000.
5. Name and discuss three possible reasons that the payback period is used to help make capital investment decisions.

6. What is the ARR? Compute the ARR for an investment that requires an initial outlay of $300,000 and promises an average net income of $100,000.

7. The NPV is the same as the profit of a project expressed in present dollars. Do you agree? Explain.

8. Explain the relationship between NPV and a firm's value.

9. What is the cost of capital? What role does it play in capital investment decisions?

10. What is the role that the required rate of return plays in the NPV model? In the IRR model?

11. Explain how the NPV is used to determine whether a project should be accepted or rejected.

12. The IRR is the true or actual rate of return being earned by the project. Do you agree or disagree? Discuss.

13. Explain what a postaudit is and how it can provide useful input for future capital investment decisions, especially those involving advanced technology.

14. Explain why NPV is generally preferred over IRR when choosing among competing or mutually exclusive projects. Why would managers continue to use IRR to choose among mutually exclusive projects?

15. Suppose that a firm must choose between two mutually exclusive projects, both of which have negative NPVs. Explain how a firm can legitimately choose between two such projects.

Multiple-Choice Exercises

12-1 Capital investments should

a. earn back their original capital outlay.
b. only be analyzed using the ARR.
c. always produce an increase in market share.
d. always be done using a payback criterion.
e. do none of the above.

12-2 To make a capital investment decision, a manager must

a. estimate the quantity and timing of cash flows.
b. assess the risk of the investment.
c. consider the impact of the investment on the firm's profits.
d. select investments with a positive NPV.
e. do all of the above.

12-3 Mutually exclusive capital budgeting projects are those that

a. if accepted or rejected do not affect the cash flows of other projects.
b. if accepted will produce a negative NPV.
c. if accepted preclude the acceptance of all other competing projects.
d. if rejected preclude the acceptance of all other competing projects.
e. if rejected imply that all other competing projects have a positive NPV.

12-4 An investment of $1,000 produces a net annual cash inflow of $500 for each of five years. What is the payback period?

a. Two years
b. One-half year
c. Unacceptable
d. Three years
e. Cannot be determined

12-5 An investment of $1,000 produces a net cash inflow of $600 in the first year and $2,000 in the second year. What is the payback period?

a. 1.67 years
b. 0.50 year
c. 2.00 years
d. 1.20 years
e. Cannot be determined

12-6 The payback period suffers from which of the following deficiencies?

a. It is a rough measure of the uncertainty of future cash flows.
b. It helps control the risk of obsolescence.
c. It ignores the time value of money.
d. It ignores the financial performance of a project beyond the payback period.
e. Both c and d.

12-7 The accounting rate of return has one specific advantage not possessed by the payback period in that it

a. considers the time value of money.
b. measures the value added by a project.
c. considers the profitability of a project beyond the payback period.
d. is more widely accepted by financial managers.
e. is always an accurate measure of profitability.

12-8 An investment of $1,000 provides an average net income of $220 with zero salvage value. Depreciation is $20 per year. The accounting rate of return using the original investment is

a. 44 percent.
b. 22 percent.
c. 20 percent.
d. 40 percent.
e. None of the above.

12-9 If the net present value is positive, it signals

a. that the initial investment has been recovered.
b. that the required rate of return has been earned.
c. that the value of the firm has increased.
d. All of the above.
e. Both a and b.

12-10 Net present value measures

a. the profitability of an investment.
b. the change in wealth.
c. the change in firm value.
d. the difference in present value of cash inflows and outflows.
e. All of the above.

12-11 Net present value is calculated by using

a. accounting income.
b. the required rate of return.
c. the IRR.
d. the future value of cash flows.
e. None of the above.

12-12 Using net present value, a project is rejected if it is

a. equal to zero.
b. positive.
c. negative.
d. less than the hurdle rate.
e. greater than the cost of capital.

12-13 If the present value of future cash flows is $1,200 for an investment that requires an outlay of $1,000, the net present value

a. is $200.
b. is $1,000.
c. is $1,200.
d. is $2,200.
e. cannot be determined.

12-14 Assume that an investment of $1,000 produces a future cash flow of $1,000. The discount factor for this future cash flow is 0.89. The net present value is

a. $0.
b. $110.
c. $2,000.
d. $911.
e. None of the above.

12-15 Which of the following is *not* true regarding the internal rate of return?

a. The IRR is the interest rate that sets the present value of a project's cash inflows equal to the present value of the project's cost.
b. The IRR is the interest rate that sets the NPV equal to zero.
c. The IRR is the most reliable of the capital budgeting methods.
d. If the IRR is greater than the required rate of return, then the project is acceptable.
e. The popularity of IRR may be attributable to the fact that it is a rate of return, a concept that is comfortably used by managers.

12-16 Using internal rate of return, a project is rejected if the internal rate of return

a. is less than the required rate of return.
b. is equal to the required rate of return.
c. is greater than the cost of capital.
d. is greater than the required rate of return.
e. produces a NPV equal to zero.

12-17 A postaudit

a. is a follow-up analysis of a capital project, once implemented.
b. compares the actual benefits with the estimated benefits.
c. evaluates the overall outcome of the investment.
d. proposes corrective action, if needed.
e. does all of the above.

12-18 Postaudits of capital projects are useful because

a. they are not very costly.
b. they help to ensure that resources are used wisely.
c. the assumptions underlying the original analyses are often invalidated by changes in the actual working environment.
d. they have no significant limitations.
e. of all of the above.

12-19 For competing projects, net present value is preferred to internal rate of return because

a. maximizing IRR may not maximize the wealth of the owners.
b. in the final analysis, total dollars earned, not relative profitability, are what count.
c. choosing the project with the largest NPV maximizes the wealth of the shareholders.
d. assuming that cash flows are reinvested at the required rate of return is more realistic than assuming that cash flows are reinvested at the computed IRR.
e. of all of the above.

12-20 Assume that there are two competing projects: A and B. Project A has a net present value of $1,000 and an internal rate of return of 15 percent; Project B has a net present value of $800 and an internal rate of return of 20 percent. Which of the following is true?

a. It is not possible to use NPV or IRR to choose between the two projects.
b. Project B should be chosen because it has a higher IRR.
c. Project A should be chosen because it has a higher NPV.
d. Neither project should be chosen.
e. None of the above.

Exercises

OBJECTIVES ① ②

CORNERSTONE 12-1

spreadsheet

Exercise 12-21 Payback Period

Each of the following situations is independent. Assume that all cash flows are after-tax cash flows.

a. Kaylin Hansen has just invested $200,000 in a book and video store. She expects to receive a cash income of $60,000 per year from the investment.
b. Kambry Day has just invested $500,000 in a new biomedical technology. She expects to receive the following cash flows over the next five years: $125,000, $175,000, $250,000, $150,000, and $100,000.
c. Emily Nabors invested in a project that has a payback period of three years. The project brings in $120,000 per year.
d. Joseph Booth invested $250,000 in a project that pays him an even amount per year for five years. The payback period is 2.5 years.

Required:
1. What is the payback period for Kaylin?
2. What is the payback period for Kambry?
3. How much did Emily invest in the project?
4. How much cash does Joseph receive each year?

OBJECTIVES ① ②

CORNERSTONE 12-2

Exercise 12-22 Accounting Rate of Return

Each of the following scenarios is independent. Assume that all cash flows are after-tax cash flows.

a. Cameron Company is considering the purchase of new equipment that will speed up the process for extracting copper. The equipment will cost $1,500,000 and have a life of five years with no expected salvage value. The expected cash flows associated with the project are as follows:

Year	Cash Revenues	Cash Expenses
1	$2,500,000	$2,000,000
2	2,500,000	2,000,000
3	2,500,000	2,000,000
4	2,500,000	2,000,000
5	2,500,000	2,000,000

b. Merlene Jensen is considering investing in one of the following two projects. Either
project will require an investment of $20,000. The expected revenues less cash
expenses for the two projects follow. Assume each project is depreciable.

Year	Project A	Project B
1	$ 6,000	$ 6,000
2	8,000	8,000
3	10,000	12,000
4	20,000	6,000
5	20,000	6,000

c. Suppose that a project has an accounting rate of return of 25 percent (based on
initial investment) and that the average net income of the project is $100,000.
d. Suppose that a project has an accounting rate of return of 50 percent and that the
investment is $200,000.

Required:
1. Compute the ARR on the new equipment that Cameron Company is considering.
2. Which project should Merlene Jensen choose based on the ARR?
3. How much did the company in scenario (c) invest in the project?
4. What is the average income earned by the project in scenario (d)?

Exercise 12-23 Net Present Value

Each of the following scenarios is independent. Assume that all cash flows are after-tax
cash flows.
a. Modinero Bank is considering the purchase of a new automated teller system. The cash
benefits will be $240,000 per year. The system costs $1,360,000 and will last 10 years.
b. Brandon Smith is interested in investing in some tools and equipment so that he
can do independent remodeling. The cost of the tools and equipment is $30,000.
He estimates that the return from owning his own equipment will be $9,000 per
year. The tools and equipment will last six years.
c. Golman Company calculated the NPV of a project and found it to be $3,550. The
project's life was estimated to be six years. The required rate of return used for the
NPV calculation was 10 percent. The project was expected to produce annual after-
tax cash flows of $10,000.

Required:
1. Compute the NPV for Moderino Bank, assuming a discount rate of 12 percent.
Should the bank buy the new automated teller system?
2. Assuming a required rate of return of 8 percent, calculate the NPV for Brandon
Smith's investment. Should he invest?
3. What was the required investment for Golman Company's project?

Exercise 12-24 Internal Rate of Return

Each of the following scenarios is independent. Assume that all cash flows are after-tax
cash flows.
a. Collins Company is considering the purchase of new equipment that will speed up
the process for producing hard disk drives. The equipment will cost $1,563,500
and have a life of five years with no expected salvage value. The expected cash flows
associated with the project follow:

Year	Cash Revenues	Cash Expenses
1	$1,500,000	$1,000,000
2	1,500,000	1,000,000
3	1,500,000	1,000,000
4	1,500,000	1,000,000
5	1,500,000	1,000,000

OBJECTIVES ① ③
CORNERSTONE 12-3

OBJECTIVES ① ④
CORNERSTONE 12-4

b.   Pamela Barker is evaluating an investment in an information system that will save $100,000 per year. She estimates that the system will last 10 years. The system will cost $521,600. Her company's cost of capital is 10 percent.

c.   Wellington Enterprises just announced that a new plant would be built in Wilmington, Delaware. Wellington told its shareholders that the plant has an expected life of 15 years and an expected IRR equal to 24 percent. The cost of building the plant is expected to be $2,400,000.

Required:

1.   Calculate the IRR for Collins Company. The company's cost of capital is 16 percent. Should the new equipment be purchased?

2.   Calculate Pamela Barker's IRR. Should she acquire the new system?

3.   What should be Wellington Enterprises expected annual cash flow from the plant?

OBJECTIVES ① ⑥   **Exercise 12-25 Net Present Value and Competing Projects**

CORNERSTONE 12-5   Heltham Medical Clinic is investigating the possibility of investing in new blood analysis equipment. Two local manufacturers of this equipment are being considered as sources of the equipment. After-tax cash inflows for the two competing projects are as follows:

spreadsheet

Year	Marson Equipment	Lawson Equipment
1	$120,000	$ 20,000
2	100,000	20,000
3	80,000	120,000
4	40,000	160,000
5	20,000	180,000

Both projects require an initial investment of $200,000. In both cases, assume that the equipment has a life of five years with no salvage value.

Required:

1.   Assuming a discount rate of 12 percent, compute the net present value of each piece of equipment.

2.   A third option has surfaced for equipment purchased from an out-of-state supplier. The cost is also $200,000, but this equipment will produce even cash flows over its five-year life. What must be the annual cash flow for this equipment to be selected over the other two? Assume a 12-percent discount rate.

OBJECTIVES ① ② ③ ④   **Exercise 12-26 Payback, Accounting Rate of Return, Net Present Value, Internal Rate of Return**

CORNERSTONE 12-1
CORNERSTONE 12-2   Wheeler Company wants to buy a numerically controlled (NC) machine to be used
CORNERSTONE 12-3   in producing specially machined parts for manufacturers of trenching machines. The out-
CORNERSTONE 12-4   lay required is $800,000. The NC equipment will last five years with no expected salvage value. The expected after-tax cash flows associated with the project follow:

Year	Cash Revenues	Cash Expenses
1	$1,300,000	$1,000,000
2	1,300,000	1,000,000
3	1,300,000	1,000,000
4	1,300,000	1,000,000
5	1,300,000	1,000,000

Required:

1.   Compute the payback period for the NC equipment.

2.   Compute the NC equipment's ARR.

3.   Compute the investment's NPV, assuming a required rate of return of 10 percent.
4.   Compute the investment's IRR.

Exercise 12-27 Payback, Accounting Rate of Return, Present Value, Net Present Value, Internal Rate of Return

OBJECTIVES ① ② ③ ④

CORNERSTONE 12-1
CORNERSTONE 12-2
CORNERSTONE 12-3
CORNERSTONE 12-4

The first two parts are related; the last three are independent of all other parts. Assume that all cash flows are after-tax cash flows.

a.   Randy Willis is considering investing in one of the following two projects. Either project will require an investment of $10,000. The expected cash flows for the two projects follow. Assume that each project is depreciable.

Year	Project A	Project B
1	$ 3,000	$3,000
2	4,000	4,000
3	5,000	6,000
4	10,000	3,000
5	10,000	3,000

b.   Calculate the ARR for each project in Requirement 1 (the expected cash flows are the difference between cash revenues and cash expenses).

c.   Wilma Golding is retiring and has the option to take her retirement as a lump sum of $225,000 or to receive $24,000 per year for 20 years. Wilma's required rate of return is 8 percent.

d.   David Booth is interested in investing in some tools and equipment so that he can do independent dry walling. The cost of the tools and equipment is $20,000. He estimates that the return from owning his own equipment will be $6,000 per year. The tools and equipment will last six years.

e.   Patsy Folson is evaluating what appears to be an attractive opportunity. She is currently the owner of a small manufacturing company and has the opportunity to acquire another small company's equipment that would provide production of a part currently purchased externally. She estimates that the savings from internal production will be $25,000 per year. She estimates that the equipment will last 10 years. The owner is asking $130,400 for the equipment. Her company's cost of capital is 10 percent.

Required:

1   What is the payback period for each of Randy Willis's projects? If rapid payback is important, which project should be chosen? Which would you choose?
2.   Which of Randy's projects should be chosen based on the ARR?
3.   Assuming that Wilma Golding will live for another 20 years, should she take the lump sum or the annuity?
4.   Assuming a required rate of return of 8 percent for David Booth, calculate the NPV of the investment. Should David invest?
5.   Calculate the IRR for Patsy Folson's project. Should Patsy acquire the equipment?

Exercise 12-28 Net Present Value, Basic Concepts

OBJECTIVE ③

CORNERSTONE 12-3

Harmony Company is considering an investment that requires an outlay of $200,000 and promises an after-tax cash inflow one year from now of $231,000. The company's cost of capital is 10 percent.

Required:

1.   Break the $231,000 future cash inflow into three components: (a) the return of the original investment, (b) the cost of capital, and (c) the profit earned on the investment. Now compute the present value of the profit earned on the investment.

2. Compute the NPV of the investment. Compare this with the present value of the profit computed in Requirement 1. What does this tell you about the meaning of NPV?

Exercise 12-29 Solving for Unknowns

Each of the following cases is independent. Assume that all cash flows are after-tax cash flows.

a. Thomas Company is investing $120,000 in a project that will yield a uniform series of cash inflows over the next four years.
b. Video Repair has decided to invest in some new electronic equipment. The equipment will have a three-year life and will produce a uniform series of cash savings. The NPV of the equipment is $1,750, using a discount rate of 8 percent. The IRR is 12 percent.
c. A new lathe costing $60,096 will produce savings of $12,000 per year.
d. The NPV of a project is $3,927. The project has a life of four years and produces the following cash flows:

| Year 1 | $10,000 | Year 3 | $15,000 |
| Year 2 | $12,000 | Year 4 | ? |

The cost of the project is two times the cash flow produced in year 4. The discount rate is 10 percent.

Required:

1. If the internal rate of return is 14 percent for Thomas Company, how much cash inflow per year can be expected?
2. Determine the investment and the amount of cash savings realized each year for Video Repair.
3. For scenario (c), how many years must the lathe last if an IRR of 18 percent is realized?
4. For scenario (d), find the cost of the project and the cash flow for year 4.

Exercise 12-30 Net Present Value versus Internal Rate of Return

A company is thinking about two different modifications to its current manufacturing process. The after-tax cash flows associated with the two investments follow:

Year	Project I	Project II
0	$(100,000)	$(100,000)
1	—	63,857
2	134,560	63,857

The company's cost of capital is 10 percent.

Required:

1. Compute the NPV and the IRR for each investment.
2. Explain why the project with the larger NPV is the correct choice for the company.

Problems

Problem 12-31 Basic Net Present Value Analysis

Camus Blalack, process engineer, knows that the acceptance of a new process design will depend on its economic feasibility. The new process is designed to improve environmental performance. On the negative side, the process design requires new equipment and an infusion of working capital. The equipment will cost $300,000, and its cash operating expenses will total $60,000 per year. The equipment will last for seven years but will need a major overhaul costing $30,000 at the end of the fifth year. At the end of seven years, the equipment will be sold for $24,000. An increase in working capital totaling $30,000 will also be needed at the beginning. This will be recovered at the end of the seven years.

On the positive side, Camus estimates that the new process will save $135,000 per year in environmental costs (fines and cleanup costs avoided). The cost of capital is 10 percent.

Required:

1. Prepare a schedule of cash flows for the proposed project. Assume that there are no income taxes.
2. Compute the NPV of the project. Should the new process design be accepted?

Problem 12-32 Net Present Value Analysis

OBJECTIVES ① ③

Uintah Communications Company is considering the production and marketing of a communications system that will increase the efficiency of messaging for small businesses or branch offices of large companies. Each unit hooked into the system is assigned a mailbox number, which can be matched to a telephone extension number, providing access to messages 24 hours a day. Up to 20 units can be hooked into the system, allowing the delivery of the same message to as many as 20 people. Personal codes can be used to make messages confidential. Furthermore, messages can be reviewed, recorded, cancelled, replied to, or deleted all during the same phone call. Indicators wired to the telephone blink whenever new messages are present.

To produce this product, a $1.1 million investment in new equipment is required. The equipment will last 10 years but will need major maintenance costing $100,000 at the end of its sixth year. The salvage value of the equipment at the end of 10 years is estimated to be $40,000. If this new system is produced, working capital must also be increased by $50,000. This capital will be restored at the end of the product's life cycle, which is estimated to be 10 years. Revenues from the sale of the product are estimated at $1.5 million per year; cash operating expenses are estimated at $1.26 million per year.

Required:

1. Prepare a schedule of cash flows for the proposed project. Assume that there are no income taxes.
2. Assuming that Uintah's cost of capital is 12 percent, compute the project's NPV. Should the product be produced?

Problem 12-33 Basic Internal Rate of Return Analysis

OBJECTIVES ① ④

Lindsey Thompson, owner of Leshow Company, was approached by a local dealer of air-conditioning units. The dealer proposed replacing Leshow's old cooling system with a modern, more efficient system. The cost of the new system was quoted at $96,660, but it would save $20,000 per year in energy costs. The estimated life of the new system is 10 years, with no salvage value expected. Excited over the possibility of saving $20,000 per year and having a more reliable unit, Lindsey requested an analysis of the project's economic viability. All capital projects are required to earn at least the firm's cost of capital, which is 10 percent. There are no income taxes.

Required:

1. Calculate the project's IRR. Should the company acquire the new cooling system?
2. Suppose that energy savings are less than claimed. Calculate the minimum annual cash savings that must be realized for the project to earn a rate equal to the firm's cost of capital.
3. Suppose that the life of the new system is overestimated by two years. Repeat Requirements 1 and 2 under this assumption.
4. Explain the implications of the answers from Requirements 1, 2, and 3.

OBJECTIVES ① ③   **Problem 12-34 Net Present Value, Uncertainty**

Eden Airlines is interested in acquiring a new aircraft to service a new route. The route will be from Dallas to El Paso. The aircraft will fly one round-trip daily except for scheduled maintenance days. There are 15 maintenance days scheduled each year. The seating capacity of the aircraft is 150. Flights are expected to be fully booked. The average revenue per passenger per flight (one-way) is $200. Annual operating costs of the aircraft follow:

Fuel	$1,400,000
Flight personnel	500,000
Food and beverages	100,000
Maintenance	400,000
Other	100,000
Total	$2,500,000

The aircraft will cost $100,000,000 and has an expected life of 20 years. The company requires a 14-percent return. Assume there are no income taxes.

Required:
1. Calculate the NPV for the aircraft. Should the company buy it?
2. In discussing the proposal, the marketing manager for the airline believes that the assumption of 100-percent booking is unrealistic. He believes that the booking rate will be somewhere between 70 percent and 90 percent, with the most likely rate being 80 percent. Recalculate the NPV by using an 80-percent seating capacity. Should the aircraft be purchased?
3. Calculate the average seating rate that would be needed so that NPV will equal zero.
4. Suppose that the price per passenger could be increased by 10 percent without any effect on demand. What is the average seating rate now needed to achieve a NPV equal to zero? What would you now recommend?

OBJECTIVES ① ② ③ ④   **Problem 12-35 Review of Basic Capital Budgeting Procedures**

spreadsheet

Dr. Whitley Avard, a plastic surgeon, had just returned from a conference in which she learned of a new surgical procedure for removing wrinkles around eyes, reducing the time to perform the normal procedure by 50 percent. Given her patient-load pressures, Dr. Avard is excited to try out the new technique. By decreasing the time spent on eye treatments or procedures, she can increase her total revenues by performing more services within a work period. Unfortunately, in order to implement the new procedure, some special equipment costing $74,000 is needed. The equipment has an expected life of four years, with a salvage value of $6,000. Dr. Avard estimates that her cash revenues will increase by the following amounts:

Year	Revenue Increases
1	$19,800
2	27,000
3	32,400
4	32,400

She also expects additional cash expenses amounting to $3,000 per year. The cost of capital is 12 percent. Assume that there are no income taxes.

Required:
1. Compute the payback period for the new equipment.
2. Compute the ARR.
3. Compute the NPV and IRR for the project. Should Dr. Avard purchase the new equipment? Should she be concerned about payback or the ARR in making this decision?

4. Before finalizing her decision, Dr. Avard decided to call two plastic surgeons who had been using the new procedure for the past six months. The conversations revealed a somewhat less glowing report than she received at the conference. The new procedure reduced the time required by about 25 percent rather than the advertised 50 percent. Dr. Avard estimated that the net operating cash flows of the procedure would be cut by one-third because of the extra time and cost involved (salvage value would be unaffected). Using this information, recompute the NPV of the project. What would you now recommend?

Problem 12-36 Net Present Value and Competing Alternatives

OBJECTIVES ① ⑥

Stillwater Designs has been rebuilding 100, 120, and 150 Kicker subwoofers that were returned for warranty action. Customers returning the subwoofers receive a new replacement. The warranty returns are then rebuilt and resold (as seconds). Tent sales are often used to sell the rebuilt speakers. As part of the rebuilding process, the speakers are demagnetized so that metal pieces and shavings can be removed. A demagnetizing (demag) machine is used to achieve this objective. A product design change has made the most recent 150 speakers too tall for the demag machine. They no longer fit in the demag machine.

Stillwater Designs has two alternatives that it is currently considering. First, a new demag machine can be bought that has a different design, eliminating the fit problem. The cost of this machine is $100,000, and it will last five years. Second, Stillwater can keep the current machine and sell the 150 speakers for scrap, using the old demag machine for the 100 and 120 speakers only. A rebuilt speaker sells for $295 and costs $274.65 to rebuild (for materials, labor, and overhead cash outlays). The $274.65 outlay includes the annual operating cash effects of the new demag machine. If not rebuilt, the 150 speakers can be sold for $17 each as scrap. There are 10,000 150 warranty returns per year. Assume that the required rate of return is 10 percent.

Required:
1. Determine which alternative is the best for Stillwater Designs by using NPV analysis.
2. Determine which alternative is best for Stillwater Designs by using an IRR analysis. Explain why NPV analysis is a better approach.

Problem 12-37 Basic Net Present Value Analysis, Competing Projects

OBJECTIVES ③ ⑥

Kildare Medical Center, a for-profit hospital, has three investment opportunities: (1) adding a wing for in-patient treatment of substance abuse, (2) adding a pathology laboratory, and (3) expanding the out-patient surgery wing. The initial investments and the net present value for the three alternatives are as follows:

	Substance Abuse	Laboratory	Out-Patient Surgery
Investment	$1,500,000	$500,000	$1,000,000
NPV	150,000	140,000	135,000

Although the hospital would like to invest in all three alternatives, only $1.5 million is available.

Required:
1. Rank the projects on the basis of NPV, and allocate the funds in order of this ranking. What project or projects were selected? What is the total NPV realized by the medical center using this approach?
2. Assume that the size of the lot on which the hospital is located makes the substance abuse wing and the out-patient surgery wing mutually exclusive. With unlimited capital, which of those two projects would be chosen? With limited capital and the three projects being considered, which projects would be chosen?
3. Form a group with two to four other students, and discuss qualitative considerations that should be considered in capital budgeting evaluations. Identify three such considerations.

OBJECTIVES ①②③④⑥ **Problem 12-38 Payback, Net Present Value, Internal Rate of Return, Intangible Benefits, Inflation Adjustment**

Foster Company wants to buy a numerically controlled (NC) machine to be used in producing specially machined parts for manufacturers of trenching machines (to replace an existing manual system). The outlay required is $3,500,000. The NC equipment will last five years with no expected salvage value. The expected incremental after-tax cash flows (cash flows of the NC equipment less cash flows of the old equipment) associated with the project follow:

Year	Cash Benefits	Cash Expenses
1	$3,900,000	$3,000,000
2	3,900,000	3,000,000
3	3,900,000	3,000,000
4	3,900,000	3,000,000
5	3,900,000	3,000,000

Foster has a cost of capital equal to 10 percent. The above cash flows are expressed without any consideration of inflation.

Required:
1. Compute the payback period.
2. Calculate the NPV and IRR of the proposed project.
3. Inflation is expected to be 5 percent per year for the next five years. The discount rate of 10 percent is composed of two elements: the real rate and the inflationary element. Since the discount rate has an inflationary component, the projected cash flows should also be adjusted to account for inflation. Make this adjustment, and recalculate the NPV. Comment on the importance of adjusting cash flows for inflationary effects.

OBJECTIVE ③ **Problem 12-39 Cost of Capital, Net Present Value**

Leakam Company's product engineering department has developed a new product that has a three-year life cycle. Production of the product requires development of a new process that requires a current $100,000 capital outlay. The $100,000 will be raised by issuing $60,000 of bonds and by selling new stock for $40,000. The $60,000 in bonds will have net (after-tax) interest payments of $3,000 at the end of each of the three years, with the principal being repaid at the end of year 3. The stock issue carries with it an expectation of a 17.5-percent return, expressed in the form of dividends at the end of each year [($7,000) in dividends is expected for each of the next three years]. The sources of capital for this investment represent the same proportion and costs that the company typically has. Finally, the project will produce after-tax cash inflows of $50,000 per year for the next three years.

Required:
1. Compute the cost of capital for the project. (*Hint:* The cost of capital is a weighted average of the two sources of capital where the weights are the proportion of capital from each source.)
2. Compute the NPV for the project. Explain why it is not necessary to subtract the interest payments and the dividend payments and appreciation from the inflow of $50,000 in carrying out this computation.

OBJECTIVES ①⑥ **Problem 12-40 Capital Investment, Advanced Manufacturing Environment**

"I know that it's the thing to do," insisted Pamela Kincaid, vice president of finance for Colgate Manufacturing. "If we are going to be competitive, we need to build this completely automated plant."

"I'm not so sure," replied Bill Thomas, CEO of Colgate. "The savings from labor reductions and increased productivity are only $4 million per year. The price tag for this factory—and it's a small one—is $45 million. That gives a payback period of more than 11 years. That's a long time to put the company's money at risk."

"Yeah, but you're overlooking the savings that we'll get from the increase in quality," interjected John Simpson, production manager. "With this system, we can decrease our waste and our rework time significantly. Those savings are worth another million dollars per year."

"Another million will only cut the payback to about nine years," retorted Bill. "Ron, you're the marketing manager—do you have any insights?"

"Well, there are other factors to consider, such as service quality and market share. I think that increasing our product quality and improving our delivery service will make us a lot more competitive. I know for a fact that two of our competitors have decided against automation. That'll give us a shot at their customers, provided our product is of higher quality and we can deliver it faster. I estimate that it'll increase our net cash benefits by another $2.4 million."

"Wow! Now that's impressive," Bill exclaimed, nearly convinced. "The payback is now getting down to a reasonable level."

"I agree," said Pamela, "but we do need to be sure that it's a sound investment. I know that estimates for construction of the facility have gone as high as $48 million. I also know that the expected residual value, after the 20 years of service we expect to get, is $5 million. I think I had better see if this project can cover our 14-percent cost of capital."

"Now wait a minute, Pamela," Bill demanded. "You know that I usually insist on a 20-percent rate of return, especially for a project of this magnitude."

Required:

1. Compute the NPV of the project by using the original savings and investment figures. Calculate by using discount rates of 14 percent and 20 percent. Include salvage value in the computation.
2. Compute the NPV of the project using the additional benefits noted by the production and marketing managers. Also, use the original cost estimate of $45 million. Again, calculate for both possible discount rates.
3. Compute the NPV of the project using all estimates of cash flows, including the possible initial outlay of $48 million. Calculate by using discount rates of 14 percent and 20 percent.
4. If you were making the decision, what would you do? Explain.

Problem 12-41 Postaudit, Sensitivity Analysis

OBJECTIVES ⑤ ⑥

Newmarge Products Inc. is evaluating a new design for one of its manufacturing processes. The new design will eliminate the production of a toxic solid residue. The initial cost of the system is estimated at $860,000 and includes computerized equipment, software, and installation. There is no expected salvage value. The new system has a useful life of eight years and is projected to produce cash operating savings of $225,000 per year over the old system (reducing labor costs and costs of processing and disposing of toxic waste). The cost of capital is 16 percent.

Required:

1. Compute the NPV of the new system.
2. One year after implementation, the internal audit staff noted the following about the new system: (1) the cost of acquiring the system was $60,000 more than expected due to higher installation costs, and (2) the annual cost savings were $20,000 less than expected because more labor cost was needed than anticipated. Using the changes in expected costs and benefits, compute the NPV as if this information had been available one year ago. Did the company make the right decision?
3. Upon reporting the results mentioned in the postaudit, the marketing manager responded in a memo to the internal auditing department indicating that revenues

Statement of Cash Flows

© Big Cheese Photo/Jupiter Images

After studying Chapter 13, you should be able to:

① Explain the basic elements of a statement of cash flows.

② Prepare a statement of cash flows by using the indirect method.

③ Calculate operating cash flows by using the direct method.

④ Prepare a statement of cash flows by using a worksheet approach.

You probably are familiar with the famous business phrase, "Cash Is King." In fact, cash is so important that it has its own financial statement—the Statement of Cash Flows. Cash flows, particularly their source and timing, are especially important for high-growth companies. **Google** is one of the fastest-growing companies in U.S. history. Many companies are pleased with double-digit growth (e.g., at least 10 percent). But from 2002 through 2006, Google's revenue grew at a triple-digit annualized rate! In addition, its stock price has skyrocketed from its initial public offering price of $85 in 2004 to over $500 per share in only a few years, making the two founders multibillionaires in their early 30s. How has Google grown at such an amazing pace, and what are some of the impacts of this growth on the company? Someone interested in answering this question could consult many sources of information, but one very helpful source is Google's Statement of Cash Flows, which is contained in its Annual Report and available for free on-line. The statement shows that Google's cash balance decreased during 2006 from a beginning balance of $3,877,174,000 to an ending balance of $3,544,671,000. However, a further breakdown of this aggregate decrease in cash provides more useful information. As will be explained in this chapter, the statement of cash flows separates cash flows into three categories: operating, investing, and financing. Google's impressive growth is reflected partly in its cash flows from operating activities. Driven by soaring sales, Google's net cash *provided* by *operating* activities more than tripled from 2004 through 2006 to $3,580,508,000. Also, the statement shows that large purchases of property and equipment, as well as significant investments in marketable and non-marketable securities, explain the company's relatively large net cash outflows, as represented by the net amount of cash *used* for *investing* activities of $6,899,150,000. Finally, the statement of cash flows indicates that the company issued a large amount of stock in 2006, over 3 million shares of which was for the purchase of YouTube, which *Time* magazine awarded its 2006 Invention of the Year. The issuance of stock was the driver of Google's net cash *provided* by *financing* activities of $2,966,398,000. Therefore, these three important categories of cash inflows and outflows—operating, investing, and financing—go a long way in helping to explain Google's business activities and its impact on the king of all measures—cash!

As illustrated in the previous paragraph, management needs to understand the sources and uses of cash within its own company to assess its financing capabilities. Management might raise a number of questions relating to cash management. For example, can the company make necessary purchases by using cash generated from operations? Will the company need to borrow all or some of the cash it needs for various purposes? If borrowing is necessary, can the debt be serviced? Can some or all of the cash be raised by issuing additional capital stock?

Answers to these questions and others like them are not available in a company's income statement or balance sheet. A third financial statement—the statement of cash flows—does provide this information. All firms that are registered with the U.S. Securities and Exchange Commission (SEC) must issue a statement of cash flows.

OBJECTIVE ①
Explain the basic elements of a statement of cash flows.

Overview of the Statement of Cash Flows

Cash Defined

Cash is defined as both currency and cash equivalents. **Cash equivalents** are highly liquid investments such as Treasury bills, money market funds, and commercial paper. Many firms, as part of their cash management programs, invest their excess cash in these short-term securities. Because of their high liquidity, these short-term investments are treated as cash for the statement of cash flows. For example, suppose that a company has $100,000 of cash and $200,000 of marketable securities on its beginning balance sheet. The total cash at the beginning of the year would be measured as $300,000.

Analytical Q&A

On the beginning balance sheet, a company reports $20,000 cash, $40,000 in Treasury bills, $30,000 in the money market, and $200,000 in accounts receivable. What is the total cash at the beginning of the year?

_____

Answer:
The total cash at the beginning of the year is $90,000. Accounts receivable is not counted as cash.

Sources and Uses of Cash

The **statement of cash flows** provides information regarding the sources and uses of a firm's cash. Activities that increase cash are sources of cash; they are referred to as **cash inflows**. Activities that decrease cash are uses of cash, referred to as **cash outflows**. The statement provides additional information by classifying cash flows into three categories.

1. Cash flows from **operating activities**.
2. Cash flows from **investing activities**.
3. Cash flows from **financing activities**.

This classification, referred to as the **activity format**, is the format that should be followed in preparing the statement of cash flows. Cornerstone 13-1 shows how activities can be classified into the three categories and identified as sources or uses of cash (shown in Exhibit 13-1 on page 560).

Noncash Exchanges

Occasionally, investing and financing activities take place without affecting cash. These are referred to as **noncash investing and financing activities**. A direct exchange of noncurrent balance sheet items may occur. For example, land may be exchanged for common stock. These noncash transactions must also be disclosed as a supplementary schedule attached to the statement. The requirement to report noncash financing and investing activity is essentially an "all-financial-resources approach." Since

HOW TO Classify Activities and Identify Them as Sources or Uses of Cash

CORNERSTONE 13–1

Information:

- Operating activities are the ongoing, day-to-day, revenue-generating activities of an organization. Typically, operating cash flows involve increases or decreases in either current assets or current liabilities. Cash inflows from operating activities come from the collection of sales revenues. Cash outflows are caused by payment for operating costs. The difference between the two produces the net cash inflow (outflow) from operations.
- Investing activities are those activities that involve the acquisition or sale of long-term assets. Long-term assets may be productive assets (e.g., acquiring new equipment) or long-term activities (e.g., acquiring stock in another company).
- Financing activities are those activities that raise (provide) cash from (to) creditors and owners. Although interest payments could be seen as financing outflows, the statement includes these payments in the operating section.

Required: Classify the following major activities as belonging to the operating, investing, or financing categories. Identify them as sources or uses of cash.
1. Issuing long-term debt
2. Paying cash dividends
3. Reporting unprofitable operations
4. Issuing capital stock
5. Reducing long-term debt
6. Retiring capital stock
7. Selling long-term assets (e.g., plant, equipment, and securities)
8. Reporting profitable operations
9. Purchasing long-term assets

Calculation:
1. Issuing long-term debt—financing, source of cash
2. Paying cash dividends—financing, use of cash
3. Reporting unprofitable operations—operating, use of cash
4. Issuing capital stock—financing, source of cash
5. Reducing long-term debt—financing, use of cash
6. Retiring capital stock—financing, use of cash
7. Selling long-term assets (e.g., plant, equipment, and securities)—investing, source of cash
8. Reporting profitable operations—operating, source of cash
9. Purchasing long-term assets—investing, use of cash

the major purpose of the statement is to provide cash flow information, the noncash nature of these transactions should be identified and highlighted in the supplementary schedule.

Methods for Calculating Operating Cash Flows

The two approaches for calculating operating cash flows are the *indirect method* and the *direct method*. The two methods differ only on how the cash flows from *operating activities* are calculated. The **indirect method** computes operating cash flows by *adjust-*

Exhibit 13–1

Sources and Uses of Cash

Sources of Cash

Operating Activities
• Collection of
  sales revenue

Investing Activities
• Sale of long-term asset

Financing Activities
• Issuance of long-term
  debt or stock

Uses of Cash

Operating Activities
• Payment of
  operating expenses

Investing Activities
• Purchase long-term asset

Financing Activities
• Retirement of
  long-term debt
• Treasury stock purchases
• Dividends

Concept Q&A

Explain why disclosing the sources and uses of cash is so important for potential users of a statement of cash flows.

Answer:

Knowing the sources of cash—especially from operating activities—provides a user with a good idea of a company's financial strength and its long-term viability. The decision to invest in a company is much safer if a potential investor—be it a bank or buyer—knows how much cash is being produced, where it is coming from, and the requirements for using cash. A firm's value is inextricably tied to its cash flows.

ing net income for items that do not affect cash flows. The **direct method** computes operating cash flows by *adjusting each line on the income statement* to reflect cash flows. For example, revenue on an accrual basis is adjusted to reflect only cash revenue. If the direct method is used, companies must also provide a supplementary schedule that shows how net income is reconciled with operating cash flows. This requirement means that direct method users must also provide the information associated with the indirect method. On the other hand, if the indirect method is used, there is no need to provide a line-by-line adjustment as found in the direct method. Not surprisingly, the indirect method is by far the most widely used.

The need to report a strong cash position for obtaining loans and equity capital may invite potential abuse. For example, at the end of a fiscal year, early deliveries of goods sold on credit (to reduce inventories) coupled with deliberate one-time special arrangements for secretive cash side payments by a third party to cover the increase in accounts receivables would show a stronger cash position than a company really has. Of course, such behaviors are deceptive and unethical. Ethical professional practices require fair, objective, and accurate reporting.

OBJECTIVE ②

Prepare a statement of cash flows by using the indirect method.

Preparation of the Statement: Indirect Method

Five basic steps are followed in preparing a statement of cash flows:

1. *Compute the change in cash for the period.* This figure is the difference between the ending and beginning cash balances shown on the balance sheets. It must equal the net cash inflow or outflow shown on the statement of cash flows.

2. *Compute the cash flows from operating activities.* Use the period's beginning and ending balance sheets and information about other events and transactions to adjust the period's income statement to an operating cash flow basis.
3. *Identify the cash flows from investing activities.* Use the period's beginning and ending balance sheets and information about other events and transactions to identify the cash flows associated with the sale and purchase of long-term assets.
4. *Identify the cash flows from financing activities.* Use the period's beginning and ending balance sheets to identify the cash flows associated with long-term debt and capital stock.
5. *Prepare the statement of cash flows based on the previous four steps.*

An example will be used to illustrate the specific details underlying the application of these five steps. Comparative balance sheets provide essential information for preparing a statement of cash flows. Exhibit 13-2 provides comparative balance sheets for the Lemmons Company.

Step One: Compute the Change in Cash Flow

Cornerstone 13-2 on page 562 shows how to compute the change in cash flow. Notice that the change in cash flow is simply the change in cash, which for Lemmons is an increase of $105,000 from 2009 to 2010. This number serves as a control figure for the statement of cash flows. The sum of the operating, investing, and financing cash flows must equal $105,000.

Exhibit 13-2

Balance Sheets: Lemmons Company

Lemmons Company
Comparative Balance Sheets
For the Years Ended December 31, 2009 and 2010

			Net Changes	
	2009	2010	Debit	Credit
Assets				
Cash	$ 70,000	$ 175,000	$105,000	
Accounts receivable	140,000	112,500		$ 27,500
Inventories	50,000	60,000	10,000	
Plant and equipment	400,000	410,000	10,000	
Accumulated depreciation	(200,000)	(210,000)		10,000
Land	200,000	287,500	87,500	
Total assets	$ 660,000	$ 835,000		
Liabilities and Stockholders' Equity				
Accounts payable	$ 120,000	$ 95,000	25,000	
Mortgage payable		100,000		100,000
Common stock	75,000	75,000		
Contributed capital in excess of par	100,000	100,000		
Retained earnings	365,000	465,000		100,000
Total liabilities and stockholders' equity	$ 660,000	$ 835,000	$237,500	$237,500

CORNERSTONE 13-2

HOW TO Compute the Change in Cash Flow

Information: From Exhibit 13–2, we extract the information on cash and cash equivalents:

Lemmons Company
Comparative Balance Sheets
For the Years Ended December 31, 2009 and 2010

			Net Changes	
Assets	2009	2010	Debit	Credit
Cash	$70,000	$175,000	$105,000	—

Required: Calculate the change in cash flow.

Calculation: The change in cash flow is the difference between ending and beginning cash balances:

$$175,000 - 70,000 = 105,000.$$

Step Two: Compute Operating Cash Flows

Income statements are prepared on an accrual basis. Thus, revenues and expenses that involve no cash inflows and outflows might be recognized. Also, cash inflows and outflows that are not recognized on the income statement might occur. The accrual income statement can be converted to an operating cash flow basis by making four adjustments to net income. Cornerstone 13-3 lists these four types of adjustments and illustrates how to calculate operating cash flows that use them. Five adjusting items are used to compute operating cash flows for Lemmons Company. These five entries exhibit each of the four types of adjustments.

Decrease in Accounts Receivable (Example of Type A Adjustment)

From Cornerstone 13-3, operating income is increased by a $27,500 decrease in accounts receivable. A decrease in accounts receivable represents a decrease in a noncash current asset. It indicates that cash collections from customers were greater than the revenues reported on the income statement by the amount of the decrease. Thus, to compute the operating cash flow, the decrease must be added to net income. To understand fully why this amount is added back to net income, consider the cash collection activity of Lemmons.

At the beginning of the year, the company reported accounts receivable of $140,000 (Exhibit 13-2). This beginning balance represents revenues recognized during 2009 but not collected. During 2010, additional operating revenues of $480,000 were earned and recognized on the income statement; Lemmons Company, therefore, had a total cash collection potential of $620,000 ($140,000 + $480,000). Since the ending balance of accounts receivable was $112,500, the company collected cash totaling $507,500 ($620,000 − $112,500). The cash collected from operations was $27,500 greater than the amount recognized on the income statement ($507,500 vs. $480,000), an amount exactly equal to the decrease in accounts receivable. Thus, the change in accounts receivable can be used to adjust revenues from an accrual to a cash basis.

Decrease in Accounts Payable and Increase in Inventories (Examples of Type B Adjustment)   Cornerstone 13-3 shows that the second adjusting item in the operating section reflects a decrease in accounts payable of $25,000 and the third an increase in inventories of $10,000. Taken together, these two items adjust the cost

HOW TO Calculate Operating Cash Flows: Indirect Method

**CORNERSTONE
13–3**

Information:

1. Four types of adjustments:
    a. Add to net income any increases in *current* liabilities and decreases in noncash *current* assets.
    b. Deduct from net income any decreases in *current* liabilities and increases in noncash *current* assets.
    c. Add to or deduct from net income the remaining net income items that do not affect cash flows (e.g., add back noncash expenses).
    d. Eliminate any income items that belong in either the investing or financing section.

2. Current assets and liabilities extracted from the comparative balance sheets for Lemmons Company (Exhibit 13-2):

**Lemmons Company
Comparative Balance Sheets
For the Years Ended December 31, 2009 and 2010**

			Net Changes	
	2009	**2010**	**Debit**	**Credit**
Current assets				
Accounts receivable	$140,000	$112,500		$27,500
Inventories	50,000	60,000	$10,000	
Current liabilities				
Accounts payable	$120,000	$95,000	$25,000	

3. The income statement for Lemmons Company:

**Lemmons Company
Income Statement
For the Year Ended December 31, 2010**

Revenues	$ 480,000
Gain on sale of equipment	20,000
Less: Cost of goods sold	(260,000)
Less: Depreciation expense	(50,000)
Less: Interest expense	(10,000)
Net income	$ 180,000

Required: Compute operating cash flows by using the indirect method.

Calculation:

Operating net income	$180,000	
Add (deduct) adjusting items:		
Decrease in accounts receivable	27,500	(Type A adjustment)
Decrease in accounts payable	(25,000)	(Type B adjustment)
Increase in inventories	(10,000)	(Type B adjustment)
Depreciation expense	50,000	(Type C adjustment)
Gain on sale of equipment	(20,000)	(Type D adjustment)
Net cash from operating activities	$202,500	

of goods sold to a cash basis. A decrease in accounts payable means that cash payments to creditors were larger than the purchases made during the period; the difference is the amount that accounts payable decreased. The total cash payment made to creditors, therefore, is equal to the purchases plus the decrease in accounts payable. Since inventories increased, purchases are larger than the cost of goods sold by the amount that inventories increased. Thus, by deducting both the decrease in accounts payable and the increase in inventories, the cost of goods sold figure is increased to reflect the cash outflow for goods during the period.

The effect of the above adjustments is best illustrated with the actual figures from Lemmons Company. From Exhibit 13-2, the following statement of costs of goods sold can be prepared. (In this statement, goods available for sale and purchases are obtained by working backwards from cost of goods sold.)

Beginning inventory	$ 50,000
Purchases	270,000
Goods available for sale	$320,000
Less: Ending inventory	(60,000)
Cost of goods sold	$260,000

Adding purchases to the beginning balance in accounts payable (from Exhibit 13–2) yields the total potential payments to creditors: $390,000 ($270,000 + $120,000). Subtracting the ending balance of accounts payable (Exhibit 13–2) from the total potential payments gives the total cash payments for the year: $295,000 ($390,000 − $95,000). By deducting the decrease in accounts payable ($25,000) and the increase in inventories ($10,000), an additional $35,000 is deducted, bringing the cost of goods sold figure from $260,000 to $295,000. This amount equals the total cash payment for goods during 2010.

Depreciation Expense (Example of Type C Adjustment)   While depreciation expense is a legitimate deduction from revenues to arrive at net income, it does not require any cash outlay. As a noncash expense, it should be added back to net income as part of the adjustment needed to produce operating cash flow.

Gain on the Sale of Equipment (Example of Type D Adjustment)   The sale of long-term assets is a nonoperating activity and should be classified in the section that reveals the firm's investing activities. Furthermore, the gain on the sale of the equipment does not reveal the total cash received—it gives only the cash received in excess of the equipment's book value. The correct procedure is to deduct the gain and report the full cash inflow from the sale in the investing section of the statement of cash flows.

Analytical Q&A

What adjustment would be made to net income for (a) an increase of $100,000 in accounts receivable, (b) an increase of $30,000 in accounts payable, and (c) a decrease in inventories of $10,000? Explain why.

Answer:

(a) Decrease net income by $100,000 because sales were recognized where cash was not collected, (b) increase net income by $30,000 because cash payments to creditors were less than purchases, and (c) increase net income by $10,000 because purchases were less than cost of goods sold because inventories decreased.

Step Three: Compute Investing Cash Flows

Investing activities include the purchase and sale of long-term assets (plant and equipment, land, and long-term securities). Cornerstone 13-4 shows how to compute investing cash flows for Lemmons Company. The company had three investing transactions in 2010. These transactions are summarized in the investing section that follows.

HOW TO Compute Investing Cash Flows

Information:

a. Equipment with a book value of $50,000 was sold for $70,000 (original purchase cost of $90,000). New equipment was purchased.

b. Information extracted from the comparative balance sheets of Lemmons Company (from Exhibit 13–2):

CORNERSTONE 13–4

Comparative Balance Sheets
For the Years Ended December 31, 2009 and 2010

Long-Term Assets	2009	2010	Net Changes Debit	Credit
Plant and equipment	$ 400,000	$ 410,000	$10,000	
Accumulated depreciation	(200,000)	(210,000)		$10,000
Land	200,000	287,500	87,500	

Required: Calculate the investing cash flows.

Calculation:

Sale of equipment	$ 70,000 [a]
Purchase of equipment	(100,000) [b]
Purchase of land	(87,500) [c]
Net cash from investing activities	$(117,500)

[a] The sale of long-tem assets is an investing activity. Thus, the receipt of the $70,000 should be reported in the investing section.

[b] There is no explicit information concerning the purchase price of equipment. The purchase price is inferred from the comparative balance sheet information as well as the information about the equipment originally costing $90,000 that was sold and removed from the books. The purchase price of the new equipment can be computed by the following procedure:

Beginning plant and equipment	$400,000
Purchase of equipment	?
Less: Sale of equipment	(90,000)
Ending balance, plant, and equipment	$410,000

The "plug figure" for the equipment purchase must be $ 100,000. (*Note:* $ 40,000 of accumulated depreciation was deducted from the books, removing the accumulated depreciation associated with the equipment that was sold, and $50,000 was added to reflect the depreciation expense for 2010, giving a net increase of $10,000.)

[c] The comparative balance sheets reveal that land was purchased for $87,500. This transaction also should appear in the investing section.

Step Four: Cash Flows from Financing

Issuance of long-term debt or capital stock can produce cash inflows; retirement of debt or stock and payment of dividends produce cash outflows. Cornerstone 13-5 shows how to compute the financing cash flows for Lemmons Company.

Step Five: Prepare the Statement of Cash Flows

The outcomes of steps 2 to 4 correspond to the individual sections needed for the statement of cash flows. Cornerstone 13-6 shows how to prepare this statement. Notice that the change in cash flow computed in step 1 from the comparative balance

**CORNERSTONE
13–5**

HOW TO Compute Financing Cash Flows

Information:
a. Net income of $180,000 was earned in 2010.
b. Extraction from comparative balance sheets (Exhibit 13-2):

Comparative Balance Sheets
For the Years Ended December 31, 2009 and 2010

			Net Changes	
	2009	**2009**	**Debit**	**Credit**
Mortgage payable		100,000		100,000
Common stock	75,000	75,000		
Contributed capital in excess of par	100,000	100,000		
Retained earnings	365,000	465,000		100,000

Required: Compute the investing cash flows for 2010.

Calculation: The cash flows associated with the financing activities of Lemmons Company are as follows:

Issuance of mortgage	$100,000[a]
Payment of dividends	(80,000)[b]
Net cash flow from financing	$ 20,000

[a]The comparative balance sheets show that the only change in long-term debt and capital stock accounts is the apparent issue of a mortgage during 2010. The proceeds from this mortgage should be shown as a source of cash in the financing section.

[b]Retained earnings, end of 2009	$365,000
Net income (2010)	180,000
Total	$545,000
Less retained earnings, end of 2010	465,000
Dividends paid in 2010	$ 80,000

Since dividends represent a return on the funds provided by stockholders, this amount should be shown in the financing section.

**CORNERSTONE
13-6**

HOW TO Prepare the Statement of Cash Flows

Information: Cornerstones 13-2 to 13-5.

Required: Prepare a statement of cash flows for Lemmons Company.

Calculation:

Lemmons Company
Statement of Cash Flows
For the Year Ended December 31, 2010

Cash flows from operating activities:	
Net income	$ 180,000
Add (deduct) adjusting items:	
Decrease in accounts receivable	27,500
Decrease in accounts payable	(25,000)
Increase in inventories	(10,000)
Depreciation expense	50,000
Gain on sale of equipment	(20,000)
Net operating cash	$ 202,500

Cash flows from investing activities:		
Sale of equipment	$ 70,000	
Purchase of equipment	(100,000)	
Purchase of land	(87,500)	
Net cash from investing activities		(117,500)
Cash flows from financing activities:		
Issuance of mortgage	$ 100,000	
Payment of dividends	(80,000)	
Net cash from financing activities		20,000
Net increase in cash		$ 105,000

**CORNERSTONE
13-6
(continued)**

sheets corresponds to the net increase in cash identified in the statement of cash flows. The computation produced by step 1 serves as a control on the accuracy of steps 2 to 4.

The Direct Method: An Alternative Approach

OBJECTIVE ③
Calculate operating cash flows by using the direct method.

The section of operating cash flows in Cornerstone 13-3 computes cash flows by adjusting net income for items that do not affect cash flows. This approach is known as the indirect method. Some individuals prefer to show operating cash flows as the difference between cash receipts and cash payments. To do so, each item on the accrual income statement is adjusted to reflect cash flows. The same adjustments and the same reasoning behind the indirect method are used to produce the operating cash flows; however, the presentation of the information is different. Each line on the income statement is adjusted to produce a cash flow income statement. Cornerstone 13-7 shows how to compute operating cash flows by using this approach, known as the direct method, using the Lemmons Company example. Either approach to computing and presenting operating cash flows may be used; which to use is a matter of preference. However, if a company chooses the direct method, it must also present the indirect method in a separate schedule.

Here's The Real Kicker

The statement of cash flows is a report required of all SEC-registered firms. Stillwater Designs, however, is not a public company and therefore is not subject to the requirement to produce a statement of cash flows. The management of Stillwater Designs does not see any value in producing this statement, and, therefore, the accounting department does not produce it. A daily cash position report is provided to management. Furthermore, it is a very easy matter to identify the source of the cash flows—either they come from operating, investing, or financing activities. Thus, if this information is ever explicitly needed, it can be provided. Interestingly, Stillwater Designs' creditors have not demanded this statement as information needed for granting loans. Income statements and balance sheets have provided the needed information. Stillwater Designs' chief accountant, Jeanne Snyder, noted that bank officers tend to be much more interested in assets that can act as collateral such as accounts receivable and inventory.

CORNERSTONE
13-7

HOW TO Calculate Operating Cash Flows by Using the Direct Method

Information:

a. Current assets and liabilities extracted from the comparative balance sheets for Lemmons Company (Exhibit 13-2):

Lemmons Company
Comparative Balance Sheets
For the Years Ended December 31, 2009 and 2010

| | | | Net Changes | |
	2009	2010	Debit	Credit
Current assets				
Accounts receivable	$140,000	$112,500		$27,500
Inventories	50,000	60,000	$10,000	
Current liabilities				
Accounts payable	$120,000	$ 95,000	$25,000	

b. The income statement for Lemmons Company:

Lemmons Company
Income Statement
For the Year Ended December 31, 2010

Revenues	$ 480,000
Gain on sale of equipment	20,000
Less: Cost of goods sold	(260,000)
Less: Depreciation expense	(50,000)
Less: Interest expense	(10,000)
Net income	$ 180,000

Required: Calculate operating cash flows by using the direct method.

Calculation:

	Income Statement	Adjustments	Cash Flows
Revenues	$ 480,000	$ 27,500[a]	$507,500
Gain on sale of equipment	20,000	(20,000)	
Less: Cost of goods sold	(260,000)	(25,000)[b]	
		(10,000)[c]	(295,000)
Less: Depreciation expense	(50,000)	50,000	
Less: Interest expense	(10,000)		(10,000)
Net income	$ 180,000		
Net operating cash			$202,500

[a]Decrease in accounts receivable.
[b]Decrease in accounts payable.
[c]Increase in inventories.

Worksheet Approach to the Statement of Cash Flows

OBJECTIVE ④
Prepare a statement of cash flows by using a worksheet approach.

As transactions increase in number and complexity, a worksheet becomes a useful and almost necessary aid in preparing the statement of cash flows. The approach minimizes confusion and allows careful consideration of all the details underlying an analysis of cash flows. One advantage of a worksheet is the fact that it uses a spreadsheet format, allowing the preparer to use a PC and spreadsheet software. Furthermore, a worksheet offers the user an efficient, logical means to organize the data needed to prepare a statement of cash flows. Although the worksheet itself is not the statement of cash flows, the statement can be easily extracted from the worksheet. The use of a worksheet is best illustrated with an example. The comparative balance sheets of Portermart Company are presented in Exhibit 13-3.

Cornerstone 13-8 shows how to prepare a worksheet for Portermart's statement of cash flows. Notice that the worksheet is divided into two major sections: one corresponding to the balance sheet classifications and one corresponding to the statement of cash flows classifications. Four columns are needed: two for the beginning and ending balances of the balance sheet and two to analyze the transactions that produced the changes in cash flows. The columns for the analysis of transactions are the focus of the worksheet approach. Generally, a debit or credit in a balance sheet column produces a corresponding credit or debit in a cash flow column. Once all changes are accounted for, the statement of cash flows can be prepared (by using the lower half of the worksheet).

Exhibit 13-3

Balance Sheets: Portermart Company

Portermart Company
Comparative Balance Sheets
For the Years Ended December 31, 2009 and 2010

	2009	2010	Net Changes Debit	Net Changes Credit
Assets				
Cash	$ 90,000	$ 183,000	$ 93,000	
Accounts receivable	55,000	60,000	5,000	
Inventory	80,000	55,000		$ 25,000
Plant and equipment	130,000	100,000		30,000
Accumulated depreciation	(65,000)	(60,000)	5,000	
Land	25,000	65,000	40,000	
Total assets	$ 315,000	$ 403,000		
Liabilities and Stockholders' Equity				
Accounts payable	$ 40,000	$ 60,000		20,000
Wages payable	5,000	3,000	2,000	
Bonds payable	30,000	20,000	10,000	
Preferred stock (no par)	5,000	15,000		10,000
Common stock	50,000	60,000		10,000
Paid-in capital in excess of par	50,000	80,000		30,000
Retained earnings	135,000	165,000		30,000
Total liabilities and stockholders' equity	$ 315,000	$ 403,000	$155,000	$155,000

**CORNERSTONE
13-8**

HOW TO Prepare a Statement of Cash Flows by Using a Worksheet Approach

Information:

1. Exhibit 13-3 (comparative balance sheets for Portermart Company).
2. Other (2010) transactions:
    a. Cash dividends of $10,000 were paid.
    b. Equipment was sold for $8,000. It had an original cost of $30,000 and a book value of $15,000. The loss is included in operating expenses.
    c. Land with a fair market value of $40,000 was acquired by issuing common stock with a par value of $10,000.
    d. One thousand shares of preferred stock (no par) were sold for $10 per share.

3. The income statement for 2010 is as follows:

Sales	$ 400,000
Less: Cost of goods sold	(250,000)
Gross margin	$ 150,000
Less: Operating expenses	(110,000)
Net income	$ 40,000

Required: Prepare a worksheet for Portermart Company.

Calculation:

Worksheet: Portermart Company

	2009	Transactions Debit	Transactions Credit	2010
Assets				
Cash	$ 90,000	(1) $93,000		$183,000
Accounts receivable	55,000	(2) 5,000		60,000
Inventory	80,000		(3) $25,000	55,000
Plant and equipment	130,000		(4) 30,000	100,000
Accumulated depreciation	(65,000)	(4) 15,000	(5) 10,000	(60,000)
Land	25,000	(6) 40,000		65,000
Total assets	$315,000			$403,000
Liabilities and stockholders' equity:				
Accounts payable	$ 40,000		(7) $20,000	$ 60,000
Wages payable	5,000	(8) $ 2,000		3,000
Bonds payable	30,000	(9) 10,000		20,000
Preferred stock (no par)	5,000		(10) 10,000	15,000
Common stock	50,000		(11) 10,000	60,000
Paid-in capital in excess of par	50,000		(11) 30,000	80,000
Retained earnings	135,000	(13) 10,000	(12) 40,000	165,000
Total liabilities and stockholders' equity	$315,000			$403,000

	2009	Transactions		2010
		Debit	**Credit**	
Operating cash flows:				
Net income		(12) $40,000		
Depreciation expense		(5) 10,000		
Loss on sale of equipment		(4) 7,000		
Decrease in inventory		(3) 25,000		
Increase in accounts payable		(7) 20,000		
Increase in accounts receivable			(2) 5,000	
Decrease in wages payable			(8) 2,000	
Cash flows from investing:				
Sale of equipment		(4) 8,000		
Cash flows from financing:				
Reduction in bonds payable			(9) 10,000	
Payment of dividends			(13) 10,000	
Issuance of preferred stock		(10) 10,000		
Net increase in cash			(1) 93,000	
Noncash investing and financing activities:				
Land acquired with common stock		(11) 40,000	(6) 40,000	

**CORNERSTONE
13-8
(continued)**

Analysis of Transactions

The summary transactions on the worksheet will be explained by examining the items on the worksheet in order of their appearance (essentially equivalent to the numerical order of the entries). The entries are developed by considering each balance sheet item and the associated supplementary information.

Change in Cash   Entry (1) identifies the total change in cash during 2010.

(1)	Cash	93,000	
	Net increase in cash		93,000

The actual cash balance increased from the beginning to the end of the year by $93,000.

Change in Accounts Receivable   Entry (2) reflects the increase in accounts receivable.

(2)	Accounts receivable	5,000	
	Operating cash		5,000

Increasing accounts receivable means that revenues were recognized on the income statement but not collected. Thus, net income must be adjusted to show that cash inflows from revenues were less by this amount.

Decrease in Inventory   Entry (3) reflects the effect of a decrease of inventory on operating cash flow.

(3)	Operating cash	25,000	
	Inventory		25,000

Operating cash should be increased since a decrease in inventory would be included in the cost of goods sold but would not represent a cash outflow.

Sale of Equipment
The sale of equipment affects two balance sheet accounts and two cash flow accounts. The effect is captured in Entry (4).

(4)	Operating Cash	7,000	
	Cash from investing activities	8,000	
	Accumulated depreciation	15,000	
	Plant and equipment		30,000

Operating cash shows an increase because the loss on the sale is a noncash expense and should be added back to net income to arrive at the correct cash provided by operating activities. The equipment is sold for $8,000. This sale produces a cash inflow that is recognized as a cash flow from investing activities. The other two entries reflect the fact that the original cost of the equipment and the accumulated depreciation have been removed from the company's books.

Depreciation Expense
Entry (5) shows an increase in operating cash flow because depreciation expense, a noncash expense, is added back to net income.

(5)	Operating cash	10,000	
	Accumulated depreciation		10,000

Although the amount of depreciation expense is not explicitly given, it can be easily computed. The net decrease in the accumulated depreciation account is $5,000 (Exhibit 13-3). The sale of the equipment decreased accumulated depreciation by $15,000 (accumulated depreciation removed is equal to original cost minus book value, or $30,000 − $15,000). Thus, the amount of depreciation expense recognized for the period must be $10,000. Depreciation expense increases accumulated depreciation—an increase of $10,000 and a decrease of $15,000 produce a net decrease of $5,000.

Land for Common Stock
Three balance sheet accounts are affected in the noncash transaction that acquires land in exchange for common stock. To balance the transactions columns, two separate entries [(6) and (11)] are needed.

(6)	Land	40,000	
	Noncash investing activities		40,000
(11)	Noncash investing activities	40,000	
	Common stock		10,000
	Paid-In capital in excess of par		30,000

Accounts Payable
Entry (7) provides the adjusting entry for an increase in accounts payable.

(7)	Operating cash	20,000	
	Accounts payable		20,000

An increase in accounts payable means that some of the purchases were not acquired through the use of cash. Accordingly, the amount of the increase needs to be added back to net income.

Wages Payable
Wages payable decreased by $2,000 during 2010. This decrease means that the company had a cash outflow $2,000 larger than the wage expense recognized on the income statement. Entry (8) reflects this $2,000 decrease.

(8)	Wages payable	2,000	
	Operating cash		2,000

Bonds Payable
Bonds payable decreased by $10,000, indicating a cash outflow belonging to the financing section. Entry (9) recognizes the reduction of debt and the associated cash outflow.

(9)	Bonds payable	10,000	
	Cash flow from financing activities		10,000

Preferred Stock   Entry (10) reflects the cash inflow that resulted from the issuance of preferred stock.

(10)	Cash flow from financing activities	10,000	
	Preferred Stock		10,000

Net Income   Net income is assigned to the operating cash flow section by entry (12).

(12)	Operating cash	40,000	
	Retained earnings		40,000

Payment of Dividends   The payment of dividends is given in entry (13).

(13)	Retained earnings	10,000	
	Cash flow from financing activities		10,000

The Final Step

Once the worksheet is completed, the final step in preparing the statement of cash flows is relatively straightforward. The lower half of the worksheet contains all of the sections needed. The debit column provides the cash inflows, and the credit column provides the cash outflows. The noncash section is an exception; either column may be used to provide the information. The only additional effort needed is to compute subtotals for each section. The statement of cash flows for Portermart Company is shown in Exhibit 13-4.

Concept Q&A

What are the advantages of a worksheet approach for preparing the statement of cash flows?

Answer:
A worksheet reduces confusion, provides a ready way to track the details of a cash flow analysis, and allows the use of spreadsheet programs.

Exhibit 13-4

Worksheet-Derived Statement of Cash Flows

Portermart Company
Statement of Cash Flows
For the Year Ended December 31, 2010

Operating cash flows:		
Net income	$40,000	
Add (deduct) adjusting items:		
Depreciation expense	10,000	
Loss on sale of equipment	7,000	
Decrease in inventory	25,000	
Increase in accounts payable	20,000	
Increase in accounts receivable	(5,000)	
Decrease in wages payable	(2,000)	
Net operating cash		$ 95,000
Cash flows from investing activities:		
Sale of equipment		$ 8,000
Cash flows from financing activities:		
Reduction in bonds payable		$(10,000)
Payment of dividends		(10,000)
Issuance of preferred stock		10,000
Total cash flow from financing		$(10,000)
Net increase in cash		$ 93,000
Investing and financing activities not affecting cash:		
Acquisition of land issuing common stock		$ 40,000

Summary of Learning Objectives

1. **Explain the basic elements of a statement of cash flows.**
   - Knowing a company's cash flows enables managers, investors, creditors, and others to assess more fully the economic strength and viability of a company by allowing the evaluation of its current cash flows and by assessing future cash flow potential.
   - The Financial Accounting Standards Board (FASB), recognizing the need for cash flow information, has recommended that all firms prepare a statement of cash flows.
   - The activity format for a statement of cash flows has three sections: cash flows from operating activities, cash flows from investing activities, and cash flows from financing activities. Noncash financing and investing activities also are reported.
   - The change in cash for a period is the difference between the beginning and ending balances of the cash account. The change in cash equivalents also is included in the change in cash.
   - Operating activities are the main revenue-generating activities engaged in by the organization.
   - Operating cash flows are computed by adjusting the period's net income for noncash expenses, accrual effects, and nonoperating revenues or expenses.
   - Investing activities involve the acquisition and sale of long-term assets.
   - Financing activities involve raising outside capital through the issuance of debt and capital stock. Financing activities also involve the retirement of debt and capital stock.

2. **Prepare a statement of cash flows by using the indirect method.**
   - Compute the change in cash flows.
   - Compute operating cash flows by *adjusting net income* for items that do not affect cash flows.
   - Identify investing cash flows.
   - Identify financing cash flows.
   - Assemble the data into a statement of cash flows.
   - Preparation of the statement relies on the beginning and ending balance sheets and information regarding other activities and events that may not be fully apparent from the balance sheets themselves.

3. **Calculate operating cash flows by using the direct method.**
   - Compute the change in cash flows.
   - Compute operating cash flows by *adjusting each line on the income statement* to reflect cash flows.
   - Identify investing cash flows.
   - Identify financing cash flows.
   - Assemble the data into a statement of cash flows.
   - Preparation of the statement relies on the beginning and ending balance sheets and information regarding other activities and events that may not be fully apparent from the balance sheets themselves.

4. **Prepare a statement of cash flows by using a worksheet approach.**
   - Worksheets can be used to organize the preparation of the statement of cash flows.
   - In addition to increased efficiency in form, worksheets offer the added convenience of the PC and spreadsheet software packages.

Cornerstone 13-1 How to classify activities and identify them as sources or uses of cash, page 559

Cornerstone 13-2 How to compute the change in cash flow, page 562

Cornerstone 13-3 How to calculate operating cash flows: indirect method, page 563

Cornerstone 13-4 How to compute investing cash flows, page 565

Cornerstone 13-5 How to compute financing cash flows, page 566

Cornerstone 13-6 How to prepare the statement of cash flows, page 566

Cornerstone 13-7 How to calculate operating cash flows by using the direct method, page 568

Cornerstone 13-8 How to prepare a statement of cash flows by using a worksheet approach, page 570

CORNERSTONES FOR CHAPTER 13

Key Terms

Activity format, 558
Cash equivalents, 558
Cash inflows, 558
Cash outflows, 558
Direct method, 560
Financing activities, 558

Indirect method, 559
Investing activities, 558
Noncash investing and financing
    activities, 558
Operating activities, 558
Statement of cash flows, 558

Review Problems

I. The following balance sheets are taken from the records of Golding Inc.:

	2009	2010
Assets:		
Cash	$130,000	$150,000
Accounts receivable	25,000	20,000
Plant and equipment	50,000	60,000
Accumulated depreciation	(20,000)	(25,000)
Land	10,000	10,000
Total assets	$195,000	$215,000
Liabilities and equity:		
Accounts payable	$ 10,000	$ 5,000
Bonds payable	8,000	18,000
Common stock	120,000	120,000
Retained earnings	57,000	72,000
Total liabilities and equity	$195,000	$215,000

Additional information is as follows:

a. Equipment costing $10,000 was purchased at year-end. No equipment was sold.
b. Net income for the year was $25,000; $10,000 in dividends were paid.

Required:
Prepare a statement of cash flows by using the indirect method.

Solution:
1. Cash flow change: $150,000 – $130,000 = $20,000
2. Operating cash flows

Operating net income	$25,000
Add (deduct):	
Decrease in accounts receivable	5,000
Depreciation expense	5,000
Decrease in accounts payable	(5,000)
Net cash from operations	$30,000

3. Cash from investing activities for purchase of equipment is $(10,000).
4. Cash from financing activities

Payment of dividends	$(10,000)
Issuance of bonds	10,000
Net cash from financing	$ 0

5.

Golding Inc.
Statement of Cash Flows
For the Year Ended 2010

Cash flows from operating activities:	
Net income	$ 25,000
Add (deduct) adjusting items:	
Decrease in accounts receivable	5,000
Depreciation expense	5,000
Decrease in accounts payable	(5,000)
Net operating cash	$ 30,000
Cash flows from investing activities:	
Purchase of equipment	(10,000)
Cash flows from financing activities:	
Payment of dividends	$(10,000)
Issuance of bonds	10,000
Net cash from financing	0
Net increase in cash	$ 20,000

II. **The following balance sheets are taken from the records of Golding Inc.:**

	2009	2010
Assets:		
Cash	$130,000	$150,000
Accounts receivable	25,000	20,000
Plant and equipment	50,000	60,000
Accumulated depreciation	(20,000)	(25,000)
Land	10,000	10,000
Total assets	$195,000	$215,000
Liabilities and equity:		
Accounts payable	$ 10,000	$ 5,000
Bonds payable	8,000	18,000
Common stock	120,000	120,000
Retained earnings	57,000	72,000
Total liabilities and equity	$195,000	$215,000

Additional information is as follows:

a.   Equipment costing $10,000 was purchased at year-end. No equipment was sold.
b.   Net income for the year was calculated as follows:

Revenues	$ 500,000
Cost of goods sold	(375,000)
Depreciation expense	(5,000)
Other expenses	(95,000)
Net income	$ 25,000

Dividends were $10,000.

Required:

Prepare a statement of operating cash flows by using the direct method.

Solution:

Cash flows from operating activities:

	Income Statement	Adjustments	Cash Flows
Revenues	$ 500,000	$5,000[a]	$ 505,000
Cost of goods sold	(375,000)		(375,000)
Depreciation expense	(5,000)	5,000[b]	
Other expenses	(95,000)	(5,000)[c]	(100,000)
Net operating cash			$ 30,000

[a]Decrease in accounts receivable.
[b]Add back depreciation (noncash expense).
[c]Decrease in accounts payable.

Discussion Questions

1. The activity format calls for three categories on the statement of cash flows. Define each category.
2. Of the three categories on the statement of cash flows, which do you think provides the most useful information? Explain.
3. Explain what is meant by the all-financial-resources approach to reporting financing and investing activities.
4. Why is it better to report the noncash investing and financing activities in a supplemental schedule rather than to include these activities on the body of the statement of cash flows?
5. What are the five steps for preparing the statement of cash flows? What is the purpose of each step?
6. What are cash equivalents? How are cash equivalents treated in preparing a statement of cash flows?
7. What are the advantages in using worksheets when preparing a statement of cash flows?
8. Explain how a company can report a positive net income and yet still have a negative net operating cash flow.
9. Explain how a company can report a loss and still have a positive net operating cash flow.
10. In computing the period's net operating cash flows, why are increases in current liabilities and decreases in current assets added back to net income?
11. In computing the period's net operating cash flows, why are decreases in liabilities and increases in current assets deducted from net income?
12. In computing the period's net cash operating flows, why are noncash expenses added back to net income?

13. Explain the reasoning for including the payment of dividends in the financing section of the statement of cash flows.

14. Explain how the statement of cash flows can be prepared by using the worksheet approach.

Multiple-Choice Exercises

13-1 Cash inflows from operating activities come from

a. payment for raw materials.
b. collection of sales revenues.
c. gains on the sale of operating equipment.
d. issuing capital stock.
e. issuing bonds.

13-2 Cash outflows from operating activities come from

a. payment for raw materials.
b. collection of sales revenues.
c. acquisition of operating equipment.
d. retirement of bonds.
e. None of the above.

13-3 Raising cash by issuing capital stock is an example of

a. an operating activity.
b. an investing activity.
c. a financing activity.
d. a noncash transaction.
e. None of the above.

13-4 Sources of cash include

a. profitable operations.
b. the issuance of long-term debt.
c. the sale of long-term assets.
d. the issuance of capital stock.
e. All of the above.

13-5 Uses of cash include

a. cash dividends.
b. the purchase of long-term assets.
c. the sale of old equipment.
d. Only a and b.
e. None of the above.

13-6 The difference between the beginning and ending cash balances shown on the balance sheet

a. is added to net income to obtain total cash inflows.
b. is deducted from net income to obtain net cash inflows.
c. serves as a control figure for the statement of cash flows.
d. is the source of all investing and financing activities.
e. Both c and d.

13-7 Which of the following adjustments helps to convert accrual income to operating cash flows?

a.   Add to net income an increase in inventories
b.   Deduct from net income a decrease in inventories
c.   Add to net income a decrease in accounts payable
d.   Deduct from income an increase in accounts payable
e.   None of the above

13-8 Which of the following adjustments to net income is needed to obtain cash flows?

a.   Elimination of gains on sale of equipment
b.   Add to net income all noncash expenses (e.g., depreciation and amortization)
c.   Add to net income any increases in current liabilities
d.   Deduct from net income any increases in inventories
e.   All of the above

13-9 A decrease in accounts receivable is added to net income to obtain operating cash flows because

a.   cash collections from customers were greater than the revenues reported.
b.   cash collections from customers were less than the revenues reported.
c.   cash collections decreased due to declining sales.
d.   cash collections increased due to increasing sales.
e.   None of the above.

13-10 An increase in inventories is deducted from net income to arrive at operating cash flow because

a.   cash payments to customers were larger than the purchases made during the period.
b.   cash payments to customers were less than the purchases made during the period.
c.   purchases are larger than the cost of goods sold by the amount that inventories increased.
d.   purchases are less than the cost of goods sold by the amount that inventories increased.
e.   All of the above.

13-11 The gain on sale of equipment is deducted from net income to arrive at operating cash flows because

a.   the sale of long-term assets is a nonoperating activity.
b.   the gain does not reveal the total cash received.
c.   all of the cash received from the sale is reported in the investing section.
d.   All of the above.
e.   None of the above.

13-12 Which of the following is an investing activity?

a.   Issuance of a mortgage
b.   Purchase of land
c.   Increase in accounts receivable
d.   Increase in inventories
e.   All of the above

Booth Manufacturing
Comparative Balance Sheets
For the Years Ended December 31, 2009 and 2010

	2009	2010
Assets		
Cash	$ 112,500	$ 350,000
Accounts receivable	350,000	281,250
Inventories	125,000	150,000
Plant and equipment	1,000,000	1,025,000
Accumulated depreciation	(500,000)	(525,000)
Land	500,000	718,750
Total assets	$1,587,500	$2,000,000
Liabilities and equity		
Accounts payable	$ 300,000	$ 237,500
Mortgage payable	—	250,000
Common stock	75,000	75,000
Contributed capital in excess of par	300,000	300,000
Retained earnings	912,500	1,137,500
Total liabilities and equity	$1,587,500	$2,000,000

Booth Manufacturing
Income Statement
For the Year Ended December 31, 2010

Revenues	$1,200,000
Gain on sale of equipment	50,000
Less: Cost of goods sold	(640,000)
Less: Depreciation expense	(125,000)
Less: Interest expense	(35,000)
Net income	$ 450,000

Required:

1. Calculate the cash flows from operations by using the indirect method.
2. Prepare a statement of cash flows.
3. Search the Internet to find a statement of cash flows. Which method was used—the indirect method or the direct method? How does the net income reported compare with the operating cash flows? To the change in cash flows?

OBJECTIVES ① ③   **Problem 13-33 Statement of Cash Flows: Direct Method**

spreadsheet

Refer to the information in **Problem 13-32**. Assume that all data are the same except that during 2010, common stock was exchanged for land with a fair market value of $60,000. This transaction changes the balance sheet for 2010 by increasing the land account by $60,000 and the capital stock accounts by $60,000.

Required:

1. Calculate the operating cash flows by using the direct method.
2. Prepare a statement of cash flows.

OBJECTIVES ② ③   **Problem 13-34 Direct and Indirect Methods**

The following balance sheets and income statement were taken from the records of Rosie-Lee Company:

	2009	2010
Assets		
Cash	$270,000	$333,000
Accounts receivable	126,000	144,000
Investments		54,000
Plant and equipment	180,000	189,000
Accumulated depreciation	(54,000)	(57,600)
Land	36,000	54,000
Total assets	$558,000	$716,400
Liabilities and equity		
Accounts payable	$ 72,000	$ 90,000
Mortgage payable	108,000	
Bonds payable		90,000
Preferred stock	36,000	
Common stock	180,000	288,000
Retained earnings	162,000	248,400
Total liabilities and equity	$558,000	$716,400

Rosie-Lee Company
Income Statement
For the Year Ended June 30, 2010

Sales	$ 920,000
Less: Cost of goods sold	(620,000)
Gross margin	$ 300,000
Less: Operating expenses	(177,600)
Net income	$ 122,400

Additional transactions were as follows:

a. Sold equipment costing $21,600 with accumulated depreciation of $16,200 for $3,600
b. Retired bonds at a price of $108,000 on December 31
c. Paid cash dividends of $36,000

Required:
1. Prepare a schedule of operating cash flows by using:
    a. The indirect method
    b. The direct method
2. Prepare a statement of cash flows by using the indirect method.

Problem 13-35, Statement of Cash Flows, Worksheet

The following balance sheets and income statement were taken from the records of Rosie-Lee Company:

OBJECTIVE ④
WORKSHEET

	2009	2010
Assets		
Cash	$270,000	$333,000
Accounts receivable	126,000	144,000
Investments		54,000
Plant and equipment	180,000	189,000
Accumulated depreciation	(54,000)	(57,600)
Land	36,000	54,000
Total assets	$558,000	$716,400

	2009	2010
Liabilities and equity		
Accounts payable	$ 72,000	$ 90,000
Mortgage payable	108,000	
Bonds payable		90,000
Preferred stock	36,000	
Common stock	180,000	288,000
Retained earnings	162,000	248,400
Total liabilities and equity	$558,000	$716,400

Rosie-Lee Company
Income Statement
For the Year Ended June 30, 2010

Sales	$ 920,000
Less: Cost of goods sold	(620,000)
Gross margin	$ 300,000
Less: Operating expenses	(177,600)
Net income	$ 122,400

Additional transactions were as follows:

a. Sold equipment costing $21,600 with accumulated depreciation of $16,200 for $3,600
b. Retired a mortgage at a price of $108,000 on December 31
c. Paid cash dividends of $36,000

Required:
Prepare a statement of cash flows by using a worksheet similar to the one shown in Cornerstone 13-8.

OBJECTIVES ① ②   **Problem 13-36 Statement of Cash Flows: Indirect Method**

Balance sheets for Brierwold Corporation follow:

	Beginning Balances	Ending Balances
Assets		
Cash	$ 100,000	$ 150,000
Accounts receivable	200,000	180,000
Inventory	400,000	410,000
Plant and equipment	700,000	690,000
Accumulated depreciation	(200,000)	(245,000)
Land	100,000	150,000
Total assets	$1,300,000	$1,335,000
Liabilities and equity		
Accounts payable	$ 300,000	$ 250,000
Mortgage payable		110,000
Preferred stock	60,000	
Common stock	240,000	280,000
Contributed capital in excess of par:		
Preferred stock	40,000	
Common stock	360,000	420,000
Retained earnings	300,000	275,000
Total liabilities and equity	$1,300,000	$1,335,000

Additional transactions were as follows:

a. Purchased equipment costing $50,000
b. Sold equipment costing $60,000 with a book value of $25,000 for $40,000
c. Retired preferred stock at a cost of $110,000 (the premium is debited to retained earnings)

d.   Issued 10,000 shares of its common stock (par value, $4) for $10 per share
e.   Reported a loss of $15,000 for the year
f.   Purchased land for $50,000

Required:
Prepare a statement of cash flows by using the indirect method.

Problem 13-37 Statement of Cash Flows, Worksheet

OBJECTIVE ④

Balance sheets and other information for Brierwold Corporation follow:

	Beginning Balances	Ending Balances
Assets		
Cash	$ 100,000	$ 150,000
Accounts receivable	200,000	180,000
Inventory	400,000	410,000
Plant and equipment	700,000	690,000
Accumulated depreciation	(200,000)	(245,000)
Land	100,000	150,000
Total assets	$1,300,000	$1,335,000
Liabilities and equity		
Accounts payable	$ 300,000	$ 250,000
Mortgage payable		110,000
Preferred stock	60,000	
Common stock	240,000	280,000
Contributed capital in excess of par:		
Preferred stock	40,000	
Common stock	360,000	420,000
Retained earnings	300,000	275,000
Total liabilities and equity	$1,300,000	$1,335,000

Additional transactions were as follows:

a.   Purchased equipment costing $50,000
b.   Sold equipment costing $60,000 with a book value of $25,000 for $40,000
c.   Retired preferred stock at a cost of $110,000 (the premium is debited to retained earnings)
d.   Issued 10,000 shares of its common stock (par value, $4) for $10 per share
e.   Reported a loss of $15,000 for the year
f   Purchased land for $50,000

Required:
1.   Prepare a statement of cash flows by using the indirect method.
2.   Prepare a statement of cash flows by using the worksheet approach.

Problem 13-38 Schedule of Operating Cash Flows: Indirect Method

OBJECTIVES ① ②

The income statement for the Mendelin Corporation is as follows:

Revenues		$ 380,000
Less: Cost of goods sold	$ 50,000	
Beginning inventory	200,000	
Ending inventory	(34,000)	(216,000)
Less: Patent amortization		(20,000)
Advertising		(12,000)
Depreciation expense		(60,000)
Wages expense		(30,000)
Insurance expense		(10,500)
Bad debt expense		(6,400)
Interest expense		(7,600)
Net income		$ 17,500

Additional information is as follows:

a.   Interest expense includes $1,800 of discount amortization
b.   The prepaid insurance expense account decreased by $2,000 during the year
c.   Accrued wages decreased by $3,000 during the year
d.   Accounts payable increased by $7,500 (this account is for purchase of merchandise only)
e.   Accounts receivable increased by $10,000 (net of allowance for doubtful accounts)

Required:
Prepare a schedule of operating cash flows by using the indirect method.

OBJECTIVES ① ②   Problem 13-39 Statement of Cash Flows, Indirect Method

The following balance sheets are taken from the records of Golding Company (numbers are expressed in thousands):

	2009	2010
Assets		
Cash	$130,000	$150,000
Accounts receivable	25,000	20,000
Plant and equipment	50,000	60,000
Accumulated depreciation	(20,000)	(25,000)
Land	10,000	10,000
Total assets	$195,000	$215,000
Liabilities and equity		
Accounts payable	$ 10,000	$ 5,000
Bonds payable	8,000	18,000
Common stock	120,000	120,000
Retained earnings	57,000	72,000
Total liabilities and equity	$195,000	$215,000

Additional information is as follows:

a.   Equipment costing $10,000,000 was purchased at year-end. No equipment was sold.
b.   Net income for the year was $25,000,000; $10,000,000 in dividends were paid.

Required:
1.   Prepare a statement of cash flows by using the indirect method.
2.   Assess Golding's ability to use cash to acquire Lemmons Company. Consider the information in Exhibit 13-2 and Cornerstone 13-6 as part of your analysis.

OBJECTIVE ②   Problem 13-40 Statement of Cash Flows

The following balance sheets were taken from the records of Blalock Company:

	2009	2010
Assets		
Cash	$150,000	$185,000
Accounts receivable	70,000	80,000
Investments		30,000
Plant and equipment	100,000	105,000
Accumulated depreciation	(30,000)	(32,000)
Land	20,000	30,000
Total assets	$310,000	$398,000

Liabilities and equity

Accounts payable	$ 40,000	$ 50,000
Bonds payable	60,000	
Mortgage payable		50,000
Preferred stock	20,000	
Common stock	100,000	160,000
Retained earnings	90,000	138,000
Total liabilities and equity	$310,000	$398,000

Additional transactions were as follows:

a. Sold equipment costing $12,000 with accumulated depreciation of $9,000 for $2,000
b. Retired bonds at a price of $60,000 on December 31
c. Earned net income for the year of $68,000; paid cash dividends of $20,000

Required:
Prepare a statement of cash flows by using the indirect method.

Problem 13-41 Statement of Cash Flows, Worksheet

OBJECTIVE ④

The following balance sheets were taken from the records of Blalock Company:

	2009	2010
Assets		
Cash	$150,000	$185,000
Accounts receivable	70,000	80,000
Investments		30,000
Plant and equipment	100,000	105,000
Accumulated depreciation	(30,000)	(32,000)
Land	20,000	30,000
Total assets	$310,000	$398,000
Liabilities and equity		
Accounts payable	$ 40,000	$ 50,000
Bonds payable	60,000	
Mortgage payable		50,000
Preferred stock	20,000	
Common stock	100,000	160,000
Retained earnings	90,000	138,000
Total liabilities and equity	$310,000	$398,000

Additional transactions were as follows:

a. Sold equipment costing $12,000 with accumulated depreciation of $9,000 for $2,000
b. Retired bonds at a price of $60,000 on December 31
c. Earned net income for the year of $68,000; paid cash dividends of $20,000

Required:
Prepare a statement of cash flows by using the worksheet approach.

Cases

Case 13-42 Direct and Indirect Methods

OBJECTIVES ② ③

The comparative balance sheets and income statement of Piura Manufacturing are shown on the following page. Additional transactions for 2010 were as follows:

a. Cash dividends of $8,000 were paid.
b. Equipment was acquired by issuing common stock with a par value of $6,000. The fair market value of the equipment is $32,000.

c.   Equipment with a book value of $12,000 was sold for $6,000. The original cost of the equipment was $24,000. The loss is included in operating expenses.

d.   Two thousand shares of preferred stock were sold for $4 per share

Piura Manufacturing
Comparative Balance Sheets
For the Years Ended June 30, 2009 and 2010

	2009	2010
Assets		
Cash	$ 72,000	$146,400
Accounts receivable	44,000	48,000
Inventory	64,000	44,000
Plant and equipment	104,000	112,000
Accumulated depreciation	(52,000)	(48,000)
Land	20,000	20,000
Total assets	$252,000	$322,400
Liabilities and equity		
Accounts payable	$ 32,000	$ 48,000
Wages payable	4,000	2,400
Bonds payable	24,000	16,000
Preferred stock (no par)	4,000	12,000
Common stock	30,000	36,000
Paid-in capital in excess of par	50,000	76,000
Retained earnings	108,000	132,000
Total liabilities and equity	$252,000	$322,400

Piura Manufacturing
Income Statement
For the Year Ended June 30, 2010

Sales	$ 320,000
Less: Cost of goods sold	(200,000)
Gross margin	$ 120,000
Less: Operating expenses	(88,000)
Net income	$ 32,000

Required:

1.   Prepare a schedule of operating cash flows by using:
     a. The indirect method
     b. The direct method
2.   Prepare a statement of cash flows using the indirect method.
3.   Prepare a statement of cash flows by using a worksheet similar to the one shown in Cornerstone 13-8.
4.   Form a group with two to four other students, and discuss the merits of the direct and indirect methods. Which do you think investors might prefer? Should the FASB require all companies to use the direct method?

Case 13-43 Management of Statement of Cash Flows, Ethical Issues

Fred Jackson, president of Bailey Company, is concerned about the company's ability to obtain a loan from a major bank. The loan is a key factor in the firm's plan to expand its operations. Demand for the firm's product is high—too high for the current production capacity to handle. Fred is convinced that a new plant is needed. Building the new plant, however, will require an infusion of new capital. Fred calls a meeting with Karla Jones, financial vice president.

   Fred: Karla, what is the status of our loan application? Do you think that the bank will approve?

Karla: Perhaps, but at this point, there is a real risk. The loan officer has requested a complete set of financials for this year and the past two years. He has indicated that he is particularly interested in the statement of cash flows. As you know, our income statement looks great for all three years, but the statement of cash flows will show a significant increase in receivables, especially for this year. It will also show a significant increase in inventory, and I'm sure that he'll want to know why inventory is increasing if demand is so great that we need another plant. Both of these effects show decreasing cash flows from operating activities.

Fred: Well, it is certainly true that cash flows have been decreasing. One major problem is the lack of operating cash. This loan will solve that problem. Bill Lawson has agreed to build the plant for the amount of the loan but will actually charge me for only 95 percent of the stated cost. We get 5 percent of the loan for operating cash. Bill is willing to pay 5 percent to get the contract.

Karla: The loan may help with operating cash flows, but we can't get the loan without showing some evidence of cash strength. We need to do something about the increases in inventory and receivables that we expect for this year.

Fred: The increased inventory is easy to explain. We had to work overtime and use subcontractors to take care of one of our biggest customers. That inventory will be gone by the first of next year.

Karla: The problem isn't explaining the inventory. The problem is that the increase in inventory decreases our operating cash flows and this shows up on the statement of cash flows. This effect coupled with the increase in receivables reveals us as being cash poor. It'll definitely hurt our chances.

Fred: I see. Well, this can be solved. The inventory is for a customer that I know well. She'll do me a favor. I'll simply get her to take delivery of the inventory early, before the end of our fiscal year. She can pay me next year as originally planned.

Karla: Fred, all that will do is shift the increase from inventory to receivables. It'll still report the same cash position.

Fred: No problem. We'll report the delivery as a cash sale, and I'll have Bill Lawson advance me the cash as a temporary loan. He'll do that to get the contract to build our new plant. In fact, we can do the same with some of our other receivables. We'll report them as collected, and I'll get Bill to cover. If he understands that this is what it takes to get the loan, he'll cooperate. He stands to make a lot of money on the deal.

Karla: Fred, this is getting complicated. The bank will have us audited each year if this loan is approved. If an audit were to reveal some of this manipulation, we could be in big trouble, particularly if the company has any trouble in repaying the loan.

Fred: The company won't have any trouble. Sales are strong, and the problem of collecting receivables can be solved, especially given the extra time that the 5 percent of the loan proceeds will provide.

Required:

1. Form a group with two to four other students. Discuss the propriety of the arrangement that Fred has with Bill Lawson concerning the disbursement of the proceeds from the loan.
2. In your group, discuss the propriety of the actions that Fred is proposing to improve the firm's statement of cash flows. Suppose that there is very little risk that the loan will not be repaid. Does this information affect your assessment?
3. Assume that Karla is subject to the Institute of Management Accountant's (IMA) code of ethics. Look up this code, and identify the standards of ethical conduct that will be violated, if any, by Karla should she agree to cooperate with Fred's scheme.
4. Using the IMA code of ethics, if you were in Karla's position, what would you do (suppose that Fred insists on implementing his plan)? Now, answer the question assuming that Fred is willing to consider alternative ways to solve the company's problems.

14

Financial Statement Analysis

© PhotoDisc/Getty Images

After studying Chapter 14, you should be able to:

① Analyze financial statements by using two forms of common-size analysis: horizontal analysis and vertical analysis.

② Explain why historical standards and industrial averages are important for ratio analysis.

③ Calculate and use liquidity ratios to assess the ability of a company to meet its current obligations.

④ Calculate and use leverage ratios to assess the ability of a company to meet its long- and short-term obligations.

⑤ Calculate and use profitability ratios to assess the extent to which a company's resources are being used efficiently.

Experience Managerial Decisions

with Apple

In response to a 2006 survey, 73 percent of college students ranked the iPod as the most "in" thing on campus—higher than anything else, including Facebook.com and specialty beverages. Not surprisingly, during the fourth quarter of 2006, **Apple** shipped 21.1 million iPods (50 percent more than the year-ago quarter), which brought the total number of iPods shipped since inception to over 100 million units! How has Apple achieved such amazing market penetration, and does it have the capability to continue this impressive trend? Several common and easily computed financial statement ratios can begin to provide an answer to this question. First, the current ratio of 2.24—a common liquidity ratio—indicates that on December 31, 2006, Apple had $2.24 of current assets for every $1.00 of current liabilities. Given that it has more current assets than current liabilities, it appears as though Apple is in a position to remain liquid and meet its short-term obligations. Apple's inventory turnover, another liquidity ratio, shows that the company turned over its inventory 63 times during the year, which also means that on average, its inventory sat on the shelf for only 5.79 days before being sold! Turning inventory into cash so quickly is very beneficial to the company because it can reinvest the cash back into the business, such as for research and development of the next generation of iPhone or iPod. Apple's debt ratio is 0.42, indicating that nearly 60 percent of its assets are financed by using equity. Interestingly, almost 90 percent of Apple's liabilities are current in nature. For example, an interested financial statement user might try to calculate the times-interest-earned ratio, another leverage ratio. However, the user would find it impossible to compute this ratio because Apple had no long-term debt in 2006 and, therefore, no interest payments on long-term debt (a key part of the times-interest-earned ratio). Rather than taking on long-term debt, and the interest associated with such debt, Apple chose to raise the capital necessary to supplement its cash from operating activities by issuing $318 million worth of stock to investors during 2006. Finally, the company's return on sales of 0.10, a profitability ratio, indicates that $0.10 of every $1.00 in sales revenue was left over as profit after accounting for all expenses. In summary, several common financial statement ratios suggest that Apple was able to perform so effectively in 2006, in part, because of its impressive ability to turn inventory into cash quickly, avoid costly long-term debt, and raise significant capital through stock issuances to investors. Therefore, the next time you download a song from the iTunes Store, you can appreciate Apple's performance on these key financial statement ratios and be thankful for its part in revolutionizing the music industry!

Financial statement analysis provides useful information for many purposes. For example, the formal analysis of financial statements can provide important input for commercial loan managers in making loan decisions. By using ratio analysis, common-size analysis, and other techniques, loan managers can assess the creditworthiness of potential customers. The formal analysis of financial statements can also provide a means to exercise control over outstanding loans.

Managers of commercial loan departments, however, are not the only ones who can benefit from analysis of financial statements. Individuals interested in investing in a company and managers of the company to whom the financial statements belong need this skill as well. Investors need to analyze financial statements to assess the attractiveness of a company as a potential investment. Managers need to analyze their own financial statements so as to assess profitability, liquidity, debt position, and progress toward organizational objectives. The analysis of financial statements is designed to reveal relationships among items on the financial statements and trends of individual items over time. By knowing these relationships and trends, users are in a better position to exercise sound judgment regarding the current or future performance of a company. The two major techniques for financial analysis are common-size analysis and ratio analysis.

Common-Size Analysis

OBJECTIVE ①
Analyze financial statements using two forms of common-size analysis: horizontal analysis and vertical analysis.

A simple first step in financial statement analysis is comparing two financial statements. For example, the income statement for this year could be compared with the income statement for last year. To make the analysis more meaningful, percentages can be used. **Common-size analysis** expresses line items or accounts in the financial statements as percentages. The two major forms of common-size analysis are horizontal analysis and vertical analysis. Exhibit 14-1 illustrates vertical and horizontal analysis.

Horizontal Analysis

Also called trend analysis, **horizontal analysis** expresses a line item as a percentage of some prior-period amount. This approach allows the trend over time to be assessed. In horizontal analysis, line items are expressed as a percentage of a base period amount. The base period can be the immediately preceding period, or it can be a period further

Exhibit 14-1

Common-Size Analysis

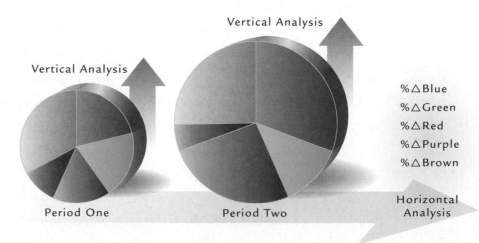

in the past. Cornerstone 14-1 shows how to prepare common-size income statements by using the first year as the base period.

Since the base year in Cornerstone 14-1 is year 1, all line amounts in subsequent years are compared with the amount in the base year. For example, year 3 sales are expressed as a percentage of year 1 sales. By comparing each subsequent amount with the base period, trends can be seen. The data reveal that sales have increased by 32 percent over the three years. With such a large increase in sales, many would expect net income likewise to experience a significant increase. The percentage analysis, however, shows that net income has shown no change from the base period. Net income has stayed flat because expenses and taxes also have increased; cost of goods sold has increased by 35 percent, operating expenses by 45 percent, and taxes by 25 percent. As a result of the percentage analysis, the manager of the company might decide to focus more attention on controlling costs.

HOW TO Prepare Common-Size Income Statements by Using Base Period Horizontal Analysis

CORNERSTONE 14-1

Information: Simpson Company provided the following income statements for its first three years of operation:

	Year 1	Year 2	Year 3
Net sales	$100,000	$120,000	$132,000
Less: Cost of goods sold	(60,000)	(75,000)	(81,000)
Gross margin	$ 40,000	$ 45,000	$ 51,000
Less:			
Operating expenses	(20,000)	(24,000)	(29,000)
Income taxes	(8,000)	(9,000)	(10,000)
Net income	$ 12,000	$ 12,000	$ 12,000

Required: Prepare common-size income statements by using year 1 as the base period.

Calculation: Year 1 is the base year. Therefore, every dollar amount in year 1 is 100 percent of itself.

Percent for a line item = (Dollar amount of line item/Dollar amount of base year line item) × 100

Percent year 1 net sales = ($100,000/$100,000) × 100 = 100%
Percent year 2 net sales = ($120,000/$100,000) × 100 = 120%
Percent year 3 net sales = ($132,000/$100,000) × 100 = 132%

	Year 1		Year 2		Year 3	
	Dollars	Percent	Dollars	Percent	Dollars	Percent
Net sales	$100,000	100%	$120,000	120.0%	$132,000	132.0%
Less: Cost of goods sold	(60,000)	100	(75,000)	125.0	(81,000)	135.0
Gross margin	$ 40,000	100	$ 45,000	112.5	$ 51,000	127.5
Less:						
Operating expenses	(20,000)	100	(24,000)	120.0	(29,000)	145.0
Income taxes	(8,000)	100	(9,000)	112.5	(10,000)	125.0
Net income	$ 12,000	100	$ 12,000	100.0	$ 12,000	100.0

Vertical Analysis   While horizontal analysis involves relationships among items *over time*, vertical analysis is concerned with relationships among items *within a particular time period*. **Vertical analysis** expresses the line item as a percentage of some other line item for the same period. With this approach, within-period relationships can be assessed. Line items on income statements often are expressed as percentages of net sales; items on the balance sheet often are expressed as a percentage of total assets. Cornerstone 14-2 shows how to perform vertical analysis with the same example used in Cornerstone 14-1. Sales is used as the base for computing percentages. Although the main purpose of vertical analysis is to highlight relationships among components of a company's financial statements, changes in these relationships over time can also be informative. For example, Cornerstone 14-1 reveals large increases in cost of goods sold and operating expenses over time. Over the three-year period, cost of goods sold has increased by 35 percent ($21,000/$60,000), and operating expenses have increased by 45 percent ($9,000/$20,000). Cornerstone 14-2

**CORNERSTONE
14-2**

HOW TO Prepare Income Statements by Using Net Sales as the Base: Vertical Analysis

Information: Simpson Company provided the following income statements for its first three years of operation:

	Year 1	Year 2	Year 3
Net sales	$100,000	$120,000	$132,000
Less: Cost of goods sold	(60,000)	(75,000)	(81,000)
Gross margin	$ 40,000	$ 45,000	$ 51,000
Less:			
Operating expenses	(20,000)	(24,000)	(29,000)
Income taxes	(8,000)	(9,000)	(10,000)
Net income	$ 12,000	$ 12,000	$ 12,000

Required: Prepare common-size income statements by using net sales as the base.

Calculation: Since the analysis is based on net sales, net sales in each year equals 100 percent of itself. Then, every line item on the income statement is figured as a percent of that year's net sales.

Percent for a line item = (Dollar amount of line item/Dollar amount of that year's sales) × 100
Percent year 1 net sales = ($100,000/($100,000) × 100 = 100%
Percent year 2 net sales = ($120,000/($120,000) × 100 = 100%
Percent year 3 net sales = ($132,000/($100,000) × 100 = 132%

	Year 1		Year 2		Year 3	
	Dollars	Percent	Dollars	Percent	Dollars	Percent
Net sales	$100,000	100%	$120,000	100.0%	$132,000	100.0%
Less: Cost of goods sold	(60,000)	60	(75,000)	62.5	(81,000)	61.4
Gross margin	$ 40,000	40	$ 45,000	37.5	$ 51,000	38.6
Less:						
Operating expenses	$ (20,000)	20	$ (24,000)	20.0	$ (29,000)	22.0
Income taxes	(8,000)	8	(9,000)	7.5	(10,000)	7.6
Net income	$ 12,000	12	$ 12,000	10.0	$ 12,000	9.1

compares these expenses with sales. This comparison reveals that much of the increase may be tied to increased sales. That is, year 1 operating expenses represented 20 percent of sales, whereas in year 3, they represented 22 percent of sales.

Percentages and Size Effects

The use of common-size analysis makes comparisons more meaningful because percentages eliminate the effects of size. For example, if one company earns $100,000 and another company earns $1 million, which is the more profitable? The answer depends to a large extent on the assets employed to earn the profits. If the first company used an investment of $1 million to earn the $100,000, then the return expressed as a percentage of dollars is 10 percent ($100,000/ $1,000,000). If the second company used an investment of $20 million to earn its $1 million, the percentage return is only 5 percent ($1,000,000/$20,000,000). By using percentages, it is easy to see that the first firm is relatively more profitable than the second.

Concept Q&A

Company A's net income is $1,000 one year and $1,500 the following year. Company B's net income is $10,000 one year and $12,000 the following year. What is the percentage increase from one year to the next for each company? Which company is doing better?

Answer:

Company A's net income has increased by 50 percent, while company B's net income has increased by 20 percent. Because percentages abstract from size, a user must exercise caution in their interpretation, particularly when the numbers involved are small. If the base is small, small changes in line items can produce large percentage changes. The percentage increase in net income is larger for company A than company B. However, company A increased its total earnings by only $500, while company B increased its earnings by $2,000.

Here's The Real Kicker

Every month, Kicker holds a company-wide meeting of all employees. In addition to the introduction of new employees and general announcements, Kicker's owner shares financial information. Then, graphs showing the trend in sales and profits are posted on the bulletin board in the break room. Employees can check trends in financial information at their leisure. This information is very important to Kicker employees because all of them are part of a comprehensive profit-sharing plan. Robust monthly sales and income will result in a bonus check to every employee that month. Yearly profits lead to another bonus check at year-end. Finally, Kicker also contributes to employees' 401(K) accounts. Since all of this is dependent on net income, each employee has a vested interest in keeping costs down and sales up.

Ratio Analysis

OBJECTIVE ②
Explain why historical standards and industrial averages are important for ratio analysis.

Ratio analysis is the second major technique for financial statement analysis. Ratios are fractions or percentages computed by dividing one account or line-item amount by another. For example, operating income divided by sales produces a ratio that measures the profit margin on sales.

Standards for Comparison

Ratios by themselves tell little about the financial well-being of a company. For meaningful analysis, the ratios should be compared with a standard. Only through comparison can someone using a financial statement assess the financial health of a company. Two standards commonly used are the past history of the company and industrial averages. Exhibit 14-2 on the following page illustrates the way a company might view both types of ratio comparison.

Exhibit 14-2

Ratio Analysis

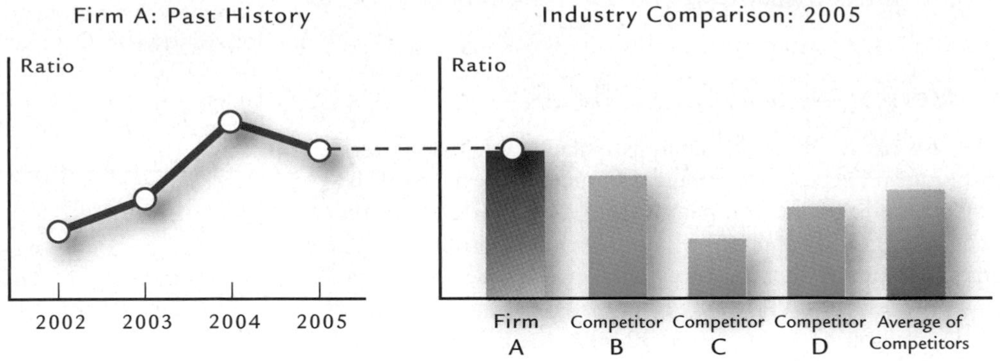

Firm A: Past History

Ratio

2002   2003   2004   2005

Industry Comparison: 2005

Ratio

Firm A   Competitor B   Competitor C   Competitor D   Average of Competitors

Past History   One way to detect progress or problems is to compare the value of a ratio over time. Doing so allows trends to be assessed. For example, ratios measuring liquidity may be dropping over time, signaling a deteriorating financial condition. The company's management can use this information to take corrective action. Investors and creditors, on the other hand, may use this information to decide whether or not to invest money in the company.

Industrial Averages   Additional insight can be gained by comparing a company's ratios with the same ratios to other companies in the same line of business. To facilitate the comparison, a number of annual publications provide industrial figures. For example, Dun and Bradstreet report the median, upper quartile, and lower quartile for 14 commonly used ratios for more than 900 lines of business. The titles and publishers of some of the more common sources of industrial ratios are as follows:

1. *Key Business Ratios*, Dun and Bradstreet
2. *Standard and Poor's Industry Survey*, Standard and Poor's
3. *Annual Statement Studies*, Robert Morris Associates
4. *The Almanac of Business and Industrial Financial Ratios*, Prentice-Hall
5. *Dow Jones-Irwin Business and Investment Almanac*, Dow Jones-Irwin

A number of online sources are useful for competitive information on a company's ratios. Some of these are:

1. http://www.bizstats.com
2. http://www.fidelity.com
3. http://moneycentral.msn.com/investor/invsub/results/compare.asp?
4. http://biz.yahoo.com/r/

Even though the industrial figures provide a useful reference point, they should be used with care. Companies within the same industry may use different accounting methods, which diminishes the validity of the average. Other problems such as small sample sizes for the industrial report, different labor markets, the impact of extreme values, and terms of sale can produce variations among companies within the same industry. The industrial statistics should not be taken as absolute norms but rather as general guidelines for purposes of making comparisons.

Classification of Ratios

Ratios generally are classified into one of three categories: liquidity, borrowing capacity or leverage, and profitability.

- **Liquidity ratios** measure the ability of a company to meet its current obligations.
- **Leverage ratios** measure the ability of a company to meet its long- and short-term obligations. These ratios provide a measure of the degree of protection provided to a company's creditors.
- **Profitability ratios** measure the earning ability of a company. These ratios allow investors, creditors, and managers to evaluate the extent to which invested funds are being used efficiently.

Some of the more common and popular ratios for each category will be defined and illustrated. Exhibits 14-3 below and 14-4 on the following page provide an income statement, a statement of retained earnings, and comparative balance sheets for Payne Company, a manufacturer of glassware. These financial statements provide the basis for subsequent analyses.

Exhibit 14-3

Income Statement and Statement of Retained Earnings for Payne Company for Year 2

Payne Company
Income Statement
For the Year Ended December 31, Year 2
(dollars in thousands)

	Amount	Percent
Net sales	$ 50,000	100.0%
Less: Cost of goods sold	(35,000)	70.0
Gross margin	$ 15,000	30.0
Less: Operating expenses	(10,000)	20.0
Operating income	$ 5,000	10.0
Less: Interest expense	(400)	0.8
Net income before taxes	$ 4,600	9.2
Less: Taxes (50%)*	(2,300)	4.6
Net income	$ 2,300	4.6

Payne Company
Statement of Retained Earnings
For the Year Ended December 31, Year 2

Balance, beginning of period	$ 5,324
Net income	2,300
Total	$ 7,624
Less: Preferred dividends	(224)
Dividends to common stockholders	(1,000)
Balance, end of period	$ 6,400

*Includes both state and federal taxes.

Exhibit 14-4

Comparative Balance Sheets for Payne Company for Years 1 and 2

Payne Company
Comparative Balance Sheets
For the Years Ended December 31, Year 1 and Year 2
(dollars in thousands)

Assets	Year 2	Year 1
Current assets:		
Cash	$ 1,600	$ 2,500
Marketable securities	1,600	2,000
Accounts receivable (net)	8,000	10,000
Inventories	10,000	3,000
Other	800	1,500
Total current assets	$22,000	$19,000
Property and equipment:		
Land	$ 4,000	$ 6,000
Building and equipment (net)	6,000	5,000
Total long-term assets	$10,000	$11,000
Total assets	$32,000	$30,000

Liabilities and Stockholders' Equity		
Current liabilities:		
Notes payable, short term	$ 3,200	$ 3,000
Accounts payable	6,400	5,800
Current maturity of long-term debt	400	400
Accrued payables	2,000	1,876
Total current liabilities	$12,000	$11,076
Long-term liabilities:		
Bonds payable, 10%	4,000	4,000
Total liabilities	$16,000	$15,076
Stockholder's equity:		
Preferred stock, $25 par, 7%	$ 3,200	$ 3,200
Common stock, $2 par	1,600	1,600
Additional paid-in capital*	4,800	4,800
Retained earnings	6,400	5,324
Total equity	$16,000	$14,924
Total liabilities and stockholders' equity	$32,000	$30,000

*For common stock only.

OBJECTIVE ③
Calculate and use liquidity ratios to assess the ability of a company to meet its current obligations.

Liquidity Ratios

Liquidity ratios are used to assess the short-term debt-paying ability of a company. If a company does not have the short-term financial strength to meet its current obligations, it is likely to have difficulty meeting its long-term obligations. Accordingly, evaluation of the short-term financial strength of a company is a good starting point in financial analysis. Although there are numerous liquidity ratios, only the most common ones will be discussed in this section. These liquidity ratios are the current ratio, quick or acid-test ratio, accounts receivable turnover ratio, and inventory turnover ratio.

Current Ratio

The **current ratio** is a measure of the ability of a company to pay its short-term liabilities out of short-term assets. The current ratio is computed by dividing the current assets by the current liabilities:

Current ratio = Current assets/Current liabilities

Since current liabilities must be paid within an operating cycle (usually within a year) and current assets can be converted to cash within an operating cycle, the current ratio provides a direct measure of the ability of a company to meet its short-term obligations. Payne Company's current ratio for year 2 is computed as follows, using data from Exhibit 14-4:

$$\text{Current} = \$22{,}000{,}000/\$12{,}000{,}000$$
$$= 1.83$$

But what does a current ratio of 1.83 mean? Does the ratio of 1.83 signal good or poor debt-paying ability? Additional information is needed to interpret it. Many creditors use the rule of thumb that a 2.0 ratio is needed to provide good debt-paying ability. Based on this assessment, Payne does not have sufficient liquidity; however, this rule has many exceptions. For example, the industrial norm might be less than 2.0. Information on the ratio's trend is also helpful. Suppose that the upper quartile, median, and lower quartile values of the current ratio for the glassware industry are 2.2, 1.7, and 1.3, respectively. Payne's current ratio of 1.83 is above the median ratio for its industry, suggesting that Payne does not have liquidity problems. More than half of the firms in its industry have lower current ratios. It is possible, however, that Payne's current ratio for year 2 is representative of what usually happens. By comparing this year's ratio with ratios for prior years, some judgment about whether or not it is representative can be made. For example, if the ratio in prior years has been reasonably stable with values in the 1.7 to 1.9 range, this year's ratio is representative. If the ratio has been declining for the past several years, the company's financial position could be deteriorating.

A declining current ratio is not necessarily bad, particularly if it is falling from a high value. A high current ratio may signal excessive investment in current resources. Some of these current resources may be more productively employed by reducing long-term debt, paying dividends, or investing in long-term assets. Thus, a declining current ratio may signal a move toward more efficient utilization of resources. But a declining current ratio coupled with a current ratio lower than that of the other firms in the industry supports the judgment that a company is having liquidity problems.

Quick or Acid-Test Ratio

For many companies, inventory represents 50 percent or more of total current assets. For example, Payne Company's inventory represents 45 percent of its total current assets. The liquidity of inventory often is less than that of receivables, marketable securities, and cash. Inventory may be slow moving, nearly obsolete, or even pledged in part to creditors. Because including inventory may produce a misleading measure of liquidity, it often is excluded in computing liquidity ratios. For similar reasons, other current assets, such as miscellaneous assets, are excluded.

The **quick** or **acid-test ratio** is a measure of liquidity that compares only the most liquid assets with current liabilities. Excluded from the quick or acid-test ratio are

Concept Q&A

This year, Bellows Company has the same level of current assets and current liabilities as last year. However, last year, current assets were 50 percent cash and accounts receivable, while this year, current assets are 75 percent inventories. How will the change in the current asset mix affect this year's current ratio? Quick (acid-test) ratio?

Answer:

The current ratio will be unaffected (i.e., this year's current ratio will equal last year's current ratio). The quick ratio will be lower this year than last year because cash and accounts receivable are lower than last year. Hint: Sometimes, it helps to put numbers into this type of a question. For example, you can choose to let last year's (as well as this year's) current assets equal $2,000 and to let last year's (as well as this year's) current liabilities equal $1,000. Then, the current ratio last year will be $2,000/$1,000 or 2. This year's current ratio is the same. The quick ratio for last year will be 1 ($1,000/$1,000), while this year's quick ratio will be 0.5 ($500/$1,000).

nonliquid current assets such as inventories. The numerator of the quick or acid-test ratio includes only the most liquid assets (cash, marketable securities, and receivables).

Quick ratio = (Cash + Marketable securities + Receivables)/Current liabilities

For Payne Company, the quick ratio is calculated as follows (using data from Exhibit 14-4 for year 2):

$$\text{Quick ratio} = (\$1{,}600{,}000 + \$1{,}600{,}000 + \$8{,}000{,}000)/\$12{,}000{,}000$$
$$= \$11{,}200{,}000/\$12{,}000{,}000$$
$$= 0.93$$

Payne's quick ratio reveals that it does not have the capability to meet its current obligations with its most liquid assets; a ratio of 1.0 is the usual standard. Payne's quick ratio is not far below the standard level, and perhaps some attention should be paid to raise it somewhat. Cornerstone 14-3 shows how to calculate the current ratio and the quick ratio.

Accounts Receivable Turnover Ratio

The extent of Payne's liquidity problem can be further investigated by examining the liquidity of its receivables, or by how long it takes the company to turn its receivables into cash. A low liquidity of receivables signals more difficulty since the quick ratio would be overstated. The liquidity of receivables is measured by the **accounts receivable turnover ratio**. This ratio is computed by dividing net sales by average accounts receivable. The average accounts receivable is used and is based on the beginning and ending balances of accounts receivable because this matches the account to the period that corresponds to the income statement measure.

Accounts receivable turnover ratio = Net sales/Average accounts receivable

**CORNERSTONE
14-3**

HOW TO Calculate the Current Ratio and the Quick (or Acid-Test) Ratio

Information: Bordner Company has current assets equal to $120,000. Of these, $15,000 is cash, $30,000 is accounts receivable, and the remainder is inventories. Current liabilities total $50,000.

Required:
1. Calculate the current ratio.
2. Calculate the quick ratio (acid-test ratio).

Calculation:
1. Current ratio = Current assets/Current liabilities
   = $120,000/$50,000
   = 2.4
2. Quick ratio = (Cash + Marketable securities + Receivables)/Current liabilities
   = ($15,000 + 0 + $30,000)/$50,000
   = 0.90

Average accounts receivable is defined as follows:

Average accounts receivable = (Beginning receivables + Ending receivables)/2

The accounts receivable turnover ratio can be taken further to determine the number of days the average balance of accounts receivable is outstanding before being converted into cash. This number is found by dividing the days in a year by the receivables turnover ratio:

Turnover in days = 365/Receivables turnover ratio

Payne Company's accounts receivable turnover is computed as follows (using data from Exhibits 14-3 and 14-4):

$$\text{Accounts receivable turnover} = \$50,000,000/\$9,000,000^*$$
$$= 5.56 \text{ times per year}$$

*Average receivables = ($10,000,000 + $8,000,000)/2.

$$\text{Accounts receivable turnover in days} = (365/5.56) = 65.6 \text{ days}$$

Payne's receivables are held for almost 66 days before being converted to cash. Whether this is good or bad depends to some extent on what other companies in the industry are experiencing. The low turnover ratio suggests a need for Payne's managers to modify credit and collection policies to speed up the conversion of receivables to cash. This need is particularly acute if a historical analysis shows a persistent problem or a trend downward. Note that net sales were used to compute the turnover ratio. Technically, credit sales should be used; however, external financial reports do not usually break net sales into credit and cash components. Consequently, if a turnover ratio is to be computed by external users, net sales must be used. For many firms, most sales are credit sales, and the computation is a good approximation. If sales are mostly for cash, liquidity is not an issue. In that case, the ratio provides a measure of the company's operating cycle. Cornerstone 14-4 shows how to calculate the average accounts receivable, the accounts receivable turnover ratio, and the accounts receivable turnover in days.

HOW TO Calculate the Average Accounts Receivable, the Accounts Receivable Turnover Ratio, and the Accounts Receivable Turnover in Days

**CORNERSTONE
14-4**

Information: Last year, Shuster Company had net sales of $750,000 and cost of goods sold of $400,000. Shuster had the following balances:

	January 1	December 31
Accounts receivable	$ 98,500	$101,500
Inventories	463,000	497,000

Required:
1. Calculate the average accounts receivable.
2. Calculate the accounts receivable turnover ratio.
3. Calculate the accounts receivable in days.

Calculation:
1. Average accounts receivables = (Beginning receivables + Ending receivables)/2
   = ($98,500 + $101,500)/2 = $100,000
2. Accounts receivable turnover ratio = Net sales/Average accounts receivable
   = $750,000/$100,000 = 7.5
3. Accounts receivable in days = Days in a year/Accounts receivable turnover ratio
   = (365/7.5) = 48.7 days

Inventory Turnover Ratio

Inventory turnover is also an important liquidity measure. The **inventory turnover ratio** is computed by dividing the cost of goods sold by the average inventory.

Inventory turnover ratio = Cost of goods sold/Average inventory

Average inventory is found as follows:

Average inventory = (Beginning inventory + Ending inventory)/2

This ratio tells an analyst how many times the average inventory turns over, or is sold, during the year. The number of days inventory is held before being sold can be computed by dividing the number of days in a year by the inventory turnover ratio:

Turnover in days = 365/Inventory turnover ratio

The inventory turnover ratio for Payne Company is computed as follows, using data from Exhibits 14-3 and 14-4:

Inventory turnover = $35,000,000/$6,500,000*
= 5.38 times per year, or every 67.8 days (365/5.38)

*Average inventory = ($3,000,000 + $10,000,000)/2.

Suppose that the glassware industry revealed the upper quartile, median, and lower quartile turnover figures in days to be 34, 57, and 79, respectively. Payne's turnover ratio is midway between the median and the lower quartile. The evidence seems to indicate that the turnover ratio is lower than it should be. A low turnover ratio may signal the presence of too much inventory or sluggish sales. More attention to inventory policies and marketing activities may be in order. Cornerstone 14-5 shows how to calculate the average inventory, the inventory turnover ratio, and the inventory turnover in days.

**CORNERSTONE
14-5**

HOW TO Calculate the Average Inventory, the Inventory Turnover Ratio, and the Inventory Turnover in Days

Information: Last year, Shuster Company had net sales of $750,000 and cost of goods sold of $400,000. Shuster had the following balances:

	January 1	December 31
Accounts receivable	$98,500	$101,500
Inventories	83,000	87,000

Required:
1. Calculate the average inventory.
2. Calculate the inventory turnover ratio.
3. Calculate the inventory turnover in days.

Calculation:
1. Average inventory = (Beginning inventory + Ending inventory)/2
= ($83,000 + $87,000)/2
= $85,000
2. Inventory turnover ratio = Cost of goods sold/Average inventory
= $400,000/$85,000
= 4.7
3. Inventory turnover in days = Days in a year/Inventory turnover ratio
= (365/4.7) = 77.7 days

Leverage Ratios

OBJECTIVE ④
Calculate and use leverage ratios to assess the ability of a company to meet its long- and short-term obligations.

When a company incurs debt, it has the obligation to repay the principal and the interest. Holding debt increases the riskiness of a company. Unlike other sources of capital (e.g., retained earnings or proceeds from the sale of capital stock), debt carries with it the threat of default foreclosure and bankruptcy if income does not meet projections. Both potential investors and creditors need to evaluate a company's debt position. A potential creditor may find that the amount of debt and debt-servicing requirements of a company make it too risky to grant further credit. Similarly, the company may be too risky for some potential investors. Leverage ratios can help an individual to evaluate a company's debt-carrying ability.

Times-Interest-Earned Ratio

The first leverage ratio uses the income statement to assess a company's ability to service its debt. This ratio, called the **times-interest-earned ratio**, is computed by dividing net income before taxes and interest by interest expense:

Times-interest-earned ratio = (Income before taxes + Interest expense)/Interest expense

Income before taxes must be recurring income; thus, unusual or infrequent items appearing on the income statement should be excluded in order to compute the ratio. Recurring income is used because it is the income that is available each year to cover interest payments. The times-interest-earned ratio for Payne Company is computed as follows, using data from Exhibit 14-3:

Times-interest-earned ratio = ($4,600,000 + $400,000)/$400,000
= $5,000,000/$400,000
= 12.5

Since the assumed upper quartile for the glassware industry is 10.0, Payne's times-interest-earned ratio is among the highest in its industry. Payne does not have a significant interest expense burden. Cornerstone 14-6 shows how to calculate the times-interest-earned ratio.

HOW TO Calculate the Times-Interests-Earned Ratio

CORNERSTONE 14-6

Information: Calvin Company provided the following income statement for last year:

Sales	$900,000
Cost of goods sold	350,000
Gross margin	$550,000
Operating expenses	270,000
Operating income	$280,000
Interest expense	15,000
Net income before taxes	$265,000
Income taxes	80,000
Net income	$185,000

Required: Calculate the times-interest-earned ratio.

Calculation:
Times-interest-earned ratio = (Income before taxes + Interest expense)/Interest expense
= ($265,000 + $15,000)/$15,000
= 18.7

Concept Q&A

Quickly estimate your total debts and your total assets. Calculate your own debt ratio. Do you expect it to change over the next five years? Why or why not?

_____

Answer:
Answers will vary.

Debt Ratio

Investors and creditors are the two major sources of capital. As the percentage of assets financed by creditors increases, the riskiness of the company increases. The **debt ratio** measures this percentage. It is computed by dividing a company's total liabilities by its total assets:

Debt ratio = Total liabilities/Total assets

Since total liabilities are compared with total assets, the ratio measures the degree of protection afforded creditors in case of insolvency. Creditors often impose restrictions on the percentage of liabilities allowed. If this percentage is exceeded, the company is in default, and foreclosure can take place. The debt ratio for Payne Company is calculated as follows, using data from Exhibit 14-4:

$$\text{Debt ratio} = \$16{,}000{,}000/\$32{,}000{,}000$$
$$= 0.50$$

Payne's debt ratio indicates that 50 percent of its assets are financed by creditors. Is this percentage good or bad? How much risk will the stockholders allow? Will creditors be willing to provide more capital? For guidance, we again turn to industrial figures. The upper quartile, median, and lower quartile figures are 0.47, 0.55, and 0.69, respectively. With respect to industrial performance, Payne's debt ratio is not out of line. In fact, Payne is close to the upper quartile figure of 0.47. This position might indicate that Payne still has the capability to use additional credit.

Another ratio useful in assessing the leverage used by a company is the debt-to-equity ratio. This ratio compares the amount of debt that is financed by stockholders. For Payne Company, the debt-to-equity ratio is calculated as follows, using data from Exhibit 14-4:

$$\text{Debt-to-equity ratio} = \text{Total liabilities/Total stockholders' equity}$$
$$\text{Debt-to-equity ratio} = \$16{,}000{,}000/\$16{,}000{,}000$$
$$= 1.00$$

Creditors would like this ratio to be relatively low, indicating that stockholders have financed most of the assets of the firm. Stockholders, on the other hand, may wish this ratio to be higher because that indicates that the company is more highly leveraged and stockholders can reap the return of the creditors' financing. Cornerstone 14-7 shows how to calculate the debt ratio and the debt-to-equity ratio.

**CORNERSTONE
14-7**

HOW TO Calculate the Debt Ratio and the Debt-to-Equity Ratio

Information: Jemell Company's balance sheet shows total liabilities of $450,000, total stockholders' equity of $300,000, and total assets of $750,000.

Required:
1. Calculate the debt ratio for Jemell Company.
2. Calculate the debt-to-equity ratio for Jemell Company.

Calculation:
1. Debt ratio = Total liabilities/Total assets
   = $450,000/$750,000
   = 0.6, or 60%
2. Debt-to-equity ratio = Total liabilities/Total stockholders' equity
   = $450,000/$300,000
   = 1.5

Profitability Ratios

OBJECTIVE ⑤
Calculate and use profitability ratios to assess the extent to which a company's resources are being used efficiently.

Investors earn a return through the receipt of dividends and appreciation of the market value of their stock. Both dividends and market price of shares are related to the profits generated by companies. Since they are the source of debt-servicing payments, profits also are of concern to creditors. Managers also have a vested interest in profits. Bonuses, promotions, and salary increases often are tied to reported profits. Profitability ratios, therefore, are given particular attention by both internal and external users of financial statements.

Return on Sales

Return on sales is the profit margin on sales. It represents the percentage of each sales dollar that is left over as net income after all expenses have been subtracted. **Return on sales** is one measure of the efficiency of a firm; it is computed by dividing net income by sales as follows:

$$\text{Return on sales} = \text{Net income/Sales}$$

Cornerstone 14-8 shows how to calculate the return on sales for Payne Company for year 2.

Return on Total Assets

Return on assets measures how efficiently assets are used by calculating the return on total assets used to generate profits. **Return on total assets** is computed by dividing net income plus the after-tax cost of interest by the average total assets:

$$\text{Return on assets} = \frac{[\text{Net income} + \text{Interest expense (1–Tax rate)}]}{\text{Average total assets}}$$

Average total assets is found as follows:

$$\text{Average total assets} = (\text{Beginning total assets} + \text{Ending total assets})/2$$

By adding back the after-tax cost of interest, this measure reflects only how the assets were employed; it does not consider the manner in which they were financed (interest expense is a cost of obtaining the assets, not a cost of *using* them). For Payne Company, the return on assets for year 2 is computed in Cornerstone 14-9.

HOW TO Calculate the Return on Sales

Information: Refer to Exhibits 14-3 and 14-4 for information on Payne Company.

Required: Calculate the return on sales.

Calculation: Return on sales = $2,300,000/$50,000,000
                              = 0.046, or 4.6%

**CORNERSTONE
14-8**

CORNERSTONE 14-9

HOW TO Calculate the Average Total Assets and the Return on Assets

Information: Refer to Exhibits 14-3 and 14-4 for information on Payne Company.

Required:
1. Calculate the average total assets.
2. Calculate the return on total assets.

Calculation:
1. Average total assets = ($30,000,000 + $32,000,000)/2
2. Return on total assets = [$2,300,000 + (0.5 × $400,000)]/$31,000,000
$$= (\$2,300,000 + \$200,000)/\$31,000,000$$
$$= \$2,500,000/\$31,000,000$$
$$= 0.0806, \text{ or } 8.06\%$$

Return on Common Stockholders' Equity

Return on total assets is measured without regard to the source of invested funds. For common stockholders, however, the return that they receive on their investment is of paramount importance. Of special interest to common stockholders is how they are being treated relative to other suppliers of capital funds. The **return on stockholders' equity** is computed by dividing net income less preferred dividends by the average common stockholders' equity; it provides a measure that can be used to compare against other return measures (e.g., preferred dividend rates and bond rates). The beginning and ending common stockholders' equity require further calculations for Payne Company because the company has preferred stock. The preferred stock must be backed out of the total equity to get the common stockholders' equity. For Payne Company, the beginning and ending common stockholders' equity are calculated as follows:

Beginning common stockholders' equity = $14,924,000 − $3,200,000
= $11,724,000

Ending common stockholders' equity = $16,000,000 − $3,200,000
= $12,800,000

Average common stockholders' equity = ($12,800,000 + $11,724,000)/2
= $12,262,000

Return on stockholders' equity is calculated as follows:

**Return on stockholders' equity = (Net income − Preferred dividends)/
Average common stockholders' equity**

Payne Company's return on stockholders' equity is computed in Cornerstone 14-10.

As we can see in Cornerstone 14-10, compared with the bond return of 10 percent and the preferred dividend rate of 7 percent, common stockholders are faring quite well. Furthermore, since the industrial average is about 14 percent, the rate of return provided to common stockholders is above average.

Earnings per Share

Investors also pay considerable attention to a company's profitability on a per-share basis. **Earnings per share** is computed by dividing net income less preferred dividends by the average number of shares of common stock outstanding during the period.

Earnings per share = (Net income − Preferred dividends)/Average common shares

HOW TO Calculate the Average Common Stockholders' Equity and the Return on Stockholders' Equity

Information: Refer to Exhibits 14-3 and 14-4 for information on Payne Company.

Required:
1. Calculate the average common stockholders' equity.
2. Calculate the return on stockholders' equity.

Calculation:
1. Average common stockholders' equity = ($11,724,000 + $12,800,000)/2
$$= \$12,262,000$$
2. Return on stockholders' equity = ($2,300,000 − $224,000)/$12,262,000
$$= \$2,076,000/\$12,262,000$$
$$= 0.1693, \text{ or } 16.93\%$$

CORNERSTONE
14-10

Average common shares outstanding is computed by taking a weighted average of the common shares for the period under study. For example, assume that a company has 8,000 common shares at the beginning of the year. At the end of the first quarter, 4,000 additional shares are issued. No other transactions take place during the period. The weighted average is computed as follows:

	Outstanding Shares	Weight	Weighted Shares
First quarter	8,000	3/12	2,000
Last three quarters	12,000	9/12	9,000
Average common shares outstanding			11,000

Cornerstone 14-11 shows how to compute earnings per share for Payne Company.

HOW TO Compute Earnings per Share

Information: Refer to Exhibits 14-3 and 14-4 for data on Payne Company.

Required:
1. Compute the dollar amount of preferred dividends.
2. Compute the number of common shares.
3. Compute earnings per share for Payne Company.

Calculation:
1. Preferred dividends = $3,200,000 × 0.07 = $224,000
   (Recall that the preferred shares pay a dividend of 7 percent as shown in Exhibit 14-4.)

2. Number of common shares = $1,600,000/$2 = 800,000
3. Earnings per share = ($2,300,000 − $224,000)/800,000
$$= \$2,076,000/800,000$$
$$= \$2.60$$

CORNERSTONE
14-11

Since the median value for the industry is about $3.47 per share, Payne's earnings per share is somewhat low and may signal a need for management to focus on increasing earnings.

Price-Earnings Ratio

The **price-earnings ratio** is found by dividing the market price per share by the earnings per share:

Price-earnings ratio = Market price per share/Earnings per share

Price-earnings ratios are viewed by many investors as important indicators of stock values. If investors believe that a company has good growth prospects, then the price-earnings ratio should be high. If investors believe that the current price-earnings ratio is low based on their view of future growth opportunities, the market price of the stock may be bid up. Cornerstone 14-12 shows how to compute the price-earnings ratio.

As Cornerstone 14-12 shows, Payne's stock is selling for 5.8 times its current earnings per share. This ratio compares with an industrial median value of 6.3. Thus, Payne's price-earnings ratio is lower than more than half of the firms in the industry.

Dividend Yield and Payout Ratios

The profitability measure called **dividend yield** is computed by dividing the dividends received per unit of common share by the market price per common share.

Dividend yield = Dividends per common share/Market price per common share

By adding the dividend yield to the percentage change in stock price, a reasonable approximation of the total return accruing to an investor can be obtained. For Payne Company, the dividend yield is computed in Cornerstone 14-13.

The **dividend payout ratio** is computed by dividing the total common dividends by the earnings available to common stockholders, as follows:

Dividend payout ratio = Common dividends/(Net income − Preferred dividends)

The payout ratio tells an investor the proportion of earnings that a company pays in dividends. Investors who prefer regular cash payments instead of returns through price appreciation will want to invest in companies with a high payout ratio; investors who prefer gains through appreciation will generally prefer a lower payout ratio. Cornerstone 14-13 shows how to compute the dividend yield and dividend payout ratio.

**CORNERSTONE
14-12**

HOW TO Compute the Price-Earnings Ratio

Information: Assume that the price per common share for Payne Company is $15.

Required: Compute the price-earnings ratio.

Calculation: Price-earnings ratio = $15/$2.60
= 5.7692, or 5.8

Note: Price-earnings ratios are typically rounded to one significant digit.

HOW TO Compute the Dividend Yield and the Dividend Payout Ratio

Information: Assume that the market price per common share is $15. Refer to Exhibits 14-3 and 14-4.

Required:
1. Compute the dividends per share.
2. Compute the dividend yield.
3. Compute the dividend payout ratio.

Calculation:
1. Dividends per share = $1,000,000/800,000 = $1.25
2. Dividend yield = $1.25/$15
   = 0.0833, or 8.33%
3. Dividend payout ratio = $1,000,000/($2,300,000 − $224,000)
   = $1,000,000/$2,076,000
   = 0.48

CORNERSTONE 14-13

Impact of the Just-in-Time Manufacturing Environment

In the new manufacturing environment, reducing inventories and increasing quality are critical activities. Both activities are essential for many companies to retain their competitive ability. Accordingly, users of financial statements should have a special interest in ratios that measure a company's progress in achieving the goals of zero inventories and total quality. As a company reduces its inventory, the inventory turnover ratio should increase dramatically. Traditionally, high inventory turnovers have had a negative connotation. It was argued that a high inventory turnover ratio might signal such problems as stockouts and disgruntled customers. In the new manufacturing environment, however, a high turnover ratio is viewed positively. High turnover is interpreted as a signal of success—of achieving the goal of zero inventories with all of the efficiency associated with that state (Chapter 11). As inventory levels drop, the current ratio also is affected. Without significant inventories, the current ratio will drop; in fact, it will approach the value of the quick ratio. Since many lenders require a 2.0 current ratio to grant and control a loan, some reevaluation of the use of this ratio is needed for customers with a just-in-time (JIT) system. It may be necessary to rely more on the quick ratio or other alternative ratios (such as cash flow divided by current maturities of long-term debt). A ratio that says something about quality also is desirable for JIT firms. The usual approach is to express quality costs as a percentage of sales. External users, however, may not have access to quality costs as a separate category. Warranty costs, returns and allowances, unfavorable materials quantity variances, and other quality costs that are readily identifiable from the financial statement can be added. This sum can then be divided by sales to give the external users some idea of the company's capability in this important area. Tracking this ratio over time will reveal the progress that the company is making. As quality improves, quality costs as a percentage of sales should decline.

The Importance of Profitability Ratios to External Users of the Financial Statements

Of course, for ratio analysis to be useful, it is critically important that the underlying financial information be accurate. The purpose of financial statements prepared for outside users is to fairly represent the underlying economic position of the firm. Many external users, such as investors in the stock market, banks, and public agencies, rely on the financial statements to provide necessary information. A look back at the past five to ten years shows many instances in which corporate heads, knowing the importance of various ratios, took unethical steps to make the information fit the desired ratio results rather than letting the ratios come from fairly generated information.

Ethics **Enron** provides an excellent example of top management's obsession with ratio "doctoring." The focus of Enron top management was the company's stock price. In order to convince the stock market that Enron was a strong company, worthy of supporting the price set by the market, Enron officials took steps to report increasing income, even when income was decreasing. Of course, when the facts about Enron's actual earnings came out, the stock price tumbled, and the company resorted to bankruptcy. The demise of this company, one of the largest companies in the United States, had serious consequences for Enron employees and investors, as well as charges being brought against certain members of the Enron management team.[1]◆

---

[1]For an excellent, and readable, description of the environment and events leading up to Enron's fall, see Bethany McLean and Peter Elkind, *The Smartest Guys in the Room: The Amazing Rise and Scandalous Fall of Enron.* New York: Penguin Books, 2003/2004.

Summary of Learning Objectives

1. Analyze financial statements by using two forms of common-size analysis: horizontal analysis and vertical analysis.
   - Common-size analysis expresses accounts or line items in financial statements as percentages.
   - Horizontal analysis compares line items from one period with another period, to assess trends. Vertical analysis compares one line item with another line item from the same time period, to assess relationships among financial statement items.
2. Explain why historical standards and industrial averages are important for ratio analysis.
   - Ratios can be compared with a standard.
   - The most common standards are historical values and industrial values.
3. Calculate and use liquidity ratios to assess the ability of a company to meet its current obligations. Exhibit 14-5 provides a summary of the ratios discussed throughout the chapter.
   - Liquidity ratios are used to assess the short-term debt-paying ability of a company. These ratios include the current ratio, the quick or acid-test ratio, accounts receivable turnover, and inventory turnover.
4. Calculate and use leverage ratios to assess the ability of a company to meet its long- and short-term obligations.
   - Leverage ratios measure the ability of a company to meet long-term debt obligations.
   - These ratios include the times-interest-earned ratio and the debt ratio.
5. Calculate and use profitability ratios to assess the extent to which a company's resources are being used efficiently.
   - Profitability ratios relate the firm's earnings to the resources used to create those earnings.
   - They include return on sales, return on total assets, earnings per share, price-earnings ratio, dividend yield, and dividend payout.

Exhibit 14-5

Summary of Important Ratios

	Formula
Liquidity ratios:	
Current ratio	Current assets/Current liabilities
Quick ratio	(Cash + Marketable securities + Receivables)/Current liabilities
Accounts receivable turnover ratio	Net sales/Average accounts receivable
Inventory turnover ratio	Cost of goods sold/Average inventory
Turnover in days	Days in a year/Receivables turnover ratio
Leverage ratios:	
Times-interest-earned ratio	(Income before taxes + Interest expense)/Interest expense
Debt ratio	Total liabilities/Total assets
Debt to equity ratio	Total liabilities/Total stockholders' equity
Profitability ratios:	
Return on sales	Net income/Sales
Return on total assets	[Net income + Interest expense (1 − Tax rate)]/Average total assets
Return on common stockholders' equity	(Net income − Preferred dividends)/Average common stockholders' equity
Earnings per share	(Net income − Preferred dividends)/Average common shares
Price-earnings ratio	Market price per share/Earnings per share
Dividend yield	Dividends per common share/Market price per common share
Dividend payout ratio	Common dividends/(Net income − Preferred dividends)

CORNERSTONES FOR CHAPTER 14

Cornerstone 14-1 How to prepare common-size income statements by using base period horizontal analysis, page 597

Cornerstone 14-2 How to prepare income statements by using net sales as the base: vertical analysis, page 598

Cornerstone 14-3 How to calculate the current ratio and the quick (or acid-test) ratio, page 604

Cornerstone 14-4 How to calculate the average accounts receivable, the accounts receivable turnover ratio, and the accounts receivable turnover in days, page 605

Cornerstone 14-5 How to calculate the average inventory, the inventory turnover ratio, and the inventory turnover in days, page 606

Cornerstone 14-6 How to calculate the times-interest-earned ratio, page 607

Cornerstone 14-7 How to calculate the debt ratio and the debt-to-equity ratio, page 608

Cornerstone 14-8 How to calculate the return on sales, page 609

Cornerstone 14-9 How to calculate the average total assets and the return on assets, page 610

Cornerstone 14-10 How to calculate the average common stockholders' equity and the return on stockholders' equity, page 611

Cornerstone 14-11 How to compute earnings per share, page 611

Cornerstone 14-12 How to compute the price-earnings ratio, page 612

Cornerstone 14-13 How to compute the dividend yield and the dividend payout ratio, page 613

Key Terms

Accounts receivable turnover ratio, 604
Common-size analysis, 596
Current ratio, 603
Debt ratio, 608
Dividend payout ratio, 612
Dividend yield, 612
Earnings per share, 610
Horizontal analysis, 596
Inventory turnover ratio, 606
Leverage ratios, 601

Liquidity ratios, 601
Price-earnings ratio, 612
Profitability ratios, 601
Quick or acid-test ratio, 603
Return on sales, 609
Return on stockholders' equity, 610
Return on total assets, 609
Times-interest-earned ratio, 607
Vertical analysis, 598

Review Problems

Shera Company just completed its second year of operations. The comparative income statements for these years are as follows:

	2009	2010
Sales revenue	$500,000	$800,000
Less cost of goods sold	300,000	464,000
Gross margin	$200,000	$336,000
Operating expense	80,000	$164,000
Interest expense	20,000	20,000
Income before taxes	$100,000	$152,000
Taxes	34,000	51,680
Net income	$ 66,000	$100,320

Selected information from the balance sheet for 2010 is also given.

Current assets	$100,000
Long-term assets	400,000
Total assets	$500,000
Current liabilities	$ 80,000
Long-term liabilities	220,000
Total liabilities	$300,000
Common stock	$100,000
Retained earnings	100,000
Total equity	$200,000

The company had 100,000 shares of stock outstanding. At the end of 2010, a share had a market value of $1.80. The shares outstanding have not changed since the original issue. Dividends of $30,000 were paid in 2010. Total assets have not changed.

Required:
1. Using 2009 as a base period, express all line items of the income statements as a percentage of the corresponding base period item.
2. Express each line item of the two income statements as a percentage of sales.
3. Comment on the trends revealed by the computations in Requirements 1 and 2.

4.   Compute the following ratios for 2010:
  a.   Current ratio
  b.   Debt ratio
  c.   Return on total assets
  d.   Times-interest-earned
  e.   Earnings per share
  f.   Dividend yield

Solution:
1.   Horizontal analysis:

	2009	Percent	2010	Percent
Sales revenue	$500,000	100.0%	$800,000	160.0%
Less cost of goods sold	300,000	100.0	464,000	154.7
Gross margin	$200,000	100.0	$336,000	168.0
Operating expense	80,000	100.0	$164,000	205.0
Interest expense	20,000	100.0	20,000	100.0
Income before taxes	$100,000	100.0	$152,000	152.0
Taxes	34,000	100.0	51,680	152.0
Net income	$ 66,000	100.0	$100,320	152.0

2.   Vertical analysis:

	2009	Percent	2010	Percent
Sales revenue	$500,000	100.0%	$800,000	100.0%
Less cost of goods sold	300,000	60.0	464,000	58.0
Gross margin	$200,000	40.0	$336,000	42.0
Operating expense	80,000	16.0	$164,000	20.6
Interest expense	20,000	4.0	20,000	2.5
Income before taxes	$100,000	20.0	$152,000	19.0
Taxes	34,000	6.8	51,680	6.5
Net income	$ 66,000	13.2	$100,320	12.5

3.   The trends reflected by both the horizontal and vertical analyses are basically favorable. Sales have increased and, with the notable exception of operating expenses, expenses have not increased as rapidly as sales and have declined as a percentage of sales. Operating expenses, however, have more than doubled from 2009 to 2010 and also have increased as a percentage of sales.

4.   Ratio computation:
  a.   Current ratio = $100,000/$80,000 = 1.25
  b.   Debt ratio = $300,000/$500,000 = 0.60
  c.   Return on total assets = [$100,320 + $20,000(0.66)]/$500,000 = 0.227 or 22.7%
  d.   Times-interest-earned ratio = $172,000/$20,000 = 8.6
  e.   Earnings per share = $100,320/100,000 = $1.003 per share
  f.   Dividend yield = $0.30/$1.80 = 0.167 or 16.7%

Discussion Questions

1.   Name the two major types of financial statement analysis discussed in this chapter.
2.   What is horizontal analysis? Vertical analysis? Should both horizontal and vertical analyses be done? Why?
3.   Explain how creditors, investors, and managers can use common-size analysis as an aid in decision making.

4. What are liquidity ratios? Leverage ratios? Profitability ratios?
5. Identify two types of standards used in ratio analysis. Explain why it is desirable to use both types.
6. What information does the quick ratio supply have that the current ratio does not?
7. Suppose that the accounts receivable turnover ratio of a company is low when compared with other firms within its industry. How would this information be useful to the managers of a company?
8. A high inventory turnover ratio provides evidence that a company is having problems with stockouts and disgruntled customers. Do you agree? Explain.
9. A loan agreement between a bank and a customer specified that the debt ratio could not exceed 60 percent. Explain the purpose of this restrictive agreement.
10. A manager decided to acquire some expensive equipment through the use of an operating lease even though a capital budgeting analysis showed that it was more profitable to buy than to lease. However, the purchase alternative would have required the issuance of some bonds. Offer some reasons that would explain the manager's choice.
11. Explain why an investor would be interested in a company's debt ratio.
12. Assume that you have been given the responsibility to invest some funds in the stock market to provide an annuity to an individual who has just retired. Explain how you might use the dividend yield and the dividend payout ratio to help you with this investment decision.
13. Explain how an investor might use the price-earnings ratio to value the stock of a company.
14. Why would investors and creditors be interested in knowing the dilutive effects of convertible securities on earnings per share?
15. Explain the significance of the inventory turnover ratio in a JIT manufacturing environment.
16. In a JIT manufacturing environment, the current ratio and the quick ratio are virtually the same. Do you agree? Why?

Multiple-Choice Exercises

14-1 A company provided income statements for the past five years. In looking at the percentage columns for each year, you notice that sales are 46 percent higher in year 5 than in year 1. The company has most likely provided

a. a horizontal analysis using the prior period as the base year.
b. a vertical analysis using sales as the base.
c. a horizontal analysis using year 1 as the base year.
d. a vertical analysis using net income as the base.
e. none of the above.

14-2 An advantage of common-size analysis is that

a. the size of dollar amounts impact the analysis.
b. larger companies will have higher common-size percentages.
c. the effects of size are eliminated.
d. it focuses only on vertical analysis.
e. it focuses only on horizontal analysis.

14-3 Fractions or percentages computed by dividing one account or line-item amount by another are called

a. ratios.
b. industry averages.
c. common-size statements.

d. dividend yields.
e. returns.

14-4 The measures of the ability of a company to meet its long- and short-term obligations are called

a.   ratios.
b.   liquidity ratios.
c.   leverage ratios.

d.   profitability ratios.
e.   percentage changes.

14-5 A company's inventory turnover in days is 80 days. Which of the following actions could help to improve that ratio?

a.   Increase in sales price
b.   Increase in manufacturing costs
c.   Reduction in cost of goods sold
d.   Reduction in average inventory
e.   All of the above

14-6 Company B shows that 46 percent of its assets are financed by creditors. Which of the following shows this result?

a.   Current ratio
b.   Times-interest-earned
c.   Return on sales

d.   Inventory turnover in days
e.   Debt ratio

14-7 Profitability ratios are used by which of the following groups?

a.   Company managers
b.   Creditors
c.   Lenders
d.   Investors
e.   All of the above

14-8 Fred and Torrie Jones are a retired couple looking for income. They are currently rebalancing their portfolio of stocks to include more with high dividends. Fred and Torrie will be most interested in which of the following?

a.   Dividend payout ratio
b.   Current ratio
c.   Return on assets
d.   Price-earnings ratio
e.   Dividend yield

14-9 A small pizza restaurant, founded and owned by the Martinelli sisters, would be expected to have which of the following?

a.   High price-earnings ratio
b.   High inventory turnover and low gross margin
c.   Low inventory turnover and high gross margin
d.   Low accounts receivable turnover and low gross margin
e.   All of the above

14-10 The after-tax cost of interest expense is used in calculating which of the following?

a.   Times-interest-earned
b.   Return on total assets
c.   Debt ratio
d.   Inventory turnover ratio
e.   All of the above

Exercises

OBJECTIVE ①
CORNERSTONE 14-1

Exercise 14-11 Horizontal Analysis

Fogel Company's income statements for two years are shown below.

Fogel Company
Income Statements
For the Years 1 and 2

	Year 1	Year 2
Sales	$ 2,000,000	$ 1,800,000
Less: Cost of goods sold	(1,400,000)	(1,200,000)
Gross margin	$ 600,000	$ 600,000
Less operating expenses:		
Selling expenses	(300,000)	(300,000)
Administrative expenses	(100,000)	(110,000)
Net operating income	$ 200,000	$ 190,000
Less: Interest expense	(50,000)	(40,000)
Income before taxes	$ 150,000	$ 150,000

Required:

Prepare a common-size income statement for year 2 by expressing each line item for year 2 as a percentage of that same line item from year 1. (Round percentages to the nearest tenth of a percent.)

OBJECTIVE ①
CORNERSTONE 14-2

Exercise 14-12 Vertical Analysis

Refer to the income statements in **Exercise 14-11**.

Required:

1. Prepare a common-size income statement for year 1 by expressing each line item as a percentage of sales revenue. (Round percentages to the nearest tenth of a percent.)
2. Prepare a common-size income statement for year 2 by expressing each line item as a percentage of sales revenue. (Round percentages to the nearest tenth of a percent.)

OBJECTIVE ①
CORNERSTONE 14-1

Exercise 14-13 Horizontal Analysis

Camellia Company's income statements for the last three years are as follows:

Camellia Company
Income Statements
For the Years 1, 2, and 3

	Year 1	Year 2	Year 3
Sales	$1,000,000	$1,200,000	$ 1,700,000
Less: Cost of goods sold	(700,000)	(700,000)	(1,000,000)
Gross margin	$ 300,000	$ 500,000	$ 700,000
Less operating expenses:			
Selling expenses	(150,000)	(220,000)	(250,000)
Administrative expenses	(50,000)	(60,000)	(120,000)
Net operating income	$ 100,000	$ 220,000	$ 330,000
Less: Interest expense	(25,000)	(25,000)	(25,000)
Income before taxes	$ 75,000	$ 195,000	$ 305,000

Required:

1. Prepare a common-size income statement for year 2 by expressing each line item for year 2 as a percentage of that same line item from year 1. (Round percentages to the nearest tenth of a percent.)

2. Prepare a common-size income statement for year 3 by expressing each line item for year 3 as a percentage of that same line item from year 1. (Round percentages to the nearest tenth of a percent.)

Exercise 14-14 Vertical Analysis

Refer to the income statements in **Exercise 14-13**.

Required:
1. Prepare a common-size income statement for year 1 by expressing each line item as a percentage of sales revenue. (Round percentages to the nearest tenth of a percent.)
2. Prepare a common-size income statement for year 2 by expressing each line item as a percentage of sales revenue. (Round percentages to the nearest tenth of a percent.)
3. Prepare a common-size income statement for year 3 by expressing each line item as a percentage of sales revenue. (Round percentages to the nearest tenth of a percent.)

OBJECTIVE ①
CORNERSTONE 14-2

Exercise 14-15 Current Ratio and Quick (Acid-Test) Ratio

Matalin Company provided the following information:

Current assets:	
Cash	$ 50,000
Accounts receivable	100,000
Inventories	138,000
Total current assets	$288,000
Current liabilities	$ 80,000

OBJECTIVE ③
CORNERSTONE 14-3

spreadsheet

Required:
1. Compute the current ratio for Matalin Company.
2. Compute the quick (acid-test) ratio for Matalin Company. (Do not round your answer.)

Exercise 14-16 Current Ratio and Quick (Acid-Test) Ratio

Nbulio Company has current assets equal to $180,000. Of these, $20,000 is cash, $40,000 is accounts receivable, and the remainder is inventories. Current liabilities total $75,000.

OBJECTIVE ③
CORNERSTONE 14-3

Required:
1. Compute the current ratio for Nbulio Company.
2. Compute the quick (acid-test) ratio for Nbulio Company.

Exercise 14-17 Average Accounts Receivable, Accounts Receivable Turnover Ratio, Accounts Receivable Turnover in Days

Calista Company had net sales of $400,000. Calista had the following balances:

OBJECTIVE ③
CORNERSTONE 14-4

	January 1	December 31
Accounts receivable	$ 82,400	$ 77,600
Inventories	113,000	107,000

Required:
1. Calculate the average accounts receivable.
2. Calculate the accounts receivable turnover ratio.
3. Calculate the accounts receivable in days.

OBJECTIVE ③
CORNERSTONE 14-4

Exercise 14-18 Average Accounts Receivable, Accounts Receivable Turnover Ratio, Accounts Receivable Turnover in Days

Franklin Company had net sales of $593,400. Franklin had the following balances:

	January 1	December 31
Accounts receivable	$ 51,400	$ 77,600
Inventories	113,000	107,000

Required:
1. Calculate the average accounts receivable.
2. Calculate the accounts receivable turnover ratio.
3. Calculate the accounts receivable in days (take your answer out to one decimal place).

OBJECTIVE ③
CORNERSTONE 14-5

Exercise 14-19 Average Inventory, Inventory Turnover Ratio, Inventory Turnover in Days

Calista Company had net sales of $400,000 and cost of goods sold of $250,000. Calista had the following balances:

	January 1	December 31
Inventories	$113,000	$107,000

Required:
1. Calculate the average inventory.
2. Calculate the inventory turnover ratio. (Round your answer to one decimal place.)
3. Calculate the inventory turnover in days. (Round your answer to one decimal place.)

OBJECTIVE ③
CORNERSTONE 14-5

spreadsheet

Exercise 14-20 Average Inventory, Inventory Turnover Ratio, Inventory Turnover in Days

Dejong Company had cost of goods sold of $1,232,000. Dejong had beginning inventory of $45,000 and ending inventory of $43,000.

Required:
1. Calculate the average inventory.
2. Calculate the inventory turnover ratio. (Round your answer to one decimal place.)
3. Calculate the inventory turnover in days. (Round your answer to one decimal place.)

OBJECTIVE ④
CORNERSTONE 14-6

Exercise 14-21 Times-Interest-Earned

Bessette Company provided the following income statement for last year:

Sales	$600,000
Cost of goods sold	350,000
Gross margin	$250,000
Operating expenses	160,000
Operating income	$ 90,000
Interest expense	15,000
Net income before taxes	$ 75,000
Income taxes	20,000
Net income	$ 55,000

Required:
Calculate the times-interest-earned ratio.

Exercise 14-22 Debt Ratio, Debt-to-Equity Ratio

Sasquall Company's balance sheet shows total liabilities of $585,000, total equity of $715,000, and total assets of $1,300,000.

Required:
1. Calculate the debt ratio for Sasquall Company.
2. Calculate the debt-to-equity ratio for Sasquall Company. (Round your answer to two decimal places.)

OBJECTIVE ④
CORNERSTONE 14-7

Exercise 14-23 Times-Interest-Earned, Debt Ratio, Debt-to-Equity Ratio

Woodall Inc. provided the following income statement for last year:

Sales	$12,600,000
Cost of goods sold	7,500,000
Gross margin	$ 5,100,000
Operating expenses	2,400,000
Operating income	$ 2,700,000
Interest expense	400,000
Net income before taxes	$ 2,300,000
Income taxes	690,000
Net income	$ 1,610,000

OBJECTIVE ④
CORNERSTONE 14-6
CORNERSTONE 14-7

Woodall's balance sheet as of December 31 last year showed total liabilities of $2,500,000, total equity of $9,500,000, and total assets of $12,000,000.

Required:
1. Calculate the times-interest-earned ratio. (Round your answer to two decimal places.)
2. Calculate the debt ratio. (Round your answer to two decimal places.)
3. Calculate the debt-to-equity ratio. (Round your answer to two decimal places.)

Exercise 14-24 Return on Sales

Refer to **Exercise 14-23** for information on Woodall, Inc.

Required:
Calculate the return on sales. (Round your answer to three decimal places.)

OBJECTIVE ⑤
CORNERSTONE 14-8

Exercise 14-25 Average Total Assets, Return on Assets

Refer to **Exercise 14-23** for information on Woodall, Inc. Woodall's total assets at the beginning of last year also equaled $12,000,000. The tax rate applicable to Woodall is 30 percent.

Required:
1. Calculate the average total assets.
2. Calculate the return on assets.

OBJECTIVE ⑥
CORNERSTONE 14-9

Exercise 14-26 Average Common Stockholders' Equity, Return on Stockholders' Equity

Haidary Inc. showed the following balances for last year:

OBJECTIVE ⑤
CORNERSTONE 14-10

	January 1	December 31
Stockholder's equity:		
Preferred stock, $100 par, 8%	$ 4,000,000	$ 4,000,000
Common stock, $3 par	3,000,000	3,000,000
Additional paid-in capital*	4,800,000	4,800,000
Retained earnings	4,000,000	4,250,000
Total equity	$15,800,000	$16,050,000

*For common stock only.

Haidary's net income for last year was $3,182,000.

Required:
1.   Calculate the average common stockholders' equity.
2.   Calculate the return on stockholders' equity.

OBJECTIVE ⑤

CORNERSTONE 14-11
CORNERSTONE 14-12

Exercise 14-27 Earnings per Share, Price-Earnings Ratio

Refer to the data in **Exercise 14-26**. The market price per share for Haidary Inc. is $51.50.

Required:
1.   Compute the dollar amount of preferred dividends.
2.   Compute the number of common shares.
3.   Compute earnings per share.
4.   Compute the price-earnings ratio. (Round to the nearest whole number.)

OBJECTIVE ⑤

CORNERSTONE 14-13

Exercise 14-28 Dividend Yield Ratio, Dividend Payout Ratio

Refer to the data in **Exercise 14-26**. The dividends paid to common stockholders for last year were $2,600,000. The market price per share of common stock is $51.50.

Required:
1.   Compute the dividends per share.
2.   Compute the dividend yield. (Round to two decimal places.)
3.   Compute the dividend payout ratio. (Round to two decimal places.)

Problems

OBJECTIVE ③

spreadsheet

Problem 14-29 Liquidity Analysis

The following selected information is taken from the financial statements of Riflen Company for its most recent year of operations:

Beginning balances:	
Inventory	$200,000
Accounts receivable	300,000
Ending balances:	
Inventory	$250,000
Accounts receivable	400,000
Cash	100,000
Marketable securities (short term)	200,000
Prepaid expenses	50,000
Accounts payable	175,000
Taxes payable	85,000
Wages payable	90,000
Short-term loans payable	50,000

During the year, Riflen Company had net sales of $2.45 million. The cost of goods sold was $1.3 million.

Required:
1.   Compute the current ratio.
2.   Compute the quick or acid-test ratio.
3.   Compute the accounts receivable turnover ratio.
4.   Compute the accounts receivable turnover in days.
5.   Compute the inventory turnover ratio.
6.   Compute the inventory turnover ratio in days.

Problem 14-30 Leverage Ratios

OBJECTIVES ② ④

spreadsheet

Timmins Company has just completed its third year of operations. The income statement is as follows:

Sales	$2,460,000
Less: Cost of goods sold	(1,410,000)
Gross profit	$1,050,000
Less: Selling and administrative expenses	(710,000)
Operating income	$ 340,000
Less: Interest expense	(140,000)
Income before taxes	$ 200,000
Less: Income taxes	(68,000)
Net income	$ 132,000

Selected information from the balance sheet is as follows:

Current liabilities	$1,000,000
Long-term liabilities	1,500,000
Total liabilities	$2,500,000
Common stock	$4,000,000
Retained earnings	750,000
Total equity	$4,750,000

Required:

1. Compute the times-interest-earned ratio.
2. Compute the debt ratio.
3. Assume that the lower quartile, median, and upper quartile values for debt and times-interest-earned ratios in Timmins's industry are as follows:

Times-interest-earned:	2.3, 5.4, 16.1
Debt:	2.4, 0.8, 0.5

How does Timmins compare with the industrial norms? Does it have too much debt?

Problem 14-31 Profitability Ratios

OBJECTIVES ② ④

The following information has been gathered for Leatroy Manufacturing:

Net income	$5,000,000
Interest expense	$400,000
Average total assets	$60,000,000
Preferred dividends	$400,000
Common dividends	$1,200,000
Average common shares outstanding	800,000
Average common stockholders' equity	$20,000,000
Market price per common share	$40

Assume that the firm has no common stock equivalents. The tax rate is 34 percent.

Required:

1. Compute the return on total assets.
2. Compute the return on common stockholders' equity.
3. Compute the earnings per share.
4. Compute the price-earnings ratio.
5. Compute the dividend yield.
6. Compute the dividend payout ratio.

OBJECTIVE ①   Problem 14-32 Horizontal Analysis

Mike Sanders is considering the purchase of Kepler Company, a firm specializing in the manufacture of office supplies. To be able to assess the financial capabilities of the company, Mike has been given the company's financial statements for the two most recent years.

Kepler Company
Comparative Balance Sheets

Assets	This Year	Last Year
Current assets:		
Cash	$ 50,000	$100,000
Accounts receivable, net	300,000	150,000
Inventory	600,000	400,000
Prepaid expenses	25,000	30,000
Total current assets	$ 975,000	$680,000
Property and equipment, net	125,000	150,000
Total assets	$1,100,000	$830,000

Liabilities and Stockholders' Equity	This Year	Last Year
Liabilities:		
Accounts payable	$ 400,000	$290,000
Short-term notes payable	200,000	60,000
Total current liabilities	$ 600,000	$350,000
Long-term bonds payable, 12%	100,000	150,000
Total liabilities	$ 700,000	$500,000
Stockholders' equity:		
Common stock (100,000 shares)	200,000	200,000
Retained earnings	200,000	130,000
Total liabilities and equity	$1,100,000	$830,000

Kepler Company
Comparative Income Statements

	This Year	Last Year
Sales	$ 950,000	$ 900,000
Less: Cost of goods sold	(500,000)	(490,000)
Gross margin	$ 450,000	$ 410,000
Less: Selling and administrative expenses	(275,000)	(260,000)
Operating income	$ 175,000	$ 150,000
Less: Interest expense	(12,000)	(18,000)
Income before taxes	$ 163,000	$ 132,000
Less: Taxes	(65,200)	(52,800)
Net income	$ 97,800	$ 79,200
Less: Dividends	(27,800)	(19,200)
Net income, retained	$ 70,000	$ 60,000

Required:

1. Compute the percentage change for each item in the balance sheet and income statement.
2. Comment on any significant trends.

OBJECTIVE ①   Problem 14-33 Vertical Analysis

Refer to the financial statements for Kepler Company in **Problem 14-32**. Round all percentages to three significant digits.

Required:

1. Express each item in the asset section of the balance sheet as a percentage of total assets for each year.
2. Express each item in the liabilities and equity section as a percentage of total liabilities and equity for each year.
3. Express each item in the income statement as a percentage of sales for each year.

Problem 14-34 Liquidity Ratios

OBJECTIVES ② ③

Refer to the financial statements for Kepler Company in **Problem 14-32**.

Required:

1. Compute the following ratios for each year:
    a. Current ratio
    b. Quick ratio
    c. Receivables turnover (in days)
    d. Inventory turnover (in days)
2. Has the liquidity of Kepler improved over the past year? Explain why industrial liquidity performance would be useful information in assessing Kepler's liquidity performance.

Problem 14-35 Leverage Ratios

OBJECTIVES ② ④

Refer to the financial statements for Kepler Company in **Problem 14-32**.

Required:

1. Compute the following for each year:
    a. The times-interest-earned ratio
    b. The debt ratio
2. Does Kepler have too much debt? What other information would help in answering this question?

Problem 14-36 Profitability Ratios

OBJECTIVES ② ⑤

Refer to the financial statements for Kepler Company in **Problem 14-32**. For last year and for the current year, the market price per share of common stock is $2.98. For last year, assets and equity were the same at the beginning and end of the year.

Required:

1. Compute the following for each year:
    a. Return on total assets
    b. Return on stockholders' equity
    c. Earnings per share
    d. Price-earnings ratio
    e. Dividend yield
    f. Dividend payout
2. Based on the analysis in Requirement 1, would you invest in the common stock of Kepler Company?

Problem 14-37 Profitability Analysis

OBJECTIVE ⑤

Albion Inc. provided the following information for its most recent year of operation. The tax rate is 40 percent.

Sales	$100,000
Cost of goods sold	$45,000
Net income	$10,500
Interest expense	$350
Assets—beginning balance	$120,000
Assets—ending balance	$126,000
Preferred dividends	$300
Common dividends (paid December 31)	$8,000
Common shares outstanding—January 1	30,000
Common shares outstanding—December 31	40,000
Average common stockholders' equity	$55,000
Market price per common share	$12

Required:
1. Compute the following:
   a. Return on sales
   b. Return on assets
   c. Return on common stockholders' equity
   d. Earnings per share
   e. Price-earnings ratio
   f. Dividend yield
   g. Dividend payout ratio
2. If you were considering purchasing stock in Albion, which of the above ratios would be of most interest to you? Explain.

OBJECTIVE ③ Problem 14-38 Analysis of Accounts Receivable and Credit Policy

Based on customer feedback, Ted Pendleton, manager of a company that produces photo supplies, decided to grant more liberal credit terms. Ted chose to allow customers to have 60 days before full payment of the account was required. From 2000 through 2002, the company's credit policy for sales on account was 2/10, n/30. In 2003, the policy of 2/10, n/60 became effective. By the end of 2005, Ted's company was beginning to experience cash flow problems. Although sales were strong, collections were sluggish, and the company was having a difficult time meeting its short-term obligations. Ted noted that the cash flow problems materialized after the credit policy was changed and wondered if there was a connection. To help assess the situation, he gathered the following data pertaining to the collection of accounts receivable (balances are end-of-year balances; the 2000 balance was the same as that in 1999):

	2000	2001	2002	2003	2004
Accounts receivable	$100,000	$120,000	$100,000	$150,000	$190,000
Net credit sales	500,000	600,000	510,000	510,000	520,000

Required:
1. Compute the number of times that receivables turned over per year for each of the five years. Also express the turnover in days instead of times per year.
2. Based on your computation in Requirement 1, evaluate the effect of the new credit policy. Include in this assessment the impact on the company's cash inflows.
3. Assume that the industry has an average receivables turnover of six times per year. If this knowledge had been available in 2002, along with knowledge of the company's receivable turnover rate, do you think that Ted Pendleton would have liberalized his company's credit policy?

OBJECTIVE ⑤ Problem 14-39 Profitability Analysis for an Investment Decision

Suppose that you are considering investing in one of two companies, each in the same industry. The most recent income statements for each company and other relevant information are as follows:

Income Statements (in thousands)

	Company A	Company B
Sales	$50,000	$40,000
Less: Cost of goods sold	(30,000)	(26,000)
Gross margin	$20,000	$14,000
Less: Selling and administrative expenses	(15,000)	(7,000)
Operating income	$ 5,000	$ 7,000
Less: Interest expense	(1,000)	(3,000)
Income before taxes	$ 4,000	$ 4,000
Less: Taxes	(1,360)	(1,360)
Net income	$ 2,640	$ 2,640
Retained earnings	8,000	6,000
	$10,640	$ 8,640
Less: Dividends	(840)	(1,040)
Ending retained earnings	$ 9,800	$ 7,600
Average total assets	$20,000,000	$22,000,000
Average common equity	$10,000,000	$13,000,000
Average common shares	1,000,000	1,200,000
Average preferred shares*	300,000	100,000
Market price per common share	$5.00	$9.80

*For both Company A and company B, the preferred dividend is $1 per share.

Required:
1. Compute the following for each company:
   a. Earnings per share
   b. Dividend yield ratio
   c. Dividend payout ratio
   d. Price-earnings ratio
   e. Return on total assets
   f. Return on common equity
2. In which of the two companies would you invest? Explain.

Cases

Case 14-40 Manipulation of Ratios and Ethical Behavior

OBJECTIVES ② ③ ④

Pete Donaldson, president and owner of Donaldson Mining Supplies, was concerned about the firm's liquidity. He had an easy time selling supplies to the local coal mines but had a difficult time collecting the receivables. He had even tried offering discounts for prompt payment. The outcome wasn't as expected. The coal mines still took as long to pay as before but took the discount as well. Although he had complained about the practice, he was told that other suppliers would provide the supplies for the same terms. Collections were so slow that he was unable to pay his own payables on time and was receiving considerable pressure from his own creditors.

The solution was a line of credit that could be used to smooth his payment patterns. Getting the line of credit was another matter, however. One bank had turned him down, indicating that he already had too much debt and that his short-term liquidity ratios were marginal. Pete had begun the business with $5,000 of his own capital and a $30,000 loan from his father-in-law. He was making interest payments of $3,000 per year to his father-in-law with a promise to pay the principal back in five years (three years from now).

While mulling over his problem, Pete suddenly saw the solution. By changing accountants, he could tell the next accountant that the $30,000 had been donated to the business and therefore would be reclassified into the equity section. This would dramatically improve the debt ratio. He would simply not disclose the $3,000 annual payment—or he could call it a dividend. Additionally, he would not tell the next accountant about the $6,000 of safety gear that was now obsolete. That gear could be added back, and the current ratio would also improve. With an improved financial statement, the next bank would be more likely to grant the needed line of credit.

Required:
1. Evaluate Pete Donaldson's ethical behavior.
2. Suppose that you have been hired as the chief finance officer for Donaldson Mining Supplies. You have been told that the $30,000 has been donated to the company. During the second week of your employment, the father-in-law drops in unexpectedly and introduces himself. He then asks you how the company is doing and wants to know if his $30,000 loan is still likely to be repaid in three years. Suppose also that same day you overhear an employee mention that the safety equipment is no longer usable because regulations now require a newer and different model.
    a. Assume that you have yet to prepare the financial statements for the loan application. What should you do?
    b. Suppose that the financial statements have been prepared and submitted to the bank. In fact, that morning, you had received a call from the bank, indicating that a decision was imminent and that the line of credit would likely be approved. What should you do under these circumstances?
3. Suppose that Pete invites you in as a consultant. He describes his problem to you. Can you think of a better solution?

OBJECTIVES ② ③ ④ ⑤   **Case 14-41 Interpreting the Meaning of Ratios from the Financial Statements**

Using the Internet, locate the most recent financial statements for two companies from the same industry. Find (or calculate) the ratios listed below, and compare the two companies. (If you cannot calculate a particular ratio, explain why.) Which company do you think is performing better? Why?

Ratios:
a. Current ratio
b. Quick ratio
c. Accounts receivable turnover ratio
d. Inventory turnover ratio
e. Turnover in days
f. Times-interest-earned ratio
g. Debt ratio
h. Debt-to-equity ratio
i. Return on sales
j. Return on total assets
k. Return on common stockholders' equity
l. Earnings per share
m. Price-earnings ratio
n. Dividend yield
o. Dividend payout ratio

Glossary

A

Absorption costing A product-costing method that assigns all manufacturing costs to units of product: direct materials, direct labor, variable overhead, and fixed overhead.

Accounting rate of return The rate of return obtained by dividing the average accounting net income by the original investment (or by average investment).

Accounts receivable turnover ratio A ratio that measures the liquidity of receivables. It is computed by dividing net sales by average accounts receivable.

Accumulating costs The way that costs are measured and recorded.

Activity analysis The process of identifying, describing, and evaluating the activities an organization performs.

Activity attributes Nonfinancial and financial information items that describe individual activities.

Activity dictionary A list of activities described by specific attributes such as name, definition, classification as primary or secondary, and activity driver.

Activity drivers Factors that measure the consumption of activities by products and other cost objects.

Activity elimination The process of eliminating non-value-added activities.

Activity flexible budgeting Predicting what activity costs will be as activity usage changes.

Activity format A format for the statement of cash flows that reports cash flows for three categories: (1) cash flows from operating activities, (2) cash flows from investing activities, and (3) cash flows from financing activities.

Activity inputs The resources consumed by an activity in producing its output (they are the factors that enable the activity to be performed).

Activity output The result or product of an activity.

Activity output measure The number of times an activity is performed. It is the quantifiable measure of the output.

Activity reduction Decreasing the time and resources required by an activity.

Activity selection The process of choosing among sets of activities caused by competing strategies.

Activity sharing Increasing the efficiency of necessary activities by using economies of scale.

Activity-based budget A budget that requires three steps: (1) the activities within an organization must be identified, (2) the demand for each activity's output must be estimated, and (3) the cost of resources required to produce this activity output must be assessed.

Activity-based costing (ABC) system A cost assignment approach that first uses direct and driver tracing to assign costs to activities and then uses drivers to assign costs to cost objects.

Activity-based management A systemwide, integrated approach that focuses management's attention on activities with the objective of improving customer value and the profit achieved by providing this value. It includes driver analysis, activity analysis, and performance evaluation, and draws on activity-based costing as a major source of information.

Actual cost system An approach that assigns actual costs of direct materials, direct labor, and overhead to products.

Adjusted cost of goods sold The cost of goods sold after all adjustments for overhead variances are made.

Administrative costs All costs associated with research, development, and general administration of the organization that cannot reasonably be assigned to either selling or production.

Allocation When an indirect cost is assigned to a cost object using a reasonable and convenient method.

Annuity A series of future cash flows.

Applied overhead Overhead assigned to production using predetermined rates.

Appraisal costs Cost incurred to determine whether products and services are conforming to requirements.

Assigning costs The way that a cost is linked to some cost object.

B

Balanced Scorecard A strategic management system that defines a strategic-based responsibility accounting system. The Balanced Scorecard translates an organization's mission and strategy into operational objectives and performance measures for four different perspectives: the financial perspective, the customer perspective, the internal business process perspective, and the learning and growth (infrastructure) perspective.

Break-even point The point where total sales revenue equals total cost; at this point, neither profit nor loss is earned.

Budget committee A committee responsible for setting budgetary policies and goals, reviewing and approving the budget, and resolving any differences that may arise in the budgetary process.

Budget director The individual responsible for coordination and directing the overall budgeting process.

Budgetary slack The process of padding the budget by overestimating costs and underestimating revenues.

Budgets Plans of action expressed in financial terms.

C

Capital budgeting The process of making capital investment decisions.

Capital investment decisions The process of planning, setting goals and priorities, arranging financing, and identifying criteria for making long-term investments.

Carrying costs The costs of holding inventory.

Cash budget A detailed plan that outlines all sources and uses of cash.

Cash equivalents Highly liquid investments such as Treasury bills, money market funds, and commercial paper.

Cash inflows Activities that increase cash and are sources of cash.

Cash outflows Activities that decrease cash and are uses of cash.

Causal factors Activities or variables that invoke service costs. Generally, it is desirable to use causal factors as the basis for allocating service costs.

Certified Internal Auditor (CIA) The CIA has passed a comprehensive examination designed to ensure technical competence and has two years' experience.

Certified Management Accountant (CMA) A certified management accountant has passed a rigorous qualifying examination, met an experience requirement, and participates in continuing education.

Certified Public Accountant (CPA) A certified accountant who is permitted (by law) to serve as an external auditor. CPAs must pass a national examination and be licensed by the state in which they practice.

Coefficient of determination (R2) The percentage of total variability in a dependent variable that is explained by an independent variable. It assumes a value between 0 and 1.

Committed fixed cost A fixed cost that cannot be easily changed.

Common costs The costs of resources used in the output of two or more services or products.

Common fixed expenses Fixed expenses that cannot be directly traced to individual segments and that are unaffected by the elimination of any one segment.

Common-size analysis A type of analysis that expresses line items or accounts in the financial statements as percentages.

Compounding of interest Paying interest on interest.

Constraints Mathematical expressions that express resource limitations.

Consumption ratio The proportion of an overhead activity consumed by a product.

Continuous budget A moving 12-month budget with a future month added as the current month expires.

Continuous improvement Searching for ways to increase the overall efficiency and productivity of activities by reducing waste, increasing quality, and reducing costs.

Contribution margin Sales revenue minus total variable cost or price minus unit variable cost.

Contribution margin income statement The income statement format that is based on the separation of costs into fixed and variable components.

Contribution margin ratio Contribution margin divided by sales revenue. It is the proportion of each sales dollar available to cover fixed costs and provide for profit.

Control The process of setting standards, receiving feedback on actual performance, and taking corrective action whenever actual performance deviates significantly from planned performance.

Control activities Activities performed by an organization to prevent or detect poor quality (because poor quality may exist).

Control costs Costs incurred from performing control activities.

Control limits The maximum allowable deviation from a standard.

Controllable costs Costs that managers have the power to influence.

Controller The chief accounting officer in an organization.

Controlling The managerial activity of monitoring a plan's implementation and taking corrective action as needed.

Conversion cost The sum of direct labor cost and overhead cost.

Core objectives and measures Those objectives and measures common to most organizations.

Cost The amount of cash or cash equivalent sacrificed for goods and/or services that are expected to bring a current or future benefit to the organization.

Cost behavior The way in which a cost changes when the level of output changes.

Cost center A division of a company that is evaluated on the basis of cost.

Cost object Any item such as products, customers, departments, projects, and so on, for which costs are measured and assigned.

Cost of capital The cost of investment funds, usually viewed as a weighted average of the costs of funds from all sources.

Cost of goods manufactured The total product cost of goods completed during the current period.

Cost of goods sold The total product cost of goods sold during the period.

Cost of goods sold budget The estimated costs for the units sold.

Cost reconciliation The final section of the production report that compares the costs to account for with the costs accounted for to ensure that they are equal.

Cost structure A company's mix of fixed costs relative to variable costs.

Costs of quality Costs incurred because poor quality may exist or because poor quality does exist.

Cost-volume-profit graph A graph that depicts the relationships among costs, volume, and profits. It consists of a total revenue line and a total cost line.

Current ratio A measure of the ability of a company to pay its short-term liabilities out of short-term assets.

Currently attainable standards Standards that reflect an efficient operating state; they are rigorous but achievable.

Customer perspective A Balanced Scorecard viewpoint that defines the customer and market segments in which the business will compete.

Customer value Realization less sacrifice, where realization is what the customer receives and sacrifice is what is given up.

Cycle time The length of time required to produce one unit of a product.

D

Debt ratio The ratio that measures the percentage of a company's risk as the percentage of its assets financed by creditors increases. It is computed by dividing a company's total liabilities by its total assets.

Decentralization The granting of decision-making freedom to lower operating levels.

Decision making The process of choosing among competing alternatives.

Decision model A specific set of procedures that, when followed, produces a decision.

Defective product A product or service that does not conform to specifications.

Degree of operating leverage (DOL) A measure of the sensitivity of profit changes to changes in sales volume. It measures the percentage change in profits resulting from a percentage change in sales.

Departmental overhead rate Estimated overhead for a single department divided by the estimated activity level for that same department.

Dependent variable A variable whose value depends on the value of another variable.

Differential cost The difference in total cost between the alternatives in a decision.

Direct costs Costs that can be easily and accurately traced to a cost object.

Direct fixed expenses Fixed costs that are directly traceable to a given segment and, consequently, disappear if the segment is eliminated.

Direct labor The labor that can be directly traced to the goods or services being produced.

Direct labor budget A budget showing the total direct labor hours needed and the associated cost for the number of units in the production budget.

Direct materials Materials that are a part of the final product and can be directly traced to the goods or services being produced.

Direct materials purchases budget A budget that outlines the expected usage of materials production and purchases of the direct materials required.

Direct method A method that allocates service costs directly to producing departments. This method ignores any interactions that may exist among support departments.

Discount factor The factor used to convert a future cash flow to its present value.

Discount rate The rate of return used to compute the present value of future cash flows.

Discounted cash flows Future cash flows expressed in present-value terms.

Discounting The act of finding the present value of future cash flows.

Discounting models Capital investment models that explicitly consider the time value of money in identifying criteria for accepting and rejecting proposed projects.

Discretionary fixed costs Fixed costs that can be changed relatively easily at management discretion.

Dividend payout ratio A ratio that is computed by dividing the total common dividends by the earnings available to common stockholders.

Dividend yield A profitability measure that is computed by dividing the dividends received per unit of common share by the market price per common share.

Double-loop feedback Information about both the effectiveness of strategy implementation and the validity of assumptions underlying the strategy.

Downstream costs Costs that occur after product manufacturing, such as marketing, distribution and customer service costs.

Driver A factor that causes or leads to a change in a cost or activity; a driver is an output measure.

Driver analysis The effort expended to identify those factors that are the root causes of activity costs.

Dysfunctional behavior Individual behavior that conflicts with the goals of the organization.

E

Earnings per share Earnings per share is computed by dividing net income less preferred dividends by the average number of shares of common stock outstanding during the period.

Ecoefficiency A view of environmental management maintaining that organizations can produce more useful goods and services while simultaneously reducing negative environmental impacts, resource consumption, and costs.

Economic order quantity (EOQ) The amount that should be ordered (or produced) to minimize the total ordering (or setup) and carrying costs.

Economic value added (EVA) A performance measure that is calculated by taking the after-tax operating profit minus the total annual cost of capital.

Ending finished goods inventory budget A budget that describes planned ending inventory of finished goods in units and dollars.

Enterprise Risk Management (ERM) A formal way for managerial accountants to identify and respond to the most important threats and business opportunities facing the organization. ERM is becoming increasingly important for long-term success.

Environmental costs Costs that are incurred because poor environmental quality exists or may exist.

Environmental detection costs Costs incurred to detect poor environmental performance.

Environmental external failure costs Costs incurred after contaminants are introduced into the environment.

Environmental internal failure costs Costs incurred after contaminants are produced but before they are introduced into the environment.

Environmental prevention costs Costs incurred to prevent damage to the environment.

Equivalent units of output Complete units that could have been produced given the total amount of manufacturing effort expended during the period.

Ethical behavior Choosing actions that are right, proper, and just.

Expenses Costs that are used up (expired) in the production of revenue.

External failure costs Costs incurred because products fail to conform to requirements after being sold to outside parties.

F

Failure activities Activities performed by an organization or its customers in response to poor quality (poor quality does exist).

Failure costs The costs incurred by an organization because failure activities are performed.

Favorable (F) variances Variances produced whenever the actual amounts are less than the budgeted or standard allowances.

FIFO costing method A process-costing method that separates units in beginning inventory from those produced during the current period. Unit costs include only current-period costs and production.

Financial accounting A type of accounting that is primarily concerned with producing information for external users.

Financial budgets The portions of the master budget that include the cash budget, the budgeted balance sheet, the budgeted statement of cash flows, and the capital budget.

Financial perspective A Balanced Scorecard viewpoint that describes the financial consequences of actions taken in the other three perspectives.

Financing activities Those activities that raise (provide) cash from (to) creditors and owners.

Fixed costs Costs that, in total, are constant within the relevant range as the level of output increases or decreases.

Fixed overhead spending variance The difference between actual fixed overhead and applied fixed overhead.

Fixed overhead volume variance The difference between budgeted fixed overhead and applied fixed overhead; it is a measure of capacity utilization.

Flexible budget A budget that can specify costs for a range of activity.

Flexible budget variance The sum of price variances and efficiency variances in a performance report comparing actual costs to expected costs predicted by a flexible budget.

Future value The value that will accumulate by the end of an investment's life if the investment earns a specified compounded return.

G

Goal congruence The alignment of a manager's personal goals with those of the organization.

Gross margin The difference between sales revenue and cost of goods sold.

H

High-low method A method for separating mixed costs into fixed and variable components by using just the high and low data points. [Note: The high (low) data point corresponds to the high (low) output level.]

Horizontal analysis Also called trend analysis, this type of analysis expresses a line item as a percentage of some prior-period amount.

I

Ideal standards Standards that reflect perfect operating conditions.

Incentives The positive or negative measures taken by an organization to induce a manager to exert effort toward achieving the organization's goals.

Independent projects Projects that, if accepted or rejected, will not affect the cash flows of another project.

Independent variable A variable whose value does not depend on the value of another variable.

Indifference point The quantity at which two systems produce the same operating income.

Indirect costs Costs that cannot be easily and accurately traced to a cost object.

Indirect method A method that computes operating cash flows by adjusting net income for items that do not affect cash flows.

Innovation process A process that anticipates the emerging and potential needs of customers and creates new products and services to satisfy those needs.

Intercept The fixed cost, representing the point where the cost formula intercepts the vertical axis.

Internal business process perspective A Balanced Scorecard viewpoint that describes the internal processes needed to provide value for customers and owners.

Internal failure costs Costs incurred because products and services fail to conform to requirements where lack of conformity is discovered prior to external sale.

Internal rate of return The rate of return that equates the present value of a project's cash inflows with the present value of its cash outflows (i.e., it sets the NPV equal to zero). Also, the rate of return being earned on funds that remain internally invested in a project.

Inventory turnover ratio A ratio that is computed by dividing the cost of goods sold by the average inventory.

Investing activities Those activities that involve the acquisition or sale of long-term assets.

Investment center A division of a company that is evaluated on the basis of return on investment.

J

Job One distinct unit or set of units for which the costs of production must be assigned.

Job-order cost sheet A subsidiary account to the work-in-process account on which the total costs of materials, labor, and overhead for a single job are accumulated.

Job-order costing system A costing system in which costs are collected and assigned to units of production for each individual job.

Joint products Products that are inseparable prior to a split-off point. All manufacturing costs up to the split-off point are joint costs.

Just-in-time (JIT) A demand-pull system whose objective is to eliminate waste by producing a product only when it is needed and only in the quantities demanded by customers.

K

Kaizen costing A cost management practice that focuses on the continuous reduction of the manufacturing costs of existing products and processes.

Kaizen standard An interim standard that reflects the planned improvement for a coming period.

Keep-or-drop decisions Relevant costing analyses that focus on keeping or dropping a segment of a business.

L

Labor efficiency variance (LEV) The difference between the actual direct labor hours used and the standard direct labor hours allowed multiplied by the standard hourly wage rate.

Labor rate variance (LRV) The difference between the actual hourly rate paid and the standard hourly rate multiplied by the actual hours worked.

Lean accounting An accounting practice that organizes costs according to the value chain by focusing primarily on the elimination of waste. The objective is to provide information to managers that support this effort and to provide financial statements that better reflect overall performance, using financial and nonfinancial information.

Learning and growth (infrastructure) perspective A Balanced Scorecard viewpoint that defines the capabilities that an organization needs to create long-term growth and improvement.

Leverage ratios Ratios that measure the ability of a company to meet its long- and short-term obligations. These ratios provide a measure of the degree of protection provided to a company's creditors.

Line positions Positions that have direct responsibility for the basic objectives of an organization.

Liquidity ratios Ratios that measure the ability of a company to meet its current obligations.

M

Make-or-buy decisions Relevant costing analyses that focus on whether a component should be made internally or purchased externally.

Management accounting The provision of accounting information for a company's internal users.

Manufacturing Cycle Efficiency (MCE) Measured as valueadded time divided by total time. The result tells the company what percentage of total time spent is devoted to actual production.

Manufacturing organization An organization that produces tangible products.

Margin The ratio of net operating income to sales.

Margin of safety The units sold, or expected to be sold, or sales revenue earned, or expected to be earned, above the break-even volume.

Markup The percentage applied to a base cost; it includes desired profit and any costs not included in the base cost.

Master budget The collection of all area and activity budgets representing a firm's comprehensive plan of action.

Materials price variance (MPV) The difference between the actual price paid per unit of materials and the standard price allowed per unit multiplied by the actual quantity of materials purchased.

Materials requisition form A source document that records the type, quantity, and unit price of the direct materials issued to each job.

Materials usage variance (MUV) The difference between the direct materials actually used and the direct materials allowed for the actual output multiplied by the standard price.

Method of least squares (regression) A statistical method to find the best-fitting line through a set of data points. It is used to break out the fixed and variable components of a mixed cost.

Mixed costs Costs that have both a fixed and a variable component.

Monetary incentives The use of economic rewards to motivate managers.

Mutually exclusive projects Projects that, if accepted, preclude the acceptance of competing projects.

Myopic behavior Managerial actions that improve budgetary performance in the short run at the expense of the long-run welfare of the organization.

N

Net present value The difference between the present value of a project's cash inflows and the present value of its cash outflows.

Noncash investing and financing activities Investing and financing activities that take place without affecting cash.

Nondiscounting models Capital investment models that identify criteria for accepting or rejecting projects without considering the time value of money.

Nonmonetary incentives The use of psychological and social rewards to motivate managers.

Non-unit-level activity drivers Factors that measure the consumption of non-unit-level activities by products and other cost objects.

Non-value-added activities All activities other than those that are absolutely essential to remain in business.

Non-value-added costs Costs that are caused either by non-value-added activities or by the inefficient performance of value-added activities.

Normal cost of goods sold The cost of goods sold before adjustment for any overhead variance.

Normal cost system An approach that assigns the actual costs of direct materials and direct labor to products but uses a predetermined rate to assign overhead costs.

O

Operating activities The ongoing, day-to-day, revenue-generating activities of an organization.

Operating assets Assets used to generate operating income, consisting usually of cash, inventories, receivables, and property, plant, and equipment. Average operating assets are found by adding together beginning operating assets and ending operating assets, and dividing the result by 2.

Operating budgets Budgets associated with the income-producing activities of an organization.

Operating income Revenues minus operating expenses from the firm's normal operations. Operating income is before-tax income.

Operating leverage The use of fixed costs to extract higher percentage changes in profits as sales activity changes. Leverage is achieved by increasing fixed costs while lowering variable costs.

Operations process A process that produces and delivers existing products and services to customers.

Opportunity cost The benefit given up or sacrificed when one alternative is chosen over another.

Ordering costs The costs of placing and receiving an order.

Overapplied overhead The amount by which applied overhead exceeds actual overhead.

Overhead A category in which all product costs, other than direct materials and direct labor, are placed.

Overhead budget A budget that reveals the planned expenditures for all indirect manufacturing items.

Overhead variance The difference between actual overhead and applied overhead.

P

Parallel processing A processing pattern in which two or more sequential processes are required to produce a finished good.

Participative budgeting An approach to budgeting that allows managers who will be held accountable for budgetary performance to participate in the budget's development.

Payback period The time required for a project to return its investment.

Performance report A report that compares the actual data with planned data.

Period costs Costs that are expensed in the period in which they are incurred; they are not inventoried.

Physical flow schedule A schedule that reconciles units to account for with units accounted for. The physical units are not adjusted for percent of completion.

Planning A management activity that involves the detailed formulation of action to achieve a particular end.

Plantwide overhead rate A single overhead rate calculated using all estimated overhead for a factory divided by the estimated activity level across the entire factory.

Postaudit A follow-up analysis of an investment decision, comparing actual benefits and costs with expected benefits and costs.

Postpurchase costs The costs of using, maintaining, and disposing of the product.

Postsales service process A process that provides critical and responsive service to customers after the product or service has been delivered.

Predetermined overhead rate An overhead rate computed using estimated data.

Present value The current value of a future cash flow. It represents the amount that must be invested now if the future cash flow is to be received assuming compounding at a given rate of interest.

Prevention costs Cost incurred to prevent defects in products or services being produced.

Price The revenue per unit.

Price (rate) variance The difference between standard price and actual price multiplied by the actual quantity of inputs used.

Price standards The price that should be paid per unit of input.

Price-earnings ratio The price-earnings ratio is found by dividing the market price per share by the earnings per share.

Prime cost The sum of direct materials cost and direct labor cost.

Private costs Environmental costs that an organization has to pay.

Process value chain The innovation, operations, and postsales service processes.

Process-costing system A costing system that accumulates production costs by process or by department for a given period of time.

Process-value analysis An approach that focuses on processes and activities and emphasizes systemwide performance instead of individual performance.

Producing departments Units within an organization responsible for producing the products or services that are sold to customers.

Product diversity The situation present when products consume overhead in different proportions.

Product (manufacturing) costs Costs associated with the manufacture of goods or the provision of services. Product costs include: direct materials, direct labor, and overhead.

Production budget A budget that shows how many units must be produced to meet sales needs and satisfy ending inventory requirements.

Production report A document that summarizes the manufacturing activity that takes place in a process department for a given period of time.

Profit center A division of a company that is evaluated on the basis of operating income or profit.

Profitability ratios Ratios that measure the earning ability of a company. These ratios allow investors, creditors, and managers to evaluate the extent to which invested funds are being used efficiently.

Profit-volume graph A graphical portrayal of the relationship between profits and sales activity in units.

Pseudoparticipation A budgetary system in which top management solicits inputs from lower-level managers and then ignores those inputs. Thus, in reality, budgets are dictated from above.

Q

Quality product (service) A product that meets or exceeds customer expectations.

Quantity standards The quantity of input allowed per unit of output.

Quick or acid-test ratio A measure of liquidity that compares only the most liquid assets to current liabilities.

R

Realized external failure costs Environmental costs caused by environmental degradation and paid for by the responsible organization.

Reciprocal method A method that simultaneously allocates service costs to all user departments. It gives full consideration to interactions among support departments.

Relevant costs Future costs that change across alternatives.

Relevant range The range of output over which an assumed cost relationship is valid for the normal operations of a firm.

Required rate of return The minimum rate of return that a project must earn in order to be acceptable. Usually corresponds to the cost of capital.

Residual income The difference between operating income and the minimum dollar return required on a company's operating assets.

Resource drivers Factors that measure the consumption of resources by activities.

Responsibility center A segment of the business whose manager is accountable for specified sets of activities.

Return on investment (ROI) The ratio of operating income to average operating assets.

Return on sales A measure of the efficiency of a firm that is computed by dividing net income by sales.

Return on stockholders' equity A measure that can be used to compare against other return measures (e.g., preferred dividend rates and bond rates). It is computed by dividing net income less preferred dividends by the average common stockholders' equity.

Return on total assets The result of dividing net income plus the after-tax cost of interest by the average total assets.

Revenue center A segment of the business that is evaluated on the basis of sales.

S

Sales budget A budget that describes expected sales in units and dollars for the coming period.

Sales mix The relative combination of products (or services) being sold by an organization.

Sarbanes-Oxley Act (SOX) Passed in 2002 in response to revelations of misconduct and fraud by several well-known firms, this legislation established stronger governmental control and regulation of public companies in the United States, from enhanced oversight (PCAOB), to increased auditor independence and tightened regulation of corporate governance.

Scattergraph method A method to fit a line to a set of data using two points that are selected by judgment. It is used to break out the fixed and variable components of a mixed cost.

Segment A subunit of a company of sufficient importance to warrant the production of performance reports.

Segment margin The contribution a segment makes to cover common fixed costs and provide for profit after direct fixed costs and variable costs are deducted from the segment's sales revenue.

Selling and administrative expenses budget A budget that outlines planned expenditures for nonmanufacturing activities.

Selling (marketing) costs Those costs necessary to market, distribute, and service a product or service.

Sell-or-process-further decision Relevant costing analysis that focuses on whether a product should be processed beyond the split-off point.

Semi-variable costs Costs that in total increase disproportionately with increases in the activity level. For example, total learning curve costs increase at a decreasing rate as output increases.

Sensitivity analysis The "what-if" process of altering certain key variables to assess the effect on the original outcome.

Sequential (or step) method A method that allocates service costs to user departments in a sequential manner. It gives partial consideration to interactions among support departments.

Sequential processing A processing pattern in which units pass from one process to another in a set order.

Service organization An organization that produces intangible products.

Services Tasks or activities performed for a customer or an activity performed by a customer using an organization's products or facilities.

Single-loop feedback Information about the effectiveness of strategy implementation.

Slope The variable cost per unit of activity usage.

Societal costs (See Unrealized external failure costs.)

Special-order decisions Relevant costing analyses that focus on whether a specially priced order should be accepted or rejected.

Split-off point The point at which products become distinguishable after passing through a common process.

Staff positions Positions that are supportive in nature and have only indirect responsibility for an organization's basic objectives.

Standard cost per unit The per-unit cost that should be achieved given materials, labor, and overhead standards.

Standard cost sheet A listing of the standard costs and standard quantities of direct materials, direct labor, and overhead that should apply to a single product.

Standard hours allowed The direct labor hours that should have been used to produce the actual output (Unit labor standard × Actual output).

Standard quantity of materials allowed The quantity of materials that should have been used to produce the actual output (Unit materials standard × Actual output).

Statement of cash flows A statement that provides information regarding the sources and uses of a firm's cash.

Static budget A budget for a particular level of activity.

Step cost A cost that displays a constant level of cost for a range of output and then jumps to a higher level of cost at some point, where it remains for a similar range of output.

Stockout costs The costs of insufficient inventory.

Strategic plan The long-term plan for future activities and operations, usually involving at least five years.

Strategy The process of choosing a business's market and customer segments, identifying its critical internal business processes, and selecting the individual and organizational capabilities needed to meet internal, customer, and financial objectives.

Sunk costs Costs for which the outlay has already been made and that cannot be affected by a future decision.

Supplies Those materials necessary for production that do not become part of the finished product or are not used in providing a service.

Support departments Units within an organization that provide essential support services for producing departments.

Sustainable development Development that meets the needs of the present without compromising the ability of future generations to meet their own needs.

T

Tangible products Goods produced by converting raw materials through the use of labor and capital inputs, such as plant, land, and machinery.

Target cost The difference between the sales price needed to achieve a projected market share and the desired per-unit profit.

Target costing A method of determining the cost of a product or service based on the price (target price) that customers are willing to pay.

Testable strategy A set of linked objectives aimed at an overall goal that can be restated into a sequence of cause-and-effect hypotheses.

Time ticket A source document by which direct labor costs are assigned to individual jobs.

Times-interest-earned ratio A leverage ratio that uses the income statement to assess a company's ability to service its debt. It is computed by dividing net income before taxes and interest by interest expense.

Total budget variance The difference between the actual cost of an input and its planned cost.

Total quality management A management philosophy in which manufacturers strive to create an environment that will enable workers to manufacture perfect (zero-defect) products.

Transfer price The price charged for goods transferred from one division to another.

Transferred-in costs Costs transferred from a prior process to a subsequent process.

Treasurer The individual responsible for the finance function; raises capital and manages cash and investments.

Turnover The ratio of sales to average operating assets.

U

Underapplied overhead The amount by which actual overhead exceeds applied overhead.

Unfavorable (U) variances Variances produced whenever the actual input amounts are greater than the budgeted or standard allowances.

Unit-level activities Activities that are performed each time a unit is produced.

Unit-level activity drivers Factors that measure the consumption of unit-level activities by products and other cost objects.

Unrealized external failure costs Environmental costs caused by an organization but paid for by society.

Upstream costs Costs that occur before product manufacturing, such as research and development and product design costs.

Usage (efficiency) variance The difference between standard quantities and actual quantities multiplied by standard price.

V

Value chain The set of activities required to design, develop, produce, market, and deliver products and services to customers.

Value-added activities Activities that are necessary for a business to achieve corporate objectives and remain in business.

Value-added costs Costs caused by value-added activities.

Variable budgets (See Flexible budget.)

Variable cost A cost that increases as output increases and decreases as output decreases.

Variable cost ratio Variable costs divided by sales revenues. It is the proportion of each sales dollar needed to cover variable costs.

Variable costing A product-costing method that assigns only variable manufacturing costs to production: direct materials, direct labor, and variable overhead. Fixed overhead is treated as a period cost.

Variable costs Costs that, in total, vary in direct proportion to changes in output within the relevant range.

Variable overhead efficiency variance The difference between the actual direct labor hours used and the standard hours allowed multiplied by the standard variable overhead rate.

Variable overhead spending variance The difference between the actual variable overhead and the budgeted variable overhead based on actual hours used to produce the actual output.

Velocity The number of units that can be produced in a given period of time (e.g., output per hour).

Vertical analysis A type of analysis that expresses the line item as a percentage of some other line item for the same period.

W

Weighted average costing method A process-costing method that combines beginning inventory costs with current-period costs to compute unit costs. Costs and output from the current period and the previous period are averaged to compute unit costs.

Work in process (WIP) The cost of the partially completed goods that are still being worked on at the end of a time period.

Z

Zero defects A quality performance standard that requires all products and services to be produced and delivered according to specifications.

Check Figures

Check Figures are given for selected problems.

Chapter 1

1-42
1. Total direct materials = $7,810
2. Income = $6,120

1-43
1. Total owed by Natalie = $30
2. Total cost for Mary = $17.50

1-44
2. Cost of goods manufactured = $224,950
3. Cost of goods sold = $226,050

1-45
1. Total product cost = $9,200,000
2. Operating income = $2,000,000
3. Gross margin = $2,860,000

1-46
1. Cost of goods manufactured = $24,725
2. Cost of goods sold = $27,160

1-47
3. Conversion cost = $173,000
5. Operating income = $90,950

1-49
3. Operating income = $332,100

1-51
2. Magazine total prime costs = $4,500
4. Income before taxes = $2,010

1-52
2. Tent sale loss = $(1,300)

Chapter 2

2-36
2. Fixed receiving cost = $6,600
3. Receiving cost for the year = $295,200

2-37
2. Receiving cost = $25,180

2-38
1. 10 months' data intercept = 3,212

2-39
2. Variable power cost = $1.13 (rounded)

2-40
2. Supplies variable rate = $6.50
4. Charge per hour = $75.69

2-41
2. Fixed rate = $1,349

2-42
2. Plan 2 unused minutes = 75
3. Plan 2 minutes used = 90

2-43
3. Variable rate = $4.50

Chapter 3

3-30
1. Break-even units = 8,000
2. Units for target profit = 11,750
4. Margin of safety in units = 2,000

3-31
2. Break-even units = 16,500

3-32
1. Break-even sales = $3,333,333
3. $94,500
5. Percent increase in operating income = 41.8%

3-33
2. Breakeven circles = 31,310
3. Increase in total contribution margin = $300,000

3-34
1. Margin of safety in units = 230,000
2. Operating income = $20,700
3. Units for target profit = 1,000,000

3-35
2. $277,778
4. Break-even point = $294,118

3-36
1. Revenue = $450,000
2. Desk lamps = 8,998
3. Operating leverage = 4.0

3-37
2. Operating income = $34,000
3. Trim kits = 32,444

3-38
1. Breakeven units = 21,429
3. Operating income = $119,900

3-39
1. Contribution margin ratio = 0.62
3. Margin of safety = $430,000
4. Contribution margin from increased sales = $4,650

3-40
1. Price = $380

Chapter 4

4-34
2. Total cost Job 62 = $126,690
4. Cost of goods sold = $253,265

4-35
1. Total = $6,752

4-36
2. Total cost of Job 37 = $3,680
4. Gross margin = $2,955

4-37
1. Overhead rate = $2
2. Department B overhead rate = $1.375

4-38
2. Department 3 overhead rate = $12.50
2. Total manufacturing cost Job 2 = $13,003

4-39
2. Ending work in process = $16,726

4-40
2. Total Job 444 = $2,750

4-41
1. Overhead rate = 175%
3. Cost of goods manufactured = $245,000

4-42
2. Applied overhead = $4,320
5. Adjusted cost of goods sold = $700,200

4-43
2. Total Job 703 = $41,220
4. Ending balance Work in Process = $40,900

4-44
1. Total Ed's Job = $234

Chapter 5

5-37
1. Equivalent units = 6,700
2. Units transferred out = 6,600
3. Units transferred out = 1,000

5-38   1. Total units to account for = 120,000
        2. Equivalent units, conversion = 104,000
        3. Unit cost = $320
        4. Cost of EWIP = $4,960,000
5-39   1. Unit cost = $320
5-40   1. Total units to account for = 80,000
        2. Equivalent units = 72,000
        3. Unit conversion cost = $1.16
5-41   1. Cost per equivalent unit = $1.16
5-42   1. Units to account for = 20,000
        2. Equivalent units = 18,500
        3. Unit cost = $0.50
        4. Cost of EWIP = $250
        5. Spoilage cost = $500
5-43   1. Unit cost = $6.20
5-44   1. Cost per equivalent unit = $5.3424
5-45   1. Total equivalent units = 521,000
        2. Unit cost = $21.19
        3. Cost of goods transferred out = $10,595,000
        5. Unit paraffin cost = $6.10
5-46   1. Unit cost = $5.74
5-47   1. Cost of units transferred out = $160,940
5-48   1. Cost of goods transferred out = $17,349
        2. Cost of goods transferred out = $23,192
5-49   1. Cost of units started and completed = $15,573
        2. Cost of units started and completed = $22,950

Chapter 6

6-42   1. Unit cost = $0.60
        2. Duffel bags = $2.40 per unit
        3. Backpacks = $1.20 per unit
6-43   1. Model B cost per unit = $1.50
        2. Model B cost per unit = $1.66
        3. Model B cost per unit = $1.86
6-44   1. Total cost = $120,000
        2. Basic unit cost = $87.50
6-45   1. Cost per patient day = $200
        2. Cost per patient day (complications) = $500
6-46   1. Average monthly fee = $6.78
        2. Cost per account (low) = $87.37
        3. Profit (high balance) = $112.50
6-47   2. Category 1 unit cost = $0.075
        3. Reduction = $2,450,000
6-48   1. Watson unit cost = $998.30
6-49   2. Potential reduction per unit = $7.10
        4. Total unit reduction potential = $8.35
        5. $12 price
6-50   1. Total non-value cost = $1,204,800
        2. Materials variance = $164,000 U
6-51   1. Cycle time = 8 minutes
        2. Cycle time = 9.6 minutes
        3. Reduction = $16.67 per binocular

Chapter 7

7-36   1. Total cash, September = $253,362
7-37   1. i. Budgeted income = $3,823,760 j. Ending cash balance
        (March) = $1,642,076
7-38   1. Total assets = $562,750
        2. Ending cash (Sept.) = $12,005
        3. Total assets = $565,605

7-40   1. Ending cash balance = $113,412
7-41   10. Income before taxes = $16,129,000

Chapter 8

8-34   1. MUV = $6,000 F
        2. LRV = $4,000 U
        3. LEV = $4,000 F
8-35   2. LEV, Cutting = $300 U
8-36   1. Standard cost per unit = $126.88
        2. LRV = $2,457.60 F
        3. Average time = 0.768 per unit
8-37   1. Standard cost (normal) = $252 per patient day
        2. MUV Cesarean = $20,000 U
        3. LEV (normal) = $3,200 U
        4. LEV = $24,000 U
8-38   1. UCL (labor) = $645,000
        2. Total liquid variance = $48,000 U
        3. LEV = $21,875 F
8-39   1. June UCL (labor) = $26,400 (quantity standard)
        2. May LRV = $6,996 F (2.3%)
8-40   1. MPV = $975 U
        2. LEV = $1,000 U
        3. LRV = $0
8-42   1. MUV = $100,000 U
        2. LEV = $24,000 U
        3. Net effect = $46,000 U

Chapter 9

9-34   1. Total direct labor hours = 18,000
        2. Total overhead = $43,950
9-35   1. Variable = $685; Fixed = $13,000,000
        2. Optimistic income = $5,750,000
9-36   1. Total = $45,613
        2. Supplies, variable = $1.40
9-37   1. Total overhead = $2,425
        2. Revised overhead = $2,495
9-39   1. Total variance = $100,000 U
        2. Total variance = $6,000 F
9-40   1. Total variance = $2,500 F
        2. Unit cost = $15.29
        3. Total (20,000 moves) = $165,000
9-41   2. Total variance = $184,360 U
9-42   1. SFOR = $3.00; SVOR = $2.00
        2. Total Fixed OH variance = $108,000 U
        3. Volume variance = $18,000 U
        4. VOH efficiency variance = $35,700 U
9-43   1. VOH efficiency = $20,000 U
        2. FOH spending = $20,000 F
9-45   3. VOH spending variance = $7,996 U
        4. 0.26667 hours per unit
9-46   1. Total variance = $40,000 U
        2. Volume variance = $15,000 U; Efficiency variance =
        $15,000 U

Chapter 10

10-26   2. Gross margin = $686,400
        4. Operating income = $575,200
        5. Absorption-costing income = $534,100

10-27   2. Ending inventory = $3,750
        3. Segment margin beauty shops = $51,000
10-28   1. (b) 0.15
        2. (c) $1,470,000
10-29   1. ROI year 3 = 6.30%
        3. Turnover = 0.75
        4. Turnover = 0.83
10-30   Turbocharger ROI = 15.2%
        3. (c) $280,480
        4. (d) $1,445,000
10-31   2. ROI = 10.34% (rounded)
        4. Margin = 9.13%
        5. EVA with investment = $122,500

Chapter 11

11-31   1. Total net benefit = $100,000
11-32   1. Cost to make = $367,000
        4. Cost to make = $514,000
11-33   2. Additional income per pound = $21.025
11-34   1. Operating income = $6,100
        2. Operating income = $16,558
        3. Total segment margin = $29,620
11-35   1. Increase Pat's income = $18,400
        2. Increase Steve's income = $15,200
11-36   2. Markup = $2,646
11-37   1. Standard contribution margin per machine hour = $20
11-38   1. Loss per box = $0.05
11-39   1. Operating profit = $40,000
11-40   1. $300,000
11-41   1. Differential amount to process further = $4,900
11-42   1. Monthly cost for Community Bank = $5,773

Chapter 12

12-31   2. NPV = $44,172
12-32   2. NPV = $184,520
12-33   1. IRR = 0.16
        2. Cash flow = $15,730
        3. Minimum CF = $18,118
12-34   1. NPV = $22,525,500
        2. NPV = ($5,291,100)
        3. Seating rate = 84%
        4. Seat rate = 77%
12-35   1. Payback = 3.13 years
        2. ARR = 10.68%
        3. IRR = 14% (approximately)
        4. NPV = $(21,009)
12-36   1. NPV = $644,470
12-38   1. Payback = 3.89 years
        2. NPV = $(89,000)
        3. NPV = $421,529

12-39   1. Cost of capital = 0.10
        2. NPV = $24,300
12-40   1. NPV (20% rate) = $(25,390,000)
        2. NPV (14%) = $4,375,200
        3. NPV (14%) = $1,375,200
12-41   1. NPV = $117,400
        2. NPV = $(29,480)
        3. NPV = $231,160
12-42   1. NPV (standard) = $190,500
        2. NPV (CAM) = $762,100
12-43   1. NPV (CAM) = $199,800
        2. NPV (Standard) = $95,450

Chapter 13

13-28   Cash from operations = $3,600
13-30   Cash from operations = $2,000
13-32   1. Cash from operations = $506,250
        2. Cash from investing = $(293,750)
13-36   1. Net operating cash = $10,000; investing = $(60,000)
13-38   1. Net operating cash = $95,800
13-39   1. Net operating cash = $30,000,000; investing = $(10,000,000)
13-40   1. Net operating cash = $80,000; investing = $(55,000)

Chapter 14

14-29   1. Current ratio = 2.5
        3. Average receivables = $350,000
        5. Average inventory = $225,000
14-30   2. Total assets = $7,250,000
14-31   1. 0.088
        3. $5.75
        5. 0.0375
14-32   1. Percent change total assets = 32.5%
14-33   1. This year percent total current assets = 88.6%
        2. Last year percent total liabilities = 60.2%
        3. This year percent net income = 10.3%
14-34   1. (b) last year = 0.714
        (d) last year turnover in days = 297.96
14-35   1. (b) last year debt ratio = 0.6024
14-36   1. (a) Last year return on total assets = 0.0853
        (f) Last year dividend payout = 0.32
14-37   1. (b) return on assets = 8.7%
14-38   1. 2001 accounts receivables turnover = 5.452004 accounts receivables turnover = 3.06
14-39   1. (a) Company A EPS = 2.34
        (b) Company B dividends per common share = $0.7833
        (e) Company A return on total assets = 0.165

Important Equations

Chapter 1

1. Total product cost = Direct materials + direct labor + overhead
2. Unit product cost = Total product cost/number of units
3. Prime cost = Direct materials + Direct labor
4. Conversion cost = Direct labor + Overhead
5. Direct materials used in production
   = Beginning inventory of materials
   + Purchases − Ending inventory of materials
6. Cost of goods manufactured = Direct materials used in production + Direct labor used in production + Manufacturing overhead costs used in production + Beginning WIP inventory − Ending WIP inventory
7. Cost of goods sold = Beginning inventory + Cost of goods manufactured − Ending inventory

Chapter 2

1. Cost formula: Total cost = Total fixed cost + (variable rate × units of output)
2. Total variable cost = Variable rate × Units of output

Chapter 3

1. Sales revenue = Price × Units sold
2. Operating income = (Price × Units sold) − (Unit variable cost × Units sold) − Fixed cost
3. Break-even point in units = Fixed cost/(Price − Unit variable cost)
4. Contribution margin ratio = Total contribution margin/Sales
   or
   = (Price − Unit variable cost)/Price
5. Variable cost ratio = Total variable cost/Sales
   or
   = Unit variable cost/Price
6. Break-even point in sales dollars = Fixed cost/Contribution margin ratio
   or
   = Fixed cost/(1 − Variable cost ratio)
7. Margin of safety = Sales − Break-even sales
8. Degree of opearting leverage = Total contribution margin /Operating income
9. Percentage change in profits = Degree of operating leverage × Percent change in sales

Chapter 4

1. Predetermined overhead rate = Estimated annual overhead /Estimated annual activity level
2. Applied overhead = Predetermined overhead rate × Actual activity usage
3. Overhead variance = Applied overhead − Actual overhead
4. Adjusted COGS = Unadjusted COGS ± Overhead variance
   (*Note*: Applied overhead > Actual overhead **means** Overapplied overhead; Applied overhead < Actual overhead **means** Underapplied overhead)
5. Departmental overhead rate = Estimated departmental overhead/Estimated departmental activity level
6. Total product cost = Total direct materials + total direct labor + Applied overhead
7. Unit product cost = Total product cost/Number of units

Chapter 7

1. Units to be produced = Expected unit sales + Units in ending inventory − Units in beginning inventory
2. Purchases = Direct materials needed for production + Desired direct materials in ending inventory − Direct materials in beginning inventory

Chapter 8

1. $MPV = (AP - SP)AQ$
2. $MUV = (AQ - SQ)SP$
3. $LRV = (AR - SR)AH$
4. $LEV = (AH - SH)SR$

Chapter 9

1. Variable overhead
   spending variance $= (AVOR \times AH) - (SVOR \times AH)$
   $= (AVOR - SVOR)AH$
2. Variable overhead efficiency variance $= (AH - SH)SVOR$
3. $SFOR$ = Budgeted fixed overhead costs/Practical capacity
4. SH_p = Unit standard × Units of practical capacity
5. $BFOH = SFOR \times SH_p$
6. $ApFOH = SFOR \times SH$
7. Total variance = Actual fixed overhead − Applied fixed overhead
   $= AFOH - ApFOH$
8. FOH spending variance $= AFOH - BFOH$
9. Volume variance = Budgeted fixed overhead − Applied fixed overhead
   $= BFOH - ApFOH$
   $= (SH_p \times SFOR) - (SH \times SFOR)$
   $= (SH_p - SH)SFOR$

Chapter 10

1. Absorption-costing product cost = Direct materials + Direct labor + Variable overhead + Fixed overhead
2. Variable-costing product cost = Direct materials + Direct labor + Variable overhead
3. ROI = Operating income/Average operating assets
   ROI = Margin × Turnover
4. Average operating assets = (Beginning operating assets + Ending operating assets)/2
5. Margin = Operating income/Sales
6. Turnover = Sales/Average operating assets
7. Residual income = Operating income − (Minimum rate of return × Average operating assets)
8. EVA = After-tax income − (Actual percentage cost of capital × Total capital employed)

Chapter 11

1. Contribution margin per unit of scarce resource
   = Contribution margin per unit /Amount of scarce resource to make one unit
2. Price using markup = Cost per unit + (Cost per unit × Markup percentage)
3. Target cost = Target price − Desired profit
4. Total inventory-related cost = Ordering cost + Carrying cost
5. Ordering cost = Number of orders per year × Cost of placing one order
6. Average number of units in inventory
   = (Maximum units in inventory − Minimum units in inventory)/2
7. Carrying cost = Average number of units in inventory × Cost of carrying one unit in inventory
8. Economic order quantity
   $$= \sqrt{\frac{(2 \times \text{Cost per order} \times \text{Annual demand in units})}{\text{Carrying cost per unit}}}$$

Chapter 12

1. $NPV = [\sum CF_t/(1 + i)^t] - I$
   $= [\sum CF_t df_t] - I$
   $= P - I$
   where
   I = The present value of the project's cost (usually the initial outlay)
   CF_t = The cash inflow to be received in period t, with $t = 1 \ldots n$
   i = The required rate of return
   t = The time period
   P = The present value of the project's future cash inflows
   df_t = $1/(1 + i)^t$, the discount factor
2. $I = \sum CF_t/(1 + i)^t$
   where $t = 1, \ldots, n$
3. $I = CF(df)$
   Solving for df, we obtain:
   $df = I / CF$
   = Investment/Annual cash flow

Cornerstones